Lecture Notes in Computer Science   12649

Advanced Research in Computing and Software Science
Subline of Lecture Notes in Computer Science

More information about this subseries at http://www.springer.com/series/7407

Esther Guerra · Mariëlle Stoelinga (Eds.)

Fundamental Approaches to Software Engineering

24th International Conference, FASE 2021
Held as Part of the European Joint Conferences
on Theory and Practice of Software, ETAPS 2021
Luxembourg City, Luxembourg, March 27 – April 1, 2021
Proceedings

 Springer

Editors
Esther Guerra
Universidad Autónoma de Madrid
Madrid, Spain

Mariëlle Stoelinga
University of Twente
Enschede, The Netherlands

Radboud University
Nijmegen, The Netherlands

ISSN 0302-9743 ISSN 1611-3349 (electronic)
Lecture Notes in Computer Science
ISBN 978-3-030-71499-4 ISBN 978-3-030-71500-7 (eBook)
https://doi.org/10.1007/978-3-030-71500-7

LNCS Sublibrary: SL1 – Theoretical Computer Science and General Issues

This Springer imprint is published by the registered company Springer Nature Switzerland AG
The registered company address is: Gewerbestrasse 11, 6330 Cham, Switzerland

ETAPS Foreword

Welcome to the 24th ETAPS! ETAPS 2021 was originally planned to take place in Luxembourg in its beautiful capital Luxembourg City. Because of the Covid-19 pandemic, this was changed to an online event.

ETAPS 2021 was the 24th instance of the European Joint Conferences on Theory and Practice of Software. ETAPS is an annual federated conference established in 1998, and consists of four conferences: ESOP, FASE, FoSSaCS, and TACAS. Each conference has its own Program Committee (PC) and its own Steering Committee (SC). The conferences cover various aspects of software systems, ranging from theoretical computer science to foundations of programming languages, analysis tools, and formal approaches to software engineering. Organising these conferences in a coherent, highly synchronised conference programme enables researchers to participate in an exciting event, having the possibility to meet many colleagues working in different directions in the field, and to easily attend talks of different conferences. On the weekend before the main conference, numerous satellite workshops take place that attract many researchers from all over the globe.

ETAPS 2021 received 260 submissions in total, 115 of which were accepted, yielding an overall acceptance rate of 44.2%. I thank all the authors for their interest in ETAPS, all the reviewers for their reviewing efforts, the PC members for their contributions, and in particular the PC (co-)chairs for their hard work in running this entire intensive process. Last but not least, my congratulations to all authors of the accepted papers!

ETAPS 2021 featured the unifying invited speakers Scott Smolka (Stony Brook University) and Jane Hillston (University of Edinburgh) and the conference-specific invited speakers Işil Dillig (University of Texas at Austin) for ESOP and Willem Visser (Stellenbosch University) for FASE. Inivited tutorials were provided by Erika Ábrahám (RWTH Aachen University) on analysis of hybrid systems and Madhusudan Parthasararathy (University of Illinois at Urbana-Champaign) on combining machine learning and formal methods.

ETAPS 2021 was originally supposed to take place in Luxembourg City, Luxembourg organized by the SnT - Interdisciplinary Centre for Security, Reliability and Trust, University of Luxembourg. University of Luxembourg was founded in 2003. The university is one of the best and most international young universities with 6,700 students from 129 countries and 1,331 academics from all over the globe. The local organisation team consisted of Peter Y.A. Ryan (general chair), Peter B. Roenne (organisation chair), Joaquin Garcia-Alfaro (workshop chair), Magali Martin (event manager), David Mestel (publicity chair), and Alfredo Rial (local proceedings chair).

ETAPS 2021 was further supported by the following associations and societies: ETAPS e.V., EATCS (European Association for Theoretical Computer Science), EAPLS (European Association for Programming Languages and Systems), and EASST (European Association of Software Science and Technology).

The ETAPS Steering Committee consists of an Executive Board, and representatives of the individual ETAPS conferences, as well as representatives of EATCS, EAPLS, and EASST. The Executive Board consists of Holger Hermanns (Saarbrücken), Marieke Huisman (Twente, chair), Jan Kofron (Prague), Barbara König (Duisburg), Gerald Lüttgen (Bamberg), Caterina Urban (INRIA), Tarmo Uustalu (Reykjavik and Tallinn), and Lenore Zuck (Chicago).

Other members of the steering committee are: Patricia Bouyer (Paris), Einar Broch Johnsen (Oslo), Dana Fisman (Be'er Sheva), Jan-Friso Groote (Eindhoven), Esther Guerra (Madrid), Reiko Heckel (Leicester), Joost-Pieter Katoen (Aachen and Twente), Stefan Kiefer (Oxford), Fabrice Kordon (Paris), Jan Křetínský (Munich), Kim G. Larsen (Aalborg), Tiziana Margaria (Limerick), Andrew M. Pitts (Cambridge), Grigore Roşu (Illinois), Peter Ryan (Luxembourg), Don Sannella (Edinburgh), Lutz Schröder (Erlangen), Ilya Sergey (Singapore), Mariëlle Stoelinga (Twente), Gabriele Taentzer (Marburg), Christine Tasson (Paris), Peter Thiemann (Freiburg), Jan Vitek (Prague), Anton Wijs (Eindhoven), Manuel Wimmer (Linz), and Nobuko Yoshida (London).

I'd like to take this opportunity to thank all the authors, attendees, organizers of the satellite workshops, and Springer-Verlag GmbH for their support. I hope you all enjoyed ETAPS 2021.

Finally, a big thanks to Peter, Peter, Magali and their local organisation team for all their enormous efforts to make ETAPS a fantastic online event. I hope there will be a next opportunity to host ETAPS in Luxembourg.

February 2021

Marieke Huisman
ETAPS SC Chair
ETAPS e.V. President

Preface

This volume contains the papers presented at FASE 2021, the 24th International Conference on Fundamental Approaches to Software Engineering. FASE 2021 was organized as part of the annual European Joint Conferences on Theory and Practice of Software (ETAPS 2021).

FASE is concerned with the foundations on which software engineering is built, including topics like software engineering as an engineering discipline, requirements engineering, software architectures, software quality, model-driven development, software processes, software evolution, search-based software engineering, and the specification, design, and implementation of particular classes of systems, such as (self-)adaptive, collaborative, intelligent, embedded, distributed, mobile, pervasive, cyber-physical, or service-oriented applications.

FASE 2021 received 51 submissions. The submissions came from the following countries (in alphabetical order): Argentina, Australia, Austria, Belgium, Brazil, Canada, China, France, Germany, Iceland, India, Ireland, Italy, Luxembourg, Macedonia, Malta, Netherlands, Norway, Russia, Singapore, South Korea, Spain, Sweden, Taiwan, United Kingdom, and United States. FASE used a double-blind reviewing process. Each submission was reviewed by three Program Committee members. After an online discussion period, the Program Committee accepted 16 papers as part of the conference program (31% acceptance rate).

FASE 2021 hosted the 3rd International Competition on Software Testing (Test-Comp 2021). Test-Comp is an annual comparative evaluation of testing tools. This edition contained 11 participating tools, from academia and industry. These proceedings contain the competition report and three system descriptions of participating tools. The system-description papers were reviewed and selected by a separate program committee: the Test-Comp jury. Each paper was assessed by at least three reviewers. Two sessions in the FASE program were reserved for the presentation of the results: the summary by the Test-Comp chair and the participating tools by the developer teams in the first session, and the community meeting in the second session.

A lot of people contributed to the success of FASE 2021. We are grateful to the Program Committee members and reviewers for their thorough reviews and constructive discussions. We thank the ETAPS 2021 organizers, in particular, Peter Y. A. Ryan (General Chair), Joaquin Garcia-Alfaro (Workshops Chair), Peter Roenne (Organization Chair), Magali Martin (Event Manager), David Mestel (Publicity Chair) and Alfredo Rial (Local Proceedings Chair). We also thank Marieke Huisman (Steering Committee Chair of ETAPS 2021) for managing the process, and Gabriele Taenzter (Steering Committee Chair of FASE 2021) for her feedback and support. Last but not least, we would like to thank the authors for their excellent work.

March 2021

Esther Guerra
Mariëlle Stoelinga

Organization

Steering Committee

Wil van der Aalst	RWTH Aachen, Germany
Jordi Cabot	ICREA - Universitat Oberta de Catalunya, Spain
Marsha Chechik	University of Toronto, Canada
Reiner Hähnle	Technische Universität Darmstadt, Germany
Reiko Heckel	University of Leicester, UK
Tiziana Margaria	University of Limerick, Ireland
Fernando Orejas	Universitat Politècnica de Catalunya, Spain
Julia Rubin	University of British Columbia, Canada
Alessandra Russo	Imperial College London, UK
Andy Schürr	Technische Universität Darmstadt, Germany
Perdita Stevens	University of Edinburgh, UK
Gabriele Taentzer	Philipps-Universität Marburg, Germany
Andrzej Wąsowski	IT University of Copenhagen, Denmark
Heike Wehrheim	Universtät Paderborn, Germany

FASE – Program Committee

João Paulo Almeida	Universidade Federal do Espírito Santo, Brazil
Étienne André	LORIA, Université de Lorraine, France
Uwe Aßmann	Technische Universität Dresden, Germany
Artur Boronat	University of Leicester, UK
Paolo Bottoni	Sapienza University of Rome, Italy
Jordi Cabot	ICREAUniversitat Oberta de Catalunya, Spain
Yu-Fang Chen	Academia Sinica, Taiwan
Philippe Collet	Université Côte d'Azur - CNRS/I3S, France
Francisco Durán	University of Málaga, Spain
Marie-Christine Jakobs	Technische Universität Darmstadt, Germany
Nils Jansen	Radboud University Nijmegen, The Netherlands
Einar Broch Johnsen	University of Oslo, Norway
Leen Lambers	Hasso-Plattner-Institut, Universität Potsdam, Germany
Yi Li	Nanyang Technological University, Singapore
Stefan Mitsch	Carnegie Mellon University, USA
Martin R. Neuhäußer	Siemens AG, Germany
Ajitha Rajan	University of Edinburgh, UK
Augusto Sampaio	Federal University of Pernambuco, Brazil
Perdita Stevens	University of Edinburgh, UK
Daniel Strüber	Radboud University Nijmegen, The Netherlands
Gabriele Taentzer	Philipps-Universität Marburg, Germany

Silvia Lizeth Tapia Tarifa	University of Oslo, Norway
Daniel Varró	McGill University, Canada
Heike Wehrheim	University of Paderborn, Germany
Anton Wijs	Eindhoven University of Technology, The Netherlands
Manuel Wimmer	Johannes Kepler University Linz, Austria
Tao Yue	Simula Research Laboratory, Norway
Steffen Zschaler	King's College London, UK

Test-Comp – Program Committee and Jury

Dirk Beyer (Chair)	LMU Munich, Germany
Gidon Ernst (Representing CMA-ES Fuzz)	LMU Munich, Germany
Marie-Christine Jakobs (Representing CoVeriTest)	TU Darmstadt, Germany
Kaled Alshmrany (Representing FuSeBMC)	U. of Manchester, UK
Sebastian Ruland (Representing HybridTiger)	TU Darmstadt, Germany
Martin Nowack (Representing KLEE)	Imperial College London, UK
Dongge Liu (Representing Legion)	U. of Melbourne, Australia
Hoang M. Le (Representing LibKluzzer)	U. of Bremen, Germany
Thomas Lemberger (Representing PRTest)	LMU Munich, Germany
Marek Chalupa (Representing Symbiotic)	Masaryk U., Czechia
Joxan Jaffar (Representing TracerX)	National U. of Singapore, Singapore
Raveendra Kumar M. (Representing VeriFuzz)	Tata Consultancy Service, India

Additional Reviewers

Antonino, Pedro
Babikian, Aren
Badings, Thom
Bubel, Richard
Búr, Márton
Cánovas Izquierdo, Javier Luis
Chang, Yun-Sheng

Clarisó, Robert
De Lara, Juan
Din, Crystal Chang
Du, Xiaoning
Gómez, Abel
Hajdu, Ákos
Haltermann, Jan

Kamburjan, Eduard
König, Jürgen
Lehner, Daniel
Lienhardt, Michael
Lin, Tzu Chi
Martens, Jan
Mey, Johannes
Morgenstern, Martin
Mukelabai, Mukelabai
Oliveira, Marcel Vinícius Medeiros
Oruc, Orcun
Osama, Muhammad
Pun, Violet Ka I.

Richter, Cedric
Sharma, Arnab
Steffen, Martin
Stolz, Volker
Suilen, Marnix
Szárnyas, Gábor
Tang, Yun
Tsai, Wei-Lun
Veeraragavan, Narasimha Raghavan
Waga, Masaki
Weinreich, Rainer
Wu, Xiuheng
Zhu, Chenguang

Contents

Test-Comp Contributions

FASE Contributions

On Benchmarking for
Concurrent Runtime Verification*

Luca Aceto[2,3] , Duncan Paul Attard[✉,1,2] ,
Adrian Francalanza[1] , and Anna Ingólfsdóttir[2]

[1] University of Malta, Msida, Malta {duncan.attard.01,afra1}@um.edu.mt
[2] Reykjavík University, Reykjavík, Iceland {luca,duncanpa17,annai}@ru.is
[3] Gran Sasso Science Institute, L'Aquila, Italy {luca.aceto}@gssi.it

Abstract. We present a synthetic benchmarking framework that targets the systematic evaluation of RV tools for message-based concurrent systems. Our tool can emulate various load profiles via configuration. It provides a multi-faceted view of measurements that is conducive to a comprehensive assessment of the overhead induced by runtime monitoring. The tool is able to generate significant loads to reveal edge case behaviour that may only emerge when the monitoring system is pushed to its limit. We evaluate our framework in two ways. First, we conduct sanity checks to assess the precision of the measurement mechanisms used, the repeatability of the results obtained, and the veracity of the behaviour emulated by our synthetic benchmark. We then showcase the utility of the features offered by our tool in a two-part RV case study.

Keywords: Runtime verification · Synthetic benchmarking · Software performance evaluation · Concurrent systems

1 Introduction

Large-scale software design has shifted from the classic monolithic architecture to one where applications are structured in terms of independently-executing asynchronous components [17]. This shift poses new challenges to the validation of such systems. Runtime Verification (RV) [9,27] is a *post-deployment* technique that is used to complement other methods such as testing [46] to assess the *functional* (*e.g.* correctness) and *non-functional* (*e.g.* quality of service) aspects of concurrent software. RV relies on instrumenting the system to be analysed with monitors, which inevitably introduce *runtime overhead* that should be kept minimal [9]. While the worst-case complexity bounds for monitor-induced overheads can be calculated via standard methods (see, *e.g.* [40,14,1,28]), *benchmarking* is, by far, the preferred method for assessing these overheads [9,27]. One reason for

* Supported by the doctoral student grant (No: 207055-051) and the TheoFoMon project (No: 163406-051) under the Icelandic Research Fund, the BehAPI project funded by the EU H2020 RISE under the Marie Skłodowska-Curie action (No: 778233), the ENDEAVOUR Scholarship Scheme (Group B, national funds), and the MIUR project PRIN 2017FTXR7S IT MATTERS.

E. Guerra and M. Stoelinga (Eds.): FASE 2021, LNCS 12649, pp. 3–23, 2021.
https://doi.org/10.1007/978-3-030-71500-7_1

this choice is that benchmarks tend to be more *representative* of the overhead observed in practice [30,15]. Benchmarks also provide a *common platform* for gauging workloads, making it possible to *compare* different RV tool implementations, or rerun experiments to *reproduce* and *confirm* existing results.

The utility of a benchmarking tool typically rests on two aspects: *(i)* the *coverage* of scenarios of interest, and *(ii)* the quality of *runtime metrics* collected by the benchmark harness. To represent scenarios of interest, benchmarking tools generally employ suites of third-party *off-the-shelf (OTS) programs* (*e.g.* [60,11,59]). OTS software is appealing because it is readily usable and inherently provides realistic scenarios. By and large, benchmarks rely on a range of OTS programs to broaden the coverage of real-world scenarios (*e.g.* DaCapo [11] uses 11 open-source libraries). Yet, using OTS programs as benchmarks poses challenges. By design, these programs do *not* expose hooks that enable harnesses to easily and accurately gather the runtime metrics of interest. When OTS software is treated as a black box, benchmarks become harder to control, impacting their ability to produce repeatable results. OTS software-based benchmarks are also limited when inducing specific edge cases—this aspect is critical when assessing the safety of software, such as runtime monitors, that are often assumed to be *dependable*. Custom-built *synthetic programs* (*e.g.* [35]) are an alternative way to perform benchmarking. These tend to be less popular due to the perceived drawbacks associated with developing such programs from scratch, and the lack of 'real-world' behaviour intrinsic to benchmarks based on OTS software. However, synthetic benchmarks offer benefits that offset these drawbacks. For example, *specialised* hooks can be built into the synthetic set-up to collect a broad range of runtime metrics. Moreover, synthetic benchmarks can also be *parametrised* to emulate variations on the same core benchmark behaviour; this is usually harder to achieve via OTS programs that implement narrow use cases.

Established benchmarking tools such as SPECjvm2008 [60], DaCapo [11], ScalaBench [59] and Savina [35]—developed for the JVM—feature extensively in the RV literature, *e.g.* see [48,19,18,54,13,45]. Apart from [45], these works assess the runtime overhead solely in terms of the *execution slowdown*, *i.e.,* the difference in running time between the system fitted with and without monitors. Recently, the International RV competition (CRV) [8] advocated for other metrics, such as *memory consumption*, to give a more qualitative view of runtime overhead. We hold that RV set-ups that target concurrency benefit from other facets of runtime behaviour, such as the *response time*, that captures the overhead between communicating components. Tangibly, this metric reflects the *perceived reactiveness* from an end-user standpoint (*e.g.* interactive apps) [50,61,58,21]; more generally, it describes the *service degradation* that must be accounted for to ensure adequate quality of service [15,39]. Arguably, benchmarking tools like the ones above (*e.g.* Savina) should provide even more. Often, RV set-ups for concurrent systems *need* to scale in response to dynamic changes, and the capacity for a benchmark to emulate *high loads* cannot be overstated. In actual fact, these loads are known to assume characteristic *profiles* (*e.g.* spikes or uniform rates), which are hard to administer with the benchmarks mentioned earlier.

The state of the art in benchmarking for concurrent RV suffers from another issue. Existing benchmarks—conceived for validating other tools—are repurposed for RV and often *fail* to cater for concurrent scenarios where RV is realistically put to use. SPECjvm2008, DaCapo, and ScalaBench lack workloads that leverage the JVM concurrency primitives [52]; meanwhile, [12] shows that the Savina microbenchmarks are essentially sequential, and that the rest of the programs in the suite are sufficiently simple to be regarded as microbenchmarks too. The CRV suite mostly targets *monolithic* software with limited concurrency, where the potential for scaling up to high loads is, therefore, severely curbed.

This paper presents a benchmarking framework for evaluating *runtime monitoring* tools written for verification purposes. Our tool focusses on component systems for asynchronous message-passing concurrency. It generates synthetic system models following the *master-slave* architecture [61]. The master-slave architecture is pervasive in distributed (*e.g.* DNS, IoT) and concurrent (*e.g.* web servers, thread pools) systems [61,29], and lies at the core of the MapReduce model [22] supported by Big Data frameworks such as Hadoop [63]. This justifies our aim to build a benchmarking tool targeting this architecture. Concretely:

- We detail the design of a *configurable benchmark* that emulates various master-slave models under commonly-observed load profiles, and gathers different metrics that give a *multi-faceted* view of runtime overhead, Sec. 2.
- We demonstrate that our synthetic benchmarks can be engineered to approximate the *realistic behaviour* of web server traffic with high degrees of precision and repeatability, Sec. 3.1.
- We present a case study that *(i)* shows how the load profiles and parametrisability of our benchmarks can produce edge cases that can be measured through our performance metrics to asses runtime monitoring tools in a *comprehensive* manner, and *(ii)* confirms that the results from *(i)* coincide with those obtained via a real-world use case using OTS software, Sec. 3.2.

2 Benchmark Design and Implementation

Our set-up can emulate a range of system models and subject them to various load types. We consider master-slave architectures, where one central process, called the *master*, creates and allocates tasks to *slave* processes [61]. Slaves work concurrently on tasks, relaying the result to the master when ready; the latter then combines these results to yield the final output. Our slaves are an *abstraction* of sets of cooperating processes that can be treated as a single unit.

2.1 Approach

We target concurrent applications that execute on a single node. Nevertheless, our design adheres to three criteria that facilitate its extension to a distributed setting. Specifically, components: *(i)* share neither a common clock, *(ii)* nor memory, and *(iii)* communicate via asynchronous messages. Our present set-up assumes that communication is reliable and components do not fail.

Load generation. Load on the system is induced by the master when it creates slave processes and allocates *tasks*. The total number of slaves in one run can be set via the parameter n. Tasks are allocated to slave processes by the master, and consist of one or more *work requests* that a slave receives, handles, and relays back. A slave terminates its execution when all of its allocated work requests have been processed *and* acknowledged by the master. The number of work requests that *can* be batched in a task is controlled by the parameter w; the *actual* batch size per slave is then drawn randomly from a normal distribution with mean $\mu = w$ and standard deviation $\sigma = \mu \times 0.02$. This induces a degree of variability in the amount of work requests exchanged between master and slaves. The master and slaves communicate *asynchronously*: an allocated work request is delivered to a slave process' incoming work queue where it is eventually handled. Work responses issued by a slave are queued and processed similarly on the master.

Load configuration. We consider *three load profiles* (see fig. 3 for examples) that determine how the creation of slaves is distributed along the load timeline t. The timeline is modelled as a sequence of *discrete logical time units* representing instants at which a new set of slaves is created by the master. *Steady* loads replicate executions where a system operates under stable conditions. These are modelled on a homogeneous Poisson distribution with *rate* λ, specifying the mean number of slaves that are created at each time instant along the load timeline with duration $t = \lceil n/\lambda \rceil$. *Pulse* loads emulate settings where a system experiences gradually increasing load peaks. The Pulse load shape is parametrised by t and the *spread*, s, that controls how slowly or sharply the system load increases as it approaches its maximum peak, halfway along t. Pulses are modelled on a normal distribution with $\mu = t/2$ and $\sigma = s$. *Burst* loads capture scenarios where a system is stressed due to load spikes; these are based on a log-normal distribution with $\mu = \ln(m^2/\sqrt{p^2 + m^2})$ and $\sigma = \sqrt{\ln(1 + p^2/m^2)}$, where $m = t/2$, and parameter p is the *pinch* controlling the concentration of the initial load burst.

Wall-clock time. A load profile created for a logical timeline t is put into effect by the master process when the system starts running. The master *does not* create the slave processes that are set to execute in a particular time unit *in one go*, since this naïve strategy risks saturating the system, deceivingly increasing the load. In doing so, the system may become overloaded not because the mean request rate is high, but because the created slaves overwhelm the master when they send their requests all at once. We address this issue by introducing the notion of *concrete time* that maps one discrete time unit in t to a real time *period*, π. The parameter π is given in milliseconds (ms), and defaults to 1000 ms.

Slave scheduling. The master process employs a scheduling scheme to distribute the creation of slaves uniformly across the time period π. It makes use of three queues: the *Order* queue, *Ready* queue, and *Await* queue, denoted by Q_O, Q_R, and Q_A respectively. Q_O is initially populated with the load profile, step ① in fig. 1a. The load profile consists of an array with t elements—each corresponding to a discrete time instant in t—where the value l of every element indicates the number of slaves to be created at that instant. Slaves, $S_1, S_2, ..., S_n$, are scheduled and created in *rounds*, as follows. The master picks the first element from Q_O

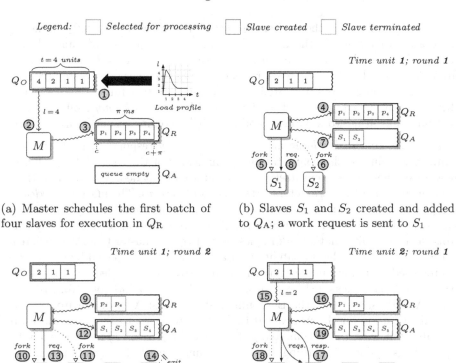

Fig. 1: Master M scheduling slave processes S_j and allocating work requests

to compute the upcoming schedule, step ②, that starts at the *current* time, c, and finishes at $c+\pi$. A series of l time points, $p_1, p_2, ..., p_l$, in the schedule period π are *cumulatively* calculated by drawing the next p_i from a normal distribution with $\mu = \lceil \pi/l \rceil$ and $\sigma = \mu \times 0.1$. Each time point stipulates a moment in *wall-clock* time when a new slave S_j is to be created; this set of time points is *monotonic*, and constitutes the Ready queue, Q_R, step ③. The master checks Q_R, step ④ in fig. 1b, and creates the slaves whose time point p_i is smaller than or equal to the current wall-clock time[4], steps ⑤ and ⑥ in fig. 1b. The time point p_i of a newly-created slave is removed from Q_O, and an entry for the corresponding slave S_j is appended to the Await queue Q_A; this is shown in step ⑦ for S_1 and S_2. Slaves in Q_A are now ready to receive work requests from the master process, *e.g.* step ⑧. Q_A is traversed by the master at this stage so that work requests can be allocated to existing slaves. The master continues processing queue Q_R in subsequent rounds, creating slaves, issuing work requests, and updating Q_R and Q_A accordingly as shown in steps ⑨–⑬

---

[4] We assume that the platform scheduling the master and slave processes is *fair*.

in fig. 1c. At any point, the master can receive responses, *e.g.* step ⑰ in fig. 1d; these are *buffered* inside the masters' incoming work queue and handled once the scheduling and work allocation phases are complete. A *fresh* batch of slaves from Q_O is scheduled by the master whenever Q_R becomes empty, step ⑮, and the described procedure is repeated. The master stops scheduling slaves when all the entries in Q_O are processed. It then transitions to *work-only* mode, where it continues allocating work requests and handling incoming responses from slaves.

Reactiveness and task allocation. Systems generally respond to load with differing rates, due to the computational complexity of the task at hand, IO, or slowdown when the system itself becomes gradually loaded. We simulate these phenomena using the parameters $\Pr(send)$ and $\Pr(recv)$. The master *interleaves* the processing of work requests to allocate them uniformly among the various slaves: $\Pr(send)$ and $\Pr(recv)$ bias this behaviour. Specifically, $\Pr(send)$ controls the probability that a work request is sent by the master to a slave, whereas $\Pr(recv)$ determines the probability that a work response received by the master is processed. Sending and receiving is *turn-based* and modelled on a Bernoulli trial. The master picks a slave S_j from Q_A and sends *at least* one work request when $X \leq \Pr(send)$, *i.e.*, the Bernoulli trial succeeds; X is drawn from a uniform distribution on the interval $[0,1]$. Further requests to the *same* slave are allocated following this scheme (steps ⑧, ⑬ and ⑳ in fig. 1) and the entry for S_j in Q_A is updated accordingly with the number of work requests remaining. When $X > \Pr(send)$, *i.e.*, the Bernoulli trial fails, the slave misses its turn, and the next slave in Q_A is picked. The master also queries its incoming work queue to determine whether a response can be processed. It dequeues one response when $X \leq \Pr(recv)$, and the attempt is repeated for the next response in the queue until $X > \Pr(recv)$. The master signals slaves to terminate once it acknowledges all of their work responses (*e.g.* step ⑭). Due to the load imbalance that may occur when the master becomes overloaded with work responses relayed by slaves, dequeuing is repeated $|Q_A|$ times. This encourages an even load distribution in the system as the number of slaves *fluctuates* at runtime.

2.2   Realisability

The set-up detailed in sec. 2.1 is easily translatable to the actor model of computation [2]. In this model, the basic units of decomposition are *actors*: concurrent entities that do not share mutable memory with other actors. Instead, they interact via *asynchronous messaging*. Each actor owns an incoming message buffer called the *mailbox*. Besides sending and receiving messages, an actor can also *fork* other child actors. Actors are uniquely addressable via a dynamically-assigned *identifier*, often referred to as the PID. Actor frameworks such as Erlang [16], Akka [55] for Scala [51], and Thespian [53] for Python [44] implement actors as *lightweight* processes to enable highly-scalable architectures that span multiple machines. The terms *actor* and *process* are used interchangeably henceforth.

Implementation. We use Erlang to implement the set-up of sec. 2.1. Our implementation maps the master and slave processes to actors, where slaves are forked by the master via the Erlang function `spawn()`; in Akka and Thespian `ActorContext.spawn()` and `Actor.createActor()` can be respectively used to the same effect. The work request queues for both master and slave processes coincide with actor mailboxes. We abstract the task computation and model work requests as Erlang messages. Slaves emulate no delay, but respond instantly to work requests once these have been processed; delay in the system can be induced via parameters $\Pr(send)$ and $\Pr(recv)$. To maximise efficiency, the Order, Ready and Await queues used by our scheduling scheme are maintained *locally* within the master. The master process keeps track of other details, such as the total number of work requests sent and received, to determine when the system should stop executing. We extend the parameters in sec. 2.1 with a *seed* parameter, r, to fix the Erlang pseudorandom number generator to output reproducible number sequences.

2.3   Measurement Collection

To give a multi-faceted view of runtime overhead, we extend the approach in [8] and, apart from the *(i)* mean *execution duration*, measured in seconds (s), we also collect the *(ii)* mean *scheduler utilisation*, as a percentage of the total available capacity, *(iii)* mean *memory consumption*, measured in GB, and, *(iv)* mean *response time (RT)*, measured in milliseconds (ms). Our definition of runtime overhead encompasses all four metrics. Measurement taking largely depends on the platform on which the benchmark executes, and one often leverages *platform-specific* optimised functionality in order to attain high levels of efficiency. Our implementation relies on the functionality provided by the Erlang ecosystem.

Sampling. We collect measurements centrally using a special process, called the *Collector*, that samples the runtime to obtain periodic snapshots of the execution environment (see fig. 2). Sampling is often necessary to induce low overhead in the system, especially in scenarios where the system components are sensitive to latency [32]. Our sampling frequency is set to 500 ms: this figure was determined empirically, whereby the measurements gathered are neither too coarse, nor excessively fine-grained such that sampling affects the runtime. Every sampling snapshot combines the four metrics mentioned above and formats them as records that are written *asynchronously* to disk to minimise IO delays.

Performance metrics. Memory and scheduler readings are gathered via the Erlang Virtual Machine (EVM). We sample scheduler—rather than CPU utilisation at the OS-level—since the EVM keeps scheduler threads momentarily spinning to remain reactive; this would inflate the metric reading. The overall system responsiveness is captured by the mean RT metric. Our Collector exposes a hook that the master uses to obtain *unique timestamps*, step ① in fig. 2. These are embedded in all work request messages the master issues to slaves. Each timestamp enables the Collector to track the time taken for a message to travel from the master to a slave and back, *including* the time it spends in the master's mailbox until dequeued, *i.e.*, the round-trip in steps ②–⑤. To efficiently compute the RT, the Collector samples the total number of messages exchanged between the master and slaves, and calculates the mean using Welford's online algorithm [62].

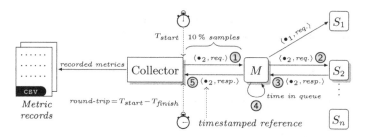

Fig. 2: Collector tracking the round-trip time for work requests and responses

3   Evaluation

We evaluate our synthetic benchmarking tool developed as described in Sec. 2 in a number of ways. In sec. 3.1, we discuss sanity checks for its measurement collection mechanisms, and assess the repeatability of the results obtained from the synthetic system executions. Crucially, sec. 3.1 provides evidence that the benchmarking tool is sufficiently expressive to cover a number of execution pro- files that are shown to emulate realistic scenarios. Sec. 3.2 demonstrates the utility of the features offered by our tool for the purposes of assessing RV tools.

Experiment set-up. We define an *experiment* to consist of ten benchmarks, each performed by running the system set-up with incremental loads. Our experiments were performed on an Intel Core i7 M620 64-bit machine with 8GB of memory, running Ubuntu 18.04 LTS and Erlang/OTP 22.2.1.

3.1   Benchmark Expressiveness and Veracity

The parameters for the tool detailed in sec. 2.1 can be configured to model a range of master-slave scenarios. However, not all of these configurations are meaningful in practice. For example, setting $\Pr(send) = 0$ does not enable the master to allocate work requests to slaves; with $\Pr(send) = 1$, this allocation is enacted sequentially, defeating the purpose of a concurrent master-slave system. In this section, we establish a set of parameter values that model experiment set- ups whose behaviour *approximates* that of master-slave systems typically found in practice. Our experiments are conducted with $n=500k$ slaves and $w=100$ work requests per slave. This generates $\approx n \times w \times$ (work requests and responses)=100M message exchanges between the master and slaves. We initially fix $\Pr(send) = \Pr(recv)=0.9$, and choose a Steady (*i.e.,* Poisson process) load profile since this features in industry-strength load testing tools such as Tsung [49] and JMeter [3]. Fig. 3 shows the load applied at each benchmark run, *e.g.* on the tenth run, the benchmark uses $\approx 5k$ slaves/s. The total loading time is set to $t = 100s$.

Measurement precision. A series of trials were conducted to select the appro- priate sampling window size for the RT. This step is crucial because it directly affects the capability of the benchmark to scale in terms of its number of slave processes and work requests. Our RT sampling of sec. 2.3 (see also fig. 2) was calibrated by taking various window sizes over numerous runs for different load profiles of $\approx 1\,\mathrm{M}$ slaves. The results were compared to the *actual* mean calculated on *all* work request and response messages exchanged between master and slaves. Window sizes close to $10\,\%$ yielded the best results ($\approx \pm 1.4\,\%$ discrepancy from the actual RT). Smaller window sizes produced excessive discrepancy; larger sizes induced noticeably higher system loads. We also cross-checked the precision of our sampling method of the scheduler utilisation against readings obtained via the Erlang Observer tool [16] to confirm that these coincide.

Experiment repeatability. Data variability affects the *repeatability* of experiments. It also plays a role when determining the number of repeated readings, k, required before the data measured is deemed *sufficiently representative*. Choosing the lowest k is crucial when experiment runs are time consuming. The *coefficient of variation* (CV)—*i.e.*, the ratio of the standard deviation to the mean, $\mathrm{CV} = \frac{\sigma}{\bar{x}} \times 100$—can be used to establish the value of k empirically, as follows. Initially, the CV_k for one batch of experiments for some number of repetitions k is calculated. The result is then compared to the $\mathrm{CV}_{k'}$ for the next batch of repetitions $k' = k + b$, where b is the step size. When the difference between successive CV metrics k' and k is sufficiently small (for some percentage ϵ), the value of k is chosen, otherwise the described procedure is repeated with k'. Crucially, this condition must hold for *all variables* measured in the experiment before k can be fixed. For the results presented next, the CV values were calculated manually. The mechanism that determines the CV automatically is left for future work.

Data variability. The data variability between experiments can be reduced by seeding the Erlang pseudorandom number generator (parameter r in sec. 2.2) with a constant value. This, in turn, tends to require fewer repeated runs before the metrics of interest—scheduler utilisation, memory consumption, RT, and execution duration—converge to an acceptable CV. We conduct experiment sets with three, six and nine repetitions. For the majority of cases, the CV for our metrics is *lower* when a fixed seed is used, by comparison to its unseeded counterpart. In fact, very low CV values for the scheduler utilisation, memory consumption, RT, and execution duration, $0.17\,\%$, $0.15\,\%$, $0.52\,\%$ and $0.47\,\%$ respectively, were obtained with three repeated runs. We thus set the number of repetitions to *three* for *all* experiment runs in the sequel. Note that fixing the seed *still* permits the system to exhibit a modicum of variability that stems from the inherent *interleaved execution* of components due to process scheduling.

Load profiles. Our tool is expressive enough to generate the load profiles introduced in sec. 2.1 (see fig. 3), enabling us to gauge the behaviour of monitoring set-ups under varying forms of loads. These loads make it possible to mock specific system scenarios that test different implementation aspects. For example, a benchmark configured with load surges could uncover buffer overflows in a particular monitoring implementation that only arise under stress when the length of the request queue exceeds some preset length.

System reactivity. The reactivity of the master-slave system correlates with the idle time of each slave which, in turn, affects the capacity of the system to *absorb*

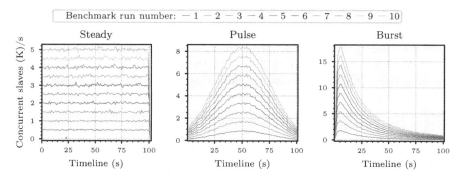

Fig. 3: Steady, Pulse and Burst load distributions of 500 k slaves for 100 s

overheads. Since this can skew the results obtained when assessing overheads, it is imperative that the benchmarking tool provides methods to control this aspect. The parameters $\Pr(send)$ and $\Pr(recv)$ regulate the speed with which the system reacts to load. We study how these parameters affect the overall performance of system models set up with $\Pr(send) = \Pr(recv) \in \{0.1, 0.5, 0.9\}$. The results are shown in fig. 4, where each metric (*e.g.* memory consumption) is plotted against the total number of slaves. At $\Pr(send) = \Pr(recv) = 0.1$, the system has the lowest RT out of the three configurations (bottom left), as indicated by the gentle linear increase of the plot. One may expect the RT to be *lower* for the system models configured with probability values of 0.5 and 0.9. However, we recall that with $\Pr(send) = 0.1$, work requests are allocated infrequently by the master, so that slaves are *often idle*, and can *readily* respond to (low numbers of) incoming work requests. At the same time, this prolongs the execution duration, when compared to that of the system set with $\Pr(send) = \Pr(recv) \in \{0.5, 0.9\}$ (bottom right). This effect of slave idling can be gleaned from the relatively lower scheduler utilisation as well (top left). Idling increases memory consumption (top right), since slaves created by the master typically remain alive for extended periods. By contrast, the plots set with $\Pr(send) = \Pr(recv) \in \{0.5, 0.9\}$ exhibit markedly gentler gradients in the memory consumption and execution duration charts; corresponding linear slopes can be observed in the RT chart. This indicates that values between 0.5 and 0.9 yield system models that: *(i)* consume reasonable amounts of memory, *(ii)* execute in respectable amounts of time, and *(iii)* maintain tolerable RT. Since master-slave architectures are typically employed in settings where high throughput is demanded, choosing values smaller than 0.5 goes against this principle. In what follows, we opt for $\Pr(send) = \Pr(recv) = 0.9$.

Emulation veracity. Our benchmarks can be configured to closely model *realistic* web server traffic where the request intervals observed at the server are known to follow a Poisson process [31,43,37]. The probability distribution of the RT of web application requests is generally right-skewed, and approximates log-normal [31,20] or Erlang distributions [37]. We conduct three experiments using *Steady loads* fixed with $n = 10k$ for $\Pr(send) = \Pr(recv) \in \{0.1, 0.5, 0.9\}$ to

Fig. 4: Performance benchmarks of system models for Pr(*send*) and Pr(*recv*)

establish whether the RT in our system set-ups resembles the aforementioned distributions. Our results, summarised in fig. 5, were obtained by estimating the parameters for a set of candidate probability distributions (*e.g.* normal, log-normal, gamma, *etc.*) using maximum likelihood estimation [56] on the RT obtained from *each* experiment. We then performed goodness-of-fit tests on these parametrised distributions using the Kolmogorov-Smirnov test, selecting the most appropriate RT fit for each of the three experiments. The fitted distributions in fig. 5 indicate that the RT of our system models follows the findings reported in [31,20,37]. This makes a strong case in favour of our benchmarking tool striking a balance between the *realism* of benchmarks based on OTS programs and the *controllability* offered by synthetic benchmarking. Lastly, we point out that fig. 5 matches the observations made in fig. 4, which show an increase in the mean RT as the system becomes more reactive. This is evident in the histogram peaks that grow shorter as Pr(*send*) = Pr(*recv*) progresses from 0.1 to 0.9.

3.2   Case Study

We demonstrate how our benchmarking tool can be used to assess the runtime overhead comprehensively via a concurrent RV case study. By controlling the benchmark parameters and subjecting the system to specific workloads, we show that our multi-faceted view of overhead reveals nuances in the observed runtime behaviour, benefitting the interpretation of empirical results. We further assess the veracity of these synthetic benchmarks against the overhead measured from a use case that considers industry-strength OTS applications.

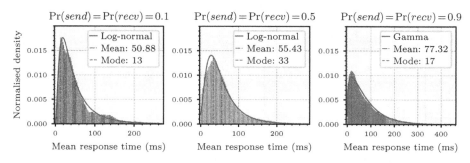

Fig. 5: Fitted probability distributions on RT for Steady loads for $n=10\text{k}$

The RV Tool We use a RV tool to objectively compare the conclusions derived from our synthetic benchmarks against those obtained from the experiment set up with the OTS applications. The tool under scrutiny targets concurrent Erlang programs [4]. It synthesises *automata-like* monitors from sHML specifications [26] and *inlines* them into the system via *code injection* by manipulating the program abstract syntax tree. Inline instrumentation underlies various other state-of-the-art RV tools, such as JavaMOP [36], MarQ [54], Java-MaC [38] and RiTHM [47]. sHML is a fragment of the Hennessy-Milner Logic with recursion [41] that can express all regular safety properties [26]. The tool augments it to handle pattern matching and data dependencies for three kinds of event patterns, namely *send* and *receive* actions, denoted by ! and ? respectively, and process *crash*, denoted by $\star$. This suffices to specify properties of both the master and slave processes, resulting in the set-up depicted in fig. 6a. For instance, the recursive property φ_{s} describes an *invariant* of the master-slave communication protocol (from the slave's point of view), stating that '*a slave processing integer successor requests should not crash*':

$$\max X.\Big(\overbrace{[\backslash Slv\star]\mathsf{ff}}^{①} \wedge \underbrace{\overbrace{[\backslash Slv?\backslash Req]}^{②.①}\big(\overbrace{[Slv\star]\mathsf{ff}}^{③.①}\wedge\overbrace{[Slv!(Req+1)]X}^{③.②}\big)}_{②}\Big) \qquad (\varphi_{\text{s}})$$

The key construct in sHML is the modal formula $[p]\varphi$, stating that *whenever* a satisfying system exhibits an event e matching pattern p, its continuation then satisfies φ. In property φ_{s}, the invariant—denoted by recursion binder $\max X$— asserts that a slave Slv does not crash, specified by sub-formula ①. It further stipulates in sub-formula ② that when a request-carrying payload, Req is received, ②.①, Slv cannot crash, ③.①, *and* if the slave replies to Req with the payload $Req+1$, the property *recurses* on variable X, ③.②. Action patterns use two types of value variables: binders, $\backslash x$, that are pattern-matched to concrete values learnt at runtime, and variable instances, x, that are bound by the respective binders and instantiated to concrete data via pattern matching at runtime. This induces the usual notion of free and bound value variables; we assume closed terms. For example, when checking property φ_s against the trace event pid?42, the analysis unfolds the sub-formula guarded by $\max X$, matching the event with the pattern $\backslash Slv?\backslash Req$ in (2.1). Variables Slv and Req are substituted with pid and 42 respectively in property φ_s, leaving the residual formula:

$$[\text{pid}\star]\textbf{ff} \wedge [\text{pid}!(42+1)]\max X. \begin{pmatrix} [\backslash Slv\star]\textbf{ff} \wedge \\ [\backslash Slv?\backslash Req]\big([Slv\star]\textbf{ff}\wedge[Slv!(Req+1)]X\big) \end{pmatrix}$$

The RV tool under scrutiny produces inlined monitor code that executes in the same process space of system components (see fig. 6a), yielding the lowest possible amount of runtime overhead. This enables us to scale our benchmarks to considerably high loads. Our experiments focus on correctness properties that are *parametric* w.r.t. to system components [7,19,54,48]: with this approach, monitors need not interact with one another and can reach verdicts independently. Verdicts are communicated by monitors to a central entity that records the expected number of verdicts in order to determine when the experiment can be stopped. The set of properties used in our benchmarks translate to monitors that loop continually to exert the maximum level of runtime overhead possible.

Fig. 6b shows the monitor synthesised from property φ_s, consisting of states Q_0, Q_1, the rejection state ✗, and inconclusive state ?. The rejection state corresponds to a *violation* of the property, *i.e.*, **ff**, whereas the *inconclusive* state is reached when the analysed trace events do not contain enough information to enable the monitor to transition to any other state. Both of these states are sinks, modelling the irrevocability of verdicts [24,26]. The modality $[\backslash Slv?\backslash Req]$ in property φ_s corresponds to the transition between Q_0 and Q_1 in fig. 6b. The monitor follows this transition when it analyses the trace event $\text{pid}_1?\text{d}_1$ exhibited by the slave with PID pid_1 when it receives data payload d_1 from the master; as a side effect, the transition binds the variable Slv to pid_1 and Req to d_1 in

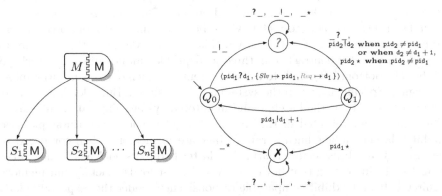

(a) Inlined runtime monitors   (b) Synthesised monitor from property φ_s

Fig. 6: Synthesised monitors instrumented with master and slave processes state Q_1. From Q_1, the monitor transitions to Q_0 only when the event $\texttt{pid}_1!\texttt{d}_2$ is analysed, where $\texttt{d}_2 = \texttt{d}_1 + 1$ and $\texttt{pid}_1$ is the slave PID (previously) bound to *Slv*. From Q_0 and Q_1, the rejection state ✗ can be reached when a crash event is analysed. In the case of Q_0, the transition to ✗ is followed for *any* crash event _⋆ (the wildcard _ denotes the *anonymous* variable). By contrast, the monitor reaches ✗ from Q_1 *only* when the slave with PID $\texttt{pid}_1$ crashes, otherwise it transitions to the inconclusive state ?. Other transitions from Q_0 and Q_1 leading to ? follow a similar reasoning. Interested readers are encouraged to consult [25,6,5] for more information on the specification logic and monitor synthesis.

Synthetic Benchmarks We set the total number of slaves to $n = 20\text{k}$ for *moderate* loads and $n = 500\text{k}$ for *high* loads; $\Pr(send) = \Pr(recv)$ is fixed at 0.9 as in sec. 3.1. These configurations generate $\approx n \times w \times$ (work requests and responses) = 4M and 100M messages respectively to produce 8M and 200M analysable trace events per run. The pseudorandom number generator is seeded with a constant value and three experiment repetitions are performed for the Steady, Pulse and Burst load profiles (see fig. 3). A loading time of $t = 100\text{s}$ is used. Our results are summarised in figs. 7 and 8. Each chart in these figures plots the particular performance metric (*e.g.* memory consumption) for the system without monitors, *i.e.*, the *baseline*, together with the overhead induced by the RV monitors.

Moderate loads. Fig. 7 shows the plots for the system set with $n = 20\text{k}$. These loads are similar to those employed by the state-of-the-art frameworks to evaluate component-based runtime monitoring, *e.g.* [57,7,10,23,48] (ours are slightly higher). We remark that none of the benchmarks used in these works consider different load profiles: they either model load on a Poisson process, or fail to specify the kind of load used. In fig. 7, the execution duration chart (bottom right) shows that, regardless of the load profile used, the running time of each experiment is comparable to the baseline. With the moderate size of 20k slaves, the execution duration on its own does not give a detailed enough view of runtime overhead, despite the fact that our benchmarks provide a broad coverage in terms of the Steady, Pulse and Burst load profiles. This trend is mirrored in the scheduler utilisation plot (top left), where both baseline and monitored system induce a constant load of $\approx 17.5\%$. On this account, we deem these results to be *inconclusive*. By contrast, our three load profiles induce different overhead for the RT (bottom left), and, to a lesser extent, the memory consumption plots (top right). Specifically, when the system is subjected to a Burst load, it exhibits a surge in the RT for the baseline and monitored system alike, at $\approx 16\text{k}$ slaves. While this is not reflected in the consumption of memory, the Burst plots do exhibit a larger—albeit linear—rate of increase in memory when compared to their Steady and Pulse counterparts. The latter two plots once again show analogous trends, indicating that both Steady and Pulse loads exact similar memory requirements and exhibit comparable responsiveness under the respectable load of 20k slaves. Crucially, the data plots in fig. 7 *do not* enable us to confidently extrapolate our results. The edge case in the RT chart for Burst plots raises the question of whether the surge in the trend observed at $\approx 16\text{k}$ remains consistent

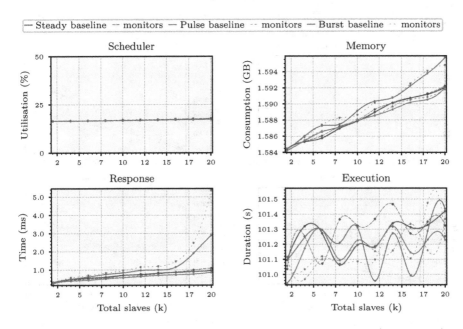

Fig. 7: Mean runtime overhead for master and slave processes (20 k slaves)

when the number of slaves goes beyond 20k. Similarly, although for a different reason, the execution duration plots do not allow us to distinguish between the overhead induced by monitors for different loads on this small scale—this occurs due to the *perturbations* introduced by the underlying OS (*e.g.* scheduling other processes, IO, *etc.*) that affect the sensitive time keeping of benchmarks.

High loads. We increase the load to $n = 500$k slaves to determine whether our benchmark set-up can adequately scale, and show how the monitored system performs under stress. The RT chart in fig. 8 indicates that for Burst loads (bottom left), the overhead induced by monitors *grows linearly* in the number of slaves. This contradicts the results in fig. 7, confirming our supposition that moderate loads may provide scant empirical evidence to extrapolate to general conclusions. However, the memory consumption for Burst loads (top right) exhibits similar trends to the ones in fig. 7. Subjecting the system to high loads renders discernible the discrepancy between the RT and memory consumption gradients for the Steady and Pulse plots that appeared to be similar under the moderate loads of 20k slaves. Considering the execution duration chart (bottom right of fig. 8) as the *sole* indicator of overhead could *deceivingly suggest* that runtime monitoring induces virtually identical overhead for the distinct load profiles of fig. 3. However, this erroneous observation is easily refuted by the memory consumption and RT plots that show otherwise. This stresses the merit of gathering multi-faceted metrics to assist in the interpretation of runtime overhead.

We extend the argument for multi-faceted views to the scheduler utilisation metric in fig. 8 that reveals a subtle aspect of our concurrent set-up. Specifically,

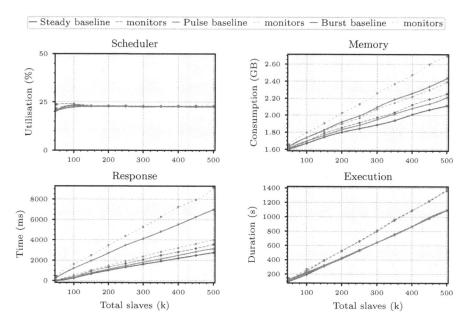

Fig. 8: Mean runtime overhead for master and slave processes (500 k slaves)

the charts show that while the execution duration, RT and memory consumption plots grow in the number of slave processes, scheduler utilisation stabilises at ≈ 22.7%. This is partly caused by the master-slave design that becomes susceptible to bottlenecks when the master is overloaded with requests [61]. In addition, the preemptive scheduling of the EVM [16] ensures that the master *shares* the computational resources of the same machine with the rest of the slaves. We conjecture that, in a distributed set-up where the master resides on a *dedicated* node, the overall system throughput may be further pushed. Fig. 8 also attests to the utility of having a benchmarking framework that scales considerably well to increase the chances of detecting potential trends. For instance, the evidence gathered earlier in fig. 7 could have misled one to assert that the RV tool under scrutiny scales poorly under Burst loads of moderate and larger sizes.

An OTS Application Use Case We evaluate the overheads induced by the RV tool under scrutiny using a third-party industry-strength web server called Cowboy [33], and show that the conclusions we draw are *in line* with those reported earlier for our synthetic benchmark results. Cowboy is written in Erlang and built on top of Ranch [34]—a socket acceptor pool for TCP protocols that can be used to develop custom network applications. Cowboy relies on Ranch to manage its socket connections, but delegates HTTP client requests to *protocol handlers* that are forked dynamically by the web server to handle each request independently. This architecture follows closely our master-slave set-up of sec. 2.1 which abstracts details such as TCP connection management and

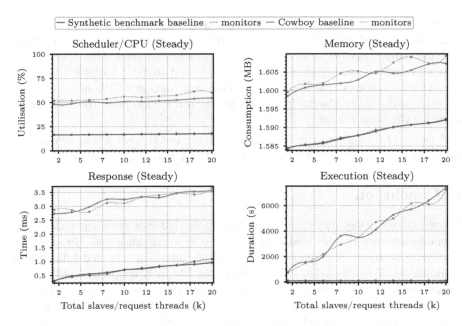

Fig. 9: Mean overhead for synthetic and Cowboy benchmarks (20 k threads)

HTTP protocol parsing. We generate load on Cowboy using the popular stress testing tool JMeter [3] to issue HTTP requests from a dedicated machine residing on the same network where Cowboy is hosted. The latter machine is the one used in the experiments discussed earlier. To emulate the typical behaviour of web clients (*e.g.* browsers) that fetch resources via multiple HTTP requests, our Cowboy application serves files of various sizes that are randomly accessed by JMeter during the benchmark. In our experiments, we monitored fragments of the Cowboy and Ranch communication protocol used to handle client requests.

Moderate loads. Fig. 9 plots our results for *Steady* loads from fig. 7, together with the ones obtained from the Cowboy benchmarks; JMeter did not enable us to reproduce the Pulse and Burst load profiles. For our Cowboy benchmarks, we fixed the total number of JMeter request threads to 20 k over the span of 100s, where each thread issued 100 HTTP requests. This configuration coincides with parameter settings used in the experiments of fig. 7. In fig. 9, the scheduler utilisation, memory consumption and RT charts (top, bottom left) show a correspondence between the baseline plots of our synthetic benchmarks and those taken with Cowboy and JMeter. This indicates that, for these metrics, our synthetic system model exhibits *analogous characteristics* to the ones of the OTS system, under the chosen load profile. The argument can be extended to the monitored versions of these systems which follow identical trends. We point out the similarity in the RT trends of our synthetic and Cowboy benchmarks, despite the fact that the latter set of experiments were conducted over a local network. This suggests that, for our single-machine configuration, the synthetic master-slave benchmarks manage to adequately capture local network conditions. The gaps separating the plots of the two experiment set-ups stem from the implementation specifics of Cowboy and our synthetic model. This discrepancy in measurements also depends on the method used to gather runtime metrics, *e.g.* JMeter cannot sample the EVM directly, and measures CPU as opposed to scheduler utilisation. The deviation in execution duration plots (bottom right) arises for the same reason.

High loads. Our efforts to run tests with 500k request threads where stymied by the scalability issues we experienced with Cowboy and JMeter on our set-up.

4   Conclusion

Concurrent RV necessitates benchmarking tools that can *scale dynamically* to accommodate considerable load sizes, and are able to provide a *multi-faceted view* of runtime overhead. This paper presents a benchmarking tool that fulfils these requirements. We demonstrate its implementability in Erlang, arguing that the design is easily instantiatable to other actor frameworks such as Akka and Thespian. Our set-up emulates various system models through configurable parameters, and scales to reveal behaviour that emerges only when software is pushed to its limit. The benchmark harness gathers different performance metrics, offering a multi-faceted view of runtime overhead that, to wit, other state-of-the-art tools do not currently offer. Our experiments demonstrate that these metrics benefit the interpretation of empirical measurements: they increase visibility that may spare one from drawing insufficiently general, or otherwise, erroneous conclusions. We establish that—despite its synthetic nature—our master-slave model faithfully approximates the mean response times observed in realistic web server traffic. We also compare the results of our synthetic benchmarks against those obtained from a real-world use case to confirm that our tool captures the behaviour of this realistic set-up. It is worth noting that, while our empirical measurements of secs. 3.1 and 3.2 depend on the implementation language, our conclusions are transferrable to other frameworks, *e.g.* Akka and Play [42].

Related work. There are other less popular benchmarks targeting the JVM besides those mentioned in sec. 1. Renaissance [52] employs workloads that leverage the concurrency primitives of the JVM, focussing on the performance of compiler optimisations similar to DaCapo and ScalaBench. These benchmarks gather metrics that measure software quality and complexity, as opposed to metrics that gauge runtime overhead. The CRV suite [8] aims to standardise the evaluation of RV tools, and mainly focusses on RV for monolithic programs. We are unaware of RV-centric benchmarks for concurrent systems such as ours. In [43], the authors propose a queueing model to analyse web server traffic, and develop a benchmarking tool to validate it. Their model coincides with our master-slave set-up, and considers loads based on a Poisson process. A study of message-passing communication on parallel computers conducted in [31] uses systems loaded with different numbers of processes; this is similar to our approach. Importantly, we were able to confirm the findings reported in [43] and [31] (sec. 3.1).

References

1. Aceto, L., Achilleos, A., Francalanza, A., Ingólfsdóttir, A., Kjartansson, S.Ö.: Determinizing Monitors for HML with Recursion. JLAMP **111**, 100515 (2020)
2. Agha, G., Mason, I.A., Smith, S.F., Talcott, C.L.: A Foundation for Actor Computation. JFP **7**(1), 1–72 (1997)
3. Apache Software Foundtation: Jmeter (2020), https://jmeter.apache.org
4. Attard, D.P.: detectEr (2020), https://github.com/duncanatt/detecter-inline
5. Attard, D.P., Cassar, I., Francalanza, A., Aceto, L., Ingólfsdóttir, A.: Introduction to Runtime Verification. In: Behavioural Types: from Theory to Tools, pp. 49–76. Automation, Control and Robotics, River (2017)
6. Attard, D.P., Francalanza, A.: A Monitoring Tool for a Branching-Time Logic. In: RV. LNCS, vol. 10012, pp. 473–481 (2016)
7. Attard, D.P., Francalanza, A.: Trace Partitioning and Local Monitoring for Asynchronous Components. In: SEFM. LNCS, vol. 10469, pp. 219–235 (2017)
8. Bartocci, E., Falcone, Y., Bonakdarpour, B., Colombo, C., Decker, N., Havelund, K., Joshi, Y., Klaedtke, F., Milewicz, R., Reger, G., Rosu, G., Signoles, J., Thoma, D., Zalinescu, E., Zhang, Y.: First International Competition on Runtime Verification: Rules, Benchmarks, Tools, and Final Results of CRV 2014. Int. J. Softw. Tools Technol. Transf. **21**(1), 31–70 (2019)
9. Bartocci, E., Falcone, Y., Francalanza, A., Reger, G.: Introduction to Runtime Verification. In: Lectures on RV, LNCS, vol. 10457, pp. 1–33. Springer (2018)
10. Berkovich, S., Bonakdarpour, B., Fischmeister, S.: Runtime Verification with Minimal Intrusion through Parallelism. FMSD **46**(3), 317–348 (2015)
11. Blackburn, S.M., Garner, R., Hoffmann, C., Khan, A.M., McKinley, K.S., Bentzur, R., Diwan, A., Feinberg, D., Frampton, D., Guyer, S.Z., Hirzel, M., Hosking, A.L., Jump, M., Lee, H.B., Moss, J.E.B., Phansalkar, A., Stefanovic, D., VanDrunen, T., von Dincklage, D., Wiedermann, B.: The DaCapo Benchmarks: Java Benchmarking Development and Analysis. In: OOPSLA. pp. 169–190 (2006)
12. Blessing, S., Fernandez-Reyes, K., Yang, A.M., Drossopoulou, S., Wrigstad, T.: Run, Actor, Run: Towards Cross-Actor Language Benchmarking. In: AGERE!@SPLASH. pp. 41–50 (2019)
13. Bodden, E., Hendren, L.J., Lam, P., Lhoták, O., Naeem, N.A.: Collaborative Runtime Verification with Tracematches. J. Log. Comput. **20**(3), 707–723 (2010)
14. Bonakdarpour, B., Finkbeiner, B.: The Complexity of Monitoring Hyperproperties. In: CSF. pp. 162–174 (2018)
15. Buyya, R., Broberg, J., Goscinski, A.M.: Cloud Computing: Principles and Paradigms. Wiley-Blackwell (2011)
16. Cesarini, F., Thompson, S.: Erlang Programming: A Concurrent Approach to Software Development. O'Reilly Media (2009)
17. Chappell, D.: Enterprise Service Bus: Theory in Practice. O'Reilly Media (2004)
18. Chen, F., Rosu, G.: Mop: An Efficient and Generic Runtime Verification Framework. In: OOPSLA. pp. 569–588 (2007)
19. Chen, F., Rosu, G.: Parametric Trace Slicing and Monitoring. In: TACAS. LNCS, vol. 5505, pp. 246–261 (2009)
20. Ciemiewicz, D.M.: What Do You mean? - Revisiting Statistics for Web Response Time Measurements. In: CMG. pp. 385–396 (2001)
21. Cornejo, O., Briola, D., Micucci, D., Mariani, L.: In the Field Monitoring of Interactive Application. In: ICSE-NIER. pp. 55–58 (2017)

22. Dean, J., Ghemawat, S.: MapReduce: Simplified Data Processing on Large Clusters. Commun. ACM **51**(1), 107–113 (2008)
23. El-Hokayem, A., Falcone, Y.: Monitoring Decentralized Specifications. In: ISSTA. pp. 125–135 (2017)
24. Francalanza, A.: A Theory of Monitors (Extended Abstract). In: FoSSaCS. LNCS, vol. 9634, pp. 145–161 (2016)
25. Francalanza, A., Aceto, L., Achilleos, A., Attard, D.P., Cassar, I., Della Monica, D., Ingólfsdóttir, A.: A Foundation for Runtime Monitoring. In: RV. LNCS, vol. 10548, pp. 8–29 (2017)
26. Francalanza, A., Aceto, L., Ingólfsdóttir, A.: Monitorability for the Hennessy-Milner Logic with Recursion. FMSD **51**(1), 87–116 (2017)
27. Francalanza, A., Pérez, J.A., Sánchez, C.: Runtime Verification for Decentralised and Distributed Systems. In: Lectures on RV, LNCS, vol. 10457, pp. 176–210. Springer (2018)
28. Francalanza, A., Xuereb, J.: On Implementing Symbolic Controllability. In: CO-ORDINATION. LNCS, vol. 12134, pp. 350–369 (2020)
29. Ghosh, S.: Distributed Systems: An Algorithmic Approach. CRC (2014)
30. Gray, J.: The Benchmark Handbook for Database and Transaction Processing Systems. Morgan Kaufmann (1993)
31. Grove, D.A., Coddington, P.D.: Analytical Models of Probability Distributions for MPI Point-to-Point Communication Times on Distributed Memory Parallel Computers. In: ICA3PP. LNCS, vol. 3719, pp. 406–415 (2005)
32. Harman, M., O'Hearn, P.W.: From Start-ups to Scale-ups: Opportunities and Open Problems for Static and Dynamic Program Analysis. In: SCAM. pp. 1–23 (2018)
33. Hoguin, L.: Cowboy (2020), `https://ninenines.eu`
34. Hoguin, L.: Ranch (2020), `https://ninenines.eu`
35. Imam, S.M., Sarkar, V.: Savina - An Actor Benchmark Suite: Enabling Empirical Evaluation of Actor Libraries. In: AGERE!@SPLASH. pp. 67–80 (2014)
36. Jin, D., Meredith, P.O., Lee, C., Rosu, G.: JavaMOP: Efficient Parametric Runtime Monitoring Framework. In: ICSE. pp. 1427–1430 (2012)
37. Kayser, B.: What is the expected distribution of website response times? (2017, last accessed, 19th Jan 2021), `https://blog.newrelic.com/engineering/expected-distributions-website-response-times`
38. Kim, M., Viswanathan, M., Kannan, S., Lee, I., Sokolsky, O.: Java-mac: A Run-Time Assurance Approach for Java Programs. FMSD **24**(2), 129–155 (2004)
39. Kshemkalyani, A.D.: Distributed Computing: Principles, Algorithms, and Systems. Cambridge University Press (2011)
40. Kuhtz, L., Finkbeiner, B.: LTL Path Checking is Efficiently Parallelizable. In: ICALP (2). LNCS, vol. 5556, pp. 235–246 (2009)
41. Larsen, K.G.: Proof Systems for Satisfiability in Hennessy-Milner Logic with Recursion. TCS **72**(2&3), 265–288 (1990)
42. Lightbend: Play framework (2020), `https://www.playframework.com`
43. Liu, Z., Niclausse, N., Jalpa-Villanueva, C.: Traffic Model and Performance Evaluation of Web Servers. Perform. Evaluation **46**(2-3), 77–100 (2001)
44. Matthes, E.: Python Crash Course: A Hands-On, Project-Based Introduction to Programming. No Starch Press (2019)
45. Meredith, P.O., Jin, D., Griffith, D., Chen, F., Rosu, G.: An Overview of the MOP Runtime Verification Framework. STTT **14**(3), 249–289 (2012)
46. Myers, G.J., Sandler, C., Badgett, T.: The Art of Software Testing. Wiley (2011)

47. Navabpour, S., Joshi, Y., Wu, C.W.W., Berkovich, S., Medhat, R., Bonakdarpour, B., Fischmeister, S.: RiTHM: A Tool for Enabling Time-Triggered Runtime Verification for C Programs. In: ESEC/SIGSOFT FSE. pp. 603–606. ACM (2013)
48. Neykova, R., Yoshida, N.: Let it Recover: Multiparty Protocol-Induced Recovery. In: CC. pp. 98–108 (2017)
49. Niclausse, N.: Tsung (2017), http://tsung.erlang-projects.org
50. Nielsen, J.: Usability Engineering. Morgan Kaufmann (1993)
51. Odersky, M., Spoon, L., Venners, B.: Programming in Scala. Artima Inc. (2020)
52. Prokopec, A., Rosà, A., Leopoldseder, D., Duboscq, G., Tuma, P., Studener, M., Bulej, L., Zheng, Y., Villazón, A., Simon, D., Würthinger, T., Binder, W.: Renaissance: Benchmarking Suite for Parallel Applications on the JVM. In: PLDI. pp. 31–47 (2019)
53. Quick, K.: Thespian (2020), http://thespianpy.com
54. Reger, G., Cruz, H.C., Rydeheard, D.E.: MarQ: Monitoring at Runtime with QEA. In: TACAS. LNCS, vol. 9035, pp. 596–610 (2015)
55. Roestenburg, R., Bakker, R., Williams, R.: Akka in Action. Manning (2015)
56. Rossi, R.J.: Mathematical Statistics: An Introduction to Likelihood Based Inference. Wiley (2018)
57. Scheffel, T., Schmitz, M.: Three-Valued Asynchronous Distributed Runtime Verification. In: MEMOCODE. pp. 52–61 (2014)
58. Seow, S.C.: Designing and Engineering Time: The Psychology of Time Perception in Software. Addison-Wesley (2008)
59. Sewe, A., Mezini, M., Sarimbekov, A., Binder, W.: DaCapo con Scala: design and analysis of a Scala benchmark suite for the JVM. In: OOPSLA. pp. 657–676 (2011)
60. SPEC: SPECjvm2008 (2008), https://www.spec.org/jvm2008
61. Tarkoma, S.: Overlay Networks: Toward Information Networking. Auerbach (2010)
62. Welford, B.P.: Note on a Method for Calculating Corrected Sums of Squares and Products. Technometrics **4**(3), 419–420 (1962)
63. White, T.: Hadoop: The Definitive Guide: Storage and Analysis at Internet Scale. O'Reilly Media (2015)

Certified Abstract Cost Analysis

Elvira Albert[1,2], Reiner Hähnle[3], Alicia Merayo[2](✉), and Dominic Steinhöfel[3,4]

[1] Instituto de Tecnología del Conocimiento, Madrid, Spain
[2] Complutense University of Madrid, Madrid, Spain. (✉ amerayo@ucm.es)
[3] Technische Universität Darmstadt, Darmstadt, Germany
[4] CISPA Helmholtz Center for Information Security, Saarbrücken, Germany

Abstract. A program containing placeholders for unspecified statements or expressions is called an abstract (or schematic) program. Placeholder symbols occur naturally in program transformation rules, as used in refactoring, compilation, optimization, or parallelization. We present a generalization of automated cost analysis that can handle abstract programs and, hence, can analyze the impact on the cost of program transformations. This kind of relational property requires provably precise cost bounds which are not always produced by cost analysis. Therefore, we certify by deductive verification that the inferred abstract cost bounds are correct and sufficiently precise. It is the first approach solving this problem. Both, abstract cost analysis and certification, are based on quantitative abstract execution (QAE) which in turn is a variation of abstract execution, a recently developed symbolic execution technique for abstract programs. To realize QAE the new concept of a cost invariant is introduced. QAE is implemented and runs fully automatically on a benchmark set consisting of representative optimization rules.

1 Introduction

We present a generalization of automated cost analysis that can handle programs containing placeholders for unspecified statements. Consider the program $Q \equiv$ "i = 0; **while** (i < t) {P; i ++;}", where P is any statement not modifying i or t. We call P an *abstract statement*; a program like Q containing abstract statements is called *abstract program*. The (exact or upper bound) cost of executing P is described by a function $\mathsf{ac_P}(\overline{x})$ depending on the variables $\overline{x}$ occurring in P. We call this function the *abstract cost* of P. Assuming that executing any statement has unit cost and that $t \geq 0$, one can compute the (abstract) cost of Q as $2 + t \cdot (\mathsf{ac_P}(\overline{x}) + 2)$ depending on $\mathsf{ac_P}$ and t. For any concrete instance of P, we can derive its concrete cost as usual and then obtain the concrete cost of Q simply by instantiating $\mathsf{ac_P}$. In this paper, we define and implement an abstract cost analysis to infer abstract cost bounds. Our implementation consists of an automatic abstract cost analysis tool and an automatic certifier for the correctness of inferred abstract bounds. Both steps are performed with an approach called *Quantitative Abstract Execution* (QAE).

Fine, but what is this good for? Abstract programs occur in program transformation rules used in compilation, optimization, parallelization, refactoring,

© The Author(s) 2021
E. Guerra and M. Stoelinga (Eds.): FASE 2021, LNCS 12649, pp. 24–45, 2021.
https://doi.org/10.1007/978-3-030-71500-7_2

etc.: Transformations are specified as rules over *program schemata* which are nothing but abstract programs. If we can perform cost analysis of abstract programs, we can *analyze the cost effect of program transformations*. Our approach is the *first method to analyze the cost impact of program transformations*.

Automated Cost Analysis. Cost analysis occupies an interesting middle ground between termination checking and full functional verification in the static program analysis portfolio. The main problem in functional verification is that one has to come up with a functional specification of the intended behavior, as well as with auxiliary specifications including loop invariants and contracts [21]. In contrast, termination is a generic property and it is sufficient to come up with a suitable term order or ranking function [6]. For many programs, termination analysis is vastly easier to automate than verification.[1]

Computation cost is not a generic property, but it is usually schematic: One fixes a class of cost functions (for example, polynomial) that can be handled. A cost analysis then must come up with parameters (degree, coefficients) that constitute a valid bound (lower, upper, exact) for all inputs of a given program with respect to a cost model (# of instructions, allocated memory, etc.). If this is performed bottom up with respect to a program's call graph, it is possible to *infer* a cost bound for the top-level function of a program. Such a cost expression is often *symbolic*, because it depends on the program's input parameters.

A central technique for inferring symbolic cost of a piece of code with high precision is *symbolic execution* (SE) [9, 25]. The main difficulty is to render SE of loops with symbolic bounds finite. This is achieved with *loop invariants* that generalize the behavior of a loop body: an invariant is valid at the loop head after arbitrarily many iterations. To infer sufficiently strong invariants automatically is generally an unsolved problem in functional verification, but much easier in the context of cost analysis, because invariants do not need to characterize functional behavior: it suffices that they permit to infer schematic cost expressions.

Abstract Execution. To infer the cost of program transformation *schemata* requires the capability of analyzing abstract programs. *This is not possible with standard SE*, because abstract statements have no operational semantics. One way to reason about abstract programs is to perform structural induction over the syntactic definition of statements and expressions whenever an abstract symbol is encountered. Structural induction is done in interactive theorem proving [7, 31] to verify, e.g., compilers. It is labor-intensive and not automatic. Instead, here we perform cost analysis of abstract programs via a recent generalization of SE called abstract execution (AE) [37,38]. The idea of AE is, quite simply, to symbolically execute a program containing abstract placeholder symbols for expressions and statements, just as if it were a concrete program. It might seem

---

[1] In theory, of course, proving termination is as difficult as functional verification. It is hard to imagine, for example, to find a termination argument for the Collatz function without a deep understanding of what it does. But automated termination checking works very well for many programs in practice.

counterintuitive that this is possible: after all, nothing is known about an abstract symbol. But this is not quite true: one can equip an abstract symbol with an *abstract* description of the behavior of its instances: a set of memory locations its behavior may depend on, commonly called *footprint* and a (possibly different) set of memory locations it can change, commonly called *frame* [21].

Cost Invariants. In automated cost analysis, one infers cost bounds often from loop invariants, ranking functions, and size relations computed during SE [3,11, 16,40]. For *abstract* programs, we need a more general concept, namely a loop invariant expressing a *valid abstract cost bound* at the beginning of any iteration (e.g., $2 + i * (\mathsf{ac_P}(\overline{x}) + 2)$ for the program Q above). We call this a *cost invariant*. This is an important technical innovation of this paper, increasing the modularity of cost analysis, because each loop can be verified and certified separately.

Relational Cost Analysis. AE allows specifying and verifying *relational* program properties [37], because one can express rule schemata. This extends to QAE and makes it possible, for the first time, to infer and to prove (automatically!), for example, the impact of program transformation on performance.

Certification. Cost annotations inferred by abstract cost analysis, i.e., cost invariants and abstract cost bounds, are automatically *certified* by a deductive verification system, extending the approach reported in [4] to abstract cost and abstract programs. This is possible because the specification (i.e., the cost bound) and the loop (cost) invariants are inferred by the cost analyzer—the verification system does not need to generate them.

To argue correctness of an abstract cost analysis is complex, because it must be valid for an infinite set of concrete programs. For this reason alone, it is useful to certify the abstract cost inferred for a given abstract program: during development of the abstract cost analysis reported here, several errors in abstract cost computation were detected—analysis of the failed verification attempt gave immediate feedback on the cause. We built a test suite of problems so that any change in the cost analyzer can be validated in the future.

Certification is crucial for the correctness of quantitative relational properties: The inferred cost invariants might not be precise enough to establish, e.g., that a program transformation does not increase cost for any possible program instance and run. This is only established at the certification stage, where relational properties are formally verified. *A relational setting requires provably precise cost bounds.* This feature is not offered by existing cost analysis methods.

2   QAE by Example

We introduce our approach and terminology informally by means of a motivating example: *Code Motion* [1] is a compiler optimization technique moving a statement not affected by a loop from the beginning of the loop body to before the loop. This code transformation should preserve behavior provided the loop is executed at least once, but can be expected to improve computation effort, i.e. *quantitative* properties of the program, such as execution time and memory

```
┌──── Program Before ─────────────────┐   ┌──── Program After ──────────────────┐
│ int i = 0;                          │   │ int i = 0;                          │
│ //@ loop_invariant i ≥ 0 && i ≤ t;  │   │ //@ assignable x;                   │
│ //@ cost_invariant                  │   │ //@ accessible t, w;                │
│     i · (ac_P (t, w) + ac_Q (t, z) + 2); │ //@ cost_footprint t, w;            │
│ //@ decreases t − i;                │   │ \abstract_statement P;              │
│ while (i < t) {                     │   │ //@ loop_invariant i ≥ 0 && i ≤ t;  │
│     //@ assignable x;               │   │ //@ cost_invariant                  │
│     //@ accessible t, w;            │   │     i · (ac_Q (t, z) + 2);          │
│     //@ cost_footprint t, w;        │   │ //@ decreases t − i;                │
│     \abstract_statement P;          │   │ while (i < t) {                     │
│     //@ assignable y;               │   │     //@ assignable y;               │
│     //@ accessible i, t, y, z;      │   │     //@ accessible i, t, y, z;      │
│     //@ cost_footprint t, z;        │   │     //@ cost_footprint t, z;        │
│     \abstract_statement Q;          │   │     \abstract_statement Q;          │
│     i++;                            │   │     i++;                            │
│ }                                   │   │ }                                   │
│ //@ assert \cost == 2 +             │   │ //@ assert \cost == 2 +             │
│     t · (ac_P (t, w) + ac_Q (t, z) + 2); │     ac_P (t, w) + t · (ac_Q (t, z) + 2); │
└─────────────────────────────────────┘   └─────────────────────────────────────┘
┌──── Preconditions and Postconditions ────────────────────────────────────────┐
│ Inputs: t, w, x, y, z   Precondition: t > 0   Postcondition: \cost_1 ≥ \cost_2 │
└───────────────────────────────────────────────────────────────────────────────┘
```

Fig. 1: Motivating example on relational quantitative properties.

consumption: The moved code block is executed just once in the transformed context, leading to less instructions (less energy consumed) and, in case it allocates memory, less memory usage. In the following we subsume any quantitative aspect of a program under the term *cost* expressed in an unspecified *cost model* with the understanding that it can be instantiated to specific cost measures, such as number of instructions, number of allocated bytes, energy consumed, etc.

To formalize code motion as a transformation rule, we describe in- and output of the transformation *schematically*. Fig. 1 depicts such a schema in a language based on JAVA. An *Abstract Statement* (AS) with identifier *Id*, declared as "\abstract_statement *Id*;", represents an arbitrary concrete statement. It is obviously unsafe to extract arbitrary, possibly non-invariant, code blocks from loops. For this reason, the AS P in question has a *specification* restricting the allowed behavior of its instances. For compatibility with JAVA we base our specification language on the *Java Modeling Language* (JML) [27]. Specifications are attached to code via structured comments that are marked as JML by an "@" symbol. JML keyword "**assignable**" defines the memory locations that may occur in the frame of an AS; similarly, "**accessible**" restricts the footprint. Fig. 1 contains further keywords explained below.

Input to QAE is the abstract program to analyze, including annotations (highlighted in light gray in Fig. 1) that express restrictions on the permitted instances of ASs. In addition to the frame and footprint, the *cost footprint* of an AS, denoted with the keyword "**cost_footprint**", is a subset of its footprint listing locations the cost expressions in AS instances may depend on. In Fig. 1, the cost footprint of AS Q excludes accessible variables i and y. Annotations highlighted in dark gray are *automatically inferred* by abstract cost analysis and are input for the certifier. As usual, loop invariants (keyword "**loop_invariant**") are needed to describe the behavior of loops with symbolic bounds. The loop invariant in Fig. 1 allows inferring the final value t of loop counter i after loop termination. To prove termination, the loop *variant* (keyword "**decreases**") is inferred.

So far, this is standard automated cost analysis [3]. The ability to *infer automatically* the remaining annotations represents our main contribution: Each AS P has an associated *abstract cost* function parametric in the locations of its footprint, represented by an abstract cost symbol ac_P. The symbol $ac_P(t, w)$ in the "**assert**" statement in Fig. 1 can be instantiated with any concrete function parametric in t, w being a valid cost bound for the instance of P. For example, for the instantiation "$P \equiv x=t+1;$" the constant function $ac_P(t, w) = 1$ is the correct *exact* cost, while $ac_P(t, w) = t$ with $t \geq 1$ is a correct *upper bound* cost.

As pointed out in Sect. 1 we require *cost invariants* to capture the cost of each loop iteration. They are declared by the keyword "**cost_invariant**". To generate them, it is necessary to infer the *cost growth* of abstract programs that bounds the number of loop iterations executed so far. In Sect. 4 we describe automated inference of cost invariants including the generation of cost growth for all loops. Our technique is compositional and also works in the presence of nested loops.

The QAE framework can express and prove quantitative relational properties. The assertions in the last lines in Fig. 1 use the expression **cost** referring to the total accumulated cost of the program, i.e., the quantitative *postcondition*. We support quantitative relational postconditions such as **cost_1** $\geq$ **cost_2**, where **cost_1**, **cost_2** refer to the total cost of the original (on the left) and transformed (on the right) program, respectively. To prove relational properties, one must be able to deduce *exact* cost invariants for loops such that the comparison of the invariants allows concluding that the programs from which the invariants are obtained fulfill the proven relational property. Otherwise, over-approximation introduced by cost analysis could make the relation for the postconditions hold, while the relational property does not necessarily hold for the programs.

To obtain a formal account of QAE with correctness guarantees we require a mathematically rigorous semantic foundation of abstract cost. This is provided in the following section.

3   (Quantitative) Abstract Execution

Abstract Execution [37, 38] extends symbolic execution by permitting abstract statements to occur in programs. Thus AE reasons about an *infinite* set of concrete programs. An abstract program contains at least one AS. The semantics of an AS is given by the set of concrete programs it represents, its set of *legal instances*. To simplify presentation, we only consider normally completing JAVA code as instances: an instance may not throw an exception, break from a loop, etc. Each AS has an *identifier* and a specification consisting of its frame and footprint. Semantically, instances of an AS with identifier P may at most write to memory locations specified in P's frame and may only read the values of locations in its footprint. All occurrences of an AS with the *same identifier* symbol have the same legal instances (possibly modulo renaming of variables, if variable names in frame and footprint specifications differ). For example, by

```
//@ assignable x,y;
//@ accessible y, z;
\abstract_statement P;
```

we declare an AS with identifier "P", which can be instantiated by programs that write at most to variables x and y, while only depending on variables y and z. The program "x=y; y=17;" is a legal instance of it, but not "x=y; y=w;", which accesses the value of variable w not contained in the footprint.

We use the shorthand $P(x, y :\approx y, z)$ for the AS declaration above. The left-hand side of ":$\approx$" is the frame, the right-hand side the footprint. Abstract programs allow expressing a second-order property such as "all programs assigning at most x, y while reading at most y, z leave the value of i unchanged". In *Hoare triple* format (where i_0 is a fresh constant not occurring in P):

$$\{i \doteq i_0\} \, P(x, y :\approx y, z); \, \{i \doteq i_0\} \qquad (*)$$

3.1 Abstract Execution with Abstract Cost

We extend the AE framework [37,38] to QAE by adding *cost specifications* that extend the specification of an AS with an annotated *cost expression*. An abstract cost expression is a function whose value may depend on any memory location in the footprint of the AS it specifies. This location set is called the *cost footprint*, specified via the **cost_footprint** keyword (see Fig. 1), and must be a subset of the footprint of the specified AS. The cost footprint for the program in $(*)$ might be declared as "$\{z\}$". It implicitly declares the abstract function $ac_P(z)$ that could be instantiated to, say, quadratic cost "z^2".

Definition 1 (Abstract Program). *A pair $\mathcal{P} = (abstrStmts, p_{abstr})$ of a set of AS declarations $abstrStmts \neq \emptyset$ and a program fragment p_{abstr} containing exactly those ASs is called* abstract program. *Each AS declaration in abstrStmts is a pair* $(P(frame :\approx footprint), ac_P(costFootprint))$, *where* P *is an identifier; frame, footprint, and costFootprint $\subseteq$ footprint are location sets.*

A concrete program fragment p is a legal instance of $\mathcal{P}$ if it arises from substituting concrete cost functions for all ac_P in abstrStmts, and concrete statements for all P in abstrStmts, where (i) all ASs are instantiated legally, i.e., by statements respecting their frame, footprint, and cost function, and (ii) all ASs with the same identifier are instantiated with the same concrete program. The semantics $[\![\mathcal{P}]\!]$ consists of all its legal instances.

The abstract program consisting of only AS P in $(*)$ with cost footprint "$\{z\}$" is formally defined as: $(\{(P(x, y :\approx y, z), ac_P(z))\}, P;)$. The program "$P^0 \equiv$ i =0; **while** (i <z) $\{x = z; i++;\}$" with cost function "$ac_P(z) = 3 \cdot z + 2$" is a legal instance: it respects frame, footprint, and cost footprint, as well as the cost function, that (assuming $z \geq 0$) can be obtained by static cost analysis of P^0.

By encoding the semantics of abstract programs in a program logic [38, Sect. 4.2] one can statically verify whether an instance is legal. It may require auxiliary specifications (invariants, contracts) of the concrete code. The property is unde-cidable, but can be proven automatically in many cases, see [38] for a discussion. A first implementation of such a check is part of the REFINITY tool (see [36], also https://www.key-project.org/REFINITY/).

3.2 Cost of Abstract Programs

Finitely executing a concrete program p starting in a state $s_0 = (p, \sigma_0)$ with an initial assignment σ_0 of p's program variables results in a finite trace of the form $t \equiv s_0 \xrightarrow{c_1} \ldots \xrightarrow{c_n} s_n$. Each state $s_i = (p_i, \sigma_i)$ consists of a program counter p_i (the remaining program to execute) and a store σ_i (the current variable assignment); each transition $s_i \xrightarrow{c_{i+1}} s_{i+1}$ updates s_i to s_{i+1} according to the effect of executing command c_{i+1} defined in the semantics of the programming language. A *complete* trace corresponds to a terminating execution, i.e., $s_n = (\epsilon, \sigma_n)$, where ϵ is the empty program and σ_n the resulting final variable assignment.

The cost of a program can be computed based on execution traces. To allow arbitrary quantitative properties, we work on a generic *cost model* $\mathcal{M}$ that assigns cost values to programming language instructions. We will compute the cost of a trace t, denoted $\mathcal{M}(t)$, by summing up the costs of the executed instructions. A straightforward measure is the number of executed instructions $\mathcal{M}_{\mathsf{instr}}$: In this cost model, instructions like "x=1;", the evaluation of the loop guard, etc., all are assigned cost 1. For example, the cost of the complete trace of "**while** $(i > 0)$ i−−;" when started with an initial store assigning the value 3 to i is 7, because "i −−;" is executed three times and the guard is evaluated four times. This can be generalized to *symbolic* execution: Executing the same program with a *symbolic* store assigning to i a symbolic initial value $i_0 \geq 0$ produces traces of cost $2 \cdot i_0 + 1$. The cost of *abstract programs*, i.e., the generalization to QAE, is defined similarly: By generalizing not merely over all initial stores, but also over all concrete instances of the abstract program.

Definition 2 (Abstract Program Cost). *Let $\mathcal{M}$ be a cost model. Let an integer-valued expression $c_{\mathcal{P}}$ consist of scalar constants, program variables, and abstract cost symbols applied to constants and variables. Expression $c_{\mathcal{P}}$ is the cost of an abstract program $\mathcal{P}$ w.r.t. $\mathcal{M}$ if for all concrete stores σ and instances $p \in [\![\mathcal{P}]\!]$ such that p terminates with a complete trace t of cost $\mathcal{M}(t)$ when executed in σ, $c_{\mathcal{P}}$ evaluates to $\mathcal{M}(t)$ when interpreting variables according to σ, and abstract cost functions according to the instantiation step leading to p. The instance of $c_{\mathcal{P}}$ using the concrete store σ is denoted $c_{\mathcal{P}}(\sigma)$.*

Example 1. We test the cost assertion in the last lines of the left program in Fig. 1 by computing the cost of a trace obtained from a fixed initial store and instances of P, Q. We use the cost model $\mathcal{M}_{\mathsf{instr}}$ and an initial store that assigns 2 to t and 0 to all other variables. We instantiate P with "x=2*t;" and Q with "y=i; y++;". Consequently, the abstract cost functions $\mathsf{ac_P}(t, w)$ and $\mathsf{ac_Q}(t, z)$ are instantiated with 1 and 2, respectively. Evaluating the postulated abstract program cost $2 + t \cdot (2 + \mathsf{ac_P}(t, w) + \mathsf{ac_Q}(t, z))$ for the concrete store and AS instantiations results in $2 + 2 \cdot (2 + 1 + 2) = 12$. Consequently, the execution trace should contain 12 transitions, which is the case.

3.3 Proving Quantitative Properties with QAE

There are two ways to realize QAE on top of the existing functional verification layer provided by the AE framework [37, 38]: (i) provide a "cost" extension to the program logic and calculus underlying AE; (ii) translate non-functional (cost) properties to functional ones. We opt for the second, as it is less prone to introduce soundness issues stemming from the addition of new concepts to the existing framework. It is also faster to realize and allows early testing.

The translation consists of three elements: (a) A global "ghost" variable "cost" (representing keyword "\cost") for tracking accumulated cost; (b) explicit encoding of a chosen cost model by suitable ghost setter methods that update this variable; (c) functional loop invariants and method postconditions expressing cost invariants and cost postconditions.

Regarding item (c), we support three kinds of cost specification. These are, descending in the order of their strength: *exact*, *upper bound*, and *asymptotic* cost. At the analysis stage, it is usually impossible to determine the best match. For this reason, there is merely one **cost_invariant** keyword, not three. However, when translating cost to functional properties, a decision has to be made. A natural strategy is to start with the strongest kind of specification, then proceed towards the weaker ones when a proof fails.

An exact cost invariant has the shape "cost $==$ *expr*", an upper bound on the invariant cost is specified by "cost $<=$ *expr*"; asymptotic cost is expressed by the idiom "asymptotic(cost) $<=$ asymptotic(*expr*)". The function "asymptotic" abstracts from constant symbols in the argument. For example, the (exact) cost postcondition of the abstract program on the right in Fig. 1 is:

$$\text{cost} \; == \; 2 + \text{ac}_P\,(t,w) + t \cdot (\text{ac}_Q\,(t,z) + 2) \tag{†}$$

Asymptotic cost would be expressed as asymptotic(cost) $<=$ asymptotic($2 +$ $\text{ac}_P\,(t,w) + t \cdot (\text{ac}_Q\,(t,z) + 2)$) where the right-hand side of the equation is equivalent to asymptotic($\text{ac}_P\,(t,w) + t \cdot (\text{ac}_Q\,(t,z))$).

Listing 2 shows the result of translating the cost invariant in Fig. 1 to a functional loop invariant (highlighted lines), using cost model $\mathcal{M}_{instr}$ in ghost setters and postconditions of AS ("**ensures**" clauses). ASs P, Q must include the ghost variable "cost" in their frame, because they update its value. The keyword **before** in the postcondition of an AS refers to the value a variable had just before executing the AS. In loops we use "inner" cost variables "iCost" tracking the cost inside the loop. When the loop terminates, we add the final value of "iCost" to "cost". After every evaluation of the guard of the loop, the cost is incremented accordingly. Using the translation in Listing 2 of the inferred annotations in Fig. 1, the AE system proves cost postcondition (†) automatically.

Apart from the translation of inferred quantitative annotations to functional AE specifications, we implemented the axiomatization of the asymptotic function and extended the AE system's *proof script* language. This made it possible to define a highly automated proof strategy for non-linear arithmetic problems generated by some cost analysis benchmarks.

4   Abstract Cost Analysis

Recall from Sect. 2 that for automatic cost certification we need to infer annotations for abstract cost invariants and cost postconditions. To achieve this, we

```
 1 //@ ghost int cost = 0;                    13 //@ decreases t − i;
 2 int i = 0;                                  14 while (i < t) {
 3 //@ set cost = cost + 1;                    15     //@ set iCost = iCost + 1;
 4                                             16     //@ assignable y, cost;
 5 //@ assignable x, cost;                     17     //@ accessible i, t, y, z;
 6 //@ accessible t, w;                        18     //@ ensures cost ==
 7 //@ ensures cost == \before(cost)           19     //@    \before(cost) + ac_Q (t, z);
 8 //@    + ac_P (t, w);                        20     \abstract_statement Q;
 9 \abstract_statement P;                       21     i ++;
10                                             22     //@ set iCost = iCost + 1;
11 //@ ghost int iCost = 0;                    23 }
12 //@ loop_invariant i ≥ 0 && i ≤ t           24 //@ set cost = cost + 1;
13 //@    && iCost == i · (ac_Q (t, z) + 2);   25 //@ set cost = cost + iCost;
```

Listing 2: Translation of cost model and cost invariants to AE.

leverage a cost analysis framework for concrete programs to the abstract setting. The presentation is structured as follows: Sect. 4.1 defines the notion of an abstract cost relation system (ACRS) used in cost analysis for the abstract setting. Sect. 4.2 details how to generate automatically inductive cost invariants for abstract programs from ACRSs. Sect. 4.3 tells how to generate cost postconditions used to prove relational properties and required to handle nested loops.

4.1 Inference of Abstract Cost Relations

There are two main cost analysis approaches: those using recurrence equations in the style of Wegbreit [39], and those based on type systems [14, 24]. Our formalization is based on the first kind, but the main ideas for extending the framework to abstract programs would be also applicable to the second. The key issue when extending a recurrences-based framework to the abstract setting is the notion of *abstract cost relation* for loops which generalizes the concept of cost recurrence equations for a loop to an abstract setting. We start with notation for loops and technical details on assumed size relations.

Loops. In our formalization we consider while-loops containing n abstract statements and m non-abstract statements. Non-abstract statements include any concrete instruction of the target language (arithmetic instructions, conditionals, method calls, ...). We assume loops L have the general outline displayed on the right. Each abstract statement has a frame specification, abstract and non-abstract statements may appear in any order, either might be empty.

```
while (G) {
    //@ accessible r_{1,1}, ..., r_{1,h_{r1}}
    //@ assignable w_{1,1}, ..., w_{1,h_{w1}}
    //@ cost_footprint c_{1,1}, ..., c_{1,h_{c1}}
    \abstract_statement A_1;
    non_abstract_statement N_1;
    ...
}
```

Size relations. We assume that for each loop sets of *size constraints* have been computed. These sets capture the size relation among the variables in the loop upon exit (called *base case*, denoted φ_B), and when moving from one iteration to the next (denoted φ_I). ASs are ignored by the size analysis. While this would be unsound in general, it will be correct under the requirements we impose in Def. 4 and with the handling of ASs in Def. 3. Size relations are available from any cost analyzer by means of a static analysis [13] that records the effect of concrete program statements on variables and propagates it through each loop iteration. In our examples, since we work on integer data, size analysis corresponds to a value analysis [10] tracking the value of the integer variables.[2]

Example 2. The size relations for the loop on the left in Fig. 1 are $\varphi_B = \{i \geq t\}$ and $\varphi_I = \{i < t, \; i' = i + 1\}$. φ_B is inferred from the loop guard and φ_I from the guard and the increment of i (primed variables refer to the value of the variable after the loop execution).

Based on pre-computed size relations, we define the cost of executing a loop by means of an *abstract cost relation system* (ACRS). This is a set of cost equations characterizing the abstract cost of executing a loop for any input with respect to a given cost model $\mathcal{M}$. Cost equations consist of a cost expression governed by size constraints containing applicability conditions for the equation (like $i < t$ in φ_I above) and size relations between loop variables (like $i' = i + 1$ in φ_I).

Definition 3 (Abstract Cost Relation System). *Let L be a loop as above with n abstract and m non-abstract statements. Let $\bar{x}$ be the set of variables accessed in L. Let φ_I, φ_B be sound size relations for L, and $\mathcal{M}$ a cost model. The ACRS for L is defined as the following set of cost equations:*

$$C(\bar{x}) = \mathsf{C_B} \qquad\qquad\qquad\qquad\qquad\qquad , \; \varphi_B$$
$$C(\bar{x}) = \sum_{j=1}^{n} \mathsf{ac_j}\left(c_{j,1}, \ldots, c_{j,h_{cj}}\right) + \sum_{i=1}^{m} \mathsf{C_{N_i}} + C(\bar{x}'), \; \varphi_I$$

where:

(1) $\mathsf{C_B} \geq 0$ *is the cost of exiting the loop (executing the base case) w.r.t. $\mathcal{M}$.*
(2) *Each* $\mathsf{ac_j}(\cdot) \geq 0$ *represents the abstract cost for the abstract statement A_j in L w.r.t. to $\mathcal{M}$. Each $\mathsf{ac_j}$ is parameterized with the variables in the cost footprint of the corresponding A_j, as it may depend on any of them.*
(3) *Each* $\mathsf{C_{N_i}} \geq 0$ *is the cost of the non-abstract statement N_i w.r.t. to $\mathcal{M}$.*
(4) *C is a recursive call.*
(5) *$\bar{x}'$ are variables $\bar{x}$ when renamed after executing the loop.*
(6) *The assignable variables $w_{j,*}$ in the $\mathsf{ac_j}$ get an unknown value in $\bar{x}'$ (denoted with "_" in the examples below).*

Ignoring the abstract statements, one can apply a complete algorithm for cost relation systems [6] to an ACRS to obtain automatically a *linear*[3] ranking function f for loop L: f is a linear, non-negative function over $\bar{x}$ that decreases strictly at every loop iteration. Function f yields directly the "//@ decreases f;" annotation required for QAE.

As in Sect. 3, the definition of ACRS assumes a generic cost model $\mathcal{M}$ and uses C to refer in a generic way to cost according to $\mathcal{M}$. For example, to infer the number of executed steps, C is set to 1 per instruction, while for memory usage C records the amount of memory allocated by an instruction.

---

[2] For complex data structures, one would need heap analyses [35] to infer size relations.
[3] There exist (more expensive) algorithms to obtain also polynomial ranking functions [5] but for the sake of efficiency we are not using them in our system.

General Case of ACRS. The definition of ACRS was simplified for presentation. The following generalizations, not requiring any new concept, are possible: (1) We assume an ACRS for a loop has only two equations, one for the base case (the guard G does not hold) and one for the iterative case (G holds). In general, there might be more than one equation for the base case, e.g., if the guard involves multiple conditions and the cost varies depending on the condition that holds on the exit. Similarly, there might be multiple equations in the iterative case, e.g., if the loop body contains conditional statements and each iteration has different cost depending on the taken branch. This issue is orthogonal to the extension to abstract cost. (2) A loop might contain method calls that in turn contain ASs. In absence of recursion, such calls can be inlined. For recursive methods, it is possible to compute the call graph and solve the equations in reverse topological order such that the abstract cost of the (inner) method calls is obtained first and then inserted into the surrounding equations. (3) The cost of code fragments not part of any loop (before, after, and in between loops) is defined as well by abstract cost equations accumulating the cost of all instructions these fragments include, just as for concrete programs. This aspect does not require changes to the framework for concrete programs, so we do not formalize it, but just illustrate it in the next example.

Example 3. The ACRSs of the programs in Fig. 1 are (left program above line, right program below):

$$C_{\text{before}}(t, x, w, y, z) = c_{\text{before}} + C_{w_0}(i, t, x, w, y, z), \qquad \{i = 0\}$$
$$C_{w_0}(i, t, x, w, y, z) = c_{B_{w_0}}, \qquad \{i \geq t\}$$
$$C_{w_0}(i, t, x, w, y, z) = c_{w_0} + \text{ac}_P(t, w) + \text{ac}_Q(t, z) + C_{w_0}(i', t, \_, w, \_, z), \ \{i' = i + 1, i < t\}$$

$$C_{\text{after}}(t, x, w, y, z) = c_{\text{after}} + \text{ac}_P(t, w) + C_{w_1}(i, t, \_, w, y, z), \qquad \{i = 0\}$$
$$C_{w_1}(i, t, x, w, y, z) = c_{B_{w_1}}, \qquad \{i \geq t\}$$
$$C_{w_1}(i, t, x, w, y, z) = c_{w_1} + \text{ac}_Q(t, z) + C_{w_1}(i', t, x, w, \_, z), \qquad \{i' = i + 1, i < t\}$$

Notation c refers to the generic cost that can be instantiated to a chosen cost model $\mathcal{M}$. Cost equation C_{before} for the first program is composed of the instructions appearing before the loop is c_{before} plus the cost of executing the while loop C_{w_0}. The size constraint fixes the initial value of i. Following Def. 3, there are two equations corresponding to the base case of the loop and executing one iteration, respectively. Observe that assignable variables in ASs have unknown values in the ACRS (according to item (6) in Def. 3). Program *after* has a similar structure. A ranking function for both loops is $t - i$ which is used to generate the annotation "//@ **decreases** t−i;" inserted just before each loop in Fig. 1.

To guarantee soundness of abstract cost analysis, it is mandatory that (i) no AS in the loop modifies any of the variables that influence loop cost, i.e., they do not *interfere with cost,* and (ii) the cost of the AS in the loop is independent of the variables modified in the loop. We call the latter ASs *cost neutral.* The first requirement is guaranteed by item (6) in Def. 3, because the value of assignable variables is "forgotten" in the equations. It is implemented, as usual in static analysis, by using a name generator for *fresh* variables. If cost depends on assignable variables in an AS, then the ACRS will not be solvable (i.e., the analysis returns "unbound cost"). The ACRS in the example contains "_" in equations that do not prevent solvability of the system nor its evaluation, because they do not interfere with cost. However, if we had "forgotten" a cost-relevant variable (such as t), we would be unable to solve or evaluate the equations: without knowing t the equation guard is not evaluable. Requirement (ii) is ensured by the following definition ensuring that variables in the cost footprint are not modified by other statements in the loop.

Definition 4 (Cost neutral AS). *Given a loop L, where*

- *$W(L)$ is the set of variables written by the non-abstract statements of L.*
- *$\texttt{Abstr}(L)$ is the set of all ASs in loop L.*
- *$Frame(\texttt{Abstr}(L))$ is the set of variables assigned by any AS $A \in \texttt{Abstr}(L)$.*
- *$CostFootprint(A)$ is the set of variables which the cost of an A depends on.*

L is a loop with cost neutral ASs if, for all $A \in \texttt{Abstr}(L)$, it is the case that $(W(L) \cup Frame(\texttt{Abstr}(L))) \cap CostFootprint(A) = \emptyset$.

The definition above constitutes a sufficient, but not necessary criterion that could be tightened by a more expensive analysis. For instance, our framework easily extends to allow conditions in the cost footprint that the concretizations of the AS must fulfill. In our example, the cost footprint might include condition $i' \geq i$, where i' is the value of i after executing the AS. This permits the abstract statement to modify i provided it does not decrease its value. Thus, the AS is not cost neutral, but the upper bound remains sound. The formalization of this generalization is left to future work.

Example 4. It is easy to check that both loops in Fig. 1 have cost neutral ASs. On the left: $W(L) = \{i\}$, $Frame(\{P, Q\}) = \{x, y\}$, $CostFootprint(P) = \{t, w\}$, and $CostFootprint(Q) = \{t, z\}$, so $(W(L) \cup Frame(\{P, Q\})) \cap CostFootprint(P) = \emptyset$, and $(W(L) \cup Frame(\{P, Q\})) \cap CostFootprint(Q) = \emptyset$. The program on the right is checked analogously.

Given a program $\mathcal{P}$ with variables $\bar{x}$ and ACRS with initial equation $C_{ini}(\bar{x})$. We denote by $eval(C_{ini}(\bar{x}), \sigma_0)$ the evaluation of the ACRS for a given initial assignment σ_0 of the variables. This is a standard evaluation of recurrence equations performed by instantiating the right-hand side of the equations with the values of the variables in σ_0 and checking the satisfiability of the size constraints (if the expression being checked or accumulated contains "_", the evaluation returns "unbound"). As usual, the process is repeated until an equation without calls is reached.

Example 5. Consider the ACRS of the left program in Fig. 1 with variables (t, x, w, y, z), initial state $\sigma_0 = (2, 0, 0, 0, 0)$, and cost model $\mathcal{M}_{inst}$ (thus c_{before}, $c_{B_{w_0}}$ and c_{w_0} take values 1, 1 and 2 respectively). The evaluation of the ACRS results in $eval(C_{ini}(t, x, w, y, z), (2, 0, 0, 0, 0)) = 6 + 2 \cdot \texttt{ac}_P(2, 0) + 2 \cdot \texttt{ac}_Q(2, 0)$.

The following theorem states soundness of the ACRS obtained by applying Def. 3 provided that all loops satisfy Def. 4.

Theorem 1 (Soundness of ACRS). *Let $\mathcal{M}$ be a cost model and $\mathcal{P}$ an abstract program whose loops satisfy Def. 4. Let $c_{\mathcal{P}}$ be the abstract cost of $\mathcal{P}$ defined as in Definition 2. Let C_{ini} be the initial equation for the ACRS obtained by Def. 3. For any initial state of the variables $\sigma_0 \in \mathbb{Z}^{n_m}$, it holds that $c_{\mathcal{P}}(\sigma_0) \leq eval(C_{ini}(\overline{x}), \sigma_0)$.*

4.2   From ACRS to Abstract Cost Invariants

Example 5 shows that ACRSs are evaluable for concrete instances. However, to enable automated QAE, we need to obtain from them *closed-form* cost invariants and postconditions, i.e., non-recursive expressions. We introduce the novel concept of *abstract cost invariant* (ACI) that enables automated, inductive proofs over cost in a deductive verification system. The crucial difference to (non-inductive) cost postconditions as inferred by existing cost analyzers is that ACIs can be proven inductively for each loop iteration. Hence, they integrate naturally into deductive verification systems that use loop invariants [21].

In contrast to ACIs, postconditions provide a bound for the cost *after* execution of the *whole* loop they refer to. Typically, a postcondition bound for a loop has the form $max\_iter * max\_cost + max\_base$, where max_iter is the maximal number of iterations of the loop, max_cost is the maximal cost of any loop iteration, and max_base is the maximal cost of executing the loop with no iterations. Instead, an ACI has the form $growth * max\_cost + max\_base$, where $growth$ counts how many times the loop has been executed and hence provides a bound after *each* loop iteration. The challenge is to design an automated technique that infers $growth$. We propose to obtain it from the ranking function:

Definition 5 (Growth). *Given a loop with ranking function $F = c + \sum_i a_i \cdot v_i$, where c and v_i are the constant and variable parts of the function, respectively, and a_i are constant coefficients. If we denote with v_i^0 the initial value of variable v_i before entering the loop, then $growth = \sum_i a_i \cdot (v_i^0 - v_i)$.*

Example 6. We look at four simple loops with ranking function *decreases* and the *growth* inferred automatically by applying Def. 5:

`int i = 0;`
`while (i < t)`
`i++;`
	`int i = t;`
	`while (i > 0)`
	`i--;`
		`int i = 0;`
		`while (i < t)`
		`i += 2;`
			`int i = t;`
			`while (i > 0)`
			`i -= 2;`

decreases $t - i$	*decreases* i	*decreases* $\frac{t-i+1}{2}$	*decreases* $\frac{i+1}{2}$
growth i	*growth* $t - i$	*growth* $\frac{i}{2}$	*growth* $\frac{t-i}{2}$

We can now define the concept of ACI that relies on abstract cost relations defined in Sect. 4.1 and growth as defined above.

Definition 6 (Abstract Cost Invariant). *Given an ACRS as in Def. 3 and its growth as in Def. 5, an abstract cost invariant is defined as follows:*
$$\mathtt{cinv}(\overline{x}) = \mathtt{C_B}^{\mathtt{max}} + growth \cdot \left(\sum_{j=1}^n \mathtt{ac_j}\left(c_{j,1}, \ldots, c_{j,h_{c_j}}\right) + \sum_{i=1}^m \mathtt{C_{N_i}}^{\mathtt{max}} \right)$$ *where $\mathtt{C_B}^{\mathtt{max}}$ stands for the maximal value that the expression $\mathtt{C_B}$ can take under the constraints φ_B, and $\mathtt{C_{N_i}}^{\mathtt{max}}$ the maximal value of $\mathtt{C_{N_i}}$ under φ_I. We generate the annotation* "**//@ cost_invariant** $\mathtt{cinv}(\overline{x})$;".

To obtain the maximal cost of a cost expression under a set of constraints, we use existing maximization procedures [5].

From Def. 6 we obtain ACIs as closed-form abstract cost expressions of the form $\texttt{abexpr} = \texttt{cexpr} \mid \texttt{ac} \mid \texttt{abexpr}_1 + \texttt{abexpr}_2 \mid \texttt{abexpr}_1 * \texttt{abexpr}_2$ where $\texttt{ac}$ represents an abstract cost function as defined in Sect. 3.1 and $\texttt{cexpr}$ is a concrete cost expression. The definition above yields linear bounds, however, the extension to infer postconditions in the subsequent section leads to polynomial expressions (of arbitrary degree).[4]

Example 7 (Abstract Cost Invariant). Consider the first loop in Example 6 (where *growth* = i) with the following frame and footprint:

> //@ **assignable** j; **accessible** i , t, j , k; **cost_footprint** k;

Using $\mathcal{M}_{\mathsf{instr}}$, the evaluation of the loop guard and the increase of i both have unit cost, so the ACRS is:

$$C(\mathsf{i},\mathsf{t},\mathsf{j},\mathsf{k}) = 1 \qquad\qquad\qquad \{\mathsf{i} \geq \mathsf{t}\}$$
$$C(\mathsf{i},\mathsf{t},\mathsf{j},\mathsf{k}) = \mathsf{ac_P}(\mathsf{k}) + 2 + C(\mathsf{i}',\mathsf{t},\_,\mathsf{k}) \quad \{\mathsf{i}' = \mathsf{i}+1,\ \mathsf{i} < \mathsf{t}\}$$

The value of the assignable variable j in the recursive call is "forgotten" (item (6) in Def. 3), but this information loss does not affect solvability of the ACRS. We obtain the following ACI: "//@ **cost_invariant** $1 + \mathsf{i} * (2 + \mathsf{ac_P}(\mathsf{k}))$;".

Example 8 (Upper Bound Abstract Cost Invariant). Sometimes an ACI is over-approximating cost, resulting in an *upper bound ACI*. To illustrate this, we add an instruction that creates an array of non-constant size "i" to the program in Example 7 and measure memory consumption instead of instruction count.

```
while (i < t) {
    a = new int[i];
    //@ assignable j;
    //@ accessible i , t, j , a, k;
    //@ cost_footprint k;
    \abstract_statement P;
    i ++;
}
```

The resulting ACRS thus accumulates cost "i" at each iteration, plus the memory consumed by the abstract statement:

$$C(\mathsf{i},\mathsf{t},\mathsf{j},\mathsf{k}) = 0, \qquad\qquad\qquad\qquad \{\mathsf{i} \geq \mathsf{t}\}$$
$$C(\mathsf{i},\mathsf{t},\mathsf{j},\mathsf{k}) = \mathsf{ac_P}(\mathsf{k}) + \mathsf{i} + C(\mathsf{i}',\mathsf{t},\_,\mathsf{k}), \quad \{\mathsf{i}' = \mathsf{i}+1, \mathsf{i} < \mathsf{t}\}$$

Now, maximizing the expression $C_{N_1} = \mathsf{i}$ under $\{\mathsf{i}' = \mathsf{i}+1, \mathsf{i} < \mathsf{t}\}$ results in $C_{N_1}{}^{\max} = \mathsf{t}-1$ and upper bound ACI "//@ **cost_invariant** $\mathsf{i} * (\mathsf{t} - 1 + \mathsf{ac_P}(\mathsf{k}))$;".

Let c_L denote the abstract cost of executing a loop L (in analogy to c_P in Def. 2, but considering only loop L rather than the whole program $\mathcal{P}$). We denote by c_I the portion of the cost in c_L up to the execution of iteration I.

Proposition 1. *Let L be a loop with variables $\bar{x}$ satisfying Def. 4, $\mathrm{cinv}(\bar{x})$ its ACI, and $\sigma_I \in \mathbb{Z}^{nm}$ be the store after performing iteration I of L. Then the following holds: (1) $\mathrm{cinv}(\bar{x})$ is true on entering the loop; (2) $c_I(\sigma_I) \leq \mathrm{cinv}(\sigma_I)$.*

---

[4] As our approach is based on a recurrences-based framework [39] that works for exponential and logarithmic expressions, the results in this section generalize to these expressions. However, the AE deductive verification system is not able to deal with them automatically at the moment, so we skip these expressions in our account.

4.3   From Cost Invariants to Postconditions

To handle programs with nested loops and to prove relational properties it is necessary to infer *cost postconditions* for abstract programs. For nested loops the cost postcondition states the abstract cost after complete execution of the inner loop and it is used to compute the invariant of the outer loop. For relational properties, the cost postconditions of two abstract programs are compared. Cost postconditions for concrete programs are obtained by upper bound solvers (e.g., COSTA [3], CoFloCo [16], APROVE [17]) that compute *max_iter*, an upper bound on the number of iterations that a loop performs. To do so, one relies on ranking functions. We do this as well, but generalize the computation of postconditions to abstract programs. The cost postcondition is obtained by substituting `growth` by `max_iter` in the formula of $cinv(\overline{x})$ in Def. 6 as follows.

Definition 7 (Cost Postcondition). *Let L be a loop, max_iter be an upper bound on the number of iterations of L. Given the ACRS for L in Def. 3, we infer the cost postcondition for L as*

$$post(\overline{x}) = C_B^{\ max} + max\_iter(\overline{x}) \cdot \left(\sum_{j=1}^{n} ac_j \left(c_{j,1}, \ldots, c_{j,h_{cj}} \right) + \sum_{i=1}^{m} C_{N_i}^{\ max} \right)$$

and generate the annotation " `//@ assert cost == post(x̄);` *".*

To infer the postcondition for a complete abstract program, we take the sum of all *cost postconditions* of its top-level loops plus the cost of the non-iterative fragments. Fig. 1 shows the cost postconditions for our running example obtained by replacing the growth i of the invariant with the bound t on the loop iterations and requiring $t \geq 0$. The generation of inductive ACIs for nested loops uses the cost postcondition of inner loops to compute the invariants of the outer ones. The following theorem states soundness of cost postconditions:

Theorem 2. *Let L be a loop over variables $\overline{x}$ satisfying Def. 4 and $post(\overline{x})$ its cost postcondition. Let $\sigma_L \in \mathbb{Z}^{m_n}$ be the store upon termination of L. Then $c_L(\sigma_L) \leq post(\sigma_L)$.*

5   Experimental Evaluation

We implemented a prototype of our approach downloadable from https://tinyurl.com/qae-impl (including required libraries). The archive contains the benchmarks of this section and additional examples as well as build and usage instructions. The prototype is a command-line implementation backed by an existing cost analysis library for (non-abstract) Java bytecode as well as the deductive verification system KeY [2] including the AE framework [37,38]. Our implementation consists of three components: (1) An extension of a cost analyzer (written in PYTHON) to handle abstract JAVA programs, (2) a conversion tool (written in JAVA) translating the output of the analyzer to a set of input files for KeY, (3) a bash script orchestrating the whole tool chain, specifically, the interplay between item (1), item (2) and the two libraries. In case of a failed certification attempt, our script offers the choice to open the generated proof in KeY for further debugging. In total, our implementation (excluding the libraries) consists of 1,802 lines of PYTHON, 703 lines of JAVA, and 389 lines of bash code (without blank lines and comments).

To assess effectiveness and efficiency of our approach, we used our QAE implementation to analyze seven typical code optimization rules using cost models $\mathcal{M}_{instr}$ (rows "1*"–"6*" in Table 1) and $\mathcal{M}_{heap}$ (rows "7*"). While $\mathcal{M}_{instr}$ counts the number of instructions, $\mathcal{M}_{heap}$ measures heap consumption. The first column identifies the benchmark ("a" refers to the original program, "b" to the transformed one), the second **P** refers to the kind of proven cost result (asymptotic "a", exact "e", upper "u"), column three shows the inferred growth function for each loop in the program (separated by "," if there are two or more loops), in the fourth column we list the cost postcondition obtained by the analysis (expressions indicating the number of loop iterations are highlighted), and columns five to eight display performance metrics. Time t_{cost}, given in milliseconds, is the time needed to perform the cost analysis. The proof generation time t_{proof} is given in seconds. We also display the time t_{check} needed for checking integrity of an already generated proof certificate. Finally, s_{proof} is the size of the generated KeY proof in terms of number of proof steps. Even though the time needed for certification is significantly higher than for cost analysis (which is to be expected), each analysis can be performed within one minute. The time to *check* a proof certificate amounts to approximately one fourth to one third of the time needed to *generate* it. We stress that all analyses are *fully automatic*.

We briefly describe the nature of each experiment: **1** is a *loop unrolling* transformation duplicating the body of a loop: each copy of the body is put inside an **if** -statement conditioned by the loop guard. Here, we had to switch to *asymptotic* cost invariants: The cost analyzer over-approximates the number of iterations of the unrolled loop, since there are different possible control flows in the body. This was automatically detected by the certifier which failed to find a proof when exact cost invariants are conjectured and succeeds with asymptotic ones. **2** is the *CodeMotion* example from Sect. 2. The result reflects the cost *decrease* in the sense that less instructions need to be executed by the transformed program. **3** implements a *LoopTiling* optimization at compiler level in which a single loop with $n \cdot m$ iterations is transformed into two nested loops, an outer one looping until n and an inner one until m. Since our cost analyzer only handles linear size expressions, the first program is written using an auxiliary parameter t that is then instantiated to value $n \cdot m$. **4** is a *SplitLoop* transformation splitting a loop with two independent parts into two separate loops. We prove that this transformation does not affect the cost up to a constant factor. **5** is an optimization combining *two loops* with the same body structure into one loop. **6** is a *three loops* example, one nested and one simple. The optimization combines the bodies of the outer loop in the nested structure and the simple loop. **7** is an *array* optimization, where an array declaration is moved in front of a loop, initializing it with an auxiliary parameter that is the sum of all the initial sizes.

	P	Cost analysis results		t_{cost} [ms]	t_{proof} [s]	t_{check} [s]	s_{proof} #nodes
		Growth	Postcondition				
1a	a	i	$t \cdot ac_P(x)$	45.0	12.9	4.3	1,784
1b	a	i	$t \cdot ac_P(x)$	53.4	23.8	5.0	3,472
2a	e	i	$2 + t \cdot (7 + ac_P(t,w) + ac_Q(t,z))$	50.0	23.3	5.7	3,692
2b	e	i	$3 + ac_P(t,w) + t \cdot (6 + ac_Q(t,z))$	42.0	19.7	5.7	3,243
3a	e	i	$2 + t \cdot (6 + ac_P(k))$	49.1	18.7	5.1	2,821
3b	e	i , j	$6 + n \cdot m \cdot (6 + ac_P(k))$	49.5	23.3	5.7	3,794
4a	e	$i + 1$	$2 + (l+1) \cdot (7 + ac_{Q1}(t,w) + ac_{Q2}(t,z))$	49.5	23.8	5.7	3,933
4b	e	$i+1 , i+1$	$2 + (l+1) \cdot (12 + ac_{Q1}(t,w) + ac_{Q2}(t,z))$	48.5	29.4	7.3	5,137
5a	e	i , j	$2 + n \cdot (6 + ac_P(y)) + m \cdot (6 + ac_P(y))$	55.1	25.3	7.1	4,795
5b	e	i	$2 + (n+m) \cdot (8 + ac_P(y))$	48.2	14.1	4.7	2,492
6a	e	$k , j , n - i$	$6 + n \cdot (m \cdot (6 + ac_P(y)) + n \cdot (5 + ac_Q(y))$	49.8	32.0	8.1	7,078
6b	e	k , j	$7 + n \cdot (m \cdot (6 + ac_P(y)) + ac_Q(y))$	49.6	24.9	6.4	4,995
7a	u	$i - 1$	$(t-1) \cdot (4 \cdot (t-1) + ac_P(y))$	51.2	15.6	5.3	2,578
7b	u	$i - 1$	$4 \cdot m + (t-1) \cdot ac_P(y)$	43.3	13.0	4.2	1,793

Table 1: Results of the experiments.

6   Related Work

The present paper builds on the original AE framework [37,38], which we extend to *Quantitative* AE. At the moment no other approach or tool is able to analyze and certify the cost of schematic programs, specifically relational properties, so a direct comparison is impossible.

Cost Analysis. There are many resource analysis tools, including: [20], based on introducing counters and inferring loop invariants; [23], based on an analysis over the depth of functional programs formalized by means of type systems. Approaches that bound the number of execution steps include [19,29], working at the level of compilers. Systems such as APROVE [17] analyze the complexity of JAVA programs by transforming them to integer transition systems; COSTA [3] and COFLOCO [16] are based on the generation of cost recurrence equations from which upper bounds can be inferred. That is also the basis of the approach we pursue to infer abstract upper bounds in Sect. 4.1, hence our technique can be viewed as a generalization of these systems. Approaches based on type systems could also be generalized to work on abstract programs by introducing abstract cost as in Sect. 4.1.

For our work it is crucial to use ranking functions to infer growth of cost invariants. Ranking functions were used to generate bounds on the number of loop iterations in several systems, but none used them to define growth: [10] obtain runtime complexity bounds via symbolic representation from ranking functions, likewise PUBS [3], LOOPUS [40], and ABC [8]. PUBS analyses all loop transitions at once, LOOPUS uses an iterative procedure where bounds are propagated from inner to outer loops, ABC deals with nested, but not sequential loops. In our work, when inferring upper bounds, we solve all transitions at once and handle nested as well as sequential loops.

Certification. Several general-purpose deductive software verification [21] tools exist, including VERYFAST [34], WHY [15], DAFNY [28], KIV [33], and KeY [2]. We use KeY, the currently only system to implement AE. *Interactive* proof assistants like Isabelle [31] or Coq [7] also support more or less expressive abstract program fragments, but lack full automation. There are dedicated approaches involving schematic programs for *specific* contexts, like regression verification [18], compilation [22, 26, 30] or derived symbolic execution rules [12].

Regarding the combination of deductive verification and cost analysis, the closest approach to ours is the integration of COSTA and KeY [4] which was realized for concrete, not abstract programs. They verify upper bounds on the cost of concrete programs by decomposing them into ranking functions and size relations which are then verified separately. Here we use the novel concept of cost invariant that allows verification of quantitative properties without decomposition. Paper [4] deals only with the global number of iterations as is common in worst-case cost analysis. Our cost invariants are designed to be inductive and propagate cost through all loop iterations. Radiček et al. [32] devise a formal framework for analyzing the relative cost of different programs (or the same program with different inputs). Compared to our approach, they target purely functional programs extended with monads representing cost, while we work with an industrial programming language. Moreover, we generally reason about the cost of *transformations*, not of a transformation applied to one *particular* program.

7   Conclusion and Future Work

We presented the first approach to analyze the cost of schematic programs with placeholders. We can infer and verify cost bounds for a potentially infinite class of programs once and for all. In particular, for the first time, it is possible to analyze and prove changes in efficiency caused by program transformations—for all input programs. Our approach supports exact and asymptotic cost and a configurable cost model. We implemented a tool chain based on a cost analyzer and a program verifier which analyzes and formally certifies abstract cost bounds in a fully automated manner. Certification is essential, because only the verifier can determine whether the bounds inferred by the cost analyzer are exact.

Our work required the new concept of an (abstract) cost invariant. This is interesting in itself, because (i) it renders the analysis of nested loops modular and (ii) provides an interface to backends (such as verifiers) that characterizes the cost of code in iterations.

Obvious future work involves extending the analyzed target language. Cost analysis and deductive verification (including AE) are already possible for a large JAVA fragment [3, 37]. More interesting—and more challenging—is the analysis of program transformations that parallelize code. The extension to larger classes of cost functions, such as logarithmic or exponential, could be realized by integrating non-linear SMT solvers into the tool chain.

Acknowledgments. This work was funded partially by the Spanish MCIU, AEI and FEDER(EU) project RTI2018-094403-B-C31, by the CM project S2018/TCS-4314 co-funded by EIE Funds of the EU and by the UCM CT42/18-CT43/18 grant.

References

1. Alfred V. Aho, Ravi Sethi, and Jeffrey D. Ullman. *Compilers: Principles, Techniques, and Tools*. Addison-Wesley, 1986.
2. Wolfgang Ahrendt, Bernhard Beckert, Richard Bubel, Reiner Hähnle, Peter H. Schmitt, and Mattias Ulbrich, editors. *Deductive Software Verification - The KeY Book - From Theory to Practice*, volume 10001 of *LNCS*. Springer, 2016.
3. Elvira Albert, Puri Arenas, Samir Genaim, German Puebla, and Damiano Zanardini. Cost analysis of object-oriented bytecode programs. *Theor. Comput. Sci.*, 413(1):142–159, 2012.
4. Elvira Albert, Richard Bubel, Samir Genaim, Reiner Hähnle, Germán Puebla, and Guillermo Román-Díez. A formal verification framework for static analysis - as well as its instantiation to the resource analyzer COSTA and formal verification tool KeY. *Software and Systems Modeling*, 15(4):987–1012, 2016.
5. Roberto Bagnara, Patricia M. Hill, and Enea Zaffanella. The Parma polyhedra library: Toward a complete set of numerical abstractions for the analysis and verification of hardware and software systems. *Sci. Comput. Program.*, 72(1-2):3–21, 2008.
6. Roberto Bagnara, Fred Mesnard, Andrea Pescetti, and Enea Zaffanella. A new look at the automatic synthesis of linear ranking functions. *Inf. Comput.*, 215:47–67, 2012.
7. Yves Bertot and Pierre Castéran. *Interactive Theorem Proving and Program Development - Coq'Art: The Calculus of Inductive Constructions*. Texts in Theoretical Computer Science. An EATCS Series. Springer, 2004.
8. Régis Blanc, Thomas A. Henzinger, Thibaud Hottelier, and Laura Kovács. ABC: algebraic bound computation for loops. In Edmund M. Clarke and Andrei Voronkov, editors, *Logic for Programming, Artificial Intelligence, and Reasoning - 16th International Conference, LPAR-16, Dakar, Senegal, April 25-May 1, 2010, Revised Selected Papers*, volume 6355 of *LNCS*, pages 103–118. Springer, 2010.
9. Robert S. Boyer, Bernard Elspas, and Karl N. Levitt. SELECT—A formal system for testing and debugging programs by symbolic execution. *ACM SIGPLAN Notices*, 10(6):234–245, June 1975.
10. Marc Brockschmidt, Fabian Emmes, Stephan Falke, Carsten Fuhs, and Jürgen Giesl. Alternating runtime and size complexity analysis of integer programs. In Erika Ábrahám and Klaus Havelund, editors, *Tools and Algorithms for the Construction and Analysis of Systems - 20th Intl. Conf., TACAS, Grenoble, France*, volume 8413 of *LNCS*, pages 140–155. Springer, 2014.
11. Marc Brockschmidt, Richard Musiol, Carsten Otto, and Jürgen Giesl. Automated termination proofs for Java programs with cyclic data. In P. Madhusudan and Sanjit A. Seshia, editors, *Computer Aided Verification - 24th International Conference, CAV 2012, Berkeley, CA, USA, July 7-13, 2012 Proceedings*, volume 7358 of *LNCS*, pages 105–122. Springer, 2012.
12. Richard Bubel, Andreas Roth, and Philipp Rümmer. Ensuring the Correctness of Lightweight Tactics for JavaCard Dynamic Logic. *Electr. Notes Theor. Comput. Sci.*, 199:107–128, 2008.
13. Patrick Cousot and Nicolas Halbwachs. Automatic discovery of linear restraints among variables of a program. In Alfred V. Aho, Stephen N. Zilles, and Thomas G. Szymanski, editors, *Conference Record of the Fifth Annual ACM Symposium on Principles of Programming Languages, Tucson, Arizona, USA, January 1978*, pages 84–96. ACM Press, 1978.

14. Karl Crary and Stephanie Weirich. Resource bound certification. In Mark N. Wegman and Thomas W. Reps, editors, *POPL 2000, Proceedings of the 27th ACM SIGPLAN-SIGACT Symposium on Principles of Programming Languages, Boston, Massachusetts, USA, January 19-21, 2000*, pages 184–198. ACM, 2000.

15. Jean-Christophe Filliâtre and Claude Marché. The Why/Krakatoa/Caduceus platform for deductive program verification. In Werner Damm and Holger Hermanns, editors, *Computer Aided Verification, 19th Intl. Conf., CAV, Berlin, Germany*, volume 4590 of *LNCS*, pages 173–177. Springer, 2007.

16. Antonio Flores-Montoya and Reiner Hähnle. Resource analysis of complex programs with cost equations. In Jacques Garrigue, editor, *Programming Languages and Systems - 12th Asian Symposium, APLAS 2014, Singapore, November 17-19, 2014, Proceedings*, volume 8858 of *LNCS*, pages 275–295. Springer, 2014.

17. Jürgen Giesl, Marc Brockschmidt, Fabian Emmes, Florian Frohn, Carsten Fuhs, Carsten Otto, Martin Plücker, Peter Schneider-Kamp, Thomas Ströder, Stephanie Swiderski, and René Thiemann. Proving termination of programs automatically with AProVE. In Stéphane Demri, Deepak Kapur, and Christoph Weidenbach, editors, *Automated Reasoning - 7th Intl. Joint Conf., IJCAR, Vienna, Austria*, volume 8562 of *LNCS*, pages 184–191. Springer, 2014.

18. Benny Godlin and Ofer Strichman. Regression Verification: Proving the Equivalence of Similar Programs. *Softw. Test., Verif. Reliab.*, 23(3):241–258, 2013.

19. Neville Grech, Kyriakos Georgiou, James Pallister, Steve Kerrison, and Kerstin Eder. Static energy consumption analysis of LLVM IR programs. *CoRR*, abs/1405.4565, 2014.

20. Sumit Gulwani, Krishna K. Mehra, and Trishul M. Chilimbi. SPEED: precise and efficient static estimation of program computational complexity. In Zhong Shao and Benjamin C. Pierce, editors, *Proceedings of the 36th ACM SIGPLAN-SIGACT Symposium on Principles of Programming Languages, POPL 2009, Savannah, GA, USA, January 21-23, 2009*, pages 127–139. ACM, 2009.

21. Reiner Hähnle and Marieke Huisman. Deductive verification: from pen-and-paper proofs to industrial tools. In Bernhard Steffen and Gerhard Woeginger, editors, *Computing and Software Science: State of the Art and Perspectives*, volume 10000 of *LNCS*, pages 345–373. Springer, 2019.

22. Reiner Hähnle and Dominic Steinhöfel. Modular, correct compilation with automatic soundness proofs. In Tiziana Margaria and Bernhard Steffen, editors, *Leveraging Applications of Formal Methods, Verification and Validation: Foundational Techniques, 8th Intl. Symp., Proc. Part I, ISoLA, Cyprus*, volume 11244 of *LNCS*, pages 424–447. Springer, 2018.

23. Jan Hoffmann and Martin Hofmann. Amortized resource analysis with polynomial potential. In Andrew D. Gordon, editor, *Programming Languages and Systems, 19th European Symposium on Programming, ESOP, Paphos, Cyprus*, volume 6012 of *LNCS*, pages 287–306. Springer, 2010.

24. John Hughes, Lars Pareto, and Amr Sabry. Proving the correctness of reactive systems using sized types. In *Proceedings of the 23rd ACM SIGPLAN-SIGACT Symposium on Principles of Programming Languages*, POPL '96, page 410–423, New York, NY, USA, 1996. Association for Computing Machinery.

25. James C. King. Symbolic execution and program testing. *Communications of the ACM*, 19(7):385–394, July 1976.

26. Sudipta Kundu, Zachary Tatlock, and Sorin Lerner. Proving Optimizations Correct Using Parameterized Program Equivalence. In *Proc. PLDI 2009*, pages 327–337, 2009.

27. Gary T. Leavens, Erik Poll, Curtis Clifton, Yoonsik Cheon, Clyde Ruby, David Cok, Peter Müller, Joseph Kiniry, Patrice Chalin, Daniel M. Zimmerman, and Werner Dietl. JML Reference Manual, May 2013. Draft revision 2344.

28. Rustan Leino. Dafny: An automatic program verifier for functional correctness. In *16th International Conference, LPAR-16, Dakar, Senegal*, pages 348–370. Springer Berlin Heidelberg, April 2010.

29. Umer Liqat, Kyriakos Georgiou, Steve Kerrison, Pedro López-García, John P. Gallagher, Manuel V. Hermenegildo, and Kerstin Eder. Inferring parametric energy consumption functions at different software levels: ISA vs. LLVM IR. In Marko C. J. D. van Eekelen and Ugo Dal Lago, editors, *Foundational and Practical Aspects of Resource Analysis - 4th Intl. Workshop, FOPARA, London, UK, Revised Selected Papers*, volume 9964 of *LNCS*, pages 81–100, 2015.

30. Nuno P. Lopes, David Menendez, Santosh Nagarakatte, and John Regehr. Practical Verification of Peephole Optimizations with Alive. *Commun. ACM*, 61(2):84–91, 2018.

31. Tobias Nipkow, Lawrence C. Paulson, and Markus Wenzel. *Isabelle/HOL - A Proof Assistant for Higher-Order Logic*, volume 2283 of *LNCS*. Springer, 2002.

32. Ivan Radiček, Gilles Barthe, Marco Gaboardi, Deepak Garg, and Florian Zuleger. Monadic refinements for relational cost analysis. *Proc. ACM Program. Lang.*, 2(POPL), December 2017.

33. Wolfgang Reif. The KIV-approach to software verification. In *KORSO - Methods, Languages, and Tools for the Construction of Correct Software*, volume 1009 of *LNCS*, pages 339–370. Springer, 1995.

34. Jan Smans, Bart Jacobs, Frank Piessens, and Wolfram Schulte. An automatic verifier for Java-like programs based on dynamic frames. In José Luiz Fiadeiro and Paola Inverardi, editors, *Fundamental Approaches to Software Engineering, 11th Intl. Conf., FASE, Budapest, Hungary*, volume 4961 of *LNCS*, pages 261–275. Springer, 2008.

35. Fausto Spoto, Fred Mesnard, and Étienne Payet. A termination analyzer for Java bytecode based on path-length. *ACM Trans. Program. Lang. Syst.*, 32(3):8:1–8:70, 2010.

36. Dominic Steinhöfel. REFINITY to Model and Prove Program Transformation Rules. In Bruno C. d. S. Oliveira, editor, *Proc. 18th Asian Symposium on Programming Languages and Systems (APLAS)*, LNCS. Springer, 2020.

37. Dominic Steinhöfel and Reiner Hähnle. Abstract execution. In Maurice H. ter Beek, Annabelle McIver, and José N. Oliveira, editors, *Formal Methods - The Next 30 Years - Third World Congress, FM 2019, Porto, Portugal, October 7-11, 2019, Proceedings*, volume 11800 of *LNCS*, pages 319–336. Springer, 2019.

38. Dominic Steinhöfel. *Abstract Execution: Automatically Proving Infinitely Many Programs*. PhD thesis, Technical University of Darmstadt, Department of Computer Science, Darmstadt, Germany, 2020.

39. Ben Wegbreit. Mechanical program analysis. *Commun. ACM*, 18(9):528–539, 1975.

40. Florian Zuleger, Sumit Gulwani, Moritz Sinn, and Helmut Veith. Bound analysis of imperative programs with the size-change abstraction (extended version). *CoRR*, abs/1203.5303, 2012.

Bootstrapping Automated Testing for RESTful Web Services

Yixiong Chen[1], Yang Yang[1], Zhanyao Lei[1],
Mingyuan Xia[2], and Zhengwei Qi[1]

[1] Shanghai Jiao Tong University, Shanghai, China
{lawischen,ylxy452782520,leizhanyao,qizhwei}@sjtu.edu.cn
[2] AppetizerIO, Shanghai, China
ken@appetizer.io

Abstract. Modern RESTful services expose RESTful APIs to integrate with diversified applications. Most RESTful API parameters are weakly typed, which greatly increases the possible input value space. This poses difficulties for automated testing tools to generate effective test cases to reveal web service defects related to parameter validation. We call this phenomenon the type collapse problem. To remedy this problem, we introduce FET (Format-encoded Type) techniques, including the FET, the FET lattice, and the FET inference to model fine-grained information for API parameters. Enhanced by FET techniques, automated testing tools can generate targeted test cases. We demonstrate Leif, a trace-driven fuzzing tool, as a proof-of-concept implementation of FET techniques. Experiment results on 27 commercial services show that FET inference precisely captures documented parameter definitions, which helps Leif to discover 11 new bugs and reduce $72\% \sim 86\%$ fuzzing time as compared to state-of-the-art fuzzers.

Keywords: Fuzz Testing · RESTful Web Service · Type Inference.

1 Introduction

The REST (Representational State Transfer) architecture [28] nowadays has dominated the design of complex web services, such as public clouds (e.g. AWS and Azure), social networking (e.g. Facebook and Twitter), and code hosting (e.g. GitHub and GitLab). Typically, a RESTful web service exposes a set of RESTful APIs. A client requests an API providing parameter values, and the service responds with data represented in some common exchange format (e.g. JSON or XML). According to a recent survey of 40 real-world popular RESTful web services [36], modern services involve an average of 64 APIs and over 20 parameters per API. Testing such an input space of possible parameter value combinatorics is challenging, and therefore automated testing is indispensable.

Since RESTful APIs are intended for applications implemented by different programming languages, API parameters are weakly typed. An investigation on 27 RESTful web services [19] shows that over 67% of the parameters are

© The Author(s) 2021
E. Guerra and M. Stoelinga (Eds.): FASE 2021, LNCS 12649, pp. 46–66, 2021.
https://doi.org/10.1007/978-3-030-71500-7_3

`string`-typed, about 32% are `number`-typed, and the remaining 1% are `boolean`-typed or `object`-typed. Overusing primitive data types significantly increases the possible input value space. For example, a `string`-typed parameter can take values varying from a specific URL to a comment about a YouTube video. This poses difficulties for generating effective test cases. Consequently, many automated REST testing tools are ineffective while RESTful web services suffer from various input-related attacks, such as integer overflow attacks and SQL injection attacks [18]. We call this phenomenon the *type collapse problem*.

The solution is to bridge the gap for automated testing tools to have a better understanding of parameters. We observe that though parameter types are weak, their values usually have distinct formats. For example, a datetime parameter may require an `ISO8601` date string. This motivates us to introduce the *FET (Format-encoded Type)* which combines *data types* and *value formats* to describe parameters in fine grains. For instance, the `SHA1` FET represents 40-digit-hex `string`-typed parameters. Furthermore, we introduce the FET lattice which hierarchically organizes a set of FETs by a partial order, along with the FET inference which seeks suitable FETs among a FET lattice for parameters in an unambiguous manner.

To manifest how to enhance automated REST testing by FET techniques, we implement Leif, a trace-driven fuzz testing tool. Leif gains fine-grained parameter information by performing FET inference on HTTP traffic and then mutates parameter values to mimic real attacks based on the inferred results. We apply Leif to real-world web services, and the experiment results are encouraging. FET techniques provide better bug-finding capability and bring 72% ∼ 86% fuzzing time reduction for Leif when compared to state-of-the-art fuzzing tools.

In particular, this paper makes the following contributions:

- We introduce FET techniques, including the FET, the FET lattice, and the FET inference, to remedy the type collapse problem and serve as a cornerstone for high-level automated testing tools.
- We implement Leif, a FET-enhanced fuzzing tool which showcases how to construct a ubiquitous FET lattice for common RESTful APIs and embed FET techniques in an existing testing workflow.
- We evaluate the accuracy of FET inference, and the result is encouraging (67% exact matches, 32% partial matches, and 1% mismatches on average).
- We evaluate Leif's bug-finding capability (11 distinct bugs detected in 27 commercial web services) as well as its testing efficiency (72% ∼ 86% fuzzing time reduction as compared to existing fuzzing tools).

The remainder of the paper is organized as follows. Section 2 analyzes the type collapse problem in detail. Section 3 introduces FET techniques to solve the type collapse problem. Section 4 introduces Leif as a proof-of-concept implementation of FET techniques. Section 5 presents the evaluation of FET techniques and Leif. Section 6 discusses related works and Section 7 concludes.

2   Motivation

It is essential for automated REST testing tools to generate test cases by filling parameters with automatically generated values. This procedure requires adequate information about parameters. Otherwise, the possible candidate space would become enormous even for one single parameter. Therefore, a majority of state-of-the-art automated testing tools focus on reducing the candidate space by sophisticated methodologies. For instance, RESTler [13] arranges multiple APIs in the producer-consumer order, and uses response data gained from the previous APIs to request the next. Chizpurfle [23] and EvoMaster [12] generate optimal candidate values based on evolutionary algorithms.

Nevertheless, the previous works have not focused on the root cause of the candidate space explosion. Since most RESTful APIs are designed for exchanging data between programs implemented by different languages (e.g., Java for mobile applications while Python for the service), only a few common *primitive data types* can be used to represent API parameters. For example, Amazon's online shopping web service takes about 2,400 parameters, among which 748 are number-typed (31%) and 1,581 are string-typed (66%) [19]. That is, types, which are supposed to be diversified, now collapse into very limited cases. Consequently, existing automated testing tools encounter a huge candidate space, e.g., solely knowing a parameter is string-typed spans a boundless candidate space from paragraphs of Shakespeare to specific datetime strings. In addition, it is difficult to pick up effective values that can pass parameter checking, then reach actual business logic, and finally trigger bugs. Figure 1 shows a code sample of a RESTful API (requires four parameters: string-typed start, string-typed end, number-typed amount, and number-typed interest). In order to generate an effective value which can reach business logic for the parameter start, a testing tool has to know it is an ISO8601 datetime string. Unfortunately, since parameters are mainly in primitive data types, this information is usually hard to obtain. Therefore, the testing tool may treat it as an ordinary string and generate arbitrary strings which are all rejected by the parameter checking and thus are basically useless.

```
1   def calculate_monthly_installment():
2     try:
3       start = parse(request.get("start"), "YYYY-MM-DDTHH:MM:SSZ")
4       end = parse(request.get("end"), "YYYY-MM-DDTHH:MM:SSZ")
5       amount = float(request.get("amount"))
6       interest = float(request.get("interest"))
7     except Exception:
8       return make_response("Invalid Parameter", 400, "Bad Request")
9     # business logic
10    ...
```

Fig. 1. A Code Sample of a RESTful API (Written in Python).

The type collapse problem is the major obstacle to obtaining adequate parameter information and leads to inefficient automated testing. Therefore, our solution is to provide a fine-grained description method for parameters by exploiting both its data type and its value format. Leveraged by such information, we are able to bootstrap and enhance automated testing techniques to gain efficiency improvement when testing RESTful web services.

3   FET Techniques

To address the type collapse problem, we introduce FET techniques, including the FET (Format-encoded Type), the FET lattice, and the FET inference. A FET models an API parameter by its data type and its value format. A FET lattice hierarchically organizes a set of FETs based on a partial order. We design FET inference algorithms to seek suitable FETs among a FET lattice for parameters, and the inferred results are the critical information for bootstrapping test case generation strategies.

3.1   Type Lattice

The idea of the FET lattice is inspired by the type lattice [24] for programming languages widely used in compilation and program analysis [33, 44, 45]. A type lattice is a *complete lattice* defined on $\langle T, \sqsubseteq \rangle$, where T is a set of data types (e.g. long in C/C++) and $\sqsubseteq$ is a partial order representing type convertibility. Every two lattice elements have a unique *least upper bound* and a unique *greatest lower bound*. An element t_j is said to *cover* another element t_i if and only if $t_i \sqsubset t_j$ but there does not exist a t_m such that $t_i \sqsubset t_m \sqsubset t_j$, where $t_i \sqsubset t_j$ means $t_i \sqsubseteq t_j$ and $t_i \neq t_j$. Type lattices can model class inheritance hierarchies for object-oriented languages. In this context, for any two elements t_i and t_j, $t_i \sqsubseteq t_j$ holds if and only if t_i inherits from or equals to t_j. Figure 2 depicts a type lattice for java.util.Collection (each vertex represents a class or an interface, and each directed edge stands for the inheritance relationship).

The type lattice is the cornerstone of type systems for modern programming languages. In static compilation, the type lattice is applied to checking value assignment and type casting for code validity [38]. In dynamic compilation, e.g., JIT (Just-in-time Compilation) [14], it is employed to predict variable types at program points, so as to remove unnecessary type checking. The type lattice is a powerful tool to ensure the correctness and efficiency of programs. However, in the context of REST, API parameters only manifest limited primitive data types due to the type collapse problem, where the type lattice is no longer sufficient.

3.2   FET Lattice

A FET lattice is defined on $\langle \Psi \subseteq T \times F, \preceq \rangle$. A FET $\psi \in \Psi$ is defined by (t_ψ, f_ψ), where $t_\psi \in T$ is a *data type*, and $f_\psi \in F$ is a *value format* or more specifically a *set* of values. $\preceq$ is a partial order that for any two FETs ψ_i and ψ_j, $\psi_i \preceq \psi_j$

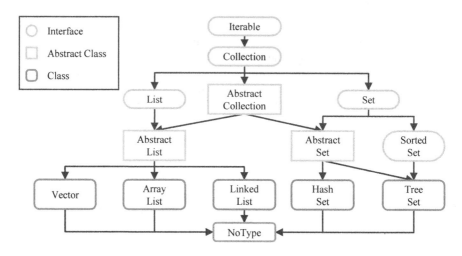

Fig. 2. A Type Lattice for the Java Collections Framework.

holds if and only if t_{ψ_i} is *type-convertible* to t_{ψ_j} and f_{ψ_i} is a *subset* of f_{ψ_j}, denoted by $t_{\psi_i} \sqsubseteq t_{\psi_j}$ and $f_{\psi_i} \subseteq f_{\psi_j}$. A FET ψ_i covered by ψ_j implies that ψ_i describes parameter features in a finer grain than ψ_j. $\psi_\top$ and $\psi_\bot$ are defined as $(\texttt{AnyType}, U)$ and $(\texttt{NoType}, \emptyset)$, where U is the set containing arbitrary values. Figure 3 depicts an example FET lattice (a FET's name describes its value format, and FETs at the same level are identically colored).

FET Acceptance for Parameter Values. Similar to type lattices, FET lattices help to determine FETs for given parameter values. To achieve this, we define that a value v is *accepted* by a FET ψ if and only if $typeof(v) \sqsubseteq t_\psi$ and $v \in f_\psi$, denoted by $\psi \in acceptance(v)$. Otherwise v is said to be *rejected* by ψ, denoted by $\psi \notin acceptance(v)$. Spontaneously, $\psi_\top$ accepts all values while $\psi_\bot$ accepts none. A value v can be accepted by more than one FET, while the *greatest lower bound* of the acceptances describes the value in the finest grain. We call such an acceptance the *minimum acceptance* of v. The *predecessors* of the minimum acceptance accept v but describe it in a coarser grain, while the *siblings* reject v but describe other similar values in the same grain. The minimum acceptance, the predecessors, and the siblings of v compose a *tree*, denoted by $\psi\text{-}tree(v)$. For example, for a $\texttt{SHA1}$ string v, its minimum acceptance (the $\texttt{SHA1}$ FET in Figure 3), the predecessors ($\texttt{Hash}$, $\texttt{String}$, and $\psi_\top$) and the siblings ($\texttt{MD5}$, and $\texttt{SHA256}$) compose the $\psi\text{-}tree(v)$.

Avoiding the Ambiguity of FET Lattices. As seen in Figure 3, if a single value is accepted by two sibling FETs (e.g. $\texttt{MD5}$ and $\texttt{SHA1}$), the minimum acceptance will fall into the trivial $\psi_\bot$. Generally, a FET lattice is said to be *ambiguous* if there exist two FETs with the *same predecessor* can both accept the *same value*. To avoid ambiguity, a validation procedure is obligatory after a FET lattice is constructed, which is to ensure the value formats of every two sibling FETs with the same data type are always disjoint.

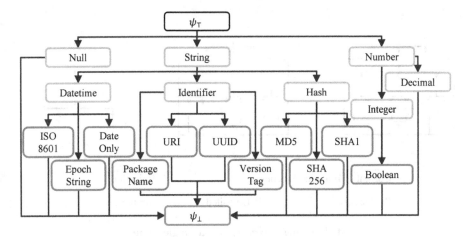

Fig. 3. An Example FET Lattice.

In practice, we specify value formats by the regular language, and provide a ubiquitous FET lattice [20] to model the most common RESTful parameters. We will elaborate FET lattice construction and verification in Section 4.2.

3.3   FET Inference

Tree-merging FET Inference.   As discussed previously, for a single value v, a unique $\psi\text{-}tree(v)$ can always be found in an unambiguous FET lattice. A RESTful API parameter usually involves multiple values in practice. Hence we give the *tree-merging FET inference*. For a parameter with values $v_1, \cdots, v_n$, the tree-merging inference is to compute $\psi\text{-}tree(v_1), \cdots, \psi\text{-}tree(v_n)$, and then merge them into one tree. The merged tree is denoted by $\psi\text{-}tree^n(V_n)$ where $V_n = \{v_1, \cdots, v_n\}$. The tree-merging inference can be described as a "find-expand-merge" procedure: (1) find the minimum acceptance for a single value v_i by performing a depth-first searching from $\psi_\top$ and add the predecessors along the searching path into the tree; (2) expand the tree by adding the siblings and then the $\psi\text{-}tree(v_i)$ is obtained; (3) repeat the step (1) and (2) for every value and merge all the trees. Step (1) and (2) are illustrated in Figure 4, and step (3) can be reduced to the DNS tree merging [25]. Assuming that the FET lattice has l levels with m FETs, the time complexity is $O(m)$ for computing one tree and $O(l)$ for merging two trees. Thus the time complexity of tree-merging FET inference for a parameter involving n values is $O(n \cdot (m + l))$.

Bitfield-boosting FET Inference.   In practice, we notice that the number of FETs m in a lattice is a constant while the number of values n is a variate (usually over 1,000). Therefore, we optimize the tree-merging FET inference based on three observations: (1) each FET can be uniquely represented by one bit in a m-bit bitfield, and therefore $\psi\text{-}trees$ can be represented by several bits in such bitfields; (2) given a minimum acceptance, its $\psi\text{-}tree$ can be uniquely

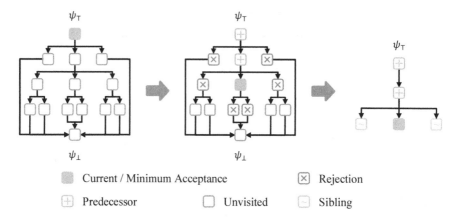

$\psi_\top$ $\psi_\top$ $\psi_\top$

$\psi_\bot$ $\psi_\bot$

| | Current / Minimum Acceptance | | ⊠ Rejection |
| | Predecessor | ☐ Unvisited | ⊟ Sibling |

Fig. 4. Inferring ψ-$tree(v_i)$ for a Single Value v_i.

determined, so the ψ-$tree$ for every FET can be computed before inference; (3) merging two ψ-$trees$ is equivalent to performing a bitwise OR operation on their corresponding bitfields.

Hence, we give the *forward computation algorithm* and the *bitfield-boosting FET inference*. The forward computation traverses the lattice in breadth-first order, assigns a unique bitfield ID per FET, and computes the ψ-$tree$, as shown in Algorithm 1. Leveraged by the forward computation, the bitfield-boosting inference only needs to find the minimum acceptance by the depth-first searching, yields the bitfield tree, and merges it into the ψ-$tree^{i-1}(V_{i-1})$, as shown in Algorithm 2. Therefore, the ψ-$tree^n(V_n)$ can be efficiently computed by a series of bitwise OR operations instead of graph computations, reducing the time complexity from $O(n \cdot (m + l))$ to $O(n \cdot m)$.

4   FET-enhanced REST Fuzzing

To manifest the utility of FET techniques, we design Leif, a FET-enhanced REST fuzzing tool, and we implement it to a command-line tool in 2,796 lines of Python code. This section elaborates the workflow of Leif, along with methodologies for collecting HTTP traffic (Section 4.1), for constructing FET lattices (Section 4.2), and for interfacing FET techniques with fuzzers (Section 4.3).

Figure 5 depicts Leif's workflow and its interaction with existing systems and tools. Leif assumes that the web service under test is already deployed on a staging server or in a production environment. The developer acquires the Leif program with a built-in FET lattice and traces HTTP traffic between the service and the clients. Then Leif identifies RESTful APIs by parsing the captured traffic and performs FET inference on parameter values. The inferred results are provided to bootstrap test case generating. Finally, Leif emits test cases and observes wrongful behaviors of the service.

Algorithm 1: The Forward Computation.

Input: A FET Lattice.

1 $ID \leftarrow 1; \quad queue \leftarrow Queue(\psi_\top);$
2 **while** $!queue.isEmpty()$ **do**
3      $current \leftarrow queue.pop();$
4      $current.ID \leftarrow ID;$
5      $ID \leftarrow ID \ll 1;$
6   **foreach** $\psi \preceq current$ **AND** $\psi \neq \psi_\bot$ **do**
7          $\lfloor \; queue.push(\psi);$

8 $\psi_\top.pTree \leftarrow 0; \quad \psi_\top.sTree \leftarrow \psi_\top.ID;$
9 $\psi_\top.tree \leftarrow \psi_\top.pTree \vee \psi_\top.sTree;$
10 $queue \leftarrow Queue(\psi_\top);$
11 **while** $!queue.isEmpty()$ **do**
12     $current \leftarrow queue.pop();$
13     $sTree \leftarrow 0;$
14   **foreach** $\psi \preceq current$ **AND** $\psi \neq \psi_\bot$ **do**
15         $\lfloor \; sTree \leftarrow sTree \vee \psi.ID;$
16   **foreach** $\psi \preceq current$ **AND** $\psi \neq \psi_\bot$ **do**
17         $\psi.pTree \leftarrow current.pTree \vee current.ID;$
18         $\psi.sTree \leftarrow sTree;$
19         $\psi.tree \leftarrow pTree \vee sTree;$
20         $\lfloor \; queue.push(\psi);$

4.1   Collecting and Parsing HTTP Traffic

As introduced in Section 3.3, the inferred result of a parameter is contributed by
its different values, and therefore the accuracy of FET inference increases when
Leif witnesses more value cases. Thus developers are expected to apply suitable
tracing methods. For example, monkey testing and scripted regression testing
are more preferred than unit testing to collect traffic. Leif takes the HAR file (an
archival format for HTTP traffic [39]), which is the standard output of network
proxies (Fiddler, MitmProxy [22], etc.), and browser inspection (e.g. Chrome,
and Safari). To identify parameters, the payload (including the headers, the
query string, and the body) of a captured request is parsed to key-value pairs
in JSON format. Due to the type collapse problem, only four data types are
present: `boolean`, `number`, `string` and `object` (including `array`). Non-object-
typed parameters are directly provided to FET inference while `object`-typed
parameters are flattened. Since a JSON object is a tree of properties, Leif flattens
it by splitting leaf properties to independent non-object-typed parameters and
assigning new keys named by their JSONPaths [29], as illustrated in Figure 6.
Then the flatten parameters are also provided to FET inference. Finally, FET
inference receives parameters for each API where each parameter has a unique
key and usually multiple values.

Algorithm 2: The Bitfield-boosting FET Inference.

Input: Parameter Values $V_n = \{v_1, \cdots, v_n\}$.
Output: $\psi\text{-}tree^n(V_n)$.

1 $\psi\text{-}tree^0(V_0) \leftarrow 0$;
2 **for** $i \leftarrow 1$ **to** n **do**
3 $\quad$ $current \leftarrow \psi_\top$;
4 $\quad$ $accepted \leftarrow true$;
5 $\quad$ **while** $accepted$ **do**
6 $\quad\quad$ $accepted \leftarrow false$;
7 $\quad\quad$ **foreach** $\psi \preceq current$ **do**
8 $\quad\quad\quad$ **if** $\psi \in acceptance(v_i)$ **then**
9 $\quad\quad\quad\quad$ $current \leftarrow \psi$;
10 $\quad\quad\quad\quad$ $accepted \leftarrow true$;
11 $\quad$ $\psi\text{-}tree^i(V_i) \leftarrow \psi\text{-}tree^{i-1}(V_{i-1}) \vee current.tree$;
12 **return** $\psi\text{-}tree^n(V_n)$;

4.2 Ubiquitous FET Lattice

Regular Expressions for Value Formats. In Leif's built-in ubiquitous FET lattice, value formats are specified by regular expressions. We choose to use the regular language rather than creating a new language to define value formats because it has many advantages in this scenario. Firstly, regular expressions are the de-facto descriptions of most string formats. Although regular expressions are context-free, they can still distinguish different value formats. Secondly, they are already familiar to developers, and therefore they are easy to construct without extra learning costs. Finally, to ensure the unambiguity of a FET lattice is to ensure the regular expression orthogonality of sibling FETs, which can be formally determined by finite automata [46].

FET Lattice Constructing and Updating. We construct the ubiquitous FET lattice by referencing popular RESTful services (e.g. Google Map, AWS, Twitter, and GitHub): (1) we crawl API documents from these services and then identify potential FETs used in these services; (2) we construct regular expressions for these FETs by referencing related RFCs (e.g. RFC3339 [35] for ISO8601, and RFC3986 [16] for URI), programming language specifications (e.g. the Java specification [34] for PackageName), and database schema definitions (e.g. the MongoDB data type definition [21] for Hash) to build a base FET lattice; (3) we apply the Bayesian regular expression generation technique [42] to discover new FETs from traffic and merge them into the base lattice; (4) we verify the unambiguity by checking the orthogonality of regular expressions for sibling FETs, using dk.brics.automaton library [37]. The verified lattice has 21 FETs organized in 5 levels, and we believe it is competent to model most of the RESTful services. If a developer has application-specific FETs (at the first usage or when major service updates take place), one can update the lattice by adding FETs via step (3) and repeat step (4) for unambiguity verification.

Fig. 5. The Workflow Architecture of Leif.

(a) The Original Parameter.   (b) The Tree Structure.   (c) The Flattening Result.

Fig. 6. An Example of Object Flattening.

Twinning FET Inference. We notice some parameters can be represented by multiple data types and are minimally accepted by distinct FETs in different data types. For example, an epoch datetime (elapsed seconds or milliseconds since 1970-01-01 00:00:00) is accepted by the EpochString FET when it is represented by string while is accepted by the Integer FET when in number. Apparently, applying type casting to such parameters is very meaningful during testing. To support this feature, we implement the *twinning FET inference*. Before a value is inferred, Leif generates its twinning value if possible. If the original value is number-typed, Leif generates a twinning string-typed value (e.g. 1589809244481 → "1589809244481") and vice versa ("1589809244481" → 1589809244481). Then both values are inferred, and the resulting two ψ-trees are merged as if Leif witnesses two independent values. By doing so, both the `Datetime` and the `Integer` FETs are included in the final $\psi\text{-}tree^n$ of an epoch datetime parameter.

4.3 FET-aware Trace-driven Fuzzing

Trace-driven fuzzing tools generate test cases by replacing parameter values of captured requests with candidate values. Therefore the success of a fuzzer mainly depends on its quality of candidate values. In conventional tools, using a larger candidate dictionary is the basic strategy to increase the opportunity for triggering bugs, yet it lengthens the fuzzing time.

On the contrary, Leif provides a small but targeted dictionary for each FET and we give several examples (corresponding to Figure 3): `Number` is tried with integer overflows (8-bit, 16-bit, 32-bit, and 64-bit overflows) with signed and unsigned values; `Datetime` is tried with year overflows (`year 2038`, and `year 10,000`), invalid dates (e.g. `2019-2-29`), and timezone tweaks; `ISO8601` is tried with omitting meta characters (`"-"`, `":"`, etc.); `URI` is tried with malformed URLs (e.g. doubling `"/"`, stripping `"protocol://"`, and unescaped characters). With each parameter tagged by a $\psi\text{-}tree^n$, Leif generates test cases by exhausting dictionaries of all the FETs in the tree. Notice that, as discussed in Section 3.2, the predecessors and the siblings of the minimum acceptance describe similar but usually invalid values. Therefore, candidates from these FETs are the most likely values which can pass parameter checking and trigger bugs. For an API with multiple parameters, Leif exhausts dictionaries for one parameter each time and tests such API by iterations of exhaustion. In this way, Leif increases the opportunity to trigger bugs and meanwhile saves the fuzzing time.

5 Evaluation

In this section, we evaluate Leif with real-world RESTful web services, and the complete dataset of our evaluation is publicly available [19]. Specifically, we design three experiments to answer the following research questions:

RQ-1 How accurately do FET inference results describe RESTful API parameters of complicated real-world web services?

RQ-2 Can Leif generate effective test cases and therefore help developers to detect web service vulnerabilities in practice?

RQ-3 Does Leif have better bug-finding capability with reduced fuzzing time when compared to existing state-of-the-art trace-driven and specification-driven fuzz testing tools?

5.1 FET Inference Accuracy Evaluation

In this experiment, we assume that API documents provided by the service developers are the *ground truth* and we validate the accuracy of FET inference by comparing the inferred results with the ground truth. We choose GitHub[3] and Twitter[4], and we randomly pick up 50 RESTful APIs (25 from each). We extract two pieces of information from document text: (1) parameter data types, as explicitly listed in the documents; (2) parameter value formats, as provided in the detailed descriptions (e.g. "This [the parameter `since`] is a timestamp in `ISO8601` format."[5]). We feed example requests gained from the documents to FET inference, compare the inferred FETs with the ground truth, and observe three levels of matching:

(1) **exact match**, the inferred FET is said to be an exact match if it has the exactly same data type and the value format as the ground truth;
(2) **partial match**, the inferred FET is said to be a partial match if it has the exact data type, but its value format is a proper superset of the ground truth;
(3) **mismatch**, for the remaining cases.

Intuitively, an exact match precisely describes a parameter such that a fuzzer can exploit it to generate the most targeted values. A partial match is benign, for it includes values that will not appear in practice, and a fuzzer may generate a small set of useless values based on a partial match. A mismatch indicates that the value format is not yet supported by the current FET lattice.

(a) FET Inference Accuracy.

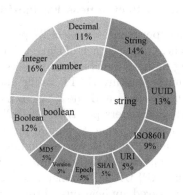

(b) Exact Match Distribution.

Fig. 7. FET Inference Accuracy Evaluation Results.

Figure 7(a) exhibits the ratios of matching on GitHub (137 parameters), Twitter (86 parameters) and the weighted average (223 parameters). In total, 149 (67%) inferred results are exact matches, and 71 (32%) are partial matches.

---

[3] https://docs.github.com/en/free-pro-team@latest/rest/reference
[4] https://developer.twitter.com/en/docs
[5] https://docs.github.com/en/free-pro-team@latest/rest/reference/gists

And we observe 3 mismatches in two cases: one is a binary-array parameter for file uploading and the other is an array of key-value pairs (e.g. [["key1", "value1"], ["key2", "value2"], ...]). Binary arrays can be supported by adding a FET ([01]* for the value format) to the current lattice, but Leif aims to detect logic-related bugs while binaries are usually logic-free but content-sensitive [43]. Therefore Leif simply does not mutate them. As for key-value pairs, they are actually two-dimensional arrays where the first dimension is immutable since it indicates the actual parameter key. We consider allowing developers to specify which special parameters are immutable in Leif's future version to support such cases. For the partial matches, we review the documents, and the top cases are application-specified formats such as comma-separated strings and PGP signatures. These formats are less common and developers can add application-specific FETs to their lattices by following the steps introduced in Section 4.2. Figure 7(b) exhibits the breakdown of exact matches (the inner ring is the distribution of the primitive data types and the outer ring is the inferred FETs) to quantify how FET inference improves parameter information. The coarse-grained number-typed (27%) and string-typed (61%) parameters are divided into much smaller slices (5% ∼ 14%). The breakdown clarifies that FET inference classifies parameters in balance, and therefore restores the collapsed types. This enables a fuzzer to generate more targeted values, which shrinks candidate space and increases the opportunity to find bugs.

5.2   Leif Effectiveness Evaluation

In this experiment, we select 27 popular mobile applications to evaluate the effectiveness of Leif. Each of them is backed by a commercial RESTful web service serving millions and billions of users. We monkey-test [30] each application for 20 minutes, capture HTTP traffic and run the full-stack Leif workflow. Table 1 lists the subjects and the services have an average of 133 RESTful APIs with over 19 parameters per API. We collect 46 requests per API on average which yields adequate request samples for inference. Leif reports 5XX HTTP responses as bugs along with the corresponding traffic. We have reached out to the service owners, reported these bugs, and validated these bugs through analysis of traffic (through API URLs, parameter key-value pairs, and response data) and analysis of the involved applications (through reverse engineering and static code analysis of APKs) to eliminate any false-positive or duplicated cases. Table 2 summarizes the 11 distinct bugs found by Leif. The testing process is fully automated which mimics how developers would use Leif as a black-box fuzzing tool in practice and our following analysis mimics how to classify bugs and locate related code lines based on Leif's testing results.

Security Bugs with Information Leakage. Bug 1, 2 and 10 are security bugs with information leakage problems. They can be reproduced by mutating the parameter appVer (VersionTag), the parameter platform (Identifier), and the parameter c.v (Integer). These bugs not only cause service crashes but also expose sensitive information to end users (potential attackers). With the exposed information, attackers can easily design specialized attacks. For example, the

Table 1. Experiment Subjects of the Effectiveness Validation.

Application Name	Category	Downloads[a]	Version	Traffic Size (MB)	# Unique APIs	# Parameters
Amazon	Shopping	205M+	18.4.0.1	213	142	2,380
Baidu	Tools	2.8B+	11.15.0.12	453	332	4,742
Bilibili	Video	220M+	5.49.0	524	219	4,338
Damai	Shopping	6.6M+	7.6.4	596	104	1,535
Dianping	Social	340M+	10.19.12	629	148	2,247
Eleme	Social	180M+	8.26.3	230	57	992
Hupu	Reading	11.1M+	7.3.26	295	229	4,446
iQiyi	Video	2.5B+	10.10.0	1,338	257	7,063
Jianshu	Reading	6.4M+	4.16.0	339	111	1,609
Jingdong	Shopping	950M+	8.3.2	514	131	1,521
Kaola	Shopping	15.3M+	4.3.5	322	252	3,848
Mafengwo	Trip	21.3M+	9.3.33	340	151	3,178
Meituan	Shopping	1.4B+	10.3.401	1,111	58	1,151
MissFresh	Shopping	16.3M+	9.6.4	348	50	719
ONE	Reading	4.8M+	4.6.2	242	53	567
Pinduoduo	Shopping	1.9B+	4.77.0	795	79	866
Qunar	Trip	330M+	8.9.28	1,246	146	1,563
Shanbay	Tools	2.91M+	4.2.6502	84	9	94
Sina News	News	110M+	7.25.1	266	53	724
Smzdm	Shopping	8.5M+	9.5.26	267	104	1,866
Sohu News	News	170M+	6.1.8	591	201	3,144
Tencent News	News	2.9B+	5.9.00	1,045	142	1,796
Tmall	Shopping	310M+	9.1.0	177	49	635
Toutiao	News	2.0B+	7.4.8	1,198	323	12,408
Tuniu	Trip	79.7M+	10.19.0	217	68	772
WUBA	Social	370M+	9.1.2	79	123	5,490
Xiaohongshu	Social	66.3M+	6.19.0	295	20	334
Total				**13,754**	**3,611**	**70,028**

[a] The statistic is from Tencent AppStore (https://sj.qq.com) up to Jan. 9th, 2020.

response data of bug 10 contains the full Java exception stack trace without any obfuscation. From the stack trace, attackers can obtain that the service uses an outdated Spring Framework[6] version which suffers from numerous security vulnerabilities [5,6,8–11]. By exploiting CVE-2020-5421 and CVE-2020-5398 [10, 11], attackers can initiate reflected file download attacks [31] to mislead users into downloading malware. And by exploiting CVE-2018-1257 [5], attackers can expose STOMP over WebSocket and then initiate denial of service attacks [17]. They can also obtain that the service uses `com.alibaba.fastjson` library[7] to deserialize user inputs. Therefore attackers can launch remote code executions by exploiting known defects in that specific library version [7,32].

Upon such cases, we suggest developers should first avoid information leakage problems by checking the service data flow, ensuring that no sensitive methods

---

[6] Spring Framework, https://spring.io/projects/spring-framework
[7] Fastjson, https://github.com/alibaba/fastjson

Table 2. Bugs Found by Leif during the Effectiveness Validation.

Bug ID	Involved Application	Status Code	API Path	Description
1	iQiyi	500	/book/register	A *private* API, served for user registration.
2	Pinduoduo	500	/cappuccino/splash	A *private* API, served for first-screen advertising.
3[a]	Sina News	500	/oauth2/getaid.json	A *deprecated public* API provided by Sina Weibo, served for user authorization.
4[a]	Sina News	503	/oauth2/getaid.json	A *deprecated public* API provided by Sina Weibo, served for user authorization.
5[b]	Smzdm	502	/integration.php	A *public* API provided by Baidu, served for inter-application integration.
6[c]	Sohu News	502	/sendacc.jsp	A *public* API provided by 53KF, served for customer service.
7[c]	Sohu News	502	/sendacc.jsp	A *public* API provided by 53KF, served for customer service.
8	Toutiao	502	/user/tab/tabs/v3	A *private* API, probably served for inter-application redirecting.
9	Toutiao	504	/user/tab/tabs/v3	A *private* API, probably served for inter-application redirecting.
10	Tuniu	500	/vip/recommend	A *private* API, served for content recommendation.
11[b]	WUBA	502	/integration.php	A *public* API provided by Baidu, served for inter-application integration.

[a] Bug 3 and bug 4 involve the same API but with different HTTP status codes.
[b] Bug 5 and bug 11 involve the same API but different applications.
[c] Bug 6 and bug 7 involve the same API path but different domain names.

(e.g., `java.lang.Exception.toString`) can be output to end users, and then diagnose security problems by analyzing server logs. Besides, they should stay alert to public vulnerability reports and timely upgrade their codebases.

Third-party API Bugs. We notice that 6 of the bugs involve APIs provided by third parties. Bug 3 and 4 involve the API for user authorization provided by Sina Weibo, a social networking platform serving over half a billion users. We decompile the Sina News APK and locate the related code lines. We find out the application uses a deprecated version of the API. When this API fails, an unhandled exception is propagated and causes the application to crash. It can be reproduced by injecting meta characters `"/.:/"` to the parameter `packagename` (`PackageName`) and to the parameter `mfp` (`Hash`). Bug 6 and 7 involve the API provided by a customer service platform. The application also suffers from the deprecated API and crashes when the API fails. Bug 5 and 11 are detected in different applications but involve the same API provided by Baidu. These two bugs can be reproduced by mutating the parameter `SdkVer` (`VersionTag`).

Using third-party APIs is very common, but they are often overlooked during testing. However, bugs in third-party code are as important as the application's own code, because they both mean application functionality failure to billions of end users. Our results show that Leif can find bugs across into third-party

APIs. We suggest that developers should capture application traffic and apply Leif to test untrusted third-party APIs. In addition, they should design proper exception handling logic for third-party code and timely upgrade to the latest API versions with known bugs fixed.

Bugs with Limited Information. We obtain very limited information from bug 8 and 9, because their responses solely contain HTTP status codes. These bugs could be as critical as the security bugs since they involve a private API and cause the service to crash. Therefore service developers can debug such APIs by following the analysis methods for the security bugs as mentioned.

5.3   Comparative Evaluation

Leif vs. Trace-driven Fuzzers. We classify Leif as a trace-driven fuzzer and we now compare it with state-of-the-art trace-driven fuzzing tools. We select BurpSuite [2], a commercial security testing fuzzer for RESTful web services, and Fuzzapi [3], an open-source general-purpose HTTP fuzzer. They provide built-in candidate dictionaries but require a series of manual configurations, including filling the URL for each API and the data type for each parameter. Therefore we only apply them to Sina News, Toutiao, and Amazon Shopping (518 unique APIs with 15,512 parameters in total). In addition, we implement NaiveFuzzer as a baseline that only understands primitive data types and randomly mutates parameter values solely based on such coarse-grained information. We construct NaiveFuzzer's candidate dictionaries by combining the dictionaries of BurpSuite and Fuzzapi.

We evaluate the bug-finding capabilities of BurpSuite, Fuzzapi, Leif, and NaiveFuzzer by comparing the number of bugs found by each tool, as reported in Figure 8(a). And we evaluate their fuzzing time by comparing the averaged number of test cases generated per parameter, as exhibited in Figure 8(b). Less generated test cases mean less test execution time, leading to the more efficient fuzzing. Considering the subjects are already well-tested before release, we believe the bug-finding capability of Leif is better than BurpSuite and Fuzzapi for Leif finds extra bugs. And NaiveFuzzer has the same capability as BurpSuite and Fuzzapi. This is because they share the same candidate space. As for fuzzing time, BurpSuite, Fuzzapi and NaiveFuzzer respectively generate $5.0\times \sim 6.7\times$, $3.6\times \sim 4.7\times$ and $6.3\times \sim 7.1\times$ test cases of Leif, indicating FET techniques bring $72\% \sim 86\%$ fuzzing time reduction.

Leif vs. Specification-driven Fuzzers. We now compare Leif with existing specification-driven fuzzers, which test RESTful web services based on parsing API specifications. We select RESTler [13], a state-of-the-art research fuzzer, and TnT-Fuzzer [4], an open-source robustness testing tool. They both require OpenAPI specifications [40] as input, but most of the subject services do not provide OpenAPI specifications. Therefore we construct OpenAPI specifications for Sina News, Toutiao, and Amazon Shopping by parsing HTTP traffic and referencing their official API documents.

We intend to run RESTler, but unfortunately neither the executable program nor the source code is available. According to the paper, RESTler only supports

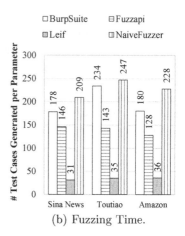

(a) Bug-finding Capabilities.   (b) Fuzzing Time.

Fig. 8. Bug-finding Capabilities and Fuzzing Time of the Evaluated Fuzzers.

primitive data types and uses a plain candidate dictionary (consisting of 0, 1, "", and "sampleString"). Yet none of the bugs found by Leif can be triggered by these values, indicating that performing RESTler would fail to detect any of the bugs. And TnT-Fuzzer generates candidate values simply based on the Python random() function (i.e. purely random fuzzing). We configure it to generate 1,000 test cases per parameter (about 5× of NaiveFuzzer and 30× of Leif). Still, TnT-Fuzzer fails to find any bugs in the three services. We conclude that the two fuzzers' effectiveness is limited by the practical hardness of finding well-written OpenAPI specifications and the quality of their candidates. These are also the main shortcomings of all specification-driven fuzzers. Besides, many modern APIs require short-lived session tokens for access control or throttling. Specification-driven fuzzers require manual configuration or even repeated re-configuration for such parameters. In contrast, it is easy for trace-driven fuzzers to achieve this requirement by mutating freshly captured requests.

6   Related Work

Model-driven Testing.   Model-driven testing [15, 26, 27, 47, 48] is usually white-box and requires using some specific modeling method (e.g. UML or DSL) through the whole lifecycle of developing, which is human-intensive and technically-limited for services across multiple servers and micro-services from different vendors. Essentially, FET techniques are also model-driven (i.e. driven by the lattice model) but only intervene in the test phase. Thus FET techniques can be practically employed to test diversified RESTful web services in black-box approaches.

Trace-driven Fuzzing.   Trace-driven fuzzing generates test cases by mutating recorded requests. Fuzzapi [3], BurpSuite [2], AppSpider [1] and Leif all fall into this category. Existing trace-driven fuzzers mainly focus on improving the ability to capture and replay HTTP traffic. However, Leif demonstrates that FET techniques provide fundamental parameter information to fuzzers, bringing the enhanced bug-finding capability and significant fuzzing time reduction.

Specification-driven Fuzzing. Another main class of fuzz testing techniques is specification-driven fuzzing, such as TnT-Fuzzer [4], EvoMaster [12], and RESTler [13], which avoids the type collapse problem by assuming developers provide well-defined specifications with detailed parameter information. However, the OpenAPI [40] is the only well-established standard up to now, yet is not widely used. A survey [41] reveals that 71% developers lack the knowledge of the OpenAPI framework. Therefore, the specification-driven fuzzing is still too idealistic for testing real-world RESTful web services. In comparison, instead of asking developers for good specifications, FET techniques generate fine-grained specifications (i.e. ψ-$trees^n$ of parameters) on its own.

Security Penetration Testing. Fuzz testing techniques are also commonly purposed for security penetration testing. Commercial security penetration tools, such as BurpSuite [2], use values of SQL injections, unescaped HTML characters, XML/JSON external entities, etc., to expose system vulnerabilities. FET techniques can also be employed in security penetration testing, as demonstrated in Section 5.2. While our main goal is not limited to security testing for RESTful web services, because FET techniques improve the value selecting strategy for general-purpose REST fuzzing.

7 Conclusion and Future Work

In this paper, we analyze the type collapse problem and propose FET techniques to remedy this problem. As a proof-of-concept, we design and implement Leif, a FET-enhanced trace-driven fuzzing tool. We demonstrate that using FET techniques greatly improves a fuzzer's understanding of parameters, resulting in more effective fuzz testing. Our experiment results show that Leif unveils 11 new bugs in application-specific web services as well as general third-party open API platforms with 72% $\sim$ 86% fuzzing time reduction.

FET techniques are capable of effectively bootstrapping automated testing tools. We believe they are also helpful for parameter validity checking because these two technical problems are isomorphic in a sense. Thus we are beginning to study how to automatically generate or enhance parameter checking code based on FET techniques for RESTful web services.

Acknowledgments

We would like to thank the anonymous reviewers for their valuable comments. This work was supported in part by National Key Research Development Program of China (No. 2016YFB1000502), National NSF of China (No. 61672344, 61525204, and 61732010), Shanghai Pujiang Program (No. 19PJ1430900), and Shanghai Key Laboratory of Scalable Computing and Systems.

References

1. AppSpider. https://www.rapid7.com/products/appspider
2. BurpSuite. https://portswigger.net/burp
3. Fuzzapi. https://github.com/Fuzzapi/fuzzapi
4. TnT-Fuzzer. https://github.com/Teebytes/TnT-Fuzzer
5. CVE-2018-1257. Available from MITRE, CVE-ID CVE-2018-1257 (Dec 6 2017), https://cve.mitre.org/cgi-bin/cvename.cgi?name=CVE-2018-1257
6. CVE-2018-1275. Available from MITRE, CVE-ID CVE-2018-1275 (Dec 6 2017), https://cve.mitre.org/cgi-bin/cvename.cgi?name=CVE-2018-1275
7. CVE-2017-18349. Available from MITRE, CVE-ID CVE-2017-18349 (Oct 23 2018), https://cve.mitre.org/cgi-bin/cvename.cgi?name=CVE-2017-18349
8. CVE-2018-15756. Available from MITRE, CVE-ID CVE-2018-15756 (Aug 23 2018), https://cve.mitre.org/cgi-bin/cvename.cgi?name=CVE-2018-15756
9. CVE-2020-5397. Available from MITRE, CVE-ID CVE-2020-5397 (Jan 3 2020), https://cve.mitre.org/cgi-bin/cvename.cgi?name=CVE-2020-5397
10. CVE-2020-5398. Available from MITRE, CVE-ID CVE-2020-5398 (Jan 3 2020), https://cve.mitre.org/cgi-bin/cvename.cgi?name=CVE-2020-5398
11. CVE-2020-5421. Available from MITRE, CVE-ID CVE-2020-5421 (Jan 3 2020), https://cve.mitre.org/cgi-bin/cvename.cgi?name=CVE-2020-5421
12. Arcuri, A.: RESTful API automated test case generation with EvoMaster. ACM Trans. Softw. Eng. Methodol. **28**(1), 3:1–3:37 (2019), https://doi.org/10.1145/3293455
13. Atlidakis, V., Godefroid, P., Polishchuk, M.: RESTler: Stateful REST API fuzzing. In: Atlee, J.M., Bultan, T., Whittle, J. (eds.) Proceedings of the 41st International Conference on Software Engineering, ICSE 2019, Montreal, QC, Canada, May 25-31, 2019. pp. 748–758. IEEE/ACM (2019), https://doi.org/10.1109/ICSE.2019.00083
14. Aycock, J.: A brief history of just-in-time. ACM Comput. Surv. **35**(2), 97–113 (2003), https://doi.org/10.1145/857076.857077
15. Baker, P., Dai, Z.R., Grabowski, J., Schieferdecker, I., Williams, C.: Model-driven Testing: Using the UML Testing Profile. Springer Science & Business Media (2007)
16. Berners-Lee, T., Fielding, R., Masinterm, L.: RFC3986: Uniform Resource Identifier (URI): Generic Syntax. Internet Engineering Task Force (Jan 2005), https://www.rfc-editor.org/info/rfc3986
17. Breslaw, D., Bekerman, D.: How Mirai uses STOMP protocol to launch DDoS attacks. Tech. rep., Imperva Inc. (Nov15 2016), https://www.imperva.com/blog/mirai-stomp-protocol-ddos/
18. Chandrashekhar, R., Mardithaya, M., Thilagam, S., Saha, D.: SQL injection attack mechanisms and prevention techniques. In: International Conference on Advanced Computing, Networking and Security. pp. 524–533. Springer (2011)
19. Chen, Y., Yang, Y., Lei, Z., Xia, M., Qi, Z.: The public dataset of Leif evaluation (Jan 2021), https://doi.org/10.6084/m9.figshare.12377150
20. Chen, Y., Yang, Y., Lei, Z., Xia, M., Qi, Z.: The ubiquitous FET lattice model and verification (Jan 2021), https://doi.org/10.6084/m9.figshare.13622720
21. Chodorow, K.: MongoDB: The Definitive Guide: Powerful and Scalable Data Storage. O'Reilly Media, Inc. (2013)
22. Cortesi, A., Hils, M., Kriechbaumer, T.: MitmProxy: A free and open source interactive HTTPS proxy (2010), https://mitmproxy.org

23. Cotroneo, D., Iannillo, A.K., Natella, R.: Evolutionary fuzzing of android OS vendor system services. Empirical Software Engineering **24**(6), 3630–3658 (2019), https://doi.org/10.1007/s10664-019-09725-6

24. Cousot, P., Cousot, R.: Abstract interpretation: A unified lattice model for static analysis of programs by construction or approximation of fixpoints. In: Graham, R.M., Harrison, M.A., Sethi, R. (eds.) Conference Record of the Fourth ACM Symposium on Principles of Programming Languages, Los Angeles, California, USA, January 1977. pp. 238–252. ACM (1977), https://doi.org/10.1145/512950.512973

25. Cox, N.: Directory Services: Design, Implementation and Management. Elsevier (2001)

26. Ed-Douibi, H., Izquierdo, J.L.C., Cabot, J.: Automatic generation of test cases for REST APIs: A specification-based approach. In: 22nd IEEE International Enterprise Distributed Object Computing Conference, EDOC 2018, Stockholm, Sweden, October 16-19, 2018. pp. 181–190. IEEE Computer Society (2018), https://doi.org/10.1109/EDOC.2018.00031

27. Fertig, T., Braun, P.: Model-driven testing of RESTful APIs. In: Gangemi, A., Leonardi, S., Panconesi, A. (eds.) Proceedings of the 24th International Conference on World Wide Web Companion, WWW 2015, Florence, Italy, May 18-22, 2015 - Companion Volume. pp. 1497–1502. ACM (2015), https://doi.org/10.1145/2740908.2743045

28. Fielding, R.: Representational state transfer. Architectural Styles and the Design of Netowork-based Software Architecture pp. 76–85 (2000)

29. Goessner, S.: JSONPath - XPath for JSON. http://goessner.net/articles/JsonPath p. 48 (2007)

30. Google: Android Monkey. https://developer.android.com/studio/test/monkey

31. Hafif, O., Spiderlabs, T.: Reflected file download: A new web attack vector. Trustwave. Retrieved March **15**, 2016 (2014), https://bit.ly/2F8YZEp

32. Hao, M.: Fastjson 1.2.68 and earlier remote code execution vulnerability threat alert. Tech. rep., NSFOCUS, Inc. (Jun 2020), https://bit.ly/3iG0jwh

33. Jensen, S.H., Møller, A., Thiemann, P.: Type analysis for JavaScript. In: Palsberg, J., Su, Z. (eds.) Static Analysis, 16th International Symposium, SAS 2009, Los Angeles, CA, USA, August 9-11, 2009. Proceedings. Lecture Notes in Computer Science, vol. 5673, pp. 238–255. Springer (2009), https://doi.org/10.1007/978-3-642-03237-0_17

34. Joy, B., Steele, G., Gosling, J., Bracha, G.: The Java language specification (2000)

35. Klyne, G., Newman, C.: RFC3339: Date and Time on the Internet: Timestamps. Internet Engineering Task Force (Jul 2002), https://www.rfc-editor.org/info/rfc3339

36. Martin-Lopez, A., Segura, S., Ruiz-Cortés, A.: A catalogue of inter-parameter dependencies in RESTful web APIs. In: Yangui, S., Rodriguez, I.B., Drira, K., Tari, Z. (eds.) Service-Oriented Computing - 17th International Conference, ICSOC 2019, Toulouse, France, October 28-31, 2019, Proceedings. Lecture Notes in Computer Science, vol. 11895, pp. 399–414. Springer (2019), https://doi.org/10.1007/978-3-030-33702-5_31

37. Møller, A., Bakic, A., Moran, J., et al.: Package dk.brics.automaton. Aarhus University (Jul 4 2017), https://www.brics.dk/automaton/

38. Møller, A., Schwartzbach, M.I.: Static program analysis. Notes. Feb (2012)

39. Morlitz, D.: HTTP archive file (May 2002), US Patent App. 09/726,985

40. OAI (OpenAPI Initiative): The OpenAPI specification. https://github.com/OAI/OpenAPI-Specification

41. Open API CSA Working Group: Open API survey report. Tech. rep., Cloud Security Alliance (Sep 2019), https://cloudsecurityalliance.org/blog/2019/09/11/open-api-survey-report/

42. Ouyang, L.: Bayesian inference of regular expressions from human-generated example strings. CoRR **abs/1805.08427** (2018), http://arxiv.org/abs/1805.08427

43. Pham, V., Böhme, M., Roychoudhury, A.: Model-based whitebox fuzzing for program binaries. In: Lo, D., Apel, S., Khurshid, S. (eds.) Proceedings of the 31st IEEE/ACM International Conference on Automated Software Engineering, ASE 2016, Singapore, September 3-7, 2016. pp. 543–553. ACM (2016), https://doi.org/10.1145/2970276.2970316

44. Raychev, V., Vechev, M.T., Krause, A.: Predicting program properties from "big code". In: Rajamani, S.K., Walker, D. (eds.) Proceedings of the 42nd Annual ACM SIGPLAN-SIGACT Symposium on Principles of Programming Languages, POPL 2015, Mumbai, India, January 15-17, 2015. pp. 111–124. ACM (2015), https://doi.org/10.1145/2676726.2677009

45. Scheurer, D., Hähnle, R., Bubel, R.: A general lattice model for merging symbolic execution branches. In: Ogata, K., Lawford, M., Liu, S. (eds.) Formal Methods and Software Engineering - 18th International Conference on Formal Engineering Methods, ICFEM 2016, Tokyo, Japan, November 14-18, 2016, Proceedings. Lecture Notes in Computer Science, vol. 10009, pp. 57–73 (2016), https://doi.org/10.1007/978-3-319-47846-3_5

46. Thompson, K.: Programming techniques: Regular expression search algorithm. Commun. ACM **11**(6), 419–422 (Jun 1968), https://doi.org/10.1145/363347.363387

47. Vu, H., Fertig, T., Braun, P.: Towards model-driven hypermedia testing for RESTful systems. In: Majchrzak, T.A., Traverso, P., Krempels, K..H., é rie Monfort, V. (eds.) Proceedings of the 13th International Conference on Web Information Systems and Technologies, WEBIST 2017, Porto, Portugal, April 25-27, 2017. pp. 340–343. SciTePress (2017), https://doi.org/10.5220/0006353403400343

48. Yuan, Q., Wu, J., Liu, C., Zhang, L.: A model driven approach toward business process test case generation. In: Liu, C., Ricca, F. (eds.) Proceedings of the 10th IEEE International Symposium on Web Systems Evolution, WSE 2010, 3-4 October 2008, Beijing, China. pp. 41–44. IEEE Computer Society (2008), https://doi.org/10.1109/WSE.2008.4655394

A Decision Tree Lifted Domain for Analyzing Program Families with Numerical Features

Aleksandar S. Dimovski [✉] [iD][1], Sven Apel[iD][2], and Axel Legay[iD][3]

[1] Mother Teresa University, 12 Udarna Brigada 2a, 1000 Skopje, North Macedonia
aleksandar.dimovski@unt.edu.mk
[2] Saarland University, Saarland Informatics Campus, E1.1, 66123 Saarbrücken, Germany
[3] Université catholique de Louvain, 1348 Ottignies-Louvain-la-Neuve, Belgium

Abstract. *Lifted (family-based) static analysis* by abstract interpretation is capable of analyzing all variants of a program family simultaneously, in a single run without generating any of the variants explicitly. The elements of the underlying lifted analysis domain are tuples, which maintain one property per variant. Still, explicit property enumeration in tuples, one by one for all variants, immediately yields combinatorial explosion. This is particularly apparent in the case of program families that, apart from Boolean features, contain also numerical features with large domains, thus giving rise to astronomical configuration spaces.

The key for an efficient lifted analysis is a proper handling of variability-specific constructs of the language (e.g., feature-based runtime tests and #if directives). In this work, we introduce a new symbolic representation of the lifted abstract domain that can efficiently analyze program families with numerical features. This makes sharing between property elements corresponding to different variants explicitly possible. The elements of the new lifted domain are constraint-based *decision trees*, where decision nodes are labeled with linear constraints defined over numerical features and the leaf nodes belong to an existing single-program analysis domain. To illustrate the potential of this representation, we have implemented an experimental lifted static analyzer, called SPLNum²Analyzer, for inferring invariants of C programs. An empirical evaluation on BusyBox and on benchmarks from SV-COMP yields promising preliminary results indicating that our decision trees-based approach is effective and outperforms the baseline tuple-based approach.

1 Introduction

Many software systems today are configurable [6]: they use *features* (or configurable options) to control the presence and absence of functionality. Different family members, called variants, are derived by switching features on and off, while the reuse of common code is maximized, leading to productivity gains, shorter time to market, greater market coverage, etc. Program families (e.g., software product lines) are commonly seen in the development of commercial embedded software, such as cars, phones, avionics, medicine, robotics, etc. Configurable

© The Author(s) 2021
E. Guerra and M. Stoelinga (Eds.): FASE 2021, LNCS 12649, pp. 67–86, 2021.
https://doi.org/10.1007/978-3-030-71500-7_4

options (features) are used to either support different application scenarios for embedded components, to provide portability across different hardware platforms and configurations, or to produce variations of products for different market segments or customers. We consider here program families implemented using #if directives from the C preprocessor CPP [20]. They use #if-s to specify in which conditions parts of code should be included or excluded from a variant. Classical program families use only Boolean features that have two values: on and off. However, Boolean features are insufficient for real-world program families, as there exist features that have a range of numbers as possible values. These features are called *numerical features* [25]. For instance, Linux kernel, BusyBox, Apache web server, Java Garbage Collector represent some real-world program families with numerical features. Analyzing such program families is very challenging, due to the fact that from only a few features, a huge number of variants can be derived.

In this paper, we are concerned with the verification of program families with Boolean and numerical features using abstract interpretation-based static analysis. *Abstract interpretation* [7,24] is a general theory for approximating the semantics of programs. It provides sound (all confirmative answers are correct) and efficient (with a good trade-off between precision and cost) static analyses of run-time properties of real programs. It has been used as the foundation for various successful industrial-scale static analyzers, such as ASTRÉE [8]. Still, the static analysis of program families is harder than the static analysis of single programs, because the number of possible variants can be very large (often huge) in practice. The simplest brute-force approach that uses a preprocessor to generate all variants of a family, and then applies an existing off-the-shelf single-program analyzer to each individual variant, one-by-one, is very inefficient [3,27]. Therefore, we use so-called *lifted* (family-based) *static analyses* [3,22,27], which analyze all variants of the family simultaneously without generating any of the variants explicitly. They take as input the common code base, which encodes all variants of a program family, and produce precise analysis results corresponding to all variants. They use a lifted analysis domain, which represents an n-fold product of an existing single-program analysis domain used for expressing program properties (where n is the number of valid configurations). That is, the lifted analysis domain maintains one property element per valid variant in tuples. The problem is that this explicit property enumeration in tuples becomes computationally intractable with larger program families because the number of variants (i.e., configurations) grows exponentially with the number of features. This problem has been successfully addressed for program families that contain only Boolean features [1,2,11], by using sharing through binary decision diagrams (BDDs). However, the fundamental limitation of existing lifted analysis techniques is that they are not able to handle numerical features.

To overcome this limitation, we present a *new, refined lifted abstract domain for effectively analyzing program families with numerical features by means of abstract interpretation*. The elements of the lifted abstract domain are constraint-based *decision trees*, where the decision nodes are labelled with linear constraints over numerical features, whereas the leaf nodes belong to a single-program analysis domain. The decision trees recursively partition the space of configurations (i.e., the space of possible combinations of feature values), whereas the program properties at the leaves provide analysis information corresponding to each partition, i.e. to the variants (configurations) that satisfy the constraints along the path to the given leaf node. The partitioning is dynamic, which means that partitions are split by feature-based tests (at #if directives), and joined when merging the corresponding control flows again. In terms of decision trees, this means that new decision nodes are added by feature-based tests and removed when merging control flows. In fact, the partitioning of the set of configurations is semantics-based, which means that linear constraints over numerical features that occur in decision nodes are automatically inferred by the analysis and do not necessarily occur syntactically in the code base.

Our lifted abstract domain is parametric in the choice of numerical property domain [7,24] that underlies the linear constraints over numerical features labelling decision nodes, and the choice of the single-program analysis domain for leaf nodes. In fact, in our implementation, we also use numerical property domains for leaf nodes, which encode linear constraints over program variables. We rely on the well-known numerical domains, such as intervals [7], octagons [23], polyhedra [10], from the APRON library [19] to obtain a concrete decision tree-based implementation of the lifted abstract domain. This way, we have implemented a *forward reachability analysis* of C program families with numerical (and Boolean) features for the automatic inference of invariants. Our tool, called SPLNUM^{2}ANALYZER[4], computes a set of possible invariants, which represent linear constraints over program variables. We can use the implemented lifted static analyzer to check invariance properties of C program families, such as assertions, buffer overflows, null pointer references, division by zero, etc [8].

In summary, we make several contributions: (1) We propose a new, parameterized lifted analysis domain based on decision trees for analyzing program families with numerical features; (2) We implement a prototype lifted static analyzer, SPLNUM^{2}ANALYZER, that performs a forward analysis of #if-enriched C programs, where numerical property domains from the APRON library are used as parameters in the lifted analysis domain; (3) We evaluate our approach for automatic inference of invariants by comparing performances of lifted analyzers based on tuples and decision trees.

2   Motivating Example

To illustrate the potential of a decision tree-based lifted domain, we consider a motivating example using the code base of the following program family SIMPLE:

---

[4] NUM^2 in the name of the tool refers to its ability to both handle NUMerical features and to perform NUMerical client analysis of SPLs (program families).

```
①    int x := 10, y := 0;
②    while (x != 0) {
③        x := x-1;
④        #if (SIZE ≤ 3) y := y+1; #else y := y-1; #endif
⑤        #if (!B) y := 0;  #else skip; #endif ⑥}
⑦    assert (y > 1);
```

The set $\mathbb{F}$ of features is $\{B, SIZE\}$, where B is a Boolean feature and $SIZE$ is a numerical feature whose domain is $[1,4] = \{1,2,3,4\}$. Thus, the set of valid configurations is $\mathbb{K} = \{B \wedge (SIZE=1), B \wedge (SIZE=2), B \wedge (SIZE=3), B \wedge (SIZE=4), \neg B \wedge (SIZE = 1), \neg B \wedge (SIZE = 2), \neg B \wedge (SIZE = 3), \neg B \wedge (SIZE = 4)\}$. The code of SIMPLE contains two #if directives, which change the value assigned to y, depending on how features from $\mathbb{F}$ are set at compile-time. For each configuration from $\mathbb{K}$, a different variant (single program) can be generated by appropriately resolving #if-s. For example, the variant corresponding to configuration $B \wedge (SIZE=1)$ will have B and $SIZE$ set to true and 1, so that the assignment y := y+1 and skip in program locations ④ and ⑤, respectively, will be included in this variant. The variant for configuration $\neg B \wedge (SIZE=4)$ will have features B and $SIZE$ set to false and 4, so the assignments y := y-1 and y := 0 in program locations ④ and ⑤, respectively, will be included in this variant. There are $|\mathbb{K}| = 8$ variants that can be derived from the family SIMPLE.

Assume that we want to perform *lifted polyhedra analysis* of SIMPLE using the *Polyhedra* numerical domain [10]. The standard lifted analysis domain used in the literature [3,22] is defined as cartesian product of $|\mathbb{K}|$ copies of the basic analysis domain (e.g. polyhedra). Hence, elements of the lifted domain are tuples containing one component for each valid configuration from $\mathbb{K}$, where each component represents a polyhedra linear constraint over program variables (x and y in this case). The lifted analysis result in location ⑦ of SIMPLE is an 8-sized tuple shown in Fig. 1. Note that the first component of the tuple in Fig. 1 corresponds to configuration $B \wedge (SIZE=1)$, the second to $B \wedge (SIZE=2)$, the third to $B \wedge (SIZE=3)$, and so on. We can see in Fig. 1 that the polyhedra analysis discovers very precise results for the variable y: $(y=10)$ for configurations $B \wedge (SIZE=1)$, $B \wedge (SIZE=2)$, and $B \wedge (SIZE=3)$; $(y=-10)$ for configuration $B \wedge (SIZE=4)$; and $(y=0)$ for all other configurations. This is due to the fact that the polyhedra domain is fully relational and is able to track all relations between program variables x and y. Using this result in location ⑦, we can successfully conclude that the assertion is valid for configurations $B \wedge (SIZE=1)$, $B \wedge (SIZE=2)$, and $B \wedge (SIZE=3)$, whereas the assertion fails for all other configurations.

If we perform lifted polyhedra analysis based on the *decision tree domain* proposed in this work, then the corresponding decision tree inferred in the final program location ⑦ of SIMPLE is depicted in Fig. 2. Notice that the inner nodes of the decision tree in Fig. 2 are labeled with *Interval* linear constraints over features (SIZE and B), while the leaves are labeled with the *Polyhedra* linear constraints over program variables x and y. Hence, we use two different numerical abstract domains in our decision trees: Interval domain [7] for expressing properties in decision nodes, and Polyhedra domain [10] for expressing properties

Fig. 1: Tuple-based invariant at location ⑦ of SIMPLE.

Fig. 2: Decision tree-based invariant at location ⑦ of SIMPLE (solid edges = true, dashed edges = false).

in leaf nodes. The edges of decision trees are labeled with the truth value of the decision on the parent node; we use solid edges for true (i.e. the constraint in the parent node is satisfied) and dashed edges for false (i.e. the negation of the constraint in the parent node is satisfied). As decision nodes partition the space of valid configurations $\mathbb{K}$, we implicitly assume the correctness of linear constraints that take into account domains of numerical features. For example, the node with constraint $(\texttt{SIZE} \leq 3)$ is satisfied when $(\texttt{SIZE} \leq 3) \wedge (1 \leq \texttt{SIZE} \leq 4)$, whereas its negation is satisfied when $(\texttt{SIZE} > 3) \wedge (1 \leq \texttt{SIZE} \leq 4)$. The constraints $(1 \leq \texttt{SIZE} \leq 4)$ represent the domain $[1, 4]$ of $\texttt{SIZE}$. We can see that decision trees offer more possibilities for sharing and interaction between analysis properties corresponding to different configurations, they provide symbolic and compact representation of lifted analysis elements. For example, Fig. 2 presents polyhedra properties of two program variables $\texttt{x}$ and $\texttt{y}$, which are partitioned with respect to features $\texttt{B}$ and $\texttt{SIZE}$. When $(\texttt{B} \wedge (\texttt{SIZE} \leq 3))$ is true the shared property is $(\texttt{y} = 10, \texttt{x} = 0)$, whereas when $(\texttt{B} \wedge \neg(\texttt{SIZE} \leq 3))$ is true the shared property is $(\texttt{y} = -10, \texttt{x} = 0)$. When $\neg\texttt{B}$ is true, the property is independent from the value of $\texttt{SIZE}$, hence a node with a constraint over $\texttt{SIZE}$ is not needed. Therefore, all such cases are identical and so they share the same leaf node $(\texttt{y} = 0, \texttt{x} = 0)$. In effect, the decision tree-based representation uses only three leafs, whereas the tuple-based representation uses eight properties. This ability for sharing is the key motivation behind the decision trees-based representation.

3   A Language for Program Families

Let $\mathbb{F} = \{A_1, \ldots, A_k\}$ be a finite and totaly ordered set of *numerical features* available in a program family. For each feature $A \in \mathbb{F}$, $\text{dom}(A) \subseteq \mathbb{Z}$ denotes the set of possible values that can be assigned to A. Note that any Boolean feature can be represented as a numerical feature $B \in \mathbb{F}$ with $\text{dom}(B) = \{0, 1\}$, such that 0 means that feature B is disabled while 1 means that B is enabled. A valid combination of feature's values represents a *configuration* k, which specifies one *variant* of a program family. It is given as a *valuation function* $k : \mathbb{F} \to \mathbb{Z}$, which is a mapping that assigns a value from $\mathrm{dom}(A)$ to each feature A, i.e. $k(A) \in \mathrm{dom}(A)$ for any $A \in \mathbb{F}$. We assume that only a subset $\mathbb{K}$ of all possible configurations are *valid*. An alternative representation of configurations is based upon propositional formulae. Each configuration $k \in \mathbb{K}$ can be represented by a formula: $(A_1 = k(A_1)) \wedge \ldots \wedge (A_k = k(A_k))$. We often abbreviate $(B = 1)$ with B and $(B = 0)$ with $\neg B$, for a Boolean feature $B \in \mathbb{F}$. The set of valid configurations $\mathbb{K}$ can be also represented as a formula: $\vee_{k \in \mathbb{K}} k$.

We define *feature expressions*, denoted $FeatExp(\mathbb{F})$, as the set of propositional logic formulas over constraints of $\mathbb{F}$ generated by the grammar:

$$\theta ::= \mathrm{true} \mid e_{\mathbb{F}_\mathbb{Z}} \bowtie e_{\mathbb{F}_\mathbb{Z}} \mid \neg\theta \mid \theta_1 \wedge \theta_2 \mid \theta_1 \vee \theta_2, \qquad e_{\mathbb{F}_\mathbb{Z}} ::= n \mid A \mid e_{\mathbb{F}_\mathbb{Z}} \oplus e_{\mathbb{F}_\mathbb{Z}}$$

where $A \in \mathbb{F}$, $n \in \mathbb{Z}$, $\oplus \in \{+, -, *\}$, and $\bowtie \in \{=, <\}$. We will use $\theta \in FeatExp(\mathbb{F})$ to write presence conditions. When a configuration $k \in \mathbb{K}$ satisfies a feature expression $\theta \in FeatExp(\mathbb{F})$, we write $k \models \theta$, where $\models$ is the standard satisfaction relation of logic. We write $[\![\theta]\!]$ to denote the set of configurations from $\mathbb{K}$ that satisfy θ, that is, $k \in [\![\theta]\!]$ iff $k \models \theta$.

Example 1. For the SIMPLE program family from Section 2, the set of features is $\mathbb{F} = \{\mathtt{B}, \mathtt{SIZE}\}$ where $\mathrm{dom}(\mathtt{SIZE}) = [1,4]$, and the set of configurations is $\mathbb{K} = \{\mathtt{B} \wedge (\mathtt{SIZE}{=}1), \mathtt{B} \wedge (\mathtt{SIZE}{=}2), \mathtt{B} \wedge (\mathtt{SIZE}{=}3), \mathtt{B} \wedge (\mathtt{SIZE}{=}4), \neg\mathtt{B} \wedge (\mathtt{SIZE}{=}1), \neg\mathtt{B} \wedge (\mathtt{SIZE}{=}2), \neg\mathtt{B} \wedge (\mathtt{SIZE}{=}3), \neg\mathtt{B} \wedge (\mathtt{SIZE}{=}4)\}$. For the feature expression $(\mathtt{SIZE} \le 3)$, we have $[\![(\mathtt{SIZE} \le 3)]\!] = \{\mathtt{B} \wedge (\mathtt{SIZE}{=}1), \mathtt{B} \wedge (\mathtt{SIZE}{=}2), \mathtt{B} \wedge (\mathtt{SIZE}{=}3), \neg\mathtt{B} \wedge (\mathtt{SIZE} = 1), \neg\mathtt{B} \wedge (\mathtt{SIZE} = 2), \neg\mathtt{B} \wedge (\mathtt{SIZE} = 3)\}$. Hence, $B \wedge (\mathtt{SIZE} = 2) \models (\mathtt{SIZE} \le 3)$ and $B \wedge (\mathtt{SIZE}{=}4) \not\models (\mathtt{SIZE} \le 3)$, where $B \wedge (\mathtt{SIZE} = 2) \in \mathbb{K}$, $B \wedge (\mathtt{SIZE}{=}4) \in \mathbb{K}$, and $(\mathtt{SIZE} \le 3) \in FeatExp(\mathbb{F})$. $\square$

We consider a simple sequential non-deterministic programming language, which will be used to exemplify our work. The program variables *Var* are statically allocated and the only data type is the set $\mathbb{Z}$ of mathematical integers. To encode multiple variants, a new compile-time conditional statement is included. The new statement "#if (θ) s #endif" contains a feature expression $\theta \in FeatExp(\mathbb{F})$ as a presence condition, such that only if θ is satisfied by a configuration $k \in \mathbb{K}$ the statement s will be included in the variant corresponding to k. The syntax is:

$$s ::= \mathtt{skip} \mid \mathtt{x} \mathtt{:=} e \mid s; s \mid \mathtt{if}\,(e)\,\mathtt{then}\,s\,\mathtt{else}\,s \mid \mathtt{while}\,(e)\,\mathtt{do}\,s \mid \texttt{\#if}\,(\theta)\,s\,\texttt{\#endif},$$
$$e ::= n \mid [n, n'] \mid \mathtt{x} \mid e \oplus e$$

where n ranges over integers, $[n, n']$ over integer intervals, $\mathtt{x}$ over program variables *Var*, and $\oplus$ over binary arithmetic operators. Integer intervals $[n, n']$ denote a random choice of an integer in the interval. The set of all statements s is denoted by *Stm*; the set of all expressions e is denoted by *Exp*.

A program family is evaluated in two stages. First, the C *preprocessor* CPP takes a program family s and a configuration $k \in \mathbb{K}$ as inputs, and produces a variant (without #if-s) corresponding to k as the output. Second, the obtained variant is evaluated using the standard single-program semantics. The first stage is specified by the projection function P_k, which is an identity for all basic statements and recursively pre-processes all sub-statements of compound

```
int x := 10, y := 0;   int x := 10, y := 0;   int x := 10, y := 0;   int x := 10, y := 0;
while (x !=0) {         while (x !=0) {        while (x !=0) {        while (x !=0) {
    x := x-1;              x := x-1;              x := x-1;              x := x-1;
    y := y+1;              y := y-1;              y := y+1;              y := y-1;
    skip; }               skip; }                y := 0; }              y := 0; }
```

(a) $P_{B \wedge (\text{SIZE}=1)}$(SIMPLE) (b) $P_{B \wedge (\text{SIZE}=4)}$(SIMPLE) (c) $P_{\neg B \wedge (\text{SIZE}=1)}$(SIMPLE) (d) $P_{\neg B \wedge (\text{SIZE}=4)}$(SIMPLE)

Fig. 3: Different variants of the program family SIMPLE from Section 2.

statements. Hence, $P_k(\texttt{skip}) = \texttt{skip}$ and $P_k(s;s') = P_k(s);P_k(s')$. The interesting case is "$\texttt{\#if } (\theta) \; s \; \texttt{\#endif}$", where statement s is included in the variant if $k \models \theta$, otherwise, s is removed [5]: $P_k(\texttt{\#if } (\theta) \; s \; \texttt{\#endif}) = \begin{cases} P_k(s) & \text{if } k \models \theta \\ \texttt{skip} & \text{if } k \not\models \theta \end{cases}$. For example, variants $P_{B \wedge (\text{SIZE}=1)}$(SIMPLE), $P_{B \wedge (\text{SIZE}=4)}$(SIMPLE), $P_{\neg B \wedge (\text{SIZE}=1)}$(SIMPLE), as well as $P_{\neg B \wedge (\text{SIZE}=4)}$(SIMPLE) shown in Fig. 3a, Fig. 3b, Fig. 3c, and Fig. 3d, respectively, are derived from the SIMPLE family defined in Section 2.

4   Lifted Analysis based on Tuples

Lifted analyses are designed by *lifting* existing single-program analyses to work on program families, rather than on individual programs. They directly analyze program families. Lifted analysis as defined by Midtgaard et. al. [22] rely on a lifted domain that is $|\mathbb{K}|$-fold product of an existing single-program analysis domain $\mathbb{A}$ defined over program variables *Var*. We assume that the domain $\mathbb{A}$ is equipped with sound operators for concretization $\gamma_\mathbb{A}$, ordering $\sqsubseteq_\mathbb{A}$, join $\sqcup_\mathbb{A}$, meet $\sqcap_\mathbb{A}$, bottom $\bot_\mathbb{A}$, top $\top_\mathbb{A}$, widening $\nabla_\mathbb{A}$, and narrowing $\triangle_\mathbb{A}$, as well as sound transfer functions for tests FILTER$_\mathbb{A}$ and forward assignments ASSIGN$_\mathbb{A}$. More specifically, FILTER$_\mathbb{A}(a : \mathbb{A}, e : Exp)$ returns an abstract element from $\mathbb{A}$ obtained by restricting a to satisfy the test e, whereas ASSIGN$_\mathbb{A}(a : \mathbb{A}, \texttt{x:=}e : Stm)$ returns an updated version of a by abstractly evaluating $\texttt{x:=}e$ in it.

Lifted Domain. The *lifted analysis domain* is defined as $\langle \mathbb{A}^\mathbb{K}, \dot{\sqsubseteq}, \dot{\sqcup}, \dot{\sqcap}, \dot{\bot}, \dot{\top} \rangle$, where $\mathbb{A}^\mathbb{K}$ is shorthand for the $|\mathbb{K}|$-fold product $\prod_{k \in \mathbb{K}} \mathbb{A}$, that is, there is one separate copy of $\mathbb{A}$ for each configuration of $\mathbb{K}$. For example, consider the tuple in Fig. 1.

Lifted Abstract Operations. Given a tuple (lifted domain element) $\overline{a} \in \mathbb{A}^\mathbb{K}$, the projection π_k selects the kth component of $\overline{a}$. All abstract lifted operations are defined by lifting the abstract operations of the domain $\mathbb{A}$ configuration-wise.

$$\overline{\gamma}(\overline{a}) = \prod_{k \in \mathbb{K}} (\gamma_\mathbb{A}(\pi_k(\overline{a}))), \qquad \overline{a_1} \dot{\sqsubseteq} \overline{a_2} \equiv \pi_k(\overline{a_1}) \sqsubseteq_\mathbb{A} \pi_k(\overline{a_2}), \text{for } \forall k \in \mathbb{K}$$
$$\overline{a_1} \dot{\sqcup} \overline{a_2} = \prod_{k \in \mathbb{K}} (\pi_k(\overline{a_1}) \sqcup_\mathbb{A} \pi_k(\overline{a_2})), \qquad \overline{a_1} \dot{\sqcap} \overline{a_2} = \prod_{k \in \mathbb{K}} (\pi_k(\overline{a_1}) \sqcap_\mathbb{A} \pi_k(\overline{a_2}))$$
$$\dot{\top} = \prod_{k \in \mathbb{K}} \top_\mathbb{A} = (\top_\mathbb{A}, \dots, \top_\mathbb{A}), \qquad \dot{\bot} = \prod_{k \in \mathbb{K}} \bot_\mathbb{A} = (\bot_\mathbb{A}, \dots, \bot_\mathbb{A})$$
$$\overline{a_1} \dot{\nabla} \overline{a_2} = \prod_{k \in \mathbb{K}} (\pi_k(\overline{a_1}) \nabla_\mathbb{A} \pi_k(\overline{a_2})), \qquad \overline{a_1} \dot{\triangle} \overline{a_2} = \prod_{k \in \mathbb{K}} (\pi_k(\overline{a_1}) \triangle_\mathbb{A} \pi_k(\overline{a_2}))$$

---

[5] Since $k \in \mathbb{K}$ is a valuation function, either $k \models \theta$ holds or $k \not\models \theta$ holds for any θ.

Lifted Transfer Functions. We now define lifted transfer functions for tests, forward assignments ($\overline{\text{ASSIGN}}$), and `#if`-s ($\overline{\text{IFDEF}}$). There are two types of tests: *expression-based tests*, denoted $\overline{\text{FILTER}}$, that occur in `while`-s and `if`-s, and *feature-based tests*, denoted $\overline{\text{FEAT-FILTER}}$, that occur in `#if`-s. Each lifted transfer function takes as input a tuple from $\mathbb{A}^{\mathbb{K}}$ representing the invariant before evaluating the statement (resp., expression) to handle, and returns a tuple representing the invariant after evaluating the given statement (resp., expression).

$$\overline{\text{FILTER}}(\overline{a}:\mathbb{A}^{\mathbb{K}}, e:Exp) = \prod_{k\in\mathbb{K}}(\text{FILTER}_{\mathbb{A}}(\pi_k(\overline{a}),e))$$

$$\overline{\text{FEAT-FILTER}}(\overline{a}:\mathbb{A}^{\mathbb{K}}, \theta:FeatExp(\mathbb{F})) = \prod_{k\in\mathbb{K}}\begin{cases}\pi_k(\overline{a}), & \text{if } k \models \theta \\ \perp_{\mathbb{A}}, & \text{if } k \not\models \theta\end{cases}$$

$$\overline{\text{ASSIGN}}(\overline{a}:\mathbb{A}^{\mathbb{K}}, \texttt{x:=}e:Stm) = \prod_{k\in\mathbb{K}}(\text{ASSIGN}_{\mathbb{A}}(\pi_k(\overline{a}),\texttt{x:=}e))$$

$$\overline{\text{IFDEF}}(\overline{a}:\mathbb{A}^{\mathbb{K}}, \texttt{\#if}\,(\theta)\,s:Stm) = \overline{[\![s]\!]}(\overline{\text{FEAT-FILTER}}(\overline{a},\theta))\,\dot\sqcup\,\overline{\text{FEAT-FILTER}}(\overline{a},\neg\theta)$$

where $\overline{[\![s]\!]}(\overline{a})$ is the lifted transfer function for statement s. $\overline{\text{FILTER}}$ and $\overline{\text{ASSIGN}}$ are defined by applying $\text{FILTER}_{\mathbb{A}}$ and $\text{ASSIGN}_{\mathbb{A}}$ independently on each component of the input tuple $\overline{a}$. $\overline{\text{FEAT-FILTER}}$ keeps those components k of the input tuple $\overline{a}$ that satisfy θ, otherwise it replaces the other components with $\perp_{\mathbb{A}}$. $\overline{\text{IFDEF}}$ captures the effect of analyzing the statement s in the components k of $\overline{a}$ that satisfy θ, otherwise it is an identity for the other components.

Lifted Analysis. Lifted abstract operators and transfer functions of the lifted analysis domain $\mathbb{A}^{\mathbb{K}}$ are combined together to analyze program families. Initially, we build a tuple $\overline{a}_{in}$ where all components are set to $\top_{\mathbb{A}}$ for the first program location, and tuples where all components are set to $\perp_{\mathbb{A}}$ for all other locations. The analysis properties are propagated forward from the first program location towards the final location taking assignments, `#if`-s, and tests into account with join and widening around `while`-s. The *soundness* of the lifted analysis based on $\mathbb{A}^{\mathbb{K}}$ follows immediately from the soundness of all abstract operators and transfer functions of $\mathbb{A}$ (proved in [22]).

Numerical Lifted Analysis The single-program analysis domain $\mathbb{A}$ can be instantiated by some of the well-known numerical property domains [24], such as Intervals $\langle I, \sqsubseteq_I \rangle$ [7], Octagons $\langle O, \sqsubseteq_O \rangle$ [26], and Polyhedra $\langle P, \sqsubseteq_P \rangle$ [10]. The elements of I are intervals of the form: $\pm x \geq \beta$, where $x \in Var, \beta \in \mathbb{Z}$; the elements of O are conjunctions of octagonal constraints of the form $\pm x_1 \pm x_2 \geq \beta$, where $x_1, x_2 \in Var, \beta \in \mathbb{Z}$; while the elements of P are conjunctions of polyhedral constraints of the form $\alpha_1 x_1 + \ldots + \alpha_k x_k + \beta \geq 0$, where $x_1, \ldots x_k \in Var, \alpha_1, \ldots, \alpha_k, \beta \in \mathbb{Z}$.

5   Lifted Analysis based on Decision Trees

We now introduce a new *decision tree* lifted domain. Its elements are disjunctions of leaf nodes that belong to an existing single-program domain $\mathbb{A}$ defined over program variables *Var*. The leaf nodes are separated by linear constraints over numerical features, organized in the decision nodes. Hence, we encapsulate the set of configurations $\mathbb{K}$ into the decision nodes of a decision tree where each top-down path represents one or several configurations that satisfy the constraints encountered along the given path. We store in each leaf node the property generated from the variants representing the corresponding configurations.

Abstract domain for decision nodes. We define the family of abstract domains for linear constraints $\mathbb{C}_\mathbb{D}$, which are parameterized by any of the numerical property domains $\mathbb{D}$ (intervals I, octagons O, polyhedra P). We use $C_I = \{\pm A_i \geq \beta \mid A_i \in \mathbb{F}, \beta \in \mathbb{Z}\}$ to denote the set of *interval constraints*, $C_O = \{\pm A_i \pm A_j \geq \beta \mid A_i, A_j \in \mathbb{F}, \beta \in \mathbb{Z}\}$ to denote the set of *octagonal constraints*, and $C_P = \{\alpha_1 A_1 + \ldots + \alpha_k A_k + \beta \geq 0 \mid A_1, \ldots A_k \in \mathbb{F}, \alpha_1, \ldots, \alpha_k, \beta \in \mathbb{Z}, \gcd(|\alpha_1|, \ldots, |\alpha_k|, |\beta|) = 1\}$ to denote the set of *polyhedral constraints*. We have $C_I \subseteq C_O \subseteq C_P$.

The set $C_\mathbb{D}$ of linear constraints over features $\mathbb{F}$ is constructed by the underlying numerical property domain $\langle \mathbb{D}, \sqsubseteq_\mathbb{D} \rangle$ using the Galois connection $\langle \mathcal{P}(C_\mathbb{D}), \sqsubseteq_\mathbb{D} \rangle \xleftrightarrow[\alpha_{C_\mathbb{D}}]{\gamma_{C_\mathbb{D}}} \langle \mathbb{D}, \sqsubseteq_\mathbb{D} \rangle$, where $\mathcal{P}(C_\mathbb{D})$ is the power set of $C_\mathbb{D}$. The abstraction function $\alpha_{C_\mathbb{D}} : \mathcal{P}(C_\mathbb{D}) \to \mathbb{D}$ maps a set of interval (resp., octagon, polyhedral) constraints to an interval (resp., an octagon, polyhedral) that represents a conjunction of constraints; the concretization function $\gamma_{C_\mathbb{D}} : \mathbb{D} \to \mathcal{P}(C_\mathbb{D})$ maps an interval (resp., an octagon, a polyhedron) that represents a conjunction of constraints to a set of interval (resp., octagonal, polyhedral) constraints. We have $\gamma_{C_\mathbb{D}}(\top_\mathbb{D}) = \emptyset$ and $\gamma_{C_\mathbb{D}}(\bot_\mathbb{D}) = \{\bot_{C_\mathbb{D}}\}$, where $\bot_{C_\mathbb{D}}$ is an unsatisfiable constraint.

The domain of decision nodes is $\mathbb{C}_\mathbb{D}$. We assume $\mathbb{F} = \{A_1, \ldots, A_k\}$ be a finite and totally ordered set of features, such that the ordering is $A_1 > A_2 > \ldots > A_k$. We impose a total order $<_{\mathbb{C}_\mathbb{D}}$ on $\mathbb{C}_\mathbb{D}$ to be the lexicographic order on the coefficients $\alpha_1, \ldots, \alpha_k$ and constant α_{k+1} of the linear constraints, such that:

$$(\alpha_1 \cdot A_1 + \ldots + \alpha_k \cdot A_k + \alpha_{k+1} \geq 0) \ <_{\mathbb{C}_\mathbb{D}} \ (\alpha_1' \cdot A_1 + \ldots + \alpha_k' \cdot A_k + \alpha_{k+1}' \geq 0)$$
$$\iff \exists j > 0. \forall i < j.(\alpha_i = \alpha_i') \wedge (\alpha_j < \alpha_j')$$

The negation of linear constraints is formed as: $\neg(\alpha_1 A_1 + \ldots \alpha_k A_k + \beta \geq 0) = -\alpha_1 A_1 - \ldots - \alpha_k A_k - \beta - 1 \geq 0$. For example, the negation of $A - 3 \geq 0$ is the constraint $-A + 2 \geq 0$ (i.e., $A \leq 2$). To ensure canonical representation of decision trees, a linear constraint c and its negation $\neg c$ cannot both appear as nodes in a decision tree. For example, we only keep the largest constraint with respect to $<_{\mathbb{C}_\mathbb{D}}$ between c and $\neg c$. For this reason, we define the equivalence relation $\equiv_{C_\mathbb{D}}$ as $c \equiv_{C_\mathbb{D}} \neg c$. We define $\langle \mathbb{C}_\mathbb{D}, <_{\mathbb{C}_\mathbb{D}} \rangle$ to denote $\langle C_\mathbb{D}/_\equiv, <_{C_\mathbb{D}} \rangle$, such that elements of $\mathbb{C}_\mathbb{D}$ are constraints obtained by quotienting by the equivalence $\equiv_{C_\mathbb{D}}$.

Abstract domain for constraint-based decision trees. A *constraint-based decision tree* $t \in \mathbb{T}(\mathbb{C}_\mathbb{D}, \mathbb{A})$ over the sets $\mathbb{C}_\mathbb{D}$ of linear constraints defined over $\mathbb{F}$ and the leaf abstract domain $\mathbb{A}$ defined over *Var* is either a leaf node $\ll a \gg$ with $a \in \mathbb{A}$, or $[\![c : tl, tr]\!]$, where $c \in \mathbb{C}_\mathbb{D}$ (denoted by $t.c$) is the smallest constraint with respect to $<_{\mathbb{C}_\mathbb{D}}$ appearing in the tree t, tl (denoted by $t.l$) is the left subtree of t representing its *true branch*, and tr (denoted by $t.r$) is the right subtree of t representing its *false branch*. The path along a decision tree establishes the set of configurations (those that satisfy the encountered constraints), and the leaf nodes represent the analysis properties for the corresponding configurations.

Example 2. The following two constraint-based decision trees t_1 and t_2 have decision nodes labelled with Interval linear constraints over the numeric feature SIZE with domain $\{1, 2, 3, 4\}$, whereas leaf nodes are Interval properties:

$$t_1 = [\![\text{SIZE} \geq 4 : \ll [y \geq 2] \gg, \ll [y = 0] \gg]\!], \quad t_2 = [\![\text{SIZE} \geq 2 : \ll [y \geq 0] \gg, \ll [y \leq 0] \gg]\!] \quad \square$$

Abstract Operations. The *concretization function* $\gamma_{\mathbb{T}}$ of a decision tree $t \in \mathbb{T}(\mathbb{C}_{\mathbb{D}}, \mathbb{A})$ returns $\gamma_{\mathbb{A}}(a)$ for $k \in \mathbb{K}$, where k satisfies the set $C \in \mathcal{P}(\mathbb{C}_{\mathbb{D}})$ of constraints accumulated along the top-down path to the leaf node $a \in \mathbb{A}$. More formally, $\gamma_{\mathbb{T}}(t) = \overline{\gamma}_{\mathbb{T}}[\mathbb{K}](t)$. The function $\overline{\gamma}_{\mathbb{T}}$ accumulates into a set $C \in \mathcal{P}(\mathbb{C}_{\mathbb{D}})$ constraints along the paths up to a leaf node, which is initially equal to the set of implicit constraints over $\mathbb{F}$, $\mathbb{K} = \vee_{k \in \mathbb{K}} k$, taking into account domains of features:

$$\overline{\gamma}_{\mathbb{T}}[C](\ll a \gg) = \prod\nolimits_{k \models C} \gamma_{\mathbb{A}}(a), \quad \overline{\gamma}_{\mathbb{T}}[C]([\![c : tl, tr]\!]) = \overline{\gamma}_{\mathbb{T}}[C \cup \{c\}](tl) \times \overline{\gamma}_{\mathbb{T}}[C \cup \{\neg c\}](tr)$$

Note that $k \models C$ is equivalent with $\alpha_{\mathbb{C}_{\mathbb{D}}}(\{k\}) \sqsubseteq_{\mathbb{D}} \alpha_{\mathbb{C}_{\mathbb{D}}}(C)$. Therefore, we can check $k \models C$ using the abstract operation $\sqsubseteq_{\mathbb{D}}$ of the numerical domain $\mathbb{D}$.

Other binary operations of $\mathbb{T}(\mathbb{C}_{\mathbb{D}}, \mathbb{A})$ are based on Algorithm 1 for *tree unification*, which finds a common refinement (labelling) of two trees t_1 and t_2 by calling function UNIFICATION$(t_1, t_2, \mathbb{K})$. It possibly adds new constraints as decision nodes (Lines 5–7, Lines 11–13), or removes constraints that are redundant (Lines 3,4,9,10,15,16). The function UNIFICATION accumulates into the set $C \in \mathcal{P}(\mathbb{C}_{\mathbb{D}})$ (initialized to $\mathbb{K}$, which represents implicit constraints satisfied by both t_1 and t_2), constraints encountered along the paths of the decision tree. This set C is used by the function isRedundant(c, C), which checks whether the linear constraint $c \in \mathbb{C}_{\mathbb{D}}$ is redundant with respect to C by testing $\alpha_{\mathbb{C}_{\mathbb{D}}}(C) \sqsubseteq_{\mathbb{D}} \alpha_{\mathbb{C}_{\mathbb{D}}}(\{c\})$. Note that the tree unification does not lose any information.

Example 3. Consider constraint-based decision trees t_1 and t_2 from Example 2. After tree unification UNIFICATION$(t_1, t_2, \mathbb{K})$, the resulting decision trees are:

$$t_1 = [\![\text{SIZE} \geq 4 : \ll [y \geq 2] \gg, [\![\text{SIZE} \geq 2 : \ll [y = 0] \gg, \ll [y = 0] \gg]\!]]\!],$$
$$t_2 = [\![\text{SIZE} \geq 4 : \ll [y \geq 0] \gg, [\![\text{SIZE} \geq 2 : \ll [y \geq 0] \gg, \ll [y \leq 0] \gg]\!]]\!]$$

Note that UNIFICATION adds a decision node for SIZE ≥ 2 to the right subtree of t_1, whereas it adds a decision node for SIZE ≥ 4 to t_2 and removes the redundant constraint SIZE ≥ 2 from the resulting left subtree of t_2. $\quad \square$

All binary operations are performed leaf-wise on the unified decision trees. Given two unified decision trees t_1 and t_2, their ordering and join are defined as:

$$\ll a_1 \gg \sqsubseteq_{\mathbb{T}} \ll a_2 \gg = a_1 \sqsubseteq_{\mathbb{A}} a_2, \quad [\![c : tl_1, tr_1]\!] \sqsubseteq_{\mathbb{T}} [\![c : tl_2, tr_2]\!] = (tl_1 \sqsubseteq_{\mathbb{T}} tl_2) \wedge (tr_1 \sqsubseteq_{\mathbb{T}} tr_2)$$
$$\ll a_1 \gg \sqcup_{\mathbb{T}} \ll a_2 \gg = \ll a_1 \sqcup_{\mathbb{A}} a_2 \gg, \quad [\![c : tl_1, tr_1]\!] \sqcup_{\mathbb{T}} [\![c : tl_2, tr_2]\!] = [\![c : tl_1 \sqcup_{\mathbb{T}} tl_2, tr_1 \sqcup_{\mathbb{T}} tr_2]\!]$$

Similarly, we compute meet, widening, and narrowing of t_1 and t_2. The top is a tree with a single $\top_{\mathbb{A}}$ leaf: $\top_{\mathbb{T}} = \ll \top_{\mathbb{A}} \gg$, while the bottom is: $\bot_{\mathbb{T}} = \ll \bot_{\mathbb{A}} \gg$.

Example 4. Consider the unified trees t_1 and t_2 from Example 3. We have that $t_1 \sqsubseteq_{\mathbb{T}} t_2$ holds, and $t_1 \sqcup_{\mathbb{T}} t_2 = [\![\text{SIZE} \geq 4 : \ll [y \geq 0] \gg, [\![\text{SIZE} \geq 2 : \ll [y \geq 0] \gg, \ll [y \leq 0] \gg]\!]]\!]$.

Algorithm 1: UNIFICATION (t_1, t_2, C)

---

1   **if** isLeaf$(t_1) \wedge$ isLeaf(t_2) **then return** (t_1, t_2);
2   **if** isLeaf$(t_1) \vee$ (isNode$(t_1) \wedge$ isNode$(t_2) \wedge t_2.c <_{\mathbb{C}_\mathbb{D}} t_1.c)$ **then**
3   **if** isRedundant$(t_2.c, C)$ **then return** UNIFICATION $(t_1, t_2.l, C)$;
4   **if** isRedundant$(\neg t_2.c, C)$ **then return** UNIFICATION $(t_1, t_2.r, C)$;
5      $(l_1, l_2) =$ UNIFICATION $(t_1, t_2.l, C \cup \{t_2.c\})$;
6      $(r_1, r_2) =$ UNIFICATION $(t_1, t_2.r, C \cup \{\neg t_2.c\})$;
7   **return** $([\![t_2.c : l_1, r_1]\!], [\![t_2.c : l_2, r_2]\!])$;
8   **if** isLeaf$(t_2) \vee$ (isNode$(t_1) \wedge$ isNode$(t_2) \wedge t_1.c <_{\mathbb{C}_\mathbb{D}} t_2.c)$ **then**
9   **if** isRedundant$(t_1.c, C)$ **then return** UNIFICATION $(t_1.l, t_2, C)$;
10   **if** isRedundant$(\neg t_1.c, C)$ **then return** UNIFICATION $(t_1.r, t_2, C)$;
11     $(l_1, l_2) =$ UNIFICATION $(t_1.l, t_2, C \cup \{t_1.c\})$;
12     $(r_1, r_2) =$ UNIFICATION $(t_1.r, t_2, C \cup \{\neg t_1.c\})$;
13   **return** $([\![t_1.c : l_1, r_1]\!], [\![t_1.c : l_2, r_2]\!])$;
14 **else**
15   **if** isRedundant$(t_1.c, C)$ **then return** UNIFICATION $(t_1.l, t_2.l, C)$;
16   **if** isRedundant$(\neg t_1.c, C)$ **then return** UNIFICATION $(t_1.r, t_2.r, C)$;
17     $(l_1, l_2) =$ UNIFICATION $(t_1.l, t_2.l, C \cup \{t_1.c\})$;
18     $(r_1, r_2) =$ UNIFICATION $(t_1.r, t_2.r, C \cup \{\neg t_1.c\})$;
19   **return** $([\![t_1.c : l_1, r_1]\!], [\![t_1.c : l_2, r_2]\!])$;

Algorithm 2: ASSIGN$_\mathbb{T}(t, \mathtt{x} := e)$

---

1   **if** isLeaf(t) **then return** $\ll$ASSIGN$_\mathbb{A}(t, \mathtt{x} := e)\gg$;
2   **return** $[\![t.c :$ ASSIGN$_\mathbb{T}(t.l, \mathtt{x} := e),$ ASSIGN$_\mathbb{T}(t.r, \mathtt{x} := e)]\!]$;

Transfer functions. The transfer functions for forward assignments (ASSIGN$_\mathbb{T}$) and expression-based tests (FILTER$_\mathbb{T}$) modify only leaf nodes of a constraint-based decision tree. In contrast, transfer functions for variability-specific constructs, such as feature-based tests (FEAT-FILTER$_\mathbb{T}$) and #if-s (IFDEF$_\mathbb{T}$) add, modify, or delete decision nodes of a decision tree. This is due to the fact that the analysis information about program variables is located in leaf nodes, while the information about feature variables is located in decision nodes.

Transfer function ASSIGN$_\mathbb{T}$ for handling an assignment $\mathtt{x} := e$ in the input tree t is described by Algorithm 2. Note that $\mathtt{x} \in Var$, and $e \in Exp$ may contain only program variables. We apply ASSIGN$_\mathbb{A}$ to each leaf node a of t, which substitutes expression e for variable $\mathtt{x}$ in a. Similarly, transfer function FILTER$_\mathbb{T}$ for handling expression-based tests $e \in Exp$ is implemented by applying FILTER$_\mathbb{A}$ leaf-wise.

Transfer function FEAT-FILTER$_\mathbb{T}$ for feature-based tests θ is described by Algorithm 3. It reasons by induction on the structure of θ (we assume negation is applied to atomic propositions). When θ is an atomic constraint over numerical features (Lines 2,3), we use FILTER$_\mathbb{D}$ to approximate θ, thus producing a set of constraints J, which are then added to the tree t, possibly discarding all paths of t that do not satisfy θ. This is done by calling function RESTRICT$(t, \mathbb{K}, J)$, which

---

Algorithm 3: FEAT-FILTER$_\mathbb{T}(t, \theta)$

---

1 **switch** θ **do**
2   **case** $(e_{\mathbb{F}_Z} \bowtie e_{\mathbb{F}_Z}) \,||\, (\neg(e_{\mathbb{F}_Z} \bowtie e_{\mathbb{F}_Z}))$ **do**
3          $J = \text{FILTER}_\mathbb{D}(\top_\mathbb{D}, \theta)$; **return** RESTRICT$(t, \mathbb{K}, J)$
4   **case** $\theta_1 \wedge \theta_2$ **do**
5   **return** FEAT-FILTER$_\mathbb{T}(t, \theta_1) \sqcap_\mathbb{T}$ FEAT-FILTER$_\mathbb{T}(t, \theta_2)$
6   **case** $\theta_1 \vee \theta_2$ **do**
7   **return** FEAT-FILTER$_\mathbb{T}(t, \theta_1) \sqcup_\mathbb{T}$ FEAT-FILTER$_\mathbb{T}(t, \theta_2)$

---

adds linear constraints from J to t in ascending order with respect to $<_{\mathbb{C}_\mathbb{D}}$ as shown in Algorithm 4. Note that θ may not be representable exactly in $\mathbb{C}_\mathbb{D}$ (e.g., in the case of non-linear constraints over $\mathbb{F}$), so FILTER$_\mathbb{D}$ may produce a set of constraints approximating it. When θ is a conjunction (resp., disjunction) of two feature expressions (Lines 4,5) (resp., (Lines 6,7)), the resulting decision trees are merged by operation meet $\sqcap_\mathbb{T}$ (resp., join $\sqcup_\mathbb{T}$). Function RESTRICT(t, C, J), described in Algorithm 4, takes as input a decision tree t, a set C of linear constraints accumulated along paths up to a node, and a set J of linear constraints in canonical form that need to be added to t. For each constraint $j \in J$, there exists a boolean b_j that shows whether the tree should be constrained with respect to j or with respect to $\neg j$. When J is not empty, the linear constraints from J are added to t in ascending order with respect to $<_{\mathbb{C}_\mathbb{D}}$. At each iteration, the smallest linear constraint j is extracted from J (Line 9), and is handled appropriately based on whether j is smaller (Line 11–15), or greater or equal (Line 17–21) to the constraint at the node of t we currently consider.

Finally, transfer function IFDEF$_\mathbb{T}$ is defined as:

$$\text{IFDEF}_\mathbb{T}(t, \texttt{\#if}\,(\theta)\,s) = [\![s]\!]_\mathbb{T}(\text{FEAT-FILTER}_\mathbb{T}(t, \theta)) \sqcup_\mathbb{T} \text{FEAT-FILTER}_\mathbb{T}(t, \neg\theta)$$

where $[\![s]\!]_\mathbb{T}(t)$ denotes the transfer function in $\mathbb{T}(\mathbb{C}_\mathbb{D}, \mathbb{A})$ for statement s.

After applying transfer functions, the obtained decision trees may contain some redundancy that can be exploited to further compress them. Function COMPRESS$_\mathbb{T}(t, C)$, described by Algorithm 5, is applied to decision trees t in order to compress (reduce) their representation. We use five different optimizations. First, if constraints on a path to some leaf are unsatisfiable, we eliminate that leaf node (Lines 9,10). Second, if a decision node contains two same subtrees, then we keep only one subtree and we also eliminate the decision node (Lines 11–13). Third, if a decision node contains a left leaf and a right subtree, such that its left leaf is the same with the left leaf of its right subtree and the constraint in the decision node is less or equal to the constraint in the root of its right subtree, then we can eliminate the decision node and its left leaf (Lines 14,15). A similar rule exists when a decision node has a left subtree and a right leaf (Lines 16,17).

Lifted analysis. The abstract operations and transfer functions of $\mathbb{T}(\mathbb{C}_\mathbb{D}, \mathbb{A})$ can be used to define the lifted analysis for program families. Tree t_{in} at the initial

---

Algorithm 4: RESTRICT (t, C, J)

---

1   **if** isEmpty(J) **then**
2   **if** isLeaf(t) **then** return t;
3   **if** isRedundant$(t.c, C)$ **then** return RESTRICT$(t.l, C, J)$;
4   **if** isRedundant$(\neg t.c, C)$ **then** return RESTRICT$(t.r, C, J)$;
5      $l = \text{RESTRICT}(t.l, C \cup \{t.c\}, J)$;
6      $r = \text{RESTRICT}(t.r, C \cup \{\neg t.c\}, J)$;
7   **return** $([t.c : l, r])$;
8 **else**
9      $j = min_{<_{\mathbb{C}_{\mathbb{D}}}}(J)$;
10   **if** isLeaf$(t) \vee (\text{isNode}(t) \wedge j <_{\mathbb{C}_{\mathbb{D}}} t.c)$ **then**
11   **if** isRedundant(j, C) **then** return RESTRICT$(t, C, J\backslash\{j\})$;
12   **if** isRedundant$(\neg j, C)$ **then** return $\ll\perp_{\mathrm{A}}\gg$;
13   **if** $j =_{\mathbb{C}_{\mathbb{D}}} t.c$ **then** (**if** b_j **then** $t = t.l$; **else** $t = t.r$) ;
14   **if** b_j **then** return $([j : \text{RESTRICT}(t, C \cup \{j\}, J\backslash\{j\}), \ll\perp_{\mathrm{A}}\gg])$;
15   **else** return $([j :\ll\perp_{\mathrm{A}}\gg, \text{RESTRICT}(t, C \cup \{j\}, J\backslash\{j\})])$;
16   **else**
17   **if** isRedundant$(t.c, C)$ **then** return RESTRICT$(t.l, C, J)$;
18   **if** isRedundant$(\neg t.c, C)$ **then** return RESTRICT$(t.r, C, J)$;
19        $l = \text{RESTRICT}(t.l, C \cup \{t.c\}, J)$;
20        $r = \text{RESTRICT}(t.r, C \cup \{\neg t.c\}, J)$;
21   **return** $([t.c : l, r])$;

---

location has only one leaf node $\top_{\mathrm{A}}$ and decision nodes that define the set $\mathbb{K}$. Note that if $\mathbb{K} \equiv true$, then $t_{in} = \top_{\mathbb{T}}$. In this way, we collect the possible invariants in the form of decision trees at all program locations.

We establish correctness of the lifted analysis based on $\mathbb{T}(\mathbb{C}_{\mathbb{D}}, \mathrm{A})$ by showing that it produces identical results with tuple-based domain $\mathrm{A}^{\mathbb{K}}$. Let $[\![s]\!]_{\mathbb{T}}$ and $\overline{[\![s]\!]}$ denote transfer functions of statement s in $\mathbb{T}(\mathbb{C}_{\mathbb{D}}, \mathrm{A})$ and $\mathrm{A}^{\mathbb{K}}$, respectively. Recall that $\overline{a}_{in} = \prod_{k\in\mathbb{K}} \top_{\mathrm{A}}$, and so $\gamma_{\mathbb{T}}(t_{in}) = \overline{\gamma}(\overline{a}_{in})$.

Theorem 1. $\gamma_{\mathbb{T}}([\![s]\!]_{\mathbb{T}}(t_{in})) = \overline{\gamma}(\overline{[\![s]\!]}(\overline{a}_{in}))$.

Proof. The proof is by induction on the structure of s. We consider the most interesting cases: #if (θ) s #endif. Transfer functions for #if are identical in both lifted domains. We only need to show that $\overline{\text{FEAT-FILTER}}(\overline{a}, \theta)$ and FEAT-FILTER$_{\mathbb{T}}(t, \theta)$ are identical. This is shown by induction on θ [13]. □

Example 5. Let us consider the code base of a program family P given in Fig. 4. It contains only one numerical feature SIZE with domain $\mathbb{N}$. The decision tree inferred at the final location ④ is depicted in Fig. 5. It uses the Interval domain for both decision and leaf nodes. Note that the constraint (SIZE < 3) does not explicitly appear in the code base, but we obtain it in the decision tree representation. This shows that partitioning of the configuration space $\mathbb{K}$ induced by decision trees is semantics-based rather than syntactic-based.

Algorithm 5: COMPRESS$_\mathbb{T}(t, C)$

---

1 **switch** t **do**
2   **case** $\ll n \gg$ **do**
3   **return** $\ll n \gg$;
4   **case** $[\![t.c : l, r]\!]$ **do**
5        $l' = $ COMPRESS$_\mathbb{T}(t.l, C \cup \{t.c\})$;
6        $r' = $ COMPRESS$_\mathbb{T}(t.r, C \cup \{\neg t.c\})$;
7   **switch** l', r' **do**
8   **case** $\ll n'_l \gg, \ll n'_r \gg$ **do**
9   **if** UNSAT$(C \cup \{t.c\})$ **then return** $\ll n'_r \gg$;
10   **if** UNSAT$(C \cup \{\neg t.c\})$ **then return** $\ll n'_l \gg$;
11   **if** $n'_l = n'_r$ **then return** $\ll n'_l \gg$;
12   **case** $[\![c_1 : l_1, r_1]\!], [\![c_2 : l_2, r_2]\!]$ *when* $c_1 = c_2 \wedge l_1 = l_2 \wedge r_1 = r_2$ **do**
13   **return** $[\![c_1 : l_1, r_1]\!]$;
14   **case** $\ll n'_l \gg, [\![c_2 : l_2, r_2]\!]$ *when* $\ll n'_l \gg = l_2 \wedge c \leq_{\mathbb{C}_\mathbb{D}} c_2$ **do**
15   **return** $[\![c_2 : l_2, r_2]\!]$;
16   **case** $[\![c_1 : l_1, r_1]\!], \ll n'_r \gg$ *when* $\ll n'_r \gg = r_1 \wedge c_1 \leq_{\mathbb{C}_\mathbb{D}} c$ **do**
17   **return** $[\![c_1 : l_1, r_1]\!]$;
18   **case** *default:* **do**
19   **return** $[\![t.c : l', r']\!]$;

```
①  int x := 0;
②  #if (SIZE ≤ 4) x := x+1; #else x := x-1; #endif
③  #if (SIZE==3 || SIZE==4) x := x-2; #endif ④
```

Fig. 4: Code base for program family P.   Fig. 5: Decision tree at loc. ④ of P.

Example 6. Let us consider the code base of a program family P' given in Fig. 6. It contains one numerical feature A with domain $[1, 4]$ and a non-linear feature expression $A * A < 9$. At program location ②, FEAT-FILTER$_\mathbb{T}(\ll x = 0 \gg, A * A < 9)$ returns an over-approximating tree $\ll x = 0 \gg$, whereas FEAT-FILTER$_\mathbb{T}(\ll x = 0 \gg, \neg(A * A < 9))$ returns $[\![A \geq 3, \ll x = 0 \gg, \ll \bot_I \gg]\!]$. In effect, we obtain an over-approximating result at the final program location ③ as shown in Fig. 7. The precise result at the program location ③, which can be obtained in case we have numerical domains that can handle non-linear constraints, is given in Fig. 8. We observe that when $\neg(A \leq 2)$, we obtain an over-approximating analysis result ($-1 \leq x \leq 1$ instead of $x = -1$) due to the over-approximation of the non-linear feature expression in the numerical domains we use. □

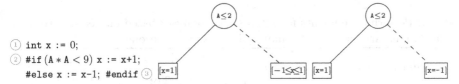

```
① int x := 0;
② #if (A * A < 9) x := x+1;
  #else x := x-1; #endif ③
```

Fig. 6: Code base for P'.

Fig. 7: Over-approximating decis. tree at loc. ③ of P'.

Fig. 8: Precise decision tree at loc. ③ of P'.

6   Evaluation

Implementation We have developed a prototype lifted static analyzer, called SPLNuM²ANALYZER, that uses lifted abstract domains of tuples $\mathbb{A}^K$ and decision trees $\mathbb{T}(\mathbb{C}_\mathbb{D}, \mathbb{A})$. The abstract domains $\mathbb{A}$ for encoding properties of tuple components and leaf nodes as well as the abstract domain $\mathbb{D}$ for encoding linear constraints over numerical features are based on intervals, octagons, and polyhedra domains. Their abstract operations and transfer functions are provided by the APRON library [19]. Our proof-of-concept implementation is written in OCAML and consists of around 6K lines of code. The current front-end of the tool accepts programs written in a (subset of) C with `#if` directives, but without `struct` and `union` types. It currently provides only a limited support for arrays, pointers, and recursion. The only basic data type is mathematical integers. SPLNuM²ANALYZER automatically infers numerical invariants in all program locations corresponding to all variants in the given family. We use delayed widening and narrowing [7,24] to improve the precision of `while`-s.

Experimental setup and Benchmarks All experiments are executed on a 64-bit Intel® Core^{TM} i7-8700 CPU@3.20GHz × 12, Ubuntu 18.04.5 LTS, with 8 GB memory, and we use a timeout value of 300 sec. All times are reported as average over five independent executions. The implementation, benchmarks, and all results obtained from our experiments are available from: https://github.com/aleksdimovski/SPLNUM2Analyzer. In our experiments, we use three instances of our lifted analysis via tuples: $\overline{\mathcal{A}}_\Pi(I)$, $\overline{\mathcal{A}}_\Pi(O)$, and $\overline{\mathcal{A}}_\Pi(P)$, and via decision trees: $\overline{\mathcal{A}}_\mathbb{T}(I)$, $\overline{\mathcal{A}}_\mathbb{T}(O)$, and $\overline{\mathcal{A}}_\mathbb{T}(P)$, which use intervals, octagons, and polyhedra domains as parameters, respectively.

SPLNuM²ANALYZER was evaluated on a dozen of C programs collected from several categories of the 8th International Competition on Software Verification (SV-COMP 2019, https://sv-comp.sosy-lab.org/2019/): `loops`, `loop-invgen` (`invgen` for short), `loop-lit` (`lit`), `termination-crafted` (`crafted`); as well as from the real-world BusyBox project (https://busybox.net). In the case of SV-COMP, we have first selected some numerical programs with integers, and then we have manually added variability (features and `#if` directives) in each of them. In the case of BusyBox, we have first selected some programs with numerical features, and then we have simplified those programs so that our tool can handle them. For example, any reference to a pointer or a library function is replaced with $[-\infty, +\infty]$. Table 1 presents characteristics of the benchmarks. We

Table 1: Performance results for lifted static analyses based on decision trees vs. tuples (which are used as baseline). All times are in seconds.

Benchmark	folder	$|\mathbb{F}|$	$|\mathbb{K}|$	LOC	$\overline{\mathcal{A}}_{\mathbb{T}}(I)$		$\overline{\mathcal{A}}_{\mathbb{T}}(O)$		$\overline{\mathcal{A}}_{\mathbb{T}}(P)$	
					TIME	IMPR.	TIME	IMPR.	TIME	IMPR.
half_2.c	invgen	2	36	60	0.010	2.4×	0.017	3.5×	0.022	4.6×
heapsort.c	invgen	2	36	60	0.036	2.2×	0.226	1.1×	0.191	2.0×
seq.c	invgen	3	125	40	0.039	9.3×	0.460	4.3×	0.164	11×
eq1.c	loops	2	36	20	0.015	3.4×	0.049	3.1×	0.052	4×
eq2.c	loops	2	25	20	0.013	1.9×	0.047	1.3×	0.040	1.9×
sum01*.c	loops	2	25	20	0.016	1.7×	0.086	1.5×	0.062	2.2×
hhk2008.c	lit	3	216	30	0.023	10×	0.153	4.5×	0.074	12.5×
gsv2008.c	lit	2	25	25	0.013	1.5×	0.035	1.2×	0.037	2×
gcnr2008.c	lit	2	25	30	0.021	2×	0.070	2.1×	0.102	2.6×
Toulouse*.c	crafted	3	125	75	0.043	6.1×	0.259	2.4×	0.175	7.6×
Mysore.c	crafted	3	125	35	0.019	3.7×	0.090	1.1×	0.056	5.4×
copyfd.c	BusyBox	1	16	84	0.013	3.9×	0.041	6.2×	0.054	5.2×
real_path.c	BusyBox	2	128	45	0.023	14×	0.077	28×	0.085	32×

list: the file name (Benchmark), the category (folder), the number of features and configurations ($|\mathbb{F}|, |\mathbb{K}|$), and lines of code (LOC).

Performance Results Table 1 shows the results of analyzing our benchmark files by using different versions of our lifted static analyses based on decision trees and on tuples. For each version of decision tree-based lifted analysis, there are two columns. In the first column, TIME, we report the running time in seconds to analyze the given benchmark using the corresponding version of lifted analysis based on decision trees. In the second column, IMPR., we report the speed up factor for each version of lifted analysis based on decision trees relative to the corresponding baseline lifted analysis based on tuples ($\overline{\mathcal{A}}_{\mathbb{T}}(I)$ vs. $\overline{\mathcal{A}}_{\Pi}(I)$, $\overline{\mathcal{A}}_{\mathbb{T}}(O)$ vs. $\overline{\mathcal{A}}_{\Pi}(O)$, and $\overline{\mathcal{A}}_{\mathbb{T}}(P)$ vs. $\overline{\mathcal{A}}_{\Pi}(P)$). The performance results confirm that sharing is indeed effective and especially so for large values of $|\mathbb{K}|$. On our benchmarks, it translates to speed ups (i.e., $\overline{\mathcal{A}}_{\mathbb{T}}(-)$ vs. $\overline{\mathcal{A}}_{\Pi}(-)$) that range from 1.1 to 4.6 times when $|\mathbb{K}| < 100$, and from 3.7 to 32 times when $|\mathbb{K}| > 100$.

Computational tractability The tuple-based lifted analysis $\overline{\mathcal{A}}_{\Pi}(-)$ may become very slow or even infeasible for very large configuration spaces $|\mathbb{K}|$. We have tested the limits of $\overline{\mathcal{A}}_{\Pi}(P)$ and $\overline{\mathcal{A}}_{\mathbb{T}}(-)$. We took a method, $\mathtt{test}_n^k()$, which contains n numerical features $\mathtt{A}_1, \ldots, \mathtt{A}_n$, such that each numerical feature $\mathtt{A}_i$ has domain $\mathrm{dom}(\mathtt{A}_i) = [0, k-1] = \{0, \ldots, k-1\}$. The body of $\mathtt{test}_n^k()$ consists of n sequentially composed #if-s of the form #if $(\mathtt{A}_i = 0)$ i := i+1 #else i := 0 #endif For example, $\mathtt{test}_2^3()$ with two features $\mathtt{A}_1$ and $\mathtt{A}_2$, whose domain is $[0, 2]$, is:

```
①    int i := 0;
②    #if (A₁ = 0) i := i+1 #else i := 0 #endif
③    #if (A₂ = 0) i := i+1 #else i := 0 #endif ④
```

$$(\begin{array}{ccc} \overset{A_1=0\wedge A_2=0}{[i=2]}, & \overset{A_1=0\wedge A_2=1}{[i=0]}, & \overset{A_1=0\wedge A_2=2}{[i=0]}, \\ \overset{A_1=1\wedge A_2=0}{[i=1]}, & \overset{A_1=1\wedge A_2=1}{[i=0]}, & \overset{A_1=1\wedge A_2=2}{[i=0]}, \\ \overset{A_1=2\wedge A_2=0}{[i=1]}, & \overset{A_1=2\wedge A_2=1}{[i=0]}, & \overset{A_1=2\wedge A_2=2}{[i=0]} \end{array})$$

Fig. 9: $\overline{\mathcal{A}}_\Pi(P)$ results at ④ of $\mathtt{test}_2^3()$. Fig. 10: $\overline{\mathcal{A}}_\mathbb{D}(P)$ results at ④ of $\mathtt{test}_2^3()$.

Subject to the chosen configuration, the variable i in location ④ can have a value in the range from value 2 when A_1 and A_2 are assigned to 0, to value 0 when $A_2 \geq 1$. The analysis results in location ④ of $\mathtt{test}_2^3()$ obtained using $\overline{\mathcal{A}}_\Pi(P)$ and $\overline{\mathcal{A}}_\mathbb{T}(P)$ are shown in Fig. 9 and Fig. 10, respectively. $\overline{\mathcal{A}}_\Pi(P)$ uses tuples with 9 interval properties (components), while $\overline{\mathcal{A}}_\mathbb{T}(P)$ uses 3 interval properties (leafs).

Table 2: The performance results of analyzing $\mathtt{test}_n^k$.

n	$k = 3$			$k = 5$			$k = 7$		
	$\overline{\mathcal{A}}_\Pi(P)$	$\overline{\mathcal{A}}_\mathbb{T}(P)$	IMPR.	$\overline{\mathcal{A}}_\Pi(P)$	$\overline{\mathcal{A}}_\mathbb{T}(P)$	IMPR.	$\overline{\mathcal{A}}_\Pi(P)$	$\overline{\mathcal{A}}_\mathbb{T}(P)$	IMPR.
5	0.164	0.137	1.2×	2.859	0.139	20.6×	19.976	0.138	144.7×
6	0.701	0.293	2.4×	23.224	0.294	79.1×	infeasible	0.299	∞×
8	17.420	1.761	9.9×	infeasible	1.765	∞×	infeasible	1.767	∞×
10	278.7	5.591	49.8×	infeasible	5.596	∞×	infeasible	5.639	∞×
11	infeasible	13.807	∞×	infeasible	13.859	∞×	infeasible	13.809	∞×
14	infeasible	327.10	∞×	infeasible	442.23	∞×	infeasible	459.19	∞×

We have generated methods $\mathtt{test}_n^k()$ by gradually increasing variability. In general, the size of tuples used by $\overline{\mathcal{A}}_\Pi(P)$ is k^n, whereas the number of leaf nodes in decision trees used by $\overline{\mathcal{A}}_\mathbb{T}(P)$ in the final program location is $n + 1$. The performance results of analyzing $\mathtt{test}_n^k$, for different values of n and k, using $\overline{\mathcal{A}}_\Pi(P)$ and $\overline{\mathcal{A}}_\mathbb{T}(P)$ are shown in Table 2. In the columns IMPR., we report the speed-up of $\overline{\mathcal{A}}_\mathbb{T}(P)$ with respect to $\overline{\mathcal{A}}_\Pi(P)$. We observe that $\overline{\mathcal{A}}_\mathbb{T}(P)$ yields decision trees that provide quite compact and symbolic representation of lifted analysis results. Since the configurations with equivalent analysis results are nicely encoded using linear constraints in decision nodes, the performance of $\overline{\mathcal{A}}_\mathbb{T}(P)$ does not depend on k, but only depends on n. On the other hand, the performance of $\overline{\mathcal{A}}_\Pi(P)$ heavily depends on k. Thus, within a timeout limit of 300 seconds, the analysis $\overline{\mathcal{A}}_\Pi(P)$ fails to terminate for $\mathtt{test}_{11}^3$, $\mathtt{test}_8^5$, and $\mathtt{test}_6^7$. In summary, we can conclude that decision trees $\overline{\mathcal{A}}_\mathbb{T}(P)$ can not only greatly speed up lifted analyses, but also turn previously infeasible analyses into feasible.

7   Related Work

Decision-tree abstract domains have been successfully used in the field of abstract interpretation recently [18,9,4,26]. Decision trees have been applied for the disjunctive refinement of Interval domain [18]. That is, each element of the new domain is a propositional formula over interval linear constraints. Segmented decision tree abstract domains has also been defined [9,4] to enable path dependent static analysis. Their elements contain decision nodes that are determined either by values of program variables [9] or by the branch (`if`) conditions [4], whereas the leaf nodes are numerical properties. Urban and Mine [26] use decision tree-based abstract domains to prove program termination. Decision nodes are labelled with linear constraints that split the memory space and leaf nodes contain affine ranking functions for proving program termination.

Recently, two main styles of static analysis have been a topic of considerable research in the SPL community: *a dataflow analysis from the monotone framework* developed by Kildall [21] that is algorithmically defined on syntactic CFGs, and *an abstract interpretation-based static analysis* developed by Cousot and Cousot [7] that is more general and semantically defined. Brabrand et. al. [3] lift a dataflow analysis from the *monotone framework*, resulting in a tuple-based lifted dataflow analysis. Another efficient implementation of the lifted dataflow analysis from the monotone framework is based on using variational data structures [27]. Midtgaard et. al. [22] have proposed a formal methodology for systematic derivation of tuple-based lifted static analyses in the *abstract interpretation framework*. A more efficient lifted static analysis by abstract interpretation obtained by improving representation via BDD domains is given in [11]. Another approach to speed up lifted analyses is by using so-called variability abstractions [14,15], which are used to derive abstract lifted analyses. They tame the combinatorial explosion of the number of configurations and reduce it to something more tractable by manipulating the configuration space. The work [5] presents a model checking technique to analyze probabilistic program families.

8   Conclusion

In this work we employ decision trees and widely-known numerical abstract domains for automatic inference of invariants in all locations of C program families that contain numerical features. In future, we would like to extend the lifted abstract domain to also support non-linear constraints [17]. An interesting direction for future work would be to explore possibilities of applying variability abstractions [14] as yet another way to speed up lifted analyses. We can also define a backward lifted analysis in combination with a preliminary forward lifted analysis to infer the necessary preconditions in order a given assertion to be satisfied or violated. The obtained preconditions in the form of linear constraints can be analyzed using model counting techniques to quantify how likely is an input or a variant to satisfy them [16,12].

References

1. Sven Apel, Hendrik Speidel, Philipp Wendler, Alexander von Rhein, and Dirk Beyer. Detection of feature interactions using feature-aware verification. In *26th IEEE/ACM International Conference on Automated Software Engineering (ASE 2011)*, pages 372–375, 2011.
2. Sven Apel, Alexander von Rhein, Philipp Wendler, Armin Größlinger, and Dirk Beyer. Strategies for product-line verification: case studies and experiments. In *35th Intern. Conference on Software Engineering, ICSE '13*, pages 482–491, 2013.
3. Claus Brabrand, Márcio Ribeiro, Társis Tolêdo, Johnni Winther, and Paulo Borba. Intraprocedural dataflow analysis for software product lines. *T. Aspect-Oriented Software Development*, 10:73–108, 2013.
4. Junjie Chen and Patrick Cousot. A binary decision tree abstract domain functor. In *Static Analysis - 22nd International Symposium, SAS 2015, Proceedings*, volume 9291 of *LNCS*, pages 36–53. Springer, 2015.
5. Philipp Chrszon, Clemens Dubslaff, Sascha Klüppelholz, and Christel Baier. Profeat: feature-oriented engineering for family-based probabilistic model checking. *Formal Aspects Comput.*, 30(1):45–75, 2018.
6. Paul Clements and Linda Northrop. *Software Product Lines: Practices and Patterns*. Addison-Wesley, 2001.
7. Patrick Cousot and Radhia Cousot. Abstract interpretation: A unified lattice model for static analysis of programs by construction or approximation of fixpoints. In *Conference Record of the Fourth ACM Symposium on Principles of Programming Languages*, pages 238–252. ACM, 1977.
8. Patrick Cousot, Radhia Cousot, Jérôme Feret, Laurent Mauborgne, Antoine Miné, David Monniaux, and Xavier Rival. The astreé analyzer. In *Programming Languages and Systems, 14th European Symposium on Programming, ESOP 2005, Proceedings*, volume 3444 of *LNCS*, pages 21–30. Springer, 2005.
9. Patrick Cousot, Radhia Cousot, and Laurent Mauborgne. A scalable segmented decision tree abstract domain. In *Time for Verification, Essays in Memory of Amir Pnueli*, volume 6200 of *LNCS*, pages 72–95. Springer, 2010.
10. Patrick Cousot and Nicolas Halbwachs. Automatic discovery of linear restraints among variables of a program. In *Conference Record of the Fifth Annual ACM Symposium on Principles of Programming Languages (POPL'78)*, pages 84–96. ACM Press, 1978.
11. Aleksandar S. Dimovski. Lifted static analysis using a binary decision diagram abstract domain. In *Proceedings of the 18th ACM SIGPLAN International Conference on Generative Programming: Concepts and Experiences, GPCE 2019*, pages 102–114. ACM, 2019.
12. Aleksandar S. Dimovski. On calculating assertion probabilities for program families. *Prilozi Contributions, Sec. Nat. Math. Biotech. Sci, MASA*, 41(1):13–23, 2020.
13. Aleksandar S. Dimovski, Sven Apel, and Axel Legay. A decision tree lifted domain for analyzing program families with numerical features (extended version). *CoRR*, abs/2012.05863, 2020.
14. Aleksandar S. Dimovski, Claus Brabrand, and Andrzej Wasowski. Variability abstractions: Trading precision for speed in family-based analyses. In *29th European Conference on Object-Oriented Programming, ECOOP 2015*, volume 37 of *LIPIcs*, pages 247–270. Schloss Dagstuhl - Leibniz-Zentrum fuer Informatik, 2015.
15. Aleksandar S. Dimovski, Claus Brabrand, and Andrzej Wasowski. Finding suitable variability abstractions for lifted analysis. *Formal Aspects Comput.*, 31(2):231–259, 2019.

16. Aleksandar S. Dimovski and Axel Legay. Computing program reliability using forward-backward precondition analysis and model counting. In *Fundamental Approaches to Software Engineering - 23rd International Conference, FASE 2020, Proceedings*, volume 12076 of *LNCS*, pages 182–202. Springer, 2020.

17. Philippe Granger. Static analysis of arithmetical congruences. *International Journal of Computer Mathematics*, 30(3-4):165–190, 1989.

18. Arie Gurfinkel and Sagar Chaki. Boxes: A symbolic abstract domain of boxes. In *Static Analysis - 17th International Symposium, SAS 2010. Proceedings*, volume 6337 of *LNCS*, pages 287–303. Springer, 2010.

19. Bertrand Jeannet and Antoine Miné. Apron: A library of numerical abstract domains for static analysis. In *Computer Aided Verification, 21st Intern. Conference, CAV 2009. Proceedings*, volume 5643 of *LNCS*, pages 661–667. Springer, 2009.

20. Christian Kästner. *Virtual Separation of Concerns: Toward Preprocessors 2.0.* PhD thesis, University of Magdeburg, Germany, May 2010.

21. Gary A. Kildall. A unified approach to global program optimization. In *Conference Record of the ACM Symposium on Principles of Programming Languages, (POPL'73)*, pages 194–206, 1973.

22. Jan Midtgaard, Aleksandar S. Dimovski, Claus Brabrand, and Andrzej Wasowski. Systematic derivation of correct variability-aware program analyses. *Sci. Comput. Program.*, 105:145–170, 2015.

23. Antoine Miné. The octagon abstract domain. *Higher-Order and Symbolic Computation*, 19(1):31–100, 2006.

24. Antoine Miné. Tutorial on static inference of numeric invariants by abstract interpretation. *Foundations and Trends in Programming Languages*, 4(3-4):120–372, 2017.

25. Daniel-Jesus Munoz, Jeho Oh, Mónica Pinto, Lidia Fuentes, and Don S. Batory. Uniform random sampling product configurations of feature models that have numerical features. In *Proceedings of the 23rd International Systems and Software Product Line Conference, SPLC 2019, Volume A*, pages 39:1–39:13. ACM, 2019.

26. Caterina Urban and Antoine Miné. A decision tree abstract domain for proving conditional termination. In *Static Analysis - 21st International Symposium, SAS 2014. Proceedings*, volume 8723 of *LNCS*, pages 302–318. Springer, 2014.

27. Alexander von Rhein, Jörg Liebig, Andreas Janker, Christian Kästner, and Sven Apel. Variability-aware static analysis at scale: An empirical study. *ACM Trans. Softw. Eng. Methodol.*, 27(4):18:1–18:33, 2018.

Finding a Universal Execution Strategy for Model Transformation Networks*

Joshua Gleitze[ID], Heiko Klare[(✉)][ID], and Erik Burger[ID]

KASTEL, Karlsruhe Institute of Technology, Karlsruhe, Germany
`joshua.gleitze@student.kit.edu`, `klare@kit.edu`, `burger@kit.edu`

Abstract. When using multiple models to describe a (software) system, one can use a network of model transformations to keep the models consistent after changes. No strategy exists, however, to orchestrate the execution of transformations if the network has an arbitrary topology. In this paper, we analyse how often and in which order transformations need to be executed. We argue why linear execution bounds are too restrictive to be useful in practice and prove that there is no upper bound for the number of necessary executions. To avoid non-termination, we propose a conservative strategy that makes execution failures easier to understand. These insights help developers and users of transformation networks to understand under which circumstances their networks can terminate. Additionally, the proposed strategy helps them to find the cause when a network cannot restore consistency.

Keywords: model consistency · model transformation networks

1 Introduction

When modelling systems, one is often confronted with the task of *model consistency*: Since model-driven development aims at separating concerns by tailoring models to the needs of the people working on the system, there are typically different models, each one capturing the parts of the system that are relevant to the model's target audience. All those models taken together should describe a coherent system and not contain contradictory information. We say that the models should be consistent. Automatic detection and resolution of inconsistencies is, however, still poorly addressed in current development processes [12].

There are different means of maintaining consistency. A popular one is to define *incremental model transformations*, which update models based on information that was changed in one of them. While there has been significant research on model transformations themselves, particularly on binary transformations, maintaining consistency of multiple models is less researched [2]. There are approaches for multiary model transformations which can transform between multiple models by means of a single transformation. Nevertheless, one will likely

---

* This work was supported by funding of the Helmholtz Association (HGF) through the Competence Center for Applied Security Technology (KASTEL).

E. Guerra and M. Stoelinga (Eds.): FASE 2021, LNCS 12649, pp. 87–107, 2021.
https://doi.org/10.1007/978-3-030-71500-7_5

also want to be able to combine multiple transformations—binary or multiary—to maintain consistency, creating a *transformation network*. Unlike using a single, overarching transformation, defining a network makes it possible to reuse modular ones. Additionally, knowledge about consistency between certain types of models is often distributed across domain experts [13]. This can be accommodated by transformation networks, because every domain expert can define transformations independently and according to their view on consistency.

To the best of the authors' knowledge, no strategy that determines an execution order of transformations to maintain consistency in a network with arbitrary topology has been presented yet. Existing work proposes, for example, defining an execution order explicitly [23, 35] or deriving a topological order [30]. Most approaches restrict the supported kinds of network topologies to such in which each transformation only needs to be executed once.

In this paper, we research properties and limitations of a universal strategy that executes a transformation network of arbitrary topology. We show that strategies that apply each transformation only once are not useful in practice. At the other end of the spectrum, we prove that not limiting the number of transformation executions does, in general, lead to non-termination. Based on the insight that a universal strategy can only operate conservatively, we derive a practicable strategy. In detail, we make the following contributions:

Formalisation *(C1)*: We formalise transformation networks and execution strategies to precisely define their expected properties.

Conservativeness Proof *(C2)*: We prove that a universal execution strategy must operate conservatively to avoid non-termination.

Strategy Design *(C3)*: We propose a strategy that improves explainability whenever no consistent models are found.

The contributions establish fundamental knowledge about the design space of network execution strategies, their undecidability, and difficulties in reducing conservativeness. The proposed strategy helps transformation network developers and users to find the reasons when an execution does not yield consistent models.

2   Problem Statement

In this section, we will further motivate our research by giving an example and clarifying its context. We provide a formalisation for transformation networks and execution strategies to generate a common understanding and formal basis for transformation network orchestration, constituting contribution *C1*.

2.1   Motivating Example

Figure 1 depicts a software project whose contributors take the roles of architects, developers and user experience (UX) designers. One person can take multiple roles, but every role has a particular view on the project and uses related tools. Architects use a UML-based tool to analyse and plan the architecture. Developers

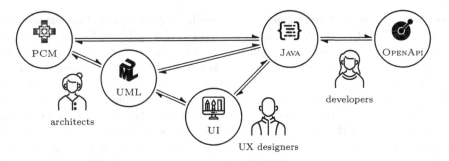

Fig. 1. Example for a transformation network in model-driven (software) development.

program the software in Java. These two models overlap: Although they cannot be derived completely from each other, the implementation should follow the architecture and architects want to see how code changes affect the architecture.

UX designers develop the UI for the software. Their designs overlap with the UML model, because, first, the software's requirements mandate certain properties of the UI, and, second, the architecture may restrict which information can be shown at which point in the interface. The UI design also overlaps with the code, since static parts of the UI can be derived from the UI model. Ideally, changes in the UI code can even be propagated back into the UI model.

The developers use OpenAPI™ [32] to exchange specifications of HTTP APIs. These specifications overlap with the parsing and serialisation code. Architects want to analyse how their architecture choices influence performance, using the Palladio Component Model (PCM) [24]. The architecture specification used in the PCM overlaps with the one defined in UML. Additionally, the PCM model contains information about performance properties and the deployment structure, which can partially be derived from the code.

Those relations can be encoded in transformations to avoid re-specification of similar information, such as the architecture in PCM and UML, to derive information, like appropriate Java stubs from OpenAPI specifications, and to preserve information consistency. Figure 1 shows the resulting transformation network. In this paper, we will find an execution strategy for such transformations, which is needed to correctly propagate changes from one model to the others.

2.2   Context

We discuss model transformation networks in a specific usage context. We assume that different roles are involved in a development project, each using some models to describe their view of the system. The models are kept consistent by model transformations. For the sake of simplicity, we only discuss *binary* transformations between two models. To foster independent specification and reuse of transformations, we assume that they are not tailor-made, but may be general-purpose. As a consequence, we cannot assume that the models or transformations are or can be aligned, for example, to ensure that their execution in a specific order always results in consistent models. Neither can we assume that the network has a certain topology. We do, however, assume that all transformations are in accordance to a well-defined overall notion of consistency (reaching a consistent state would be impossible otherwise). This means that all requirements we pose on the transformations must only concern a transformation itself. A requirement like "no transformation overwrites the result of another" would not fit our context.

We require that transformations are *synchronising* [4], i.e., that they can deal with the situation that both of their models have been changed. This is essential to find an execution strategy: When propagating changes in a transformation network that contains cycles, it will inevitably happen that both models that are connected by a transformation will be changed. In addition, the well-researched *bidirectional* transformations only change one of the models [28] and could in such a situation be forced to overwrite changes to yield a consistent result. This assumption also enables concurrent modifications by different project members.

2.3 Formalisation

We are not concerned with how models are structured, so we simply resort to defining a universe $\mathbb{M}$ that contains all models. First, we define the kind of transformations that we use:

Definition 1. *A synchronising binary transformation (syncx) $\vec{t}$ is a function that updates two models:*

$$\vec{t} \colon (\mathbb{M} \times \mathbb{M}) \to (\mathbb{M} \times \mathbb{M})$$

A syncx' image consists of fixed points:

$$\forall a \in \mathbb{M} \, \forall b \in \mathbb{M} : \vec{t}\big(\vec{t}(a, b)\big) = \vec{t}(a, b)$$

The universe of all syncx for $\mathbb{M}$ is called $\mathbb{T}$.

This formalisation is a simplification sufficient for the purposes of this paper. In practice, transformations will, for example, be allowed to indicate an error instead of being required to always produce appropriate new models.

In comparison to existing formalisms [28], there is no consistency relation in the definition of a syncx. For our purposes, the consistency relation is not part of a syncx, but rather encoded implicitly in the syncx' behaviour. We assume that the transformations are correct and hippocratic [28] with regard to their implicit consistency relation and can then recover the relation:

Definition 2. *The consistency relation $R_{\vec{t}}$ of syncx $\vec{t}$ is given by:*

$$R_{\vec{t}} = \big\{ (a, b) \mid \vec{t}(a, b) = (a, b) \big\}$$

This paper focuses on transformation networks that are created when combining multiple syncx:

Definition 3. *A transformation network $N =: ((V, E), T)$ consists of a directed, connected, self-loop-free graph $G = (V, E)$ and a syncx assignment $T \colon E \to \mathbb{T}$. Any two vertices $\{a, b\} \subseteq V$ have at most one edge between them: $(a, b) \in E \implies (b, a) \notin E$. The universe of all model transformation networks for $\mathbb{M}$ is called $\mathbb{U}$.*

A transformation network captures the topology and the used transformations. There is no inherent reason to exclude multigraphs or self-loops. We use this simpler definition because it makes it easier to argue about the networks without restricting expressiveness. We use directed edges instead of undirected ones to provide a notion of the "left" and "right" model for a syncx. The edges' direction does not indicate anything about the direction of change propagation. We will usually regard the network as given and try to find suitable model assignments:

Definition 4. *For a transformation network $N =: ((V, E), T)$, a model assignment M is a function $M : V \to \mathbb{M}$.*

Naturally, we are particularly interested in model assignments that are consistent with the transformations:

Definition 5. *For a transformation network $N =: ((V, E), T)$, a model assignment M is consistent if, and only if*

$$\forall (a, b) \in E : (M(a), M(b)) \in R_{T(a,b)}$$

The set of all consistent model assignments for N is called R_N.

We use the following additional notation in this paper:

- "$A \to B$" for the set of functions from set A to set B
- "f: $A \twoheadrightarrow B$" for a partial function f from A to B
- "$f(x) = \bot$" to mean that a partial function f is not defined at x
- "Im(f)" to denote the image of a function f

2.4 Problem Description

Our goal is to find an algorithm that, given a transformation network $N =: ((V, E), T) \in \mathbb{U}$ and a model assignment M, finds a consistent model assignment M' by applying transformations in Im(T). We call such an algorithm a "(transformation network) execution strategy". It is "universal" if it is parametrised by and thus defined for every network.

Definition 6. *A universal execution strategy determines an order (i.e., a permutation with duplicates) of transformations in Im(T) for a given transformation network $N =: ((V, E), T) \in \mathbb{U}$ and model assignment $M \in (V \to \mathbb{M})$. It realises a partial function $S : \mathbb{U} \times (V \to \mathbb{M}) \twoheadrightarrow (V \to \mathbb{M})$.*

An execution strategy finds a new model assignment only by executing the transformations of the network, as more precisely defined by Klare et al. [15, Definition 8]. If $S(N, M) \neq \bot$, we say that the strategy "resolves" N and M. If $S(N, M) = \bot$, we say that the strategy fails. We have further requirements:

Requirement 1. *An execution strategy must be correct:*

$$\forall N =: ((V, E), T) \in \mathbb{U} \ \forall M \in (V \to \mathbb{M}) : S(N, M) \in R_N \cup \{\bot\}$$

Requirement 2. *An execution strategy must be hippocratic:*

$$\forall N =: ((V, E), T) \in \mathbb{U} \ \forall M_c \in R_N : S(N, M_c) = M_c$$

An execution strategy will not always be able to find a consistent new model assignment (i.e., there will be some N, M such that $S(N, M) = \bot$). First, there may not be a consistent model assignment at all (i.e., $R_N = \emptyset$). Second, there may be a consistent model assignment but no execution order of the transformations that yields that assignment [30, 16]. We call such inputs "unresolvable" [30]. Conversely, if there is an execution order of the transformations that yields a consistent model assignment, we call the inputs "resolvable".

An execution strategy may even fail for resolvable inputs: The execution strategy may not "find" a consistent model assignment, even though it is reachable. For example, the strategy may abort before having executed the transformations often enough, or finding the assignment might require an order of execution which the strategy does not consider. We call such a strategy "conservative":

Definition 7. *An execution strategy S is* conservative *if it is correct and if there can be resolvable inputs N, M with $S(N, M) = \bot$.*

The higher the probability that an execution strategy yields a result for resolvable inputs (we also say the lower its "level of conservativeness"), the more useful the strategy will be. It is, however, also desirable that the strategy is predictable, meaning that one can determine beforehand for which inputs the strategy will succeed. For example, it would be useful to know whether a strategy yields a result for a given network for *any* resolvable model assignment. Informally speaking, we would like to have an "easy-to-check" criterion for transformation networks determining whether this is the case. An even better criterion could be applied to a single syncx, such that the strategy can resolve all inputs with a network of syncx that fulfil the criterion. This would be ideal for the motivated context of independently developing and freely combining syncx to a network.

To summarise, we aim to find a correct, hippocratic execution strategy that is able to keep models consistent via transformation networks. The strategy should succeed for realistic inputs with a high probability. Additionally, we aim to find criteria that determine the cases in which the strategy will succeed.

3   Related Work

Approaches for restoring model consistency have been subject to intensive research, surveyed by Macedo et al. [21]. Model transformations are a well-researched option, and several tools and languages have been developed to support them [27, 18, 25]. Research has, however, mainly focused on consistency between two models, which also concerns theoretical properties like *termination* as one of the properties that we investigate for the execution of transformation networks [7]. Maintaining consistency between more than two models has recently gained more attention, especially in terms of a dedicated Dagstuhl seminar [2]. The central approaches of multiary transformations and networks of binary transformations can be distinguished. In Section 1, we have discussed that multiary transformations are complex to specify, whereas networks of binary transformations have limited expressiveness [30], which does, however, not seem to be practically relevant [2].

Multiary Transformations: Different approaches for multiary transformations have been proposed. QVT-R [22] supports multidirectionality already by design, but ambiguities in the standard limit practical applicability [20]. Triple Graph Grammars (TGGs) [26] are bidirectional specifications, which are well-suited for model transformations [1]. Extensions of TGGs to multiple models called Multi Graph Grammars (MGGs) [17] and Graph Diagram Grammars [34, 33] consider the specification of multidirectional rules. All these approaches, however, require the transformation developer to know about and be able to express the relations between all involved models, which we reasonably excluded by assumption.

Auxiliary Models: Not all multiary relations can be expressed by sets of binary ones. Adding one auxiliary model makes it, however, theoretically possible to express arbitrary multiary relations by binary ones [30]. Some work discussed which kinds of relations can be expressed with such an approach and how they can be formalised in the lenses framework [5, 31]. Other work discussed how composing such auxiliary models to express commonalities of models can be achieved [14]. Such auxiliary models actually encode a multiary transformation in a model together with binary transformations to the models to keep consistent, resulting in the same challenges as for transformation network. In consequence, our work on transformation networks is also required and applicable there.

Binary Transformations: Although they cannot express all multiary relations, there are arguments in favour of using networks of modular transformations, especially binary ones: They are easier to develop when domain knowledge is distributed [13] and they are easier to comprehend by a single developer [2, 30]. Additionally, binary transformations are researched well and a variety of tools supporting different kinds of specifying them exist [27, 18, 25, 21]. Most formalisms and tools consider *bidirectional* transformations, whereas networks require synchronising transformations, as motivated in Section 2.2. Non-synchronising transformations can, however, be adapted to become synchronising [37].

Transformation Chains: Transformation chains combine transformations to derive low-level models from high-level ones across intermediate representations. Languages like FTG+PM [19] and UniTI [35] enable the specification of such chains. Transformation chains are, however, only a special case of general transformation networks. Etien et al. consider specific properties of transformation chains. They investigate how conflicts in terms of results depending on the execution order can be detected [8]. These results do, however, not aim to relieve developers from the task of finding an execution order manually, as we do in this paper.

Transformation Composition: Transformation composition techniques are a means to build networks of binary transformations. They can be separated into internal, white-box approaches [36], and external techniques, which consider transformations as black-boxes. Our contributions can be seen as an external composition technique. However, composition usually considers transformations between the same rather than different types of models. From a theoretical perspective (see Section 2.3) this could be treated equally by not distinguishing models by their metamodels. Practical approaches, however, consider transformations between specific metamodels rather than arbitrary models.

Fig. 2. Example yielding inconsistent models after executing each transformation once. Numbers in italics indicate the order in which changes are performed.

Execution Strategies: Di Rocco et al. [3] describe a simple strategy for orchestrating transformations, but make strong assumptions requiring that each of them is only applied once. Stevens [30] proposes a strategy that also executes each transformation only once in one direction. It includes a notion of authoritative models, which are not allowed to be changed, and does not consider synchronising transformations. Likewise, Stevens [29] proposes to find an *orientation model* defining in which direction transformations are executed. If, however, several transformations modify the same model, the approach leaves it to the developer to determine an execution order after which all consistency relations hold. Such strategies are only correct if the network is a tree, or if no transformations interfere with each other. We present a simple scenario in which this is already too limiting in Section 4.1. We overcome this limitation by executing transformations more than once and thereby letting them "negotiate" a result even if they interfere, which yields a *universal* execution strategy for arbitrary network topologies.

4   Design Space

We approach the possibilities for designing an execution strategy by looking at how often it executes syncx in the worst case. We consider the two extremes of executing every syncx at most once and executing them an unlimited number of times, and find that neither of them will do: While the first one is too limiting, the second one cannot guarantee termination. As a consequential insight, a universal execution strategy needs to be *conservative*, introduced as contribution *C2*.

4.1   One Execution per Transformation

Several proposed strategies execute every transformation in a network at most once [30, 35]. Since we expect that transformations are developed independently, and are thus not necessarily aligned (see Section 2.2), restricting the number of executions to one per transformation would, however, limit the possible combinations of them, and models could not be kept consistent in desirable scenarios. We give an example for this in the following.

$$\begin{array}{ccccccc} \overset{\tilde{i}_2}{\underset{}{\rightleftharpoons}} & \overset{\tilde{i}_4}{\underset{}{\rightleftharpoons}} & \cdots & \overset{\tilde{i}_n}{\underset{}{\rightleftharpoons}} & \overset{\tilde{i}_1}{\underset{}{\rightleftharpoons}} & \overset{\tilde{i}_3}{\underset{}{\rightleftharpoons}} & \cdots & \overset{\tilde{i}_{n-1}}{\underset{}{\rightleftharpoons}} \end{array}$$

$(1) \rightleftharpoons (0) \rightleftharpoons \cdots \rightleftharpoons (0) \rightleftharpoons (0) \rightleftharpoons \cdots \rightleftharpoons (0)$

Fig. 3. A transformation network with n transformations reacting to each other.

We use the example of Section 2.1, and focus on the UML, Java and OpenAPI models to consider the scenario visualised in Figure 2: An architect creates a new UML interface and applies an execution strategy that executes every transformation once. First, the UML-to-Java syncx creates an appropriate interface in Java. The OpenAPI-to-Java syncx recognises that the interface should be exposed via an HTTP API and creates a matching endpoint in the OpenAPI model. Additionally, it creates a stub implementation with parsing and serialisation code in Java. The stub implementation classes can, however, not be propagated back to UML, because the UML-to-Java syncx has already been executed.

We see that if we limit the number of executions to one per transformation, transformations cannot propagate back the changes that other transformations have made. However, in the context described in Section 2.2, it is necessary that transformations are able to "react" to the changes made by other transformations. This offers, for instance, separation of concerns: The logic for a certain aspect of consistency can be put in only one transformation and other transformations will propagate it throughout the network. Without such a mechanism, all aspects of consistency would need to be implemented in all transformations. This would cause duplication of logic and reduce reusability of transformations, which would be impractical and contradicts our assumption of independent development. If we added the logic for creating implementations of relevant Java interfaces to the UML-to-Java syncx, then it would implicitly assume the presence of the Java-to-OpenAPI syncx. It could, thus, not be easily reused in networks where the Java-to-OpenAPI syncx is not used.

We can generalise the previous example: Let the model universe be the natural numbers: $\mathbb{M} = \mathbb{N}_0$. Let further for any $1 \leq j \leq n$ the syncx $\tilde{i}_j$ be defined as

$$\tilde{i}_j \colon (a, b) \mapsto \begin{cases} (m+1, m+1) & \text{if } m = j \\ (m, m) & \text{else} \end{cases} \quad \text{with } m := \max\{a, b\}$$

$\tilde{i}_j$ sets both models to the higher number of the two, except if that number is j. Then $\tilde{i}_j$ increments the result by one. This is an abstraction of syncx "reacting" to each other: The $\tilde{i}_j$s seek to set all models to the same value, except that after $\tilde{i}_{j-1}$ was executed, $\tilde{i}_j$ changes its behaviour and increments the value by one.

We now construct the transformation network N_n for $n = 2k, k \in \mathbb{N}^+$ (see Figure 3) with n indicating the number of syncx within the network, and examine how many executions it requires:

$$T_n = (i, i+1) \mapsto \begin{cases} \tilde{i}_{2i} & \text{if } i \leq \frac{n}{2} \\ \tilde{i}_{2i-n-1} & \text{else} \end{cases}$$

$$N_n = (([1, n+1], \{(i, i+1) \mid i \in [1, n]\}), T_n)$$

Lemma 1. $\ddot{i}_n$ *must be executed at least n times to resolve N_n with the initial model assignment*

$$M_1 : i \mapsto \begin{cases} 1 & \text{if } i = 1 \\ 0 & \text{else} \end{cases}$$

Proof. The only reachable model assignment that is consistent is $M_n : i \mapsto n$. It is reached by having every $\ddot{i}_j$ increment the highest number in the model assignment by one if that highest number currently is j. All transformations incrementing even numbers are on one side of $\ddot{i}_n$ (except for $\ddot{i}_n$ itself), all transformations incrementing uneven numbers are on the other side. Thus, the currently highest number must be propagated to the other side of $\ddot{i}_n$ at least $n-1$ times. Additionally, $\ddot{i}_n$ must increment $n - 1$ to n. ☐

Theorem 1. *For any execution strategy that uses $\mathcal{O}(1)$ executions of each transformation, there are inputs that the execution strategy cannot resolve.*

Proof. Follows directly from Lemma 1. ☐

The example network in Figure 2 is a simplification of a realistic transformation scenario, which we generalised to the network N_n. In consequence of Theorem 1, we can expect that transformation networks can, in general, not be resolved with $\mathcal{O}(1)$ executions of each transformation.

4.2   Unlimited Executions

We now consider an execution strategy that executes transformations as long as they still change models, and terminates once no more changes occur. This overcomes the shortcoming that we observed with limiting the number of executions to a constant; we will, however, see that we cannot guarantee termination of such an execution strategy. By simulating Turing machines with transformation networks, we prove that it is undecidable whether the strategy will terminate.

Given a Turing machine TM over some alphabet Σ, we construct a transformation network $N_{\mathrm{TM}} =: ((V, E), T_{\mathrm{TM}})$ and a model assignment $M_{\mathrm{TM},x}$ that are resolvable if, and only if, TM halts on input $x \in \Sigma^*$. We assume that TM contains no self-loops as well as no cycles of length 2, i.e., that each transition and each sequence of two transitions changes the state of TM. This is without loss of generality, since duplication and triplication of each state resolves such self-loops and cycles, respectively. The constructed models consist of a timestamp, the tape content and the tape position (i.e., $\mathbb{M} = \mathbb{N}_0 \times \Sigma^* \times \mathbb{N}_0$). The network N_{TM} has TM's states as vertices and exactly one directed edge (in arbitrary direction) between each pair of states having a transition between them. The transformations increment the timestamp, change the tape content and update the tape position according to TM's transition if, and only if, the source model's timestamp is higher than the target model's timestamp. More formally, let $\mathrm{Tr}(a, b) \subseteq \Sigma \times \{-1, 0, 1\} \times \Sigma$ be the transitions defined between the states a

and b (with -1, 0 and 1 indicating the head movements "left", "stay" and "right"). We define T_{TM} with $w|_{p \leftarrow r} := w[0 \mathbin{..} p-1] \cdot r \cdot w[p+1 \mathbin{..} |w|-1]$ such that:

$$\forall (a,b) \in E : T_{\text{TM}}(a,b)(\alpha =: (t_a, w_a, p_a), \beta =: (t_b, w_b, p_b))$$

$$= \begin{cases} (\alpha, (t_a+1, w_a|_{p_a \leftarrow r}, p_a+d)) & \text{if } t_a > t_b \wedge \exists\, (w_a[p_a], d, r) \in \text{Tr}(a,b) \\ ((t_b+1, w_b|_{p_b \leftarrow r}, p_b+d), \beta) & \text{if } t_a < t_b \wedge \exists\, (w_b[p_b], d, r) \in \text{Tr}(b,a) \\ (\alpha, \beta) & \text{else} \end{cases}$$

Let s be the initial state of TM. We set

$$M_{\text{TM},x} : v \mapsto \begin{cases} (1, x, 0) & \text{if } v = s \\ (0, \varepsilon, 0) & \text{else} \end{cases}$$

Lemma 2. *Executing the transformations of N_{TM}, with initial model assignment $M_{\text{TM},x}$, until no transformations change the model assignment anymore terminates if, and only if, TM halts on input x. If executing the transformations terminates with the final model assignment M_f, then the model with the highest timestamp in $\text{Im}(M_i)$ contains $\text{TM}(x)$ as tape content.*

Proof. We can see by induction over the model assignments M_i, $i \in \mathbb{N}_0$ created while executing the transformations:

1. There is exactly one $v \in V$ such that the model $M_i(v) =: (t, x, p)$ has the highest timestamp t of all models in $\text{Im}(M_i)$.
2. There is at most one edge $(a,b) \in E$ whose transformation is inconsistent, i.e., $(M_i(a), M_i(b)) \notin R_{T_{\text{TM}}(a,b)}$. This follows from the definitions of TM and the last executed transformation. Additionally, $a = v$ or $b = v$, because otherwise there would have been two transformations to which models in $\text{Im}(M_{i-1})$ are inconsistent. We assume without loss of generality $a = v$.
3. If (a,b) exists, then $m' := M_{i+1}(b)$ will contain the same tape content and the same tape position as would result if TM was executed one step from state v with tape content x and tape position p. Additionally, m' will be the model with the highest timestamp of all models in $\text{Im}(M_{i+1})$.
4. (a,b) does not exist if, and only if, TM would halt in state v with tape content x and tape position p. □

Theorem 2. *Let $\mathcal{S}$ be an execution strategy that executes transformations until a consistent model assignment is reached. There are inputs for which it can not be decided whether $\mathcal{S}$ will terminate.*

Proof. It follows from Lemma 2 that deciding whether $\mathcal{S}$ terminates could decide the halting problem for a universal Turing machine. □

Even worse, this construction makes it unlikely that we will find a practicable criterion that ensures success of an execution strategy like we have motivated in Section 2.4. Because we want the criterion to apply to a single syncx, it would need to restrict the syncx so much that it makes building a network simulating

Turing machines out of the syncx impossible. But since the definition of the syncx in $\mathrm{Im}(T_{\mathrm{TM}})$ is structurally simple, it seems unlikely that a syncx fulfilling the hypothetical criterion would still be apt for most practical use cases.

We could avoid undecidability if we restricted the models' size. The models could then no longer store an unbounded tape and, thus, only simulate space-restricted Turing machines. There is, however, no reasonable bound for a *necessary* model size, to which they could be limited. In consequence, determining a universal space bound for models would be an arbitrary and thus impractical restriction.

Finally, one could question whether it is relevant if an execution strategy can be guaranteed to terminate. Execution strategies will be used to tell users whether changes they made can be incorporated into the other models automatically. In consequence, users should reliably and timely get a response. We might compare this situation to merging changes in version control systems. There, users also want a reliable and timely response on whether their changes could be incorporated automatically, or whether they need to resolve conflicts manually.

5   Proposed Strategy

As a consequence of the previous findings, every universal execution strategy will be *conservative*: there will be inputs for which it fails, even though there would have been an execution order leading to a consistent model assignment. In this section, we discuss how to find an appropriate execution order and bound, and finally present the "explanatory strategy", constituting contribution *C3*.

5.1   Execution Order: Providing Explainability

Increasing the number of transformation executions an execution strategy permits, lowers its level of conservativeness. In contrast, the effects of different orders in which transformations can be executed are not as easy to categorise. The authors developed a model transformation network simulator [11], whose source code is available at GitHub [10]. It allows to construct transformation networks and to define execution strategies, which can be applied step by step. All examples presented in this paper are also modelled in the simulator. For each examined systematic execution order, such as a depth-first or breadth-first selection, the authors found categories of networks on which the order performed worse than another one in terms of conservativeness. In consequence, conservativeness is not a good sole criterion to evaluate orders by.

We know that a universal execution strategy will inevitably be conservative, i.e., possibly fail for resolvable inputs. In practice, it will be important how well an execution strategy provides explainability in such cases, i.e., helps users to understand where and why the strategy failed with the selected execution order. The order plays a decisive role in this regard, which is why we focus on finding a strategy that improves the order. Imagine, for instance, that the strategy executed transformations in an arbitrary order until some limit is reached. Users might then be confronted with a situation where all transformations have been executed, but the last model assignment is only consistent with some of them. There would be no clear pattern and little clues for users where to start investigating the failure's cause. To improve explainability, the authors thus propose the following principle for an execution order:

Principle 1. *Ensure consistency among the transformations that have already been executed before executing a transformation that has not been executed yet.*

Since a syncx can change both models, executing it may results in models that are inconsistent with the syncx that have been executed previously. Following Principle 1, these inconsistencies should be addressed first. In effect, a strategy applying the principle will maintain a subnetwork of syncx with a consistent model assignment and try to expand the subnetwork transformation by transformation.

To exemplify how Principle 1 provides *explainability*, suppose that an execution strategy applying that principle fails after having executed the set of syncx $E \subseteq \mathbb{T}$. Let $\bar{t} \in E$ be the last syncx that was executed for its first time. The strategy can then inform users that integrating $\bar{t}$ into the subnetwork induced by E failed. Furthermore, it can inform users that a result that is consistent with the syncx in $E \setminus \{\bar{t}\}$ exists. By that, users gain valuable information for handling the error: First, when trying to understand the error, they can ignore any syncx that is not in E. Second, some aspect of consistency that is present in the consistency relation realised by $\bar{t}$, but absent in the consistency relations realised by the syncx in $E \setminus \{\bar{t}\}$, hinders the strategy from creating a consistent result. Third, when users try to find a consistent model assignment manually, they can start with the consistent result that exists for $E \setminus \{\bar{t}\}$ instead of having to start from scratch.

5.2   Execution Bound: Reacting to Each Other

As we have seen, we need to restrict the number of transformation executions with a function in $\omega(m)$ (m being the number of syncx in the input network). Such a limit must be reasonable to support most practical use cases: Not allowing enough transformation executions reduces the usefulness of the strategy since not all useful networks can be resolved. Allowing too many executions might make the strategy run for a long time before aborting, without adding much value.

In Section 4.1, we have motivated that syncx should be able to "react" to each other. We have seen that this excludes any bound in $\mathcal{O}(1)$ for the number of executions per transformation, but to guarantee termination we can also not allow transformations to react to each other indefinitely. If a syncx $\bar{t}$ changes the models and the other already executed syncx have reacted to those changes by adapting the models to be consistent with them as well, $\bar{t}$ should not react by changing the models again. Because if $\bar{t}$ changed the models again, this could easily result in executing the same sequences of transformations repeatedly and there would likely be no consistent result.

We call transformations that behave in the described way *N-converging*. This is not a property of a syncx on its own but relative to its network N. Thus, it cannot be achieved just by proper construction of an individual transformation.

Algorithm 1. The explanatory strategy in pseudocode.

---

1 **Procedure** *propagate* (network, changes):

2   executed ← ∅

3   accumulatedChanges ← changes

4   **Invariant:** accumulatedChanges applied to network consistent to executed

5   **while** network.*contains* (candidate | candidate ∉ executed
        ∧ accumulatedChanges.*adjacentTo* (candidate)) **do**

6   candidateChanges ← candidate.*execute* (accumulatedChanges)

7   subnetwork ← network.*edgeInducedSubgraph* (executed)

8   propagationChanges ←
            propagate (subnetwork, accumulatedChanges ∪ candidateChanges)

9   candidateChanges ← candidate.*execute* (propagationChanges)

10   **if** candidateChanges.*adjacentToAny* (executed) **then**
                // Only happens if candidate is not network-converging

11   *fail* (executed, propagationChanges)

12   accumulatedChanges ← propagationChanges ∪ candidateChanges

13   executed ← executed ∪ candidate

14   **return** accumulatedChanges

There is, unfortunately, also no simple way to check it statically. Nevertheless, it captures the sensible expectation for transformations explained above. We yield an execution bound for a strategy by only requiring it not to fail if all syncx are N-converging. We will see how this execution bound behaves in combination with Principle 1 in the subsequently presented execution strategy.

Definition 8. *Let* $N =: (G, T)$ *be a transformation network. A syncx* $\bar{t} \in \mathrm{Im}(T)$ *is* N-converging *if for every initial model assignment and each subset of the syncx* $T_p \subseteq \mathrm{Im}(T)$ *with* $\bar{t} \in T_p$ *the resulting model assignment is consistent to* $\bar{t}$ *whenever* $\bar{t}$ *has been executed after a sequence of the syncx in* T_p *that contains each permutation of those syncx as a (not necessarily continuous) subsequence.*

We only require that the sequence of transformation executions contains each permutation, but allow other executions in between. As an example, assume a network N of N-converging syncx $\bar{t}_1$, $\bar{t}_2$ and $\bar{t}_3$. After executing them in the order $\bar{t}_1 \bar{t}_2 \bar{t}_3 \bar{t}_1 \bar{t}_2 \bar{t}_3$, the current model assignment may still be inconsistent with $\bar{t}_1$ because $\bar{t}_1$ was not executed after the order $\bar{t}_3 \bar{t}_2$. After executing $\bar{t}_1$ once more, the resulting model assignment must now be consistent with all syncx: $\bar{t}_1$ was executed after the two orders of other syncx $\bar{t}_2 \bar{t}_3$ and $\bar{t}_3 \bar{t}_2$. Likewise, $\bar{t}_2$ was executed after $\bar{t}_1 \bar{t}_3$ and $\bar{t}_3 \bar{t}_1$, and $\bar{t}_3$ was executed after $\bar{t}_1 \bar{t}_2$ and $\bar{t}_2 \bar{t}_1$.

5.3   The Explanatory Strategy

We now turn to a concrete strategy that realises the discussed design choices. Algorithm 1 gives pseudocode for such a strategy, which we call the "explanatory

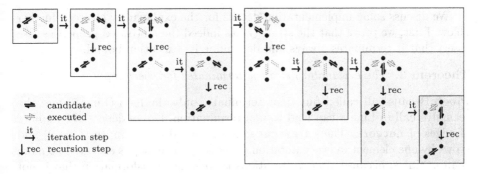

Fig. 4. Exemplary execution of the explanatory strategy for a change in the topmost model, depicting the iterations (horizontal) and recursion steps (vertical).

strategy". At a high level, it acts like this: Given a changed model assignment, the strategy picks the next **candidate** syncx to execute. After executing the candidate, the strategy calls itself on the **subnetwork** formed by the already executed syncx. By that, it propagates the changes of the last execution throughout the **subnetwork** and ensures that they are consistent with the **executed** syncx. Finally, the strategy executes the initial candidate again to ensure that the changes added during the subnetwork propagation are consistent with the **candidate**. If that repeated execution of the **candidate** generates new changes in any model that is kept consistent by an already executed syncx, the execution fails, because the **candidate** does not fulfil the definition of being *N-converging*, as we will see in the following. In that case, the procedure returns the already **executed** syncx to which consistency was restored by the also returned changes in order to support a user in examining the reasons for the strategy to fail. If the models are consistent with the **candidate**, the strategy picks the next one. In effect, the strategy realises Principle 1 in a recursive fashion and ensures that each permutation of all yet executed syncx is executed at every recursion level.

Figure 4 depicts an exemplary execution of the strategy for a network with four models and four transformations. We assume that after an initially consistent state of the models, the topmost one was modified. We can see that each recursion only treats the **subnetwork** of previously executed transformations. Hence, the **network** gets smaller at each recursion level.

Unlike the formalisation in Section 2.3, the presented algorithm is based on changes instead of model states. Changes contain information that cannot be recovered by comparing model states [6]. Thus in practice, we want to support change-based execution. The algorithm also uses changes to determine potential candidates for the next transformation to execute: It only picks candidates that are adjacent to a model that was changed. The input **changes** describe all changes that occurred since the last model assignment M that was known to be consistent. The procedure returns **accumulatedChanges** that, when applied to M, yield a new model assignment M'. For our formalisation, M' is the algorithm's output.

We discuss some implementation details for the explanatory strategy further below. First, we prove that the strategy has indeed the motivated properties. We assert that it terminates always and determine its execution bound.

Theorem 3. *The explanatory strategy terminates for every input.*

Proof. Because all called functions terminate, only the loop (Line 5) and the recursive call in Line 8 can lead to non-termination. Let m denote the number of edges of `network`. The set `executed` is initialised to be empty (Line 2) and grows by one element in every iteration of the loop. The loop is executed no more than m times, because after m iterations there is no transformation that is not in `executed` and, thus, the loop condition cannot be fulfilled.

The recursive call receives a network that is smaller than `network` in terms of edges, because it does not contain the current `candidate`. If `network` is empty, then the algorithm will not enter the loop and not make a recursive call. Hence, the recursive stack never gets higher than m. □

Theorem 4. *The explanatory strategy executes syncx at most $\mathcal{O}(2^m)$ times.*

Proof. Let $T(m)$ denote the number of syncx executions the algorithm invokes for a `network` with m edges. The set `executed` is initialised to be empty and grows by one syncx every loop iteration (Line 13). It follows that the recursive call in Line 8 receives a network that is one syncx larger each time. Thus, we find

$$T(0) = 0, \; T(m) = 2m + \sum_{i=0}^{m-1} T(i) = 2 + 2\,T(m-1) = 2\,(2^m - 1) \in \mathcal{O}(2^m)\,\square$$

Next, we show that the strategy fulfils the fundamental Requirements 1 and 2 regarding correctness and hippocraticness, which we defined in Section 2.4.

Theorem 5. *The explanatory strategy is correct.*

Proof. Assume the contrary, i.e., that the strategy produces a model assignment M for network N such that $M \notin R_N$. That means that there is an edge $(a, b) \in E$ such that $(M(a), M(b)) \notin R_{\vec{t}}$, where $\vec{t} := T(a, b)$. We distinguish these cases:

1. $\vec{t}$ was never executed. Then `accumulatedChanges` never contained any change adjacent to a or b (Line 5). Since the initial `changes` were relative to a consistent model assignment, we know that $(M(a), M(b)) \in R_{\vec{t}}$.
2. $\vec{t}$ was executed and no other transformation adjacent to a or b was executed afterwards. Then $(M(a), M(b)) \in R_{\vec{t}}$ per definition.
3. $\vec{t}$ was executed and another transformation $\vec{u}$ adjacent to a or b was executed afterwards. Because $\vec{u}$ was executed after $\vec{t}$, $\vec{t}$ was in `executed` when $\vec{u}$ was the `candidate`. So $\vec{t}$'s last execution was in the recursion after $\vec{u}$'s first execution in Line 6. Afterwards, $\vec{u}$ was only executed in Line 9. If $\vec{u}$ would have changed $M(a)$ or $M(b)$, the strategy would have raised a failure. Hence, $M(a)$ and $M(b)$ are the same as after the execution of $\vec{t}$, and $(M(a), M(b)) \in R_{\vec{t}}$.

All cases lead to a contradiction. □

Theorem 6. *The explanatory strategy is hippocratic.*

Proof. The strategy only produces changes by executing syncx, which, per definition, only generate changes if the models are not in their consistency relations.   □

Finally, we verify that we have indeed realised Principle 1 and that the strategy does not fail for a network N of only N-converging transformations.

Theorem 7. *The explanatory strategy ensures consistency among the transformations that have already been executed before executing a transformation that has not been executed yet (see Principle 1).*

Proof. After the recursive call in Line 8, the current model assignment is consistent with all **executed** syncx (Theorem 5) and no changes to models adjacent to an executed syncx are allowed.   □

Theorem 8. *If the input* **network** *of the explanatory strategy consists only of* **network**-*converging syncx, then the explanatory strategy does not fail.*

Proof. First, we note that when calling the algorithm on a **network** with m transformations, the first $m-1$ iterations of the loop act identically to executing the algorithm on a network without the last **candidate**. Second, we note that the second part of the loop condition, "**accumulatedChanges**.*adjacentTo*(**candidate**)" (Line 5), does not change the algorithm's result apart from controlling the order in which the syncx are executed. If any syncx was never executed because of this condition, then executing it would not have changed any model. Hence, we assume w.l.o.g. that all syncx in **network** will get executed.

Now we show the following, stronger statement by induction over the number m of edges in **network**: "After running the explanatory strategy, the sequence of executed syncx contains each permutation of those syncx (not necessarily continuously)". Since the transformations are **network**-converging and because of our first note above, proving this statement shows that the condition leading to a failure (Line 10) will never evaluate to true. The statement is trivially true for $m=1$. Assume that the statement is true for all networks of size $1 \leq n < m$ but not true for a network of size m. That means that after executing the last iteration of the loop, there is an order o of the m syncx in **network** in which they have not been executed yet. Let $\tilde{t}$ be the **candidate** of the last iteration. Let j be the index of $\tilde{t}$ in o. Per induction assumption, the order $o[1] \ldots o[j-1]$ has been executed in the previous iterations of the loop. Afterwards, $\tilde{t}$ was executed in Line 6. Per induction assumption, the order $o[j+1] \ldots o[m]$ has been executed in the recursive call (Line 8) of the last iteration. This happened after Line 6. Hence, the transformations have been executed in the order o. This is a contradiction.   □

The explanatory strategy only guarantees to produce a consistent model assignment if all syncx are N-converging. We can, unfortunately, not provide an approach to achieve N-convergence by construction or to determine N-convergence. We have, however, also discussed that every universal execution strategy needs to operate conservatively and thus fails in certain cases. Thus, even if a network N

contains syncx that are not N-converging, the explanatory strategy still operates conservatively and at least fails based on the notion of a sensible and well-defined property. In addition, the exponential worst-case performance of the strategy is no limitation, because it does only represent a bound to ensure termination. In cases in which the strategy terminates, we expect the repeated execution of each syncx to perform only few changes in reaction to the changes made by other syncx, as otherwise they are unlikely to be N-converging. The interested reader can try out the explanatory strategy using the previously mentioned simulator [11].

In its current formulation, the explanatory strategy does not prevent the syncx from overwriting the initial user changes. This seems inappropriate, as user changes should usually not be reverted. Other authors address this issue by forbidding changes to models that have been edited by users [3, 30, 29], called "authoritative models". There are, however, practical use cases where such changes should be allowed—the example in Section 4.1 is one of them. An option would be to let the strategy fail as soon as a syncx execution overwrites a user change.

6   Conclusion

In this paper, we have discussed influencing factors for designing a universal execution strategy for model transformation networks. Such a strategy orchestrates transformations to create a consistent set of models. It involves determining an order to execute the transformations in, and a bound for the number of executions. We have proven that every universal execution strategy that always terminates needs to be conservative, i.e., it will fail for certain cases in which an execution order of transformations that yields a consistent solution exists. We have argued that providing explainability in cases where an execution strategy fails should be a central design goal. As a result, we have proposed the *explanatory strategy*, which is proven correct and terminates for every input. Additionally, it improves explainability of failures and has a well-defined bound for the number of transformation executions to ensure a reasonable level of conservativeness.

We have formalised our findings on execution bounds and the behaviour of the proposed execution strategy to prove the insights and expected properties of the strategy. In consequence, this paper provides fundamental knowledge about the design space and relevant design goals of transformation network execution strategies. While the statements on correctness and well-definedness are proven, those on the usefulness of the strategy were derived by argumentation. To improve evidence of the results, the authors plan to apply the strategy to realistic use cases, involving larger networks of more complex transformations.

Furthermore, the authors want to examine how the strategy can be further optimised: It might, e.g., be improved by backtracking and trying further candidate transformations, or by selecting the next candidate more carefully. Since early executed transformations will be executed most often, starting with those that will most unlikely cause conflicts might be beneficial. Finally, this paper assumes transformations to be binary. Since the presented strategy does not require this, future research could investigate transferability to multiary transformations.

References

1. Anjorin, A., Rose, S., Deckwerth, F., and Schürr, A.: "Efficient Model Synchronization with View Triple Graph Grammars". In: Modelling Foundations and Applications, pp. 1–17. Springer International Publishing (2014)
2. Cleve, A., Kindler, E., Stevens, P., and Zaytsev, V.: "Multidirectional Transformations and Synchronisations (Dagstuhl Seminar 18491)". Dagstuhl Reports 8(12), 1–48 (2019)
3. Di Rocco, J., Di Ruscio, D., Heinz, M., Iovino, L., Lämmel, R., and Pierantonio, A.: "Consistency Recovery in Interactive Modeling". In: 3rd International Workshop on Executable Modeling co-Located with ACM/IEEE 20th International Conference on Model Driven Engineering Languages and Systems. Vol-2019, pp. 116–122. CEUR-WS.org (2017)
4. Diskin, Z., Gholizadeh, H., Wider, A., and Czarnecki, K.: "A Three-Dimensional Taxonomy for Bidirectional Model Synchronization". Journal of Systems and Software 111, 298–322 (2016)
5. Diskin, Z., König, H., and Lawford, M.: "Multiple Model Synchronization with Multiary Delta Lenses". In: Fundamental Approaches to Software Engineering, pp. 21–37. Springer International Publishing (2018)
6. Diskin, Z., Xiong, Y., Czarnecki, K., Ehrig, H., Hermann, F., and Orejas, F.: "From State- to Delta-Based Bidirectional Model Transformations: The Symmetric Case". In: Model Driven Engineering Languages and Systems, pp. 304–318. Springer Berlin Heidelberg (2011)
7. Ehrig, H., Ehrig, K., Lara, J. de, Taentzer, G., Varró, D., and Varró-Gyapay, S.: "Termination Criteria for Model Transformation". In: Fundamental Approaches to Software Engineering, pp. 49–63. Springer Berlin Heidelberg (2005)
8. Etien, A., Aranega, V., Blanc, X., and Paige, R.F.: "Chaining Model Transformations". In: First Workshop on the Analysis of Model Transformations, pp. 9–14. ACM (2012)
9. Etien, A., Muller, A., Legrand, T., and Blanc, X.: "Combining Independent Model Transformations". In: 2010 ACM Symposium on Applied Computing, pp. 2237–2243. ACM (2010)
10. Gleitze, J.: GitHub: Transformation Network Simulator, (2021). https://github.com/jGleitz/transformationnetwork-simulator (visited on 01/14/2021)
11. Gleitze, J.: Transformation Network Simulator, (2021). https://jgleitz.github.io/transformationnetwork-simulator (visited on 01/14/2021)
12. Guissouma, H., Klare, H., Sax, E., and Burger, E.: "An Empirical Study on the Current and Future Challenges of Automotive Software Release and Configuration Management". In: 2018 44th Euromicro Conference on Software Engineering and Advanced Applications, pp. 298–305. IEEE (2018)
13. Klare, H.: "Multi-model Consistency Preservation". In: 21st ACM/IEEE International Conference on Model Driven Engineering Languages and Systems: Companion Proceedings, pp. 156–161. ACM (2018)
14. Klare, H., and Gleitze, J.: "Commonalities for Preserving Consistency of Multiple Models". In: 22nd ACM/IEEE International Conference on Model Driven Engineering Languages and Systems Companion, pp. 371–378. IEEE (2019)
15. Klare, H., Kramer, M.E., Langhammer, M., Werle, D., Burger, E., and Reussner, R.: "Enabling consistency in view-based system development – The Vitruvius approach". Journal of Systems and Software 171 (2020)

16. Klare, H., Syma, T., Burger, E., and Reussner, R.: "A Categorization of Interoperability Issues in Networks of Transformations". In: 12th International Conference on Model Transformations. Journal of Object Technology (2019)

17. Königs, A., and Schürr, A.: "MDI: A Rule-based Multi-document and Tool Integration Approach". Software and Systems Modeling 5(4), 349–368 (2006)

18. Kusel, A., Etzlstorfer, J., Kapsammer, E., Langer, P., Retschitzegger, W., Schoenboeck, J., Schwinger, W., and Wimmer, M.: "A Survey on Incremental Model Transformation Approaches". In: Workshop on Models and Evolution co-located with ACM/IEEE 16th International Conference on Model Driven Engineering Languages and Systems. Vol-1090, pp. 4–13. CEUR-WS.org (2013)

19. Lúcio, L., Mustafiz, S., Denil, J., Vangheluwe, H., and Jukss, M.: "FTG+PM: An Integrated Framework for Investigating Model Transformation Chains". In: SDL 2013: Model-Driven Dependability Engineering, pp. 182–202. Springer Berlin Heidelberg (2013)

20. Macedo, N., Cunha, A., and Pacheco, H.: "Towards a Framework for Multi-Directional Model Transformations". In: 3rd International Workshop on Bidirectional Transformations. Vol-1133. CEUR-WS.org (2014)

21. Macedo, N., Jorge, T., and Cunha, A.: "A Feature-Based Classification of Model Repair Approaches". IEEE Transactions on Software Engineering 43(7), 615–640

22. Object Management Group (OMG): "Meta Object Facility (MOF) 2.0—Query/View/Transformation Specification", Version 1.3 (2016)

23. Pilgrim, J. von, Vanhooff, B., Schulz-Gerlach, I., and Berbers, Y.: "Constructing and Visualizing Transformation Chains". In: Model Driven Architecture – Foundations and Applications, pp. 17–32. Springer Berlin Heidelberg (2008)

24. Reussner, R.H., Becker, S., Happe, J., Heinrich, R., Koziolek, A., Koziolek, H., Kramer, M., and Krogmann, K.: "Modeling and Simulating Software Architectures – the Palladio Approach". MIT Press (2016)

25. Samimi-Dehkordi, L., Zamani, B., and Kolahdouz-Rahimi, S.: "Bidirectional Model Transformation Approaches – A Comparative Study". In: 6th International Conference on Computer and Knowledge Engineering, pp. 314–320. IEEE (2016)

26. Schürr, A.: "Specification of graph translators with triple graph grammars". In: Graph-Theoretic Concepts in Computer Science, pp. 151–163. Springer Berlin Heidelberg (1995)

27. Stevens, P.: "A Landscape of Bidirectional Model Transformations". In: Generative and Transformational Techniques in Software Engineering II, pp. 408–424. Springer Berlin Heidelberg (2008)

28. Stevens, P.: "Bidirectional Model Transformations in QVT: Semantic Issues and Open Questions". Software and Systems Modeling 9(1), 7 (2010)

29. Stevens, P.: "Connecting software build with maintaining consistency between models: towards sound, optimal, and flexible building from megamodels". Software and Systems Modeling 19(4), 935–958 (2020)

30. Stevens, P.: "Maintaining consistency in networks of models: bidirectional transformations in the large". Software and Systems Modeling 19(1), 39–65 (2020)

31. Stünkel, P., König, H., Lamo, Y., and Rutle, A.: "Multimodel Correspondence through Inter-Model Constraints". In: 2nd International Conference on Art, Science, and Engineering of Programming Companion, pp. 9–17. ACM (2018)

32. The Linux Foundation: OpenAPI Initiative, (2021). https://www.openapis.org/ (visited on 01/14/2021)

33. Trollmann, F., and Albayrak, S.: "Extending Model Synchronization Results from Triple Graph Grammars to Multiple Models". In: Theory and Practice of Model Transformations, pp. 91–106. Springer International Publishing (2016)
34. Trollmann, F., and Albayrak, S.: "Extending Model to Model Transformation Results from Triple Graph Grammars to Multiple Models". In: Theory and Practice of Model Transformations, pp. 214–229. Springer International Publishing (2015)
35. Vanhooff, B., Ayed, D., Van Baelen, S., Joosen, W., and Berbers, Y.: "UniTI: A Unified Transformation Infrastructure". In: Model Driven Engineering Languages and Systems, pp. 31–45. Springer Berlin Heidelberg (2007)
36. Wagelaar, D., Tisi, M., Cabot, J., and Jouault, F.: "Towards a General Composition Semantics for Rule-Based Model Transformation". In: Model Driven Engineering Languages and Systems, pp. 623–637. Springer Berlin Heidelberg (2011)   ˙
37. Xiong, Y., Song, H., Hu, Z., and Takeichi, M.: "Synchronizing Concurrent Model Updates Based on Bidirectional Transformation". Software and Systems Modeling 12(1), 89–104 (2013)

Image Sources

paintingred: "Default Avatar Headshot Icons", found on Vecteezy.
https://www.vecteezy.com/vector-art/141712-default-avatar-headshot-icons.
Vecteezy Free License.

Object Management Group: UML logo.
https://www.uml.org/index.htm.
Trademark.

Palladio logo.
https://sdqweb.ipd.kit.edu/wiki/File:Palladio-Logo-stilisiert-vektor.pdf.
Authorized use.

The Linux Foundation: OpenAPI™ logo.
https://github.com/OAI/OpenAPI-Style-Guide/blob/master/graphics/
vector/OpenAPI_Logo_Black.svg. Trademark.

Freepik: "Computer".
https://www.flaticon.com/free-icon/computer_1077701.
Flaticon Basic License.

CoVEGI: Cooperative Verification via Externally Generated Invariants

Jan Haltermann*(✉)📙 and Heike Wehrheim📙

Department of Computer Science, Paderborn University, Paderborn, Germany
jfh@mail.upb.de, wehrheim@upb.de

Abstract. Software verification has recently made enormous progress due to the development of novel verification methods and the speed-up of supporting technologies like SMT solving. To keep software verification tools up to date with these advances, tool developers keep on integrating newly designed methods into their tools, almost exclusively by re-implementing the method within their own framework. While this allows for a conceptual re-use of methods, it nevertheless requires novel implementations for every new technique.

In this paper, we employ *cooperative verification* in order to avoid re-implementation and enable usage of novel tools as black-box components in verification. Specifically, cooperation is employed for the core ingredient of software verification which is *invariant generation*. Finding an adequate loop invariant is key to the success of a verification run. Our framework named CoVEGI allows a master verification tool to delegate the task of invariant generation to one or several specialized helper invariant generators. Their results are then utilized within the verification run of the master verifier, allowing in particular for crosschecking the validity of the invariant. We experimentally evaluate our framework on an instance with two masters and three different invariant generators using a number of benchmarks from SV-COMP 2020. The experiments show that the use of CoVEGI can increase the number of correctly verified tasks without increasing the used resources.

Keywords: Cooperation, Software Verification, Invariant Generation

1 Introduction

Recent years have seen a major progress in software verification as for instance witnessed by the annual competition on software verification SV-COMP [2]. This success is on the one hand due to advances in SAT and SMT solving and on the other hand due to novel verification methods like interpolation in model checking [36], automata-based software verification [31] or property directed reachability [16]. Still, automatic verification remains a complex and error-prone task. In particular, it is often the case that one tool can verify a particular class

---

* This author was partially supported by the German Research Foundation (DFG) under contract WE2290/13-1.

E. Guerra and M. Stoelinga (Eds.): FASE 2021, LNCS 12649, pp. 108–129, 2021.
https://doi.org/10.1007/978-3-030-71500-7_6

of programs, but fails to verify other classes (or even gives incorrect answers), whereas it is the reverse situation for another tool. Moreover, to keep their tools up to date with novel techniques, tool developers keep on integrating them by re-implementation within their framework.

An approach for changing this unsatisfactory situation is *cooperative verification* (for an overview see [13]). Cooperative verification builds on the idea of letting tools (and thus techniques) cooperate on verification tasks, thereby leveraging the tool's individual strengths. In particular, cooperative verification aims at *black box* combinations of tools, using existing tools off-the-shelf without re-implementation. While this sounds like a natural idea, its realization poses a number of challenges, the major one being the *exchange* and *usage* of analysis information. For cooperation, tools are required to produce (partial) results which other tools can understand and employ in their verification run. With conditional model checking [7], the first proposal of an exchange *format* for verification results was made. A conditional model checker outputs its (potentially partial) result in the form of a *condition* which can be read by other conditional model checkers in order to complete the verification task. Since verification tools normally do not understand conditions, *reducers* [23,9] have been proposed to bring conditions back into a form understandable by verifiers, namely into (residual) programs describing the so far unverified program part. This allows the result of a conditional model checker to be made usable by arbitrary other verifiers. A second type of existing result usage is the *validation* of tool's results [4,34], similar to proof-carrying code [37]. Both of these types are sequential forms of cooperation: a first verifier starts and a second verifier continues, either by completing or by validating a first result.

In this paper, we propose CoVEGI, a cooperation framework which complements these existing approaches by a new type of cooperation. Conceptually, this framework (depicted in Figure 1) consists of a *master verifier* and a number of *helper invariant generators*. The master verifier has the overall control on the verification process and can *delegate* tasks to helpers as well as *continue* its own verification process with (partial) results provided by helpers. The helpers run in parallel as black boxes without cooperation. The task to be delegated is an integral part of software verification, namely *invariant generation*. The framework allows cooperation via outsourcing the task of invariant generation, leveraging the strength of specialized invariant generation tools.

Like for other types of cooperation, the question of the exchange format for results comes up. Here, we have chosen *correctness witnesses* [3] for this purpose. Correctness witnesses are employed in witness validation and certify a verifier's result stating the correctness of a program. These witnesses are particularly well suited for our intended usage, because their format is standardized and a number of verifiers already produce correctness witnesses. To account for the incooperation of helper verifiers not producing witnesses, our framework also foresees the inclusion of *adapters* transforming invariants into correctness witnesses. We provide an implementation of two such adapters. Witnesses are then *injected* into the verification run of the master. For stating the task to be solved by invariant

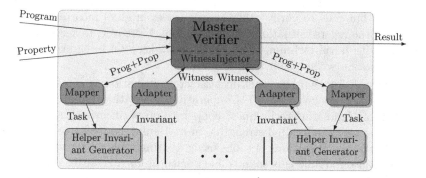

Fig. 1: Cooperative verification via externally generated invariants

generators we furthermore require *mappers* transforming program and property to be proven into a task format understandable by the helper tools. Figure 1 depicts our framework for cooperative verification via externally generated invariants. The framework can be arbitrarily configured with different masters and helpers, provided that suitable adapters and mappers are given.

We have implemented CoVEGI within the CPACHECKER framework [10] and have employed different configurations of it as master verifier. As helpers we have chosen publicly available verification tools, some producing and one not producing witnesses. We have then experimentally evaluated 14 different combinations of master and helper on benchmarks of the annual competition of software verification SV-COMP [2]. The experiments show an improvement over the verification capabilities of the master tool, without incurring significant overhead. In some cases, the verification time is even decreased in cooperative verification.

Summarizing, we make the following contributions.

- We propose a framework for cooperative software verification based on a master-helper architecture using externally generated invariants.
- We construct 14 different instantiations of the framework using 2 masters and 3 helpers, running both helpers in isolation as well as in parallel.
- For the inclusion of helper verifiers, we implement two adapters, one transforming invariants expressed in the LLVM IR language[1] into correctness witnesses, the other bringing a generated witness into the right format.
- We carry out an extensive experimental evaluation demonstrating the effectiveness and efficiency of collective invariant generation.

2   Fundamentals

We aim at the cooperative verification of programs written in GNU C, focusing on the validation of safety properties. To be able to define safety properties, a

---

[1] https://llvm.org/docs/LangRef.html

formal representation of programs as well as their semantics is needed. Thus we briefly introduce the syntax and semantics of programs which we consider here.

We follow the notation of Beyer et al. [6] describing programs as *control-flow automata* (CFAs). A CFA is basically a control-flow graph with edges annotated with program statements. More formally, a program is represented as a control-flow automaton $C = (L, l_0, G)$, consisting of a set of program locations L, an initial location $l_0 \in L$ and the control-flow edges $G, G \subseteq L \times Op \times L$. The set Op contains all possible operations on integer variables[2] present in the program, namely conditions (as of conditionals and loops), assignments, method calls and return statements. Figure 2(a) shows a C-program taken from the SV-COMP benchmarks[3], and Figure 2(b) its corresponding CFA. The program also contains a special *error* label, used for encoding the property to be verified. The verification task for this program is to show the non-reachability of the error label at location 9, i.e., for our example program the verifier has to prove that y equals n after the loop which is true (since n is unsigned).

For the semantics, we start by defining program states. Let Var denote the set of all integer variables occurring in programs, $BExp$ the set of boolean expressions and $AExp$ the set of arithmetic expressions over Var. Then a *state* σ of the program is a mapping from the variables to the integers, i.e., $\sigma : Var \to \mathbb{Z}$. We lift the mapping to also contain the evaluation of arithmetic and boolean expressions so that σ maps $AExp$ to $\mathbb{Z}$ and $BExp$ to $\mathbb{B}$. A finite *program path* π is a sequence of *transitions* $\langle \sigma_0, l_0 \rangle \xrightarrow{g_0} \langle \sigma_1, l_1 \rangle \cdots \xrightarrow{g_{n-1}} \langle \sigma_n, l_n \rangle$, such that σ_0 assigns 0 to all variables, l_n is a leaf in the CFA and $(l_i, g_i, l_{i+1}) \in G$ holds for each transition $\langle \sigma_i, l_i \rangle \xrightarrow{g_i} \langle \sigma_{i+1}, l_{i+1} \rangle$ in π. Infinite program paths are defined analogeously. As for state changes in paths: If g_i is a boolean expression, method call or return statement, then $\sigma_i = \sigma_{i+1}$ holds. If g_i is an assignment $x = a$, where $a \in AExp$, then $\sigma_{i+1} = \sigma_i[x \mapsto \sigma_i(a)]$. Finally, we denote all paths of a program represented by a CFA C by $paths(C)$.

Here, we are interested in verifying safety properties of programs given as CFAs. For the purpose of this paper, we define a *safety property* P as a pair of a location $\ell \in L$ and a boolean condition $\varphi \in BExp$. There can be multiple safety properties required to hold in a program. For our example program of Figure 2 the property is $(8, n = y)$. For the verifier this is encoded in the form

```
8:   if (!(n==y))
9:       Error: return 1;
```

A CFA (or program) C *violates a safety property* $P = (\ell, \varphi)$ when the program reaches location ℓ in a state which does not satisfy φ. More formally, P is violated by C, if there is some path $\pi \in paths(C)$, $\pi = \langle \sigma_0, l_0 \rangle \xrightarrow{g_0} \langle \sigma_1, l_1 \rangle \cdots \xrightarrow{g_{n-1}} \langle \sigma_n, l_n \rangle$ and some i, $0 \leq i \leq n$, such that $l_i = \ell$ and $\sigma_i(\varphi) = false$.

---

[2] In our formalization, we use integer variables only, the implementation covers C programs.

[3] https://github.com/sosy-lab/sv-benchmarks

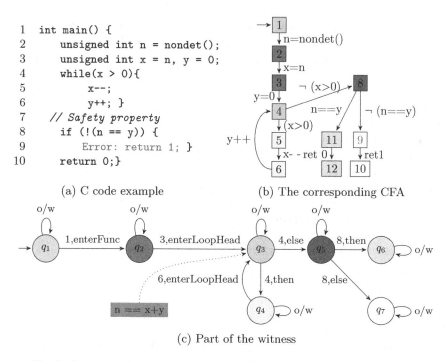

```
1   int main() {
2       unsigned int n = nondet();
3       unsigned int x = n, y = 0;
4       while(x > 0){
5           x--;
6           y++; }
7       // Safety property
8       if (!(n == y)) {
9           Error: return 1; }
10      return 0;}
```

(a) C code example   (b) The corresponding CFA

(c) Part of the witness

Fig. 2: An example program, its control flow automaton and one witness

Cooperatively verifying safety of programs is achieved in our framework via external (loop) invariant generation. Syntactically, a *loop invariant* is a boolean expression associated to a loop head. A loop invariant needs to hold (1) before the first loop execution and (2) after each loop execution. The expression $n = x + y$, for instance, is a loop invariant for the program in Figure 2(a), associated to the loop head at location 4. This loop invariant facilitates verification, because in conjunction with the negated loop condition and information about initial variable values it ensures n to be equal to y after the loop. Other valid loop invariants would be $x \geq 0$ or $n = 3 \Rightarrow y \leq 5$, which however all do not help in proving the safety property. Especially the loop invariant *true* does not provide any information. Thus, we call it a *trivial invariant*.

As stated before, we chose *witnesses* (more specifically, correctness witnesses) as exchange format during collective invariant generation. Formally, a witness is a finite state automaton in which transitions are labelled with so called *source code guards* and states can be equipped with boolean expressions. When all these boolean expressions are either *true* or *false*, we call the witness *trivial*. Source code guards are of the form location,type where type can be then, else, enterFunc and enterLoopHead. The guard o/w (otherwise) is used if a source code line does not match the other guards present. Via these labels we can match transitions of the automaton with edges in the CFA. Syntactically, correctness witnesses are stored in an XML format and consist of two parts:

(1) general information like the program associated with the witness, and (2) a GraphML representation of the witness automaton. More information and a formal specification of correctness witnesses can be found in [3].

In Figure 2(c), we see a correctness witness for our example program. State q_3 is reached by transitions labelled 3,enterLoopHead or 6,enterLoopHead and thus corresponds to the loop head at program location 4. Associated with this state is the invariant $n = x + y$.

3   Concept

In this section, we introduce our novel concept of **Co**operative **V**erification via **E**xternally **G**enerated **I**nvariants (CoVEGI), shown in Figure 1. The framework contains two sorts of main components: Master verifiers (one) and helper invariant generators (several). Next, we state some requirements on and explain the functionality of these components as well as their cooperation.

3.1   Components of the CoVEGI-Framework

The most important component of the framework is the master verifier, which we build out of an existing verifier. The master is responsible for coordinating the verification process and can, if needed, request support from the second type of components, the helpers, in the form of invariants as described by correctness witnesses. Hence, the master is also steering the cooperation.

In the following, we explain the two sorts of main components in more detail:

Master Verifier A *master verifier* gets as input the program C as CFA and a safety property P. It computes as output a boolean answer b, stating whether the property holds, and possibly (but not necessarily) provides an overall witness ω. To be able to process the provided support in form of invariants stored inside of correctness witnesses, a master is required to implement an internal function called *injectWitness*. The function loads a witness, extracts the invariants present in it and injects them into the analysis of the master verifier. The witness injection can either happen before (re-)starting the analysis or during runtime.

Helper Invariant Generator A *helper invariant generator* gets as input the program C as CFA and a safety property P. It computes as output a set of invariants, stored in a verification witness ω'. The generated invariants are neither required to be helpful for the master verifier nor to be correct. Thus, helper invariant generators are also allowed to generate trivial invariants or invariant candidates which might turn out to be wrong.

We can neither expect existing verification tools which we wish to use as helpers to be able to work on CFAs, nor to understand the safety property or to produce witnesses. Hence, we foresee two further sorts of components in our framework:

Table 1: Overview of the configuration options available

Name	Description	Values
restartMaster	restart the master after invariant generation	boolean
termAfterFirstInv	use first witness only	boolean
timerM	max. time for master until requestsForHelp is send	time(s)
timeoutH	max. time for helpers to generate an invariant	time(s)

Mapper A *mapper* transforms the safety property specification inside the program into the desired input format of the helper. A mapper basically conducts some simple syntactic code replacements. For instance, for our running example some helpers might instead require the safety property to be written as assert(n==y); or as if(!(n==y)) {verifier_error();}.

Adapter An *adapter* generates a correctness witness out of the computed loop invariants of a helper. Furthermore, some helper invariant generators work on intermediate representations (IR) of the C-language (e.g. LLVM) or intermediate verification languages (e.g. Boogie). Then, the computed invariants (formulated in terms of IR-variables) first of all need to be translated back to the namespace of the C-program. An adapter for LLVM is explained in more detail in Section 3.4.

3.2   Cooperation within CoVEGI

After having explained the individual components, we define their interaction in the framework. In this paper, we focus on the *parallel* execution of several helpers which implement complementary approaches so that we can leverage their individual strengths. Algorithm 1 describes the form of cooperation. It is steered by several user configurable options which fix aspects like time and resource limits of master and helpers. Table 1 summarizes the configuration options. We next describe them in detail.

Master options The following aspects of the master's behavior need to be fixed: First, when to delegate tasks to helpers, and second, how to continue the verification process after invariant generation. For the delegation, we let the master verifier run until it requests support, which can be checked by inspecting the master's flag requestsForHelp. The master gets a configurable timelimit (called timerM) after which it is expected to send this request. By adding such an explicit request for help, we allow the master to send a request for other reasons (besides the timer) in the future. Then, after invariant generation, the master can either be freshly restarted or continued (option restartMaster).

Helper option When at least two helpers run in parallel, eventually one of them first computes a witness. We can then either (1) directly stop the other helpers, or (2) wait for all to complete before injecting witnesses into the master. This option is called termAfterFirstInv.

Algorithm 1 CoVEGI-algorithm

Input: C   ▷ *CFA*
        P   ▷ *safety property*
        M   ▷ *master*
        Helpers   ▷ *set of helpers*
        conf   ▷ *configuration*
Output: ω ▷ *witness*
        b   ▷ *result*

1: M.start(C, P, conf.timerM);
2: wait until (M.requestsForHelp $\lor$ M.hasSolution());
3: **if** (M.hasSolution()) **then**
4:    **return** M.getSolution();
5: **for each** H $\in$ Helpers **do parallel**   ▷ *run helpers in parallel*
6:    H.start(C, P, conf.timeoutH);
7:    wait until (H.timedout() $\lor$ H.hasSolution() $\lor$ H.stopped());
8:    **if** (H.hasSolution() $\land$ nonTrivial(H.getSolution())) **then**
9:       witnesses := witnesses $\cup$ H.getSolution();
10:      **if** (conf.termAfterFirstInv) **then**
11:         **for each** H' $\in$ helpers $\setminus \{$ H $\}$ **do parallel**
12:            H'.stop();   ▷ *stop other helpers*
13: **if** (M.hasSolution()) **then**
14:    **return** M.getSolution();
15: **if** (witnesses $\neq \emptyset$) **then**   ▷ *invariants found*
16:    **if** (conf.restartMaster) **then**
17:       M.stop();
18:    M.inject(witnesses);   ▷ *inject witnesses into master*
19:    **if** (conf.restartMaster) **then**
20:       M.start(C,P, ∞);
21: join(M);   ▷ *wait for M to finish*
22: **return** M.getSolution();

Timeouts Finally, similar to the master, we can set a specific timeout for the helpers which fixes how long they are allowed to try to generate invariants. The timeout option is called `timeoutH`.

Next, we explain the CoVEGI algorithm shown in Algorithm 1 in detail. We assume that master and helpers run as threads and can be started and stopped. We furthermore employ methods `wait` for waiting until some condition is achieved and `join` for waiting for a specific thread to complete.

Initially, the master verifier is started without any helper invariant generators running in parallel (line 1), providing the opportunity to verify programs on its own. It runs standalone until it requests for help (either due to not being able to solve the problem alone or due to hitting its timer) or until it computes a result which is subsequently returned (line 3). Afterwards all helpers are started in parallel (lines 5 and 6). They also run until they reach their timeout, a solution is found or they are stopped. Their solutions (invariants) are inserted into the witness set (line 9). Depending on option `termAfterFirstInv`, either all but the first finished helper are stopped or it is waited until all helpers either computed a solution or ran into their timeout. If invariants (witnesses) have been computed, these are injected into the master (line 18). If the `restartMaster` option is set, the master needs to be stopped before injection and restarted afterwards. Then the master continues and completes its verification (without any further request for help) and the result is finally returned.

Example 1. To explain the framework's functionality, we demonstrate the CoV-EGI algorithm on the example presented in Figure 2(a). Assume that we instantiate the framework with a master verifier and four helper invariant generators, that are used in parallel[4]. Moreover, we configure the framework as follows: We set `restartMaster` to true, `terminateAfterFirstInv` to false, `timerM` to 50 seconds and `timeoutH` to 300 seconds.

Initially, the master verifier runs standalone and after 50 seconds runtime it requests help. The master runs in parallel with the four helper invariant generators being called. Let us assume that the first helper returns only trivial invariants (after 10s), the second one the invariant $n \geq y$ (after 50s), the third one the invariant $n = x + y$ (after 100s) and the fourth the invariant $n - x - y = 0$ (after 500s). The trivial invariant is ignored (see check in line 8) and when the second helper returns a solution, the third and fourth helper are still not stopped, due to the chosen configuration. The algorithm waits until the third helper computes the invariant and the fourth (only being able to compute an invariant after 500s) hits the timeout after 300s. Then the master is stopped, the invariants $n \geq y$ and $n = x + y$ are injected and the master is restarted. The master verifier can use both invariants and might now compute the correct result.

3.3   Witness Injection

As master verifiers need to offer witness injection, we explain a possible procedure for predicate abstraction and k-induction, which are the two techniques we use as masters during the evaluation. For both, the invariants are extracted from the witness and then added to the analysis information already computed by the master verifier. Both analyses store their analysis information in an *abstract reachability graph* (ARG). Broadly speaking, an ARG is a CFA equipped with predicates. More formally, an ARG is a finite state automaton, where nodes, called *abstract states*, consist among others of analysis information (i.e. predicates) and program locations. Two nodes within an ARG are connected if their program locations are connected within the CFA. Note that a program location may occur in multiple abstract states, e.g. when the analysis unrolls a loop. Hence, witness injection has to update all the abstract states for whose program location the witness contains an invariant.

Predicate Abstraction. We use a predicate abstraction technique [11], conducting predicate refinement using a CEGAR (counter example guided ab-

---

[4] In [29] is is shown that more than two helpers does not practically make sense.

Fig. 3: Workflow of an adapter for an helper working on an IR

straction refinement) scheme [20] with lazy-abstraction [33] and Craig interpolation [32].

Witness Injection: The predicate abstraction maintains, for each abstract state, one set of available predicates (called *precision*) and one set of valid predicates. Witness injection is realized by extracting all predicates and the corresponding locations from the invariants. If these predicates contain conjunctions of clauses, these are furthermore split up and inserted individually. Splitting predicates increases the performance due to the fact that SMT solvers perform better on many small predicates than on few larger ones[5]. These predicates are added to the precision of abstract states corresponding to the locations specified in the witness. Thereby, the predicates are used during the next abstraction performed by the analysis. The abstraction function itself guarantees that only predicates from the candidate set being valid at the current location are used. Thus, invalid invariants are ignored. This procedure can also be used when restarting predicate abstraction, by adding the predicates from the witness to the initial precision of the abstract states corresponding to the locations specified in the witness (which is empty otherwise).

k-Induction. The basic idea of k-induction [25] is to generalize bounded model checking (BMC) [14] via induction. After proving k-bounded program executions safe using BMC, a generalization is aimed for. Therefore, it generates auxiliary invariants that are continuously refined using a CEGAR based analysis [5]. These invariants are combined with the information generated by BMC and generalized to a safety proof by successfully conducting an induction step.

Witness Injection: For both cases, adding invariants into a running analysis or adding before restarting, we make use of the same idea: Whenever a witness is made available to the analysis, the encoded predicates and the program locations are added as candidates to the set of auxiliary invariants, generated by the analysis. New elements in this set are periodically checked for validity by k-induction. Thereby, valid externally generated invariants are conjoined with the predicates stored in the analysis abstract states, corresponding to the invariants location. Invalid invariants are thus ignored.

3.4   Adapter for LLVM-based Helper Invariant Generators

Next, we exemplify an adapter for helper invariant generators working on LLVM, following the general construction depicted in Figure 3. Often, tools associates invariants to LLVM basic blocks. A basic block is a code fragment having a single

---

[5] This has been reported by tool developers and has also shown in our experiments.

entry location (the first) and a single exit location (in general the last location of the block). To construct a witness containing the invariants, we need to translate them and find the matching C-code location for the basic block. For both, we use the LLVM-IR equipped with debug information, using the compiler with launch parameter -g. Thereby, we obtain the IR-code fragment of the program in Figure 2(a), shown in simplified form and containing the most important debug information as comments. The example contains two basic blocks, entry and _bb.

```
1        entry:
2        v1 = bitcast i32 (...)* @nondet to i32 ()*      ▷n
3        v2 = icmp eq i32 v1, 0
4        br i1 v2, label %error, label %_bb
5
6        _bb:
7        v3 = phi i32 [0, %entry], [v6, %_bb]             ▷y
8        v4 = phi i32 [v1, %entry], [v5, %_bb]            ▷x
9        v5 = add i32 v4, -1
10       v6 = add i32 v3, 1
11       v7 = icmp eq i32 v5, 0
12       br i1 v7, label %error, label %_bb      ▷line 4
```

The helper invariant generator computes the invariant $v1 - v4 - v3 = 0$ for the example and associates it with the basic block _bb. At first, we need to transform the variables from the IR to C-variables occurring in the program. In this example we can use the debug information, as shown in comments in the code. In general, a more sophisticated procedure is needed since LLVM-IR uses a three address code. Therein, complex expressions are split into several statements using intermediate variables which are resolved to C-expressions.

Afterwards, the transformed invariant needs to be associated with the correct location in the C-code. We analyze the LLVM IR program structure to map the basic blocks back to C-locations. In the example, the block _bb is identified as being the loop of the program, thus the invariant is mapped to the loop head. For this, we employed some basic functions provided by PHASAR [41] in our adapter. Finally, we construct the CFA of the C-program, store the invariants at the nodes and convert the equipped CFA to a verification witness.

4   Evaluation

In the following, we evaluate different instantiations of CoVEGI. We focus on both effectiveness and efficiency, generally aiming at checking whether the use of CoVEGI can increase the number of correctly solved verification tasks within the same resource limits. A more detailed evaluation of CoVEGI can be found in an extended pre-print [29].

4.1   Research Questions

In the evaluation, we were interested in the following three research questions.

Table 2: Summary of tools used as helpers

Tool	Techniques	Mapper	Adapter
SeaHorn	generation and solving constrained horn clauses	✗	✔
Ultimate-Automizer	predicate abstraction, automata, path-based refinement	✗	(✔)
VeriAbs	portfolio of 4 different sequential compositions	✗	✗

RQ1. Can collective invariant generation increase the effectiveness of the master verifier? *Evaluation plan:* We let the framework run with a single invariant generator and compare the results to a standalone run of the master verifier.

RQ2. Does cooperation impact the overall efficiency of the verification? *Evaluation plan:* We compare the run time of CoVEGI with one helper against the two master verifiers running standalone.

RQ3. Does it pay off to run two invariant generators in parallel? *Evaluation plan:* We let the framework run with two invariant generators and compare the results to a run, where only a single invariant generator is used.

4.2 Experimental Setup

Tools. To be able to evaluate the performance of our framework CoVEGI, we instantiated it with predicate abstraction and k-induction as master verifiers and three helpers, using existing off-the-shelf invariant generation tools. We based the implementation of our CoVEGI algorithm on CPACHECKER[6] 1.9.1. To the best of our knowledge, there are no standalone and publicly available invariant generators, that generate invariants for both, global and local variables, without doing a full verification. To be able to evaluate CoVEGI, we decided to use off-the-shelf verifiers as invariant generators instead, by only using the generated invariants. We thus looked at current and past participants of the annual competition of software verification SV-COMP [2] for invariant generation. We chose the tools SEAHORN [28], ULTIMATEAUTOMIZER [30] and VERIABS [1]. Both ULTIMATEAUTOMIZER and VERIABS achieved excellent results in this year's SV-COMP, being the reason to chose them. As third tool we use SEAHORN, a verification tool neither currently participating in the SV-COMP nor producing witnesses. It operates on the LLVM intermediate representation, therefore we used the adapter exemplified in Section 3.4. The three helper invariant generators are used as black-boxes and employ verification techniques complementary to those of both the other helpers and the two masters. An overview of the techniques employed in these tools is given in Table 2. The table also states whether the helpers require mappers and adapters. For VERIABS and ULTIMATEAUTOMIZER we used the versions as used in the SV-COMP 2020[7]. Due to the fact that there is no precompiled binary of SEAHORN, we employ the docker

---

[6] https://github.com/sosy-lab/cpachecker, Revision (8646a85)

[7] https://gitlab.com/sosy-lab/sv-comp/archives-2020/tree/master/2020

Table 3: Comparison of the two master verifiers running standalone and using a single helper.

Tool -	k-induction				predicate abstr.			
Combination	alone	+SH	+UA	+VA	alone	+SH	+UA	+VA
correct overall	146	148	158	**163**	116	122	**132**	125
correct true	102	104	114	**119**	78	84	**94**	87
correct false	44	44	44	44	38	38	38	38
additional true	-	+3	+13	**+19**	-	+6	**+16**	+9
additional false	-	0	0	0	-	0	0	0
uniquely solved	1	0	8	15	0	0	6	3

container of the latest version[8]. All three helper invariant generators are used in their default configuration.

During evaluation, we used the following default configurations for our own framework: We set `termAfterFirstInv` and `restartMaster` to true, setting the `timerM` to 50s[9] and the `timeoutH` to 300s. In general, we will use the abbreviations SH for SEAHORN, UA for ULTIMATEAUTOMIZER and VA for VERIABS.

Verification Tasks. The verification tasks used are taken from the set of SV-COMP 2020 benchmarks[10]. As we are interested in finding suitable loop invariants, we selected all tasks from the category ReachSafety-Loops. To obtain a more broad distribution of tasks, we randomly selected 55 additional tasks from the categories ProductLines, Recursive, Sequentialized, ECA, Floats and Heap, yielding in total 342 tasks.

Computing Resources. We conducted the evaluation on three virtual machines, each having an Intel Xeon E5-2695 v4 CPU with eight cores and a frequency of 2.10 GHz and 16GB memory, running an Ubuntu 18.04 LTS with Linux Kernel 4.15. We run our experiments using the same setting as in the SV-COMP, giving each task 15 minutes of CPU-time on 8 cores and 15GB of memory. We employed BENCHEXEC guaranteeing these resource-limitations [12].

Availability. Our tool and all experimental data are available[11].

4.3   Experimental Results

We implemented the CoVEGI-framework as proof-of-concept in the CPA-CHECKER-framework. For this, we had to extend the existing implementations of k-induction and predicate abstraction with witness injection. For the helper invariant generators we did not change a single line of code, only adding adapters if needed. Integrating helpers like VERIABS, not requiring an adapter or a mapper, can be done within a few lines of code. Although the implementation is a proof-of-concept, this shows that the presented framework works in practice

---

[8] suggested by the developers; used docker seahorn/seahorn-llvm5 (4c01c1d)
[9] Which has turned out to be a preferable value, as we explain in [29]
[10] https://github.com/sosy-lab/sv-benchmarks/releases/tag/svcomp20
[11] https://covercig.github.io/covegi/

and is applicable to all kinds of off-the-shelf helper invariant generators, those producing verification witnesses as well as those generating invariants in IR.

RQ1 (Effectiveness). To evaluate whether a master verifier benefits from the support of a helper, we execute a combination of a master and a helper in the default configuration and compare it to the master running standalone. Here, we are interested in the number of *correct* verification results, i.e., the verifier correctly reporting the safety property to be fulfilled (result *true*) or not (result *false*). Running standalone, k-induction can correctly solve 146 of the verification tasks, predicate abstraction 116.

Table 3 gives the results of this experiment. In the table we see the overall number of correct results, the number of correct *true* and correct *false* results plus the number of tasks additionally solved when using a helper and uniquely solved by the configuration. Through the cooperative invariant generation, the performance of both masters is increased. As expected, this applies to verification tasks with fulfilled safety property only, i.e., the invariant generators can help in proving a property to hold, but cannot help in refuting properties (as they correctly do not generate invariants in these cases). Besides the additionally solved tasks, there is also one (for SH and UA) and two (for VA) tasks, respectively, which cannot be correctly solved anymore. In these cases, the master consumes most of the CPU time available, hence sharing resources in cooperation with the helpers results in a timeout.

> On our data set, the total number of correctly solved tasks using CoVEGI increases by 12% for k-induction and 14% for predicate abstraction as master.

RQ2 (Efficiency). Next, we evaluate the efficiency of CoVEGI, analyzing the CPU time spend solving the verification tasks. As CoVEGI eventually shares the CPU time between master and helpers, we expect that more time is needed to compute a correct result after the helper is started.

Figure 4 shows two quantile plots of the verification runs, 4(a) with k-induction and 4(b) with predicate abstraction as master. A datapoint (x, y) in the plot means that the verifier computes the x-fastest correct results in at most y seconds. As CoVEGI instances behave like masters standalone in the first 50 seconds, we only show results *not* solved within these 50 seconds. We see that for tasks requiring a low amount of time, all instances (including the master alone) require a similar amount of CPU time. For tasks requiring more time, CoVEGI is actually often faster, the extreme being predicate abstraction as master which alone is unable to solve more difficult tasks in the given time.

We exemplarily also compared the CPU time of k-induction standalone with CoVEGI using VERIABS as helper *per task*. It turns out that sharing does only slightly impact the runtime, as shown in Figure 5. The scatter plot compares the CPU time of k-induction standalone as master and k-induction supported by VERIABS, in case both tools solved the task correctly. A datapoint (x, y) means that k-induction standalone takes x seconds to solve the task and in combination with VERIABS y seconds. The red dashed box contains all tasks solved within 50 seconds, where both tools behave equally, since the master does not request for

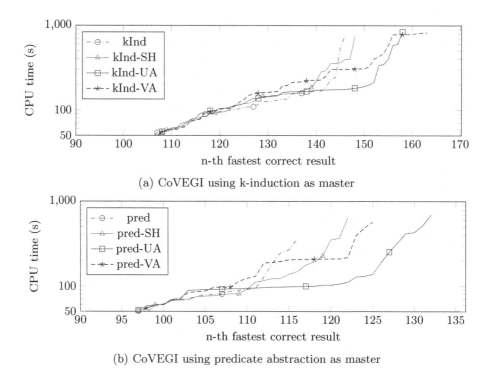

(a) CoVEGI using k-induction as master

(b) CoVEGI using predicate abstraction as master

Fig. 4: Quantile plots for CoVEGI using different single helpers.

help in these cases. We see some tasks for which helping increased the runtime, but also some for which it decreased it. In most of the cases, the CPU time used by CoVEGI is not significantly higher.

Finally, we compare the average CPU time needed to correctly solve a task. Table 4 shows the average time needed for all tasks and – in brackets – for the correctly solved tasks only. We observe that the runtime increases when only looking at correctly solved tasks (in particular for VERIABS), however, when considering all tasks the CPU time is even decreased. The latter effect is due to the number of timeouts of the master decreasing when cooperating with helpers. Concluding, we can make the following observation.

> On our dataset, collaborative invariant generation does not negatively impact the effectiveness; in some cases we even see small improvements.

RQ3 (Combination of helpers). In RQ3, we were interested in finding out (a) whether it is beneficial to run two invariant generators in parallel, and (b) if yes, which pair is best for this. We thus studied the number of correctly solved tasks using the three possible pairs of helpers, each running two helpers in parallel. Table 5 shows the results.

Fig. 5: Scatter plot for kInd and kInd-VA

Table 4: Total CPU time for all tasks and average CPU time taken for a correct answer in brackets, both in seconds.

Master	kInd	Pred
standalone	491.000	479.000
	(50)	(30)
+SH	489.000	468.000
	(63)	(39)
+UA	477.000	454.000
	(68)	(51)
+VA	482.000	470.000
	(107)	(49)

Table 5: Number of correctly solved tasks using different forms of cooperation with two or three helpers running in parallel.

Master	+SH-UA	+SH-VA	+UA-VA	+SH-UA-VA
k-induction	153	156	**163**	154
predicate abstr.	130	130	**136**	129

For checking whether parallel execution of helpers is beneficial, these numbers need to be compared against those for a single helper as given in Table 3. We see that predicate abstraction benefits from using two helpers, especially using ULTIMATEAUTOMIZER and VERIABS. Using CoVEGI with these tools perfectly combines their strengths, thereby increasing the number of correctly solved tasks in total by 17%. In contrast, it turns out that for k-induction none of the combinations of two helpers outperforms CoVEGI using VERIABS only. For ULTIMATEAUTOMIZER and VERIABS as helpers, the total number does not change, only the set of solved tasks. For instance, nearly 50% of the additional tasks solved by kInd-UA-VA are not solved using kInd-UA and vice versa. This result is based on the fact that they have to share the available CPU time in the combination. Hence, tasks that are solved using one of them as helper alone could not be solved anymore in a combination because of timeouts. This phenomenon is even more an issue when running all three helpers in parallel.

The combination of all three helpers solves only 154 tasks correctly for k-induction and 129 for predicate abstraction. In addition, we evaluated different values for parameter `timeoutH` in [29], whereas it turns out that waiting for all helpers to finish does not increase the number of correctly solved tasks.

> On our dataset, CoVEGI can increase the total number of correctly solved tasks using UA and VA in parallel; in general waiting for the other tool to also finish its computation does not pay off.

4.4   Threads to Validity

We have conducted our evaluation using a random sample of tasks as well as those in the category Loops. Although this guarantees some diversity, our findings may not completely carry over to arbitrary real-world programs.

The experiments are conducted using the reliable framework BENCHEXEC on identical machines with same resource limitations, guaranteeing comparable results. As SEAHORN is used within a docker-container, its CPU usage however cannot be measured by BENCHEXEC. We therefore measured this externally, rounded it up and added it to the measured CPU time, obtaining a lower bound for the correctly solved tasks. Thereby, all results stay valid, especially of the best performing instantiations of CoVEGI, as they do not use SEAHORN.

Our implementation of CoVEGI relies on the correctness of the used master verifiers and helpers (which are given) as well as on the adapters (which we build). An incorrectly translated invariant may however influence the performance only negatively. Both master verifiers used as well as ULTIMATEAUTOMIZER and VERIABS are participating in the annual SV-COMP, hence they might be tuned to the tasks employed. This does however not influence the validity of the results since our interest is in the *additional* number of tasks solved by cooperation, not the solved ones per se.

5   Related work

In this paper, we presented a framework for cooperative verification via collective invariant generation. The idea of collaboration for verification by combining known techniques has been widely employed before. For instance, there are combinations of verification with testing approaches [21,22,26,18,19,24] and with approaches for invariant generation [40,27,39,15,17]. The latter combinations are conducted in a *white box* manner using strong coupling between the components, making the addition of a new approach a challenging task. Our framework conceptually decouples the invariant generation from the verification, making it more flexible. In addition, using a black box integration with defined exchange formats allows us to easily exchange or integrate new approaches.

There are also existing concepts for collaboration between different techniques in a *black-box* manner. Conditional model checking is a technique for sequentially composing different model checkers, sharing information between the tools in form of conditions [7]. Beyer and Jakobs developed a concept for combining model checking with testing [8]. Although both approaches enable cooperation, none combines a verification tool and tools for invariant generation.

We next shortly discuss three approaches which are conceptually closer to our framework. Frama-C is a framework for code analysis, aiming for analyzing industrial size code [35]. The framework contains different plugins, each implementing a verification or testing technique. The plugins can exchange information in form of ASCL source code annotations. Within Frama-C, the analyzers can collaborate by being either sequentially or parallelly composed. For this, partial results produced by an analysis can be completed by a second one or several partial results computed in parallel are composed to a complete result. Frama-C offers the general possibility to define cooperation between existing plugins. To the best of our knowledge, Frama-C does however not provide a conceptual collaboration of a verification approach and tools for invariant generation driven by the verification approach's demand for support.

The approach of using continuously refined invariants for k-induction [5] uses a lightweight dataflow analysis which can be considered to be a helper for verification. Therein, the supporting invariant generator runs in parallel to the k-induction analysis. Compared to our framework, the main difference is the form of cooperation used. Beyer et al. use a white-box integration for the cooperation between k-induction and the invariant generator, building hardly wired connections between both analyses and sharing the information *inside* the tool. Thus, integrating external tools is hard to achieve. Moreover, the approach is designed to work for k-induction only. Note that an analogeous approach is proposed by Brain et al. [17].

Pauck and Wehrheim proposed CoDiDroid, a framework for cooperative taint flow analysis for Android apps [38]. Within their framework, different analysis tools with specialized capabilities are combined as black-boxes. CoDiDroid is however tailored to the needs of Android taint flow analysis, thus the exchanged information differs. Thus CoDiDroid is not able to orchestrate or exchange information on safety analysis with shared invariant generation.

To summarize, there are a lot of existing approaches for cooperative verification, but most of them are white-box combinations, and the existing black-box combinations are not general enough to allow for collective invariant generation.

6 Conclusion

In this paper, we have presented a novel form of black box cooperation for software verification via externally generated invariants. Within the configurable framework named CoVEGI, the so called master verifier steering the verification process is able to delegate the task of invariant generation to one or several helper invariant generators.

We implemented CoVEGI within the CPACHECKER framework using k-induction and predicate abstraction as master analysis supported by three existing helpers SeaHorn, UltimateAutomizer and VeriAbs. Our evaluation on a set of SV-COMP verification tasks shows that CoVEGI increases the number of correctly solved tasks without increasing the overall verification time. The best combination of helpers, UltimateAutomizer and VeriAbs in parallel, yields an increase of 12% for k-induction and 17% for predicate abstraction.

Next, we plan to enhance the cooperation by analyzing the behavior of the master in order to identify an optimal point to request for help. Moreover, extending CoVEGI by additionally taking error traces found by the helper into account is also scheduled. In addition, we intend to investigate whether a selection of helpers on the basis of the given verification task is beneficial.

References

1. Afzal, M., Asia, A., Chauhan, A., Chimdyalwar, B., Darke, P., Datar, A., Kumar, S., Venkatesh, R.: Veriabs : Verification by abstraction and test generation. In: ASE. pp. 1138–1141. IEEE (2019). https://doi.org/10.1109/ASE.2019.00121
2. Beyer, D.: Software verification with validation of results - (report on SV-COMP 2017). In: Legay, A., Margaria, T. (eds.) TACAS. LNCS, vol. 10206, pp. 331–349. Springer, Berlin, Heidelberg (2017). https://doi.org/10.1007/978-3-662-54580-5_20
3. Beyer, D., Dangl, M., Dietsch, D., Heizmann, M.: Correctness witnesses: exchanging verification results between verifiers. In: Zimmermann, T., Cleland-Huang, J., Su, Z. (eds.) FSE. pp. 326–337. ACM, New York, NY, USA (2016). https://doi.org/10.1145/2950290.2950351
4. Beyer, D., Dangl, M., Dietsch, D., Heizmann, M., Stahlbauer, A.: Witness validation and stepwise testification across software verifiers. In: Nitto, E.D., Harman, M., Heymans, P. (eds.) ESEC/FSE. pp. 721–733. ACM, New York, NY, USA (2015). https://doi.org/10.1145/2786805.2786867
5. Beyer, D., Dangl, M., Wendler, P.: Boosting k-induction with continuously-refined invariants. In: Kroening, D., Pasareanu, C.S. (eds.) CAV. LNCS, vol. 9206, pp. 622–640. Springer, Cham (2015). https://doi.org/10.1007/978-3-319-21690-4_42
6. Beyer, D., Gulwani, S., Schmidt, D.A.: Combining model checking and data-flow analysis. In: Clarke, E.M., Henzinger, T.A., Veith, H., Bloem, R. (eds.) Handbook of Model Checking, pp. 493–540. Springer (2018). https://doi.org/10.1007/978-3-319-10575-8_16
7. Beyer, D., Henzinger, T.A., Keremoglu, M.E., Wendler, P.: Conditional model checking: a technique to pass information between verifiers. In: Tracz, W., Robillard, M.P., Bultan, T. (eds.) FSE. p. 57. ACM (2012). https://doi.org/10.1145/2393596.2393664
8. Beyer, D., Jakobs, M.: Coveritest: Cooperative verifier-based testing. In: Hähnle, R., van der Aalst, W.M.P. (eds.) FASE. LNCS, vol. 11424, pp. 389–408. Springer (2019). https://doi.org/10.1007/978-3-030-16722-6_23
9. Beyer, D., Jakobs, M., Lemberger, T., Wehrheim, H.: Reducer-based construction of conditional verifiers. In: Chaudron, M., Crnkovic, I., Chechik, M., Harman, M. (eds.) ICSE. pp. 1182–1193. ACM (2018). https://doi.org/10.1145/3180155.3180259
10. Beyer, D., Keremoglu, M.E.: CPAchecker: A tool for configurable software verification. In: Gopalakrishnan, G., Qadeer, S. (eds.) CAV. LNCS, vol. 6806, pp. 184–190. Springer, Berlin, Heidelberg (2011). https://doi.org/10.1007/978-3-642-22110-1_16
11. Beyer, D., Keremoglu, M.E., Wendler, P.: Predicate abstraction with adjustable-block encoding. In: Bloem, R., Sharygina, N. (eds.) FMCAD. pp. 189–197. IEEE, Washington, DC, USA (2010), http://ieeexplore.ieee.org/document/5770949/
12. Beyer, D., Löwe, S., Wendler, P.: Reliable benchmarking: requirements and solutions. Int. J. Softw. Tools Technol. Transf. **21**(1), 1–29 (2019). https://doi.org/10.1007/s10009-017-0469-y
13. Beyer, D., Wehrheim, H.: Verification artifacts in cooperative verification:survey and unifying component framework. In: Margaria, T., Steffen, B. (eds.) ISoLA. LNCS, vol. 12476, pp. 143–167. Springer (2020). https://doi.org/10.1007/978-3-030-61362-4_8
14. Biere, A., Cimatti, A., Clarke, E.M., Strichman, O., Zhu, Y.: Bounded model checking. Advances in Computers **58**, 117–148 (2003). https://doi.org/10.1016/S0065-2458(03)58003-2

15. Blanchet, B., Cousot, P., Cousot, R., Feret, J., Mauborgne, L., Miné, A., Monniaux, D., Rival, X.: A static analyzer for large safety-critical software. In: Cytron, R., Gupta, R. (eds.) PLDI. pp. 196–207. ACM (2003). https://doi.org/10.1145/781131.781153

16. Bradley, A.R.: Sat-based model checking without unrolling. In: Jhala, R., Schmidt, D.A. (eds.) VMCAI. LNCS, vol. 6538, pp. 70–87. Springer (2011). https://doi.org/10.1007/978-3-642-18275-4_7

17. Brain, M., Joshi, S., Kroening, D., Schrammel, P.: Safety verification and refutation by k-invariants and k-induction. In: Blazy, S., Jensen, T.P. (eds.) SAS. LNCS, vol. 9291, pp. 145–161. Springer (2015). https://doi.org/10.1007/978-3-662-48288-9_9

18. Christakis, M., Müller, P., Wüstholz, V.: Collaborative verification and testing with explicit assumptions. In: Giannakopoulou, D., Méry, D. (eds.) FM. LNCS, vol. 7436, pp. 132–146. Springer, Berlin, Heidelberg (2012). https://doi.org/10.1007/978-3-642-32759-9_13

19. Christakis, M., Müller, P., Wüstholz, V.: Guiding dynamic symbolic execution toward unverified program executions. In: Dillon, L.K., Visser, W., Williams, L. (eds.) ICSE. pp. 144–155. ACM, New York, NY, USA (2016). https://doi.org/10.1145/2884781.2884843

20. Clarke, E.M., Grumberg, O., Jha, S., Lu, Y., Veith, H.: Counterexample-guided abstraction refinement for symbolic model checking. J. ACM 50(5), 752–794 (2003). https://doi.org/10.1145/876638.876643

21. Csallner, C., Smaragdakis, Y.: Check 'n' crash: combining static checking and testing. In: Roman, G., Griswold, W.G., Nuseibeh, B. (eds.) ICSE. pp. 422–431. ACM, New York, NY, USA (2005). https://doi.org/10.1145/1062455.1062533

22. Csallner, C., Smaragdakis, Y., Xie, T.: DSD-Crasher: A hybrid analysis tool for bug finding. TOSEM 17(2), 8:1–8:37 (2008). https://doi.org/10.1145/1348250.1348254

23. Czech, M., Jakobs, M., Wehrheim, H.: Just test what you cannot verify! In: Egyed, A., Schaefer, I. (eds.) FASE. LNCS, vol. 9033, pp. 100–114. Springer, Berlin, Heidelberg (2015). https://doi.org/10.1007/978-3-662-46675-9_7

24. Daca, P., Gupta, A., Henzinger, T.A.: Abstraction-driven concolic testing. In: Jobstmann, B., Leino, K.R.M. (eds.) VMCAI. LNCS, vol. 9583, pp. 328–347. Springer, Berlin, Heidelberg (2016). https://doi.org/10.1007/978-3-662-49122-5_16

25. Donaldson, A.F., Haller, L., Kroening, D., Rümmer, P.: Software verification using k-induction. In: Yahav, E. (ed.) SAS. LNCS, vol. 6887, pp. 351–368. Springer (2011). https://doi.org/10.1007/978-3-642-23702-7_26

26. Ge, X., Taneja, K., Xie, T., Tillmann, N.: Dyta: dynamic symbolic execution guided with static verification results. In: Taylor, R.N., Gall, H.C., Medvidovic, N. (eds.) ICSE. pp. 992–994. ACM, New York, NY, USA (2011). https://doi.org/10.1145/1985793.1985971

27. Gupta, A., Rybalchenko, A.: Invgen: An efficient invariant generator. In: Bouajjani, A., Maler, O. (eds.) CAV. LNCS, vol. 5643, pp. 634–640. Springer (2009). https://doi.org/10.1007/978-3-642-02658-4_48

28. Gurfinkel, A., Kahsai, T., Komuravelli, A., Navas, J.A.: The seahorn verification framework. In: Kroening, D., Pasareanu, C.S. (eds.) CAV. LNCS, vol. 9206, pp. 343–361. Springer (2015). https://doi.org/10.1007/978-3-319-21690-4_20

29. Haltermann, J., Wehrheim, H.: Cooperative Verification via Collective Invariant Generation. arXiv e-prints arXiv:2008.04551 (2020), https://arxiv.org/abs/2008.04551

30. Heizmann, M., Chen, Y., Dietsch, D., Greitschus, M., Hoenicke, J., Li, Y., Nutz, A., Musa, B., Schilling, C., Schindler, T., Podelski, A.: Ultimate automizer and the search for perfect interpolants - (competition contribution). In: Beyer, D., Huisman, M. (eds.) TACAS. LNCS, vol. 10806, pp. 447–451. Springer (2018). https://doi.org/10.1007/978-3-319-89963-3_30

31. Heizmann, M., Hoenicke, J., Podelski, A.: Software model checking for people who love automata. In: Sharygina, N., Veith, H. (eds.) CAV. LNCS, vol. 8044, pp. 36–52. Springer (2013). https://doi.org/10.1007/978-3-642-39799-8_2

32. Henzinger, T.A., Jhala, R., Majumdar, R., McMillan, K.L.: Abstractions from proofs. In: Jones, N.D., Leroy, X. (eds.) POPL. pp. 232–244. ACM, New York, NY, USA (2004). https://doi.org/10.1145/964001.964021

33. Henzinger, T.A., Jhala, R., Majumdar, R., Sutre, G.: Lazy abstraction. In: Launchbury, J., Mitchell, J.C. (eds.) POPL. pp. 58–70. ACM, New York, NY, USA (2002). https://doi.org/10.1145/503272.503279

34. Jakobs, M., Wehrheim, H.: Certification for configurable program analysis. In: Rungta, N., Tkachuk, O. (eds.) SPIN. pp. 30–39. LNCS, ACM, New York, NY, USA (2014). https://doi.org/10.1145/2632362.2632372

35. Kirchner, F., Kosmatov, N., Prevosto, V., Signoles, J., Yakobowski, B.: Frama-c: A software analysis perspective. Formal Asp. Comput. **27**(3), 573–609 (2015). https://doi.org/10.1007/s00165-014-0326-7

36. McMillan, K.L.: Interpolation and model checking. In: Clarke, E.M., Henzinger, T.A., Veith, H., Bloem, R. (eds.) Handbook of Model Checking, pp. 421–446. Springer (2018). https://doi.org/10.1007/978-3-319-10575-8_14

37. Necula, G.C.: Proof-carrying code. In: Lee, P., Henglein, F., Jones, N.D. (eds.) POPL. pp. 106–119. ACM Press, New York, NY, USA (1997). https://doi.org/10.1145/263699.263712

38. Pauck, F., Wehrheim, H.: Together strong: cooperative Android app analysis. In: Dumas, M., Pfahl, D., Apel, S., Russo, A. (eds.) ASE. pp. 374–384. ACM (2019). https://doi.org/10.1145/3338906.3338915

39. Rocha, W., Rocha, H., Ismail, H., Cordeiro, L.C., Fischer, B.: Depthk: A k-induction verifier based on invariant inference for C programs - (competition contribution). In: Legay, A., Margaria, T. (eds.) TACAS. LNCS, vol. 10206, pp. 360–364 (2017). https://doi.org/10.1007/978-3-662-54580-5_23

40. Sankaranarayanan, S., Sipma, H.B., Manna, Z.: Scalable analysis of linear systems using mathematical programming. In: Cousot, R. (ed.) VMCAI. LNCS, vol. 3385, pp. 25–41. Springer (2005). https://doi.org/10.1007/978-3-540-30579-8_2

41. Schubert, P.D., Hermann, B., Bodden, E.: Phasar: An inter-procedural static analysis framework for C/C++. In: Vojnar, T., Zhang, L. (eds.) TACAS. LNCS, vol. 11428, pp. 393–410. Springer (2019). https://doi.org/10.1007/978-3-030-17465-1_22

Engineering Secure Self-Adaptive Systems with Bayesian Games

Nianyu Li[1]([✉]), Mingyue Zhang[2], Eunsuk Kang[3], and David Garlan[4]

[1] Peking University, Beijing, China nianyu_li@pku.edu.cn
[2] Peking University, Beijing, China mingyuezhang@pku.edu.cn
[3] Carnegie Mellon University, Pittsburgh, USA eunsukk@andrew.cmu.edu
[4] Carnegie Mellon University, Pittsburgh, USA garlan@cs.cmu.edu

Abstract. Security attacks present unique challenges to self-adaptive system design due to the adversarial nature of the environment. Game theory approaches have been explored in security to model malicious behaviors and design reliable defense for the system in a mathematically grounded manner. However, modeling the system as a single player, as done in prior works, is insufficient for the system under partial compromise and for the design of fine-grained defensive strategies where the rest of the system with autonomy can cooperate to mitigate the impact of attacks. To deal with such issues, we propose a new self-adaptive framework incorporating Bayesian game theory and model the defender (i.e., the system) at the granularity of *components*. Under security attacks, the architecture model of the system is translated into a *Bayesian multi-player game*, where each component is explicitly modeled as an independent player while security attacks are encoded as variant types for the components. The optimal defensive strategy for the system is dynamically computed by solving the pure equilibrium (i.e., adaptation response) to achieve the best possible system utility, improving the resiliency of the system against security attacks. We illustrate our approach using an example involving load balancing and a case study on inter-domain routing.

1 Introduction

A self-adaptive system is designed to be capable of modifying its structure and behavior at run time in response to changes in its environment and the system itself (e.g., variability in system performance, deployment cost, internal faults, and system availability) [9,12]. One of the major challenges in self-adaptive systems is managing *uncertainty*; i.e., the system should be capable of making appropriate planning decisions despite limited observations about its environment. Achieving *security* in presence of uncertainty is particularly challenging due to the adversarial nature of the environment [17,13]: (1) to avoid detection, a typical attacker may attempt to remain hidden while carrying out its actions, and so accurately estimating its objectives and capabilities can be difficult, and (2) the attacker actively attempts to cause as much harm as possible to the system, and so a typical "average case" analysis may not be appropriate for making optimal defensive decisions [28].

E. Guerra and M. Stoelinga (Eds.): FASE 2021, LNCS 12649, pp. 130–151, 2021.
https://doi.org/10.1007/978-3-030-71500-7_7

Various game-theoretic approaches have been explored in the security community for modeling interactions between the system and attackers as a *game* between a group of *players* (i.e., system and multiple attackers, each as one player) and computing optimal strategies (i.e., Nash Equilibrium) for the system to minimize the impact of possible attacks and improve its resiliency against them [40,15,19,28]. These methods can be used to (1) model adversarial behaviors by malicious attackers [19], and (2) design reliable defense for the system by using underlying incentive mechanisms to balance perceived risks in a mathematically grounded manner [15]. In particular, a type of game-theoretic method called *Bayesian games* [25] is designed to explicitly encode and reason about uncertainty in the information that players have (e.g., partial knowledge about each other's actions and objectives).

Prior works in security that leverage game theory [40,15,19,28] have treated the system as an independent player (i.e., defender) in the game. However, such a monolithic approach that involves abstracting the entire system as a single player might be insufficient for capturing certain practical scenarios, where only one part of the system is compromised while the remaining system components may co-operate each other to mitigate the impact of an on-going attack.

In this paper, we argue that compared to a coarse one-player abstraction of a system, modeling the defender under security attacks at the granularity of *components* is more expressive, in that it allows the design of fine-grained defensive strategies for the system under partial compromise. In particular, we advocate a security modeling approach where an attack is modeled as the anomalous behavior of a system component that deviates from its expected behavior, as an alternative to a conventional approach where attackers themselves are modeled as separate players.

To this end, we propose a novel approach to improving the resiliency of self-adaptive systems against security attacks by leveraging game theory. In particular, we propose a new self-adaptive framework that leverages *multi-players Bayesian games* at the granularity of *components* at the system architecture level. Specifically, in our approach, each major system component is modeled separately as an independent player. Under an attack, one or more components with vulnerabilities might be exploited by an attacker to deliberately perform harmful actions (i.e., turning into a malicious type). Different types of attacks that these components might be subject to are encoded as different *types* of game players, encoding uncertainty in the attack being carried out. The rest of the components are then modeled as forming a coalition to mitigate the impact of the malicious actions by those compromised components.

To perform a security analysis, a model of the system architecture and component attacks are translated into a mathematical Bayesian game structure. Then, the adaptive defensive strategy for the system is dynamically computed by solving a pure equilibrium, to achieve the best possible system utility under all assignments of the components to their possible types (i.e., in the presence of security attacks).

Our main contributions are summarized as follows:

- A self-adaptive framework that incorporates Bayesian game theory to improve the resiliency of the system under potential security attacks;
- An approach to modeling the system under attacks as a multi-player game with potentially uncooperative players at the granularity of components and the use of equilibrium as an optimal adaptation response;
- A demonstration of the applicability of our approach through an example with load-balancing scenarios and a case study involving a network routing application with a proposed dynamic programming algorithm.

2   Background

2.1   Running Example

As a running example, we adopt Znn.com, a hypothetical news website that has been used as a representative system for the application of self-adaptive systems [10,11]. In a typical workflow, given a request from a client, the web server fetches appropriate content (in form of text) from its back-end database and generates a web page containing a visualization of the text. Furthermore, the system also provides an optional service with multimedia

Fig. 1: Running Example.

content (e.g., images, videos). This service involves additional computation on the server side, but also brings in more revenue compared to the requests with only text. With R_M and R_T being the revenue, C_M and C_T being the computation of one response to a user request with the media content and with only text content, respectively, we assume that $R_M > R_T > 0$ and $C_M > C_T > 0$.

In order to support multiple servers, a *LoadBalancer* is added to distribute the requests from the users to a pool of servers, as shown in Figure 1. The cost of each server is proportional to its load due to, such as potential high response time since companies such as Amazon, eBay, and Google claim that increased user perceived response time results in revenue loss [33]. To be more specific, the cost per server is denoted by $(S_i - T)^2/K$ where S_i is the current occupied load for server i, depending on the request serving mode (i.e., $S_i = D_i C_T$ in text only while $S_i = D_i C_M$ in multi-media mode where D_i is the number of requests distributed to server i); T is the threshold beyond which the response time would be affected; K is a constant used to adjust the cost ratio.

The goal of the self-adaptive system is to maximize the difference between revenue and cost.

$$U = R_M x_M + R_T x_T - \sum_{i=1}^{3} (S_i \leq T \; ? \; 0 \; : \; (S_i - T)^2/K) \qquad (1)$$

where x_M and x_T are the numbers of responses with media and text content, respectively; the penalty is the sum of the cost for all three servers.

Suppose that some of the servers are vulnerable to various attacks such as password guessing, SQL injection, command injection, etc [1]. The information collected from the web server, however, cannot fully demonstrate its compromise due to, e.g., the deficiencies of scanning tools, but with uncertainty. As shown in the Figure, *Server2* could be potentially attacked with a 20% probability while *Server3* is with a higher probability of 50%. These two servers, if compromised in reality, might perform harmful actions controlled by the attackers to achieve their objectives, rendering the loss of system reward. Here we assume the malicious strategies of simply discarding all the distributed user requests. The reward of attacks is denoted by the system loss, i.e., subtracting the maximum reward the system could achieve from the reward under attacks, leading to a zero-sum game.

2.2 Bayesian Game Theory

Game theory is the application of mathematical analysis of individual and cooperative behaviors between players that follow a certain strategy to satisfy their self-interests [21,38]. A *Bayesian* game is a type of game in which players have incomplete information about the other players [25]. For example, a player may not know the exact type (e.g., malicious or good) associated with a unique payoff function of the other players, but instead, have beliefs about these types. These beliefs are represented by a probability distribution over the possible types. More formally, Bayesian games or *incomplete information games* are defined as follows:

Definition 1. *A Bayesian game is a tuple* $BG = \langle P, A, \Theta, U, \rho \rangle$

- *A set of n players P;*
- *A set of (joint) actions* $A = A_1 \times ... \times A_n$*, where* A_i *denotes a finite set of actions available to player* P_i*;*
- *A set of types for each player* $i : \theta_i \in \Theta_i$*;*
- *A payoff function for each player* $i : u_i(a_1, ..., a_n; \theta_1, ..., \theta_n)$*, determined by the types of all players and actions they choose;*
- *A (joint) probability distribution* $\rho(\theta_1, ..., \theta_n)$ *over types.*

Importantly, throughout the Bayesian games, we assume that the assignment of types to players is private information, while the priori type probability distribution, the action spaces and the payoff functions are assumed to be common knowledge. A player's strategy can be pure (i.e., take a deterministic action) or mixed (i.e., randomly choose an action according to some probability distribution). A strategy for player i is $s_i : \Theta_i \times A_i \to [0, 1]$, and $\forall \theta \in \Theta_i, \sum_{a \in A_i} s_i(a|\theta) = 1$. The strategy is pure if it satisfies that $\forall \theta \in \Theta_i, \exists a \in A_i, s_i(a|\theta) = 1$, also denoted as $s_i : \Theta_i \to A_i$.

Definition 2. *(Bayesian Nash Equilibrium Strategy) Given a joint strategy for all players* $\vec{s}^* = [s_1^*, ..., s_n^*]$*,* $\vec{s}^*$ *is the Bayesian Nash equilibrium strategy if for any player i, it satisfies that:*

$$s_i^* = \arg \max_{s_i \in S(\theta_i)} \sum_{\vec{\theta}_{-i}} \rho(\vec{\theta}_{-i}|\theta_i) \mathbb{E}_{\vec{a}_{-i} \sim \vec{s}_{-i}^*, a_i \sim s_i} [u_i(a_i, \vec{a}_{-i}; \theta_i, \vec{\theta}_{-i})]$$

where $\vec{a}_{-i} = [a_1, ..., a_{i-1}, a_{i+1}, ..., a_n]$*,* $\vec{\theta}_{-i} = [\theta_1, ..., \theta_{i-1}, \theta_{i+1}, ..., \theta_n]$*,* $\vec{s}_{-i}^* = [s_1^*, ...s_{i-1}^*, s_{i+1}^*, ..., s_n^*]$*,* $S(\theta_i)$ *is the set of all possible strategies for agent i under*

θ_i, and $\rho(\vec{\theta}_{-i}|\theta_i)$ *is the conditional probability representing the player i's belief about other players' types under type* θ_i.

Bayesian Nash equilibrium is a set of strategies, one for each type of player. It is the best strategy that maximizes his or her payoff to other players' equilibrium strategies. In a Nash equilibrium, there is no player who can improve his profit by unilaterally modifying his strategy if the actions of the rest are fixed [25,21].

3   Self-Adaptive Framework Incorporating Bayesian Game Theory

Security attacks are usually associated with a high degree of uncertainty where the defender may know little about the identity of the attackers nor fully understand their technical effect on the system. A Bayesian game is a game in which players have incomplete information about the other players, appropriate for modeling and dealing with the attacks with uncertainty. In this section, we propose a new type of self-adaptive framework incorporating Bayesian Game. Adaptation behaviors build on the Nash equilibrium from unexpected attacks and are achieved by elaborating the widely adopted mechanism of the MAPE-

Fig. 2: Self-Adaptive Framework.

K (Monitoring, Analysis, Planning, Execution, Knowledge) loop [27,43], shown in Figure 2.

Knowledge. Knowledge Base requires the system developers or domain experts to specify (1) the component and connector model of the managed subsystem and its action space for each component, (2) system objectives usually defined as the quality attributes quantified by the utility, and (3) component vulnerabilities with potential behavior deviations that can be exploited by the potential attacks. Other necessary information such as the history information of system behaviors and environment information are saved in Knowledge Base and can be updated for the sake of self-adaptation.

Monitor. Events generated in the managed subsystem or environment indicating the execution of system actions or natural changes in the environmental factors are received. Monitor gathers and synthesizes the on-going attacks information through sensors and saves information in the Knowledge Base. For our example, events such as plenty of user request loss or command injection can indicate a potential attack on the web server.

Analyzer. During speculative analysis, conditions of the environment/managed subsystem representing violations or better satisfaction of goals that can arise based on the input from Monitor are identified. The Analyzer performs analysis and further checks whether certain components are attacked with probabilities; potential deviated malicious actions are identified; the rewards for the attack are estimated, based on the knowledge about component vulnerabilities and system objectives. Such attack probabilities can be analyzed with a statistical combination of all feasible scenarios along with expert judgment [16,24]. A typical example is that both Server2 and Server3 are analyzed to be compromised and discarding user requests with a certain probability, reducing the system utility.

Planner. Planner generates a workflow of adaptation actions aiming to counteract violations of system goals or better achieving goals. It consists of one or a set of actions to be enacted by automatically solving the Multi-player Bayesian Game transformed with the input of potential attacks from the Analyzer and architectural model of the managed subsystem along with the system objectives, which is elaborated in Section 4. For each security situation, it generates an equilibrium if one exists as the adaptation to respond to unexpected attacks, or prompts for a change in the design of the system if the violation cannot be handled. Distributing more percentage of a user request to the normal server while decreasing the percentage to those with a high probability of compromise as well as adjusting the fidelity level for servers could be feasible actions for Znn.com Website under security attacks.

Executor. During execution, the strategies from the adaptation equilibrium are enacted on the managed subsystem through actuators. Typical examples could be setting the distribution percentage of user percentage in *LoadBalancer* for each server.

In the next part, we focus on planning activity with Bayesian game theory. We assume adequate monitoring in place, sufficient analysis methods on potential attacks with uncertainties based on observation and historical information, as well as an execution environment through which selected adaptation strategies are enacted.

4   Bayesian Game Through Model Transformation

In this section, we start by defining the system under attacks and transforming the system architecture and on-going attacks into a component-based multi-player Bayesian game. Solving the game with equilibrium is to find the adaptation strategy. Then, we present the analysis results on our running example.

Component-based System. A system component is an independent and replaceable part of a system (e.g., a process, program) that fulfills a clear function in the context of a well-defined architecture. Typical examples are the *LoadBalancer* and servers in Figure 1. Components forming architectural structures affect different quality attributes. For example, quality attributes of user satisfaction (i.e., revenue) and the costs (i.e., penalty) identified in the Znn Website example are influenced by the actions of all four components and characterized as utility functions as shown in Eq.(1) mapping them to utility values.

Definition 3. *A system can be formally defined as a tuple $S = \langle C, A, Q \rangle$.*

- *C is a set of components;*
- *A is a set of joint actions $A = A_1 \times ... \times A_n$, where A_i denotes a finite set of actions available to component i;*
- *Q is a set of quality attributes a system is interested in; for each Q_x, a subset of components $SubC_x \subseteq C$ could contribute to this quality attribute;*

Each component is trying to make the right reaction to maximize the system utility, essentially like a rational player in the game theory. Naturally, a system under normal operation could be viewed as a cooperative game dealing with how coalitions interact. Each component is denoted as an independent player and these interacting components/players form a coalition. For instance, in the running example, the *LoadBalancer* and three servers collaborate to achieve the goals together, i.e., maximizing the system reward with revenue and penalty. Specifically, the *LoadBalancer* should assign more user requests to those servers with low computation usage, like the waiting queue in the bank, while the server should adjust the fidelity level according to its current load. A high load may lead to the text only content to decrease the cost while the server with low usage can provide media content to promote the revenue.

Modeling Utility as Payoffs. The payoff among those players is allocated by the utility from quality attributes. It is straightforward for developers to design a system-level payoff function (e.g., the revenue and penalty in Section 2.1). However, due to the different roles of the components and the complex relationship between them, it is complicated and sometimes untraceable to manually design an appropriate component-level payoff function. To solve this problem, we use the *Shapley Value Method*, a solution concept of fairly distributing both gains and costs to several players working in coalition proportional to their marginal contributions [37,36], to automatically decompose the system-level utility into the component-level payoff. *Shapley Value Method* applies primarily in situations when the contributions of each player are unequal, but each player works in cooperation with each other to obtain the payoff. Given the component set C, and a system-level utility function v, the payoff for a component i is:

$$\phi_i(C, v) = \frac{1}{|C|!} \sum_{C' \subseteq C \setminus \{i\}} |C'|!(|C| - |C'| - 1)![v(C' \cup \{i\}) - v(C')] \quad (2)$$

where $|C|$ is the number of components in the set; $C \setminus \{i\}$ is the set C excluding component i; $v(C')$ values the expected system-level utility when the system only consists of the component set C'.

The following is a typical example of system utility allocation with the *Shapley Value Method* for the Znn website. To simplify the illustration, we consider the situation where *Server2* and *Server3* are indeed compromised, the *LoadBalancer* chooses the strategy equally distributing user requests to *Server1* and *Server2* (i.e., the requests distributed to *Server1*, *Server2* and *Server3* are 50, 50 and 0 respectively), and *Server1* selects the text only mode. Besides, the total unprocessed requests in the setting are 100, which is assumed to be the full load of a server serving only text, with $R_M = 1.6$, $R_T = 1, T = 50$, and $K = 25$ in Eq.(1). The computation capacity of a unit of text and media is 1 and 1.4 (i.e., C_M and C_T) respectively. Thus, the system utility in this situation is $U_{system} = 50$ (i.e., $50 \times 1 - (50 \times 1 - 50)^2/25$ with the remaining 50 requests discarded by malicious *Server2*). The *cooperative* player set consisting of *LoadBalancer* and *Server1* share this utility while *Server2* and *Server3* fight on behalf of the attacks' interests, thus not being considered in the coalition neither allocated the payoff from the system utility.

Based on Eq.(2), we need the following two cases of coalitions for Shapley Value calculation: (1) If there is only the *LoadBalancer* without *Server1* in the coalition, the utility of the system $U_{LoadBalancer}$ is 0 due to no requests process from *Server1* neither from malicious *Server2*; (2) If there is only *Server1* without *LoadBalancer* distributing user requests, the requests are randomly passed among three servers, i.e., the requests distributed to *Server1*, *Server2* and *Server3* are 34, 33 and 33 respectively, and the utility of the system for this coalition $U_{server1}$ is 34 (i.e., $34 \times 1 - 0$). This is because malicious *Server2* and *Server3* do not return any feedback. As a result, $\phi_{LoadBalancer}(C, v) = 1/2(U_{system} - U_{server1} + U_{loadbalancer}) = 8$ and $\phi_{Server1}(C, v) = 1/2(U_{system} - U_{LoadBalancer} + U_{server1}) = 42$. Therefore,the payoff to player *LoadBalancer* and *Server1* are 8 and 42 respectively. Meanwhile, attacks' utility, the difference between system utility and the highest utility the system could achieve without attacks (i.e., equally distributing user requests to three servers and each server choosing multi-media mode in this setting with value $160 = 100 \times 1.6 - 0$) is equally divided for two malicious players. In other words, both *Server2* and *Server3* is allocated payoff $55 = (160-50)/2$. Following the aforementioned allocation process, each player obtains a unique payoff under different attack situations and strategies from the *Shapley Value Method* based on their roles contributing to marginal system utility.

Component-based Attacks. A system under security attacks is also defined as a tuple $SAS = \langle C, A, Q, ATT \rangle$. Instead of modeling an attacker or several attackers with possible complex behaviors over different parts of the system, we model the on-going attacks ATT the system is enduring at the component level since the vulnerabilities of the components as well as their potential behavior deviations are comparatively easy to observe. ATT can be obtained by synthesizing the information from Monitor and Analyzer as described in Section 3.

Definition 4. *The security attacks on the system is formally defined as a tuple* $ATT = \langle C_{att}, A_{att}, P_{att}, R_{att} \rangle.$

- C_{att} *is the set of components affected by the attacks;*
- $A_{att} = A_{att1} \times ... \times A_{attm}$ *where* A_{atti} *denotes the set of actions controlled by attacks on compromised component i;*
- $P_{att} = \{p_1, ..., p_m\}$ *is a set of probability where* p_i *is the probability of component i being successfully compromised;*
- R_{att} *is the reward for attacks.*

Translation into a Bayesian game With the definition of the system on the component level and the definition of the attacks ATT, a system under security attacks is converted into a non-cooperative Bayesian game by the following steps:

1. Each component in the system $c \in C$, such as *LoadBalancer* and three servers in the running example, is separately modeled as an independent player;
2. The components potentially affected by attacks $C_{att} \subseteq C$ is associated with two types (e.g., *Server2* and *Server3* can be *normal* or *malicious* in the simplified Znn website scenario) while the remaining components $C - C_{att}$, i.e., *LoadBalancer* and *Server1*, are deterministic in *normal* type;
3. The probability distribution for a player i over two types is $\rho(p_i, 1 - p_i)$ as defined in P_{att}. One typical example for *Server2* is $\rho(0.8, 0.2)$ and for *Server3* $\rho(0.5, 0.5)$;
4. The action space of player i under security attacks is the union of both its normal actions and those malicious actions controlled by attacks (i.e., $A_i \cup A_{atti}$). *Server2* can serve user requests either with text only or multimedia content as a normal player, or maliciously discard them with the intention of attacks;
5. The payoff for players in normal type is allocated with system utility by the *Shapley Value Method*, while components in malicious type performing harmful actions is assigned with utility the on-going attacks obtain by achieving their own goals. This assignment could be simple average distribution or *Shapley Value Method* if the malicious players are treated as another coalition;
6. The game constructed is put into a game solver, to find a Nash equilibrium, which, in essence, is the best reaction for the system to potential attacks.

Note that this definition can be easily extended for the situation where a component is simultaneously compromised by different attackers with multiple types. Besides, the game solver we adopted in this work is *Gambit* [35], a collection of tools for building game models, computing game equilibrium and analyzing game results, to efficiently model the Bayesian game translated by the above steps and automatically figure out the equilibrium strategy as the adaptation response.

4.1   Analysis Results for Znn.com Example

In this subsection, we demonstrate how our approach can produce adaptation decisions under security attacks for Znn website to enhance the system utility. In particular, we exploit the Bayesian game model by following the aforementioned steps and generate the equilibrium. To explore different attack scenarios, we statically analyze a discretized region of the state space, which is projected over two dimensions that vary the malicious probability (i.e., *probability_S2* and *probability_S3*) of *Server2* and *Server3* respectively (with values in the range $[0, 1]$). Each state of the discrete set requires a solution of the game with the Nash Equilibrium that quantifies the best utility the system could obtain. The experiment takes less than one minute to generate all the results, as shown in Figure 3, and for each state, the solution generation time is negligible. To set up the experiment, we assume there are 100 user requests - the maximum load of a server in text only mode - with $R_M = 1.6$, $R_T = 1$, $x_M = 1.4$, $x_T = 1$, $T = 50$, and $X = 25$ in Eq.(1). Additionally, we adopt the probabilistic model checking method as the benchmark [11,7,32] and compare our Bayesian Game theory method with it in terms of the system utility.

Figure 3 (a) illustrates the percentage of user requests distributed to *Server1* from the strategy for the *LoadBalancer* in equilibrium. As expected, the percentage of *Server1* increases progressively with the increasing malicious probability of *Server2* and *Server3* as more user requests are supposed to be processed by a server under normal operation. In particular, we observed that the user percentage is around one third when both *Server2* and *Server3* are functioning normally (i.e., both *probability_S2* and *probability_S3* are 0), with *LoadBalancer* equally delivering the user requests since none of the servers is compromised. Moreover, the percentage for *Server1* reaches around 84% when the other two servers are fully compromised. In this situation, *LoadBalancer* does not deliver all user requests to *Server1*; otherwise *Server1* may be overloaded with the increasing costs due to high response time which in turn outweigh its benefits of request processing.

Fig. 3: Results for Znn Website: (a) percentage of user requests to *Server1*; (b) percentage of user requests to *Server2*; (c) strategies for *Server1*; (d) system utility with game theory approach; (e) delta utility between Bayesian game theory approach and probabilistic model checking approach.

Figure 3 (b) describes the percentage of user request that *LoadBalancer* delivers to *Server2* in the equilibrium. We can also observe that user requests to *Server2* are negatively proportional to its malicious probability. Particularly, user requests are 50 when probability *probability_S2* is 0 while *Server3* is fully malicious (i.e., *probability_S3*=1) where *LoadBalancer* should equally distribute the user request to both *Server1* and *Server2*. Figure 3 (c) presents the strategy in equilibrium for *Server1*. The states in which text content is provided are indicated by red triangles, whereas the multimedia strategies for *Server1* are denoted by white rectangles. As we can see, red points are in the upper right corner where malicious probabilities of *Server2* and *Server3* are greater than 50%, which means that they are very likely compromised. Therefore, *LoadBalancer* distributes as many user requests as possible to *Server1*, thus *Server1* choosing to provide text only content in avoid of overloading. Otherwise, *Server1* can provide multimedia content in less load condition to promote user satisfaction with higher revenue.

Figure 3 (d) illustrates the maximum utility the system can achieve under various attack situations. In particular, we observe that the utility reaches around 160 when all three servers are cooperative and is progressively decreased with the increasing malicious probability of *Server2* and *Server3*. This is consistent with the fact that the system utility is deteriorated under security attack. To compare the system utility in game theory with existing methods, we adopt probabilistic model checking [29] as the comparison standard to formally model the running example and synthesize the adaptation strategy maximizing its expectation of the utility by reasoning about reward-based properties [11,7,32]. Figure 3 (e) presents the delta between two approaches (i.e., system utility with game theory approach minus the utility with the probabilistic model checking approach). Without security attacks, the adaptation decision generated by the two approaches achieve the same utility. However, with the increasing malicious probability of *Server2* and *Server3*, game theory approach outperforms, providing the better response to make up for the utility loss due to security attack, and the average delta is 10.54, i.e., 15 percent outperforming with the average utility 80.39 achieved by game theory.

5   Evaluation – Routing Games

To evaluate our approach and assess its applicability for validation, we consider a case study on an interdomain routing application. We first define the game (Section 5.1) and propose a dynamic programming algorithm to solve the equilibrium by decomposing the problem into smaller and tractable sub games (Section 5.2). The results are present (Section 5.3) with a sensitivity analysis, illustrating how the system can choose a robust strategy effective for a range of threat landscapes, and a utility analysis by quantifying the defender's utility with Bayesian game compared to a greedy solution within the security context.

A routing system is usually composed of smaller networks called nodes as shown in Figure 4. Since not all nodes are directly connected, packets often have to traverse several nodes and the task of ensuring connectivity between nodes is called interdomain routing [30,31]. Each node could be owned by economic entities (Microsoft, AT&T, etc.) and might be compromised by the attacker at any time. Therefore, it is natural to

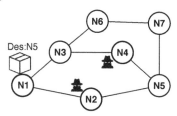

Fig. 4: Routing Scenario.

consider interdomain routing from a game-theoretic point of view. Specifically, game players are source nodes located on a network, aiming to send a package (i.e., starting at $N1$) to a unique destination node (i.e., $N5$). The interaction between players is dynamic and complex – asynchronous, sequential, and based on partial information - and the best strategy for each player as the adaptation response is updated as needed.

5.1   Game Definition for Interdomain Routing

The interdomain routing system is described below with the component-based definition.

- The components set for the interdomain routing is $C = \{N1, N2, ..., N7\}$;
- The action space for each node is to deliver the package at hand to its neighboring nodes. Typical example is $A_{N1} = \{toN2, toN3\}$;
- The only quality attribute this network needs to be concerned with is the time delivering the package to its destination as we assume there is no case of package loss. Specifically, we consider the delivery time is proportional to the distance denoted by hops between nodes. Its utility function is encoded using a formula that enables the quantification of the utility of a given state and defined as $U_{system} = 10 - \#hops$. Usually, the longer time, the lower utility and the maximum utility system could achieve under normal operations for this network is 8 with two hops $\langle N1 \; N2 \; N5 \rangle$;

Currently, $N2$ and $N4$ are analyzed to be potentially attacked based on the historical package delivery record, deliberately sending the package in the opposite direction, extending the delivery time. The game definition with the security attacks is summarized below.

- The player set for the game is $C = \{N1, N2, ..., N7\}$. The set of affected components by the attack includes $N2$ and $N4$, i.e., $C_{att} = \{N2, \; N4\}$;
- The action set for all players, including malicious ones controlled by attacks, is delivering the package to its neighboring nodes.
- The set of types for potential attacked component node includes "normal" and "malicious" (i.e., $\theta_{N2} \in \{normal, \; malicious\}$, $\theta_{N4} \in \{normal, \; malicious\}$).
- The payoff for all the normal players is allocated by the system utility with the *Shapley Value Method* (i.e., $U_{system} \div |normal \; players|$, equally allocated in this case since all of the nodes in this network is not cut vertex with the same importance). For example. each node is awarded 8/7 if none of them is attacked. The utility for the ongoing attacks on two components is the utility loss from the system's best response without attack, rendering a case of zero-sum game.
- The probability distribution for both component $N2$ and $N4$ could be, e.g., 50%/50% split (i.e., $\rho_{N2, N4}(normal, malicious) = (0.5, 0.5)$).

5.2   Dynamic Programming Algorithm

In practice, a network might be complex and each node could have hundreds of neighboring nodes. It is impractical to directly build a game tree, in the component level with a large number of players (each with a massive action set), and solve such a network in a reasonable time. To deal with the complexity of network nature, we propose an algorithm inspired by dynamic programming to effectively solve the generated Bayesian game for this class of routing problems.

The algorithm 1 for routing game has as input a routing network N – consisting of a starting point s of package delivery and a destination point d. To carry out dynamic programming, the algorithm uses a set $subG$ to store the set of nodes which have been processed with their best reactive strategy. $subG$ is initialized as an empty set (line 1) and added with node d (line 2) since d does not need the strategy to transmit the package. The algorithm starts by iterating all the nodes in the distance $disValue$ (line 5), initialized by 1 (line 3). For example, $N2$, $N4$ and $N7$ are qualified in the first iteration. Each node is checked whether it is potentially attacked (i.e., $uncertain(n)$ in line 6). For those uncertain nodes (e.g., $N2$ and $N4$), they might affect the strategy of their prior nodes (line 7) (e.g., $N1$ and $N3$), which shall be added to $todoS$ (line 8), to be processed to update their strategy due to its neighboring uncertainty. A typical example is that node $N3$ might trade off the delivery between $N4$ and $N6$ even though $N4$ is in the shortest path from $N3$ to $N5$, however, could deliberately send the package back controlled by the attack. If the node is not in $todoS$ to be updated (line 11), it is directly added to the $setG$ (line 12) as the best strategy for such benign node is passing the package down to its adjacent node along the shortest path. In this routing scenario, $N2$, $N4$ and $N7$ is added to $subG$ as their strategies in equilibrium with normal type is easily determined.

After iterating all the nodes in $disValue$ 1, each node in $todoS$ (line 15) is checked whether it satisfies the condition (line 16) where all its neighboring nodes (i.e., $i \in adj(n)$) closer to destination (i.e., $dis(i,d) == dis(n) - 1$) have been solved with their best strategies (i.e., in $subG$), to build a sub-game. As shown in the example, though both $N1$ and $N3$ are prior to an uncertain node, their strategy update is postponed as $N6$ is not in $subG$ yet, which affects the sub-game generation for $N3$, in turn delaying the sub-game construction for $N1$.

An exemplified subgame construction (line 17) starting from $N3$ is illustrated in Fig 5 when all conditions are satisfied. The stochastic behavior of those potentially compromised nodes can be modeled by introducing a nature (or chance player), who moves according to the probability distribution (e.g., 50%/50% split), randomly determining whether attacks on $N2$ and $N4$ are successful. Then, $N3$ can choose an action passing to the one from the set of its adjacent nodes, i.e., $N6$ or $N4$. Here, $N3$ is a normal node aware of that the package is transmitted from $N1$ and it is not necessary to consider a rollback to $N1$. The game is ended after $N3$'s action as we

Fig. 5: Sub-Game for N3.

can prune the following branches: 1) to $N6$, the remaining route sequence is $N7$ and $N5$ by default as their best strategy have been solved (i.e., $N6$ delivers the package to $N7$, which in turn forwards to $N5$); 2) to $N4$, with $N4$ forwarding to $N5$ if it is normal while backing to $N3$ in malicious type. When the game terminates, each player gets a unique payoff following different branches. As

Algorithm 1 Dynamic Programming Algorithm to Solve Routing Game.

1: $setG \Leftarrow \emptyset$
2: $addNode(d, setG)$
3: $disValue \Leftarrow 1$
4: **repeat**
5:    **for all** $n \in N$ *and* $dis(n, d) == disValue$ **do**
6:       **if** $uncertain(n) == true$ **then**
7:          **for all** $n_p \in adj(n)$ *and* $dis(n_p, d) == disValue + 1$ **do**
8:             $addNode(n_p, todoS)$
9:          **end for**
10:      **end if**
11:      **if** $n \notin todoS$ **then**
12:         $addNode(n, setG)$
13:      **end if**
14:   **end for**
15:   **for all** $n \in todoS$ **do**
16:      **if** $\forall i \in adj(n)$ *and* $dis(i, d) == dis(n) - 1$ *and* $i \in sutG$ **then**
17:         $gambitTree \Leftarrow buildGame(n, d)$
18:         $equilibria \leftarrow solve(gamebitTree)$
19:         $removeNode(n, todoS)$
20:         $addNode(n, setG)$
21:      **end if**
22:   **end for**
23:   $disValue \Leftarrow disValue + 1$
24: **until** $s \in subG$

shown in the left most rectangle all the players (including $N2$ and $N4$ as they are benign collaborating nodes) equally share the system utility value 6 with 3 hops from $N3$ to $N5$ plus the shortest path from $N1$ to $N3$. However, on the rightmost branch, only five players ruling out $N2$ and $N4$ is allocated with the system utility 4. The system utility is resulting from 6 hops if $N3$ decides to deliver the package to $N4$ as the nature problematically chooses the malicious type for $N4$, which sends the package back to $N3$ to maximize the attack's utility. Once $N3$ receives the package from $N4$, it redelivers the package to $N6$ because $N3$ as a good player does not repeatedly send it back. To this end, $N2$ and $N4$ is uniformly allocated the delta (i.e., 4) between the utility system obtained (i.e., 4) and the maximum utility system could obtain (i.e., 8) as the payoff. The payoff of the remaining branches can also be calculated accordingly.

After that, a pure Nash equilibrium is generated by solving this sub-game (line 18) with Gambit software tools [35], and the best strategy for the node is updated according to the equilibrium. By solving the sub-game for $N3$, the strategy for $N3$ in the equilibrium is to deliver the package to $N6$, as the potential detriment on delayed delivery time to $N4$ due to attacks is greater than its comparative advantage of the shortest path. Thus, this node with the solved strategy is removed from $todoS$ (line 19) and absorbed in $setG$ (line 21). Once all the nodes in the distance of $disValue$ from the destination have been iterated and all the nodes in *todoS* satisfying conditions are computed for their best strategy, the algorithm increment the value of *disValue* one unit (line 23) and continue, until the starting point *s* is in the set *setG* (line 24).

5.3   Experiment Setup & Results

We demonstrate how our Bayesian game approach combined with the proposed dynamic programming algorithm can produce adaptation decisions about how to forward packages for each node in the routing example. Similar to the experiment results found on the Znn website, we statically analyzed a discretized region of the state space which represented different attack scenarios (i.e., malicious probability of $N2$ and $N4$). The entire experiment setup of the network structure is exactly shown in Figure 4. In addition, we also adopted a greedy algorithm for this routing application as the benchmark, and compared the system utility between these two approaches to demonstrate the superiority of game theory under security attacks. The experiment for the whole state space with Bayesian approach takes less than one minute and the solution generation time for each state is negligible.

Fig. 6: Results for interdomain route example: (a) Expected route in equilibrium; (b) System utility with game theory approach; (c) Delta between system utility from game theory approach and utility from greedy algorithm.

Figure 6 (a) presents the results of the strategy selection (i.e., expected package sequence) over two dimensions that correspond to the malicious probability of $N2$ and $N4$, respectively. Red triangle points denote that the strategy for $N1$ is $N2$, extending the range of *Probability_N2* to around $[0, 0.50]$. This is because when the chance of $N2$ coming under attack is less than 0.50, $N1$ should pass the package to $N2$, since $N2$ is in the shortest path to the destination; otherwise, $N1$ delivers the package to $N3$. Similarly, when the malicious probability of $N4$ is less than 0.35, the strategy for $N3$ reaching equilibrium is to deliver the package to $N4$ (i.e., blue square points), since the benefits of a short delivery time outweigh the potential detriment. For the remaining situations denoted by the black circle points, $N1$ passes the package to $N3$, which in turn forwards it to $N6$.

Figure 6 (b) describes the utility the system could obtain for the attacked components' equilibrium strategies. As expected, when the *Probability_N2* is greater than 50% and *Probability_N4* greater than 35% (i.e., black circle points in Figure 6 (a)), the utility system can gain is 6 as there are 4 hops in the expected sequence ⟨$N1$ $N3$ $N6$ $N7$ $N5$⟩). This plot also shows that the system utility increases progressively with decreasing probability of the compromised $N2$ and $N4$. When the *probability_N2* is 0, the expected utility increases to 8 (i.e., two hops in $\langle N1\ N2\ N5 \rangle$). Similarly, the utility reaches 7 with *probability_N4* 0 (i.e., three hops in $\langle N1\ N3\ N4\ N5 \rangle$).

Furthermore, we adopted a baseline that generates strategies for each node in a non-repeating fashion, passing the package to the adjacent node along the shortest path to the destination. The aim of this was to compare the utility between two different approaches dealing with security attacks. For the network as shown in Figure 4, the baseline firstly picks up the shortest path sequence $\langle N1\ N2\ N5 \rangle$. If $N2$ is compromised and sends the package back, $N1$ redelivers it to $N3$ instead of $N2$ since the package is received from $N2$. The system utility for the greedy algorithm is the expected value, the weighted average of utility for paths in different attack situations. Figure 6 (c) shows the delta between the utility produced by our game theory method and the utility produced by the baseline. During security attacks, we can see that the utility from the game theory approach is always higher than the greedy approach under security attacks. The delta is much more noticeable, especially in the situations where $N2$ and $N4$ are highly likely to be compromised (i.e., *Probability_N2* and *Probability_N4* close to 1). This is because game theory approaches can help the defenders to trade off the gains and losses due to perceived risks.

In summary, based on the preliminary results of our experiment, our game theory approach in the component level applies to self-adaptive applications. To adopt our approach, attacks information, such as various types with probabilities as well as its payoff, shall be provided from the *Analyzer*, to construct a Bayesian game based on system architectural structures. The results have also shown that game theory can enhance the performance of the system, especially when a potential attack is more likely to happen. In these situations, game theory approaches could help the defenders balance perceived risks by using underlying incentive mechanisms, and figure out the best response as the adaptation to be executed on the network using proven mathematics. Besides, our proposed dynamic programming algorithm is specific to this kind of application to optimize the game solving. Another potential application is the multi-agent finding (MAPF) problem where a spatial position in a path can be viewed as a node in the network [39,3]. Other optimization techniques might be adopted or customized for different applications with complicated game structures.

6 Related Work

Self-adaptive systems under security attacks need to make adaptation decisions as a response to a detected threat or to deviations from security goals and requirements [18]. Lorenzoli et al. [34] proposed a technique that could observe values at relevant program points and identified the execution contexts leading to a software failure so that mechanisms can be enabled for preventing future occurrences of failures of the same type. Bailey et al. [4] generated Role Based Access Control (RBAC) models to provide assurances for adaptations against insider threats. RBAC technique was also applied to cloud computing environment to provide appropriate security services according to the security level and dynamic changes of the common resources [44]. Tsigkanos et al. [41] explored the use of Bigraphical Reactive Systems to perform speculative threat analysis through model checking. Burmester et al. [5] described a threat model to incorporate typical characteristics of systems, such as survivability to abnormal behavior and possibility to recover after critically vulnerable states are reached. Dimkov et al. [14] discussed insider threats that span physical, cyber and social domains and present a framework Portunes integrating all three security domains to describe attacks. Nashif et al. [2] presented a multi-level intrusion detection system to detect network attacks within three levels of granularities and proactively protected against them by employing a fusion decision algorithm. Although, there are many different ways of dealing with security attacks in self-adaptive systems, it is notable that the application of game theory, with the characteristic of modeling the adversarial nature of security attacks and designing reliable defense with proven mathematics, has not gained the deserved attention.

Different sorts of games have been employed to study the actions of the defender and attacker. Dijk et al. [42] presented a two-player game that reasons about security scenarios where an attacker with uncertainty about its actions may periodically gain full control of an asset, with each side trying to maintain control as much as possible. An extension work by Farhang et al. [19] explicitly modeled the information gains for the attackers as they control assets, improving attacker's capability. Based on these work, Kinneer et al. [28] additionally considered multiple attacker types with different goals and capabilities by Bayesian Game. Instead of modeling the attackers as independent players, our work models the attacks on the component level, focusing on the defender modeling at the architecture level and possible deviations of component behaviors. Cámara et al. [6,8] adopted a game-theoretic perspective and model the system as turn-based stochastic multi-player games between different players where players can either cooperate to achieve the same goal or compete to achieve their own goals. In addition, Glazier et al. [23] used game-based approach to automatically reason and synthesize strategies for meta-manager by explicitly considering alternate potential future state, thus improving the performance of a collection of autonomic systems against a defined quality objective. Though, some of these existing works concern about competitive behaviors in a system when some components cannot be controlled and even behave according to conflicting goals with respect to other components in the system. None of them, to the best of our knowledge, proposed to model the Bayesian game in an architecture/component level and captured multiple attacks as component's variant types as well as the uncertainty due to unsuccessful compromise.

Game theory is also increasingly applied to network security. Frigault et al. [20] measured the network security in a dynamic environment with dynamic Bayesian networks-based model to incorporate temporal factors. Charles et al. [26] developed a packet forwarding game model under imperfect private monitoring. Their equilibria rely on the probability of cooperation after observing a defection, similar to our routing games in the evaluation. However, they looked at this problem from the perspective of network nodes, without considering the situation of being attacked and how to allocate rewards from the system utility for multiple components from the architecture perspective as illustrated in this work.

7   Conclusion and Future Work

In this paper, we have proposed a new framework for self-adaptive systems by adopting Bayesian game theory and modeled the system under security attacks as a multi-player game. An optimal adaptation strategy for responding to attacks is generated by computing the equilibrium to the game. One limitation is that we validate our approach on a simulated rather than an actual system, and we plan to further evaluate the applicability and scalability of the approach using case studies involving real systems. A second limitation is the simplification of the amount of uncertainty, such as restricting the number of component types under attacks and assuming the payoffs with zero-sum game, which might be more complex in the real world security landscape. Rather, we attempted to convey the idea of transforming the system architecture consisting of multiple components under attacks into a Bayesian game. While the equilibrium is sensitive to the probability distribution over types (i.e., malicious probability), sensitivity analysis are useful when the probability cannot be determined by the analysis with precision but lies within a known range. In addition, modeling attacks on component level, though more monitorable and easy to handle, cannot depict those attacks with highly motivated and capable adversaries willing to devote significant time and continuous attack to facilitate their malicious goals, known as advanced persistent threats (APTs) [28].

Moreover, we adopt pure equilibrium as the adaptation response. However, in practice, there will likely be multiple equilibria and no guarantee of uniqueness. While this is an area for future work, one possible way to overcome this is to choose the equilibrium with highest utility for the system. Another limitation, and a topic for future work, is that mixed equilibrium is another common solution for game theory. Its interpretation on system behaviors could be various and allows generation of different types of defense strategies for the system, which can be explored for different applications. For example, if the mixed strategy for N1 in routing game is choosing N2 and N3 in 50%/50% split as shown in Figure 4, we can consider that N1 may equally distribute its packages to N2 and N3 if multiple packages exist, or deliver its packages to N3 for the current time and to N2 next time. Also, the Bayesian games for these two examples were manually created by following the framework into the input language of the Gambit tool, to solve the equilibrium. In future, we are planning to construct the game in an automated way by supporting an architecture description interchange language, such as Acme [22].

Acknowledgements

The research is partially supported by the National Natural Science Foundation of China under Grant Nos. 61620106007 and 61751210, award N00014172899 from the Office of Naval Research and the NSA under Award No. H9823018D0008.

References

1. Web server and its types of attacks. https://www.greycampus.com/opencampus/ \ethical-hacking/web-server-and-its-types-of-attacks. Accessed: 2010-09-30.
2. Y. Al-Nashif, A. A. Kumar, S. Hariri, Y. Luo, F. Szidarovsky, and G. Qu. Multi-level intrusion detection system (ml-ids). In *2008 International Conference on Autonomic Computing*, pages 131–140, 2008.
3. Ofra Amir, Guni Sharon, and Roni Stern. Multi-agent pathfinding as a combinatorial auction. In *The Twenty-Ninth AAAI Conference on Artificial Intelligence (AAAI)*, pages 2003–2009, 2015.
4. Christopher Bailey, Lionel Montrieux, Rogério de Lemos, Yijun Yu, and Michel Wermelinger. Run-time generation, transformation, and verification of access control models for self-protection. In *9th International Symposium on Software Engineering for Adaptive and Self-Managing Systems, SEAMS 2014, Proceedings, Hyderabad, India, June 2-3, 2014*, pages 135–144, 2014.
5. Mike Burmester, Emmanouil Magkos, and Vassilios Chrissikopoulos. Modeling security in cyber-physical systems. *Int. J. Crit. Infrastructure Prot.*, 5(3-4):118–126, 2012.
6. Javier Cámara, Gabriel A. Moreno, and David Garlan. Stochastic game analysis and latency awareness for proactive self-adaptation. In *9th International Symposium on Software Engineering for Adaptive and Self-Managing Systems, SEAMS 2014, Proceedings, Hyderabad, India, June 2-3, 2014*, pages 155–164, 2014.
7. Javier Cámara, Gabriel A. Moreno, and David Garlan. Reasoning about human participation in self-adaptive systems. In *10th IEEE/ACM International Symposium on Software Engineering for Adaptive and Self-Managing Systems, SEAMS, Florence, Italy, May 18-19, 2015*, pages 146–156, 2015.
8. Javier Cámara, Gabriel A. Moreno, David Garlan, and Bradley R. Schmerl. Analyzing latency-aware self-adaptation using stochastic games and simulations. *ACM Trans. Auton. Adapt. Syst.*, 10(4):23:1–23:28, 2016.
9. Betty H. C. Cheng and et al. Software engineering for self-adaptive systems: A research roadmap. In *Software Engineering for Self-Adaptive Systems [outcome of a Dagstuhl Seminar]*, pages 1–26, 2009.
10. Shang-Wen Cheng, David Garlan, and Bradley R. Schmerl. Evaluating the effectiveness of the rainbow self-adaptive system. In *2009 ICSE Workshop on Software Engineering for Adaptive and Self-Managing Systems, SEAMS 2009, Vancouver, BC, Canada, May 18-19, 2009*, pages 132–141, 2009.
11. J. Cámara, D. Garlan, G.A. Moreno, and B. Schmerl. Chapter 7 - evaluating trade-offs of human involvement in self-adaptive systems. In Ivan Mistrik, Nour Ali, Rick Kazman, John Grundy, and Bradley Schmerl, editors, *Managing Trade-Offs in Adaptable Software Architectures*, pages 155 – 180. Morgan Kaufmann, Boston, 2017.
12. Rogério de Lemos and et al. Software engineering for self-adaptive systems: A second research roadmap. In *Software Engineering for Self-Adaptive Systems II - International Seminar, Dagstuhl Castle, Germany, October 24-29, 2010 Revised Selected and Invited Papers*, pages 1–32, 2010.
13. Premkumar T. Devanbu and Stuart G. Stubblebine. Software engineering for security: a roadmap. In *22nd International Conference on on Software Engineering, Future of Software Engineering Track, ICSE 2000, Limerick Ireland, June 4-11, 2000*, pages 227–239, 2000.

14. Trajce Dimkov, Wolter Pieters, and Pieter H. Hartel. Portunes: Representing attack scenarios spanning through the physical, digital and social domain. In *Automated Reasoning for Security Protocol Analysis and Issues in the Theory of Security - Joint Workshop, ARSPA-WITS 2010, Paphos, Cyprus, March 27-28, 2010. Revised Selected Papers*, pages 112–129, 2010.

15. Cuong T. Do, Nguyen H. Tran, Choong Seon Hong, Charles A. Kamhoua, Kevin A. Kwiat, Erik Blasch, Shaolei Ren, Niki Pissinou, and Sundaraja Sitharama Iyengar. Game theory for cyber security and privacy. *ACM Comput. Surv.*, 50(2):30:1–30:37, 2017.

16. Dmitry Dudorov, David Stupples, and Martin Newby. Probability analysis of cyber attack paths against business and commercial enterprise systems. In *2013 European Intelligence and Security Informatics Conference, Uppsala, Sweden, August 12-14, 2013*, pages 38–44, 2013.

17. Ahmed M. Elkhodary and Jon Whittle. A survey of approaches to adaptive application security. In *2007 ICSE Workshop on Software Engineering for Adaptive and Self-Managing Systems, SEAMS 2007, Minneapolis Minnesota, USA, May 20-26, 2007*, page 16, 2007.

18. Mahsa Emami-Taba. A game-theoretic decision-making framework for engineering self-protecting software systems. In *Proceedings of the 39th International Conference on Software Engineering, ICSE 2017, Buenos Aires, Argentina, May 20-28, 2017 - Companion Volume*, pages 449–452, 2017.

19. Sadegh Farhang and Jens Grossklags. Flipleakage: A game-theoretic approach to protect against stealthy attackers in the presence of information leakage. In *Decision and Game Theory for Security - 7th International Conference, GameSec 2016, New York, NY, USA, November 2-4, 2016, Proceedings*, pages 195–214, 2016.

20. Marcel Frigault, Lingyu Wang, Anoop Singhal, and Sushil Jajodia. Measuring network security using dynamic bayesian network. In *Proceedings of the 4th ACM Workshop on Quality of Protection, QoP 2008, Alexandria, VA, USA, October 27, 2008*, pages 23–30, 2008.

21. Drew Fudenberg and Jean Tirole. *Game Theory*. MIT press, 1991.

22. David Garlan, Robert T. Monroe, and David Wile. Acme: an architecture description interchange language. In *Proceedings of the 1997 conference of the Centre for Advanced Studies on Collaborative Research, November 10-13, 1997, Toronto, Ontario, Canada*, page 7, 1997.

23. Thomas J. Glazier and David Garlan. An automated approach to management of a collection of autonomic systems. In *IEEE 4th International Workshops on Foundations and Applications of Self* Systems, FAS*W@SASO/ICCAC 2019, Umea, Sweden, June 16-20, 2019*, pages 110–115, 2019.

24. M. Hajizadeh, T. V. Phan, and T. Bauschert. Probability analysis of successful cyber attacks in sdn-based networks. In *2018 IEEE Conference on Network Function Virtualization and Software Defined Networks (NFV-SDN)*, pages 1–6, 2018.

25. John C Harsanyi. Games with incomplete information played by bayesian players, i-iii. *Management Science*, 50(12):1804–1817, 2004.

26. Charles A. Kamhoua, Niki Pissinou, Alan Busovaca, and Kia Makki. Belief-free equilibrium of packet forwarding game in ad hoc networks under imperfect monitoring. In *29th International Performance Computing and Communications Conference, IPCCC 2010, 9-11 December 2010, Albuquerque, NM, USA*, pages 315–324, 2010.

27. Jeffrey O. Kephart and David M. Chess. The vision of autonomic computing. *IEEE Computer*, 36(1):41–50, 2003.

28. Cody Kinneer, Ryan Wagner, Fei Fang, Claire Le Goues, and David Garlan. Modeling observability in adaptive systems to defend against advanced persistent threats. In *Proceedings of the 17th ACM-IEEE International Conference on Formal Methods and Models for System Design, MEMOCODE 2019, La Jolla, CA, USA, October 9-11, 2019*, pages 10:1–10:11, 2019.

29. Marta Kwiatkowska, Gethin Norman, and David Parker. *Probabilistic Model Checking: Advances and Applications*, pages 73–121. Springer International Publishing, Cham, 2018.

30. Hagay Levin, Michael Schapira, and Aviv Zohar. Interdomain routing and games. In *Proceedings of the 40th Annual ACM Symposium on Theory of Computing, Victoria, British Columbia, Canada, May 17-20, 2008*, pages 57–66, 2008.

31. Hagay Levin, Michael Schapira, and Aviv Zohar. Interdomain routing and games. *SIAM J. Comput.*, 40(6):1892–1912, 2011.

32. Nianyu Li, Sridhar Adepu, Eunsuk Kang, and David Garlan. Explanations for human-on-the-loop: A probabilistic model checking approach. In *Proceedings of the 15th International Symposium on Software Engineering for Adaptive and Self-managing Systems (SEAMS)*, 2020. To appear.

33. Wyatt Lloyd, Michael J. Freedman, Michael Kaminsky, and David G. Andersen. Stronger semantics for low-latency geo-replicated storage. In *Proceedings of the 10th USENIX Symposium on Networked Systems Design and Implementation, NSDI 2013, Lombard, IL, USA, April 2-5, 2013*, pages 313–328, 2013.

34. Davide Lorenzoli, Leonardo Mariani, and Mauro Pezzè. Towards self-protecting enterprise applications. In *ISSRE 2007, The 18th IEEE International Symposium on Software Reliability, Trollhättan, Sweden, 5-9 November 2007*, pages 39–48, 2007.

35. Richard D. McKelvey, Andrew M. McLennan, and Theodore L. Turocy. Gambit: Software tools for game theory, version 16.0.1, 2018-02. http://www.gambit-project.org.

36. Martin J. Osborne and Ariel Rubinstein. A course in game theory. *MIT Press Books*, 1, 1994.

37. Lloyd S Shapley. A value for n-person games. *In Contributions to the Theory of Games*, vol. 2, 1953.

38. Yoav Shoham and Kevin Leyton-Brown. *Multiagent systems: Algorithmic, game-theoretic, and logical foundations.* Cambridge University Press, 2008.

39. Roykrong Sukkerd, Reid Simmons, and David Garlan. Tradeoff-focused contrastive explanation for mdp planning, 2020.

40. Milind Tambe. *Security and Game Theory - Algorithms, Deployed Systems, Lessons Learned.* Cambridge University Press, 2012.

41. Christos Tsigkanos, Liliana Pasquale, Carlo Ghezzi, and Bashar Nuseibeh. On the interplay between cyber and physical spaces for adaptive security. *IEEE Trans. Dependable Secur. Comput.*, 15(3):466–480, 2018.

42. Marten van Dijk, Ari Juels, Alina Oprea, and Ronald L. Rivest. Flipit: The game of "stealthy takeover". *J. Cryptology*, 26(4):655–713, 2013.

43. Danny Weyns, M. Usman Iftikhar, and Joakim Söderlund. Do external feedback loops improve the design of self-adaptive systems? a controlled experiment. In *Proceedings of the 8th International Symposium on Software Engineering for Adaptive and Self-Managing Systems, SEAMS 2013, San Francisco, CA, USA, May 20-21, 2013*, pages 3–12, 2013.

44. Youngmin Jung and Mokdong Chung. Adaptive security management model in the cloud computing environment. In *2010 The 12th International Conference on Advanced Communication Technology (ICACT)*, volume 2, pages 1664–1669, 2010.

An Abstract Contract Theory for Programs with Procedures*

Christian Lidström$^{(\boxtimes)}$ and Dilian Gurov

KTH Royal Institute of Technology, Stockholm, Sweden
{clid,dilian}@kth.se

Abstract. When developing complex software and systems, *contracts* provide a means for controlling the complexity by dividing the responsibilities among the components of the system in a hierarchical fashion. In specific application areas, dedicated *contract theories* formalise the notion of contract and the operations on contracts in a manner that supports best the development of systems in that area. At the other end, *contract meta-theories* attempt to provide a systematic view on the various contract theories by axiomatising their desired properties. However, there exists a noticeable gap between the most well-known contract meta-theory of Benveniste et al. [5], which focuses on the design of embedded and cyber-physical systems, and the established way of using contracts when developing general software, following Meyer's design-by-contract methodology [18]. At the core of this gap appears to be the notion of *procedure*: while it is a central unit of composition in software development, the meta-theory does not suggest an obvious way of treating procedures as components.

In this paper, we provide a first step towards a contract theory that takes procedures as the basic building block, and is at the same time an instantiation of the meta-theory. To this end, we propose an abstract contract theory for sequential programming languages with procedures, based on *denotational semantics*. We show that, on the one hand, the specification of contracts of procedures in *Hoare logic*, and their procedure-modular verification, can be cast naturally in the framework of our abstract contract theory. On the other hand, we also show our contract theory to fulfil the axioms of the meta-theory. In this way, we give further evidence for the utility of the meta-theory, and prepare the ground for combining our instantiation with other, already existing instantiations.

1 Introduction

Contracts. Loosely speaking, a *contract* for a software or system component is a means of specifying that the component obliges itself to guarantee a certain behaviour or result, provided that the user (or client) of the component obliges itself to fulfil certain constraints on how it interacts with the component.

---

* This work has been funded by the Swedish Governmental Agency for Innovation Systems (VINNOVA) under the AVerT project 2018-02727.

E. Guerra and M. Stoelinga (Eds.): FASE 2021, LNCS 12649, pp. 152–171, 2021.
https://doi.org/10.1007/978-3-030-71500-7_8

One of the earliest inspirations for the notion of software contracts came from the works of Floyd [10] and Hoare [15]. One outcome of this was *Hoare logic*, which is a way of assigning meaning to sequential programs *axiomatically*, through so-called Hoare triples. A Hoare triple $\{P\}S\{Q\}$ consists of two assertions P and Q over the program variables, called the pre-condition and post-condition, respectively, and a program S. The triple states that if the pre-condition P holds prior to executing S, then, if execution of S terminates, the post-condition Q will hold upon termination. With the help of additional, so-called *logical variables*, one can specify, with a Hoare triple, the desired relationship between the final values of certain variables (such as the return value of a procedure) and the initial values of certain other variables (such as the formal parameters of the procedure).

This style of specifying contracts has been advocated by Meyer [18], together with the design methodology Design-by-Contract. A central characteristic of this methodology is that it is well-suited for *independent implementation and verification*, where software components are developed independently from each other, based solely on the contracts, and without any knowledge of the implementation details of the other components.

Contract Theories. Since then, many other contract theories have emerged, such as Rely/Guarantee reasoning [16,22] and a number of Assume/Guarantee contract theories [4,6]. A contract theory typically formalises the notion of contract, and develops a number of operations on contracts that support typical design steps. This in turn has lead to a few developments of contract *meta-theories* (e.g. [5,2,8]), which aim at unifying these, in many cases incompatible, contract theories. The most comprehensive, and well-known, of these, is presented in Benveniste et al. [5], and is concerned specifically with the design of cyber-physical systems. Here, all properties are derived from a most abstract notion of a contract. The meta-theory focuses on the notion of contract *refinement*, and the operations of contract *conjunction* and *composition*. The intention behind refinement and composition is to support a top-down design flow, where contracts are decomposed iteratively into sub-contracts; the task is then to show that the composition of the sub-contracts refines the original contract. These operations are meant to enable *independent development* and *reuse* of components. In addition, the operation of conjunction is intended to allow the superimposition of contracts over *the same* component, when they concern different aspects of its behaviour. This also enables *component reuse*, by allowing contracts to reveal only the behaviour relevant to the different use cases.

Motivation and Contribution. The meta-theory of Benveniste et al. focuses on the design of embedded and cyber-physical systems. However, there exists a noticeable gap between this meta-theory and the way contracts are used when developing general software following Meyer's design-by-contract methodology. At the core of this gap appears to be the notion of *procedure*[1]. While the proce-

---

[1] We use the term "procedure", rather than "function" or "method", to refer to the well-known control abstraction mechanism of imperative programming languages.

dure is a central unit of composition in software development, the meta-theory does not suggest an obvious way of treating procedures as components. This situation is not fully satisfactory, since the software components of most embedded systems are implemented with the help of procedures (a typical C-module, for instance, would consist of a main function and a number of *helper* functions), and their development should ideally follow the same design flow as that of the embedded system as a whole.

In this paper we provide a first step towards a contract theory that takes procedures as the basic building block, and at the same time respects the axioms of the meta-theory. Our contract theory is abstract, so that it can be instantiated to any procedural language, and similarly to the meta-theory, is presented at the semantics level only. Then, in the context of a simplistic imperative programming language with procedures and its denotational semantics, we show that the specification of contracts of procedures in *Hoare logic*, and their procedure-modular verification, can be cast in the framework of our abstract contract theory. We also show that our contract theory is an instance of the meta-theory of Benveniste et al. With this we expect to contribute to the bridging of the gap mentioned above, and to give a formal justification of the design methodology supported by the meta-theory, when applied to the software components of embedded systems. Several existing contract theories have already been shown to instantiate the meta-theory. In providing a contract theory for procedural programs that also instantiates it, we increase the value of the meta-theory by providing further evidence for its universality. In addition, we prepare the theoretical ground for combining our instantiation with other instantiations, which may target components not to be implemented in software.

Our theoretical development should be seen as a proof-of-concept. In future work it will need to be extended to cover more programming language features, such as object orientation, multi-threading, and exceptions.

Related Work. Software contracts and operations on contracts have long been an area of intensive research, as evidenced, e.g., by [1]. We briefly mention some works related to our theory, in addition to the already mentioned ones.

Reasoning from multiple Hoare triples is studied in [21], in the context of unavailable source code, where new properties cannot be derived by re-verification. In particular, it is found that two Hoare-style rules, the standard rule of consequence and a generalised normalisation rule, are sufficient to infer, from a set of existing contracts for a procedure, any contract that is semantically entailed.

Often-changing source code is a problem for contract-based reasoning and contract reuse. In [13], abstract method calls are introduced to alleviate this problem. Fully abstract contracts are then introduced in [7], allowing reasoning about software to be decoupled from contract applicability checks, in a way that not all verification effort is invalidated by changes in a specification.

The relation between behavioural specifications and assume/guarantee-style contracts for modal transition systems is studied in [2], which shows how to build a contract framework from any specification theory supporting composition and refinement. This work is built on in [9], where a formal contract framework based on temporal logic is presented, allowing verification of correctness of contract refinement relative to a specific decomposition.

A survey of behavioural specification languages [14] found that existing languages are well-suited for expressing properties of software components, but it is a challenge to express how components interact, making it difficult to reason about system and architectural level properties from detailed design specifications. This provides additional evidence for the gap between contracts used in software verification and contracts as used in system design.

Structure. The paper is organised as follows. Section 2 recalls the concept of contract based design and the contract meta-theory considered in the present paper. In Section 3 we present a denotational semantics for programs with procedures, including a semantics for contracts for use in procedure-modular verification. Next, Section 4 presents our abstract contract theory for sequential programs with procedures. Then, we show in Section 5 that our contract theory fulfils the axioms of the meta-theory, while in Section 6 we show how the specification of contracts of procedures in Hoare logic and their procedure-modular verification can be cast in the framework of our abstract contract theory. We conclude with Section 7.

2   Contract Based Design

This section describes the concept of *contract based design*, and motivates its use in cyber-physical systems development. We then recall the contract meta-theory by Benveniste et al. [5].

2.1   Contract Based Design of Cyber-Physical Systems

Contract based design is an approach to systems design, where the system is developed in a top-down manner through the use of contracts for components, which are incrementally assembled so that they preserve the desired system-wide properties. Contracts are typically described by a set of *assumptions* the component makes on its environment, and a set of *guarantees* on the component's behaviour, given that it operates in an environment adhering to the assumptions [5].

Present-day cyber-physical systems, such as those found in the automotive, avionics and other industries, are extremely complex. Products assembled by Original Equipment Manufacturers (OEMs) often consist of components from a number of different suppliers, all using their own specialised design processes, system architectures, development platforms, and tools. This is also true inside the OEMs, where there are different teams with different viewpoints of the system, and their own design processes and tools. In addition, the system itself has several different aspects that need to be managed, such as the architecture, safety and security requirements, functional behaviour, and so on. Thus, a rigorous design framework is called for that can solve these design-chain management issues.

Contract based design addresses these challenges through the principles, at the specification level, of *refinement* and *abstraction*, which are processes for managing the design flow between different layers of abstraction, and *composition* and *decomposition*, which manage the flow at the same level of abstraction. Generally, when designing a system, at the top level of abstraction there will be an overall system specification (or contract). This *top-level contract* is then refined, to provide a more concrete contract for the system, and decomposed, in order to obtain contracts for the sub-systems, and to separate the different viewpoints of the system. A system design typically iterates the decomposition-and-refinement process, resulting in several layers of abstraction, until contracts are obtained that can be directly implemented, or for which implementations already exist. An important requirement on this methodology of hierarchical decomposition and refinement of contracts is that it must guarantee that when the low-level components implement their concrete contracts, and are combined to form the overall system, then the top-level, abstract, contract shall hold.

Furthermore, a contract framework in particular needs to support *independent development* and *component reuse*. That is, specifications for components, and their operations, must allow for components and specifications to be independently designed and implemented, and to be used in different parts of the system, each with their own assumptions on how the other components, the environment, behave. This is achieved through the principle operations on contracts: *refinement, composition,* and *conjunction.*

Refinement allows one to extract a contract at the appropriate level of abstraction. A desired property of refinement is that components which have been designed with reference to the more abstract (i.e., weaker) contract do not need to be re-designed after the refinement step. That is, in the early stages of development an OEM may have provided a weak contract for some subsystem to an external supplier, which implemented a component relying on this contract. As development of the system progresses, and the contract is refined, the component supplied externally should still operate according to its guarantees without needing to be changed, when instead assuming the new, refined, contract.

Composition enables one to combine contracts of different components into a contract for the larger subsystem obtained when combining the components. Again, a desirable property is that other components relying on one or more of the individual contracts, can, after composition of the contracts, assume the new contract and still perform its guarantees, without being re-designed, thus ensuring that subsystems can be independently implemented.

Finally, contract conjunction is another way of combining contracts, but now for the different viewpoints of a single component. This allows one to separate a contract into several different, finer contracts for the same component, revealing just enough information for each particular system that depends on it, so that it can be reused in different parts of the system, or in entirely different systems.

2.2   A Contract Meta-Theory

We consider the meta-theory described in [5]. The stated purpose of the meta-theory has been to distil the notion of a contract to its essence, so that it can be used in system design methodologies without ambiguities. In particular, the meta-theory has been developed to give support for design-chain management, and to allow *component reuse* and *independent development*. It has been shown that a number of concrete contract theories instantiate it, including assume/guarantee-contracts, synchronous Moore interfaces, and interface theories. To our knowledge, this is the only meta-theory of its purpose and scope.

We now present the formal definitions of the concepts defined in the meta-theory, and the properties that they entail. The meta-theory is defined only in terms of semantics, and it is up to particular concrete instantiations to provide a syntax.

Components. The most basic concept in the meta-theory is that of a *component*, which represents any concrete part of the system. Thus, we have an abstract component universe $\mathbb{M}$ with components $m \in \mathbb{M}$. Over pairs of components, we have a *composition* operation $\times$. This operation is partially defined, and two components m_1 and m_2 are called *composable* when $m_1 \times m_2$ is defined. In such cases, we call m_1 an *environment* for m_2, and vice versa. In addition, component composition must be both commutative and associative, in order to ensure that different components can be combined in any order.

Typically, components are *open*, in the sense that they contain functionality provided by other components, i.e., their environment. The environment in which a component is to be placed is often unknown at development time, and although a component cannot restrict it, it is designed for a certain context.

Contracts. In the meta-theory, the notion of *contract* is defined in terms of sets of components. The contract universe $\mathbb{C} \stackrel{\text{def}}{=} 2^{\mathbb{M}} \times 2^{\mathbb{M}}$ consists of contracts $\mathcal{C} = (E, M)$, where E and M are the sets of *environments* and *implementations* of $\mathcal{C}$, respectively. Importantly, each pair $(m_1, m_2) \in E \times M$ must be composable. This definition is intentionally abstract. The intuition is that contracts separate the responsibilities of a component from the expectations on its environment. Moreover, contracts are best seen as *weak specifications* of components: they should expose just enough information to be adequate for their purpose.

For a component m and a contract $\mathcal{C} = (E, M)$, we shall sometimes write $m \models^E \mathcal{C}$ for $m \in E$, and $m \models^M \mathcal{C}$ for $m \in M$. A contract $\mathcal{C}$ is said to be *consistent* if it has at least one implementation, and *compatible* if it has at least one environment.

Contract refinement. For two contracts $\mathcal{C}_1 = (E_1, M_1)$ and $\mathcal{C}_2 = (E_2, M_2)$, $\mathcal{C}_1$ is said to *refine* $\mathcal{C}_2$, denoted $\mathcal{C}_1 \preceq \mathcal{C}_2$, iff $M_1 \subseteq M_2$ and $E_2 \subseteq E_1$. As an axiom of the meta-theory, it is required that the greatest lower bound with respect to refinement exists, for all subsets of $\mathbb{C}$. Table 1 summarises the important properties of refinement and the other operations on contracts that a concrete

Table 1. Properties that hold in theories that adhere to the meta-theory.

#	Property
1	*Refinement.* When $\mathcal{C}_1 \preceq \mathcal{C}_2$, every implementation of $\mathcal{C}_1$ is also an implementation of $\mathcal{C}_2$.
2	*Shared refinement.* Any contract refining $\mathcal{C}_1 \wedge \mathcal{C}_2$ also refines $\mathcal{C}_1$ and $\mathcal{C}_2$. Any implementation of $\mathcal{C}_1 \wedge \mathcal{C}_2$ is a shared implementation of $\mathcal{C}_1$ and $\mathcal{C}_2$. Any environment for $\mathcal{C}_1$ and $\mathcal{C}_2$ is an environment for $\mathcal{C}_1 \wedge \mathcal{C}_2$.
3	*Independent implementability.* Compatible contracts can be independently implemented.
4	*Independent refinement.* For all contracts $\mathcal{C}_i$ and $\mathcal{C}'_i, i \in I$, if $\mathcal{C}_i, i \in I$ are compatible and $\mathcal{C}'_i \preceq \mathcal{C}_i, i \in I$ hold, then $\mathcal{C}'_i, i \in I$ are compatible and $\bigotimes_{i \in I} \mathcal{C}'_i \preceq \bigotimes_{i \in I} \mathcal{C}_i$
5	*Commutativity, sub-associativity.* For any finite sets of contracts $\mathcal{C}_i, i = 1, \ldots, n$, $\mathcal{C}_1 \otimes \mathcal{C}_2 = \mathcal{C}_2 \otimes \mathcal{C}_1$ and $\bigotimes_{1 \leq i < n} \mathcal{C}_i \preceq (\bigotimes_{1 \leq i < n} \mathcal{C}_i) \otimes \mathcal{C}_n$ holds.
6	*Sub-distributivity.* The following holds, if all contract compositions in the formula are well defined: $((\mathcal{C}_{11} \wedge \mathcal{C}_{21}) \otimes (\mathcal{C}_{12} \wedge \mathcal{C}_{22})) \preceq ((\mathcal{C}_{11} \otimes \mathcal{C}_{12}) \wedge (\mathcal{C}_{21} \otimes \mathcal{C}_{22}))$

contract theory needs to possess in order to be considered an instance of the meta-theory.

Contract conjunction. The *conjunction* of two contracts $\mathcal{C}_1$ and $\mathcal{C}_2$, denoted $\mathcal{C}_1 \wedge \mathcal{C}_2$, is defined as their greatest lower bound w.r.t. the refinement order. (The intention is that $(E_1, M_1) \wedge (E_2, M_2)$ should equal $(E_1 \cup E_2, M_1 \cap M_2)$; however, this cannot be taken as the definition since not every such pair necessarily constitutes a contract.) Then, we have the three desirable properties of conjunction listed in Table 1, which together are referred to as *shared refinement*.

Contract composition. The *composition* of two contracts $\mathcal{C}_1 = (E_1, M_1)$ and $\mathcal{C}_2 = (E_2, M_2)$, denoted $\mathcal{C}_1 \otimes \mathcal{C}_2 = (E, M)$, is defined when every two components $m_1 \in M_1$ and $m_2 \in M_2$ are composable, and must then be the least contract, w.r.t. the refinement order, satisfying the following conditions:

(i) $m_1 \in M_1 \wedge m_2 \in M_2 \Rightarrow m_1 \times m_2 \in M$;
(ii) $e \in E \wedge m_1 \in M_1 \Rightarrow m_1 \times e \in E_2$; and
(iii) $e \in E \wedge m_2 \in M_2 \Rightarrow e \times m_2 \in E_2$.

If all of the above is satisfied, then properties 3-6 of Table 1 hold. The intention is that composing two components implementing $\mathcal{C}_1$ and $\mathcal{C}_2$ should yield an implementation of $\mathcal{C}_1 \otimes \mathcal{C}_2$, and composing an environment of $\mathcal{C}_1 \otimes \mathcal{C}_2$ with an implementation of $\mathcal{C}_1$ should result in a valid environment for $\mathcal{C}_2$, and vice versa. This is important in order to enable independent development.

3   Denotational Semantics of Programs and Contracts

In this section we summarise the background needed to understand the formal developments later in the paper. First, we recall the standard denotational semantics of programs with procedures on a typical toy programming language.

Next, we summarise Hoare logic and contracts, and provide a semantic justification of procedure-modular verification, also based on denotational semantics.

3.1   The Denotational Semantics of Programs with Procedures

This section sketches the standard presentation of denotational semantics for procedural languages, as presented in textbooks such as [23,19]. This semantics is the inspiration for the definition of components in our abstract contract theory in Section 4.1. We start with a simplistic programming language not involving procedures, and add procedures later to the language.

The following toy sequential programming language is typically used to present the denotational semantics of imperative languages:

$$S ::= \text{skip} \mid \mathsf{x} := \mathsf{a} \mid S_1; S_2 \mid \text{if } b \text{ then } S_1 \text{ else } S_2 \mid \text{while } b \text{ do } S$$

where S ranges over statements, a over arithmetic expressions, and b over Boolean expressions.

To define the denotational semantics of the language, we define the set **State** of program states. A state $s \in$ **State** is a mapping from the program variables to, for simplicity, the set of integers.

The *denotation* of a statement S, denoted $[\![S]\!]$, is typically given as a partial function **State** $\hookrightarrow$ **State** such that $[\![S]\!](s) = s'$ whenever executing statement S from the initial state s terminates in state s'. In case that executing S from s does not terminate, the value of $[\![S]\!](s)$ is undefined. The definition of $[\![S]\!]$ proceeds by induction on the structure of S. For example, the meaning of sequential composition of statements is usually captured with relation composition, as given by the equation $[\![S_1; S_2]\!] \overset{\text{def}}{=} [\![S_1]\!] \circ [\![S_2]\!]$. For the treatment of the remaining statements of the language, the reader is referred to [23,19].

The definition of denotation captures through its type (as a partial function) that the execution of statements is deterministic. For non-deterministic programs, the type of denotations is relaxed to $[\![S]\!] \subseteq$ **State** $\times$ **State**; then, $(s, s') \in [\![S]\!]$ captures that there is an execution of S starting in s that terminates in s'. For technical reasons that will become clear below, we shall use this latter denotation type in our treatment.

Note that we could alternatively have chosen **State**$^+$ as the denotational domain, and most results would still hold in the context of finite-trace semantics. However, we chose to develop the theory with a focus on Hoare-logic and deductive verification. In fact, the domain **State** $\times$ **State** can be seen as a special case of finite traces. In future work, we will also investigate concrete contract languages based on this semantics, and extend the theory for that context.

Procedures and Procedure Calls. To extend the language and its denotational semantics with procedures and procedure calls, we follow again the approach of [23], but adapt it to an "open" setting, where some called procedures might not be declared. We consider programs in the context of a finite set $\mathcal{P}$ of procedure names (of some larger, "closed" program), and a set of *procedure declarations* of the form proc p is S_p, where $p \in \mathcal{P}$. Further, we extend the toy programming language with the statement call p.

Listing 1.1. An even-odd toy program.

```
proc even is if n = 0 then r := 1 else (n := n - 1; call odd);
proc odd  is if n = 0 then r := 0 else (n := n - 1; call even)
```

As an example, Listing 1.1 shows a (closed) program in the toy language, implementing two mutually recursive procedures. The procedures check whether the value of the global variable n is even or odd, respectively, and assign the corresponding truth value to the variable r.

Due to the (potential) recursion in the procedure declarations, the denotation of call p, and thus of the whole language, cannot be defined by structural induction as directly as before. We therefore define, for any set $P \subseteq \mathcal{P}$ of procedure names, the set $\mathbf{Env}_P = P \to 2^{\mathbf{State} \times \mathbf{State}}$ of *procedure environments*, each environment $\rho \in \mathbf{Env}_P$ thus providing a denotation for each procedure in P.

Let $\mathbf{Env} \stackrel{\text{def}}{=} \bigcup_{P \subseteq \mathcal{P}} \mathbf{Env}_P$ be the set of all procedure environments. We define a partial order relation $\sqsubseteq$ on procedure environments, as follows. For any two procedure environments $\rho \in \mathbf{Env}_P$ and $\rho' \in \mathbf{Env}_{P'}$, $\rho \sqsubseteq \rho'$ if and only if $P \subseteq P'$ and $\forall p \in P.\ \rho(p) \subseteq \rho'(p)$.

Recall that a *complete lattice* is a partial order, every set of elements of which has a greatest lower bound (*glb*) within the domain of the lattice (see, e.g., [23]). It is easy to show that for any $P \subseteq \mathcal{P}$, $(\mathbf{Env}_P, \sqsubseteq)$ is a complete lattice, since a greatest lower bound will exist within $\mathbf{Env}_P$. Then, the least upper bound (*lub*) $\rho_1 \sqcup \rho_2$ of any two function environments $\rho_1 \in \mathbf{Env}_{P_1}$ and $\rho_2 \in \mathbf{Env}_{P_2}$ also exists, and is the environment $\rho \in \mathbf{Env}_{P_1 \cup P_2}$ such that $\forall p \in P_1 \cup P_2.\ \rho(p) = \rho_1(p) \cup \rho_2(p)$.

We will sometimes need a procedure environment that maps every procedure in P to $\mathbf{State} \times \mathbf{State}$, and we shall denote this environment by $\rho_P^\top$.

Next, for sets of procedures, we shall need the notion of *interface*, which is a pair (P^-, P^+) of disjoint sets of procedure names, where $P^+ \subseteq \mathcal{P}$ is a set of *provided* (or declared) procedures, and $P^- \subseteq \mathcal{P}$ a set of *required* (or called, but not declared) ones.

Then, we (re)define the notion of denotation of statements S in the context of a given interface (P^-, P^+) and environments $\rho^- \in \mathbf{Env}_{P^-}$ and $\rho^+ \in \mathbf{Env}_{P^+}$, and denote it by $[\![S]\!]_{\rho^-}^{\rho^+}$. In particular, we define $[\![$call $p]\!]_{\rho^-}^{\rho^+}$ as $\rho^-(p)$ when $p \in P^-$ and as $\rho^+(p)$ when $p \in P^+$.

Intuitively, the denotation of a call to a procedure should be equal to the denotation of the body of the latter. We therefore introduce, given an environment $\rho^- \in \mathbf{Env}_{P^-}$, the function $\xi : \mathbf{Env}_{P^+} \to \mathbf{Env}_{P^+}$ defined by $\xi(\rho^+)(p) \stackrel{\text{def}}{=} [\![S_p]\!]_{\rho^-}^{\rho^+}$ for any $\rho^+ \in \mathbf{Env}_{P^+}$ and $p \in P^+$, and consider its fixed points. By the Knaster-Tarski Fixed-Point Theorem (as stated, e.g., in [23]), since $(\mathbf{Env}_{P^+}, \sqsubseteq)$ is a complete lattice and ξ is monotonic, ξ has a least fixed-point ρ_0^+.

Finally, we define the notion of *standard denotation* of statement S in the context of a given interface (P^-, P^+) and environment $\rho^- \in \mathbf{Env}_{P^-}$, denoted $[\![S]\!]_{\rho^-}$, by $[\![S]\!]_{\rho^-} \stackrel{\text{def}}{=} [\![S]\!]_{\rho^-}^{\rho_0^+}$, where ρ_0^+ is the least fixed-point defined above.

For example, for the closed program in Listing 1.1, we have an interface with $P^+ = \{even, odd\}$ and $P^- = \varnothing$. Then, $(s, s') \in [\![S_{even}]\!]_{\rho^-}^{\rho^+}$ if either $s(n) = 0$ and $s' = s[r \mapsto 1]$, or else if $s(n) > 0$ and $(s[n \mapsto s(n) - 1], s') \in \rho^+(odd)$. The denotation $[\![S_{odd}]\!]_{\rho^-}^{\rho^+}$ is analogous. The resulting least fixed-point ρ_0^+ is such that $(s, s') \in [\![S_{even}]\!]_{\rho^-}$, or equivalently $(s, s') \in [\![S_{even}]\!]_{\rho^-}^{\rho_0^+}$, whenever $s(n) \geq 0$, and either $s(n)$ is even and then $s'(n) = 0$ and $s'(r) = 1$, or else $s(n)$ is odd and then $s'(n) = 0$ and $s'(r) = 0$. The standard denotation $[\![S_{odd}]\!]_{\rho^-}$ of odd is analogous.

3.2   Hoare Logic and Contracts

In this section we summarise the denotational semantics of Hoare logic and the semantic justification of procedure-modular verification, as developed by the second author in [12]. These formalisations serve as the starting point for the definition of contracts in our contract theory developed in Section 4.2.

Hoare Logic. The basic judgement of Hoare logic [15] is the Hoare triple, written $\{P\}S\{Q\}$, where P and Q are assertions over the program state, and S is a program statement. The Hoare triple signifies that if the statement S is executed from a state that satisfies P (called the pre-condition), and if this execution terminates, then the final state of the execution will satisfy Q (called the post-condition). Additionally, so-called *logical variables* can be used within a Hoare triple, to specify the desired relationship between the values of variables after execution and the values of variables before execution. The values of the program variables are defined by the notion of state; to give a meaning to the logical variables we shall use *interpretations* $\mathcal{I}$. We shall write $s \models_{\mathcal{I}} P$ to signify that the assertion P is true w.r.t. state s and interpretation $\mathcal{I}$. The formal validity of a Hoare triple is denoted by $\models_{par} \{P\}S\{Q\}$, where the subscript signifies that validity is in terms of *partial correctness*, where termination of the execution of S is not required.

An example of a Hoare triple, stating the desired behaviour of procedure odd from Listing 1.1, is shown below, where we use the logical variable n_0 to capture to the value of n prior to execution of odd:

$$\{n \geq 0 \wedge n = n_0\} \; S_{odd} \; \{(n_0 \bmod 2 = 0 \Rightarrow r = 0) \wedge (n_0 \bmod 2 = 1 \Rightarrow r = 1)\} \quad (1)$$

Procedure *even* is specified analogously.

Hoare logic comes with a proof calculus for reasoning in terms of Hoare triples, consisting of proof rules for the different types of statements of the programming language. An example is the rule for sequential composition:

$$\frac{\{P\}\,S_1\,\{R\} \qquad \{R\}\,S_2\,\{Q\}}{\{P\}\,S_1; S_2\,\{Q\}} \quad \text{COMPOSITION}$$

which essentially states that if executing S_1 from any state satisfying P terminates (if at all) in some state satisfying R, and executing S_2 from any state satisfying R terminates (if at all) in some state satisfying Q, then it is the case that executing the composition $S_1; S_2$ from any state satisfying P terminates (if at all) in some state satisfying Q. The proof system is sound and relatively complete w.r.t. the denotational semantics of the programming language (see, e.g., [23,19]).

Hoare Logic Contracts. One can view a Hoare triple $\{P\}S\{Q\}$ as a *contract* $C = (P, Q)$ imposed on the program S. In many contexts it is meaningful to separate the contract from the program; for instance, if the program is yet to be implemented. In our earlier work [12], we gave such contracts a denotational semantics as follows:

$$[\![C]\!] \stackrel{\text{def}}{=} \{(s, s') \mid \forall \mathcal{I}. (s \models_{\mathcal{I}} P \Rightarrow s' \models_{\mathcal{I}} Q)\} \tag{2}$$

The rationale behind this definition is the following desirable property: a program *meets* a contract whenever its denotation is subsumed by the denotation of the contract, i.e., $S \models_{par} C$ if and only if $[\![S]\!] \subseteq [\![C]\!]$.

For example, for the contract C_{odd} induced by (1) we have that $(s, s') \in [\![C_{odd}]\!]$ if and only if either $s(n) < 0$, or else $s'(r) = 0$ if $s(n)$ is even and $s'(r) = 1$ if $s(n)$ is odd. The denotation of C_{even} is analogous.

The Denotational Semantics of Programs with Procedure Contracts. Let S be a program with procedures, and let every declared procedure $p \in \mathcal{P}$ be equipped with a procedure contract C_p. *Procedure-modular verification* refers to techniques that verify every procedure in isolation. The key to this is to handle procedure calls by using the contract of the called procedure rather than its body (i.e., by *contracting* rather than by *inlining* [7]). In [12], a semantic justification of this is given by means of a *contract-relative* denotational semantics of statements. The intuition behind this semantics is that procedure calls are given a meaning through the denotation of the contract of the called procedure, rather than through the denotation of its body.

The contract-relative denotational semantics of a statement S, denoted $[\![S]\!]^{cr}$, is defined with the help of the *contract environment* ρ_c that is induced by the procedure contracts, i.e., $\rho_c(p) \stackrel{\text{def}}{=} [\![C_p]\!]$ for all $p \in \mathcal{P}$, as $[\![S]\!]^{cr} \stackrel{\text{def}}{=} [\![S]\!]_{\rho_c}$. Notice that this definition does not involve solving any recursive equations (i.e., finding fixed points), and gives rise to a contract-relative notion of when a statement meets a contract, namely $S \models_{par}^{cr} C$ if and only if $[\![S]\!]^{cr} \subseteq [\![C]\!]$. This is exactly the correctness notion that is the target of procedure-modular verification. As shown in [12], this notion is *sound* w.r.t. the original notion $S \models_{par} C$, in the sense that $S \models_{par}^{cr} C$ entails $S \models_{par} C$. In other words, verifying a program procedure-modularly establishes that the program is correct w.r.t. its contract in the standard sense.

For example, the contract-relative semantics of S_{even} is such that $(s, s') \in [\![S_{even}]\!]^{cr}$ if either $s(n) < 0$, or $s(n) = 0$ and $s' = s[r \mapsto 1]$, or else $s'(r) = 1$

if $s(n)$ is even and $s'(r) = 0$ if $s(n)$ is odd. The contract-relative semantics of S_{odd} is analogous. Then, it is easy to check that both $S_{even} \models^{cr}_{par} C_{even}$ and $S_{odd} \models^{cr}_{par} C_{odd}$ hold.

4 An Abstract Contract Theory

This section presents an abstract contract theory for programs with procedures. The theory builds on the basic notion of *denotation* as a binary relation over states. As we will show later, it is both an abstraction of the denotational semantic view on programs with procedures and procedure contracts presented in Sections 3.1 and 3.2, and an instantiation of the meta-theory described in Section 2.2.

4.1 Components

In the context of a concrete programming language, we view a component as a module, consisting of a collection of procedures that are *provided* by the module. The module may call *required* procedures that are external to the module. The way the provided procedures transform the program state upon a call depends on how the required procedures transform the state. We take this observation as the basis of our abstract setting, in which state transformers are modelled as denotations (i.e., as binary relations over states). A component will thus be simply a mapping from denotations of the required procedures to denotations of the provided ones, both captured through the notion of procedure environments.

The contract theory is abstract, in that it is not defined for a particular programming language, and may be instantiated with any procedural language. As with the meta-theory, the abstract contract theory is also defined only on the semantic level.

Recall the notions and notation from Section 3.1. A component *interface* $I = (P^-, P^+)$ is a pair of disjoint, finite sets of procedure names, of the required and the provided ones, respectively.

Definition 1 (Component). *A component m with interface $I_m = (P^-_m, P^+_m)$ is a mapping $m : \mathbf{Env}_{P^-_m} \to \mathbf{Env}_{P^+_m}$.*

Let $\mathcal{M}$ denote the universe of all components over $\mathcal{P}$.

We assume that any system is built up from a set of *base components*, the simplest components from which more complex components are then obtained by composition. The base components must be *monotonic* functions over the lattice defined in Section 3.1.

When $P^-_m = \varnothing$, we shall identify m with an element of $\mathbf{Env}_{P^+_m}$. In other words, when a component is *closed*, i.e., is not dependent on any external procedures, the provided environment is constant.

Definition 2 (Component composability). *Two components m_1 and m_2 are composable iff $P^+_{m_1} \cap P^+_{m_2} = \varnothing$.*

When defining the composition of two components, particular care is required in the treatment of procedure names that are provided by one of the components while required by the other. Let $\mu x.\ f(x)$ denote the least fixed-point of a function f, when it exists.

Definition 3 (Component composition). *Given two composable components* $m_1 : \mathbf{Env}_{P_{m_1}^-} \to \mathbf{Env}_{P_{m_1}^+}$ *and* $m_2 : \mathbf{Env}_{P_{m_2}^-} \to \mathbf{Env}_{P_{m_2}^+}$, *their composition is defined as a mapping* $m_1 \times m_2 : \mathbf{Env}_{P_{m_1 \times m_2}^-} \to \mathbf{Env}_{P_{m_1 \times m_2}^+}$ *such that:*

$$P_{m_1 \times m_2}^+ \stackrel{\text{def}}{=} P_{m_1}^+ \cup P_{m_2}^+$$

$$P_{m_1 \times m_2}^- \stackrel{\text{def}}{=} (P_{m_1}^- \cup P_{m_2}^-) \setminus (P_{m_1}^+ \cup P_{m_2}^+)$$

$$m_1 \times m_2 \stackrel{\text{def}}{=} \lambda \rho_{m_1 \times m_2}^- \in \mathbf{Env}_{P_{m_1 \times m_2}^-}.\ \mu\rho.\ \chi_{m_1 \times m_2}^+(\rho)$$

where $\chi_{m_1 \times m_2}^+ : \mathbf{Env}_{P_{m_1 \times m_2}^+} \to \mathbf{Env}_{P_{m_1 \times m_2}^+}$ *is defined, in the context of a given* $\rho_{m_1 \times m_2}^- \in \mathbf{Env}_{P_{m_1 \times m_2}^-}$, *as follows. Let* $\rho_{m_1 \times m_2}^+ \in \mathbf{Env}_{P_{m_1 \times m_2}^+}$, *and let* $\rho_{m_1}^- \in \mathbf{Env}_{P_{m_1}^-}$ *be the environment defined by:*

$$\rho_{m_1}^-(p) \stackrel{\text{def}}{=} \begin{cases} \rho_{m_1 \times m_2}^+(p) & \text{if } p \in P_{m_1}^- \cap P_{m_2}^+ \\ \rho_{m_1 \times m_2}^-(p) & \text{if } p \in P_{m_1}^- \setminus P_{m_2}^+ \end{cases}$$

and let $\rho_{m_2}^- \in \mathbf{Env}_{P_{m_2}^-}$ *be defined symmetrically. We then define:*

$$\chi_{m_1 \times m_2}^+(\rho_{m_1 \times m_2}^+)(p) \stackrel{\text{def}}{=} \begin{cases} m_1(\rho_{m_1}^-)(p) & \text{if } p \in P_{m_1}^+ \\ m_2(\rho_{m_2}^-)(p) & \text{if } p \in P_{m_2}^+ \end{cases}$$

In the above definition, $\chi_{m_1 \times m_2}^+$ represents the denotations of the procedure *bodies* of the procedures provided by the two composed components, given denotations of procedure *calls* to the same procedures. The choice of least fixed-point will be crucial for the proof of Theorem 2(i) in Section 4.2 below.

The definition is well-defined, in the sense that the stated least fixed-points exist, and the resulting components are monotonic functions.

Theorem 1. *Component composition is well-defined.*

The existence of a least fixed-point follows from the Knaster-Tarski Fixed-Point Theorem, as stated, e.g., in [23]. It can then be shown, by structural induction, that composition is well-defined. For lack of space, the proofs of all theorems, some of which are conceptually not very involved but rather verbose, are omitted here. The full proofs can be found in the accompanying technical report [17].

4.2   Denotational Contracts

We now define the notion of denotational contracts c in the style of *assume/guarantee contracts* [4,6]. Contracts shall also be given interfaces.

Definition 4 (Denotational contract). *A denotational contract c with interface $I_c = (P_c^-, P_c^+)$ is a pair (ρ_c^-, ρ_c^+), where $\rho_c^- \in \mathbf{Env}_{P_c^-}$ and $\rho_c^+ \in \mathbf{Env}_{P_c^+}$.*

The intended interpretation of the environment pair is as follows: *assuming* that the denotation of every called procedure $p \in P_c^-$ is subsumed by $\rho_c^-(p)$, then it is *guaranteed* that the denotation of every provided procedure $p' \in P_c^+$ is subsumed by $\rho_c^+(p')$.

Definition 5 (Contract implementation). *A component m with interface $I_m = (P_m^-, P_m^+)$ is an implementation for, or implements, a contract $c = (\rho_c^-, \rho_c^+)$ with interface $I_c = (P_c^-, P_c^+)$, denoted $m \models c$, iff $P_c^- \subseteq P_m^-$, $P_m^+ \subseteq P_c^+$, and $m(\rho_c^- \sqcup \rho_{P_m^- \backslash P_c^-}^\top) \sqsubseteq \rho_c^+$.*

The reason for not requiring the interfaces to be equal is that we aim at a subset relation between components implementing a contract and those implementing a refinement of said contract, in the meta-theory instantiation.

For a mapping $h : A \to B$ and set $A' \subseteq A$, let $h_{|A'}$ denote as usual the restriction of h on A'.

Definition 6 (Contract environment). *A component m is an environment for contract c iff, for any implementation m' of c, m and m' are composable, and $\forall \rho_{m \times m'}^- \in \mathbf{Env}_{P_{m \times m'}^-} . \ (m \times m')(\rho_{m \times m'}^-)_{|P_c^+} \sqsubseteq \rho_c^+$.*

Intuitively, an environment of a contract c is then a component such that when it is composed with an implementation of c, the composition will operate satisfactorily with respect to the guarantee of the contract.

We will now define the refinement relation, and the conjunction and composition operations, on contracts.

Definition 7 (Contract refinement). *A contract c refines contract c', denoted $c \preceq c'$, iff $\rho_{c'}^- \sqsubseteq \rho_c^-$ and $\rho_c^+ \sqsubseteq \rho_{c'}^+$, where $\sqsubseteq$ is the partial order relation defined in Section 3.1.*

The refinement relation reflects the intention that if a contract c refines another contract c', then any component implementing c should also implement c'.

Definition 8 (Contract conjunction). *The conjunction of two contracts $c_1 = (\rho_{c_1}^-, \rho_{c_1}^+)$ and $c_2 = (\rho_{c_2}^-, \rho_{c_2}^+)$ is the contract $c_1 \wedge c_2 \overset{\text{def}}{=} (\rho_{c_1}^- \sqcup \rho_{c_2}^-, \rho_{c_1}^+ \sqcap \rho_{c_2}^+)$, where $\sqcup$ and $\sqcap$ are the lub and glb operations of the lattice, respectively.*

This definition is consistent with the intention that any contract that refines $c_1 \wedge c_2$ should also refine c_1 and c_2 individually. The interface of $c_1 \wedge c_2$ is then $I_{c_1 \wedge c_2} = (P_{c_1}^- \cup P_{c_2}^-, P_{c_1}^+ \cap P_{c_2}^+)$. Note that while this is the interface in general, conjunction of contracts is typically used to merge different viewpoints of *the same* component, and in that case $I_{c_1} = I_{c_2} = I_{c_1 \wedge c_2}$.

Definition 9 (Contract composability). *Two contracts $c_1 = (\rho_{c_1}^-, \rho_{c_1}^+)$ and $c_2 = (\rho_{c_2}^-, \rho_{c_2}^+)$ with interfaces $I_{c_1} = (P_{c_1}^-, P_{c_1}^+)$ and $I_{c_2} = (P_{c_2}^-, P_{c_2}^+)$ are composable if: (i) $P_{c_1}^+ \cap P_{c_2}^+ = \varnothing$, (ii) $\forall p \in P_{c_1}^- \cap P_{c_2}^+ . \ \rho_{c_2}^+(p) \subseteq \rho_{c_1}^-(p)$, and (iii) $\forall p \in P_{c_2}^- \cap P_{c_1}^+ . \ \rho_{c_1}^+(p) \subseteq \rho_{c_2}^-(p)$.*

The conditions for composability ensure that the mutual guarantees of the two contracts meet each other's assumptions.

Definition 10 (Contract composition). *The composition of two composable contracts $c_1 = (\rho_{c_1}^-, \rho_{c_1}^+)$ and $c_2 = (\rho_{c_2}^-, \rho_{c_2}^+)$, with interfaces $I_{c_1} = (P_{c_1}^-, P_{c_1}^+)$ and $I_{c_2} = (P_{c_2}^-, P_{c_2}^+)$, respectively, is the contract $c_1 \otimes c_2 \stackrel{\text{def}}{=} (\rho_{c_1 \otimes c_2}^-, \rho_{c_1}^+ \sqcup \rho_{c_2}^+)$, where:*

$$\rho_{c_1 \otimes c_2}^- \stackrel{\text{def}}{=} (\rho_{c_1}^- \sqcap \rho_{c_2}^-)\big|_{(P_{c_1}^- \cup P_{c_2}^-) \setminus (P_{c_1}^+ \cup P_{c_2}^+)}$$

The interface of $c_1 \otimes c_2$ is $I_{c_1 \otimes c_2} = ((P_{c_1}^- \cup P_{c_2}^-) \setminus (P_{c_1}^+ \cup P_{c_2}^+), P_{c_1}^+ \cup P_{c_2}^+)$.

Theorem 2. *For any composable contracts c_1 and c_2, and any implementations $m_1 \models c_1$ and $m_2 \models c_2$, m_1 and m_2 are composable, and $c_1 \otimes c_2$ is the least contract (w.r.t. refinement order) for which the following properties hold:*

(i) $m_1 \times m_2 \models c_1 \otimes c_2$,
(ii) if m is an environment to $c_1 \otimes c_2$, then $m_1 \times m$ is an environment to c_2,
(iii) if m is an environment to $c_1 \otimes c_2$, then $m \times m_2$ is an environment to c_1.

5   Connection to Meta-Theory

In this section we show that the abstract contract theory presented in Section 4 instantiates the meta-theory described in Section 2.2.

In our instantiation of the meta-theory, we consider as the abstract component universe $\mathbb{M}$ the same universe of components $\mathcal{M}$ as defined in Section 4.1. To distinguish the contracts of the meta-theory from those of the abstract theory, we shall always denote the former by $\mathcal{C}$ and the latter by c. Recall that a contract $\mathcal{C}$ is a pair (E, M), where $E, M \subseteq \mathcal{M}$. The formal connection between the two notions is established with the following definition.

Definition 11 (Induced contract). *Let c be a denotational contract. It induces the contract $\mathcal{C}_c = (E_c, M_c)$, where $E_c \stackrel{\text{def}}{=} \{m \in \mathcal{M} \mid m$ is an environment for $c\}$ and $M_c \stackrel{\text{def}}{=} \{m \in \mathcal{M} \mid m \models c\}$.*

Since contract implementation requires that the implementing component's provided functions are a subset of the contract's provided functions, every component m such that $P_m^+ \cap P_c^+ = \varnothing$ is composable with every component in M_c.

The definitions of implementation, refinement and conjunction of denotational contracts make this straightforward definition of induced contracts possible, so that it directly results in refinement as set membership and conjunction as lub w.r.t. the refinement order.

Theorem 3. *The contract theory of Section 4 instantiates the meta-theory of Benveniste et al. [5], in the sense that composition of components is associative and commutative, and for any two contracts c_1 and c_2:*

(i) $c_1 \preceq c_2$ iff $\mathcal{C}_{c_1}$ refines $\mathcal{C}_{c_2}$ according to the definition of the meta-theory,

(ii) $C_{c_1 \wedge c_2}$ *is the conjunction of* C_{c_1} *and* C_{c_2} *as defined in the meta-theory, and*
(iii) $C_{c_1 \otimes c_2}$ *is the composition of* C_{c_1} *and* C_{c_2} *as defined in the meta-theory.*

The proof is straightforward, since many definitions of the contract theory are deliberately similar to their counterparts in the meta-theory.

Let us now return to our example from Section 3. When applying Contract Based Design, contracts at the more abstract level will be decomposed into contracts at the more concrete level. So, for our example, we might have at the top level a contract $c = (\rho_c^-, \rho_c^+)$ with interface $(\varnothing, \{even, odd\})$, where $\rho_c^- = \varnothing$, and where $\rho_c^+ \in \mathbf{Env}_{P_c^+}$ maps *even* to the set of pairs (s, s') such that whenever $s(n)$ is non-negative and even, then $s'(r) = 1$, and when $s(n)$ is non-negative and odd, then $s'(r) = 0$, and maps *odd* in a dual manner. This contract could then be decomposed into two contracts c_{even} and c_{odd}, so that $\rho_{c_{even}}^+(even) \stackrel{\text{def}}{=} \rho_c^+(even)$ and $\rho_{c_{even}}^-(odd) \stackrel{\text{def}}{=} \rho_c^+(odd)$, and c_{odd} is analogous. Then, we would have $c_{even} \otimes c_{odd} \preceq c$, and for any two components m_{even} and m_{odd} such that $m_{even} \models c_{even}$ and $m_{odd} \models c_{odd}$, it would hold that $m_{even} \times m_{odd} \models c$.

6   Connection to Programs with Procedures

In this section we discuss how our abstract contract theory from Section 4 relates to programs with procedures as presented in Section 3.1, and how it relates to Hoare logic and procedure-modular verification as presented in Section 3.2.

First, we define how to abstract the denotational notion of procedures into components in the abstract theory, based on the function ξ from Section 3.1.

Definition 12 (From procedure sets to components). *For any set of procedures* P^+, *calling procedures* P', *we define the component* $m : \mathbf{Env}_{P_m^-} \to \mathbf{Env}_{P_m^+}$, *where* $P_m^- \stackrel{\text{def}}{=} P' \setminus P_m^+$ *and* $P_m^+ \stackrel{\text{def}}{=} P^+$, *so that* $\forall \rho_m^- \in \mathbf{Env}_{P_m^-}. \forall p \in P_m^+. m(\rho_m^-)(p) \stackrel{\text{def}}{=} [\![S_p]\!]_{\rho_m^-}$.

As the next result shows, procedure set abstraction and component composition commute. Together with commutativity and associativity of component composition, this means that the initial grouping of procedures into components is irrelevant, and that one can start with abstracting each individual procedure into a component.

Theorem 4. *For any two disjoint sets of procedures* P_1^+ *and* P_2^+, *abstracted individually into components* m_1 *and* m_2, *respectively, and* $P_1^+ \cup P_2^+$ *abstracted into component* m, *it holds that* $m_1 \times m_2 = m$.

The result is a direct consequence of Definition 12, Definition 3, and the well-known Bekić's Lemma [3] about simultaneous fixed-points.

Component abstraction example. Let us illustrate the theorem on our even-odd example (however, the example does not really illustrate Bekić's Lemma, since the two procedures do not call themselves).

By Definition 12, the procedure set $\{even\}$ is abstracted into component $m_{even} : \mathbf{Env}_{\{odd\}} \to \mathbf{Env}_{\{even\}}$ with interface $(\{odd\}, \{even\})$, so that $\forall \rho^- \in \mathbf{Env}_{\{odd\}}.\ m(\rho^-)(even) = [\![S_{even}]\!]_{\rho^-}$. By definition, $[\![S_{even}]\!]_{\rho^-}$ is equal to $[\![S_{even}]\!]_{\rho^-}^{\rho_0^+}$, where ρ_0^+ is the least fixed point of $\xi : \mathbf{Env}_{\{even\}} \to \mathbf{Env}_{\{even\}}$ defined by $\xi(\rho^+)(even) \overset{\text{def}}{=} [\![S_{even}]\!]_{\rho^-}^{\rho^+}$ for any $\rho^+ \in \mathbf{Env}_{\{even\}}$. Notice, however, that procedure $even$ does not have any calls to itself, so $[\![S_{even}]\!]_{\rho^-}^{\rho_0^+}$ does not really depend on ρ^+. Then, for any $\rho^- \in \mathbf{Env}_{\{odd\}}$, $(s, s') \in m(\rho^-)(even)$ if either $s(n) = 0$ and $s' = s[r \mapsto 1]$, or else if $s(n) > 0$ and $(s[n \mapsto s(n)-1], s') \in \rho^-(odd)$.

Similarly, the procedure set $\{odd\}$ is abstracted into component $m_{odd} : \mathbf{Env}_{\{even\}} \to \mathbf{Env}_{\{odd\}}$ with interface $(\{even\}, \{odd\})$, so that $\forall \rho^- \in \mathbf{Env}_{\{even\}}.$ $m(\rho^-)(odd) = [\![S_{odd}]\!]_{\rho^-}$. Then, for any $\rho^- \in \mathbf{Env}_{\{even\}}$, $(s, s') \in m(\rho^-)(odd)$ if either $s(n) = 0$ and $s' = s[r \mapsto 0]$, or else if $s(n) > 0$ and $(s[n \mapsto s(n) - 1], s') \in \rho^-(even)$.

Now, applying Definition 12 to the whole (closed) program yields a component $m : \mathbf{Env}_\varnothing \to \mathbf{Env}_{\{even, odd\}}$ with interface $(\varnothing, \{even, odd\})$, so that $\forall \rho^- \in \mathbf{Env}_\varnothing.\ \forall p \in \{even, odd\}.\ m(\rho^-)(p) = [\![S_p]\!]_{\rho^-}$. Recall the denotations $[\![S_{even}]\!]_{\rho^-}$ and $[\![S_{odd}]\!]_{\rho^-}$ from the end of Section 3.1.

Components m_{even} and m_{odd} are composable, and by Definition 3, their composition has (the same) interface $(\varnothing, \{even, odd\})$, and is (also) a mapping $m_{even} \times m_{odd} : \mathbf{Env}_\varnothing \to \mathbf{Env}_{\{even, odd\}}$.

Finally, note that function $\chi_{m_{even} \times m_{odd}}^+ : \mathbf{Env}_{\{even, odd\}} \to \mathbf{Env}_{\{even, odd\}}$ is exactly the function ξ in the context of the interface $(\varnothing, \{even, odd\})$. This can be seen by first noting that since $\mathbf{Env}_\varnothing = \varnothing$, we have that $\chi_{m_{even} \times m_{odd}}^+$ only depends on its arguments. Furthermore, for all $\rho^+ \in \mathbf{Env}_{\{even, odd\}}$, if $\rho_{odd}^+ \overset{\text{def}}{=} \rho^+_{|\{odd\}}$ and $\rho_{even}^+ \overset{\text{def}}{=} \rho^+_{|\{even\}}$ we have that, since $odd \in P_{even}^- \cap P_{odd}^+$, then $\chi_{m_{even} \times m_{odd}}^+(\rho^+)(even) = m_{even}(\rho_{odd}^+)(even) = [\![S_{even}]\!]_{\rho_{odd}^+} = [\![S_{even}]\!]^{\rho^+} = \xi(\rho^+)(even)$. Similarly $\chi_{m_{even} \times m_{odd}}^+(\rho^+)(odd) = \xi(\rho^+)(odd)$. We therefore have $m_{even} \times m_{odd} = m$.

We now define how to abstract Hoare logic contracts into denotational contracts, in terms of the contract environment ρ_c defined in Section 3.2.

Definition 13 (From Hoare logic contracts to denotational contracts).
For a procedure p with Hoare logic contract C_p, calling other procedures P^-, we define the denotational contract $c_p = (\rho_{c_p}^-, \rho_{c_p}^+)$ with interface $P_{c_p}^+ \overset{\text{def}}{=} \{p\}$ and $P_{c_p}^- \overset{\text{def}}{=} P^-$, so that $\rho_{c_p}^+(p) \overset{\text{def}}{=} \rho_c(p)$, and $\forall p' \in P^-.\ \rho_{c_p}^-(p') = \rho_c(p')$.

In this way, conceptually, denotational contracts become assume/guarantee-style specifications over Hoare logic procedure contracts: assuming that all (external) procedures called by a procedure p transform the state according to their Hoare logic contracts, procedure p obliges itself to do so as well.

We now show that if a procedure implements a Hoare logic contract, then the abstracted component will implement the abstracted contract, and vice versa. Together with Theorem 4, this result allows the *procedure-modular verification* of abstract components.

Theorem 5. *For any procedure p with procedure contract C_p, abstracted into component m_p with contract c_p, we have $S_p \models^{cr}_{par} C_p$ iff $m_p \models c_p$.*

The result follows mainly from Definitions 12 and 13, and the denotational semantics given in Section 3.

Returning to the example from Sections 3 and 5, we can abstract the procedure set $\{even\}$ into component m_{even}, with interface $(\{odd\}, \{even\})$, which would be a function $\mathbf{Env}_{\{odd\}} \to \mathbf{Env}_{\{even\}}$, and $\forall \rho^- \in \mathbf{Env}_{\{odd\}}.\ m(\rho^-)(even)$ $= [\![S_{even}]\!]_{\rho^-}$. The denotational contracts c_{even} and c_{odd} resulting from the decomposition shown in Section 5, would be exactly the abstraction of the Hoare Logic contracts C_{even} and C_{odd} shown in Section 3.2. They would both be part of the contract environment used in procedure-modular verification, for example when verifying that $S_{even} \models^{cr}_{par} C_{even}$, which would entail $m_{even} \models c_{even}$. Thus, by applying standard procedure-modular verification at the source code level, we prove the top-level contract c proposed in Section 5.

7 Conclusion

We presented an abstract contract theory for procedural languages, based on denotational semantics. The theory is shown to be an instance of the meta-theory of [5], and at the same time an abstraction of the standard denotational semantics of procedural languages. We believe that our contract theory can be used to support the development of cyber-physical and embedded systems by the design methodology supported by the meta-theory, allowing the individual procedures of the embedded software to be treated as any other system component. The work also strengthens the claims of the meta-theory of distilling the notion of contracts to its essence, by showing that it is applicable also in the context of procedural programs and deductive verification. Finally, this work serves as a preparation for combining our contract theory for procedural programs with other instantiations of the meta-theory. In future work we plan to investigate the utility of our contract theory on real embedded systems taken from the automotive industry, where not all components are procedural programs, or even software (cf. our previous work, e.g., [11]). We also plan to extend our toy imperative language with additional features, such as procedure parameters and return values. Furthermore, we plan to extend the contract theory to capture program traces by developing a finite-trace semantics, to enable its use in the specification and verification of temporal properties. Lastly, we plan to combine our contract theory with an existing contract theory for hybrid systems [20].

References

1. Abadi, M., Lamport, L.: Composing specifications. ACM Trans. Program. Lang. Syst. **15**(1), 73–132 (Jan 1993). https://doi.org/10.1145/151646.151649
2. Bauer, S., David, A., Hennicker, R., Larsen, K., Legay, A., Nyman, U., Wasowski, A.: Moving from specifications to contracts in component-based design. In: Fundamental Approaches to Software Engineering. pp. 43–58 (2012). https://doi.org/10.1007/978-3-642-28872-2_3
3. Bekić, H.: Definable operation in general algebras, and the theory of automata and flowcharts. In: Programming Languages and Their Definition - Hans Bekić (1936-1982). Lecture Notes in Computer Science, vol. 177, pp. 30–55. Springer (1984). https://doi.org/10.1007/BFb0048939
4. Benveniste, A., Caillaud, B., Ferrari, A., Mangeruca, L., Passerone, R., Sofronis, C.: Multiple viewpoint contract-based specification and design. In: Formal Methods for Components and Objects. vol. 5382, pp. 200–225 (10 2007). https://doi.org/10.1007/978-3-540-92188-2_9
5. Benveniste, A., Caillaud, B., Nickovic, D., Passerone, R., Raclet, J.B., Reinkemeier, P., Sangiovanni-Vincentelli, A., Damm, W., Henzinger, T.A., Larsen, K.G.: Contracts for System Design, vol. 12. Now Publishers (2018). https://doi.org/10.1561/1000000053
6. Benvenuti, L., Ferrari, A., Mangeruca, L., Mazzi, E., Passerone, R., Sofronis, C.: A contract-based formalism for the specification of heterogeneous systems. In: 2008 Forum on Specification, Verification and Design Languages. pp. 142–147 (09 2008). https://doi.org/10.1109/FDL.2008.4641436
7. Bubel, R., Hähnle, R., Pelevina, M.: Fully abstract operation contracts. In: Leveraging Applications of Formal Methods, Verification and Validation. Specialized Techniques and Applications. pp. 120–134 (2014). https://doi.org/10.1007/978-3-662-45231-8_9
8. Chen, T., Chilton, C., Jonsson, B., Kwiatkowska, M.: A compositional specification theory for component behaviours. In: Programming Languages and Systems. pp. 148–168. Springer Berlin Heidelberg (2012). https://doi.org/10.1007/978-3-642-28869-2_8
9. Cimatti, A., Tonetta, S.: Contracts-refinement proof system for component-based embedded systems. Science of Computer Programming **97** (2015). https://doi.org/10.1016/j.scico.2014.06.011
10. Floyd, R.W.: Assigning meanings to programs. Mathematical aspects of computer science **19**, 19–32 (1967). https://doi.org/10.1007/978-94-011-1793-7_4
11. Gurov, D., Lidström, C., Nyberg, M., Westman, J.: Deductive functional verification of safety-critical embedded c-code: An experience report. In: Proceedings of FMICS-AVoCS 2017. Lecture Notes in Computer Science, vol. 10471, pp. 3–18. Springer (2017). https://doi.org/10.1007/978-3-319-67113-0_1
12. Gurov, D., Westman, J.: A Hoare Logic Contract Theory: An Exercise in Denotational Semantics, pp. 119–127. Springer International Publishing, Cham (2018). https://doi.org/10.1007/978-3-319-98047-8_8
13. Hähnle, R., Schaefer, I., Bubel, R.: Reuse in software verification by abstract method calls. In: Automated Deduction – CADE-24. vol. 7898, pp. 300–314 (06 2013). https://doi.org/10.1007/978-3-642-38574-2_21
14. Hatcliff, J., Leavens, G.T., Leino, K.R.M., Müller, P., Parkinson, M.: Behavioral interface specification languages. ACM Comput. Surv. **44**(3) (Jun 2012). https://doi.org/10.1145/2187671.2187678

15. Hoare, C.A.R.: An axiomatic basis for computer programming. Commun. ACM **12**(10), 576–580 (Oct 1969). https://doi.org/10.1145/363235.363259
16. Jones, C.: Specification and design of (parallel) programs. In: Proceedings Of IFIP'83. vol. 83, pp. 321–332 (01 1983)
17. Lidström, C., Gurov, D.: An abstract contract theory for programs with procedures (full version). CoRR **abs/2101.06087** (2021), https://arxiv.org/abs/2101.06087
18. Meyer, B.: Applying "design by contract". IEEE Computer **25**(10), 40–51 (1992). https://doi.org/10.1109/2.161279
19. Nielson, H.R., Nielson, F.: Semantics with Applications: An Appetizer. Springer-Verlag, Berlin, Heidelberg (2007). https://doi.org/10.1007/978-1-84628-692-6
20. Nyberg, M., Westman, J., Gurov, D.: Formally proving compositionality in industrial systems with informal specifications. In: Margaria, T., Steffen, B. (eds.) Leveraging Applications of Formal Methods, Verification and Validation: Applications. pp. 348–365. Springer International Publishing, Cham (2020). https://doi.org/10.1007/978-3-030-61467-6_22
21. Owe, O., Ramezanifarkhani, T., Fazeldehkordi, E.: Hoare-style reasoning from multiple contracts. In: Integrated Formal Methods - 13th International Conference. Lecture Notes in Computer Science, vol. 10510, pp. 263–278. Springer (2017). https://doi.org/10.1007/978-3-319-66845-1_17
22. van Staden, S.: On rely-guarantee reasoning. In: Mathematics of Program Construction. pp. 30–49. Springer International Publishing, Cham (2015). https://doi.org/10.1007/978-3-319-19797-5_2
23. Winskel, G.: The Formal Semantics of Programming Languages: An Introduction. MIT Press, Cambridge, MA, USA (1993). https://doi.org/10.7551/mitpress/3054.001.0001

Paracosm: A Test Framework for Autonomous Driving Simulations

Rupak Majumdar[1], Aman Mathur[1] ✉, Marcus Pirron[1], Laura Stegner[2], and Damien Zufferey[1]

[1] MPI-SWS, Kaiserslautern, Germany {`rupak, mathur, mpirron, zufferey`}`@mpi-sws.org`
[2] University of Wisconsin, Madison, USA `stegner@wisc.edu`

Abstract. Systematic testing of autonomous vehicles operating in complex real-world scenarios is a difficult and expensive problem. We present PARACOSM, a framework for writing systematic test scenarios for autonomous driving simulations. PARACOSM allows users to programmatically describe complex driving situations with specific features, e.g., road layouts and environmental conditions, as well as reactive temporal behaviors of other cars and pedestrians. A systematic exploration of the state space, both for visual features and for reactive interactions with the environment is made possible. We define a notion of test coverage for parameter configurations based on combinatorial testing and low dispersion sequences. Using fuzzing on parameter configurations, our automatic test generator can maximize coverage of various behaviors and find problematic cases. Through empirical evaluations, we demonstrate the capabilities of PARACOSM in programmatically modeling parameterized test environments, and in finding problematic scenarios.

Keywords: Autonomous driving · Testing · Reactive programming.

1 Introduction

Building autonomous driving systems requires complex and intricate engineering effort. At the same time, ensuring their reliability and safety is an extremely difficult task. There are serious public safety and trust concerns [63], aggravated by recent accidents involving autonomous cars [48]. Software in such vehicles combine well-defined tasks such as trajectory planning, steering, acceleration and braking, with underspecified tasks such as building a semantic model of the environment from raw sensor data and making decisions using this model. Unfortunately, these underspecified tasks are critical to the safe operation of autonomous vehicles. Therefore, testing in large varieties of realistic scenarios is the only way to build confidence in the correctness of the overall system.

Running real tests is a necessary, but slow and costly process. It is difficult to reproduce corner cases due to infrastructure and safety issues; one can neither run over pedestrians to demonstrate a failing test case, nor wait for specific weather and road conditions. Therefore, the automotive industry tests

E. Guerra and M. Stoelinga (Eds.): FASE 2021, LNCS 12649, pp. 172–195, 2021.
https://doi.org/10.1007/978-3-030-71500-7_9

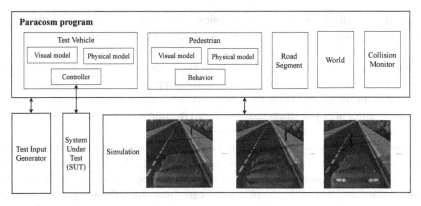

Fig. 1: A PARACOSM program consists of parameterized reactive components such as the test vehicle, the environment, road networks, other actors and their behaviors, and monitors. The test input generation scheme guarantees good coverage over the parameter space. The test scenario depicted here shows a test vehicle stopping for a jaywalking pedestrian.

autonomous systems in virtual simulation environments [21, 26, 53, 61, 68, 72]. Simulation reduces the cost per test, and more importantly, gives precise control over all aspects of the environment, so as to test corner cases.

A major limitation of current tools is the lack of customizability: they either provide a GUI-based interface to design an environment piece-by-piece, or focus on bespoke pre-made environments. This makes the setup of varied scenarios difficult and time consuming. Though exploiting parametricity in simulation is useful and effective [10, 23, 31, 67], the cost of environment setup, and navigating large parameter spaces, is quite high [31]. Prior works have used bespoke environments with limited parametricity. More recently, programmatic interfaces have been proposed [27] to make such test procedures more systematic. However, the simulated environments are largely still fixed, with no dynamic behavior.

In this work, we present PARACOSM, a programmatic interface that enables the design of *parameterized environments* and *test cases*. Test parameters control the environment and the behaviors of the actors involved. PARACOSM supports various test input generation strategies, and we provide a notion of coverage for these. Rather than computing coverage over intrinsic properties of the system under test (which is not yet understood for neural networks [39]), our coverage criteria is over the space of test parameters. Figure 1 depicts the various parts of a PARACOSM test. A PARACOSM program represents a family of tests, where each instantiation of the program's parameters is a concrete test case.

PARACOSM is based on a synchronous reactive programming model [13, 35, 40, 70]. Components, such as road segments or cars, receive streams of inputs and produce streams of outputs over time. In addition, components have graphical assets to describe their appearance for an underlying visual rendering engine and physical properties for an underlying physics simulator. For example, a vehicle in PARACOSM not only has code that reads in sensor feeds and outputs steering angle or braking, but also has a textured mesh representing its shape, position and orientation in 3D space, and a physics model for its dynamical behavior. A PARACOSM configuration consists of a composition of several components. Using a set of system-defined components (road segments, cars, pedestrians, etc.) combined using expressive operations from the underlying reactive programming model, users can set up complex temporally varying driving scenarios. For example, one can build an urban road network with intersections, pedestrians and vehicular traffic, and parameterize both, environment conditions (lighting, fog), and behaviors (when a pedestrian crosses a street).

Streams in the world description can be left "open" and, during testing, PARACOSM automatically generates sequences of values for these streams. We use a coverage strategy based on *k-wise combinatorial coverage* [14, 38] for discrete variables and *dispersion* for continuous variables. Intuitively, k-wise coverage ensures that, for a programmer-specified parameter k, all possible combinations of values of any k discrete parameters are covered by tests. Low dispersion [57] ensures that there are no "large empty holes" left in the continuous parameter space. PARACOSM uses an automatic test generation strategy that offers high coverage based on random sampling over discrete parameters and *deterministic* quasi-Monte Carlo methods for continuous parameters [49, 57].

Like many of the projects referenced before, our implementation performs simulations inside a game engine. However, PARACOSM configurations can also be output to the OPENDRIVE format [7] for use with other simulators, which is more in-line with the current industry standard. We demonstrate through various case studies how PARACOSM can be an effective testing framework for both qualitative properties (crash) and quantitative properties (distance maintained while following a car, or image misclassification).

Our main contributions are the following: (I) We present a programmable and expressive framework for programmatically modeling complex and parameterized scenarios to test autonomous driving systems. Using PARACOSM one can specify the environment's layout, behaviors of actors, and expose parameters to a systematic testing infrastructure. (II) We define a notion of test coverage based on combinatorial k-wise coverage in discrete space and low dispersion in continuous space. We show a test generation strategy based on fuzzing that theoretically guarantees good coverage. (III) We demonstrate empirically that our system is able to express complex scenarios and automatically test autonomous driving agents and find incorrect behaviors or degraded performance.

2   Paracosm through Examples

We now provide a walkthrough of PARACOSM through a testing example. Suppose we have an autonomous vehicle to test. Its implementation is wrapped into a parameterized class:

```
AutonomousVehicle(start, model, controller) {
    void run(...) { ... } }
```

where the **model** ranges over possible car models (appearance, physics), and the **controller** implements an autonomous controller. The goal is to test this class in many different driving scenarios, including different road networks, weather and light conditions, and other car and pedestrian traffic. We show how PARACOSM enables writing such tests as well as generate test inputs automatically.

A *test configuration* consists of a composition of *reactive objects*. The following is an outline of a test configuration in PARACOSM, in which the autonomous vehicle drives on a road with a pedestrian wanting to cross. We have simplified the API syntax for the sake of clarity and omit the enclosing `Test` class. In the code segments, we use ':' for named arguments.

```
1  // Test parameters
2  light = VarInterval(0.2, 1.0) // value in [0.2, 1.0]
3  nlanes = VarEnum({2,4,6}) // value is 2, 4 or 6
4  // Description of environment
5  w = World(light:light, fog:0)
6  // Create a road segment
7  r = StraightRoadSegment(len:100, nlanes:nlanes)
8  // The autonomous vehicle controlled by the SUT
9  v = AutonomousVehicle(start:..., model:..., controller:...)
10 // Some other actor(s)
11 p = Pedestrian(start:..., model:..., ...)
12 // Monitor to check some property
13 c = CollisionMonitor(v)
14 // Place elements in the world
15 run_test(env: {w, r, v, p}, test_params: {light, nlanes},
          monitors: {c}, iterations: 100)
```

An instantiation of the reactive objects in the test configuration gives a *scene*—all the visual elements present in the simulated world. A *test case* provides concrete inputs to each "open" input stream in a scene. A test case determines how the scene evolves over time: how the cars and pedestrians move and how environment conditions change. We go through each part of the test configuration in detail below.

Reactive Objects. The core abstraction of PARACOSM is a *reactive object*. Reactive objects capture geometric and graphical features of a physical object, as well as their behavior over time. The behavioral interface for each reactive object has a set of *input* streams and a set of *output* streams. The evolution of the world is computed in steps of fixed duration which corresponds to events in a predefined `tick` stream. For streams that correspond to physical quantities updated by the physics simulator, such as position and speeds of cars, etc., appropriate events are generated by the underlying physics simulator.

Input streams provide input values from the environment over time; output streams represent output values computed by the object. The object's constructor sets up the internal state of the object. An object is updated by event triggered computations. PARACOSM provides a set of assets as base classes. Autonomous driving systems naturally fit reactive programming models. They consume sensor input streams and produce actuator streams for the vehicle model. We differentiate between static *environment* reactive objects (subclassing

Fig. 2: Reactive streams represented by a marble diagram. A change in the value of test parameters **nlanes** or **light** changes the environment, and triggers a change in the corresponding sensor (output) stream **camera**.

Geometric) and dynamic *actor* reactive objects (subclassing Physical). Environment reactive objects represent "static" components of the world, such as road segments, intersections, buildings or trees, and a special component called the *world*. Actor reactive objects represent components with "dynamic" behavior: vehicles or pedestrians. The world object is used to model features of the world such as lighting or weather conditions. Reactive objects can be *composed* to generate complex assemblies from simple objects. The composition process can be used to connect static components structurally–such as two road segments connecting at an intersection. Composition also connects the behavior of an object to another by binding output streams to input streams. At run time, the values on that input stream of the second object are obtained from the output values of the first. Composition must respect geometric properties—the runtime system ensures that a composition maintains invariants such as no intersection of geometric components. We now describe the main features in PARACOSM, centered around the test configuration above.

Test Parameters. Using test variables, we can have general, but constrained streams of values passed into objects [59]. Our automatic test generator can then pick values for these variables, thereby leading to different test cases (see Figure 2). There are two types of parameters: continuous (VarInterval) and discrete (VarEnum). In the example presented, **light** (light intensity) is a continuous test parameter and **nlanes** (number of lanes) is discrete.

World. The World is a pre-defined reactive object in PARACOSM with a visual representation responsible for atmospheric conditions like the light intensity, direction and color, fog density, etc. The code segment

```
w = World(light:light, fog:0)
```

parameterizes the world using a test variable for light and sets the fog density to a constant (0).

Road Segments. In our example, StraightRoadSegment was parameterized with the number of lanes. In general, PARACOSM provides the ability to build complex road networks by connecting primitives of individual road segments and intersections. (A detailed example is presented in our Technical Report [43].)

It may seem surprising that we model static scene components such as roads as reactive objects. This serves two purposes. First, we can treat the number of lanes in a road segment as a constant input stream that is set by the test case, allowing parameterized test cases. Second, certain features of static objects can also change over time. For example, the coefficient of friction on a road segment may depend on the weather condition, which can be a function of time.

Autonomous Vehicles & System Under Test (SUT). `AutonomousVehicle`, as well as other actors, extends the `Physical` class (which in turn subclasses `Geometric`). This means that these objects have a visual as well as a physical model. The visual model is essentially a textured 3D mesh. The physical model contains properties such as mass, moments of inertia of separate bodies in the vehicle, joints, etc. This is used by the physics simulator to compute the vehicle's motion in response to external forces and control input. In the following code segment, we instantiate and place our test vehicle on the road:

```
v = AutonomousVehicle(start:r.onLane(1, 0.1), model:
    CarAsset(...), controller:MyController(...))
```

The `start` parameter "places" the vehicle in the world (in relative coordinates). The `model` parameter provides the implementation of the geometric and physical model of the vehicle. The `controller` parameter implements the autonomous controller under test. The internals of the controller implementation are not important; what is important is its interface (sensor inputs and the actuator outputs). These determine the input and output streams that are passed to the controller during simulation. For example, a typical controller can take sensor streams such as image streams from a camera as input and produce throttle and steering angles as outputs. The PARACOSM framework "wires" these streams appropriately. For example, the rendering engine determines the camera images based on the geometry of the scene and the position of the camera and the controller outputs are fed to the physics engine to determine the updated scene. Though simpler systems like OPENPILOT [15] use only a dashboard-mounted camera, autonomous vehicles can, in general, mix cameras at various mount points, LiDARs, radars, and GPS. PARACOSM can emulate many common types of sensors which produce streams of data. It is also possible to integrate new sensors, which are not supported out-of-the-box, by implementing them using the game engine's API.

Other Actors. A test often involves many actors such as pedestrians, and other (non-test) vehicles. Apart from the standard geometric (optionally physical) properties, these can also have some pre-programmed behavior. Behaviors can either be only dependent on the starting position (say, a car driving straight on the same lane), or be dynamic and reactive, depending on test parameters and behaviors of other actors. In general, the reactive nature of objects enables complex scenarios to be built. For example, here, we specify a simple behavior of a pedestrian crossing a road. The pedestrian starts crossing the road when a car is a certain distance away. In the code segments below, we use '_' as shorthand for a lambda expression, i.e., "`f(_)`" is the same as "`x => f(x)`".

```
Pedestrian(value start, value target, carPos, value dist,
    value speed) extends Geometric {
  ... // Initialization
  // Generate an event when the car gets close
  trigger = carPos.Filter( abs(_ - start) < dist )
  // target location reached
  done = pos.Filter( _ == target )
  // Walk to the target after trigger fires
  tick.SkipUntil(trigger).TakeUntil(done).foreach( ... /*
    walk with given speed */ )
}
```

Monitors and Test Oracles. PARACOSM provides an API to provide qualitative and quantitative temporal specifications. For instance, in the following example, we check that there is no collision and ensure that the collision was not trivially avoided because our vehicle did not move at all.

```
// no collision
CollisionMonitor(AutonomousVehicle v) extends Monitor {
  assert(v.collider.IsEmpty()) }
// cannot trivially pass the test by staying put
DistanceMonitor(AutonomousVehicle v, value minD) extends
    Monitor {
  pOld = v.pos.Take(1).Concat(v.pos)
  D = v.pos.Zip(pOld).Map( abs(_ - _) ).Sum()
  assert(D >= minD)
}
```

The ability to write monitors which read streams of system-generated events provides an expressive framework to write temporal properties, something that has been identified as a major limitation of prior tools [31]. Monitors for metric and signal temporal logic specifications can be encoded in the usual way [18,33].

3   Systematic Testing of Paracosm Worlds

3.1   Test Inputs and Coverage

Worlds in PARACOSM directly describe a parameterized family of tests. The testing framework allows users to specify various strategies to generate input streams for both, static, and dynamic reactive objects in the world.

Test Cases. A *test* of *duration* T executes a configuration of reactive objects by providing inputs to every open input stream in the configuration for T ticks. The inputs for each stream must satisfy const parameters and respect the range constraints from VarInterval and VarEnum. The runtime system manages the scheduling of inputs and pushing input streams to the reactive objects. Let In denote the set of all input streams, and $\mathsf{In} = \mathsf{In}_D \cup \mathsf{In}_C$ denote the partition of In into *discrete* streams and *continuous* streams respectively. Discrete streams take their value over a finite, discrete range; for example, the color of a car, the number of lanes on a road segment, or the position of the next pedestrian (left/right) are discrete streams. Continuous streams take their values in a continuous (bounded) interval. For example, the fog density or the speed of a vehicle are examples of continuous streams.

Coverage. In the setting of autonomous vehicle testing, one often wants to explore the state space of a parameterized world to check "how well" an autonomous vehicle works under various situations, both qualitatively and quantitatively. Thus, we now introduce a notion of coverage. Instead of structural coverage criteria such as line or branch coverage, our goal is to cover the parameter space. In the following, for simplicity of notation, we assume that all discrete streams take values from $\{0,1\}$, and all continuous streams take values in the real interval $[0,1]$. Any input stream over bounded intervals—discrete or continuous—can be encoded into such streams. For discrete streams, there are finitely many tests, since each co-ordinate is Boolean and there is a fixed number of co-ordinates. One can define the coverage as the fraction of the number of vectors tested to the total number of vectors. Unfortunately, the total number of vectors is very high: if each stream is constant, then there are already 2^n tests for n streams. Instead, we consider the notion of *k-wise testing* from combinatorial testing [38]. In k-wise testing, we fix a parameter k, and ask that every interaction between every k elements is tested. Let us be more precise. Suppose that a test vector has N co-ordinates, where each co-ordinate can get the value 0 or 1. A set of tests A is a *k-wise covering family* if for every subset $\{i_1, i_2, \ldots, i_k\} \subseteq \{1, \ldots, N\}$ of co-ordinates and every vector $v \in \{0,1\}^k$, there is a test $t \in A$ whose restriction to the $i_1, \ldots, i_k$ is precisely v.

For continuous streams, the situation is more complex: since any continuous interval has infinitely many points, each corresponding to a different test case, we cannot directly define coverage as a ratio (the denominator will be infinite). Instead, we define coverage using the notion of *dispersion* [49, 57]. Intuitively, dispersion measures the largest empty space left by a set of tests. We assume a (continuous) test is a vector in $[0,1]^N$: each entry is picked from the interval $[0,1]$ and there are N co-ordinates. Dispersion over $[0,1]^N$ can be defined relative to sets of neighborhoods, such as N-dimensional balls or axis-parallel rectangles. Let us define $\mathcal{B}$ to be the family of N-dimensional axis-parallel rectangles in $[0,1]^N$, our results also hold for other notions of neighborhoods such as balls or ellipsoids. For a neighborhood $B \in \mathcal{B}$, let $vol(B)$ denote the volume of B. Given a set $A \subseteq [0,1]^N$ of tests, we define the *dispersion* as the largest volume neighborhood in $\mathcal{B}$ without any test:

$$\text{dispersion}(A) = \sup\{vol(B) \mid B \in \mathcal{B} \text{ and } A \cap B = \emptyset\}$$

A lower dispersion means better coverage.

Let us summarize. Suppose that a test vector consists of N_D discrete co-ordinates and N_C continuous co-ordinates; that is, a test is a vector (t_D, t_C) in $\{0,1\}^{N_D} \times [0,1]^{N_C}$. We say a set of tests A is (k, ε)-*covering* if

1. for each set of k co-ordinates $\{i_1, \ldots, i_k\} \subseteq \{1, \ldots, N_D\}$ and each vector $v \in \{0,1\}^k$, there is a test $(t_D, t_C) \in \{0,1\}^{N_D} \times [0,1]^{N_C}$ such that the restriction of t_D to the co-ordinates $i_1, \ldots, i_k$ is v; and
2. for each $(t_D, t_C) \in A$, the set $\{t_C \mid (t_D, t_C) \in A\}$ has dispersion at most ϵ.

3.2   Test Generation

The goal of our default test generator is to maximize (k, ϵ) for programmer-specified number of test iterations or ticks.

k-Wise Covering Family. One can use explicit construction results from combinatorial testing to generate k-wise covering families [14]. However, a simple way to generate such families with high probability is random testing. The proof is by the probabilistic method [4] (see also [44]). Let A be a set of $2^k(k \log N - \log \delta)$ uniformly randomly generated $\{0,1\}^N$ vectors. Then A is a k-wise covering family with probability at least $1 - \delta$.

Low Dispersion Sequences. It is tempting to think that uniformly generating vectors from $[0,1]^N$ would similarly give low dispersion sequences. Indeed, as the number of tests goes to infinity, the set of randomly generated tests has dispersion 0 almost surely. However, when we fix the number of tests, it is well known that uniform random sampling can lead to high dispersion [49,57]; in fact, one can show that the dispersion of n uniformly randomly generated tests grows asymptotically as $O((\log \log n/n)^{\frac{1}{2}})$ almost surely. Our test generation strategy is based on *deterministic quasi-Monte Carlo sequences*, which have much better dispersion properties, asymptotically of the order of $O(1/n)$, than the dispersion behavior of uniformly random tests. There are many different algorithms for generating quasi-Monte Carlo sequences deterministically (see, e.g., [49,57]). We use *Halton sequences*. For a given ϵ, we need to generate $O(\frac{1}{\epsilon})$ inputs via Halton sampling. In Section 4.2, we compare uniform random and Halton sampling.

Cost Functions and Local Search. In many situations, testers want to optimize parameter values for a specific function. A simple example of this is finding higher-speed collisions, which intuitively, can be found in the vicinity of test parameters that already result in high-speed collisions. Another, slightly different case is (greybox) fuzzing [5,55], for example, finding new collisions using small mutations on parameter values that result in the vehicle narrowly avoiding a collision. Our test generator supports such *quantitative* objectives and *local search*. A quantitative monitor evaluates a cost function on a run of a test case. Our test generation tool generates an initial, randomly chosen, set of test inputs. Then, it considers the scores returned by the Monitor on these samples, and performs a local search on samples with the highest/lowest scores to find local optima of the cost function.

4   Implementation and Tests

4.1   Runtime System and Implementation

PARACOSM uses the Unity game engine [69] to render visuals, do runtime checks and simulate physics (via PhysX [16]). Reactive objects are built on top of UniRx [36], an implementation of the popular Reactive Extensions framework [56]. The game engine manages geometric transformations of 3D objects and offers easy to use abstractions for generating realistic simulations. Encoding behaviors and monitors, management of 3D geometry and dynamic checks are implemented using the game engine interface. The project code is available at: https://gitlab. mpi-sws.org/mathur/paracosm.

A simulation in PARACOSM proceeds as follows. A test configuration is specified as a subclass of the `EnvironmentProgramBaseClass`.Tests are run by invoking the `run_test` method, which receives as input the reactive objects that should be instantiated in the world as well as additional parameters relating to the test. The `run_test` method runs the tests by first initializing and placing the reactive objects in the scene using their 3D mesh (if they have one) and then invoking a reactive engine to start the simulation. The system under test is run in a separate process and connects to the simulation. The simulation then proceeds until the simulation completion criteria is met (a time-out or some monitor event).

Output to Standardized Testing Formats. There have been recent efforts to create standardized descriptions of tests in the automotive industry. The most relevant formats are OPENDRIVE [7] and OPENSCENARIO (only recently finalized) [8]. OPENDRIVE describes road structures, and OPENSCENARIO describes actors and their behavior. PARACOSM currently supports outputs to OPENDRIVE. Due to the static nature of the specification format, a different file is generated for each test iteration/configuration.

4.2   Evaluation

We evaluate PARACOSM with respect to the following research questions (**RQs**):
RQ 1: Does PARACOSM's programmatic interface enable the easy design of test environments and worlds?
RQ 2: Do the test input generation strategies discussed in Section 3 effectively explore the parameter space?
RQ 3: Can PARACOSM help uncover poor performance or bad behavior of the SUT in common autonomous driving tasks?

Methodology. To answer **RQ 1**, we develop three independent environments rich with visual features and other actors, and use the variety generated with just a few lines of code as a proxy for ease of design. To answer **RQ 2**, we use coverage maximizing strategies for test inputs to all the three environments/case studies. We also use and evaluate cost functions and local search based methods. To answer **RQ 3**, we test various neural network based systems and demonstrate

Table 1: An overview of our case studies. Note that even though the Adaptive Cruise Control study has 2 discrete parameters, we calculate k-wise coverage for 3 as the 2 parameters require 3 bits for representation.

	Road segmentation	Jaywalking pedestrian	Adaptive Cruise Control
SUT	VGGNet CNN [62]	NVIDIA CNN [12]	NVIDIA CNN [12]
Training	191 images	403 image & car control samples	1034 image & car control samples
Test params	3 discrete	2 continuous	3 continuous & 2 discrete
Test iters	100	100, 15s timeout	100, 15s timeout
Monitor	Ground truth	Scored Collision	Collision & Distance
Coverage	$k = 3$ with probability ~ 1	$\epsilon = 0.041$	$\epsilon = 0.043$, $k = 3$ with probability ~ 1

(a) A good test with all parameter values same as the training set (true positive: 89%, false positive: 0%).

(b) A bad test with all parameter values different from the training set (true positive: 9%, false positive: 1%).

Fig. 3: Example results from the road segmentation case study. Pixels with a green mask are segmented by the SUT as a road.

how PARACOSM can help uncover problematic scenarios. A summary of the case studies presented here is available in Table 1. In our Technical Report [43], we present more case studies, specifically experiments on many pre-trained neural networks, busy urban environments and studies exploiting specific testing features of PARACOSM.

4.3   Case Studies

Road segmentation Using PARACOSM's programmatic interface, we design a long road segment with several vehicles. The vehicular behavior is to drive on their respective lanes with a fixed maximum velocity. The test parameters are the number of lanes ({2, 4}), number of cars in the environment ({0, 5}) and light conditions ({*Noon, Evening*}). Noon lighting is much brighter than the evening. The direction of lighting is also the opposite. We test a deep CNN called VGGNet [62], that is known to perform well on several image segmentation benchmarks. The task is road segmentation, i.e., given a camera image, identifying which pixels correspond to the road. The network is trained on 191 dashcam images

Table 2: Summary of results of the road segmentation case study. Each combination of parameter values is presented separately, with the parameter values used for training in bold. We report the SUT's average true positive rate (% of pixels corresponding to the road that are correctly classified) and false positive rate (% of pixels that are not road, but incorrectly classified as road).

# lanes	# cars	Lighting	# test iters	True positive (%)	False positive (%)
2	**5**	**Noon**	12	70%	5.1%
2	5	Evening	14	53.4%	22.4%
2	0	Evening	12	51.4%	18.9%
2	0	Noon	12	71.3%	6%
4	5	Evening	10	60.4%	7.1%
4	5	Noon	16	68.5%	20.2%
4	0	Evening	13	51.5%	7.1%
4	0	Noon	11	83.3%	21%

Table 3: Results for the jaywalking pedestrian case study.

Testing strategy	Dispersion (ϵ)	% fail	Max. collision
Random	0.092	7%	10.5 m/s
Halton	0.041	10%	11.3 m/s
Random+opt/collision	0.109	13%	11.1 m/s
Halton+opt/collision	0.043	20%	11.9 m/s
Random+opt/almost failing	0.126	13%	10.5 m/s
Halton+opt/almost failing	0.043	13%	11.4 m/s

captured in the test environment with fixed parameters (2 lanes, 5 cars, and *Noon* lighting), recorded at the rate of one image every $1/10^{th}$ second, while manually driving the vehicle around (using a keyboard). We test on 100 images generated using PARACOSM's default test generation strategy (uniform random sampling for discrete parameters). Table 2 summarizes the test results. Tests with parameter values far away from the training set are observed to not perform so well. As depicted in Figure 3, this happens because varying test parameters can drastically change the scene.

Jaywalking pedestrian. We now test over the environment presented in Section 2. The environment consists of a straight road segment and a pedestrian. The pedestrian's behavior is to cross the road at a specific walking speed when the autonomous vehicle is a specific distance away. The walking speed of the pedestrian and the distance of the autonomous vehicle when the pedestrian starts crossing the road are test parameters. The SUT is a CNN based on NVIDIA's behavioral cloning framework [12]. It takes camera images as input, and produces the relevant steering angle or throttle control as output. The SUT is trained on 403 samples obtained by driving the vehicle manually and recording the camera and corresponding control data. The training environment has pedestrians crossing the road at various time delays, but always at a fixed walking speed (1 m/s). In order to evaluate **RQ 2** completely, we evaluate the default coverage maximizing sampling approach, as well as explore two quantitative objectives: first, maximizing the collision speed, and second, finding new failing cases around samples that *almost* fail. For the default approach, the `CollisionMonitor` as presented in Section 2 is used. For the first quantitative objective, this `CollisionMonitor`'s code is prepended with the following calculation:

```
// Score is speed of car at time of collision
coll_speed = v.speed.CombineLatest(v.collider, (s,c) => s)
    .First()
```

The score `coll_speed` is used by the test generator for optimization. For the second quantitative objective, the `CollisionMonitor` is modified to give high scores to tests where the distance between the autonomous vehicle and pedestrian is very small:

```
CollisionMonitor(AutonomousVehicle v, Pedestrian p)
    extends Monitor {
    minDist = v.pos.Zip(p.pos).Map(1/abs(_-_)).Min()
    coll_score = v.collider.Map(0)
    // Score is either 0 (collision) or 1/minDist
    score = coll_score.DefaultIfEmpty(minDist)
    assert(v.collider.IsEmpty())
}
```

We evaluate the following test input generation strategies: (i) Random sampling (ii) Halton sampling, (iii) Random or Halton sampling with local search for the two quantitative objectives. We run 100 iterations of each strategy with a 15 second timeout. For random or Halton sampling, we sample 100 times. For the quantitative objectives, we first generate 85 random or Halton samples, then choose the top 5 scores, and finally run 3 simulated annealing iterations on each of these 5 configurations. Table 3 presents results from the various test input generation strategies. Clearly, Halton sampling offers the lowest dispersion (highest coverage) over the parameter space. This can also be visually confirmed from the plot of test parameters (Figure 4). There are no big gaps in the parameter space. Moreover, we find that test strategies optimizing for the first objective are successful in finding more collisions with higher speeds. As these techniques perform simulated annealing repetitions on top of already failing tests, they also find more failing tests overall. Finally, test strategies using the second objective are also successful in finding more (newer) failure cases than simple Random or Halton sampling.

Adaptive Cruise Control. We now create and test in an environment with our test vehicle following a car (lead car) on the same lane. The lead car's behavior is programmed to drive on the same lane as the test vehicle, with a certain maximum speed. This is a very typical driving scenario that engineers test their implementations on. We use 5 test parameters: the initial lead of the lead car to

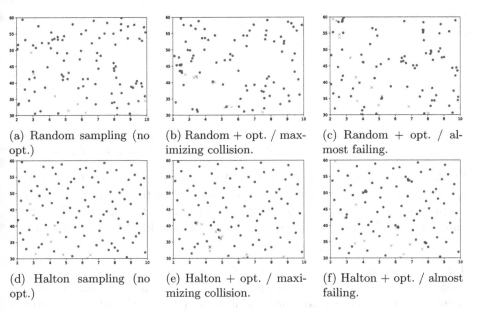

(a) Random sampling (no opt.)

(b) Random + opt. / maximizing collision.

(c) Random + opt. / almost failing.

(d) Halton sampling (no opt.)

(e) Halton + opt. / maximizing collision.

(f) Halton + opt. / almost failing.

Fig. 4: A comparison of the various test generation strategies for the jaywalking pedestrian case study. The X-axis is the walking speed of the pedestrian (2 to 10 m/s). The Y-axis is the distance from the car when the pedestrian starts crossing (30 to 60 m). Passing tests are labelled with a green dot. Failing tests (tests with a collision) are marked with a red cross.

the test vehicle ($[8m, 40m]$), the lead car's maximum speed ($[3m/s, 8m/s]$), density of fog[3] in the environment ($[0, 1]$), number of lanes on the road ($\{2, 4\}$), and color of the lead car ($\{Black, Red, Yello, Blue\}$). We use both, CollisionMonitor [4] and DistanceMonitor, as presented in Section 2. A test *passes* if there is no collision and the autonomous vehicle moves atleast 5 m during the simulation duration (15 s).

We use PARACOSM's default test generation strategy, i.e., Halton sampling for continuous parameters and Random sampling for discrete parameters (no optimization or fuzzing). The SUT is the same CNN as in the previous case study. It is trained on 1034 training samples, which are obtained by manually driving behind a red lead car on the same lane of a 2-lane road with the same maximum velocity (5.5 m/s) and no fog.

The results of this case study are presented in Table 4. Looking at the discrete parameters, the number of lanes does not seem to contribute towards a risk of collision. Surprisingly, though the training only involves a Red lead car, the results appear to be the best for a Blue lead car. Moving on to the continuous

---

[3] 0 denotes no fog and 1 denotes very dense fog (exponential squared scale).
[4] the monitor additionally calculates the mean distance of the test vehicle to the lead car during the test, which is used for later analysis.

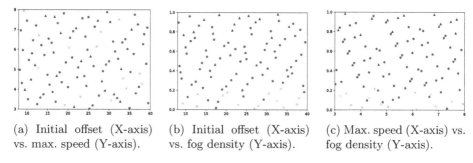

(a) Initial offset (X-axis) vs. max. speed (Y-axis).

(b) Initial offset (X-axis) vs. fog density (Y-axis).

(c) Max. speed (X-axis) vs. fog density (Y-axis).

Fig. 5: Continuous test parameters of the Adaptive Cruise Control study plotted against each other: the initial offset of the lead car (8 to 40 m), the lead car's maximum speed (3 to 8 m/s) and the fog density (0 to 1). Green dots, red crosses, and blue triangles denote passing tests, collisions, and inactivity respectively.

Table 4: Parameterized test on Adaptive Cruise Control, separated for each value of discrete parameters, and low and high values of continuous parameters. A test *passes* if there are no collisions and no inactivity (the overall distance moved by the test vehicle is more than 5 m. The average offset (in m) maintained by the test vehicle to the lead car (for passing tests) is also presented.

	Discrete parameters						Continuous parameters					
	Num. lanes		Lead car color				Initial offset (m)		Speed (m/s)		Fog density	
	2	4	Black	Red	Yellow	Blue	< 24	≥ 24	< 5.5	≥ 5.5	< 0.5	≥ 0.5
Test iters	54	46	24	22	27	27	51	49	52	48	51	49
Collisions	7	7	3	3	6	2	6	8	8	6	12	0
Inactivity	12	4	4	4	6	2	9	7	9	7	1	15
Offset (m)	42.4	43.4	46.5	48.1	39.6	39.1	33.7	52.7	38.4	47.4	36.5	49.8

parameters, the fog density appears to have the most significant impact on test failures (collision or vehicle inactivity). In the presence of dense fog, the SUT behaves pessimistically and does not accelerate much (thereby causing a failure due to inactivity). These are all interesting and useful metrics about the performance of our SUT. Plots of the results projected on to continuous parameters are presented in Figure 5.

4.4   Results and Analysis

We now summarize the results of our evaluation with respect to our **RQ**s:

RQ 1: All the three case studies involve varied, rich and dynamic environments. They are representative of tests engineers would typically want to do, and we parameterize many different aspects of the world and the dynamic behavior of its components. These designs are at most 70 lines of code. This provides confidence in PARACOSM's ability of providing an easy interface for the design of realistic test environments.

RQ 2: Our default test generation strategies are found to be quite effective at exploring the parameter space systematically, eliminating large unexplored gaps, and at the same time, successfully identifying problematic cases in all the three case studies. The jaywalking pedestrian study demonstrates that optimization and local search are possible on top of these strategies, and are quite effective in finding the relevant scenarios. The adaptive cruise control study tests over 5 parameters, which is more than most related works, and even guarantees good coverage of this parameter space. Therefore, it is amply clear that PARACOSM's test input generation methods are useful and effective.

RQ 3: The road segmentation case study uses a well-performing neural network for object segmentation, and we are able to detect degraded performance for automatically generated test inputs. Whereas this study focuses on static image classification, the next two, i.e., the jaywalking pedestrian and the adaptive cruise control study uncover poor performance on simulated driving, using a popular neural network architecture for self driving cars. Therefore, we can safely conclude that PARACOSM can find bugs in various different kinds of systems related to autonomous driving.

4.5 Threats to Validity

The *internal validity* of our experiments depends on having implemented our system correctly and, more importantly, trained and used the neural networks considered in the case studies correctly. For training the networks, we followed the available documentation and inspected our examples to ensure that we use an appropriate training procedure. We watched some test runs and replays of tests we did not understand. Furthermore, our implementation logs events and we also capture images, which allow us to check a large number of tests.

In terms of threats to external validity, the biggest challenge in this project has been finding systems that we can easily train and test in complex driving scenarios. Publicly available systems have limited capabilities and tend to be brittle. Many networks trained on real world data do not work well in simulation. We therefore re-train these networks in simulation. An alternative is to run fewer tests, but use more expensive and visually realistic simulations. Our test generation strategy maximizes coverage, even when only a few test iterations can be performed due to high simulation cost.

5 Related Work

Traditionally, test-driven software development paradigms [9] have advocated testing and mocking frameworks to test software early and often. Mocking frameworks and mock objects [42,47] allow programmers to test a piece of code against an API specification. Typically, mock objects are stubs providing outputs to explicitly provided lists of inputs of simple types, with little functionality of the actual code. Thus, they fall short of providing a rich environment for autonomous driving. PARACOSM can be seen as a mocking framework for reactive, physical systems embedded in the 3D world. Our notion of constraining streams is inspired by work on declarative mocking [59].

Testing Cyber-Physical Systems. There is a large body of work on automated test generation tools for cyber-physical systems through heuristic search of a high-dimensional continuous state space. While much of this work has focused on low-level controller interfaces [6,17,19,20,25,60] rather than the system level, specification and test generation techniques arising from this work—for example, the use of metric and signal temporal logics or search heuristics—can be adapted to our setting. More recently, test generation tools have started targeting autonomous systems under a simulation-based semantic testing framework similar to ours. In most of these works, visual scenarios are either fixed by hand [1,2,10,22,27,29,66,67], or are constrained due to the model or coverage criteria [3,45,50]. These analyses are shown to be preferable to the application of random noise on the input vector. Additionally, a simulation-based approach filters benign misclassifications from misclassifications that actually lead to bad or dangerous behavior. Our work extends this line of work and provides an expressive language to design parameterized environments and tests. AsFault [29] uses random search and mutation for procedural generation of road networks for testing. AC3R [28] reconstructs test cases from accident reports.

To address problems of high time and infrastructure cost of testing autonomous systems, several simulators have been developed. The most popular is Gazebo [26] for the ROS [54] robotics framework. It offers a modular and extensible architecture, however falls behind on visual realism and complexity of environments that can be generated with it. To counter this, game engines are used. Popular examples are TORCS [72], CARLA [21], and AirSim [61] Modern game engines support creation of realistic urban environments. Though they enable visually realistic simulations, and enable detection of infractions such as collisions, the environments themselves are difficult to design. Designing a custom environment involves manual placement of road segments, buildings, and actors (as well as their properties). Performing many systematic tests is therefore time-consuming and difficult. While these systems and PARACOSM share the same aims and much of the same infrastructure, PARACOSM focuses on procedural design and systematic testing, backed by a relevant coverage criteria.

Adversarial Testing. Adversarial examples for neural networks [32,64] introduce perturbations to inputs that cause a classifier to classify "perceptually identical" inputs differently. Much work has focused on finding adversarial examples in the context of autonomous driving as well as on training a network to be robust to perturbations [11,30,46,51,71]. Tools such as DEEPXPLORE [52], DEEPTEST [65], DEEPGAUGE [41], and SADL [37] define a notion of coverage for neural networks based on the number of neurons activated during tests compared against the total number of neurons in the network and activation during training. However, these techniques focus mostly on individual classification tasks and apply 2D transformations on images. In comparison, we consider the closed-loop behavior of the system and our parameters directly change the world rather than apply transformations post facto. We can observe, over time, that certain vehicles are not detected, which is more useful to testers than a single misclassification [31]. Furthermore, it is already known that structural coverage criteria may not be an effective strategy for finding errors in classification [39]. We use coverage metrics on the test space, rather than the structure of the neural network. Alternately, there are recent techniques to verify controllers implemented as neural networks through constraint solving or abstract interpretation [24, 30, 34, 58, 71]. While these tools do not focus on the problem of autonomous driving, their underlying techniques can be combined in the test generation phase for PARACOSM.

6 Future Work and Conclusion

Deploying autonomous systems like self-driving cars in urban environments raises several safety challenges. The complex software stack processes sensor data, builds a semantic model of the surrounding world, makes decisions, plans trajectories, and controls the car. The end-to-end testing of such systems requires the creation and simulation of whole worlds, with different tests representing different world and parameter configurations. PARACOSM tackles these problems by (i) enabling procedural construction of diverse scenarios, with precise control over elements like road layout, physical and visual properties of objects, and behaviors of actors in the system, and (ii) using quasi-random testing to obtain good coverage over large parameter spaces.

In our evaluation, we show that PARACOSM enables easy design of environmnents and automated testing of autonomous agents implemented using neural networks. While finding errors in sensing can be done with only a few static images, we show that PARACOSM also enables the creation of longer test scenarios which exercise the controller's feedback on the environment. Our case studies focused on *qualitative* state space exploration. In future work, we shall perform *quantitative* statistical analysis to understand the sensitivity of autonomous vehicle behavior on individual parameters.

In the future, we plan to extend PARACOSM's testing infrastructure to also aid in the training of deep neural networks that require large amounts of high quality training data. For instance, we show that small variations in the environment result in widely different results for road segmentation. Generating data is a time consuming and expensive task. PARACOSM can easily generate labelled data for static images. For driving scenarios, we can record a user manually driving in a parameterized PARACOSM environment and augment this data by varying parameters that should not impact the car's behavior. For instance, we can vary the color of other cars, positions of pedestrians who are not crossing, or even the light conditions and sensor properties (within reasonable limits).

Acknowledgements This research was funded in part by the Deutsche Forschungsgemeinschaft project 389792660-TRR 248 and by the European Research Council under the Grant Agreement 610150 (ERC Synergy Grant ImPACT).

References

1. Abbas, H., O'Kelly, M., Rodionova, A., Mangharam, R.: Safe at any speed: A simulation-based test harness for autonomous vehicles. In: 7th Workshop on Design, Modeling and Evaluation of Cyber Physical Systems (CyPhy17) (October 2017)

2. Abdessalem, R.B., Nejati, S., Briand, L.C., Stifter, T.: Testing vision-based control systems using learnable evolutionary algorithms. In: Proceedings of the 40th International Conference on Software Engineering. p. 1016–1026. ICSE '18, Association for Computing Machinery, New York, NY, USA (2018). https://doi.org/10.1145/3180155.3180160, https://doi.org/10.1145/3180155.3180160

3. Alexander, R., Hawkins, H., Rae, A.: Situation coverage – a coverage criterion for testing autonomous robots (02 2015)

4. Alon, N., Spencer, J.H.: The Probabilistic Method. Wiley-Interscience series in discrete mathematics and optimization, Wiley (2004)

5. American Fuzzy Loop: Technical "whitepaper" for afl-fuzz, http://lcamtuf.coredump.cx/afl/technical_details.txt, accessed: 2019-08-23

6. Annpureddy, Y., Liu, C., Fainekos, G.E., Sankaranarayanan, S.: S-TaLiRo: A tool for temporal logic falsification for hybrid systems. In: TACAS 11. Lecture Notes in Computer Science, vol. 6605, pp. 254–257. Springer (2011)

7. Association for Advancement of international Standardization of Automation and Measuring Systems (ASAM): Opendrive (2018), http://www.opendrive.org/index.html, accessed: 2019-08-21

8. Association for Advancement of international Standardization of Automation and Measuring Systems (ASAM): Openscenario (2018), http://www.opendrive.org/index.html, accessed: 2019-08-21

9. Beck, K.L.: Test Driven Development: By Example. Addison-Wesley Professional (2002)

10. Ben Abdessalem, R., Nejati, S., Briand, L.C., Stifter, T.: Testing advanced driver assistance systems using multi-objective search and neural networks. In: Proceedings of the 31st IEEE/ACM International Conference on Automated Software Engineering (ASE). pp. 63–74 (2016)

11. Bhagoji, A.N., He, W., Li, B., Song, D.: Exploring the space of black-box attacks on deep neural networks. CoRR **abs/1712.09491** (2017), http://arxiv.org/abs/1712.09491

12. Bojarski, M., Del Testa, D., Dworakowski, D., Firner, B., Flepp, B., Goyal, P., Jackel, L.D., Monfort, M., Muller, U., Zhang, J., et al.: End to end learning for self-driving cars. arXiv preprint arXiv:1604.07316 (2016)

13. Caspi, P., Pilaud, D., Halbwachs, N., Plaice, J.: Lustre: A declarative language for programming synchronous systems. In: Conference Record of the Fourteenth Annual ACM Symposium on Principles of Programming Languages, Munich, Germany, January 21-23, 1987. pp. 178–188 (1987)

14. Colbourn, C.J.: Combinatorial aspects of covering arrays. Le Matematiche **59**(1,2), 125–172 (2004), https://lematematiche.dmi.unict.it/index.php/lematematiche/article/view/166

15. comma.ai: openpilot: open source driving agent (2016), https://github.com/commaai/openpilot, accessed: 2018-11-13

16. Coporation, N.: Physx (2008), https://developer.nvidia.com/gameworks-physx-overview, accessed: 2018-11-13

17. Deshmukh, J., Jin, X., Kapinski, J., Maler, O.: Stochastic local search for falsification of hybrid systems. In: ATVA. pp. 500–517. Springer (2015)
18. Deshmukh, J.V., Donzé, A., Ghosh, S., Jin, X., Juniwal, G., Seshia, S.A.: Robust online monitoring of signal temporal logic. Formal Methods in System Design **51**(1), 5–30 (2017). https://doi.org/10.1007/s10703-017-0286-7, https://doi.org/10.1007/s10703-017-0286-7
19. Deshmukh, J.V., Horvat, M., Jin, X., Majumdar, R., Prabhu, V.S.: Testing cyber-physical systems through bayesian optimization. ACM Trans. Embedded Comput. Syst. **16**(5), 170:1–170:18 (2017). https://doi.org/10.1145/3126521, https://doi.org/10.1145/3126521
20. Donzé, A.: Breach, A Toolbox for Verification and Parameter Synthesis of Hybrid Systems, pp. 167–170. Springer (2010)
21. Dosovitskiy, A., Ros, G., Codevilla, F., Lopez, A., Koltun, V.: CARLA: An open urban driving simulator. In: Proceedings of the 1st Annual Conference on Robot Learning. pp. 1–16 (2017)
22. Dreossi, T., Donzé, A., Seshia, S.A.: Compositional falsification of cyber-physical systems with machine learning components. In: NASA Formal Methods - 9th International Symposium, NFM 2017. Lecture Notes in Computer Science, vol. 10227, pp. 357–372. Springer (2017)
23. Dreossi, T., Jha, S., Seshia, S.A.: Semantic adversarial deep learning **10981**, 3–26 (2018). https://doi.org/10.1007/978-3-319-96145-3_1, https://doi.org/10.1007/978-3-319-96145-3_1
24. Dutta, S., Chen, X., Jha, S., Sankaranarayanan, S., Tiwari, A.: Sherlock - A tool for verification of neural network feedback systems: demo abstract. In: Ozay, N., Prabhakar, P. (eds.) Proceedings of the 22nd ACM International Conference on Hybrid Systems: Computation and Control, HSCC 2019, Montreal, QC, Canada, April 16-18, 2019. pp. 262–263. ACM (2019). https://doi.org/10.1145/3302504.3313351, https://doi.org/10.1145/3302504.3313351
25. Fainekos, G.: Automotive control design bug-finding with the S-TaLiRo tool. In: ACC 2015. p. 4096 (2015)
26. Foundation, O.S.R.: Vehicle simulation in gazebo, http://gazebosim.org/blog/vehicle%20simulation, accessed: 2019-08-23
27. Fremont, D.J., Dreossi, T., Ghosh, S., Yue, X., Sangiovanni-Vincentelli, A.L., Seshia, S.A.: Scenic: A language for scenario specification and scene generation. In: Proceedings of the 40th ACM SIGPLAN Conference on Programming Language Design and Implementation. pp. 63–78. PLDI 2019, ACM, New York, NY, USA (2019). https://doi.org/10.1145/3314221.3314633, http://doi.acm.org/10.1145/3314221.3314633
28. Gambi, A., Huynh, T., Fraser, G.: Generating effective test cases for self-driving cars from police reports. In: Dumas, M., Pfahl, D., Apel, S., Russo, A. (eds.) Proceedings of the ACM Joint Meeting on European Software Engineering Conference and Symposium on the Foundations of Software Engineering, ESEC/SIGSOFT FSE 2019, Tallinn, Estonia, August 26-30, 2019. pp. 257–267. ACM (2019). https://doi.org/10.1145/3338906.3338942, https://doi.org/10.1145/3338906.3338942
29. Gambi, A., Müller, M., Fraser, G.: Automatically testing self-driving cars with search-based procedural content generation. In: Zhang, D., Møller, A. (eds.) Proceedings of the 28th ACM SIGSOFT International Symposium on Software Testing and Analysis, ISSTA 2019, Beijing, China, July 15-19, 2019. pp. 318–328. ACM (2019). https://doi.org/10.1145/3293882.3330566, https://doi.org/10.1145/3293882.3330566

30. Gehr, T., Mirman, M., Drachsler-Cohen, D., Tsankov, P., Chaudhuri, S., Vechev, M.T.: AI2: safety and robustness certification of neural networks with abstract interpretation. In: 2018 IEEE Symposium on Security and Privacy, S&P 2018. pp. 3–18. IEEE (2018)

31. Gladisch, C., Heinz, T., Heinzemann, C., Oehlerking, J., von Vietinghoff, A., Pfitzer, T.: Experience paper: Search-based testing in automated driving control applications. In: Proceedings of the 34th IEEE/ACM International Conference on Automated Software Engineering (ASE). pp. 26–37 (2019)

32. Goodfellow, I.J., Shlens, J., Szegedy, C.: Explaining and harnessing adversarial examples. CoRR **abs/1412.6572** (2014), http://arxiv.org/abs/1412.6572

33. Ho, H., Ouaknine, J., Worrell, J.: Online monitoring of metric temporal logic. In: Runtime Verification RV 2014. Lecture Notes in Computer Science, vol. 8734, pp. 178–192. Springer (2014)

34. Huang, X., Kwiatkowska, M., Wang, S., Wu, M.: Safety verification of deep neural networks. In: Majumdar, R., Kuncak, V. (eds.) Computer Aided Verification - 29th International Conference, CAV 2017, Heidelberg, Germany, July 24-28, 2017, Proceedings, Part I. Lecture Notes in Computer Science, vol. 10426, pp. 3–29. Springer (2017). https://doi.org/10.1007/978-3-319-63387-9_1, https://doi.org/10. 1007/978-3-319-63387-9_1

35. Hudak, P., Courtney, A., Nilsson, H., Peterson, J.: Arrows, robots, and functional reactive programming. In: Advanced Functional Programming, 4th International School, AFP 2002, Oxford, UK, August 19-24, 2002, Revised Lectures. Lecture Notes in Computer Science, vol. 2638, pp. 159–187. Springer (2002). https://doi.org/10.1007/978-3-540-44833-4_6, https://doi.org/10. 1007/978-3-540-44833-4_6

36. Kawai, Y.: Unirx: Reactive extensions for unity (2014), https://github.com/ neuecc/UniRx, accessed: 2018-11-13

37. Kim, J., Feldt, R., Yoo, S.: Guiding deep learning system testing using surprise adequacy. In: Proceedings of the 41st International Conference on Software Engineering. pp. 1039–1049. ICSE '19, IEEE Press, Piscataway, NJ, USA (2019). https://doi.org/10.1109/ICSE.2019.00108, https://doi.org/10.1109/ICSE. 2019.00108

38. Kuhn, D.R., Kacker, R.N., Lei, Y.: Combinatorial testing. In: Laplante, P.A. (ed.) Encyclopedia of Software Engineering, pp. 1–12. CRC Press (Nov 2010)

39. Li, Z., Ma, X., Xu, C., Cao, C.: Structural coverage criteria for neural networks could be misleading. In: Sarma, A., Murta, L. (eds.) Proceedings of the 41st International Conference on Software Engineering: New Ideas and Emerging Results, ICSE (NIER) 2019, Montreal, QC, Canada, May 29-31, 2019. pp. 89–92. IEEE / ACM (2019), https://dl.acm.org/citation.cfm?id=3339171

40. Liberty, J., Betts, P.: Programming Reactive Extensions and LINQ. Apress (2011)

41. Ma, L., Juefei-Xu, F., Zhang, F., Sun, J., Xue, M., Li, B., Chen, C., Su, T., Li, L., Liu, Y., Zhao, J., Wang, Y.: Deepgauge: Multi-granularity testing criteria for deep learning systems. In: Proceedings of the 33rd ACM/IEEE International Conference on Automated Software Engineering. pp. 120–131. ASE 2018, ACM, New York, NY, USA (2018). https://doi.org/10.1145/3238147.3238202, http://doi.acm.org/ 10.1145/3238147.3238202

42. Mackinnon, T., Freeman, S., Craig, P.: Endo-testing: Unit testing with mock objects. In: eXtreme Programming and Flexible Processes in Software Engineering - XP2000 (2000)

43. Majumdar, R., Mathur, A.S., Pirron, M., Stegner, L., Zufferey, D.: Paracosm: A language and tool for testing autonomous driving systems. CoRR **abs/1902.01084** (2019), http://arxiv.org/abs/1902.01084

44. Majumdar, R., Niksic, F.: Why is random testing effective for partition tolerance bugs? PACMPL **2**(POPL), 46:1–46:24 (2018)

45. Majzik, I., Semeráth, O., Hajdu, C., Marussy, K., Szatmári, Z., Micskei, Z., Vörös, A., Babikian, A.A., Varró, D.: Towards system-level testing with coverage guarantees for autonomous vehicles. In: 2019 ACM/IEEE 22nd International Conference on Model Driven Engineering Languages and Systems (MODELS). pp. 89–94 (2019). https://doi.org/10.1109/MODELS.2019.00-12

46. Mirman, M., Gehr, T., Vechev, M.: Differentiable abstract interpretation for provably robust neural networks. In: International Conference on Machine Learning (ICML) (2018), https://www.icml.cc/Conferences/2018/Schedule?showEvent=2477

47. Mockito: Tasty mocking framework for unit tests in java, http://site.mockito.org, accessed: 2019-08-23

48. National Transportation Safety Board: Collision between vehicle controlled by developmental automated driving system and pedestrian, tempe, arizona, march 18, 2018. Highway Accident Report NTSB/HAR-19/03, National Transportation Safety Board (November 2019)

49. Niederreiter, H.: Random number generation and quasi-Monte Carlo methods. SIAM (1992)

50. O'Kelly, M., Sinha, A., Namkoong, H., Tedrake, R., Duchi, J.C.: Scalable end-to-end autonomous vehicle testing via rare-event simulation. Advances in Neural Information Processing Systems **31**, 9827–9838 (2018)

51. Papernot, N., McDaniel, P., Goodfellow, I., Jha, S., Celik, Z.B., Swami, A.: Practical black-box attacks against machine learning. In: Proceedings of the 2017 ACM on Asia Conference on Computer and Communications Security - ASIA CCS 17. ACM (2017). https://doi.org/10.1145/3052973.3053009, https://doi.org/10.1145/3052973.3053009

52. Pei, K., Cao, Y., Yang, J., Jana, S.: Deepxplore: Automated whitebox testing of deep learning systems. In: Proceedings of the 26th Symposium on Operating Systems Principles, Shanghai, China, October 28-31, 2017. pp. 1–18. ACM (2017). https://doi.org/10.1145/3132747.3132785, https://doi.org/10.1145/3132747.3132785

53. Pomerleau, D.: ALVINN: An autonomous land vehicle in a neural network. In: NIPS 88: Neural Information Processing Systems (1988)

54. Quigley, M., Conley, K., Gerkey, B., Faust, J., Foote, T., Leibs, J., Wheeler, R., Ng, A.: Ros: an open-source robot operating system. In: ICRA workshop on open source software (2009)

55. Rawat, S., Jain, V., Kumar, A.J.S., Cojocar, L., Giuffrida, C., Bos, H.: Vuzzer: Application-aware evolutionary fuzzing. In: NDSS (2017)

56. ReactiveX: Reactivex, http://reactivex.io/, accessed: 2019-08-23

57. Rote, G., Tichy, R.: Quasi-Monte-Carlo methods and the dispersion of point sequences. Mathematical and Computer Modelling **23**, 9–23 (1996)

58. Ruan, W., Huang, X., Kwiatkowska, M.: Reachability analysis of deep neural networks with provable guarantees. In: Lang, J. (ed.) Proceedings of the Twenty-Seventh International Joint Conference on Artificial Intelligence, IJCAI 2018, July 13-19, 2018, Stockholm, Sweden. pp. 2651–2659. ijcai.org (2018). https://doi.org/10.24963/ijcai.2018/368, https://doi.org/10.24963/ijcai.2018/368

59. Samimi, H., Hicks, R., Fogel, A., Millstein, T.: Declarative mocking. In: ISSTA 2013. pp. 246–256. ACM (2013)
60. Sankaranarayanan, S., Fainekos, G.: Falsification of temporal properties of hybrid systems using the cross-entropy method. In: HSCC 12. pp. 125–134. ACM (2012)
61. Shah, S., Dey, D., Lovett, C., Kapoor, A.: Airsim: High-fidelity visual and physical simulation for autonomous vehicles. In: Field and Service Robotics (2017), https://arxiv.org/abs/1705.05065
62. Simonyan, K., Zisserman, A.: Very deep convolutional networks for large-scale image recognition. CoRR **abs/1409.1556** (2014)
63. Stewart, L., Musa, M., Croce, N.: Look no hands: self-driving vehicles' public trust problem (2019), https://www.weforum.org/agenda/2019/08/self-driving-vehicles-public-trust/, accessed: 2021-01-18
64. Szegedy, C., Zaremba, W., Sutskever, I., Bruna, J., Erhan, D., Goodfellow, I.J., Fergus, R.: Intriguing properties of neural networks. CoRR **abs/1312.6199** (2013)
65. Tian, Y., Pei, K., Jana, S., Ray, B.: Deeptest: Automated testing of deep-neural-network-driven autonomous cars. In: Proceedings of the 40th International Conference on Software Engineering. pp. 303–314. ACM (2018)
66. Tuncali, C.E., Fainekos, G., Prokhorov, D., Ito, H., Kapinski, J.: Requirements-driven test generation for autonomous vehicles with machine learning components. arXiv preprint arXiv:1908.01094 (2019)
67. Tuncali, C.E., Fainekos, G.E., Ito, H., Kapinski, J.: Sim-atav: Simulation-based adversarial testing framework for autonomous vehicles. In: Proceedings of the 21st International Conference on Hybrid Systems: Computation and Control (part of CPS Week), HSCC 2018, Porto, Portugal, April 11-13, 2018. pp. 283–284. ACM (2018). https://doi.org/10.1145/3178126.3187004, http://doi.acm.org/10.1145/3178126.3187004
68. Udacity: Self-driving car simulator, https://github.com/udacity/self-driving-car-sim, accessed: 2019-08-23
69. Unity3D: Unity game engine, https://unity3d.com/, accessed: 2019-08-23
70. Wan, Z., Hudak, P.: Functional reactive programming from first principles. In: Proceedings of the 2000 ACM SIGPLAN Conference on Programming Language Design and Implementation (PLDI), Vancouver, Britith Columbia, Canada, June 18-21, 2000. pp. 242–252. ACM (2000). https://doi.org/10.1145/349299.349331, https://doi.org/10.1145/349299.349331
71. Wicker, M., Huang, X., Kwiatkowska, M.: Feature-guided black-box safety testing of deep neural networks. In: Beyer, D., Huisman, M. (eds.) Tools and Algorithms for the Construction and Analysis of Systems - 24th International Conference, TACAS 2018, Held as Part of the European Joint Conferences on Theory and Practice of Software, ETAPS 2018, Thessaloniki, Greece, April 14-20, 2018, Proceedings, Part I. Lecture Notes in Computer Science, vol. 10805, pp. 408–426. Springer (2018). https://doi.org/10.1007/978-3-319-89960-2_22, https://doi.org/10.1007/978-3-319-89960-2_22
72. Wymann, B., Espié, E., Guionneau, C., Dimitrakakis, C., Coulom, R., Sumner, A.: TORCS, The Open Racing Car Simulator. http://www.torcs.org (2014)

Compositional Analysis of Probabilistic Timed Graph Transformation Systems*

Maria Maximova ⓘ (✉), Sven Schneider ⓘ, and Holger Giese ⓘ

University of Potsdam, Hasso Plattner Institute, Potsdam, Germany
{maria.maximova,sven.schneider,holger.giese}@hpi.de

Abstract. The analysis of behavioral models is of high importance for cyber-physical systems, as the systems often encompass complex behavior based on e.g. concurrent components with mutual exclusion or probabilistic failures on demand. The rule-based formalism of probabilistic timed graph transformation systems is a suitable choice when the models representing states of the system can be understood as graphs and timed and probabilistic behavior is important. However, model checking PTGTSs is limited to systems with rather small state spaces.

We present an approach for the analysis of large-scale systems modeled as probabilistic timed graph transformation systems by systematically decomposing their state spaces into manageable fragments. To obtain qualitative and quantitative analysis results for a large-scale system, we verify that results obtained for its fragments serve as overapproximations for the corresponding results of the large-scale system. Hence, our approach allows for the detection of violations of qualitative and quantitative safety properties for the large-scale system under analysis. We consider a running example in which we model shuttles driving on tracks of a large-scale topology and for which we verify that shuttles never collide and are unlikely to execute emergency brakes. In our evaluation, we apply an implementation of our approach to the running example.

Keywords: cyber-physical systems, graph transformation systems, qualitative analysis, quantitative analysis, probabilistic timed systems, compositional analysis, model checking

1 Introduction

Real-time cyber-physical systems often emit a complex behavior based on e.g. concurrent components with mutual exclusion or probabilistic failures on demand. Consequently, modeling formalisms for capturing such systems must suitably support the modeling of their complex behaviors. In such a model driven approach, the analysis of behavioral models w.r.t. a provided specification is vital to ensure overall soundness of the resulting system.

---

* Funded by the Deutsche Forschungsgemeinschaft (DFG, German Research Foundation) - 241885098, 148420506.

E. Guerra and M. Stoelinga (Eds.): FASE 2021, LNCS 12649, pp. 196–217, 2021.
https://doi.org/10.1007/978-3-030-71500-7_10

Fig. 1: Occurrence of single FT with border and core in LST (left) and five occurrences of three FTs in LST overlapping in their borders (right).

The rule-based transformation of graphs is a suitable choice when the models representing states of the system can be understood as graphs. In particular, the formalism of probabilistic timed graph transformation systems (PTGTSs) extends the standard rule-based transformation of graphs such that timed and probabilistic behavior is covered by supporting (a) non-deterministic choice among steps, (b) probabilistic choice among step results, and (c) steps representing the passage of time.

A model checking approach for PTGTSs w.r.t. probabilistic metric temporal properties was introduced in [19]. However, also this model checking approach is limited to systems with rather small state spaces due to the state space explosion problem. As a workaround, a selected set of small examples may be considered hopefully capturing all system-specific challenges to establish trust that the model exhibits the required safe behavior and that unwanted behavior is sufficiently unlikely. However, it cannot be excluded that the considered small examples do not reveal all the threatening behavior.

We present a decomposition-based approach for the analysis of large-scale systems modeled as PTGTSs to rule out violations of qualitative and quantitative safety properties.

As a first step, we capture the underlying static large-scale topology (short LST) of a large-scale system as a subgraph that is not changed by graph transformation, describe how a fragment topology (short FT) can be embedded into such an LST (see the left part of Figure 1), and specify how multiple such embeddings of FTs can overlap in their borders (see the right part of Figure 1).

As a second step, based on the decomposition described by such embeddings, we construct for each FT an adapted PTGTS. Such an adapted PTGTS is then ensured to (a) exhibit the same behavior on the non-overlapped part of the FT (named *core*) and to (b) simulate all possible behaviors that can happen for any occurrence of the FT in an LST. To obtain the mentioned simulation, we include modifications of the rules of the original PTGTS operating on the border of an FT into the adapted PTGTS. With this direct relationship between behaviors on the FTs and the LST, we obtain that the likelihood of an unwanted or forbidden graph pattern in one of the adapated PTGTS is an upper bound for its likelihood in its embedding in the large-scale PTGTS.

As a last step, exploiting our decomposition to counter the state space explosion problem, we apply the model checking approach from [19] to the PT-

GTSs constructed for the FTs employing its reduction to probabilistic timed automata (PTA) instead of applying the model checking approach directly to the PTGTS modeling the large-scale system.

To illustrate our approach, we consider a running example in which we model shuttles driving on tracks of an LST and for which we verify that shuttles never collide and are unlikely to execute emergency brakes. In our evaluation, we apply an implementation of our approach to the running example.

The idea to decompose a system into subsystems or to compose it from subsystems for the analysis has been studied intensively [25] but our suggested compositional approach has distinguishing characteristics. Firstly, the vast majority of approaches (like process algebras or similar models) assume that the modeling formalism supports the composition/decomposition as a first class concept such that compositional analysis techniques are directly applicable as the subsystem models cover all possible behaviors in all contexts. In contrast, we do not rely on a built-in decomposition operator but rather allow for a flexible derivation of an LST decomposition in terms of FTs, overlappings, and a suitable overapproximation on the border, which are not predefined by the modeling formalism.

Secondly, several approaches rely on a protocol-like specification of how the decomposed subsystems interact, while in our approach the overapproximation is derived systematically from the PTGTS model that does not necessarily provide such a protocol-like specification already. The compositional analysis approach for graph transformation systems (GTSs) from [24, 11] defines explicit interfaces, which are used to consider whether the behavior of two independent graphs glued via these interfaces (requiring that local transitions are compatible) cover jointly all global transitions. Moreover, in further approaches, protocols for the roles of collaborations and ports of components have been assumed. For example, in [14], the idea to overapproximate the environment and border is explored for timed automata with explicit models of the roles in form of protocol automata. This idea has been combined with dynamic collaborations in [12, 13] captured by timed GTSs (TGTSs) and their analysis via inductive invariant checking [3, 4]. Later on, this approach has been extended to role, component, and collaboration behavior, which is captured by TGTSs and hybrid GTSs in [5] and [2], respectively. However, as opposed to the presented approach, in all these cases an explicit concept of interface is assumed to separate parts that are analyzed in isolation.

This paper is structured as follows. In section 2, we introduce our running example from the domain of cyber-physical systems. In section 3, we recapitulate the necessary preliminaries related to PTA and PTGTSs also presenting the modeling of our running example. In section 4, we discuss the decomposition of static substructures of large-scale systems. In section 5, we present our decomposition-based approach allowing to split the model checking problem into more manageable parts. In section 6, we present an evaluation of the conceptual results for our running example. Finally, in section 7, we close the paper with a conclusion and an outlook on planned future work.

2   Running Example

We now informally introduce a scenario (based on the RailCab project [23]) of autonomous shuttles driving on an LST, which serves as a running example in the remainder of this paper. Based on this introduction, we will discuss how we model this shuttle scenario as a PTGTS in the next section.

In the considered shuttle scenario, a track topology containing a large number of tracks of approximately equal length is given. Tracks are connected to the adjacent tracks via directed connections building in this manner track sequences. Two track sequences can be joined together (i.e., can end up in a common track with two predecessors) leading to a *join* fragment topology (see FT8 in Figure 4a) or can split up from a common track (i.e., a common track has then two successor tracks) leading to a *fork* fragment topology (see FT7 in Figure 4a). Moreover, depots may have a directed connection to a track allowing shuttles to enter or exit the track topology. Shuttles, which are always located on a single track, may be in mode *DRIVE*, *STOP*, or *BRAKE*. Being in mode *DRIVE*, shuttles drive to the next track (respecting the direction of the connection between the tracks) with a certain velocity, which may be slow ($[3,4]$ time units per track) or fast ($[2,3]$ time units per track). Regularly, shuttles change into mode *STOP*, which allows them to avoid coming too close to other shuttles. Moreover, shuttles should slow down before entering a track with a construction site on it. However, shuttles noticing the construction site too late have to execute an emergency brake thereby changing into the mode *BRAKE*. To reduce the likelihood of such emergency brakes, yellow traffic lights are installed a few tracks ahead of such construction sites to indicate to shuttles that they should slow down. After construction sites, green traffic lights may be installed permitting shuttles to increase their velocity. However, we also consider failures on demand where a traffic light that is passed by a shuttle is not recognized or, for some other reason, not appropriately taken into account by the shuttle. We assume a failure probability of 10^{-6} for this case assuming that the failure does not only depend on the visual observation by the train driver but also depends on a failure of the backup system.

In our running example, *static* elements are the tracks, depots, installed traffic lights, and construction sites as well as connections between these elements. The PTGTS modeling the behavior of the described scenario never changes this underlying LST. Complementary, *dynamic* elements are shuttles, their attributes, their connections to tracks of the LST as well as the attributes of traffic lights. Note that we use later a grammar to generate admissible LSTs.

For the considered shuttle scenario, we are interested in various properties. Firstly, we need to verify that the behavior of the system never gets temporally stuck in a state where no steps (discrete steps of e.g. driving shuttles or timed steps) are enabled. Secondly, we need to verify whether the rules have been constructed in a way ensuring the absence of collisions between shuttles (i.e., two shuttles should not be on a common track). Thirdly, emergency brakes should be improbable at a local level for a single shuttle but also at the global level for the entire LST and its possible numerous number of shuttles.

(a) Type graph

(b) Invariant

(c) DPO diagram

(d) Example of a PTA

(e) Atomic propositions

(f) The rule *SetSlow*: a shuttle may *successfully* decrease its velocity by setting its time per track to $[3,4]$ (where only the lower end of the interval is stored in the graph) with probability $1 - 10^{-6}$ or may *fail* to decrease its velocity with probability 10^{-6}. Setting the *active* attribute to $\perp$ ensures that the rule cannot be applied twice.

(g) The rule *ConstructionSiteBrake*: a shuttle with high velocity ($[2,3]$ time units per track where only the lower end of the interval is stored in the graph) needs to execute an emergency brake to ensure that the track with a construction site on it is not entered with a too high velocity.

Fig. 2: Details for our running example, DPO diagram, and PTA example.

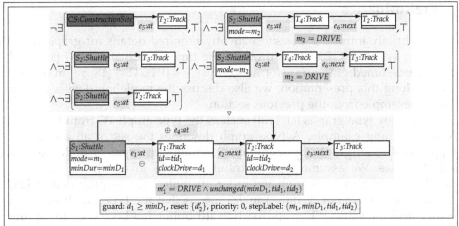

(a) The rule *Drive*: a shuttle may drive to the next track where the application condition is used to rule out situations that on the next track is a construction site or that the considered shuttle comes too close to another shuttle.

(b) The rule *DriveEnterFast*: adaptation of the rule *Drive* for the case that a new shuttle enters the current fragment topology with a high velocity (the similar rule for a shuttle with a low velocity has been omitted here for brevity) from a context track belonging to another fragment topology.

(c) The rule *DriveExit1*: adaptation of the rule *Drive* for the case that a shuttle drives onto the last track of the current fragment topology.

(d) The rule *DriveExit2*: adaptation of the rule *Drive* for the case that a shuttle exits the current fragment topology towards a track belonging to another fragment topology.

Fig. 3: The rule *Drive* and the three adapted rules *DriveEnterFast*, *DriveExit1*, and *DriveExit2* for fragment topologies where parts of the application condition of the rule *Drive* are omitted due to the overlay specification of the running example.

3 Preliminaries

We now briefly introduce the subsequently required details for graph transformation systems (GTSs) [10], probabilistic timed automata (PTA) [17], and probabilistic timed graph transformation systems (PTGTSs) [18, 19] in our notation. Along this presentation, we also discuss the modeling details for our running example from the previous section.

We employ type graphs (cf. [10]) such as the type graph TG from Figure 2a for our running example. A type graph describes the set of all admissible (typed attributed) graphs by mentioning the allowed types of nodes, edges, and attributes. We assume typed attributed graphs in which attributes are specified using a many sorted first-order attribute logic as proposed in [21] (the attribute constraint $\bot$ (false) in TG means that the type graph does not restrict attribute values). This approach to attribution has been used to capture constraints on attributes in graph conditions in [27] and to describe attribute modifications in [22, 28].

Graph transformation is then performed by applying a graph transformation rule (short rule) $\rho = (\ell : K \hookrightarrow L, r : K \hookrightarrow R)$ consisting of two monomorphisms (i.e., all components of the morphisms are injective). The rule specifies that the graph elements in $L - \ell(K)$ are to be deleted, the graph elements in K are to be preserved, and the graph elements in $R - r(K)$ are to be added during graph transformation. Such a rule is applied to a graph G for a given match $m : L \hookrightarrow G$ resulting in a graph G'' by constructing the double pushout (DPO) diagram (see Figure 2c) where the first and the second pushout squares describe the removal and the addition of graph elements specified in the rule, respectively. Moreover, a rule may additionally contain an application condition ϕ (denoted by $\rho = (\ell, r, \phi)$) to rule out certain matches specifying e.g. graph elements that may not be connected to graph elements matched by m. For further details on the graph transformation approach, we refer to [10].

PTA [17] combine the use of clocks to capture real-time phenomena and probabilism to approximate/describe the likelihood of outcomes of certain steps. A PTA such as the one in Figure 2d consists of (a) a set of locations with a distinguished initial location such as ℓ_0, (b) a set of clocks such as c_0 (which are initially set to 0), (c) an assignment of a set of atomic propositions (APs) such as $\{done\}$ to each location (for subsequent analysis of e.g. reachability properties), (d) an assignment of constraints on its clocks to each location as invariants such as $c_0 \leq 3$, and (e) a set of probabilistic timed edges each consisting of (e1) a single source location, (e2) at least one target location, (e3) a clock constraint such as $c_0 \geq 2$ specifying as a guard when the edge is enabled based on the current values of the clocks, (e4) for each target location a probability such as 0.5 that this target is reached (the sum of all the probabilities for the target locations of the edge must add up to 1 as a probability distribution is required), and (e5) for each target location a set of clocks such as $\{c_0\}$ to be reset to 0 when that target location is reached.

States of a PTA are given by pairs (ℓ, v) where ℓ is a location and v is the variable valuation mapping each clock of the PTA to a real number. Nondeterminism arises in PTA since a step for advancing time as well as multiple steps applying rules may be enabled in a single state. The logic PTCTL [17] then allows to specify properties such as "what is the worst-case probability that the PTA reaches a location labeled with the AP *done* within 5 time units", which can be analyzed by the PRISM model checker [16]. For the example PTA from Figure 2d, the given condition is satisfied with probability 0.75 since the nondeterminism of the PTA would be resolved (by a so-called adversary) such that the PTA first takes a step to ℓ_1 without letting time pass and then performs the probabilistic step (up to two times after waiting for not longer than 2 time units) until it reaches the location ℓ_2 labeled with the AP *done* (the probabilistic step cannot be taken a third time due to the requirement of at most 5 time units in the quoted property above).

PTGTSs have been introduced in [18, 19] as a probabilistic real-time extension of GTSs. It has been shown that PTGTSs can be translated to PTA and, hence, PTGTSs can be understood as a high-level language for PTA as discussed below in more detail and can be analyzed using PRISM as well.

Similarly to PTA, a PTGTS state is given by a pair (G, v) of a graph and a clock valuation. The initial state is given by a distinguished initial graph and a valuation setting all clocks to 0. In our running example, each attribute of type *clockDrive* of a *Track* node (cf. Figure 2a) represents one clock. Invariants and APs are specified for PTGTSs by means of graph conditions as in Figure 2b and Figure 2e, respectively, for our running example. We use the single invariant $INV_{driving}$ requiring that shuttles in mode *DRIVE* cannot be on a track longer than the value of their *minDur* (minimal duration) attribute plus 1. Moreover, we consider three APs to specify properties that we want to analyze later on. The AP $AP_{unexpectedVelocity}$ is used to detect graphs in which a shuttle does not have an expected velocity of $[2, 3]$ or $[3, 4]$ time units per track where only the lower end of the interval is stored in the graph in the *minDur* attribute. The AP $AP_{collision}$ is used to detect graphs in which two shuttles are on a common track to capture their collision. Finally, the AP AP_{braked} is used to detect graphs in which a shuttle has just executed an emergency brake.

PTGT rules of a PTGTS then correspond to edges of a PTA and contain (a) a left-hand side graph L, (b) an attribute constraint on the clock attributes contained in L to capture a guard, (c) a natural number describing a priority where higher numbers denote higher priorities, and (d) a nonempty set of tuples of the form $(\ell : K \hookrightarrow L, r : K \hookrightarrow R, \phi, C, p)$ where (ℓ, r, ϕ) is an underlying GT rule with application condition ϕ[1], C is a set of clock attributes contained in L to be reset, and p is a real-valued probability from $[0, 1]$ where the probabilities of all such tuples must add up to 1. See Figure 2f, Figure 2g, and Figure 3a for three PTGT rules *SetSlow*, *ConstructionSiteBrake*, and *Drive* from our running example where the last two PTGT rules have a unique underlying GT rule with probability 1 and where the first PTGT rule has a higher priority as well as two underlying GT rules with probabilities 10^{-6} and $1 - 10^{-6}$. For the PTGT rules *ConstructionSiteBrake* and *Drive*, we depict the graphs L, K, and

---

[1] The underlying GT rule may not delete or add clock attributes.

R in a single graph (subsequently called *LKR*-graph) where graph elements to be removed and to be added are annotated with $\ominus$ and $\oplus$, respectively. In the PTGT rule *SetSlow*, no graph elements are removed or added (i.e., the graphs L and R of the underlying GT rules coincide). Nevertheless, for this PTGT rule, we depict the two right-hand side morphisms r_1 and r_2 as they describe PTGT steps with different attribute modifications and probabilities. Also, the PTGT rules *ConstructionSiteBrake* and *Drive* have application conditions, which are depicted left to the $\triangleright$ symbol or above the $\triangledown$ symbol. The attribute preconditions and attribute modifications are given for each PTGT rule in the red box below the *LKR*-graph (or are split into multiple red boxes as for the PTGT rule *SetSlow*). In these attribute preconditions and attribute modifications, unprimed (primed) variables denote the values of attributes before (after) GT rule application. Note that if variables are not changed by the GT rule application, we denote this using the operator *unchanged* (see e.g. Figure 2g where $unchanged(minD_1, tid_1, tid_2)$ denotes that the variables $minD_1$, tid_1, and tid_2 remain unchanged). Moreover, further information about the PTGT rule (i.e., the guard and the priority) but also further information about the probabilistic choices (i.e., the sets of clocks to be reset and probabilities) are depicted in gray boxes. Lastly, we also allow to annotate a PTGT step in the induced state space with (a) a name chosen for the probabilistic choice such as *success* and *failure* in Figure 2f and (b) the values of the variables contained in the list stepLabel (which may contain variables from L and R).

When comparing PTA and PTGTSs, we observe that PTA edges are either enabled for the current valuation or not whereas PTGT rules may be applicable for many matches at the same time (e.g. allowing to apply the *Drive* for one of multiple shuttles). Priorities used in PTGTSs can be encoded in GTSs (including PTGTSs) by adding the left-hand side graphs of rules with higher priorities as negative application conditions to all rules with a lower priority. Similarly, priorities, if integrated into PTA, could be encoded by refining the guards. However, for our running example, we can exchange the underlying track topology without effort, while this would require a fundamental adaptation of the corresponding PTA. Also, as in [19], we observe in section 6 that small PTGTSs result in PTA of considerable size and we therefore conclude that PTGTSs are typically much more concise compared to PTA.

4   Decomposition of Large-Scale Topologies

We now present our decomposition-based approach to analyze a PTGTS $\mathcal{S}_0$ modeling a large-scale cyber-physical system along the lines of the informal presentation from the introduction. For our running example, such a PTGTS is given by an initial graph typed over the type graph from Figure 2a that is restricted later on in a suitable way, 13 PTGT rules of which we present three in Figure 2f, Figure 2g, and Figure 3a (further rules are given in [20, Appendix]), the invariant from Figure 2b, and the three APs from Figure 2e.

(a) FTs for our running example where the red arrows indicate points for topology (de)composition.

(b) Rule *Merge* for binary overlapping of two instances of FTs.

(c) Decomposition $M = \{m_1, m_2, m_3\}$ of an LST w.r.t. FT1–FT8.

Underlying GT rule ρ of the PTGTS $\mathcal{S}_0$

Step of $\mathcal{S}_0$ from G to G''

Step of $\mathcal{S}_i$ from F_i to F_i''

Underlying GT rule ρ_i of the PTGTS $\mathcal{S}_i$

(d) Correspondence of the graph transformation based steps between the large-scale system $\mathcal{S}_0$ and one of its fragment systems $\mathcal{S}_i$, which are preserving the respective static structure given by $\overline{G}$ and $\overline{F}_i$.

Fig. 4: FTs for our running example, rule *Merge*, example for topology composition, and correspondence between steps in the large-scale system and a fragment system.

As a first step, we identify a substructure of the initial graph of S_0 that is static in the sense that this substructure is preserved and also never extended throughout all PTGT steps of S_0. For large-scale cyber-physical systems such as our running example, the existence of such a static substructure may be justified by a logical or spatial distribution. The embedding of a static substructure $\overline{G}$ in a given graph G is then captured by a monomorphism $\kappa : \overline{G} \hookrightarrow G$ describing how $\overline{G}$ is embedded into G. As a special case, such an embedding κ can be derived for arbitrary graphs G by a monomorphism $\kappa_{TG} : \overline{TG} \hookrightarrow TG$ describing how the given type graph TG is restricted to a smaller type graph $\overline{TG}$. That is, $\overline{G}$ then contains only those elements from G that are typed over the smaller type graph $\overline{TG}$. For our running example, we restrict the type graph TG from Figure 2a to such a smaller type graph $\overline{TG}$ by removing the *Shuttle* node with its attributes, the *at* edge connected to the *Shuttle* node, and the *active* attributes from the *TLYellow* and *TLGreen* nodes. The graphs $\overline{G}$ obtained from graphs G of S_0 using this restriction are then called *large-scale topologies* (LSTs) and contain for our running example a track topology with depots, traffic lights, and construction sites. Note that the fact that such an underlying LST is indeed preserved and never extended by arbitrary rule applications can be verified (at least for our running example) by inspecting each rule individually using the technique of 1-induction [9, 26].

As a second step, we now introduce the notion of a decomposition of the LST into a small set of (constrained) *fragment topologies* (FTs). Such (constrained) FTs are given by (a) a graph that is typed over the type graph used for the LST and (b) a graph condition describing constraints on how the graph of the FT may be embedded into graphs of S_0. Moreover, an *overlapping specification* o is required to describe how the *embeddings* α_i of the graphs of two FTs may overlap in the LST. Such an overlapping specification is given by a set of spans $(o_1 : O \hookrightarrow \overline{T}_1, o_2 : O \hookrightarrow \overline{T}_2)$ where O is the *permitted overlapping graph* that is embedded into the two FTs. A decomposition of an LST (in the following definition, we simply consider the LST contained in the initial graph G_0 of S_0) is then given by embeddings of selected FTs into the LST (cf. Figure 1) such that the overlapping specification is satisfied (the constraints of the FTs are checked for S_0 later on). In applications, to reduce the state space explosion problem for the model checking phase later on, it is advantageous to employ a low number of small FTs that are strictly constrained and are allowed to overlap in a manageable number of ways.

Definition 1 (Decomposition of LST). *If*

- *S_0 is a PTGTS with initial state $s_0 = (G_0, v_0)$,*
- *$\kappa : \overline{G}_0 \hookrightarrow G_0$ is a monomorphism identifying the LST of S_0 contained in G_0,*
- *$\mathcal{F}$ is a set of (constrained) FTs of the form $(\overline{F}_i, \phi_i)$,*
- *$o((\overline{F}_1, \phi_1), (\overline{F}_2, \phi_2)) \subseteq \{(o_1, o_2) \mid o_1 : O \hookrightarrow \overline{F}_1, o_2 : O \hookrightarrow \overline{F}_2\}$ is an overlapping specification, which describes how two FTs from $\mathcal{F}$ may overlap,*
- *M is a list of tuples of the form $(\overline{F}, \phi, \alpha)$ where $(\overline{F}, \phi) \in \mathcal{F}$ and $\alpha : \overline{F} \hookrightarrow \overline{G}_0$,*
- *the monomorphisms in M respect the overlapping specification o, i.e., (see [20] for a visualization) for all $(\overline{F}_1, \phi_1, \alpha_1 : \overline{F}_1 \hookrightarrow \overline{G}_0), (\overline{F}_2, \phi_2, \alpha_2 : \overline{F}_2 \hookrightarrow \overline{G}_0) \in M$ there*

is some pair $(o_1 : O \hookrightarrow \overline{F}_1, o_2 : O \hookrightarrow \overline{F}_2) \in o((\overline{F}_1, \phi_1), (\overline{F}_2, \phi_2))$ *such that for the pushout* $(g_1 : \overline{F}_1 \hookrightarrow P, g_2 : \overline{F}_2 \hookrightarrow P)$ *of* (o_1, o_2) *(i.e., the overlapping of* $\overline{F}_1$ *and* $\overline{F}_2$ *w.r.t.* (o_1, o_2)*) there is some* $h : P \hookrightarrow G_0'$ *such that* $\alpha_1 = h \circ g_1$ *and* $\alpha_2 = h \circ g_2$.

then M *is a decomposition of the LST of* S_0 *w.r.t.* κ, $\mathcal{F}$, *and* o.   ◆

To provide a better intuition for this definition, we now present the decomposition of the LST considered for our running example.

Example 1 (Decomposition for Running Example). Let $\mathcal{F}$ contain the constrained FTs (FT$i, \phi_i$) for $1 \leq i \leq 8$ where each FTi is given in Figure 4a (here we use an abbreviated notation where D, T, Y, G, and CS are the obvious abbreviations for the node types of the type graph) and where ϕ_i states in each case that shuttles must have a velocity of $[2, 3]$ or $[3, 4]$ time units per track.[2]

Let $o((\overline{F}_1, \phi_1), (\overline{F}_2, \phi_2))$ be the overlapping specification stating that overlappings $(o_1 : O \hookrightarrow \overline{F}_1, o_2 : O \hookrightarrow \overline{F}_2)$ of two FTs are always (for any of the 8×8 combinations) of the form $O = T_1 \rightarrow T_2 \rightarrow T_3$ where T_1 and T_3 are mapped to a *Track* node in $\overline{F}_1$ and $\overline{F}_2$ with an entering and an exiting red arrow by o_1 and o_2, respectively.

An example of a decomposition of an LST employing the previously mentioned FTs and overlapping specification is given in Figure 4c where three FTs are embedded into an LST. To be appropriate later on, the decomposition must ensure that all tracks of the LST are covered by embedding morphisms to which *Shuttle* nodes may be connected (e.g. due to *Shuttle* nodes in the initial graph of S_0 or due to connected *Depot* nodes from which *Shuttle* nodes may enter the LST). In fact, the eight chosen FTs limit the reasoning for our running example to LSTs that can be decomposed using these FTs.   ◊

In general, we consider the two use cases: (a) a given PTGTS with underlying LST is to be analyzed and (b) LSTs are to be constructed based on the selected and analyzed FTs. Both use cases are supported but require a different handling. For the use case (a) a parsing of the LST w.r.t. the given FTs and overlapping specification must be performed to obtain a decomposition of the LST. Efficient parsing algorithms have been devised for the special case of hyperedge replacement (HR) grammars (which require that nodes are not deleted) in [8, 6, 7]. A suitable graph transformation based grammar for our running example with 25 rules is given in [20, Appendix]. For the use case (b) in which we need to construct some LST, we may employ node deleting rules. For our running example, consider the rule *Merge* from Figure 4b that can be used to iteratively overlap two FTs starting with a disjoint union of copies of FTs. The rule *Merge* overlaps two instances of three successive *Track* nodes following the overlapping specification where the application condition ensures that the rule is applied at entry and exit points also excluding the possibility that the six matched *Track* nodes belong to an instance of FTi using $\neg \phi_{\mathrm{FT}i}$.

---

[2] For each FT from Figure 4a, this constraint can be formalized as a graph condition.

5   Overapproximation of Behavior

The decompositions of LSTs introduced in the previous section are now used as a foundation to establish a behavioral relationship between a given PTGTS S_0 and n PTGTs S_i that operate on the instances of FTs that are embedded into the LST of S_0 according to the given LST decomposition.

For this purpose, we extend the structural embeddings given by the α monomorphisms from FTs to the LST in Definition 1 to embeddings of the entire graph (including the static but also the dynamic parts) of a state of some S_i called *fragment topology state (FTS)* into the entire graph of a state of S_0 called *large-scale state (LSS)*. Consider the left middle square in Figure 4d where the embedding α_i together with the FT and LST embeddings κ_i and κ is complemented with an embedding e_i of the FTS F_i into the LSS G. Note that e_i must be an extension of α_i in the sense that the square commutes (i.e., $\kappa \circ \alpha_i = e_i \circ \kappa_i$ is required). Also, $e_i \circ \kappa_i$ must satisfy the constraint ϕ_i of the FT used for S_i.

To simplify our presentation, we assume that the PTGTS S_0 (as in our running example) only employs APs of the form $\exists(f : \emptyset \hookrightarrow P, \top)$, invariants of the form $\neg\exists(f : \emptyset \hookrightarrow P, \top)$, and application conditions in PTGT rules that are conjunctions of graph conditions of the form $\neg\exists(f : \emptyset \hookrightarrow P, \top)$ for some graph P. This restriction simplifies the identification of parts of FTSs and LSSs that are considered for an evaluation of such graph conditions.

As a next step, we present a decomposition relation, which establishes a relationship between S_0 and the PTGTSs S_i in terms of embedding monomorphisms κ, α_i, e_i, and κ_i for all reachable states of S_0. Moreover, the decomposition relation requires that (a) the timed and discrete steps of S_0 can be mimicked by each affected S_i and (b) that discrete steps performed by some PTGTS S_i in isolation on a part of the LST where the FT $\overline{F}_i$ does not overlap with the FT $\overline{F}_j$ of another PTGTS S_j with $i \neq j$ can be mimicked by S_0. That is, the decomposition relation is a simulation for the steps performed by S_0 and a bisimulation on those steps that are performed in isolation by a single PTGTS S_i. Also, to allow to derive results for S_0 from a model checking based analysis of the PTGTSs S_i, we require a set of APs $\mathcal{A}$ that is part of the APs of S_0 and of each S_i. Based on this set $\mathcal{A}$, the decomposition relation also requires that only those FTSs and LSSs are related that satisfy the same sets of APs in $\mathcal{A}$. For our running example, this set will contain all three APs of S_0 (see Figure 2e). Finally, we require that the initial states of S_0 and the n PTGTSs S_i are covered by the decomposition relation.

Definition 2 (Decomposition Relation). *Given*

- (PTGTS FOR LARGE-SCALE SYSTEM) S_0 *is a PTGTS with initial LSS* $s_0 = (G_0, v_0)$ *where the LST is identified via* $\kappa_0 : \overline{G}_0 \hookrightarrow G_0$ *(and preserved by all steps of the PTGTS),*
- (PTGTSs FOR FTs) *for each* $1 \leq i \leq n$: S_i *is a PTGTS with initial FTS* $s_{0,i} = (F_{0,i}, v_{0,i})$ *where the underlying FT is identified via* $\kappa_i : \overline{F}_{0,i} \hookrightarrow F_{0,i}$ *(and preserved by all steps of the PTGTS),*

- (PRESERVED ATOMIC PROPOSITIONS) $\mathcal{A}$ is a set of APs contained in each $\mathcal{S}_i$, and
- (DECOMPOSITION OF THE LST) M is a decomposition of size n of the LST of $\mathcal{S}_0$ w.r.t. κ_0, $\mathcal{F} = \{\overline{F}_{0,i} \mid 1 \leq i \leq n\}$, and some overlapping specificiation o (cf. Definition 1).

S is a decomposition relation between $\mathcal{S}_0$ and $(\mathcal{S}_1, \ldots, \mathcal{S}_n)$ containing tuples of the form $((G, v), \kappa : \overline{G} \hookrightarrow G, w)$ where (G, v) is a state of $\mathcal{S}_0$, κ identifies the LST of G, and w is a tuple of length n of tuples of the form $(s_i, \overline{F}_i, \phi_i, \alpha_i, \kappa_i, e_i)$ when the following items are satisfied.

1. (ELEMENTS OF DECOMPOSITION RELATION) The relation S explains how the FTS of the PTGTS $\mathcal{S}_i$ is embedded into the LSS of $\mathcal{S}_0$, i.e., (see Figure 4d) if $((G, v), \kappa : \overline{G} \hookrightarrow G, w) \in S$ and $((F_i, v_i), \overline{F}_i, \phi_i, \alpha_i, \kappa_i, e_i)$ is the ith element of w, then $s_i = (F_i, v_i)$ is a state of $\mathcal{S}_i$, $(\overline{F}_i, \phi_i, \alpha_i)$ is the ith element of M, $\kappa_i : \overline{F}_i \hookrightarrow G'$ (embedding of FT into LST), $e_i : F_i \hookrightarrow G$ (embedding of FTS into LSS), $e_i \circ \kappa_i$ satisfies ϕ_i, and $\kappa \circ \alpha_i = e_i \circ \kappa_i$ (embedding e_i is an extension of embedding κ_i),

2. (CONSISTENT VALUATIONS) The clock valuations of each FTS agree with the LSS, i.e., if $((G, v), \kappa : \overline{G} \hookrightarrow G, w) \in S$, $((F_i, v_i), \overline{F}_i, \phi_i, \alpha_i, \kappa_i, e_i) \in w$, and $\kappa_i(c_i) = c$, then $v_i(c_i) = v(c)$.

3. (INITIAL STATES RELATED) The initial LSS of $\mathcal{S}_0$ is related, i.e., $(s_0, \kappa_0, w) \in S$ for some w where the ith element $(s_i, \overline{F}_i, \phi_i, \alpha_i, \kappa_i, e_i)$ of w satisfies $s_i = s_{0,i}$.

4. (ATOMIC PROPOSITIONS) The labeling with APs is in agreement w.r.t. $\mathcal{A}$, i.e., if $((G, v), \kappa : \overline{G} \hookrightarrow G, w) \in S$, $ap = \exists(f : \emptyset \hookrightarrow P, \top) \in \mathcal{A}$, the monomorphism $k : P \hookrightarrow G$ shows that ap is satisfied by G, then there is some $1 \leq i \leq n$ such that $((F_i, v_i), \overline{F}_i, \phi_i, \alpha_i, \kappa_i, e_i)$ is the ith element of w, and there is some $k_i : P \hookrightarrow F_i$ showing that ap is satisfied by F_i and $k = e_i \circ k_i$.

5. (BISIMULATION OF TIMED STEPS) If $((G, v), \kappa : \overline{G} \hookrightarrow G, w) \in S$ and $\mathcal{S}_0$ has a timed step (not involving a PTGTS rule) from (G, v) to $(G, v + \delta)$ then there is some $((G, v + \delta), w') \in S$ where w' is obtained pointwise from w by applying the corresponding timed step to each $((F_i, v_i), \overline{F}_i, \phi_i, \alpha_i, \kappa_i, e_i) \in w$ resulting in $((F_i, v_i + \delta), \overline{F}_i, \phi_i, \alpha_i, \kappa_i, e_i)$ and vice versa for a common timed step of each $\mathcal{S}_i$ of duration δ.

6. (SIMULATION OF STRUCTURAL STEPS OF $\mathcal{S}_0$ BY $\mathcal{S}_i$) if
   - $((G, v), \kappa : \overline{G} \hookrightarrow G, w) \in S$ and
   - $\mathcal{S}_0$ performs the structural step from (G, v) to (G'', v'') using an underlying GT rule $\rho = (\ell : K \hookrightarrow L, r : K \hookrightarrow R, \phi_{ac})$ given in Figure 4d where, since the step of $\mathcal{S}_0$ preserves the LST, there are unique $\kappa' : \overline{G} \hookrightarrow G'$ and $\kappa'' : \overline{G} \hookrightarrow G''$ such that $\hat{\ell} \circ \kappa' = \kappa$ and $\kappa'' = \hat{r} \circ \kappa'$, then
   - $((G'', v''), \kappa'' : \overline{G} \hookrightarrow G, w'') \in S$ for some w'' that is obtained pointwise from w by adapting each tuple $((F_i, v_i), \overline{F}_i, \phi_i, \alpha_i, \kappa_i, e_i) \in w$ into a resulting tuple $((F_i'', v_i''), \overline{F}_i, \phi_i, \alpha_i, \kappa_i'', e_i'')$ as follows. If $m(L) \cap e_i(F_i) = \emptyset$, then all components of the tuple remain unchanged. Otherwise, the PTGTS $\mathcal{S}_i$ must simulate the step and the tuple needs the updating described in the following steps.
     - There must be a step of $\mathcal{S}_i$ as given in Figure 4d from F_i to F_i'' for some underlying rule $\rho_i = (\ell_i : K_i \hookrightarrow L_i, r_i : K_i \hookrightarrow R_i, \phi_{ac,i})$ with the same probability and priority as ρ.

- Since the step of $\mathcal{S}_i$ preserves the FT, there are unique $\kappa_i' : \overline{F}_i \hookrightarrow F_i'$ and the required $\kappa_i'' : \overline{F}_i \hookrightarrow F_i''$ such that $\hat{\ell}_i \circ \kappa_i' = \kappa_i$ and $\kappa_i'' = \hat{r}_i \circ \kappa_i'$.
- The step of $\mathcal{S}_i$ must allow for $e_i' : F_i' \hookrightarrow G'$ and $e_i'' : F_i'' \hookrightarrow G''$ such that $\hat{\ell} \circ e_i' = e_i \circ \hat{\ell}_i$ and $\hat{r} \circ e_i' = e_i'' \circ \hat{r}_i$.

7. (SIMULATION OF STRUCTURAL STEPS OF $\mathcal{S}_i$ ON ITS CORE BY $\mathcal{S}_0$) if
   - $((G, v), \kappa : \overline{G} \hookrightarrow G, w) \in S$,
   - $((F_i, v_i), \overline{F}_i, \phi_i, \alpha_i, \kappa_i, e_i) \in w$,
   - $\mathcal{S}_i$ performs the structural step from (F_i, v_i) to (F_i'', v_i'') using an underlying GT rule $\rho_i = (\ell_i : K_i \hookrightarrow L_i, r_i : K_i \hookrightarrow R_i, \phi_{ac,i})$ given in Figure 4d where, since the step of $\mathcal{S}_i$ preserves the FT, there are unique $\kappa_i' : \overline{F}_i \hookrightarrow F_i'$ and $\kappa_i'' : \overline{F}_i \hookrightarrow F_i''$ such that $\hat{\ell}_i \circ \kappa_i' = \kappa_i$ and $\kappa_i'' = \hat{r}_i \circ \kappa_i'$,
   - $e_i(m_i(L_i))$ does not overlap with any $e_j(F_j)$ for $i \neq j$, then
   - there is some $((G'', v''), \kappa'' : \overline{G} \hookrightarrow G, w'') \in S$ for some G'', v'', κ'', and w'' as follows.
     - There must be a step of $\mathcal{S}_0$ as given in Figure 4d from G to G'' for some underlying rule $\rho = (\ell : K \hookrightarrow L, r : K \hookrightarrow R, \phi_{ac})$ with the same probability and priority as ρ_i.
     - Since the step of $\mathcal{S}_0$ preserves the LST, there are unique $\kappa' : \overline{G} \hookrightarrow G'$ and the required $\kappa'' : \overline{G} \hookrightarrow G''$ such that $\hat{\ell} \circ \kappa' = \kappa$ and $\kappa'' = \hat{r}_i \circ \kappa'$.
     - The step of $\mathcal{S}_0$ must allow for $e_i' : F_i' \hookrightarrow G'$ and $e_i'' : F_i'' \hookrightarrow G''$ such that $\hat{\ell} \circ e_i' = e_i \circ \hat{\ell}_i$ and $\hat{r} \circ e_i' = e_i'' \circ \hat{r}_i$.
     - Finally, w'' is obtained from w by only adapting the above chosen tuple $((F_i, v_i), \overline{F}_i, \phi_i, \alpha_i, \kappa_i, e_i)$ into the tuple $((F_i'', v_i''), \overline{F}_i, \phi_i, \alpha_i, \kappa_i'', e_i'')$.   ◆

We now state that decomposition relations allow for the simulation of each path of the PTGTS $\mathcal{S}_0$ by the PTGTSs $\mathcal{S}_i$.

Lemma 1 (Existence of Simulating Paths). *If S is a decomposition relation between $\mathcal{S}_0$ and $(\mathcal{S}_1, \ldots, \mathcal{S}_n)$, and π is a path of length m in $\mathcal{S}_0$ from the initial state to a state s_m, then, for each $1 \leq i \leq n$, there is a path π_i of $\mathcal{S}_i$ (of length $k_i \leq m$) ending in a state s_{i,k_i} such that $(s_m, \kappa, w) \in S$ for some κ and w where the ith element of w is of the form $(s_{i,k_i}, \overline{F}_i, \phi_i, \alpha_i, \kappa_i, e_i)$. Moreover, the probability of each such path π_i is at least as high as the probability of the path π. See [20] for the proof.*

We now state that a PTGTS satisfies a safety property given by an AP, when safety w.r.t. this AP can be established for each $\mathcal{S}_i$.

Theorem 1 (Safety Verification). *If S is a decomposition relation between $\mathcal{S}_0$ and $(\mathcal{S}_1, \ldots, \mathcal{S}_n)$ w.r.t $\mathcal{A}$ and $ap \in \mathcal{A}$, then $\mathcal{S}_0$ is safe w.r.t. the occurrence of an ap-labeled graph when (for each $1 \leq i \leq n$) $\mathcal{S}_i$ is safe w.r.t. the occurrence of an ap-labeled graph. Moreover, the probability of an occurrence of an ap-labeled graph from some state s in $\mathcal{S}_0$ is smaller than the probability of an occurrence of an ap-labeled graph from some S-related state s_i in $\mathcal{S}_i$. See [20] for the proof.*

We now apply the proposed methodology of establishing a behavioral relationship between the PTGTS $\mathcal{S}_0$ and the PTGTSs $\mathcal{S}_i$ to our running example. For this purpose, we now describe how the FTS of each $\mathcal{S}_i$ is embedded into the LSS of $\mathcal{S}_0$ and, based on this embedding, how the $\mathcal{S}_i$ is derived from $\mathcal{S}_0$.

Example 2 (Construction of Embeddings and Simulating PTGTSs). Firstly, the embeddings e_i of FTSs into the LSS are obtained as extensions of the structural embeddings κ_i by also matching (a) all *Shuttle* nodes (with their attributes) that are connected to *Track* nodes contained in the FT via *next* edges and (b) all *active* attributes of *TLYellow* and *TLGreen* nodes contained in the FT. This extension also naturally applies to the initial state of S_0. Clearly, two embeddings e_i and e_j (for $i \neq j$) only overlap in elements of their FTs but not in the additionally matched dynamic elements.

Secondly, we adapt the given PTGTS S_0 to obtain for each of the eight FTs one PTGTS S_i by (a) changing the initial graph to the source of e_i capturing the FT as well as the additional dynamic elements of the initial state of S_0 connected to it, (b) adding eight rules for overapproximating the behavior of S_0 on the tracks that may overlap with tracks of other FTs. For the latter point, we observe that all but three of the rules of S_0 (including *SetSlow* and *ConstructionSiteBrake* from Figure 2) are never applicable on the parts of FTs that may overlap with other FTs (i.e., borders of FTs). The remaining three rules are *Drive* from Figure 3a as well as two similar rules for stopping the shuttle that we do not consider in detail here. Three of the four derived rules for rule *Drive* are given in Figure 3.

The additional rule *DriveEnterFast* is used to simulate *Drive* steps where a shuttle in S_0 drives from a track not covered by S_i to a track covered by S_i. The rule *DriveEnterFast* is essentially constructed by omitting the source track T_1 from the rule *Drive*, by adding the shuttle with one of the two expected velocities (the other velocity results in the omitted rule *DriveEnterSlow*)[3], and by omitting application conditions that may not be satisfied due to the overlapping specification and the structure of FTs.

Similarly, the additional rules *DriveExit1* and *DriveExit2* are constructed from rule *Drive* to allow for the simulation of the two steps in which a shuttle in S_0 drives using rule *Drive* on two tracks covered by S_i to a track not covered by S_i. These two rules are then constructed similarly, by omitting the tracks T_3 (for *DriveExit1*) and T_3 and T_4 (for *DriveExit2*) from rule *Drive* as these are not covered by the S_i, by removing the shuttle with its attributes in rule *DriveExit2*, by omitting application conditions that may not be satisfied due to the overlapping specification and the structure of FTs, and by omitting application conditions that refer to the removed tracks.

Note that these additional rules overapproximate the behavior that is possible in S_0 as they may be used when analyzing S_i also when no corresponding shuttle in S_0 is able to enter the FT or when rule *Drive* would be disabled due to the omitted application conditions for the case of rules *DriveExit1* and *DriveExit2*.   ◊

For our running example, we now describe the construction of a suitable decomposition relation relying on the LST decomposition introduced before.

---

[3] Here, we rely on the constraints on the eight FTs (cf. Example 1) requiring that the AP $AP_{unexpectedVelocity}$ is never labeled in the large-scale system S_0.

Lemma 2 (Existence of Decomposition Relation for Running Example). *For the PTGTS S_0 of our running example with an arbitrary initial LST such that M is a decomposition of that LST w.r.t. some monomorphism κ, the set of eight FTs, and the overlapping specification o from Example 1 there is a decomposition relation S between S_0 and the n PTGTSs S_i from Example 2. See [20] for the proof.*

Based on this decomposition relation and Theorem 1, we can obtain the desired overapproximation result for S_0 for the qualitative safety w.r.t. collisions and the quantitative unlikeliness of emergency brakes.

Corollary 1 (Qualitative and Quantitative Safety for Running Example). S_0 *exhibits no collisions when this is the case for each S_i. Moreover, emergency brakes are performed in S_0 with a probability not higher than the probability of such an occurrence in any S_i.*

Note that we only need to analyze one PTGTS for each of the eight permitted FTs w.r.t. the occurrence of collisions and the probability of emergency brakes.

6 Evaluation

To analyze the eight PTGTSs constructed for our running example in section 5 (see Table 1 for the results), we have employed the methodology from [19] generating the state spaces for these PTGTSs without timed steps and then generated the corresponding PTA from these state spaces. We then restricted these PTA to timed automata (TA) essentially removing the information on probabilities, applied UPPAAL [15] to determine the edges of the TA that can never be applied due to unsatisfiable guards, and removed the corresponding edges from the previously generated PTA. The entire analysis using our prototypical implementation required less than three days on a machine using up to 250 GB memory where the state space generation required most of the time. However, there is a vast potential for optimizations regarding memory consumption (by only storing subsequently relevant information on states and steps) and runtime (by facilitating concurrency during state space generation).

Firstly, using UPPAAL, we have verified that each of the eight TA (hence, also the eight PTA) have no reachable deadlock (where also timed steps are disabled). Hence, we obtain that the PTGTS S_0 also does not contain this particular modeling error since, using the decomposition relation, we also obtain that every deadlock reachable in S_0 can be reached analogously in each S_i.

Secondly, we have observed that the obtained PTA do not label any location with $AP_{unexpectedVelocity}$ or $AP_{collision}$. For $AP_{unexpectedVelocity}$ this means that the additional rules such as *DriveEnterFast* and *DriveEnterSlow* for overapproximating the steps of entering shuttles entirely cover all possible velocities of shuttles. For $AP_{collision}$ this means that Corollary 1 implies that the PTGTS S_0 with an LST constructed in the described way from the eight FTs is safe w.r.t. the occurrence of collisions.

Thirdly, to verify that yellow traffic lights suitably slow down the shuttles before construction sites, we have identified locations ℓ_i in the resulting PTA

fragment topology	states	steps	collisions	max. probability for violating the velocity limit at a construction site
FT1	9	18	0	0
FT2	335	693	0	0
FT3	216	503	0	0
FT4	109 379	312 915	0	1×10^{-6}
FT5	106 122	284 102	0	1×10^{-12}
FT6	12 473	31 812	0	0
FT7	4048	16 314	0	0
FT8	121 953	452 340	0	0

Table 1: Results of our evaluation for the running example

that are labeled with AP_{braked} (occurring only in FT4 and FT5). In each case, we were able to track using a custom analysis algorithm (since the PRISM model checker was too slow for the large PTA at hand) the shuttle backwards over all possible paths leading to such a location ℓ_i up to the step where the shuttle entered the FT. We then determined the maximal probability of any such path obtaining a worst-case emergency brake probability of 10^{-6} and 10^{-12} for any entering shuttle in FT4 and FT5, respectively. On the one hand, FT5 is thereby verified to be quantitatively more desirable compared to FT4. On the other hand, Corollary 1 implies that installations of yellow traffic lights as in FT4 and FT5 suitably decrease the likelihood of emergency brakes also for S_0. However, the probabilities that some shuttle executes an emergency brake in a given time span in FT4/FT5 (obtained by combining the maximal throughput of shuttles for FT4/FT5 with the worst-case probability obtained for FT4/FT5) can be expected to be too coarse upper bounds when the maximal throughput is not to be expected for the real system.

7 Conclusion and Future Work

We presented an analysis approach for large-scale systems modeled as PT-GTSs for which model checking is not feasible. In this approach, we rely on a decomposition of an underlying static large-scale topology into fragment topologies of manageable size. Model checking is then applied for each fragment topology and an adaptation of the PTGTS to such a fragment topology. We thereby determine (a) overapproximations of reachability properties important for qualitative safety properties and (b) upper bounds for probabilistic reachability properties important for quantitative safety properties.

As future work, we intend to extend our analysis to fairness properties and conditions of the metric temporal graph logic (MTGL) [29]. Also, to cover further aspects of the RailCab project [23], we will develop more general decomposition schemes where dynamic components (such as connected shuttles driving in convoys) may be covered by multiple fragment topologies. Lastly, to further evaluate applicability of our approach, we intend to apply it to other case studies as e.g. the one discussed in [1].

References

[1]   Paolo Baldan, Andrea Corradini, and Barbara König. "Static Analysis of Distributed Systems with Mobility Specified by Graph Grammars—A Case Study". In: *Proc. of Int. Conf. on Integrated Design & Process Technology*. Ed. by Ehrig, Krämer, et al. SDPS, 2002.

[2]   Basil Becker. "Architectural modelling and verification of open service-oriented systems of systems". PhD thesis. Hasso-Plattner-Institut für Softwaresystemtechnik, Universität Potsdam, 2014. URL: http://opus.kobv.de/ubp/volltexte/2014/7015/.

[3]   Basil Becker, Dirk Beyer, Holger Giese, Florian Klein, and Daniela Schilling. "Symbolic invariant verification for systems with dynamic structural adaptation". In: *28th International Conference on Software Engineering (ICSE 2006), Shanghai, China, May 20-28, 2006*. Ed. by Leon J. Osterweil, H. Dieter Rombach, and Mary Lou Soffa. ACM, 2006, pp. 72–81. DOI: 10.1145/1134285.1134297.

[4]   Basil Becker and Holger Giese. "On Safe Service-Oriented Real-Time Coordination for Autonomous Vehicles". In: *11th IEEE International Symposium on Object-Oriented Real-Time Distributed Computing (ISORC 2008), 5-7 May 2008, Orlando, Florida, USA*. IEEE Computer Society, 2008, pp. 203–210. DOI: 10.1109/ISORC.2008.13.

[5]   Basil Becker, Holger Giese, and Stefan Neumann. *Correct dynamic service-oriented architectures : modeling and compositional verification with dynamic collaborations*. Tech. rep. 29. Hasso Plattner Institute at the University of Potsdam, 2009.

[6]   Frank Drewes, Berthold Hoffmann, and Mark Minas. "Formalization and correctness of predictive shift-reduce parsers for graph grammars based on hyperedge replacement". In: *J. Log. Algebraic Methods Program.* 104 (2019), pp. 303–341. DOI: 10.1016/j.jlamp.2018.12.006.

[7]   Frank Drewes, Berthold Hoffmann, and Mark Minas. "Graph Parsing as Graph Transformation - Correctness of Predictive Top-Down Parsers". In: *Graph Transformation - 13th International Conference, ICGT 2020, Held as Part of STAF 2020, Bergen, Norway, June 25-26, 2020, Proceedings*. Ed. by Fabio Gadducci and Timo Kehrer. Vol. 12150. Lecture Notes in Computer Science. Springer, 2020, pp. 221–238. DOI: 10.1007/978-3-030-51372-6_13.

[8]   Frank Drewes, Berthold Hoffmann, and Mark Minas. "Predictive Top-Down Parsing for Hyperedge Replacement Grammars". In: *Graph Transformation - 8th International Conference, ICGT 2015, Held as Part of STAF 2015, L'Aquila, Italy, July 21-23, 2015. Proceedings*. Ed. by Francesco Parisi - Presicce and Bernhard Westfechtel. Vol. 9151. Lecture Notes in Computer Science. Springer, 2015, pp. 19–34. DOI: 10.1007/978-3-319-21145-9_2.

[9]   Johannes Dyck. "Verification of Graph Transformation Systems with k-Inductive Invariants". PhD thesis. University of Potsdam, Hasso Plattner Institute, Potsdam, Germany, 2020. DOI: 10.25932/publishup-44274.

[10]   Hartmut Ehrig, Karsten Ehrig, Ulrike Prange, and Gabriele Taentzer. *Fundamentals of Algebraic Graph Transformation*. Springer-Verlag, 2006.

[11]   Amir Hossein Ghamarian and Arend Rensink. "Generalised Compositionality in Graph Transformation". In: *Graph Transformations - 6th International Conference, ICGT 2012, Bremen, Germany, September 24-29, 2012. Proceedings*. Ed. by Hartmut Ehrig, Gregor Engels, Hans-Jörg Kreowski, and Grzegorz Rozenberg. Vol. 7562. Lecture Notes in Computer Science. Springer, 2012, pp. 234–248. DOI: 10.1007/978-3-642-33654-6_16.

[12]   Holger Giese. "Modeling and Verification of Cooperative Self-adaptive Mechatronic Systems". In: *Reliable Systems on Unreliable Networked Platforms - 12th Monterey Workshop 2005, Laguna Beach, CA, USA, September 22-24, 2005. Revised Selected Papers*. Ed. by Fabrice Kordon and Janos Sztipanovits. Vol. 4322. Lecture Notes in Computer Science. Springer, 2005, pp. 258–280. DOI: 10.1007/978-3-540-71156-8_14.

[13]   Holger Giese and Wilhelm Schäfer. "Model-Driven Development of Safe Self-optimizing Mechatronic Systems with MechatronicUML". In: *Assurances for Self-Adaptive Systems - Principles, Models, and Techniques*. Ed. by Javier Cámara, Rogério de Lemos, Carlo Ghezzi, and Antónia Lopes. Vol. 7740. Lecture Notes in Computer Science. Springer, 2013, pp. 152–186. DOI: 10.1007/978-3-642-36249-1_6.

[14]   Holger Giese, Matthias Tichy, Sven Burmester, and Stephan Flake. "Towards the compositional verification of real-time UML designs". In: *Proceedings of the 11th ACM SIGSOFT Symposium on Foundations of Software Engineering 2003 held jointly with 9th European Software Engineering Conference, ESEC/FSE 2003, Helsinki, Finland, September 1-5, 2003*. Ed. by Jukka Paakki and Paola Inverardi. ACM, 2003, pp. 38–47. DOI: 10.1145/940071.940078.

[15]   Eun-Young Kang, Dongrui Mu, and Li Huang. "Probabilistic Verification of Timing Constraints in Automotive Systems Using UPPAAL-SMC". In: *Integrated Formal Methods - 14th International Conference, IFM 2018, Maynooth, Ireland, September 5-7, 2018, Proceedings*. Ed. by Carlo A. Furia and Kirsten Winter. Vol. 11023. Lecture Notes in Computer Science. Springer, 2018, pp. 236–254. DOI: 10.1007/978-3-319-98938-9_14.

[16]   Marta Z. Kwiatkowska, Gethin Norman, and David Parker. "PRISM 4.0: Verification of Probabilistic Real-Time Systems". In: *Computer Aided Verification - 23rd International Conference, CAV 2011, Snowbird, UT, USA, July 14-20, 2011. Proceedings*. Ed. by Ganesh Gopalakrishnan and Shaz Qadeer. Vol. 6806. Lecture Notes in Computer Science. Springer, 2011, pp. 585–591. ISBN: 978-3-642-22109-5. DOI: 10.1007/978-3-642-22110-1_47.

[17]   Marta Z. Kwiatkowska, Gethin Norman, Jeremy Sproston, and Fuzhi Wang. "Symbolic Model Checking for Probabilistic Timed Automata". In: *Formal Techniques, Modelling and Analysis of Timed and Fault-Tolerant Systems, Joint International Conferences on Formal Modelling and Analysis of Timed Systems, FORMATS 2004 and Formal Techniques in Real-Time and Fault-Tolerant Systems, FTRTFT 2004, Grenoble, France, September 22-24,*

2004, *Proceedings*. Ed. by Yassine Lakhnech and Sergio Yovine. Vol. 3253. Lecture Notes in Computer Science. Springer, 2004, pp. 293–308. ISBN: 3-540-23167-6. DOI: 10.1007/978-3-540-30206-3_21.

[18]   Maria Maximova, Holger Giese, and Christian Krause. "Probabilistic timed graph transformation systems". In: *Graph Transformation - 10th International Conference, ICGT 2017, Held as Part of STAF 2017, Marburg, Germany, July 18-19, 2017, Proceedings*. Ed. by Juan de Lara and Detlef Plump. Vol. 10373. Lecture Notes in Computer Science. Springer, 2017, pp. 159–175. ISBN: 978-3-319-61469-4. DOI: 10.1007/978-3-319-61470-0_10.

[19]   Maria Maximova, Holger Giese, and Christian Krause. "Probabilistic timed graph transformation systems". In: *J. Log. Algebr. Meth. Program.* 101 (2018), pp. 110–131. DOI: 10.1016/j.jlamp.2018.09.003.

[20]   Maria Maximova, Sven Schneider, and Holger Giese. *Compositional Analysis of Probabilistic Timed Graph Transformation Systems*. Tech. rep. 133. Potsdam, Germany: Hasso Plattner Institute at the University of Potsdam, 2021.

[21]   Fernando Orejas. "Symbolic graphs for attributed graph constraints". In: *J. Symb. Comput.* 46.3 (2011), pp. 294–315. DOI: 10.1016/j.jsc.2010.09.009.

[22]   Fernando Orejas and Leen Lambers. "Lazy Graph Transformation". In: *Fundam. Inform.* 118.1-2 (2012), pp. 65–96. DOI: 10.3233/FI-2012-706.

[23]   *RailCab Project*. URL: https://www.hni.uni-paderborn.de/cim/projekte/railcab.

[24]   Arend Rensink. "Compositionality in Graph Transformation". In: *Automata, Languages and Programming, 37th International Colloquium, ICALP 2010, July 6-10, Bordeaux, France, 2010, Proceedings, Part II*. Ed. by Samson Abramsky, Cyril Gavoille, Claude Kirchner, Friedhelm Meyer auf der Heide, and Paul G. Spirakis. Vol. 6199. Lecture Notes in Computer Science. Springer, 2010, pp. 309–320. DOI: 10.1007/978-3-642-14162-1_26.

[25]   Willem P. de Roever, Hans Langmaack, and Amir Pnueli, eds. *Compositionality: The Significant Difference, International Symposium, COMPOS'97, Bad Malente, Germany, September 8-12, 1997. Revised Lectures*. Vol. 1536. Lecture Notes in Computer Science. Springer, 1998. ISBN: 3-540-65493-3. DOI: 10.1007/3-540-49213-5.

[26]   Sven Schneider, Johannes Dyck, and Holger Giese. "Formal Verification of Invariants for Attributed Graph Transformation Systems Based on Nested Attributed Graph Conditions". In: *Graph Transformation - 13th International Conference, ICGT 2020, Held as Part of STAF 2020, Bergen, Norway, June 25-26, 2020, Proceedings*. Ed. by Fabio Gadducci and Timo Kehrer. Vol. 12150. Lecture Notes in Computer Science. Springer, 2020, pp. 257–275. DOI: 10.1007/978-3-030-51372-6_15.

[27]   Sven Schneider, Leen Lambers, and Fernando Orejas. "Automated reasoning for attributed graph properties". In: *STTT* 20.6 (2018), pp. 705–737. DOI: 10.1007/s10009-018-0496-3.

[28]   Sven Schneider, Maria Maximova, Lucas Sakizloglou, and Holger Giese. "Formal Testing of Timed Graph Transformation Systems using Metric Temporal Graph Logic". In: *STTT* (2019). Accepted.

[29]   Sven Schneider, Lucas Sakizloglou, Maria Maximova, and Holger Giese. "Optimistic and Pessimistic On-the-fly Analysis for Metric Temporal Graph Logic". In: *Graph Transformation - 13th International Conference, ICGT 2020, Held as Part of STAF 2020, Bergen, Norway, June 25-26, 2020, Proceedings*. Ed. by Fabio Gadducci and Timo Kehrer. Vol. 12150. Lecture Notes in Computer Science. Springer, 2020, pp. 276–294. DOI: 10.1007/978-3-030-51372-6_16.

Efficient Bounded Model Checking
of Heap-Manipulating Programs
using Tight Field Bounds

Pablo Ponzio[1,3]✉, Ariel Godio[2], Nicolás Rosner[*],
Marcelo Arroyo[1], Nazareno Aguirre[1,3] and Marcelo F. Frias[2,3]

[1] University of Río Cuarto, Río Cuarto, Argentina
{pponzio,marcelo.arroyo,naguirre}@dc.exa.unrc.edu.ar
[2] Buenos Aires Institute of Technology (ITBA), Buenos Aires, Argentina
{agodio,mfrias}@itba.edu.ar
[3] National Council for Scientific and Technical Research (CONICET), Buenos Aires,
Argentina

Abstract. Software model checkers are able to exhaustively explore different bounded program executions arising from various sources of nondeterminism. These tools provide statements to produce non-deterministic values for certain variables, thus forcing the corresponding model checker to consider *all* possible values for these during verification. While these statements offer an effective way of verifying programs handling basic data types and simple structured types, they are inappropriate as a mechanism for nondeterministic generation of pointers, favoring the use of insertion routines to produce dynamic data structures when verifying, via model checking, programs handling such data types.

We present a technique to improve model checking of programs handling heap-allocated data types, by taming the explosion of candidate structures that can be built when non-deterministically initializing heap object fields. The technique exploits precomputed *relational bounds*, that disregard values deemed invalid by the structure's type invariant, thus reducing the state space to be explored by the model checker. Precomputing the relational bounds is a challenging costly task too, for which we also present an efficient algorithm, based on incremental SAT solving. We implement our approach on top of the CBMC bounded model checker, and show that, for a number of data structures implementations, we can handle significantly larger input structures and detect faults that CBMC is unable to detect.

1 Introduction

SAT-based bounded model checking [7] is an automated software analysis technique, consisting of appropriately encoding a program as a propositional formula in such a way that its satisfying valuations correspond to program defects, such

---

[*] Nicolás Rosner was affiliated with the University of Buenos Aires, Buenos Aires, Argentina at the time of contribution to this work.

© The Author(s) 2021
E. Guerra and M. Stoelinga (Eds.): FASE 2021, LNCS 12649, pp. 218–239, 2021.
https://doi.org/10.1007/978-3-030-71500-7_11

as violations of assertions, uncaught exceptions and memory leaks. Satisfying valuations of the obtained propositional formulas can be automatically searched for by resorting to SAT solving, exploiting the constant advances in this analysis technology. SAT-based bounded model checking achieves full automation in program verification at the cost of completeness: it limits the number of times that loops are allowed to be executed to a user provided loop unwinding bound. This in turn limits the data that the program can manipulate, which is constrained to the program parameters, and what the program can allocate in its bounded executions. Hence, although the approach is capable of exploring a huge number of execution traces, it cannot prove program correctness due to its bounded nature. Nevertheless, it is very useful for bug finding, and is able to support fully-fledged higher-level programming languages [8].

A tool based on bounded model checking over SAT is CBMC [20]. It supports all of ANSI-C, including programs handling pointers and pointer arithmetic. The tool is able to exhaustively explore many user-bounded program executions resulting from various sources of non-determinism, including scheduling decisions and the assignment of values to program variables. To achieve this, CBMC provides statements to produce non-deterministic values for certain variables, forcing the model checker to consider *all* possible values for these variables during verification. These statements enable program verification on *all* legal inputs, by assigning these inputs values within their corresponding (legal) domains. While this mechanism is effective for the verification of programs manipulating basic data types and simple structured types, it is disabled as a feature for the generation of pointers. This issue forces the user to provide an ad-hoc environment to verify programs handling dynamic data structures. In fact, a typical, convenient mechanism to verify programs handling heap-allocated linked structures using CBMC and similar tools, is to non-deterministically build such structures using insertion routines [19, 22, 11].

The aforementioned approach, while effective, has its scalability tied to how complex the insertion routines are, and how many of these are actually needed. Indeed, there are many linked structures whose domain of valid structures cannot be built only via insertion operations (e.g., red-black trees and node caching linked lists require insertions as well as removals, in order to reach all bounded valid structures). In this paper, we study an alternative technique for verifying, using CBMC, programs handling heap-allocated linked structures. The approach essentially consists of building a pool of objects with nondeterministically initialized fields, which are then used for nondeterministically building structures. The rapid explosion in the number of generated linked structures is tamed by exploiting precomputed bounds for fields, that disregard values deemed invalid by the structure's assumed properties, such as datatype invariants and routine preconditions. This leaves us the additional problem of precomputing these bounds, a computationally costly task on its own. We then present a novel algorithm for these precomputations, based on incremental SAT solving, making the whole process fully automated.

```
avl_init(t);
int size = nondet_int();
__CPROVER_assume(size>=0 && size<=MAX_SIZE);
for (int i = 0; i < size; i++) {
    int value = nondet_int();
    __CPROVER_assume(value >= MIN_VAL && value < MAX_VAL);
    avl_insert(t, value);
}
int r_value = nondet_int();
__CPROVER_assume(r_value >= MIN_VAL && r_value < MAX_VAL);
avl_remove(t, r_value);
__CPROVER_assert(avl_repok(t));
```

Fig. 1: Verification of AVL remove, building structures by multiple insertions.

We perform an experimental evaluation on a benchmark of data structure implementations, showing that the use of field bounds contributes significantly to improve both memory consumption and verification running times (including the precomputations), allowing CBMC to consider larger structures as well as to detect faults that could not be detected without their use.

2   A Motivating Example

Let us start by describing a particular verification scenario, that will serve the purpose of motivating our approach. Suppose that we have an implementation of dictionaries, based on AVL trees; furthermore, we would like to verify that the **remove** operation on this structure preserves the structure's invariant, i.e., after a removal is performed, the resulting structure is still a valid AVL tree (acyclic, with every node having at most one parent, sorted, and balanced). Moreover, let us assume that, besides operation avl_remove, we have AVL's avl_init, avl_insert and avl_repok, the latter being a routine that checks whether a given structure satisfies the AVL invariant, as described above. In order to perform the desired verification, we can proceed by building the program shown in Figure 1. Notice how this program:

– employs CBMC primitives to nondeterministically decide how many values, and which values to insert in/remove from the tree (appropriately constrained by constants MAX_SIZE, MIN_VAL and MAX_VAL),
– uses an AVL insertion routine to produce the insertions, and
– uses an avl_repok routine, which checks the AVL invariant on the linked structure rooted at t.

When running CBMC on this program, if loops are unwound enough and no violation of the assertion is obtained, then we have verified that, within the provided bounds, **remove** indeed preserves the invariant.

The above traditional approach to verifying linked structures using CBMC and similar tools [19, 22, 11] has its efficiency tied to how complex the involved routines are, in particular the insertion routine(s) (the avl_remove routine, being verified, cannot be avoided).

```
t = nondet_avl(MAX_SIZE, MIN_VAL, MAX_VAL);      avlnode* nondet_avl(int size,
__CPROVER_assume(avl_repok(t));                     int min_val,
int r_value = nondet_int();                         int max_val) {
__CPROVER_assume(r_value >= MIN_VAL              avlnode *n = malloc(sizeof(avlnode) * size);
   && r_value < MAX_VAL);                         avlnode *result = NULL;
avl_remove(t, r_value);                           if (nondet_bool())
__CPROVER_assert(avl_repok(t));                      // root is null
                                                     return result;
                                                  result = n[0]; // root is n0
                                                  n[0]->left = NULL;
                                                  if (nondet_bool())
                                                     n[0]->left = n[1];
                                                  n[0]->right = NULL;
                                                  if (nondet_bool())
                                                     n[0]->right = n[1];
                                                  else if (nondet_bool())
                                                     n[0]->right = n[2];
                                                  ...
                                                  return result;
                                              }
```

Fig. 2: Verification of AVL remove, nondeterministically building linked structs

An alternative approach, employed by some symbolic execution-based model checkers, notably [3, 23], consists of creating a pool of nodes, whose fields are nondeterministically set, and which are also nondeterministically used to build data structures. The process is illustrated in Figure 2. The key is in the use of a routine nondet_avl(), which encapsulates the generation of the linked structure. A fragment of this routine is shown at the right of Figure 2. Notice how this routine will generate invalid structures, e.g., cyclic ones. The avl_repok(t) assumption after the generation will take care of disregarding these invalid structures for verification. Notice how our manually written example generation routine is avoiding to use any node besides n[0] as the root, or any node but n[1] as n[0]->left, thus avoiding some isomorphic structures and obvious cycles, but it does not avoid nodes from having more than one parent, nor it seems to take into account the tree's balancedness. Of course, we have other alternatives when writing the nondeterministic generation routine nondet_avl. We may produce a generation routine that, based solely on the fields of the nodes involved in the structure and their types, produces all possible structures, leaving the work of filtering out valid ones to the assume(avl_repok(t)) part of the program. We can also write a sophisticated generation routine specifically tailored for AVL trees, that already takes into account (most) invalid values for each node field, and thus mostly produces valid structures. The first option has as an advantage that it is *generic*, and thus can be made part of an automated verification technique, at the cost of being, intuitively, less efficient; the second (and our example), on the other hand, has in principle to be manually produced, and is more error prone, since we may be disregarding some valid values making the verification bounded incomplete, but is intuitively more efficient.

The technique we present in this paper consists of automatically producing the second kind of generation routines. We will start with the first kind of generation, and automatically decide which values for each field of each node can be safely removed, when we can establish that they do not participate in valid structures (i.e., structures satisfying the corresponding structure invariant). This additional problem of deciding when a value for a node field's domain can be safely removed is solved using a novel algorithm, presented in this paper, which uses incremental SAT solving.

3   Tight Field Bounds

Tight field bounds are based on a relational semantics of structures' fields in program states. The relational semantics of structures is based on interpreting a field f at a given program state as the set of pairs $\langle id, v \rangle$ relating the identifier id (representing a unique reference to some data object o in the heap) with the value v in the field f of o at that state (i.e., o->f $= v$ in the state). Then, each program state corresponds to a set of (functional) binary relations, one per field of the structures involved in the program. For example, the program state containing the binary tree depicted at the left of Fig. 3 are represented by the following relations:

$$\texttt{left} = \{\langle N0, N1 \rangle \ \langle N1, N3 \rangle\}, \quad \texttt{right} = \{\langle N0, N2 \rangle \ \langle N1, N4 \rangle, \langle N2, N5 \rangle\} \quad (1)$$

For analysis techniques that must consider all possible state configurations that satisfy some given property, we may reduce this relational semantics by considering *tight field bounds*. Intuitively, for a field f and a property α, its tight field bound on α is the union of f's representation across all program states that satisfy α. Tight field bounds have been used to reduce the number of variables and clauses in propositional representations of relational heap encodings for Java automated analyses [14, 13, 2], and in symbolic execution based model checking to prune parts of the symbolic execution search tree constraining nondeterministic options [15, 26] (see section 6 for a more detailed description of these previous applications). Tight field bounds are computed from *assumed* properties, and can be employed to restrict structures in states that are assumed to satisfy such properties, i.e. *precondition* states. In our case, we will use the invariant of the structure, as opposed to stronger preconditions, so that these can be reused across several routines of the same structure.

Definition 1. *Let f be a field of structure T_1 with type T_2. Let i and j be the scopes for types T_1 and T_2, respectively. Let $A = \{a_1, \ldots, a_i\}$ be the identifiers for data objects of type T_1, and let $B = \{b_1, \ldots, b_j\}$ be the identifiers for data objects of type T_2. Given an identifier k, o_k denotes the corresponding data object. The tight field bound for field f is the smallest relation $U_f \subseteq A \times (B + Null)$ satisfying: $\langle x, y \rangle \in U_f$ iff there exists a valid heap instance I in which o_x->$f = o_y$.*

By *scope* we mean the limit in the number of objects, ranges for numerical types, and maximum depth in loop unwinding, as in [17, 12]. An important assumption we make for analysis is that structure invariants do not refer to the specific heap addresses of data objects, and in particular that these do not

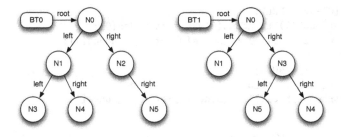

Fig. 3: Two valid binary trees.

use pointer arithmetic. Therefore, permuting data object identifiers on a valid instance still yields a valid instance (i.e., permuting the actual locations of data objects in the heap is irrelevant for invariant satisfaction). This is most times the case, and is indeed the case in all the examples that we will present in Section 5. This is an important assumption because it enables us to add an additional implicit invariant: *symmetry breaking*. This has an important impact in the size of tight field bounds, since they get greatly reduced when isomorphic structures are removed. We use a symmetry breaking procedure that removes all symmetries. For details, we refer the reader to [14, 13].

4   A Technique for Nondeterministic Generation of Dynamic Structures

We are now ready to describe the technique for nondeterministic generation of dynamic structures, used to verify programs handling such data using CBMC. The technique requires:

- the program p(T x) to be analyzed;
- a description of the structure of type T, which in the dynamic case, typically consists of a struct or set of structs (that are dynamically allocated);
- a boolean program repok(T x), that (operationally) decides whether a given instance x is valid, i.e., satisfies the structure's invariant, or not; and
- a tight field bound B_f for every field f in T and the scope n to use for bounded model checking of p.

The first three are necessary information; for the last one we present later on in the paper an algorithm to compute tight bounds, from the other three.

The technique starts by building a routine nondet_T(), that produces and returns structures of type T. The routine works as follows. First, for every (pointer) type Tt involved (including T), we start by allocating n (the scope) data objects:

```
Tt *tt_nodes = malloc(sizeof(Tt) * n);
```

Then, for every structure pointer type Ts (for which we already allocated n data objects) and field f of type Tt in Ts, we build the following nondeterministic assignment:

```
ts_nodes[0]->f = NULL;
if (nondet_bool()) ts_nodes[0]->f = tt_nodes[0];
else if (nondet_bool()) ts_nodes[0]->f = tt_nodes[1];
...
ts_nodes[1]->f = NULL;
if (nondet_bool()) ts_nodes[1]->f = tt_nodes[0];
else if (nondet_bool()) ts_nodes[1]->f = tt_nodes[1];
...
```

Finally, nondet_T() ends by returning either NULL or t_nodes[0] (no other non-null node is necessary, due to symmetry breaking). Using nondet_T(), we build the following verification harness for p:

```
T x = nondet_T();
__CPROVER_assume(repok(x));
p(x);
__CPROVER_assert(repok(x));
```

Of course the last assertion can be replaced by any expected property of p.

We now turn our attention to the use of tight field bounds to reduce non-determinism in nondet_T(). For every structure Ts and field f with type Tt declared in Ts, if $\langle N_i^{Ts} N_j^{Tt} \rangle$ does not belong to the tight bound B_f, then we remove from nondet_T() the line:

```
if (nondet_bool()) ts_nodes[i]->f = tt_nodes[j];
```

To illustrate the benefits of using tight field bounds in this setting, compare the two (semantically equivalent) nondet_avl() methods in Figure 4 for building AVLs with size at most 4. At the left of Figure 4, we show the code for the approach that considers all the feasible assignments to nodes' fields within the scope (many assignments not displayed due to the lack of space). With precomputed tight field bounds we can discard a significant number of these assignments, that are not allowed due to the bounds, as shown at the right of Figure 4. Notice that, among many others, all self-loops in nodes are discarded by the bounds.

4.1   Computing Tight Field Bounds

For the rest of this section we assume a fixed structure T, with fields $f_1, \ldots, f_m$ and representation invariant repok, and a fixed scope k. Tight field bounds for T can be automatically computed from assumed properties such as invariants and preconditions. These properties must be expressed in a language amenable to automated analysis, reducible to SAT-based analysis in our case. We employ the automated translation of the definition of T and its repok to a propositional formula implemented in the TACO tool [14, 13]. We also assume a symmetry breaking predicate is created by this translation, forcing canonical orderings of heap nodes in structures (see [14, 13] for a careful description of how these symmetry-breaking predicates are automatically built). We discuss below the

```
avlnode* nondet_avl() {                      avlnode* nondet_avl() {
  avlnode *n = malloc(sizeof(avlnode)*4);      avlnode *n = malloc(sizeof(avlnode)*4);
  if (nondet_bool())                           if (nondet_bool()) return NULL;
    return NULL;                                avlnode *result = n[0];
  avlnode *result = n[0];                       // assignments to n[0]'s fields
  // assignments to n[0]'s fields              n[0]->left = NULL;
  n[0]->left = NULL;                           if (nondet_bool())
  if (nondet_bool())                             n[0]->left = n[1];
    n[0]->left = n[0];                          n[0]->right = NULL;
  else if (nondet_bool())                      if (nondet_bool())
    n[0]->left = n[1];                            n[0]->right = n[1];
  else if (nondet_bool())                      else if (nondet_bool())
    n[0]->left = n[2];                            n[0]->right = n[2];
  else if (nondet_bool())                      n[0]->height = 1;
    n[0]->left = n[3];                         if (nondet_bool())
  n[0]->right = NULL;                            n[0]->height = 2;
  if (nondet_bool())                           else if (nondet_bool())
    n[0]->right = n[0];                           n[0]->height = 3;
  else if (nondet_bool())                      // assignments to n[1]'s fields
    n[0]->right = n[1];                        n[1]->left = NULL;
  else if (nondet_bool())                      if (nondet_bool())
    n[0]->right = n[2];                           n[1]->left = n[3];
  else if (nondet_bool())                      n[1]->right = NULL;
    n[0]->right = n[3];                        if (nondet_bool())
  n[0]->height = 0;                              n[1]->right = n[3];
  if (nondet_bool())                           n[1]->height = 1;
    n[0]->height = 1;                          if (nondet_bool())
  else if (nondet_bool())                        n[1]->height = 2;
    n[0]->height = 2;                          // assignments to n[2]'s fields
  else if (nondet_bool())                      n[2]->left = NULL;
    n[0]->height = 3;                          if (nondet_bool())
  // assignments to n[1], n[2] and n[3]'s        n[2]->left = n[3];
  // fields follow a similar pattern to        n[2]->right = NULL;
  // n[0]'s and are ommited                    if (nondet_bool())
  return result;                                 n[2]->right = n[3];
}                                              n[2]->height = 1;
                                               if (nondet_bool())
                                                 n[2]->height = 2;
                                               // assignments to n[3]'s fields
                                               n[3]->left = NULL;
                                               n[3]->right = NULL;
                                               n[3]->height = 1;
                                               return result; }
```

Fig. 4: Building AVLs with size at most 4. Left: all feasible assignments to node's fields. Right: only assignments deemed feasible by tight field bounds

parts of the translation that are important for the understanding of our approach, and refer the reader to the literature for additional details [14, 13].

Let f be a field of T with type T'. Let $A = a_1, \ldots, a_k$ and $B = b_1, \ldots, b_k$ be the identifiers for data objects of type T and T' within scope k, respectively. This bounded field is then a relation $f \subseteq A \times (B + null)$. The propositional encoding of f consists of boolean variables $f_{i,j}$, $0 \leq i, j < k$, such that $f_{i,j} = True$ in a instance I if and only if the value of f for object a_i is equal to object b_j (i.e. a_i->$f = b_j$) in I (the original translation has variables representing a_i->$f = null$, we omit these here to simplify the presentation).

As an example, Figure 5 below shows the propositional variables representing all the feasible values of binary trees' left and right fields for scope 6, in tabular form. In the tables, object identifiers are named N_i $(0 \leq i < 6)$, variables $l_{i,j}$ $(0 \leq i,j < 6)$ denote N_i->$left = N_j$ (similarly, $r_{i,j}$ denote N_i->$right = N_j$).

left	N_0	N_1	$\ldots$	N_5
N_0	$l_{0,0}$	$l_{0,1}$	$\ldots$	$l_{0,5}$
N_1	$l_{1,0}$	$l_{1,1}$	$\ldots$	$l_{1,5}$
$\vdots$	$\vdots$	$\vdots$	$\ddots$	$\vdots$
N_5	$l_{5,0}$	$l_{5,1}$	$\ldots$	$l_{5,5}$

right	N_0	N_1	$\ldots$	N_5
N_0	$r_{0,0}$	$r_{0,1}$	$\ldots$	$r_{0,5}$
N_1	$r_{1,0}$	$r_{1,1}$	$\ldots$	$r_{1,5}$
$\vdots$	$\vdots$	$\vdots$	$\ddots$	$\vdots$
N_5	$r_{5,0}$	$r_{5,1}$	$\ldots$	$r_{5,5}$

Fig. 5: Propositional encodings of binary trees' `left` and `right` fields for a scope of 6

In this way, the binary tree at the left of Figure 3, whose relational representation is given in equation 1, is defined exactly by setting the following variables to true (and all the remaining variables to false):

$$\texttt{left} = \{l_{0,1}, l_{1,3}\}, \quad \texttt{right} = \{r_{0,2}, r_{1,4}, r_{2,5}\} \tag{2}$$

As each propositional variable in the encoding of a field represents exactly the fact that a single pair of objects belongs to the field, in the following we will speak of these two notions (propositional variables and pairs of objects related by a field) interchangeably. In fact, as our approach operates with propositional formulas (needed for exploiting incremental SAT solving), the tight field bounds will be represented and computed in terms of propositional variables. It is straightforward to see that if variable $f_{i,j}$ belongs to the tight field bound for field f, then $\langle a_i, b_j \rangle$ is a feasible pair in the relational semantics (and is infeasible if $f_{i,j}$ does not belong to the tight field bound).

It is worth noticing that deciding if there exists a structure with a particular field value, say a_i->$f = b_j$, can be accomplished by querying the solver about the satisfiability of a formula consisting of a propositional encoding of the structure and the invariant (`prop_repok`), the propositional encoding of the symmetry breaking predicate (`prop_sbpred`), and the corresponding variable $f_{i,j}$:

$$\texttt{prop\_repok} \wedge \texttt{prop\_sbpred} \wedge f_{i,j} \tag{3}$$

In case the satisfiability verdict is true, the valuation returned by the solver corresponds to a *valid* (in the sense that it satisfies the invariant) memory heap, containing pair $\langle a_i, b_j \rangle$ in the relational representation of f. Also, from the valuation we can retrieve for each field f all the (true) variables that represent pairs of objects related by f in that particular heap.

The formula above can be used to compute tight bounds, determining what are the infeasible variables $f_{i,j}$ (and hence the corresponding pairs in the fields' semantics), in states that satisfy the invariant. In [14], the infeasible variables are determined using a top-down algorithm. In the algorithm therein, the field semantics is initially set, for a field of type B declared in structure A, to $A \times$

$(B \cup \{null\})$. From this fully populated initial semantics, each pair is checked for feasibility. Pairs found to be infeasible are removed from the bound. Adopting this top-down approach for computing tight field bounds leads to feasibility checks (a large number of these) that are *independent* from one another, thus making it amenable to distributed processing. Moreover, a pair can be removed from the bound as soon as it is deemed infeasible, which can be exploited to compute tight field bounds "non-exhaustively", e.g., dedicating a certain time to the computation of tight field bounds, and taking the obtained tight field bound for improving SAT analysis, regardless of whether the tight bound is the *tightest* (it converged to removing all infeasible pairs) or not. The latter can be achieved thanks to the fact that, in the top-down approach, intermediate bounds are also tight bounds [14, 13]. As each SAT query in this top-down approach is independent from the rest, the algorithm does not exploit the incremental capabilities of modern SAT solvers.

Let us present our approach to compute tight field bounds. As opposed to the technique in [14], our algorithm operates in a *bottom-up* fashion. In our presentation below, we assume a `propEncoding` method that takes the `repok`, a symmetry breaking predicate `sbpred`, and the scopes `scope`, and returns an `encoding` object. Its `getPropositionalFormula` method creates and returns a CNF propositional formula, encoding the `repok` and `sbpred` for the given `scope`. Also, the `encoding`'s `getVars(f)` method returns all the propositional variables in the encoding of field f (see Figure 5). The algorithm uses an *incremental* SAT solver, represented by a module `solver`, with the following routines:

- `load`: receives as argument a propositional formula in CNF and loads it into the solver.
- `addClause`: (incrementally) adds a clause to the current formula in the solver for future solving invocations.
- `solve`: calls the SAT-solving procedure, deciding whether the formula currently loaded in the solver is satisfiable (SAT) or not.
- `getModel`: if the formula is satisfiable, it returns the valuation produced by the SAT-solver. The truth value of a variable `v` in the model can be retrieved by invoking `getValue(v)`.

The pseudocode of our algorithm is shown in Figure 6. Line 3 builds a propositional `encoding` using the `repok`, the symmetry breaking predicate `sbpred` and the `scopes`. The CNF propositional formula produced by the `encoding` object is then loaded into the `solver` in Line 4. Lines 5-7 initialize sets $vars\_f_1, \ldots,$ $vars\_f_m$, each containing all the propositional variables in the encoding of the corresponding fields $f_1, \cdots, f_m$. As opposed to the top-down algorithm proposed in [14], which initialized fields' semantics as binary relations containing all pairs, the bottom-up algorithm starts with empty sets $feasible\_f_1, \ldots, feasible\_f_m$ (lines 8-10). $feasible\_f_1, \ldots, feasible\_f_m$ are used by the algorithm to store partial bounds for the corresponding fields $f_1, \cdots, f_m$, and will be iteratively extended with the true variables in instances returned by the SAT solver.

A crucial step in our algorithm is performed at line 12, where the current formula loaded in the SAT solver is extended, exploiting incremental SAT solving [16], with a progress-ensuring constraint on heap fields. Here, we add a clause that consists of the disjunction of all the variables in the encoding of fields that have not been previously added to the $\texttt{feasible\_f}_1, \ldots, \texttt{feasible\_f}_m$ sets. The purpose of is to ensure that instances returned by $\texttt{solver.solve()}$ in Line 13 contain at least one pair that does not belong to the sets already held in $\texttt{feasible\_f}_1, \ldots, \texttt{feasible\_f}_m$. Intuitively, by adding the clause in line 12, the call to $\texttt{solver.solve()}$ in line 13 can be interpreted as *"find a valid heap instance of the data structure that can be used to extend at least one of the current bounds in $\texttt{feasible\_f}_1, \ldots, \texttt{feasible\_f}_m$"*. If such an instance exists, it is returned by the $\texttt{solver.getModel()}$ method, and stored in the $\texttt{model}$ variable in line 14. The variables that are true in $\texttt{model}$ are then added to the $\texttt{feasible\_f}_1, \ldots, \texttt{feasible\_f}_m$ sets in lines 15-19. The loop terminates when $\texttt{feasible\_f}_1, \ldots, \texttt{feasible\_f}_m$ cannot be augmented any further (lines 20, 21), in which case, as we prove below, these sets hold tight field bounds and are returned by the algorithm (line 24).

As an example, assume we are computing tight field bounds for binary trees, and that the invocation to $\texttt{solver.solve()}$ returned the instance at the left of Figure 3. Then, the variables in sets *left* and *right* shown in equation 2 will be added to $\texttt{feasible\_left}$ and $\texttt{feasible\_right}$, respectively, in lines 15-19. Notice that this forces an instance with at least one variable not in the $\texttt{left}$ or $\texttt{right}$ sets to be returned by $\texttt{solver.solve()}$ in the next iteration.

It is worth noticing the importance of the progress-ensuring constraint in line 12, being encoded as a clause. This is what enables the possibility of using *incremental SAT solving* [16] in our tight bounds computation. Essentially, incremental SAT solvers allow one to append further constraints after each satisfying valuation is found, as long as these are in CNF. These constraints are conjoined with the main (CNF) formula, and used in computing the "next" satisfying instance without having to restart the solving process (which is a very time consuming process). Also, this allows the solver to exploit the learned clauses (that summarize the conflicts found by the solver in the search of satisfying valuations) to help accelerate subsequent queries [10]. Notice that, if the new constraints were not in CNF, the whole resulting formula would have to be translated to CNF and the SAT process restarted from scratch.

Theorem 1 proves our algorithm terminates and computes tight field bounds.

Theorem 1. *Algorithm 6 terminates and returns valid tight field bounds.*

Proof. Termination easily follows from the following two facts: *(i)* for given bounds on data domains of the structure under analysis and limited by *scopes*, the number of pairs that can be added to a field bound is a finite number; and *(ii)* each while-loop iteration either adds at least an extra pair to the bounds, or otherwise returns *unsat*, in which case the loop terminates.

To prove that the algorithm yields tight field bounds, we proceed as follows. Notice that at each iteration, and for any field f_i, the bound associated to field f_i ($\texttt{feasible\_f}_i$) is a subset of the corresponding tight bound, i.e., contains only feasible variables: the initial bound ($\emptyset$) is obviously a subset of the tight

```
1   procedure bottom−up(repok, sbpred, scopes)
2   begin
3     encoding = propEncoding(repok, sbpred, scopes)
4     solver.load(enconding.getPropositionalFormula())
5     vars_f₁ = enconding.getVars(f₁)
6     ...
7     vars_fₘ = enconding.getVars(fₘ)
8     feasible_f₁ = {}
9     ...
10    feasible_fₘ = {}
11    while True do
12      solver.addClause(⋁_{j∈1,..,m, v∈(vars_fⱼ\feasible_fⱼ)} v)
13      if solver.solve() = SAT then
14        model = solver.getModel()
15        feasible_f₁ = feasible_f₁ ∪
16            {v | v <− vars_f₁ and model.getValue(v) = True}
17        ...
18        feasible_fₘ = feasible_fₙ ∪
19            {v | v <− vars_fₘ and model.getValue(v) = True}
20      else  \\ UNSAT
21        break
22      fi
23    done
24    return feasible_f₁, ..., feasible_fₘ
25  end
```

Fig. 6: Bottom-up algorithm for tight field bounds computation

bound, and bounds are extended only by adding variables extracted from valid structures (i.e., each loop iteration produces a valid expansion). An inductive argument allows us to conclude that, on termination, the bound associated to field f_i (feasible_f_i) is a subset of the tight bound. We will now show that feasible_f_i is the tight field bound. Let us suppose that, once the algorithm terminates, bound feasible_f_i is not tight, i.e., there exists a variable $v_{w,z}$ that does not belong to feasible_f_i. Then, there must exist a canonical (i.e., satisfying symmetry breaking) instance I of repok within scopes, in which o_w->$f_i = o_z$. Therefore, I satisfies repok, sbpred, and $v_{w,z} = True$, contradicting the fact that the algorithm had terminated. Therefore, all variables excluded from feasible_f_i are infeasible, making this bound tight.

As opposed to the top-down algorithm for tight bounds introduced in [14, 13] Algorithm 6 only provides useful information once it terminates – intermediate bounds cannot be used to improve analysis. Moreover, whereas the top-down approach lends itself well to parallelization (as we mentioned before, it implies a large number of independent SAT queries, that can be solved in a distributed manner), it is not obvious how one would reasonably distribute our new bottom-up computation. Nevertheless, as we will show in Section 5, the sequential Algorithm 6 and its optimizations (i.e. the usage of incremental SAT-solving) are substantially faster than the parallel, distributed, top-down approach.

5   Evaluation

Our first experimental evaluation assesses the impact of tight field bounds in verification of code handling linked structures using CBMC. The evaluation is based on a benchmark of collection implementations, previously used for tight field bounds computation in [14, 13], composed of data structures with increasingly complex invariants:

- an implementation of sequences based on singly linked lists (LList);
- a List implementation (from Apache Commons.Collections), based on circular doubly-linked lists (AList);
- a List implementation (from Apache Commons Collections), based on node caching linked lists (CList);
- a Set implementation (from java.util) based on red-black trees (TSet);
- an implementation of AVL trees obtained from the case study used in [4] (AVL); and
- an implementation of binomial heaps used as part of a benchmark in [28] (BHeap).

Experiments in this section were run on workstations with Intel Core i7 4790 processor, 8Mb Cache, 3.6Ghz (4 Turbo), and 16 Gb of RAM, running GNU/Linux. The incremental SAT solver used was Minisat 2.2.0. We denote by OOM that the 16GB of memory were exhausted, and by OOM+ that the 16GB where exhausted while CBMC was preprocessing; in this latter case no numbers of clauses or variables were produced by CBMC. Timeout was set for these experiments to 1 hour.

Table 1 reports, for the most relevant routines of each of the data structures in our benchmark, the verification running times with the underlying decision procedure running times discriminated in seconds, as well as the number of clauses and variables (expressed in thousands) in the CNF formulas corresponding to each of the verification tasks, for several scopes (S). Since we checked whether the routines preserved the corresponding structure's invariant, we did not consider for the experiments those routines that did not modify the structure (these trivially preserve the invariant). We assessed three different approaches:

- Build*: use of verification harnesses based on insertion routines (see Fig. 1),
- Gen&Filter (generate and filter): non-deterministic generation of data structures without tight field bounds (as illustrated in Fig. 4), using a traditional symmetry breaking algorithm to discard isomorphic structures [14] (we do not discuss this here due to space reasons),
- TFB: our introduced approach, which incorporates tight field bounds into the previous to discard irrelevant non-deterministic assignments of field values (as illustrated in Fig. 4).

Some remarks on the results are in order. Table 1 shows that in all analyzed routines, the TFB approach allowed us to analyze larger scopes for which the other input generation techniques exhausted the allotted time or memory. TFB was able to analyze larger scopes than Gen&Filter in 7 out of 12 cases (remarkably, by at least 6 in AList, at least 3 in CList and at least 2 in AVL), and in 8 out of 12 cases with respect to Build* (by at least 4 in all 8 cases). Routine extractMin in structure BHeap is particularly interesting: it contains a bug first found in [14] that can only be exhibited by an input with at least 13 nodes. Gray cells mark experiments in which the bug was detected by CBMC. Notice in particular that Build* does not scale well enough to find this bug.

Our second evaluation is devoted to tight field bounds computation, in comparison with the top-down approach presented in [14]. We re-ran the TACO experiments as reported in [13] on the same hardware we used for our own experiments for a fair comparison. Original scripts and configurations were preserved. All distributed experiments were run on a cluster of 9 PCs (one being the master) of the same characteristics as described above. Each distributed experiment was run 3 times; the reported timing is the average thereof. All times are given in wall-clock seconds. A timeout (TO) is set at 18,000 seconds (5 hours), for tight bounds computation. Our bottom up tight field bounds technique is non-parallel, and was run on a single workstation. Table 2 summarizes the results of our experiments regarding tight bounds computation. We compared the running times of computing tight field bounds using the distributed technique from [14] and our non-parallel presented algorithm, for scopes 10, 12, 15, 17 and 20, reporting the following:

- TACO(||): The parallel wall-clock time required to compute tight field bounds with TACO, the tool subsuming the top-down tight bounds approach [14,13].
- TACO(s): The TACO *sequentialized* time, i.e., the sum of times over all the Minisat solvings performed by the TACO distributed algorithm.
- BU: The time the bottom-up algorithm (Alg. 6) requires to compute tight field bounds.
- speedup(||): The speed-up achieved by BU when compared to the distributed TACO time reported as TACO(||).
- Speedup(s): The speed-up achieved by BU when compared to the sequentialized TACO time reported as TACO(s).

The speed-ups obtained by Alg. 6 are, in comparison with the distributed approach in [14], in general very good. In particular, in all experiments but AVL with scope 20, the running time of our sequential bottom-up approach (BU) is already below the wall-clock time of (parallel) TACO. For AVL trees with scope 20, the only experiment where BU performed slower than TACO, the achieved speed up is 0.6X. This means that running BU on a single workstation does not even take twice as long as running TACO(||) on 32 processors (4 cores in 8 slave machines used for distributed computation). Second, it is worth noticing that structures with strong invariants (e.g., BHeap) intuitively lead to "small" tight field bounds; a bottom-up approach then, as we explained earlier, is particularly well suited for tight bounds computation for these structures, since the process

Table 1: Dynamic data structure verification in CBMC: TFB versus Build* and Gen&Filter. Verification and solving times in seconds, clauses and variables in thousands

Routine	S	Build*			Gen&Filter			TFB		
		Time(Solv)	Clauses	Vars	Time(Solv)	Clauses	Vars	Time(Solv)	Clauses	Vars
SList										
insBack	18	10(5)	705	2,236	11(5)	248	1,157	10(4)	188	916
	19	12(6)	797	2,524	13(6)	275	1,288	11(4)	206	1,015
	20	14(7)	898	2,836	16(7)	303	1,428	13(5)	226	1,122
remove	18	10(6)	629	2,004	14(9)	247	1,154	11(6)	201	967
	19	13(8)	715	2,274	23(16)	275	1,288	13(7)	221	1,075
	20	14(9)	809	2,567	20(12)	303	1,431	15(8)	243	1,190
AList										
addLast	13	2(1)	146	628	9(7)	235	947	3(2)	184	738
	14	2(1)	164	704	TO	267	1,082	3(2)	206	827
	20	6(4)	292	1,285	–	–	–	8(6)	357	1,459
remInd	14	5(3)	255	1,099	1168(1166)	352	1,444	8(6)	307	1,270
	15	6(5)	287	1,238	TO	400	1,645	10(8)	346	1,431
	20	17(14)	471	2,058	–	–	–	27/24	568	2,387
CList										
addLast	6	407(402)	2,471	9,937	2(1)	109	430	1(1)	103	402
	7	TO	3,754	15,158	2(1)	133	527	2(1)	122	482
	17	–	–	–	1423(1419)	527	2,188	10(7)	411	1,692
	18	–	–	–	TO	583	2,425	10(7)	449	1,853
	20	–	–	–	–	–	–	14(10)	530	2,195
remove	6	490(486)	1,750	6,994	4(3)	258	1,002	4(3)	247	958
	7	TO	2,755	11,066	8(3)	356	1,395	5(4)	332	1,298
	15	–	–	–	2820(2812)	2,151	8,642	60(52)	1,768	7,103
	16	–	–	–	TO	2,537	10,202	102(93)	2,067	8,315
	20	–	–	–	–	–	–	219(201)	3,578	14,454
AVL										
insert	1	114(105)	13,724	58,613	19(17)	2,232	9,593	7(5)	712	3,006
	2	OoM+	–	–	69(62)	7,011	30,138	21(15)	1,665	7,125
	3	–	–	–	203(182)	19,230	82,602	57(38)	3,414	14,745
	4	–	–	–	OoM+	–	–	169(114)	7,005	30,500
	5	–	–	–	–	–	–	411(266)	13,818	60,663
	6	–	–	–	–	–	–	OoM	26,981	119,475
delete	2	94(87)	10,874	46,271	11(10)	1,227	5,257	4(3)	421	1,777
	3	OoM+	–	–	39(34)	3,844	16,491	11(8)	823	3,487
	4	–	–	–	118(105)	10,522	45,120	40(29)	2,351	10,058
	5	–	–	–	OoM	26,768	114,697	108(81)	3,823	16,387
	7	–	–	–	–	–	–	1171/1011	14,365	62,154
	8	–	–	–	–	–	–	OoM+	–	–
TSet										
add	1	158(104)	11,849	43,627	20(16)	2,093	8,076	10(7)	980	3,811
	2	OoM+	–	–	63(62)	5,609	21,908	37(27)	3,043	11,961
	4	–	–	–	362(314)	23,538	93,122	206(160)	12,042	47,960
	5	–	–	–	OoM+	–	–	386(305)	18,270	73,206
	6	–	–	–	–	–	–	OoM+	–	–
remove	2	128(85)	9,708	34,998	10(7)	1,029	3,934	9(7)	1,000	3,825
	3	OoM	28,268	107,255	23(19)	2,074	8,039	22(17)	2,016	7,818
	9	–	–	–	828/761	22,881	91,143	760/699	22,698	90,434
	10	–	–	–	OoM	29,724	118,620	OoM	29,548	117,943
BHeap										
insert	5	188(181)	17,620	75,858	35(32)	2,722	11,679	32(28)	2,627	11,297
	6	OoM	27,217	117,396	56(50)	3,852	16,522	47(42)	3,717	15,972
	13	–	–	–	640/603	18,480	78,795	523/487	17,827	76,142
	14	–	–	–	OoM	21,645	92,214	OoM	20,967	89,456
extrMin	5	157(152)	14,713	63,329	26(23)	2,015	8,603	24(21)	1,930	8,267
	6	OoM	23,511	101,429	44(39)	3,022	12,905	40(35)	2,914	12,474
	12	–	–	–	487(459)	14,254	60,615	441(414)	13,921	59,285
	13	–	–	–	576	17,094	72,634	535	16,711	71,102

of computing bounds by discovering and adding new elements to a partial bound until nothing new can be discovered, quickly converges to termination in these

Table 2: Tight field bounds computation times and achieved speed-ups.

LList	S10	S12	S15	S17	S20
TACO(‖)	7.5	10.7	29.0	42.6	66.1
TACO(s)	122.0	231.8	777.4	1204.7	1932.5
BU	1.3	2.0	3.4	5.3	11.5
speedup(‖)	5.7X	5.3X	8.3X	8.0X	5.7X
speedup(s)	91.7X	114.1X	224.6X	227.7X	166.8X
AList	**S10**	**S12**	**S15**	**S17**	**S20**
TACO(‖)	15.9	29.8	73.0	120.3	2174.8
TACO(s)	381.4	807.9	2153.8	3638.0	67936.0
BU	2.0	2.5	4.9	8.6	16.1
speedup(‖)	7.6X	11.8X	14.7X	13.9X	134.9X
speedup(s)	184.2X	319.3X	435.9X	423.0X	4217.0X
CList	**S10**	**S12**	**S15**	**S17**	**S20**
TACO(‖)	35.6	64.2	110.7	176.3	4634.6
TACO(s)	981.1	1881.9	3331.1	5386.0	145106.0
BU	2.4	4.5	12.0	54.5	2831.2
speedup(‖)	14.6X	14.0X	9.2X	3.2X	1.6X
speedup(s)	402.0X	410.8X	276.8X	98.7X	51.2X
AVL	**S10**	**S12**	**S15**	**S17**	**S20**
TACO(‖)	64.6	141.9	465.9	2437.7	5939.5
TACO(s)	1893.7	4323.3	14645.6	77536.6	187161.0
BU	8.1	23.0	111.4	1078.0	8562.2
speedup(‖)	7.8X	6.1X	4.1X	2.2X	0.6X
speedup(s)	231.2X	187.3X	131.4X	71.9X	21.8X
TSet	**S10**	**S12**	**S15**	**S17**	**S20**
TACO(‖)	76.0	145.6	258.2	872.8	2335.4
TACO(s)	2434.9	4411.4	8005.7	27538.8	74134.6
BU	4.8	10.3	39.1	168.6	527.6
speedup(‖)	15.6X	14.0X	6.5X	5.1X	4.4X
speedup(s)	458.9X	425.4X	204.4X	163.2X	140.4X
BHeap	**S10**	**S12**	**S15**	**S17**	**S20**
TACO(‖)	115.9	188.3	345.0	1119.7	3224.0
TACO(s)	3505.6	5747.1	10759.1	35409.9	102496.0
BU	4.4	9.1	23.8	80.7	243.9
speedup(‖)	26.0X	20.4X	14.4X	13.8X	13.2X
speedup(s)	786.0X	625.3X	452.0X	438.6X	420.1X

cases. Third, some structures with relatively weak invariants also had good running times (AList, in particular), when compared to other case studies. Although the invariants in these cases are weaker, which intuitively would lead to more expensive tight bounds computations, these structures have fewer fields, so the state space to be covered to compute tight bounds is significantly smaller than that of more complex structures.

All the experiments in this section can be reproduced following the instructions available at [1].

Threats to Validity. Our experimental evaluation is limited to data structures. From the vast domain of data structures, we have selected a few ones that we consider representative for several reasons: they are often used as case studies in the evaluation of other software analysis tools [6, 9, 18, 28], their invariants have varied complexity (which is a dimension that affects tight bounds' size, and thus their computation), some are acyclic and others are not (which shows that the encoding we make in CBMC is quite general), etc. We consider this is a good menu, representative of a wider class of data structures.

Our approach to capture both the Build* and Gen&Filter strategies might have accidentally favored our technique. We tried different alternatives for capturing Build* and Gen&Filter, in particular with different ways of writing the repOK routines (which affected running times). We took the best alternative found for each case, to perform the comparison. In the case of Build*, we took the smallest number of builder routines that guaranteed producing *all* (bounded) structures, since this is a factor that impacts running times. All structures with the exception of CList and TSet required just the add routine, while these two also needed a remove routine, to guarantee generation of all structures.

Regarding variance across cluster runs, different schedulings indeed yield slightly different timings. Since the granularity of individual analyses is fine, differences are typically small. However, they grow with the scope (e.g., usually smaller than 5% for scope sizes below 10, but up to 15% for the largest sizes). We used the average of 3 runs to reduce the effect of variance in the experiments.

Finally, we did not prove our implementations correct, so our results may be affected by errors in our implementations. We checked consistency of the results across different techniques and tools to confirm that bounds were correctly computed, and verification was bounded complete in all cases.

6   Related Work

Automated analysis of code handling dynamic data structures has been the focus of various lines of research, including separation logic based approaches [5], approaches based on combinations of testing and static analysis [22], various forms of model checking including explicit state model checking [27], symbolic execution based model checking [23] and SAT-based verification [14, 13]. The approach that we refer to as Build*, producing nondeterministic structures by using insertion routines, has been used in some of these approaches, including [22, 11]. The "generate & filter" mechanism, on the other hand, is more often employed in modular (assume-guarantee) verification. In particular, the *lazy initialization* approach, whose symmetry breaking we borrowed for "generate & filter" in this paper is used in [19], among others. However, in SAT-based bounded model checking, with tools such as [20], "generate & filter" is not reported as an analysis option for dynamic data structures. The use of tight bounds to improve analysis has been used previously to improve test generation and bounded verification for JML-annotated Java programs [14, 13]. The setting is however different from that of CBMC, due to the relational program (and heap state) semantics, which enabled them to exploit tight bounds directly at the propositional encoding level. Tight bounds have also been used for improving symbolic execution based model checking [15, 26]. Again, the context is different, since these approaches that essentially "walk" the code (either concretely or symbolically), can exploit tight bounds more deeply [26], also obtaining greater profits.

We have also reported a novel technique to *compute* tight bounds. This algorithm is inspired in the work of [24] about black-box test input generation using SAT. Our work is also closely related to [14, 13]. The approach to compute tight field bounds presented in [14, 13] as part of the TACO tool, performs a very large number of independent SAT queries to compute bounds, and thus requires a cluster of workstations to do so effectively (we compared with this approach in the paper). Another alternative approach to compute tight field bounds is presented in [25], but requires structure specifications to be provided in a Separation Logic flavor [21] to compute field bounds.

7   Conclusions

We have investigated the use of tight field bounds in the context of SAT-based bounded model checking, more concretely, in (assume-guarantee) verification of C code, using CBMC. We showed that, in this context, and in particular in the verification of programs dealing with linked structures, an approach based on nondeterministically generating structures, and then "filtering out" ill-formed ones, can be more efficient than the more traditional approach of repeatedly using data structure builders, especially when tight bounds are exploited. We have performed a number of experiments that confirm that this alternative approach allows CBMC to consider larger input sizes as well as to detect bugs that could not be detected without using bounds.

Since the approach depends on precomputing tight field bounds, we have also studied this problem, providing a novel algorithm for tight field bound computation. Tight field bounds have proved useful for a number of different analyses, but computing them is costly, and previous field bound computation approaches that performed reasonably did so at the expense of relying on a cluster of workstations to perform the task, or were only applicable to a limited set of class invariants, expressible in separation logic. Thus, while tight field bounds proved to have a deep impact in the previously mentioned automated software analysis techniques, their use has been severely undermined by the necessity of a cluster of computers for their effective computation, or the availability of specifications in separation logic. The algorithm presented in this article allows one to compute tight field bounds on a single workstation more efficiently than the distributed approach on a cluster of 8 quad-core, and therefore makes tight field bounds computation both practical and worthwhile, as part of the above mentioned analyses.

References

1. Website and replication package for Efficient Bounded Model Checking of Heap-Manipulating Programs using Tight Field Bounds. https://sites.google.com/view/bmc-bounds.

2. Pablo Abad, Nazareno Aguirre, Valeria S. Bengolea, Daniel Alfredo Ciolek, Marcelo F. Frias, Juan P. Galeotti, Tom Maibaum, Mariano M. Moscato, Nicolás Rosner, and Ignacio Vissani. Improving test generation under rich contracts by tight bounds and incremental SAT solving. In *Sixth IEEE International Conference on Software Testing, Verification and Validation, ICST 2013, Luxembourg, Luxembourg, March 18-22, 2013*, pages 21–30. IEEE Computer Society, 2013.

3. Saswat Anand, Corina S. Pasareanu, and Willem Visser. JPF-SE: A symbolic execution extension to java pathfinder. In Orna Grumberg and Michael Huth, editors, *Tools and Algorithms for the Construction and Analysis of Systems, 13th International Conference, TACAS 2007, Held as Part of the Joint European Conferences on Theory and Practice of Software, ETAPS 2007 Braga, Portugal, March 24 - April 1, 2007, Proceedings*, volume 4424 of *Lecture Notes in Computer Science*, pages 134–138. Springer, 2007.

4. Jason Belt, Robby, and Xianghua Deng. Sireum/topi LDP: a lightweight semi-decision procedure for optimizing symbolic execution-based analyses. In Hans van Vliet and Valérie Issarny, editors, *Proceedings of the 7th joint meeting of the European Software Engineering Conference and the ACM SIGSOFT International Symposium on Foundations of Software Engineering, 2009, Amsterdam, The Netherlands, August 24-28, 2009*, pages 355–364. ACM, 2009.

5. Josh Berdine, Cristiano Calcagno, Byron Cook, Dino Distefano, Peter W. O'Hearn, Thomas Wies, and Hongseok Yang. Shape analysis for composite data structures. In Werner Damm and Holger Hermanns, editors, *Computer Aided Verification, 19th International Conference, CAV 2007, Berlin, Germany, July 3-7, 2007, Proceedings*, volume 4590 of *Lecture Notes in Computer Science*, pages 178–192. Springer, 2007.

6. Chandrasekhar Boyapati, Sarfraz Khurshid, and Darko Marinov. Korat: automated testing based on java predicates. In Phyllis G. Frankl, editor, *Proceedings of the International Symposium on Software Testing and Analysis, ISSTA 2002, Roma, Italy, July 22-24, 2002*, pages 123–133. ACM, 2002.

7. Edmund M. Clarke, Armin Biere, Richard Raimi, and Yunshan Zhu. Bounded model checking using satisfiability solving. *Formal Methods Syst. Des.*, 19(1):7–34, 2001.

8. Edmund M. Clarke, Daniel Kroening, and Flavio Lerda. A tool for checking ANSI-C programs. In Kurt Jensen and Andreas Podelski, editors, *Tools and Algorithms for the Construction and Analysis of Systems, 10th International Conference, TACAS 2004, Held as Part of the Joint European Conferences on Theory and Practice of Software, ETAPS 2004, Barcelona, Spain, March 29 - April 2, 2004, Proceedings*, volume 2988 of *Lecture Notes in Computer Science*, pages 168–176. Springer, 2004.

9. Greg Dennis, Felix Sheng-Ho Chang, and Daniel Jackson. Modular verification of code with SAT. In Lori L. Pollock and Mauro Pezzè, editors, *Proceedings of the ACM/SIGSOFT International Symposium on Software Testing and Analysis, ISSTA 2006, Portland, Maine, USA, July 17-20, 2006*, pages 109–120. ACM, 2006.

10. Niklas Eén and Niklas Sörensson. An extensible sat-solver. In Enrico Giunchiglia and Armando Tacchella, editors, *Theory and Applications of Satisfiability Testing,*

6th International Conference, SAT 2003. Santa Margherita Ligure, Italy, May 5-8, 2003 Selected Revised Papers, volume 2919 of *Lecture Notes in Computer Science*, pages 502–518. Springer, 2003.

11. Stephan Falke, Florian Merz, and Carsten Sinz. LLBMC: improved bounded model checking of C programs using LLVM - (competition contribution). In Nir Piterman and Scott A. Smolka, editors, *Tools and Algorithms for the Construction and Analysis of Systems - 19th International Conference, TACAS 2013, Held as Part of the European Joint Conferences on Theory and Practice of Software, ETAPS 2013, Rome, Italy, March 16-24, 2013. Proceedings*, volume 7795 of *Lecture Notes in Computer Science*, pages 623–626. Springer, 2013.

12. Marcelo F. Frias, Juan P. Galeotti, Carlos López Pombo, and Nazareno Aguirre. Dynalloy: upgrading alloy with actions. In Gruia-Catalin Roman, William G. Griswold, and Bashar Nuseibeh, editors, *27th International Conference on Software Engineering (ICSE 2005), 15-21 May 2005, St. Louis, Missouri, USA*, pages 442–451. ACM, 2005.

13. Juan P. Galeotti, Nicolás Rosner, Carlos Gustavo López Pombo, and Marcelo F. Frias. TACO: efficient sat-based bounded verification using symmetry breaking and tight bounds. *IEEE Trans. Software Eng.*, 39(9):1283–1307, 2013.

14. Juan P. Galeotti, Nicolás Rosner, Carlos López Pombo, and Marcelo F. Frias. Analysis of invariants for efficient bounded verification. In Paolo Tonella and Alessandro Orso, editors, *Proceedings of the Nineteenth International Symposium on Software Testing and Analysis, ISSTA 2010, Trento, Italy, July 12-16, 2010*, pages 25–36. ACM, 2010.

15. Jaco Geldenhuys, Nazareno Aguirre, Marcelo F. Frias, and Willem Visser. Bounded lazy initialization. In Guillaume Brat, Neha Rungta, and Arnaud Venet, editors, *NASA Formal Methods, 5th International Symposium, NFM 2013, Moffett Field, CA, USA, May 14-16, 2013. Proceedings*, volume 7871 of *Lecture Notes in Computer Science*, pages 229–243. Springer, 2013.

16. John N. Hooker. Solving the incremental satisfiability problem. *J. Log. Program.*, 15(1&2):177–186, 1993.

17. Daniel Jackson. *Software Abstractions - Logic, Language, and Analysis*. MIT Press, 2006.

18. Daniel Jackson and Mandana Vaziri. Finding bugs with a constraint solver. In Debra J. Richardson and Mary Jean Harold, editors, *Proceedings of the International Symposium on Software Testing and Analysis, ISSTA 2000, Portland, OR, USA, August 21-24, 2000*, pages 14–25. ACM, 2000.

19. Sarfraz Khurshid, Corina S. Pasareanu, and Willem Visser. Generalized symbolic execution for model checking and testing. In Hubert Garavel and John Hatcliff, editors, *Tools and Algorithms for the Construction and Analysis of Systems, 9th International Conference, TACAS 2003, Held as Part of the Joint European Conferences on Theory and Practice of Software, ETAPS 2003, Warsaw, Poland, April 7-11, 2003, Proceedings*, volume 2619 of *Lecture Notes in Computer Science*, pages 553–568. Springer, 2003.

20. Daniel Kroening and Michael Tautschnig. CBMC - C bounded model checker - (competition contribution). In Erika Ábrahám and Klaus Havelund, editors, *Tools and Algorithms for the Construction and Analysis of Systems - 20th International Conference, TACAS 2014, Held as Part of the European Joint Conferences on Theory and Practice of Software, ETAPS 2014, Grenoble, France, April 5-13, 2014. Proceedings*, volume 8413 of *Lecture Notes in Computer Science*, pages 389–391. Springer, 2014.

21. Huu Hai Nguyen, Cristina David, Shengchao Qin, and Wei-Ngan Chin. Automated verification of shape and size properties via separation logic. In Byron Cook and Andreas Podelski, editors, *Verification, Model Checking, and Abstract Interpretation, 8th International Conference, VMCAI 2007, Nice, France, January 14-16, 2007, Proceedings*, volume 4349 of *Lecture Notes in Computer Science*, pages 251–266. Springer, 2007.

22. Aditya V. Nori, Sriram K. Rajamani, SaiDeep Tetali, and Aditya V. Thakur. The yogiproject: Software property checking via static analysis and testing. In Stefan Kowalewski and Anna Philippou, editors, *Tools and Algorithms for the Construction and Analysis of Systems, 15th International Conference, TACAS 2009, Held as Part of the Joint European Conferences on Theory and Practice of Software, ETAPS 2009, York, UK, March 22-29, 2009. Proceedings*, volume 5505 of *Lecture Notes in Computer Science*, pages 178–181. Springer, 2009.

23. Corina S. Pasareanu, Willem Visser, David H. Bushnell, Jaco Geldenhuys, Peter C. Mehlitz, and Neha Rungta. Symbolic pathfinder: integrating symbolic execution with model checking for java bytecode analysis. *Autom. Softw. Eng.*, 20(3):391–425, 2013.

24. Pablo Ponzio, Nazareno Aguirre, Marcelo F. Frias, and Willem Visser. Field-exhaustive testing. In Thomas Zimmermann, Jane Cleland-Huang, and Zhendong Su, editors, *Proceedings of the 24th ACM SIGSOFT International Symposium on Foundations of Software Engineering, FSE 2016, Seattle, WA, USA, November 13-18, 2016*, pages 908–919. ACM, 2016.

25. Pablo Ponzio, Nicolás Rosner, Nazareno Aguirre, and Marcelo F. Frias. Efficient tight field bounds computation based on shape predicates. In Cliff B. Jones, Pekka Pihlajasaari, and Jun Sun, editors, *FM 2014: Formal Methods - 19th International Symposium, Singapore, May 12-16, 2014. Proceedings*, volume 8442 of *Lecture Notes in Computer Science*, pages 531–546. Springer, 2014.

26. Nicolás Rosner, Jaco Geldenhuys, Nazareno Aguirre, Willem Visser, and Marcelo F. Frias. BLISS: improved symbolic execution by bounded lazy initialization with SAT support. *IEEE Trans. Software Eng.*, 41(7):639–660, 2015.

27. Willem Visser and Peter C. Mehlitz. Model checking programs with java pathfinder. In Patrice Godefroid, editor, *Model Checking Software, 12th International SPIN Workshop, San Francisco, CA, USA, August 22-24, 2005, Proceedings*, volume 3639 of *Lecture Notes in Computer Science*, page 27. Springer, 2005.

28. Willem Visser, Corina S. Pasareanu, and Radek Pelánek. Test input generation for java containers using state matching. In Lori L. Pollock and Mauro Pezzè, editors, *Proceedings of the ACM/SIGSOFT International Symposium on Software Testing and Analysis, ISSTA 2006, Portland, Maine, USA, July 17-20, 2006*, pages 37–48. ACM, 2006.

Effects of Program Representation on Pointer Analyses — An Empirical Study

Jyoti Prakash[(✉)1] , Abhishek Tiwari[2] , and Christian Hammer[1]

[1] University of Potsdam, Potsdam, Germany
jyotiprakash1@acm.org, c.hammer@acm.org
[2] National University of Singapore, Singapore, Singapore
tiwari@comp.nus.edu.sg

Abstract Static analysis frameworks, such as *Soot* and *Wala*, are used by researchers to prototype and compare program analyses. These frameworks vary on heap abstraction, modeling library classes, and underlying intermediate program representation (IR). Often, these variations pose a threat to the validity of the results as the implications of comparing the same analysis implementation in different frameworks are still unexplored. Earlier studies have focused on the precision, soundness, and recall of the algorithms implemented in these frameworks; however, little to no work has been done to evaluate the effects of program representation. In this work, we fill this gap and study the impact of program representation on pointer analysis. Unfortunately, existing metrics are insufficient for such a comparison due to their inability to isolate each aspect of the program representation. Therefore, we define two novel metrics that measure these analyses' precision after isolating the influence of class-hierarchy and intermediate representation. Our results establish that the minor differences in the class hierarchy and IR do not impact program analysis significantly. Besides, they reveal the sources of unsoundness that aid researchers in developing program analysis.

Keywords: Pointer Analysis, Java, Program Analysis, Empirical Studies

1 Introduction

Researchers have proposed various approaches to enhance the precision and soundness of static analyses [6, 9, 10, 14, 17, 26, 30, 31]. They use program analysis frameworks to prototype and evaluate their algorithms. A program analysis based on declarative specifications (a growingly popular implementation paradigm) uses these frameworks to extract fundamental dataflow relations and feeds them as the ground facts to a Datalog engine.

Program analysis frameworks, primarily Soot and Wala, are being increasingly adopted in program analysis [11, 31, 40]. These frameworks provide APIs, which abstract internal program representation. However, program representation in these frameworks is heterogeneous in many aspects. A few of those are:

© The Author(s) 2021
E. Guerra and M. Stoelinga (Eds.): FASE 2021, LNCS 12649, pp. 240–261, 2021.
https://doi.org/10.1007/978-3-030-71500-7_12

- *Intermediate Representation (IR).* The intermediate language for program representation is an abstraction of the object code (bytecode) or source code. It removes syntactic sugar from the language and transforms it into a (minimal) core language. Thus, analysis developers can focus on the core language features to define their analysis.
- *Modeling of libraries in analysis scope.* Real-life applications are seldomly developed from scratch; instead, they reuse library modules. Whole-program analyses consider these libraries for soundness in terms of the class-hierarchy, which forms the analyses' scope. Users can tune the scope to favor scalability over soundness.
- *Heap Modeling.* Heap modeling is the technique to model dynamic heap allocation statically. Precise heap modeling is undecidable; therefore, analyses use approximations to keep it decidable [20]. Apart from these approximations, optimization may choose to keep a low memory footprint at the cost of precision and soundness.

These factors influence the precision, scalability, soundness of the analyses, and at the same time, impede a fair comparison of analyses. Earlier research (Späth et al. [29]) was concerned about the validity of results when comparing two analyses frameworks. Reif et al. consider the comparison of different frameworks "bogus" [21] at the outset. Although many earlier works have proposed techniques to enhance scalability and precision, little to no work was done on how program representation influences program analyses. As a result, a comparison of new analyses with existing analyses suffers from a threat to validity that might have been overlooked. In this work, we fill the gap with an empirical study of these aspects of program analysis frameworks.

We choose pointer analysis for this study. Pointer analysis computes the heap locations referred by program variables and builds the foundation for many others, such as alias analysis, type-state, or program slicing. To evaluate intermediate representation and library modeling, we choose Doop, a *state-of-the-art* pointer analysis framework and compare its analysis for different frontends. For the third aspect, heap modeling, we compare the pointer analysis of *Wala*'s (a *state-of-the-art* program analysis) framework with *Doop* using *Wala*'s frontend, i.e., leveraging the identical intermediate representation.

A challenging aspect of this work is that the existing notions of precision for pointer analysis were insufficient. The computation of these metrics does not isolate single aspects of pointer analysis but rather combines all effects. For example, the average points-to set size is influenced by all three of the aforementioned aspects. It is difficult to determine the effect of each aspect by only looking at the score. In this work, we counteract this problem by introducing metrics that isolate a particular aspect under study and nullifies the effect of others. Therefore, we define two novel metrics in section 3.1, one for measuring the effects of libraries to enable a fair comparison among frameworks. To the best of our knowledge, it is the first study that evaluates the impact of program representation on pointer analysis. Precisely, in this paper, we make the following contributions:

- We defined two metrics for evaluating each aspect in isolation, one for modeling of library classes, the other for IR.
- We evaluated the differences in library modeling and found that these have little influence on program analyses. Additionally, we discovered sources of unsoundness in these frameworks.
- We evaluated the precision for different IRs and found that they have no impact on the precision of *virtual* method call elimination.
- We empirically found differences in heap abstractions even for analyses claiming the same levels of context-sensitivity regarding the types of heap objects.

In summary, our empirical study dispels the threats to the validity of the results of existing works posed by these differences of frameworks. It also discovers novel sources of unsoundness and imprecision in existing frameworks that provide suggestions that users/developers of these frameworks could incorporate into their analyses. Although we focus on pointer analysis in the paper, our results are, in principle, generalizable to many other static analyses, as the findings presented in this paper also hold for these. We have made the artifacts available on https://github.com/jpksh90/pointeval to facilitate reproduction.

2   Background and Motivation

The goal of pointer analysis is to determine which objects a variable may refer (point) to at runtime. A *points-to set* is a static approximation of this question, which maps variables to objects that are allocated on the heap (heap objects). More precisely, if V is the set of variables in a program, and H is the set of heap objects, then $points\text{-}to : V \rightarrow \mathcal{P}(H)$. $points\text{-}to(v)$ returns the set of heap objects in H referred by v.

Doop is a framework that exclusively focuses on pointer analysis, defines the analysis' inference rules in Datalog [41], and is in active development. It supports tuning of the analysis to adapt for various factors of precision (and scalability). Doop leverages the program synthesizer Soufflé [12, 22] to resolve *points-to* according to the inference rules and the ground facts, which are derived directly from the program.

Wala [37] and Soot [28] are general-purpose program analyzers providing some pre-defined analyses and APIs for the development of custom analyses. Wala comes with various pre-defined pointer analyses [39], some of which feature novel optimizations to enhance scalability.

A *context-sensitive analysis* improves a pointer analysis' precision by discerning method calls based on their calling contexts. Popular notions of contexts are based on method callsites [23] (*callsite-sensitive*), invoking objects (*object-sensitive*) [19], or hybrids thereof [13].

In the sequel, we explain the need for this study by exemplifying the three factors that influence the results of pointer analyses.

Listing 1.1: Factory Method

```
1 public class Factory {
2     public static void main(String args[]) {
3         AInt a = AInt.getInstance(5);
4         AInt b = AInt.getInstance(7); } }
5 class AInt {
6     private Integer a; //... getter, setter and constructor
7     public static AInt getInstance(int x) {
8             return new AInt(x); //allocation a@8
9 }}
```

Listing 1.2: Soot IR for the *main* method in Listing 1.1

```
1 public class Factory extends java.lang.Object {
2     //constructor
3   public static void main(java.lang.String[]) {
4         java.lang.String[] r0;
5         AInt r1, r2;
6         r0 := @parameter0: java.lang.String[];
7         r1 = staticinvoke <AInt: AInt getInstance(int)>(5);
8         r2 = staticinvoke <AInt: AInt getInstance(int)>(7);
9         return; } }
```

2.1   Intermediate Representation

Many program analyses tools leverage an *intermediate representation* (IR) instead of the actual source or bytecode for analysis. IRs remove syntactic sugar from the source code and make it amenable to analysis by focussing on the fundamental operations. Popular strategies for IR generation are based on three-address code or *static single assignment* (SSA) form [4]. By default, the Soot framework uses a three-address-based IR (*Jimple*) [35], while Wala uses a SSA-based IR [38]. Both IRs are register-based [36,38], and hence introduce synthetic variables to mimic the stack-based Java bytecode. *Doop* can be configured to leverage either *Jimple* or *Wala*'s IR as a frontend for program representation.

Consider the code example in Listing 1.1 and its Jimple IR depicted in Listing 1.2. The *main* method declaration (line 2) translates to the almost identical line 3 in the IR, whose parameter is translated to the variable *@parameter0* (line 6). Due to the additional local variable *r0* (line 4), the single main method argument translates to two variables in the IR. The invocations of the static method *getInstance* (lines 3 and 4 of Listing 1.1) are translated to the corresponding operation code *staticinvoke* with the method name and arguments. The newly allocated objects returned from these factory method invocations are stored in the variables *r1* and *r2*.

Wala's IR generation differs significantly from Soot (see Listing 1.3). As an SSA-based IR, it does not assign names to method parameters and variables but ordinal numbers (starting from '*1*') called *variable numbers* (we prepend '*v*' to these numbers for clarity). Thus, the receiver object (*this* reference in Java), or the first parameter in the case of a static method is (silently) assigned

Listing 1.3: Wala IR for the *main* method in Listing 1.1

```
1 Factory.main([Ljava/lang/String;)V
2 5 = invokestatic < Application , LAInt ,
      getInstance(I)LAInt; > 3 @1 exception:4
3 8 = invokestatic < Application , LAInt ,
      getInstance(I)LAInt; > 6 @7 exception:7
4 return
```

Listing 1.4: Snapshot of pointer analysis results from Doop with different IR

```
1 // Variables in main method with ****Wala****
2 < <<main method array>> <Factory: void
     main(java.lang.String[])>/v1
3 // Variables in main method with ****Soot****
4 > <<main method array>>    <Factory: void
     main(java.lang.String[])>/@parameter0
5 > <<main method array>>    <Factory: void
     main(java.lang.String[])>/10#_0
```

the number $v1$. Further method parameters are assigned subsequent variable numbers, succeeded by local variables. Again, the static method calls to the method *getInstance* are translated to *invokestatic*, where $v3$ and $v6$ hold the (implicitly defined) constant arguments 6 and 7. The objects returned from the factory method invocations are stored in the variables $v5$ and $v8$. Potential exceptions thrown in the invoked methods are stored in $v4$ or $v7$, respectively.

The differences in program representation influence the metrics of pointer analysis: We analyzed Listing 1.1 context-insensitively with Doop, using Jimple and Wala's IR. The results are shown in Listing 1.4: The main method parameter object «main method array» is referred by one variable in Wala (line 2) but two variables in Soot (lines 4– 5). Even though the average points-to set size is 1 for all variables in Listing 1.4, we found noticeable differences in the average points-to set sizes in other program's analyses, with Soot's frontend the average size of the points-to set being 2.07 for 3328 variables, and 1.95 for 2298 variables using Wala's—Jimple again created more variables than Wala. These subtle differences in program representation affect the average points-to set size, and it is unclear whether these two numbers are in fact comparable. In this work, we aim to investigate the impact of IRs on the precision and scalability of the analysis (Section 4.3).

2.2 Static modeling of libraries

As a whole program analysis, a pointer analysis does not only requires knowledge of the program to be analyzed but also the library classes, especially those related to the runtime. For example, a whole program analysis of a Java application would require the runtime libraries, such as those in *rt.jar*, and other dependent libraries, bundled with the application. Analysis frameworks such as Soot and Wala construct the class hierarchy based on all classes present in libraries and the application. They can also remove "irrelevant" classes, favoring scalability over soundness. Interestingly, we found cases where some frontends do not load all of the required classes, which induces discrepancies when comparing the analyses.

Consider the program shown in Listing 1.1. To corroborate our intuition, we analyzed this program context-insensitively with Soot's and Wala's frontends. Using the former front-end, Doop loads 3,837 classes and computes the analysis with an average points-to set size of 2.07. With Wala's front-end, it loads 19,927 (~5×) classes for analysis with an average points-to set size of 1.95. Further investigating the types of heap objects, we found that Doop with Wala's IR contains objects of the class *java.security.PrivilegedActionException*, which is absent in the analysis with Soot. Note that our simple program contains no instance of that type, so it must stem from analyzing libraries. In another instance, Soot loads the classes from *javax.crypto*, whereas Wala does not. In this research, we examine the imprecise modeling and discover possible implications on precision and soundness (sections 4.1 and 4.2).

2.3   Heap Abstraction

Heap abstraction is an important aspect of pointer analysis and determines how object allocations are statically represented in the analysis. One simple approach is to create a unique representation for each object allocation site in the program (*allocation site abstraction*). However, at runtime allocation sites can be executed more than once, creating several objects that are then represented by the same abstract value. As an example, consider the object allocation (line 8) of Listing 1.1, represented via a single abstract object, say *a@8*. In the *main* method the newly allocated objects returned by *getInstance* are captured by the variables *a* and *b*, which would both refer to the abstract object, *a@8* in the result of the pointer analysis. Thus, *a* and *b* are spuriously considered *aliases* (i.e., referring to the same object.) This imprecision stems from ignoring the calling-context of *getInstance* (*context-insensitive heap abstraction*).

A *context-sensitive heap abstraction* (a.k.a *heap cloning*) discerns the abstract[3] heap-objects based on the calling context, associating the calling context with the heap object to distinguish the allocations in a pair ⟨*allocation site, call stack*⟩. Thus the allocation at line 8 is represented as two heap objects, ⟨*a@8*, 3⟩ and ⟨*a@8*, 4⟩. Without loss of generality, the length of the call stack can be increased to any finite number, lest the analysis be undecidable. All *state-of-the-art* pointer analysis frameworks offer *context-sensitive heap abstraction* with a finite context length.

The discussion above demonstrates how the choice of heap abstraction can (potentially) influence pointer analysis. Therefore, in this work, we study the frameworks' heap abstractions. We conducted a preliminary study to gain initial insights and to validate our intuition, and context-sensitively analyzed Listing 1.1 with a *one-call-site context-sensitivity* in Doop with Wala's IR, and the *one-call-site sensitive* analysis of the Wala framework. Both of these analyses

---

[3] In the sequel we will reference abstract heap objects as heap objects for brevity.

use a context-sensitive heap abstraction with context length of one. In spite of that, Wala creates 17 objects while Doop creates 133 objects (~7×). The average points-to set size varies between 1.55 for the analysis provided by Wala and 1.62 for Doop with Wala's IR[4]. Thus, we can see that even with the same level of sensitivity in heap abstraction (and IR), analysis results depend on the framework used. Manual inspection revealed that Wala selectively uses the context-sensitive heap abstraction, applying contextual heap abstraction only to non-library classes while treating the library's objects context-insensitively. Out of the 17 heap objects, Wala uses context-sensitivity for only 6 objects. In contrast, Doop leverages context-sensitivity for all heap objects, including the library's objects. These initial insights motivated us to analyze the influence of heap abstraction on precision and scalability in more detail in Section 4.4.

To summarize, the parameters for program analysis such as IR (Section 2.1), static modeling of libraries (Section 2.2), and heap abstraction (Section 2.3) affect the precision and scalability of a pointer analysis. Based on initial insights, we analyze the influence of the mentioned parameters using different frameworks, frontends, and on a larger and diverse set of benchmark applications.

3   Methodology

3.1   Metrics Used

The precision of a pointer analysis has been defined in numerous ways in the literature. Some of the metrics for precision available in the literature are the average size of the points-to sets, the number of call-graph edges, and the number of resolved virtual calls. These metrics are not clearly superior to one another but rather tailored to specific clients, for example, the latter is leveraged by compilers in *devirtualization* of virtual method calls.

All of these metrics reflect how precisely the analysis computes the points-to sets (sets of heap objects referred by a variable). For example, whether or not a virtual call can be resolved depends on the heap objects' types in the points-to set of the target variable. If there is only one type (or subtypes thereof that do not redefine the virtual method) then the virtual call is resolvable. Therefore, the precision of a client analysis depends on how precisely the points-to set for each variable in the program can be resolved, in other words, how low the value of the average points-to set size is. An average size close to one is considered the hallmark of pointer analysis [27].

Therefore, we leverage the wide-spread metric of average points-to set size for our evaluation, i.e., the ratio of the total sizes of the points-to sets to the total number of local variables [26, 34]. It permits a client-agnostic comparison of the pointer analysis, which generalizes our evaluation results to any specific analysis. We refer to the average points-to set size as *precision* in this paper. Note that the actual precision of the analysis is inversely connected to the average points-to

---

[4] Note that due to context-sensitive analysis, the average points-to set size is better than that mentioned in sections 2.2 and 2.1.

set size: A lower precision value (i.e. average points-to set size) implies a higher precision of the computed analysis result, as precise analyses aim at excluding unrealizable (at runtime) allocation sites from the points-to sets of variables.

An IR may create many synthetic variables, among other reasons for method parameters or for ϕ-nodes at control-flow joins of SSA-form. For example, three-address code re-uses the same variable in assignments in the *if* and *else* blocks of a conditional. However, SSA-based IRs insert a synthetic variable in a ϕ-node at the control-flow join to select one of the distinct variables of the respective blocks. The presence of synthetic variables in IRs impedes the comparison of different analyses using the average points-to set size, as averages depend on the (unequal) number of variables. Therefore, we devise heuristics to establish comparability of our metrics for different IRs.

Another challenge in this work is inferring the impact of each analysis parameter on its precision. Computed at the end of the analysis, the average points-to set size loses information on the contribution of a particular aspect of pointer analysis. Therefore, we require a fine-grained metric to quantify the precision for each parameter. We propose two such techniques, one for the class hierarchy and the other for the intermediate representation.

Class Hierarchy The analysis of the program's class hierarchy builds the foundation for inferring relevant variables and heap allocations. However, each framework leverages a particular strategy to infer classes that contribute to the program's semantics. Adding irrelevant classes to the class hierarchy may manifest into a synthetically precise analysis, as these classes add to the total number of variables (which will all be pointing to an empty set), thus potentially decreasing the average size of points-to sets. Some of these variables and heap allocations are not part of the actual code executed at runtime, but rather arise out of an imperfect model of the program analysis framework's frontend. Here, we study the variables and heap objects stemming from the additional classes exclusive to a framework.

We first instrument the *Doop* framework to log the class hierarchies and compare the class hierarchies obtained using Soot and Wala as frontends, which yields the classes exclusive to each of the frameworks. CH_{soot} and CH_{wala} denotes the set of classes in the class hierarchies of Soot and Wala respectively. $CH_{common} = CH_{soot} \cap CH_{wala}$ is the set of classes common to both frameworks. We define *CH-precision* in terms of the average points-to set size restricted to variables defined in methods of CH_{common}.

Definition 1. CH-Precision *(CP). Let* V_f^c *be the set of variables defined in methods of* CH_{common} *for the frontend* $f \in \{soot, wala\}$, *and* $H_f^c(v) = \{h \mid h \in points\text{-}to(v), v \in V_f^c\}$. *CH-Precision is the ratio of* H_f^c *and* V_f^c, *i.e.,*

$$CP_f = \frac{\sum\limits_{v \in V_f^c} H_f^c(v)}{|V_f^c|}$$

If an analysis does not contain any exclusive classes or all of their variables (and corresponding heap objects) belong to the types present in the set of exclusive classes, CH-precision equals the average points-to set size.

Intermediate Representation (IR) The choice of IR determines a program's representation but retains the program's semantics, particularly with respect to heap allocations. Thus, different IR's can differ in the number of variables but will not introduce additional heap objects (e.g. Listing 1.4).A fundamental difference between Soot's Jimple and Wala's SSA-based IR is that SSA creates unique variables for each variable definition, while three-address code does not. Rendering our precision metric comparable for structurally different IRs is challenging, as tracking which variables correspond to each other is technically involved and may not be unique. Therefore, we rely on a heuristic to determine comparable variables. We motivate the heuristics considering two different IRs for the *main* method in Listing 1.1. Jimple (Listing 1.2) defines four variables, r0 – r2, and `parameter0`, while Wala's IR (Listing 1.3) defines three variables: v1 (implicit, not shown in the listing), v5, v8.

Definition 2. *Defm denotes the set of variables defined in a method.*
$Defm(m, ir) = \bigcup_{s_i \in S_{m,ir}} def(s_i)$, *where $S_{m,ir}$ is the set of statements in method m for ir, $def(s_i)$ the variables defined in s_i.*

Definition 3. Interesting Method. *A method m is interesting if $|Defm(m, wala)| \neq |Defm(m, jimple)|$ and m is defined in class $C \in CH_{common}$, i.e., the number of variables defined in the method with the same signature vary for different IRs. $\mathcal{M}$ denotes the set of interesting methods.*

To determine the set of interesting methods ($\mathcal{M}$) we leverage the logs from pointer analyses and segregate the variables in the logs according to the declaring method (m). If the sizes of the corresponding sets differ for a method m, it is considered interesting. ($\mathcal{M}$ is confined to the set of methods defined in CH_{common} to exclude the exclusive classes.) Subsequently, we determine the points-to relation for the variables in $\mathcal{M}$.

Simple average of the heap objects and number of variables is insufficient for comparing the precision of the analysis between two IRs. Differences in class hierarchies and aliasing generates new variables, which makes the ratio incomparable if the heap objects are not same. To circumvent this problem, we combine average points-to set size with ideas from virtual call resolution. The number of virtual call sites in a program is identical irrespective of the differences in program representation (caused by aliasing and redundant variables). Therefore, we receive a fair comparison if we restrict the average point-to set size to the target variables of virtual method calls. We define a new metric, *average devirtualized heap objects* (H_v^f), which is the ratio of the total size of points-to sets of target variables at the virtual call sites to the number of virtual call sites.

Definition 4. Average devirtualized heap objects *(H_v^f). For the set of virtual call-sites C in the IR of a framework f and $V_{C,f}$ as the set of invoking variables* at C, let $H_v = $ *points-to*(v) *be the set of heap objects referred by* $v \in V_{C,f}$. *Average devirtualized heap objects is*

$$H_v^f = \frac{\sum\limits_{v \in V_{C,f}} points\text{-}to(v)}{|C|}$$

Based on the above discussion, we formulate and answer the following research questions:

RQ1. How does the class hierarchy vary with the benchmarks?
RQ2. How do differences in class hierarchies affect the precision of analyses?
RQ3. How do the choice of IR affect the precision of the analysis?
RQ4. How do the heap abstractions differ between pointer analysis frameworks?

4   Evaluation

We use Doop version *4.20.7-67* and *Wala* version *1.5.0*. For RQ1-RQ3, we invoked Doop with the following analysis options: `1-call-site-sensitive`, `1-object-sensitive`, `2-call-site-sensitive+heap`, `2-object-sensitive+ heap`. Specific options used in our study for each research questions are described in their respective sections. We use the DaCapo [2] (version 9.12-bach) benchmarks, a standardized suite of open-source Java applications, for our study.

4.1   RQ1: Class hierarchy differences with benchmarks

We captured the class hierarchies considered by the analyses to determine the differences. We instrumented *Doop* to log the classes considered during a (context-insensitive) analysis, which yields the complete class hierarchy. In order to investigate whether the class hierarchy depends on the frontend, we performed this experiment with Soot and Wala as frontend[5]. Table 1 lists the differences in the class hierarchies using Soot and Wala. On an average, Wala exclusively contains ˜13,994 classes in its class hierarchy. The number of classes exclusive to Wala range from 12,524 (Xalan) to 16,707 (Tradebeans). Soot's class hierarchy on average contains 26 classes not present in Wala's, ranging from zero to 62.

In the case of PMD and H3, Soot's class hierarchy contains only a single additional class, Jython has an additional 2 classes. Eclipse, Lusearch, and Luindex contain 62, 53, 53 additional classes, respectively. In the remaining cases the class hierarchy in Soot is strictly a subset of Wala's. In next RQ, we will study the impact of these additional classes on the precision and scalability of the analysis.

4.2   RQ2: Precision differences with class hierarchy

---

[5] Note that Soot and Wala provide options to exclude certain classes from analysis (to, e.g., exclude library classes). For a fair comparison we ignore this feature and compute the whole class hierarchy including libraries.

Table 1: Difference in classes considered by Soot and Wala. Last two columns show the extra classes loaded by Soot and Wala respectively.

	#classes analyzed		Extra classes	
Benchmark	Wala	Soot	Soot	Wala
Avrora	21,997	9,204	0	12,793
Batik	23,461	10,739	12	12,734
Eclipse	25,718	9,813	62	15,967
H2	21,007	8,042	1	12,966
Jython	23,323	10,411	2	12,914
Lusearch	20,469	4,671	53	15,851
Luindex	20,479	4,681	53	15,851
PMD	21,315	8,517	1	12,799
SunFlow	20,677	7,847	0	12,830
Tradebeans	20,658	3,951	0	16,707
Xalan	22,688	10,164	0	12,524

Study Setup   We have used the *var-points-to* relation, which maps all variables and context pairs to their resolved pairs of heap-object and context. We select those variables that originate from classes common to both frameworks (Section 4.1) and query their points-to information. We then compute the *CH − Precision* based on Definition 1.

Results   Table 2 presents the results of the analysis (for one-callsite, one-object, and two-object context-sensitivity) for the objects and variables belonging to exclusive classes present in Wala (only non-zero values included). Note that the two-object sensitive analysis did not terminate for Eclipse and Jython, therefore, these are not presented in the table. In one-callsite and one-objects analysis, Table 2 lists six out of eleven benchmarks contain variables that belong to the exclusive class hierarchy. The remaining benchmark applications show no differences in the number of variables and heap-objects, despite the presence of additional classes. It demonstrates that the additional classes loaded by the these frameworks have no influence on the precision of these benchmarks.

The third and fourth columns of Table 2 list the number of variables (in principle, variable-context pairs) and heap objects belonging to the set of exclusive classes, respectively. In all analyses, all but one benchmark have a higher average points-to set size for exclusive variables than the general average. Tradebeans only creates 3 additional heap objects with Wala' frontend, therefore the analyses are almost identical for both frontends. The average points-to sets for exclusive classes for bigger benchmarks such as Eclipse and Jython are outliers, showing very high averages. Still, the contribution of exclusive classes' heap objects and variables is negligible compared with the total heap objects of these benchmarks.

The eighth and ninth columns depict the CH-precision and the original precision for the analyses. We observe that the CH-precision is slightly lower than the precision for all benchmarks but tradebeans, which originates from the addi-

Table 2: Differences in precision in the presence of additional objects in class hierarchy (Wala). HO denotes the sum of number of heap objects in *points-to* set. CP_{wala} is the precision score for variables in CH_{common}.

Analysis	Benchmark	Exclusive classes			Original			CP_{wala}
		Vars.	HO	Average	Vars.	HO	Precision	
1CS	avrora	19	297	15.63	96,680	883,798	9.141	9.140
	eclipse	453	171,071	377.64	1,231,854	61,556,548	49.970	49.850
	h2	31	321	10.35	78,154	639,202	8.178	8.177
	jython	35	17,682	505.2	289,244	8,000,917	27.661	27.603
	tradebeans	3	3	1	59,853	549,391	9.179	9.179
	xalan	39	2,466	63.23	147,488	1,911,750	12.962	12.948
1OS	avrora	19	14,844	781.26	82,972	404,231	4.871	4.694
	eclipse	388	329,008	847.95	1,053,618	46,337,474	43.979	43.683
	h2	31	2747	88.61	59,800	220,058	3.679	3.635
	jython	35	147,214	4,206.11	573,823	22,152,008	38.604	38.35
	tradebeans	3	4	1.33	45,807	154,883	3.381	3.381
	xalan	39	13,831	354.64	199,404	1,576,762	7.907	7.839
2OS	avrora	19	1752	92.21	119,805	348,368	2.907	2.893
	h2	31	1195	38.54	82,795	242,667	2.930	2.917
	tradebeans	3	4	1.33	57,200	197,808	3.458	3.458
	xalan	55	4268	77.6	362,885	1,733,576	4.777	4.766

Table 3: Differences in precision in the presence of additional objects in class hierarchy for Eclipse (Soot).

		Variables	Heap Objects	CP_{soot}	Original
1-call-site	Exclusive Classes	786	3331	44.95	-
	Original	1.5M	68.5M	-	44.92
1-object	Exclusive Classes	1020	4130	44.90	-
	Original	1.3M	60.8M	-	44.87

tional heap objects and variables. These primarily belong to the internal libraries such as *sun.util, sun.util.resources* (discussed later).

With the Soot frontend (Table 3), the *CH-Precision* differs from *Precision* only for the benchmark Eclipse, for the other benchmarks the analysis does not contain any objects where the type belongs to the exclusive classes of the frontend. However, it is difficult to compare the precision of Soot v/s Wala on CH-Precision score due to differing variable numbers for the same benchmark application.

Finding 1: *Differences in class-hierarchy negligibly impact the pointer analysis precision (and thus client analyses).*

Soundness In our observation, the Wala frontend takes the internal Java libraries into account. We find heap objects belonging to libraries such as *sun.nio.fs, sun.util.resources, sun.security,* and *sun.nio.cs*, which are internal libraries used by the JVM. Soot, on the other hand, does not model these libraries for analysis.

Comparing the class hierarchies of the analyses using Soot and Wala, we observed that the class hierarchy using Soot as frontend is a subset of Wala's for all

Table 4: Total (for each framework) and interesting (section 4.3) methods $\mathcal{M}$.

Benchmark	1-CS			1-OS			2-OS		
	Soot	Wala	$\mathcal{M}$	Soot	Wala	$\mathcal{M}$	Soot	Wala	$\mathcal{M}$
Avrora	3651	3678	3194	3642	3669	3187	3615	3642	3159
Batik	3407	3415	3006	3398	3406	2999	3285	3293	2895
Eclipse	20339	20281	18723	20261	20204	18655	Timed out		
H2	3041	3091	2673	3027	3075	2661	2985	3029	2616
Jython	8482	8531	7672	8447	8494	7643	Timed out		
Lusearch	2449	2457	2135	2440	2448	2128	2414	2422	2103
Luindex	3524	3532	3132	3514	3522	3124	3466	3474	3081
PMD	4587	4596	4131	4577	4586	4124	4418	4427	3978
Sunflow	8369	8384	7514	8335	8350	7475	7740	7754	6928
Tradebeans	2442	2406	2083	2433	2397	2076	2407	2371	2051
Xalan	4607	5701	4125	4597	5678	4115	4502	5503	4031

benchmarks except Eclipse. This suggests that analyses with Soot are as sound as analyses with Wala for all benchmarks except Eclipse. Eclipse is a compelling case: Its analysis using Soot contains heap objects and variables that belong to the internal libraries of Eclipse, such as *org.eclipse.core.internal.runtime.PerformanceStatsProcessor*, while the analyses with Wala does not report these objects. However, results from the analyses with Wala contain heap objects from the internal libraries such as *sun.util.**, which are not present using Soot. It shows that the class hierarchy model is unsound in both frontends, as both lack some of the classes loaded by these benchmark applications at runtime.

> *Our study reveals that library modeling in both Soot and Wala is unsound even for (non-native) Java objects, shown by the presence of heap-objects belonging to the exclusive classes of Soot and Wala.*

4.3   RQ3: Precision for IR varies with the framework

Study Setup The study setup is similar to Section 4.2. We use the application's var-points-to sets, i.e., the relation of variables and heap objects excluding the library objects. From the results of the three analysis sensitivities, we extract the set of interesting methods ($\mathcal{M}$, Def. 3) and compute the average devirtualized heap objects score for the virtual calls in interesting methods. We use the Jimple IR (`--no-ssa` option in Doop), and Wala's IR (`--wala-fact-gen` option in Doop) for evaluation.

Results Table 4 reports the number of interesting methods and total methods resolved using both frontends. Note that the number of interesting method is identical for both frameworks for the same type of context-sensitivity. The number of reachable methods in each analysis differs, just as the number of distinct methods signatures discovered in each framework (columns Soot, Wala in 1-CS, 1-OS, 2-OS[6]). However, deriving a relationship between those is impossible, as

---

[6] We excluded 2-CS for its large file sizes.

Table 5: Results for IR. Third and fifth columns are the number of heap objects. Fourth and sixth columns are the number of virtual calls. Last two columns lists the average devirtualized heap objects (H_v^f) for Soot and Wala respectively.

		Soot		Wala		H_v^f	
Analysis	Benchmark	Heap Objs.	Virt. Calls	Heap Objs.	Virt. Calls	Soot	Wala
1 call-site	Avrora	7,684	3499	7759	3499	2.20	2.22
sensitive	Batik	2,645	1588	2702	1588	1.67	1.70
	Eclipse	7.7M	56.8K	7.9M	56.8K	136.33	139.24
	H2	1,936	1,434	1,988	1,434	1.35	1.39
	Jython	662K	9,286	656K	9,283	71.33	70.67
	Lusearch	1,667	1,139	1,674	1,139	1.46	1.47
	Luindex	8,090	4408	8,098	4,408	1.84	1.84
	PMD	8,518	3,527	8,708	3,527	2.42	2.47
	Sunflow	4,741	2,088	4,627	2,088	2.27	2.22
	Tradebeans	1,638	1,114	1,649	1,106	1.47	1.49
	Xalan	43K	5,832	55K	5,850	7.45	9.44
1 object	Avrora	6,561	3,498	6,563	3,498	1.88	1.88
sensitive	Batik	1,673	1,587	1,709	1,587	1.05	1.08
	Eclipse	2.9M	56.7K	3.0M	56.8K	51.61	53.53
	H2	1,218	1,433	1,258	1,433	0.85	0.88
	Jython	3.5K	9,272	3.6K	9,269	386.79	389.20
	Lusearch	958	1,138	964	1,138	0.84	0.85
	Luindex	4,530	4,407	4,552	4,407	1.03	1.03
	PMD	7,369	3,527	7,518	3,527	2.09	2.13
	Sunflow	2,978	2,088	2,864	2,088	1.43	1.37
	Tradebeans	928	1,113	938	1,105	0.83	0.85
	Xalan	99K	5,830	106K	5,810	17.11	18.33
2 object	Avrora	8,561	3,459	8,563	3,459	2.47	2.48
sensitive	Batik	1,257	1,567	1,275	1,567	0.80	0.81
	H2	1,288	1,433	1,307	1,433	0.90	0.91
	Luindex	5,210	4,363	5,215	4,363	1.19	1.20
	Lusearch	948	1,138	954	1,138	0.83	0.84
	PMD	7,271	3,496	7,398	3,496	2.08	2.12
	Sunflow	2,342	2,088	2,324	2,088	1.12	1.11
	Tradebeans	919	1,113	929	1,105	0.83	0.84
	Xalan	214K	5,791	215K	5,771	36.97	37.36

analyses such as one-call-site and one-object are not comparable. In all cases, we observed that the majority (~90%) of the methods are interesting. Therefore, we cannot ignore the significance of this aspect.

> *Interesting methods are difficult to ignore because of their sheer presence in the benchmarks applications.*

Table 5 presents the differences in the average devirtualized heap objects for Jimple and Wala IR. Although the number of variables and abstract heap locations are dependent on the IR, we did not observe many differences between those when restricting ourselves to target variables of virtual method calls, which corresponds to our intuition. The differences in the H_v^f values for both IRs

Table 6: Differences Soot IR v/s Wala IR for Xalan

Methods	Wala	Soot	Actual
org.apache.xalan.transformer.TransformerImpl.transformNode()	✔	✘	✔
Exceptions	✔	✘	✔
org.apache.xalan.xsltc.trax.TransformerFactoryImpl.setFeature()	✘	✔	✔
MethodResolver.getConstructor()	✔	✘	✔
xerces.xml.dtd.XMLDTDLoader()	✔	✘	—
org.apache.xpath.getSourceTree()	✔	✘	✔

Listing 1.5: Differences in types of heap objects created in both analysis

```
1 (Wala)  sun.misc.URLClassPath$Loader
2 (Wala)  java.util.zip.ZipError
3 (Soot)  javax.xml.transform.FactoryFinder$ConfigurationError
```

are negligible except for three larger benchmarks, Jython, Eclipse, and Xalan. Overall, the values from Soot IR were smaller than those of Wala, implying that *devirtualization* in Soot is either slightly more precise or slightly less sound than in Wala, however, the differences are minor in the majority of the cases. In conclusion, the choice of IR shows little to no impact on the precision of pointer analysis. In the sequel, we describe one such case study where the difference in H_v^f is approximately two, which is a significant figure as compared to others.

> **Finding 2**: *IR has negligible impact on the precision of pointer analysis at least for the devirtualization client.*

Case Study—Xalan To further investigate the differences, we chose *Xalan* using a one-call-site analysis as the H_v^f values for Soot (7.45) and Wala (9.44) display the highest difference among all benchmarks. The number of heap objects in both cases differs significantly, with Soot having 43K heap objects, and Wala having 55K heap objects for a comparable number of virtual calls (5,832 vs. 5,850).

To examine the heap objects, we collected their class types. We observed that the types of some of these objects belongs to the classes in $CH_{soot} \setminus CH_{common}$ or $CH_{wala} \setminus CH_{common}$. Listing 1.5 depicts the differences in heap objects created by these frameworks.

We also discovered (potential) sources of imprecision and unsoundness in both analyses. Table 6 lists methods and exceptions missed by both Soot and Wala frameworks. Note that these methods and exceptions belong to the common class hierarchy. We observed that Wala has precise exception modeling compared to Soot. For other virtual methods invocations, we compared the runtime call-graph to the static call-graph. In our observation, both Wala and Soot are unsound, as demonstrated by the absence of certain method calls in the call-graph for both analyses. In addition, Wala imprecisely includes `xerces.xml.dtd.XMLDTDLoader()` into its call-graph (which at least in our experiments was not executed at runtime).

> *Apart from reflection, imprecise/unsound virtual call resolution also induces imprecision/unsoundness into the analysis.*

4.4 RQ4: Heap abstractions in pointer analysis frameworks

In this section, we compare Doop's analysis using Wala's frontend with Wala's own analysis. We omit the comparison with the Soot framework as it leverages IRs different from Wala's and thus would not be comparable.

Study Setup We compare the one-call-site sensitive with context-sensitive heap abstraction (unique heap objects for each call-site, heap cloning) analysis available in the

Table 7: Number of Heap objects

Benchmark	#Heap Objects		#Types	
	Doop	Wala	Doop	Wala
avrora	2,504	28,235	751	3,256
batik	1,699	16,724	537	1,938
h2	1,467	16,688	482	1,934
lusearch	1,242	16,274	551	1,898
luindex	1,901	19,343	404	2,250
pmd	2,398	31,774	734	2,498
sunflow	4,424	16,688	1,196	1,934
tradebeans	1,230	16,734	405	1,937
xalan	3,874	18,174	1,003	2,078

Wala framework with a one-call-site with one-level heap abstraction in Doop, and set the time budget to 7 hours. Analyses with a higher level of call-site sensitivity were not scalable in the Wala framework and therefore, we do not leverage those. Other optimizations in Wala, such as the use of object-sensitivity only for collection objects, are not comparable to the object-sensitive analysis available in Doop. Therefore, we also choose to ignore it. To handle reflective calls in Wala, we use the option REFLECTIONS.FULL. In what follows, we present the results of our study. We first present the differences in the number of heap objects and, subsequently, delve into its implications.

Differences in the heap objects For evaluation, we extracted the heap-objects created in Wala's and Doop's analyses and observe huge differences in the number of heap objects created. Intuitively, using the same level of heap-sensitivity (heap-cloning) should create the same number of heap objects. However, in certain cases, the number of heap objects in Wala exhibits a factor of ~14 compared to those in Doop (columns 2 and 3 in 7). (Note that eclipse and jython are elided, as the analyses did not terminate within the time budget owing to the large file size (~100GB).) Therefore, the heap abstractions of these analyses are not comparable, although superficially they look similar.

> *Subtle optimizations also manifests into imprecise heap modeling even though, at the outset, they look similar.*

To investigate this further, we compared the the types of the heap objects. Our study shows that the set of types are not even consistent using the same frontend! In many cases the types of objects analyzed by Wala is approximately four times those in Doop (columns 4 and 5 in Table 7). The differences in heap abstraction for application level objects build the reason for this.

Application level objects Application level objects, i.e., the heap objects created due to allocations within the program (rather than libraries.) In three out of eleven benchmarks we observe that Doop's analysis is lacking application level classes that Wala reports. We found corresponding allocations on a manual inspection of the source code. For example, in *avrora*, the analysis in Wala allocates heap objects of *BRNE_builder* [8], which are not present in Doop's. Similar cases can be found in *PMD* and *Xalan*. However, owing to the limitations of the program representation, we could not determine the precise reason for the unsoundness. Pointer analysis uses an IR based on a control flow graph (CFG) rather than source code. Being a lower level representation of the program source code the IR mangles variables names. Therefore, a one-to-one correspondence between the IR's variables and variables in source code is not trivial.

Finding 3: *Heap modeling is not similar even for allocations within the application scope. Wala handles application levels objects more precisely than Soot in our evaluation.*

---

5   Threats to Validity

Naturally, the technique used relies on the precise handling of reflection calls and other dynamic features of the languages such as dynamic proxies. Other than that, handling of native calls could alleviate the unsoundness of the analyses. Analysis of native calls could infer the native objects in JVM missed by the Soot framework. Here, we have used the TamiFlex framework for handling reflection calls. Other approaches have improved the reflection handling [10,15–18,25]. To convince ourself, we experimented with one of the *state-of-the-art* techniques, i.e., reflection with matching substring resolution [10]. However, we did not find any significant differences in results. Another limitation of this study is the unsoundness from ignoring the native library calls in static analyses. Few of the sources of unsoundness discovered stem from the native calls. Recently, Fourtounis et al. [7] proposed a technique for resolving native calls in Java. However, at the time of writing this paper, the technique was not available. Further, our analysis in Section 4.3 is based on test-cases which may not reflect all possible executions of an application.

Our study also involves hours of manual evaluation which can be subject to bias. To counteract it, we did a manual inspection of the source code, especially for the sources of unsoundness. We had rerun the benchmark applications with valid inputs to determine to compare and reassert that the objects are actually allocated during runtime.

6   Related Work

Pointer analysis tools Pointer analysis has garnered significant interest in the last decades, focussing on scalability, precision, and soundness. The Doop system used in this paper results from years of research on declarative-style pointer analysis [1,3,10,24,26]. Similarly, the Wala framework was a result of an industrial project and, unlike Doop, follows an imperative paradigm. The underlying program representation comes with many prior assumptions mentioned. In this work, we study the effects of these assumptions on program analysis.

Empirical studies on pointer analysis Recent empirical studies focussed on the soundness limitations from dynamic features of languages in existing pointer analyses and call-graph construction as pointer analysis and call-graph construction are closely related static analyses and are mutually dependent. Dietrich et al. [5] proposed automated and manual techniques to generate unsoundness oracles to test static analysis. Sui et al. [32] present the causes of unsoundness in static analysis frameworks (Soot, Wala, and Doop) due to the dynamic features of languages. Rief et al. [21] did a comprehensive study, focussed on features in Java 9, for call-graph generation algorithms and expose the problems in the *state-of-the-art* esp. related to method calls in the Java runtime. Our work is orthogonal: we evaluate the influence of program representation on program analyses. Here, we rather focus on the program representation in static analysis frameworks and also the unsoundness arising out of it. Our study is also extensible for Java 9.

Sui et al. [33] evaluated the *recall* of call-graph construction and present how it impacts the algorithms in practice. Their evaluation expose the problems in the *state-of-the-art* esp. related to method calls in the Java runtime. Our unsoundness results concur with theirs. Here, we have focussed on program representation rather than the dynamic features of the language, which are hard to analyze for static analyzers. Further, our work features two novel metrics apart from the standard *precision* and *recall*, to measure the impact of different aspects of program representation.

7   Conclusion

This paper reports the effects of program representation on program analysis. Our metrics makes it possible to compare implementations leveraging different frontends. We find that differences in program representation have negligible impact on the precision of the pointer analysis. In addition, we also discovered novel sources of unsoundness and imprecision in the program analysis. Our results also demonstrate that the promised heap abstraction are practically not similar, even though they may appear so on a birds eye view. Since pointer analysis builds the foundation of many static analyses, we conjecture the results generalize these, as well.

References

1. Antoniadis, T., Triantafyllou, K., Smaragdakis, Y.: Porting doop to souflé;: A tale of inter-engine portability for datalog-based analyses. In: Proceedings of the 6th ACM SIGPLAN International Workshop on State Of

the Art in Program Analysis. pp. 25–30. SOAP 2017, ACM, New York, NY, USA (2017). https://doi.org/10.1145/3088515.3088522, http://doi.acm.org/10.1145/3088515.3088522

2. Blackburn, S.M., Garner, R., Hoffmann, C., Khang, A.M., McKinley, K.S., Bentzur, R., Diwan, A., Feinberg, D., Frampton, D., Guyer, S.Z., Hirzel, M., Hosking, A., Jump, M., Lee, H., Moss, J.E.B., Phansalkar, A., Stefanović, D., VanDrunen, T., von Dincklage, D., Wiedermann, B.: The dacapo benchmarks: Java benchmarking development and analysis. In: Proceedings of the 21st Annual ACM SIGPLAN Conference on Object-oriented Programming Systems, Languages, and Applications. pp. 169–190. OOPSLA '06, ACM, New York, NY, USA (2006). https://doi.org/10.1145/1167473.1167488, http://doi.acm.org/10.1145/1167473.1167488

3. Bravenboer, M., Smaragdakis, Y.: Strictly declarative specification of sophisticated points-to analyses. In: Proceedings of the 24th ACM SIGPLAN Conference on Object Oriented Programming Systems Languages and Applications. pp. 243–262. OOPSLA '09, ACM, New York, NY, USA (2009). https://doi.org/10.1145/1640089.1640108, http://doi.acm.org/10.1145/1640089.1640108

4. Cytron, R., Ferrante, J., Rosen, B.K., Wegman, M.N., Zadeck, F.K.: Efficiently computing static single assignment form and the control dependence graph. ACM Trans. Program. Lang. Syst. 13(4), 451–490 (Oct 1991). https://doi.org/10.1145/115372.115320

5. Dietrich, J., Sui, L., Rasheed, S., Tahir, A.: On the construction of soundness oracles. In: Proceedings of the 6th ACM SIGPLAN International Workshop on State Of the Art in Program Analysis. pp. 37–42. SOAP 2017, Association for Computing Machinery, New York, NY, USA (2017). https://doi.org/10.1145/3088515.3088520, https://doi.org/10.1145/3088515.3088520

6. Fourtounis, G., Triantafyllou, L., Smaragdakis, Y.: Identifying java calls in native code via binary scanning. In: Proceedings of the 29th ACM SIGSOFT International Symposium on Software Testing and Analysis. pp. 388–400. ISSTA 2020, Association for Computing Machinery, New York, NY, USA (2020). https://doi.org/10.1145/3395363.3397368, https://doi.org/10.1145/3395363.3397368

7. Fourtounis, G., Triantafyllou, L., Smaragdakis, Y.: Identifying java calls in native code via binary scanning. In: Proceedings of the 29th ACM SIGSOFT International Symposium on Software Testing and Analysis. pp. 388–400. ISSTA 2020, Association for Computing Machinery, New York, NY, USA (2020). https://doi.org/10.1145/3395363.3397368, https://doi.org/10.1145/3395363.3397368

8. GitHub: https://github.com/cmorty/. https://github.com/cmorty/avrora/blob/222ea1645b67bc40429881526555d19bced4a590/src/avrora/arch/avr/AVRInstrBuilder.java (August 2020), (Accessed on 05.08.2020)

9. Grech, N., Fourtounis, G., Francalanza, A., Smaragdakis, Y.: Heaps don't lie: Countering unsoundness with heap snapshots. Proc. ACM Program. Lang. 1(OOPSLA) (Oct 2017). https://doi.org/10.1145/3133892, https://doi.org/10.1145/3133892

10. Grech, N., Kastrinis, G., Smaragdakis, Y.: Efficient Reflection String Analysis via Graph Coloring. In: Millstein, T. (ed.) 32nd European Conference on Object-Oriented Programming (ECOOP 2018). Leibniz International Proceedings in Informatics (LIPIcs), vol. 109, pp. 26:1–26:25.

Schloss Dagstuhl–Leibniz-Zentrum fuer Informatik, Dagstuhl, Germany (2018). https://doi.org/10.4230/LIPIcs.ECOOP.2018.26, http://drops.dagstuhl.de/opus/volltexte/2018/9231

11. Grech, N., Smaragdakis, Y.: P/taint: Unified points-to and taint analysis. Proc. ACM Program. Lang. **1**(OOPSLA), 102:1–102:28 (Oct 2017). https://doi.org/10.1145/3133926, http://doi.acm.org/10.1145/3133926

12. Jordan, H., Scholz, B., Subotić, P.: Soufflé: On synthesis of program analyzers. In: Chaudhuri, S., Farzan, A. (eds.) Computer Aided Verification. pp. 422–430. Springer International Publishing, Cham (2016), https://doi.org/10.1007/978-3-319-41540-6_23

13. Kastrinis, G., Smaragdakis, Y.: Hybrid context-sensitivity for points-to analysis. In: Proceedings of the 34th ACM SIGPLAN Conference on Programming Language Design and Implementation. p. 423–434. PLDI '13, Association for Computing Machinery, New York, NY, USA (2013). https://doi.org/10.1145/2491956.2462191, https://doi.org/10.1145/2491956.2462191

14. Li, Y., Tan, T., Møller, A., Smaragdakis, Y.: A principled approach to selective context sensitivity for pointer analysis. ACM Trans. Program. Lang. Syst. **42**(2) (May 2020). https://doi.org/10.1145/3381915, https://doi.org/10.1145/3381915

15. Li, Y., Tan, T., Sui, Y., Xue, J.: Self-inferencing reflection resolution for java. In: Jones, R. (ed.) ECOOP 2014 – Object-Oriented Programming. pp. 27–53. Springer Berlin Heidelberg, Berlin, Heidelberg (2014), https://doi.org/10.1007/978-3-662-44202-9_2

16. Li, Y., Tan, T., Xue, J.: Effective soundness-guided reflection analysis. In: Blazy, S., Jensen, T. (eds.) Static Analysis. pp. 162–180. Springer Berlin Heidelberg, Berlin, Heidelberg (2015), https://doi.org/10.1007/978-3-662-48288-9_10

17. Li, Y., Tan, T., Xue, J.: Understanding and analyzing java reflection. ACM Trans. Softw. Eng. Methodol. **28**(2) (Feb 2019). https://doi.org/10.1145/3295739, https://doi.org/10.1145/3295739

18. Liu, J., Li, Y., Tan, T., Xue, J.: Reflection analysis for java: Uncovering more reflective targets precisely. In: 2017 IEEE 28th International Symposium on Software Reliability Engineering (ISSRE). pp. 12–23 (2017), https://doi.org/10.1109/ISSRE.2017.36

19. Milanova, A., Rountev, A., Ryder, B.G.: Parameterized object sensitivity for points-to analysis for java. ACM Trans. Softw. Eng. Methodol. **14**(1), 1–41 (Jan 2005). https://doi.org/10.1145/1044834.1044835, https://doi.org/10.1145/1044834.1044835

20. Ramalingam, G.: The undecidability of aliasing. ACM Trans. Program. Lang. Syst. **16**(5), 1467–1471 (Sep 1994). https://doi.org/10.1145/186025.186041, http://doi.acm.org/10.1145/186025.186041

21. Reif, M., Kübler, F., Eichberg, M., Helm, D., Mezini, M.: Judge: Identifying, Understanding, and Evaluating Sources of Unsoundness in Call Graphs. In: Proceedings of the 28th ACM SIGSOFT International Symposium on Software Testing and Analysis (to appear). ISSTA 2019 (2019). https://doi.org/10.1145/3293882.3330555, http://dx.doi.org/10.1145/3293882.3330555

22. Scholz, B., Jordan, H., Subotić, P., Westmann, T.: On fast large-scale program analysis in datalog. In: Proceedings of the 25th International Conference on Compiler Construction. pp. 196–206. CC 2016, ACM, New York, NY, USA (2016). https://doi.org/10.1145/2892208.2892226, http://doi.acm.org/10.1145/2892208.2892226

23. Sharir, M., Pnueli, A.: Two approaches to interprocedural data flow analysis. New York Univ. Comput. Sci. Dept., New York, NY (1978), https://cds.cern.ch/record/120118

24. Smaragdakis, Y., Balatsouras, G.: Pointer analysis. Found. Trends Program. Lang. **2**(1), 1–69 (Apr 2015). https://doi.org/10.1561/2500000014, http://dx.doi.org/10.1561/2500000014

25. Smaragdakis, Y., Balatsouras, G., Kastrinis, G., Bravenboer, M.: More sound static handling of java reflection. In: Feng, X., Park, S. (eds.) Programming Languages and Systems - 13th Asian Symposium, APLAS 2015, Pohang, South Korea, November 30 - December 2, 2015, Proceedings. Lecture Notes in Computer Science, vol. 9458, pp. 485–503. Springer (2015). https://doi.org/10.1007/978-3-319-26529-2_26, https://doi.org/10.1007/978-3-319-26529-2_26

26. Smaragdakis, Y., Bravenboer, M., Lhoták, O.: Pick your contexts well: Understanding object-sensitivity. In: Proceedings of the 38th Annual ACM SIGPLAN-SIGACT Symposium on Principles of Programming Languages. pp. 17–30. POPL '11, ACM, New York, NY, USA (2011). https://doi.org/10.1145/1926385.1926390, http://doi.acm.org/10.1145/1926385.1926390

27. Smaragdakis, Y., Kastrinis, G.: Defensive Points-To Analysis: Effective Soundness via Laziness. In: Millstein, T. (ed.) 32nd European Conference on Object-Oriented Programming (ECOOP 2018). Leibniz International Proceedings in Informatics (LIPIcs), vol. 109, pp. 23:1–23:28. Schloss Dagstuhl–Leibniz-Zentrum fuer Informatik, Dagstuhl, Germany (2018). https://doi.org/10.4230/LIPIcs.ECOOP.2018.23, http://drops.dagstuhl.de/opus/volltexte/2018/9228

28. Soot: Soot - a framework for analyzing and transforming java and android applications (Jan 2019), http://sable.github.io/soot/

29. Späth, J., Ali, K., Bodden, E.: Ideal: Efficient and precise alias-aware dataflow analysis. In: 2017 International Conference on Object-Oriented Programming, Languages and Applications (OOPSLA/SPLASH). ACM Press (Oct 2017), https://doi.org/10.1145/3133923

30. Späth, J., Ali, K., Bodden, E.: Context-, flow-, and field-sensitive data-flow analysis using synchronized pushdown systems. Proc. ACM Program. Lang. **3**(POPL), 48:1–48:29 (2019). https://doi.org/10.1145/3290361, https://doi.org/10.1145/3290361

31. Späth, J., Do, L.N.Q., Ali, K., Bodden, E.: Boomerang: Demand-driven flow- and context-sensitive pointer analysis for java. In: Krishnamurthi, S., Lerner, B.S. (eds.) 30th European Conference on Object-Oriented Programming, ECOOP 2016, July 18-22, 2016, Rome, Italy. LIPIcs, vol. 56, pp. 22:1–22:26. Schloss Dagstuhl - Leibniz-Zentrum für Informatik (2016). https://doi.org/10.4230/LIPIcs.ECOOP.2016.22, https://doi.org/10.4230/LIPIcs.ECOOP.2016.22

32. Sui, L., Dietrich, J., Emery, M., Rasheed, S., Tahir, A.: On the soundness of call graph construction in the presence of dynamic language features - a benchmark and tool evaluation. In: Ryu, S. (ed.) Programming Languages and Systems. pp. 69–88. Springer International Publishing, Cham (2018), https://doi.org/10.1007/978-3-030-02768-1_4

33. Sui, L., Dietrich, J., Tahir, A., Fourtounis, G.: On the recall of static call graph construction in practice. In: Proceedings of the ACM/IEEE 42nd International Conference on Software Engineering. p. 1049–1060. ICSE '20, Association for Computing Machinery, New York, NY, USA (2020). https://doi.org/10.1145/3377811.3380441, https://doi.org/10.1145/3377811.3380441

34. Tan, T., Li, Y., Xue, J.: Efficient and precise points-to analysis: Modeling the heap by merging equivalent automata. In: Proceedings of the 38th ACM SIGPLAN Conference on Programming Language Design and Implementation. pp. 278–291. PLDI 2017, Association for Computing Machinery, New York, NY, USA (2017). https://doi.org/10.1145/3062341.3062360

35. Vallée-Rai, R., Co, P., Gagnon, E., Hendren, L., Lam, P., Sundaresan, V.: Soot - a java bytecode optimization framework. In: Proceedings of the 1999 Conference of the Centre for Advanced Studies on Collaborative Research. p. 13. CASCON '99, IBM Press (1999), https://dl.acm.org/doi/10.5555/781995.782008

36. Vallée-Rai, R., Gagnon, E., Hendren, L., Lam, P., Pominville, P., Sundaresan, V.: Optimizing java bytecode using the soot framework: Is it feasible? In: Watt, D.A. (ed.) Compiler Construction. pp. 18–34. Springer Berlin Heidelberg, Berlin, Heidelberg (2000), https://doi.org/10.1007/3-540-46423-9_2

37. WALA: Watson libraries for program analysis (Jan 2019), http://wala.sourceforge.net/wiki/index.php/Main_Page

38. Wala: Intermediate representation (IR) (Aug 2020), https://github.com/wala/WALA/wiki/Intermediate-Representation-(IR)

39. Wala: Pointer analysis (Aug 2020), https://github.com/wala/WALA/wiki/Pointer-Analysis

40. Wei, F., Roy, S., Ou, X., Robby: Amandroid: A precise and general inter-component data flow analysis framework for security vetting of android apps. ACM Trans. Priv. Secur. **21**(3) (Apr 2018). https://doi.org/10.1145/3183575, https://doi.org/10.1145/3183575

41. Wikipedia: Datalog (Jan 2019), https://en.wikipedia.org/wiki/Datalog

Keeping Pace with the History of Evolving Runtime Models

Lucas Sakizloglou[ID][✉], Matthias Barkowsky[ID], and Holger Giese[ID]

Hasso Plattner Institute, University of Potsdam, Potsdam, Germany
<name>.<surname>@hpi.de

Abstract. Structural runtime models provide a snapshot of the constituents of a system and their state. Capturing the history of runtime models, i.e., previous snapshots, has been shown to be useful for a number of aims. Handling, however, history at runtime poses important challenges to tool support. We present the INTEMPO tool which is based on the ECLIPSE Modeling Framework and encodes runtime models as graphs. Key features of INTEMPO, such as, the integration of temporal requirements into graph queries, the in-memory storage of the model, and a systematic method to contain the model's memory consumption, intend to address issues which seemingly place limitations on the available tool support. INTEMPO offers two operation modes which support both runtime and postmortem application scenarios.

Keywords: runtime models · time-awareness · temporal graph queries

1 Introduction to InTempo

A (structural) *Runtime Model* (RTM) provides a snapshot of the constituents of a system and their state [3]. RTMs are typically employed in the context of *Self-adaptive Systems* (SAS) [4], where a feedback loop adapts the system behavior at runtime in response to external or internal stimuli, the latter represented as model fragments in the RTM and detected via the execution of model queries.

Encoding an RTM as a graph enables detection via *graph queries*, which specify a sought (graph) pattern. Such an encoding conforms to a *metamodel* which restricts the structure of model instances and defines types of vertices, edges, and attributes. Formally, these concepts rely on *typed, attributed graph transformation* [6] where graphs are typed over a *type graph*.

Capturing the *history* of RTMs, i.e., previous snapshots, may be useful for a number of aims such as the detection of recurrent behavior or postmortem analysis [3,8]. However, handling history at runtime poses important challenges to tool support. Tools are required to enable the specification and timely execution of queries with *temporal requirements*, i.e., requirements on the evolution of patterns over multiple snapshots. Timely execution is crucial for SAS, where a loop may depend on query results before planning and performing adaptations.

Faced with these challenges, the available tool support is seemingly limited either by the lack of support for direct specification of temporal requirements in graph queries [5] or by the on-disk representation of the model [8,11] that introduces an overhead on execution times in runtime settings, e.g., in SAS.

E. Guerra and M. Stoelinga (Eds.): FASE 2021, LNCS 12649, pp. 262–268, 2021.
https://doi.org/10.1007/978-3-030-71500-7_13

We present the INTEMPO (INcremental queries with TEMPOral requirements) tool (available online at [13]) which is based on the eponymous querying scheme in [15] and aims at mitigating these limitations. INTEMPO introduces ITQL, a language for the specification of *temporal graph queries*, which allow for the expression of temporal requirements. The core functionality of INTEMPO executes a query over an in-memory RTM which captures information about previous snapshots, called *Runtime Model with History* (RTM^H), and returns the pattern occurrences in the RTM^H that satisfy the specified temporal requirements. IN-TEMPO is implemented in the ECLIPSE Modeling Framework (EMF) [7] and can be used either via the ECLIPSE user interface or via an API. The latter enables INTEMPO results to be utilized by other tools, e.g., a SAS feedback loop.

INTEMPO offers two operation modes intended for different application scenarios (see Figure 1 for an illustration). The *RTM^{H}Analysis* (Section 2) constitutes the core functionality of INTEMPO and executes a user-specified ITQL query (in a file with *.itql* extension—required extensions are in parentheses in Figure 1) over a user-provided RTM^H, i.e., a persisted instance of an EMF model (in the standard *xmi* format). This mode returns the query results for the given RTM^H. Query results are kept in-between analyses and are updated by each RTM^{H}Analysis, which is also known as *incremental (query) execution*. The RTM^{H}Analysis is intended to be used in settings where query results can be further utilized at runtime. For instance, a SAS feedback loop may use INTEMPO to detect problems formulated as patterns, similarly to [9]. Subsequently, the query results may be utilized to plan adaptations which address these problems.

The *LogAnalysis* operation mode (Section 3) assumes that, instead of being captured by an RTM^H, past and present data about the system have been captured in an event log. INTEMPO introduces E2P, a specification language that allows for the mapping of event types to corresponding modifications of model fragments, i.e, nodes, edges, and attributes. As input, LogAnalysis requires the ITQL query, the log (with comma-separated values), and the E2P mapping. It then processes the log and maintains an internal RTM^H which it uses to perform RTM^{H}Analysis upon every event. LogAnalysis is intended for postmortem scenarios. Thus, it returns the results that were valid after each RTM^{H}Analysis sorted by the log timestamps, which affords a global, yet detailed, view on the evolution of the system state.

INTEMPO is capable of containing the data accumulation in the RTM^H by systematically discovering and discarding data that is obsolete with respect to a given timestamp, i.e., not relevant to future query executions—this capability is presented in detail in [15]. Note that an implicit requirement of both operation modes is that the metamodel of the analyzed system has been encoded as an EMF Ecore model and is available in ECLIPSE (gray input in Figure 1).

Fig. 1: INTEMPO Execution Modes and Exemplary Application Scenarios

Exemplary Application To demonstrate the features and operation of INTEMPO we rely on an example drawn from the case-study conducted in [15]. Based on real-world smart medical environments, the case-study envisions a Smart Healthcare System (SHS) where

Fig. 2: SHS Metamodel

certain medical procedures are automated and performed by devices, such as a smart pump administering medicine or a sensor tracking patient data and diagnoses—as otherwise a clinician would be doing. Data collected from the SHS are aggregated and recorded in medical (event) logs.

INTEMPO requires a metamodel which has been instrumented such that all nodes have at least two attributes named `cts` and `dts`, which capture the time point of creation, respectively deletion, of the node in the system. As an example, see the metamodel of our SHS in Figure 2. Note that to encode `cts` and `dts` for edges in EMF, the respective edges would have to be modeled as nodes. Technically, an RTM^H is an instance of such a metamodel. See G$_3$ in Figure 3 for an example based on the SHS metamodel: The RTM^H reflects that a node of type `Sensor` that is attached to the patient with `id=1` has been activated and thus has been added to the SHS at timestamp 3. The sensor `status` reflects that the patient has been diagnosed with sepsis. The value ∞ reflects that a `dts` for this node has not been set, i.e., the node is still present in the modeled system.

2   RTM^H Analysis

This section presents an exemplary query in ITQL which it then uses to demonstrate the RTM^H Analysis. It concludes with technical details.

InTempo Query Language (ITQL) Formally, a temporal graph query q is characterized by a (graph) pattern p and an *application condition ac*, denoted $q = (p, ac)$. A match m corresponds to an occurrence of p in the RTM^H. In order for m to be valid, it must satisfy the ac. ITQL supports the formulation of ac in the *Metric Temporal Graph Logic* (MTGL) [10] which supports operators such as negation ($\neg$), existential quantification ($\exists$), conjunction ($\wedge$), and the *metric*, i.e, interval-based, temporal operators *until* (U_I, where I is a time interval over $\mathbb{R}_0^+$) and *since* (S_I), as well as abbreviations such as *eventually*, i.e., $\Diamond_I \exists n = true\, U_I \exists n$, where n is a graph pattern and *true* is always satisfied. MTGL also supports the *nesting* of patterns to *bind* graph elements in outer conditions and relate them to inner (nested) conditions, i.e., elements common to two patterns n_1 and n_2 refer to the same element in the RTM^H.

MTGL is able to express real-time properties such as *"every patient diagnosed with sepsis, must eventually within 5 time units be given the proper drug"* (adjusted from the medical guideline in [14]). In an RTM^H of the SHS, IN-TEMPO can find violations of the property above by executing the ITQL query $q_1 = (n_1, \kappa)$, with κ the MTGL formula $\neg(\Diamond_{[0,5]} \exists n_2)$ and n_1, n_2 patterns representing a sepsis diagnosis and drug administration respectively. The query searches for matches of n_1 in the RTM^H that satisfy κ, i.e., for patients that,

Fig. 3: Exemplary Medical Log and Corresponding RTM^H G_3 and G_9

although diagnosed with sepsis, did not receive a drug within the designated time. In INTEMPO, each match is associated with a *temporal validity*, i.e., a set of time intervals for which, based on the overlap among the `cts` and `dts` of the matched elements and the interval for which `ac` is satisfied, the match is valid. ITQL also allows for the definition of OCL constraints [12] on sought patterns.

Output The ITQL specification for the query q_1 is shown in Figure 4. Performing RTM^{H}Analysis for the query q_1 on the RTM^H G_9 of Figure 3 returns one match, since there is indeed no `Pump` attached to the `SHS`, i.e., a match for n_2, within five time units after a `Sensor` was activated, i.e., a match for n_1 was found. The temporal validity interval $[3,4]$ is returned together with the match. The match, i.e., violation, is indeed valid only for that interval since after timestamp 4, a match for n_2 starts to exist within five time units of a match for n_1. If the API of INTEMPO is used, the

```
($n1 , !(true U[0,5] E $n2))

declarations{
  n1{shs:SHS
    s:Sensor
    shs -ownedSensors-> s
    [OCL:"s.status='sepsis'"]}

  n2{shs:SHS
    s:Sensor
    u:Pump
    shs -ownedPumps-> u
    shs -ownedSensors-> s
    [OCL:"u.status='drug'"]}
}
```

Fig. 4: Example query in ITQL

query returns the match of the n_1 pattern, i.e., the EMF objects, together with the temporal validity. In case INTEMPO is used via the UI it displays a message box in ECLIPSE with the following message: `SHS@0[] Sensor@3[status=sepsis] [[3,4]]`. Note that "@" precedes the `cts` of an object and values within square brackets are attributes of the object.

Technical Details For the execution of temporal graph queries, INTEMPO employs the operationalization framework presented in [15]. The framework supports the decomposition of a query into a suitable ordering of simpler sub-queries which is executed bottom-up. The outermost query computes the overall result. For pattern-matching, INTEMPO employs the *Story Diagram Interpreter* from [1] which uses heuristics shown to reduce the pattern-matching effort. INTEMPO provides an XTEXT [2] editor for ITQL which supports completion suggestions for element types and validation of the query syntax.

3 LogAnalysis

This section demonstrates the LogAnalysis operation mode which assumes that data from past states have been captured as events in a log. INTEMPO offers the capability to process the system changes and, upon each change, obtain an updated RTM^H which is then used internally to perform RTM^{H}Analysis.

Events-to-Patterns (E2P) Specification Language The mapping of log events (which encapsulate system changes) to prescribed modifications on an RTM^H is facilitated by E2P. An E2P specification consists of mappings between events and actions that should be performed on an RTM^H. E2P supports five actions

```
init:{adds shs:SHS}

"sepsis diagnosis":{
    adds s:Sensor [status="sepsis" id=
    *p2]
    adds-ref shs -ownedSensors-> s}

"drug administration":{
    adds u:Pump [status="drug" id=*p2]
    adds-ref shs -ownedPumps-> u}
```

Fig. 5: E2P Example for SHS

(formulated as verbs): *adds*, to add a node and optionally assign values to the added node's attributes; *adds-ref*, to add an edge between two nodes; *modifies*, to modify the attribute values of a node; *deletes* and *deletes-ref*, to delete a node, respectively an edge, from the RTM^H. To accommodate linked data, E2P allows for the *indexing* of added nodes so that later events can refer to modifications that have been processed earlier. An example of an E2P mapping from an exemplary log in Figure 3 (left) to the corresponding elements of the SHS is shown in Figure 5. Note that edge types, e.g. OwnedPumps, are not depicted in Figure 3.

As an example, the event **drug administration** from the medical log in Figure 3 corresponds to the following changes to the (internal) RTM^H: a Pump is created; its attribute **status** is set to "drug" and its attribute id takes the value of the second field after the event name (expressed by the special $*p$ token), i.e., the id field in the log of Figure 3. By default, the **cts** is set to the value of the event field that is next to the event name, i.e., the **ts** field in Figure 3. The *init* statement is used to initialize the RTM^H and the **cts** of nodes within is set to zero. To increase the readability of specifications, an explicit assignment for the **dts** may be omitted: Unless there is an attribute assignment, the **dts** of all nodes is set to the maximum value supported.

Output LogAnalysis provides a view on the matches *per event timestamp*. Performing LogAnalysis on the query q_1 and the log of Figure 3 would return:

```
@3 SHS@0[] Sensor@3[status=sepsis] [[3,∞]]
@9 SHS@0[] Sensor@3[status=sepsis] [[3,4]]
```

First, the **sepsis diagnosis** event is processed which makes the internal RTM^H be identical to G_3 in the same figure. The query is executed using RTM^H Analysis and returns a match, i.e., violation, since at that moment a match for n_2 does not exist in the graph. The temporal validity is equal to $[3,∞]$, i.e., the match is valid from time point 3 onward. Next, the **drug administration** event is processed which leads to G_9. The result of RTM^H Analysis for G_9 is the same as the result described in Section 2.

Technical Details In LogAnalysis the query execution framework monitors the RTM^H for changes and, upon every change, recomputes the matches. Previous matches are kept in-between executions and therefore the query is executed incrementally. Similarly to ITQL, E2P is supported by an XTEXT editor that offers syntax validation and completion suggestions for element types.

4   Conclusion and Future Work

We presented INTEMPO, an EMF tool which enables the specification and incremental execution of temporal graph queries over a runtime model with history. The latter can be either provided as input or obtained by an event log. INTEMPO stands out from relevant tools owing to the integration of temporal requirements into graph queries, the in-memory representation of the model, and the systematic measures to contain memory consumption despite the accumulation of temporal data. Moreover, INTEMPO offers input editors with features that aim at helping the user, e.g. syntax validation. In the future, besides streamlining INTEMPO, we plan to perform extensive evaluation and comparisons with other tools. Moreover, we plan to explore the utilization of INTEMPO in self-adaptation scenarios where the history of the system is required.

References

1. Barkowsky, M., Giese, H.: Hybrid search plan generation for generalized graph pattern matching. JLAMP **114**, 100563 (2020)
2. Bettini, L.: Implementing domain-specific languages with Xtext and Xtend. Packt Publishing Ltd (2016)
3. Bencomo N., Goetz S., and Song H.: Models@ run. time: a guided tour of the state of the art and research challenges. SoSyM **18**.5 (2019)
4. Brun, Y., Di Marzo Serugendo, G., Gacek, C., Giese, et al.:Software engineering for self-adaptive systems, pp. 48–70. Heidelberg (2009) Springer
5. Búr, M., Szilágyi, G., Vörös, A., Varró, D.: Distributed graph queries over models@run.time for runtime monitoring of cyber-physical systems. STTT **22**(1)
6. Ehrig, H., Prange, U., Taentzer, G.: Fundamental Theory for Typed Attributed Graph Transformation. ICGT Berlin, Heidelberg (2004) Springer
7. Eclipse Foundation: Eclipse modeling framework (EMF) (Aug 2020), https://www.eclipse.org/modeling/emf/, accessed: 2020-10-11
8. García-Domínguez, A., Bencomo, N., Parra-Ullauri, J.M., García-Paucar, L.H.: Querying and Annotating Model Histories with Time-Aware Patterns. MODELS. pp. 194–204 (2019) ACM/IEEE
9. Ghahremani, S., Giese, H., Vogel, T.: Efficient utility-driven self-healing employing adaptation rules for large dynamic architectures. ICAC (2017)
10. Giese, H., Maximova, M., Sakizloglou, L., Schneider, S.: Metric Temporal Graph Logic over Typed Attributed Graphs. FASE, (2019) Springer
11. Gómez, A., Cabot, J., Wimmer, M.: TemporalEMF: A temporal metamodeling framework. ER, vol. 11157, pp. 365–381. (2018) Springer
12. Kleppe, A., Warmer, J.: An introduction to the object constraint language (OCL). In: TOOLS p. 456 (2000)
13. MDELab: InTempo Homepage, http://www.hpi.uni-potsdam.de/giese/public/mdelab/mdelab-projects/intempo/, accessed: 2021-01-19
14. Rhodes, A., Evans, L.E., Alhazzani, W., Levy, M.M., et al.: Surviving sepsis campaign: International guidelines for management of sepsis and septic shock: 2016. Intensive care medicine **43**(3), 304–377 (2017)
15. Sakizloglou, L., Ghahremani, S., Barkowsky, M., Giese, H.: A scalable querying scheme for memory-efficient runtime models with history. MoDELS pp. 175–186. (2020) ACM/IEEE

SpecTest: Specification-Based Compiler Testing

Richard Schumi[✉] and Jun Sun

Singapore Management University, Singapore, Singapore

{rschumi,junsun}@smu.edu.sg

Abstract. Compilers are error-prone due to their high complexity. They are relevant for not only general purpose programming languages, but also for many domain specific languages. Bugs in compilers can potentially render all programs at risk. It is thus crucial that compilers are systematically tested, if not verified. Recently, a number of efforts have been made to formalise and standardise programming language semantics, which can be applied to verify the correctness of the respective compilers. In this work, we present a novel specification-based testing method named SpecTest to better utilise these semantics for testing. By applying an executable semantics as test oracle, SpecTest can discover deep semantic errors in compilers. Compared to existing approaches, SpecTest is built upon a novel test coverage criterion called semantic coverage which brings together mutation testing and fuzzing to specifically target less tested language features. We apply SpecTest to systematically test two compilers, i.e., the Java compiler and the Solidity compiler. SpecTest improves the semantic coverage of both compilers considerably and reveals multiple previously unknown bugs.

Keywords: Mutation testing · Compiler testing · K framework · Formal semantics · Rare language features

1 Introduction

Compilers must be thoroughly tested (if not verified) for multiple reasons. First, compilers are essential for the software ecosystem. Their correctness is a prerequisite for program correction. That is, a compiler bug might propagate to all produced programs. Second, compilers are error-prone due to their high complexity. Their main functionality is to convert source code to executable machine code. They often provide additional features, like code optimisation or debug utilities. A variety of compilers has been written for countless languages. Modern compilers like GCC, javac, and LLVM are overwhelmingly complicated (e.g., GCC has more than 7M lines of code and OpenJDK has more than 11M [20]). Although some of them have been used for decades, they may still be buggy [54,55].

Recently, there have been numerous efforts on formalising and standardising programming language semantics, such as K-Java [24], C semantics [29], KJS [47], or KSolidity [34,44], which readily serve as a specification of the respective compilers. Usually, these executable semantics are accompanied by manually crafted unit tests. Such tests are however designed to test the semantics rather than the compliance of the compiler to the language semantics. In this work, we aim to better utilise these semantics by automatically generating test programs with a novel coverage criterion that facilitates systematic compiler testing.

Multiple approaches have been recently proposed to test compilers. Most of them successfully found compiler bugs. For instance, the EMI project discovered

© The Author(s) 2021

E. Guerra and M. Stoelinga (Eds.): FASE 2021, LNCS 12649, pp. 269–291, 2021.

https://doi.org/10.1007/978-3-030-71500-7_14

more than 1600 bugs in GCC and LLVM [53]. Another study has revealed bugs in the Java compiler by comparing different javac and JVM versions [27]. For the relatively new Solidity (smart contract) language, many crashes were found through fuzzing [28]. Moreover, bugs in compilers may be exploited by attackers. For example, prior to version 0.5.0, the Solidity compiler had an uninitialised storage pointer vulnerability that affected many smart contracts on Ethereum. A honey pot named *OpenAddressLottery* was designed to exploit this vulnerably and steal ether (i.e., digital money in Ethereum). There are hundreds or even thousands of programming languages according to different sources [30] and many new ones emerge every year. For example, various new general purpose or domain-specific languages have been developed recently, such as Rust, Kotlin, Solidity, and Move.

Compiler testing is an ongoing research field. Next, we briefly review existing approaches according to how they address the following two problems.

1. The test generation problem: how are test cases (i.e., programs with specific inputs) selected and generated?
2. The oracle problem: how are testing results deemed successful or failure?

Existing compiler testing approaches solve the test generation problem mainly through two ways, by generating programs according to a grammar that specifies the syntax of a language [49,31,23], or by mutating existing seed programs [40,55,41]. For the former, due to a huge search space, additional selection criteria must be applied to selectively generate test cases for compilers, such as standard code coverage criteria like statement coverage. For the latter, existing mutation strategies are often limited by the 'weak' oracles (as we will discuss shortly) employed by the approach, e.g., mutating to introduce 'dead' code. Generally, approaches which generate complicated syntax focus more on parsing errors instead of errors in the semantics. For the oracle problem, existing proposals mainly have three oracles. The first oracle is one that only flags a test failure if the program is incompilable or leads to crashes [28]. The second oracle flags a test failure if certain algebraic properties are violated. For instance, the algebraic property adopted in the EMI approach [55] is that mutating unreachable code does not change the execution result. We remark that these two oracles are 'weak' as they are unable to detect simple semantic errors such as $3 + 4 = 8$. The third, stronger oracle is one that checks whether the output of a test program is consistent with a reference, which could be a second compiler (i.e., differential testing [45]), or an abstract specification like a state machine [35,36]. This oracle requires a reference, which is not always feasible. Furthermore, it is limited to bugs which result in inconsistencies between the compiled program and the reference. Last but not least, existing approaches do not provide a good adequacy measurement on the progress of compiler testing. Often measurements, like code coverage, are used as an indicator, but they have the limitation that they need access to the compiler code, and achieving full code coverage is challenging.

In this work, we present a novel specification-based testing method called SpecTest for compiler testing. SpecTest differs from existing approaches in the following aspects. First, SpecTest is built upon a strong oracle, i.e., an executable language specification that can predict the expected output of test programs. This strong oracle enables us to detect semantic errors, i.e., bugs that are related to the semantics. Such bugs may also originate from the runtime environment. Hence, SpecTest is not just limited to classical compiler bugs. Second, SpecTest offers a testing adequacy measurement in term of semantic coverage and has a built-in mutation-based test case generation method which aims to achieve high semantic coverage. The semantic coverage measures the number of language semantic rules that are covered by existing test cases. The test case generation method mutates the seed programs accordingly to maximise the coverage of the language semantics, e.g., by introducing less-tested language features into these programs. Compared to measuring the code coverage of a compiler, our semantic coverage has the added value that it does not need access to the compiler code, and it specifically targets semantic bugs.

Given a language semantics (in the form of a set of small-step operational semantic rules), SpecTest executes fully automatically. We have implemented SpecTest for two compilers, i.e., the Java compiler and the Solidity compiler and tested the language features that are supported by our applied semantics [24,44]. The results of the evaluation were promising. SpecTest successfully increases the semantic coverage for both compilers, and identified many bugs and issues that helped the compiler and specification developers.

To sum up, we make the following technical contributions.

- We propose a semantic coverage criterion for measuring the adequacy of compiler testing.
- We introduce a novel compiler testing method that uses an executable language specification as an oracle.
- We demonstrate the applicability and generality of SpecTest by applying it to two compilers.

The paper is structured as follows. Sect. 2 explains our method and discusses the required components in detail. In Sect. 3, we present our evaluation with two compilers. Next, we review related work in Sect. 4 and conclude in Sect. 5.

2   Method

In this section, we outline how SpecTest works. In particular, we present its high-level design, highlight relevant details of its components, and explain the workflow step by step using an example.

2.1   Overall Design

The overall workflow of SpecTest is depicted in Fig. 1. In the following, we introduce the tasks briefly before diving into the details of the main components.

(1) A set of user-provided seed programs are given as input to *a program fuzzer* one by one, which generates a set of test inputs for each program with the intention to cover as many program paths as possible. A program and the associated test inputs form a test case that is the basis for the next phase, the test execution and evaluation. (2) The program is compiled with the compiler

and executed with test inputs generated by the fuzzer. The final state (i.e., variable valuations) is obtained as the program execution result. (3) *An executable language semantics* is executed with the same program and the same inputs, through firing a set of structural operational semantic (SOS) rules. The final state is ob-

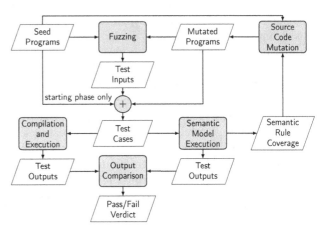

Fig. 1: Overview of the data flow of SpecTest

tained as the semantic execution result. During the semantic execution, we monitor how frequent each SOS rule is fired in order to identify rarely fired rules. (4) The results of the program and semantic execution are compared in order to assess whether the program (built by a compiler) produces an output which is consistent with the language semantics. If the results are inconsistent, the test case is flagged as a failure. The failure may be either due to a bug in the compiler (or the execution environment of the program, e.g., JVM) or in the language semantics. (5) We rank the SOS rules according to the number of times they are fired and identify the ones which are least fired. Each SOS rule is typically associated with one language feature and thus we are able to systematically identify language features which are least tested. With the information, *a program mutator* mutates the seed programs so that the corresponding language features are introduced systematically into the programs. In contrast to classical mutation testing [33], which ensures the quality of test suites, we apply mutations to generate more and better test cases. (6) We then repeat from step (1), and the process continues until a user-specified timeout is triggered. The output of SpecTest includes a set of passed/failed test cases as well as a report on the semantic coverage, i.e., the number of times each SOS rule is fired.

It should be noticed that there are three main components in SpecTest, i.e., the executable program semantics which serves as oracle, the program fuzzer, and the program mutator. We present details of these components in the following.

2.2   The Oracle

The oracle is an executable semantics of the programming language. That is, the oracle encodes the language semantics in the form of small-step SOS rules. Given a program (and necessary inputs for the program), the oracle is capable of executing the program according to the language semantics to produce the expected output, without going through the compiler to be tested.

Creating an executable semantics for a programming languages is not trivial. It requires experience as well as effort. Nonetheless, it is desirable to have one

```
rule I1 + I2 => I1 +Int I2
rule if ( true) S else _ => S
rule [Allocate-Global-NonArrayType]:
<k> #allocate(N, CN, #varInfo(X:Id, E:Value, T:NonArrayType, #storage, L)) =>
     . ...</k>
<account>
   <acctID> N </acctID> <contractName> CN </contractName>
   <acctEnv> CONTEXT:Map => CONTEXT[X <- #storedVar(Slot +Int 1, T, #storage,
       1)] </acctEnv>
   <acctStorage> STORAGE:Map => STORAGE[Slot +Int 1 <- E] </acctStorage>
   <acctSlots> Slot => Slot +Int 1 </acctSlots> ...
</account>
```

Fig. 2: Example SOS rules for Solidity [44]

because it provides a reliable way to check the correctness of compilers, and it will save time and effort in the long term since it effectively reveals ambiguities, inconsistencies and incompleteness. Many researchers have realised the importance of executable language semantics and have built foundations that we can work with, like the K framework [50], Redex [37], or Ott [51]. There are already executable semantics for many programming languages, like C, JAVA, JavaScript, or Solidity, which represent a strong oracle for compiler testing.

It is conceivable and in fact confirmed by our experiments that the oracle itself can be buggy due to human errors in encoding the language semantics or due to ambiguity in the language semantics in the first place. However, even a potentially buggy executable semantics is much better than none for the following reasons. First, during the above-mentioned process, SpecTest is able to identify bugs in the oracle, which helps to improve the language semantics. Second, bugs in the semantics are overall less likely compared to compiler bugs since the compiler must not only implement the semantics but also handle sophisticated code optimisations, which are known to be error-prone.

In this work, we apply the K framework [50] as a basis for our oracle. The K framework provides convenient notations for defining language semantics or type systems based on rewriting rules, configurations, and computations. It comes with a range of supporting tools, like a parser, an interpreter, or a program verifier, which enable the execution of the specifications. In short, it combines the functionality of both the compiler and the runtime environment. Encoding small-step SOS rules in the K framework is relatively straightforward. For example, Fig. 2 shows three (simplified) rules defined for Solidity (i.e., a language for programming smart contracts) programs. In particular, the first rule shows how simple addition should behave for Integers, given the existing k construct for addition +Int. The second example is a rule for an if conditional statement, where the condition is true and the result is the then-branch. Not all rules are simple though. The third example is a rule for the storage allocation of a global non-array variable. In general, the rules become more complex for sophisticated language features such as concurrency or higher order functions.

In this work, we adopt and extend the K semantics for Java [24] and Solidity [34,44] to implement SpecTest. The K semantics for Solidity, called KSolidity, has currently 304 rules. The K semantics for Java, called K-Java, has 1385 rules. K-Java was developed for an earlier version of Java (1.4) and some rules are deprecated or unreachable. Our extension to these existing efforts concerned mainly two aspects, i.e., extending them with proper interface and conversion so that they work with other components in SpecTest; and introducing a measurement feature for semantic coverage. For example, we enhanced the coverage engine of the old K version for K-Java, and we added a visualisation of the covered rules.

Given a test case (in the form of a program with inputs), the executable semantics is used as follows. First, the test case is executed using the built-in execution engine of the K framework which fires the SOS rules one by one. The final variable valuations are captured as the result of the test case. For instance, for Solidity, we capture all the persistent states in the blockchain network (which includes addresses, their balances and the values of storage variables). This testing result is turned into an assertion in the test case. The test case with the assertion is then executed using the compiled program. If the assertion fails (e.g., the value of at least one variable is different), a bug is revealed.

Simply applying the above-mentioned steps to test compilers would not be comprehensive. That is, existing seed programs often use a limited set of common language features and thus would not be able to test the compiler extensively. In fact, our experience on testing the Solidity compiler with existing smart contracts suggests that many smart contracts are suspiciously similar. As a result, the test cases would only exercise a limited set of semantic rules and thus would miss those bugs in the part of the Solidity compiler that encodes the remaining semantic rules. While collecting a large set of seed programs would likely be helpful, the larger problem at stake is whether there could be a certain quantitative measurement on the comprehensiveness of the test cases and whether we can use the measurement to guide the generation of new test cases? SpecTest's answer to this question lies in the design of the mutator and the fuzzer.

2.3   The Mutator

Due to the high complexity of modern compilers, it is important that a meaningful coverage criterion is applied for compiler testing. Existing approaches either are not concerned with coverage or they use coverage criteria which are not ideal for compiler testing. Hence, we introduce our novel semantic coverage.

Definition 1. *Given R is the set of all semantic rules of our specification, T is the set of our given test programs, I_t is the set of all possible inputs for the test program $t \in T$, and $cover(t, i, r)$ is a predicate that is true when there exists a test program t and a test input $i \in I_t$ for t and they are able to fire the semantic rule r of our specification; our semantic coverage can be defined as follows:*

$$\forall r \in R : \exists t \in T : \exists i \in I_t : cover(t, i, r)$$

This means that to achieve semantic coverage (or at least increase it), it is not only important that we have good test programs, but also the test inputs for these programs are essential. In order to produce good test programs, we apply our mutations that inject language features to specifically target the uncovered rules as we will explain in detail in the following. The coverage of all rules $r \in R$ would give us full semantic coverage, but in reality this is often infeasible, hence we also depict it as the percentage of rules that are covered.

In SpecTest, we achieve high semantics coverage with the following two synergistic parts. First, we design and implement a mutator which systematically introduces less-exercised language features into the test programs automatically. Second, we design and apply powerful fuzzing techniques to generate program inputs to exercise all statements including the less-used features in the test programs. The latter can be achieved with fuzzers optimised for existing code coverage criteria such as branch or statement coverage.

We believe that a comprehensive test suite for a compiler must cover all relevant aspects of the language semantics, and semantic coverage offers such a measurement. The above definition simply measures whether a rule is fired or not. It might be meaningful to further measure the context in which each SOS rule is fired (as certain bugs might only be triggered when a rule is fired in a certain context), which we leave as future work.

To achieve high semantic coverage, SpecTest employs a two-part solution. Given the oracle's feedback on which SOS-rules are not fired (or least fired), the language features which are associated with the SOS rules are identified. This is straightforward as each SOS rule is associated with a specific language construct. For instance, when the first rule of Fig. 2 is not fired, then this would highlight that our test programs contain no addition between Integer variables. Next, the mutator takes the information and systematically mutates the seed programs to introduce these less-tested language constructs.

The mutator is a code mutation engine which is designed to automatically mutate a given source program to generate new programs (i.e., test cases for the compiler). Existing mutation approaches [38,41,55] for compiler testing already applied mutators to generate test programs, but they mutate based on simple algebraic rules and are not systematic. For instance, equivalence modulo inputs (EMI) [41] works by injecting code into seed programs with the aim to achieve a high difference in the control- and data-flow compared to the original seed program in order to produce diverse test programs. In comparison, our mutator is designed to maximise semantic coverage.

Implementing the mutator is not trivial. For SpecTest, the mutators for Solidity and Java were implemented based on existing parsers through code instrumentation. That is, given a language feature and a source program, the mutator first parses the source program to build an AST. Afterwards, it identifies potential locations in the AST for introducing the features. Lastly, it systematically applies a mutation strategy specifically designed for the language constructs to inject them at all possible or specific pre-defined locations. In the following, we introduce three mutation strategies as examples.

We investigated features that were specific for Solidity. For example, one mutation introduces modifiers for functions, which define conditions that must hold when a function is executed. Listing 1.1 shows a smart contract with modifiers written in the Solidity language. Unlike traditional programs, smart contracts cannot be modified once they are deployed on the blockchain. As a result, their correctness is crucial. So is the correctness of the compiler since the compiled programs are deployed on the blockchain. Furthermore, the Solidity compiler

```
 1 contract AccessRestriction {
 2  address public owner = msg.sender;
 3  //default modifier:
 4  modifier onlyBy(address account){
 5   require(msg.sender==account, "Sender
         not authorized");
 6   _; } //injected modifier:
 7  modifier cgskst(address value){
 8   require(value == address(0x0),"");
 9   _; } //injected modifier:
10  modifier cbhsmo(address value){
11   require(value == address(0x0),"");
12   _; } //injected modifier:
13  modifier nlwxmv(address value){
14   require(value == address(0x0),"");
15   _;
16  }//Make newOwner the contract owner:
17  function changeOwner(address newOwner
        ) public onlyBy(owner) cgskst(
        address(0x0)) cbhsmo(address(0x0
        )) nlwxmv(address(0x0)){
18    owner = newOwner;
19 }}
```

Listing 1.1: Simple modifier example

```
bibt4QkDIfJ: {
 bsJxhbtSJBu: {
  bHhq23OwDjZ: { try {
   bEdqZ33tKi9: {
    bVm9tCxbul4: {
     if (i >= 5){ break; }
     break bEdqZ33tKi9;
    } }
  }catch(RuntimeException e){
   bQ2yucCPLQr: {
    System.out.print("X");
    break bQ2yucCPLQr;
} } } } }
```

Listing 1.2: Labelled block mutation

```
contract Test {
 function testFunc(int a)
  public pure returns (int) {
  int result = a + a++;
  //produces 3 when a is 1
  return result;
} }
```

Listing 1.3: Simple contract example

has been under rapid development and there are unique language features with sometimes confusing semantics. Thus, it is a good target for evaluating the effectiveness of SpecTest. In this example, the modifier onlyBy ensures that the function changeOwner can only be called when the address of the contract owner is used. By integrating various dummy modifiers (Lines 7, 10 & 13) into our seed contracts and by adding them to functions (Line 17), we noticed that an older version of the Solidity compiler crashed in some cases, when more than a certain number of modifiers are used. Such a case is difficult to find with normal tests, since it is rare to use multiple modifiers for a function. Given that a less-fired SOS rule is concerned with the modifier construct in Solidity, to introduce modifiers, the mutator scans through the AST for function declarations. For each function declaration, the mutator randomly adds one or more modifiers.

We also introduced specific mutations for Java. For example, our experiments showed that semantic rules associated with labels were not fired. Hence, we introduced mutations that target these rules, e.g., a mutation that injects labelled blocks, which is a special and rarely used feature that allows an immediate exit of a block with a break statement. This mutation is illustrated in Listing 1.2, where we injected labelled blocks and breaks (with these labels) into a seed program.

Both for Solidity and Java, we noticed that there are various rules in the K specifications (i.e., 11 rules Java and 17 for Solidity) concerning mathematical expressions that were not covered, e.g., computations with hex-values. In order to cover these rules and to cover unusual usages in different contexts, we relied on a random approach in contrast to the other mutations where we injected code at specific places. We developed mutations that produce a variety of mathematical expressions combining various language features, like operations containing variables with different data types, hexadecimal, octal or binary literals, pre- and postfix increment/decrement (++/--), bitwise and bitshift operators, various combinations of unary operators and arrays. A simplified example of a mutation produced with this strategy is shown in Listing 1.3. It can be seen that the increment operators (++) is used in an unusual context within a mathematical expression. Our experiments showed that the computation produced unexpected results, i.e., we found an issue with the computation order that caused the increment to be executed first, although it should be executed last [19].

2.4 The Fuzzer

By injecting specific language features into the seed programs, the mutator increases the likelihood of firing uncovered or poorly covered SOS rules during the test execution. The fuzzer is a fuzzing engine which generates test inputs for a given program. The generation is based on optimization (e.g., using genetic algorithms). One of the required inputs for the fuzzer is a set of seed source programs. Such source programs are often abundant. For instance, there are thousands of Solidity programs (contracts) on EtherScan.io. The fuzzer takes these contracts as input and generates test inputs for each contract. During this process, the fuzzer sets up a test blockchain network, deploys the contracts, and generates a sequence of transactions which invoke functions.

For Solidity, we applied an existing smart contract fuzzer called sFuzz [46] that works with a new adaptive fuzzing technique for maximising the branch coverage. sFuzz uses an optimised version of a technique called American Fuzzy Lop (AFL) [59], for producing inputs that can achieve a high branch coverage. It includes various test oracles for the detection of general vulnerabilities, like Integer overflows, or smart contract specific vulnerabilities, like a gasless send [48]. We applied sFuzz to maximise the coverage of our test programs to cover our injected features. For our injected features, the coverage was usually easily achieved. However, for other cases or to minimise the test inputs, it might be necessary to customise the fuzzer to specifically target newly added language features. For example, during the mutation, we can record which parts of the contracts have been mutated and prioritise those parts during fuzzing. For Java, we did not apply a fuzzer, because the majority of our seed programs were simple in nature. A single run produced full coverage in almost all cases.

3   Evaluation

We have implemented SpecTest for two compilers, a compiler for a general purpose language (Java) and one for a new domain-specific language (Solidity). In the following, we design multiple experiments to systematically answer the following research questions (RQ).

- *RQ1: How effective is our proposed method in finding bugs or inconsistencies?* This is important since the primary aim of SpecTest is to provide a systematic way of generating a test suite for identifying compiler bugs.
- *RQ2: What kind of bugs and inconsistencies can be found?* To further motivate the usage of SpecTest, it makes sense to point out what issues can be found. In particular, we would like to check whether indeed there are compiler bugs associated with less-fired SOS rules.

- *RQ3: To what extent can the coverage of rules within the language specification be increased with specific mutations?* The semantic rule coverage is one of the core aspects of SpecTest for finding bugs. Therefore, it is important to investigate to which extent we can increase this coverage.
- *RQ4: How much effort is it to apply SpecTest?* When a tester is considering a testing method, the effort usually plays a big role. To create a good basis for a decision, we discuss the effort of applying SpecTest to two compilers.

3.1   Test Setting

As seed programs, we used existing tests cases of K-Java [24] and KSolidity [34,44]. KSolidity is still under development, which means that we could not test all features or a large set of contracts, but it was already sufficiently developed to support many interesting cases. K-Java supports most features of Java 8, but it also has limitations, i.e., it was implemented in an old version of the K framework, which did not focus on performance. Hence, we used seed programs without imports of libraries. We do not regard this as a limitation since small programs have advantages, e.g., they are easier to debug and it reduces the time for test case minimisation. Moreover, it is well-known that many bugs can be revealed by small test cases [32], which are also common in traditional testing.

For Solidity, we had 37 seed programs that were part of the KSolidity project due to its early stage. Hence, it makes sense to apply SpecTest since it enables the generation of more test programs in a systematic way. Our mutator for Solidity is written with about 5,300 lines of Java code. In each test run, we applied one of our mutations (or in some cases also combinations) to the seed programs. We applied sFuzz to the mutated contracts and then converted the resulting test cases in a usable form for KSolidity. We primarily tested the Solidity compiler version 0.5.13, but initially also older versions. In some cases, we had to apply Truffle tests [21] (v5.1.10) and for debugging we used Remix [18], which facilitates a step-by-step exploration of the contract bytecode.

For Java, we applied 756 seed programs and our mutator has about 6,100 lines of code. The mutations were similar as explained before. In contrast to Solidity, we did not need a sophisticated fuzzer since the mutated Java programs were covered easily. Our focus was Java 13 (openjdk 13, 2019-09-17, RE build 13+33-Ubuntu-1), but we also tested older versions (11 and 8). For the mutator, we applied JavaParser 3.14.3 for parsing the programs and for injecting mutations.

The experiments for Solidity were performed on a Dell X1 Carbon with an Intel i7-8565U CPU with four 1.80GHz cores and 16 GB RAM, for Java on a PC with an Intel i7-7700 CPU with four 3.60GHz cores and 64 GB RAM.

3.2   Experiment Result

We ran more than 30,000 test cases for Java, which had a total execution time of about three weeks. For Solidity, we ran more than 50,000 test cases with a total execution time of about two weeks. Details about the distribution of the run time will follow below. The execution times are not exact numbers, since the experiments sometimes were stuck due to out of memory exceptions, not enough space, etc. Unfortunately, we could not fully resolve such issues, because many mutations inject features with random aspects into the diverse seed programs. This caused various unpredictable situations, like endless loops or too large data structures. By adopting our mutator, we greatly reduced the number of such situations, but we could not remove all rare cases.

RQ1: How effective is our proposed method in finding bugs or inconsistencies? We discovered issues and bugs both for Solidity and Java. Some of these issues were not found within the compiler or the runtime environment, but within the language semantics. Fixing such issues is also essential, since improving the specification is an important aspect of testing.

In total, we found six issues for the Solidity compiler [19,10], two were related to error/warning messages [7,13], and three of the other issues might have the same cause, i.e., the execution order. For KSolidity, we found eight issues, six of them were related to unimplemented features. For Java, we found four issues with the compiler [2,5], two of which were concerned with error messages [6,12], and we discovered 13 issues with K-Java [14,15,11,9,8,3,1,16] (eight issues or bugs, one warning related issue, and four minor issues, like a wrong output representation [16]). More details about the different types of issue follow below.

Our experiments showed that SpecTest is able to reveal issues, inconsistencies and bugs. These issues were not only found in the compiler, but also in language semantics (which are developed independently by other groups with dedicated effort). One might argue that finding bugs/issues in the language semantics is not as meaningful as finding bugs in the compiler. We believe that it is also crucial to ensure the robustness of the semantics since in general the quality of the tests or specification are essential for the overall robustness of software. SpecTest was able to find various inconsistencies and bugs in the specifications, which is important for the specification developers, as well as issues in the compilers. We have spent effort on confirming our findings and out of the 31 issues, we submitted 19 to the corresponding git repositories and reported the other issues to the developers or to a bug reporting system. For 13 issues, we received a confirmation or the developers mentioned that they will investigate and fix them.

An aspect that might have limited the effectiveness, is that we did not fully apply our method for Java, since we only tested simple seed programs and did not use fuzzing. We believe that the issues we found still showed that our method was reasonably effective, even though we only partially applied it. Using the full extend of SpecTest for Java might require a more powerful specification, which is a potential topic for future work. Moreover, it should be mentioned that KSolidity is still being developed and not as stable as the Solidity compiler (or runtime environment), since much more effort was invested into its development. This is similar for K-Java, and Java in general is robust due to its maturity.

RQ2: What kind of bugs and inconsistencies can be found? We categorise our findings into three categories as illustrated in Table 1, i.e., (1) normal issues, bugs and missing features, (2) issues related to warning or error messages, and (3) minor inconsistencies or issues, like a small discrepancy in the output, e.g.,

-0e+00.0 instead of -0.0 [16]. Additionally, we differentiate whether the origin of an issue was the compiler or the specification, as illustrated by the rows of Table 1.

Table 1: Found semantics and compiler issues

	Solidity	KSolidity	Java	K-Java
Normal issue or bug	4	8	2	8
Warning or error message related issues	2	-	2	1
Minor issues	-	-	-	4
Total	6	8	4	13

The most interesting issues that we found were the ones concerning the wrong computation order in Solidity. The cause of these issues were actual semantic errors within the compiler. Moreover, we also found various issues with error or warning messages. Such issues might seem trivial, but it is important to fix them since meaningless error messages can cause a huge waste of debugging effort. The bugs we found in the specifications had multiple sources, like the syntax parser, wrong semantic rules, partially implemented rules, or rules applied in a wrong context. Although K-Java and KSolidity had already many manual tests, we showed that SpecTest was able to discover many inconsistencies and bugs. In the following, we present example issues from the mentioned categories.

Solidity Findings. One of the issues [19] that SpecTest identified was that there were wrong results, when we tested expressions with different assignment operators. The behaviour can be observed in the following example, where the increment operator is applied at first, but should be applied in the end.

```
int a = 2;      a *= 1 + a++; //results in 9 but should be 6
```

A potential cause might be a wrong computation order. This issue was found since some SOS rules for assignment operators were uncovered. By creating mutations that target these rules, we could generate expressions like in the example which led to the discovery of the issue since the oracle predicted a different result.

An inconsistency regarding an error message [13] was revealed when we tested computations with different data types. As illustrated below, we discovered that it is possible to add int variables with different bit sizes, but an error is produced if an int_const is added to an int variable with a smaller bit size.

```
int8 a = 10; int16 b = 234;
int c = b + a; // works
int c = 234 + a;//TypeError: Oper. + incompatible with types int_const & int8
```

In this case, our oracle performed the computation without an error, but the Solidity compiler produced a type error. For KSolidity, we found an incorrect overflow behaviour for computations, and that there is no support for numerous language features, like increment operators.

Additionally, we applied our Solidity truffle tests to the Conflux blockchain [17], which is a new alternative for Ethereum. It basically can be seen as another runtime environment for Solidity contracts. With our tests, we were able to reveal a bug in the testing environment that resulted in incorrect results when we injected formulas with unary and bitwise operators [4].

Java findings. Our experiments showed that there is an inconsistency [1,2] when casts from double and long variables to Integers are performed. These casts are handled differently by Java when an overflow occurs, i.e., in the following code the results will be the maximum Integer for the double cast and bits will be cut off for the long cast. In K-Java both casts produce the same result, i.e., bits will be cut off. Although this behaviour is documented in the language specification and already others were wondering about this issue, we believe that the approach of K-Java is more consistent, and we are still waiting for a comment of the Java team about the motivation to handle these cases differently.

```
System.out.println(((int)2147483648L));  // -2147483648
System.out.println(((int)2147483648.0));  //  2147483647
```

A problem we found for the Java compiler [6] is a missing error message when a computation with a long and a double variable is performed. Normally, an incompatible types error is produced as illustrated in the following code, but the error does not occur when the same computation is done with an += operator.

```
long a = 1L + 0.1 * 3L; // produces error: incompatible types: possible lossy
long b = 1L;            //                  conversion from double to long
b += 0.1 * 3L;          // no error is produced
```

We discovered that K-Java has an issue with the modulo operator [14]. The computation is wrong for all negative doubles and floats, i.e., it produces inconsistent values compared to Java and compared to the same computation with Integer values. This is illustrated in the following examples.

```
System.out.println("-8   %  3  = "+(-8   %  3));  //K-Java and Java return -2
System.out.println("-8.0 %  3.0= "+(-8.0 %  3));  //K-Java 1.0 Java -2.0
System.out.println(" 8   % -3  = "+( 8   % -3));  //K-Java and Java return 2
System.out.println(" 8.0 % -3.0= "+( 8.0 % -3.0));//K-Java -4.0 Java 2.0
```

In general, we found most issues, when we injected mathematical expressions into the seed programs. This was an interesting finding for us, since these expressions are a major component of all programming languages, and we assumed it would be straightforward to develop a specification for them. However, it turned out that many interesting and ambiguous situations can occur when various combinations of operators, variables and literals are tested.

RQ3: Can SpecTest effectively improve semantic coverage? The objective of SpecTest is to systematically generate a test suite for achieving better semantic coverage. In order to evaluate the coverage, we conducted the following experiments. We identified the semantic rules that were least covered by the existing tests for Solidity and Java, and then applied SpecTest systematically (with specific mutators) and measured the improvement in terms of semantic coverage.

First, we evaluated the semantic coverage criterion that is achievable with the original seed programs of K-Java and KSolidity to have a reference value for the comparison with the mutated test programs. Table 2 shows a comparison of the coverage from the original test cases from K-Java to our mutated test cases. The rule coverage of this early version of the K framework of K-Java is rudimentary. Hence, we could only measure the covered lines and characters of the rule files, and many of these files were already fully covered due to redundant or unreachable rules. Nevertheless, we were able to identify various uncovered rules in four of the files, and we produced mutations that covered these rules.

KSolidity was built with a new version of the K framework, which has a better measurement of the rule coverage. Since the development of KSolidity is still ongoing, we focused on the completed features, like conditions, loops, arrays, structs, simple transactions, or mathematical expressions, and managed to increase the coverage. Even with just these features, we found meaningful bugs. The coverage improvements compared to the original seed programs are illustrated in Table 3. There were partially implemented features which could not be fully covered. The coverage of the completed features was considerably improved.

Table 2: Comparison of the covered rules between the K-Java tests (Default) and our mutated test cases

File	Default		Mutants		Difference	
	Char	Line	Char	Line	Char	Line
folding.k	93.04	93.89	93.04	93.89	-	-
unfolding.k	91.84	94.55	91.84	94.55	-	-
process-class-decs.k	89.07	92.95	89.07	92.95	-	-
expressions.k	72.30	78.74	86.58	89.92	14.28	11.18
process-comp-units.k	83.39	86.03	83.39	86.03	-	-
static-init.k	81.20	82.35	81.20	82.35	-	-
process-class-members.k	80.65	83.53	80.65	83.53	-	-
statements.k	80.51	82.38	80.51	82.38	-	-
new-instance.k	79.59	82.41	79.59	82.41	-	-
method-invoke.k	79.44	80.74	79.44	80.74	-	-
api-core.k	61.77	63.37	78.74	81.82	16.97	18.45
var-lookup.k	77.52	79.41	77.52	79.41	-	-
process-type-names.k	76.56	75.76	76.56	75.76	-	-
expressions-classes.k	73.03	65.00	73.03	65.00	-	-
process-local-classes.k	67.62	72.12	67.62	72.12	-	-
process-anonymous-classes.k	66.79	81.52	66.79	81.52	-	-
arrays.k	62.07	66.90	62.07	66.90	-	-
api-threads.k	35.51	39.04	41.43	47.01	5.92	7.97
syntax-conversions.k	40.65	42.42	40.65	42.42	-	-
literals.k	29.19	34.31	38.73	42.72	9.54	8.40

We have shown that our mutations can increase the rule coverage both for K-Java and KSolidity. Our close investigation shows that the increase in coverage requires non-trivial programs (e.g., programs that specifically include missing language features) which are unlikely to be generated without our mutator. It is worth mentioning that writing mutations for the uncovered rules lead to the discovery of many issues. Moreover, the mutations that targeted specific semantic rules or language features could generally increase the coverage instantaneously with a single test, but we still applied them to all seed programs, and we also used general mutation operators to produce mutants for many different situations.

RQ4: How much effort is it to apply SpecTest? To answer this question, we analysed the effort required to apply and implement SpecTest for Java and Solidity. It consists of two parts, the effort of applying SpecTest once it is developed, and the implementation effort. The latter one consists of three parts, the effort for developing the oracle, the mutator and the fuzzer. The goal of this analysis is to understand how generalisable SpecTest is to a new programming language.

Applying SpecTest after the implementation has the following timing requirements. Both for Solidity and Java, the mutant generation took only a few seconds. For Solidity, we set a timeout of 2 min per contract for fuzzing and it took on average 24 min to finish all 37 contracts. Usually, 40–45 test cases were created by the fuzzer (normally multiple per contract depending on the mutation). Most test cases were executed by KSolidity within a minute, but there were outliers which did not terminate even after hours. Hence, we used a timeout of 5 min. On average, the testing time of KSolidity was 37 min (when five runs with different mutations were considered). For Java, we did not apply a fuzzer due to the simplicity of the seed programs. We executed the 756 test programs directly with K-Java, which took on average 3 hours and 51 min for an introduced mutation (for five runs with different mutation types).

We now discuss our development efforts and the time requirements of the implementation of SpecTest for a new language. In our case, the most effort went into the development of the mutator and the supporting tooling, like translators. The implementations for both Solidity and Java took about two to three months each. It

Table 3: Comparison of the covered rules between the original KSolidity tests (Default) and our mutated test cases

File	Default	Mutants	Difference
function.k	86.21	86.21	-
expression.k	92.31	95.38	3.08
solidity-syntax.k	62.50	72.12	9.62
statement.k	92.86	92.86	-
contract.k	94.12	94.12	-
driver.k	49.15	49.15	-
solidity.k	50.00	50.00	-

should be noted that this time depends on the availability of existing tools, like a language parser or fuzzer. For this work, we relied on pre-existing language specifications, which helped to reduce the overall effort, but as mentioned they came with limitations, which caused additional efforts. Writing a specification for a new programming language is not trivial. Based on past experiences, we assume that it takes about six to 12 months depending on the complexity of the language. Given the many recent efforts on developing executable language semantics, we believe that SpecTest provides a good way to better utilise these existing specifications for systematic compiler testing.

To summarise, the implementation effort of SpecTest is about two to three work months mainly for the mutator, if there is an existing specification and a fuzzer. The application of our method in terms of run time is about a few hours for a single mutation. Further increasing the number of seed programs, and performing a reasonable number of mutations increases this time to a couple of days or weeks, when the tests are only executed on one machine. Even though this seems like a lot of effort, we believe our method is still worthwhile, since it will pay off eventually, especially considering all the effort that can be required for releasing a new compiler version, when serious bugs are discovered. Moreover, our method can be easily accelerated by distributing it to multiple machines.

As mentioned before, the implementation effort for our method was about two to three work months. This is about the time that is needed for the mutator and for other minor tools. It does not include the effort for creation of the language specification or the fuzzer. There are already many existing fuzzers that could be adopted for new programming languages, and also numerous language specifications. We especially want to recommend our method for all languages with pre-existing specifications (or when similar specifications exist) since then there is only a small implementation effort, which will soon be mitigated by the advantages of SpecTest. Even when there are no pre-existing specifications for a language, we highly recommend to create one and to adopt our method, since it will save time in the long term.

An effort that should not be underestimated is the time for analysing bugs. It can be troublesome and to find the cause of a bug, due to the complexity of the test cases, i.e., it sometimes took us hours or even days. In such cases, it can be helpful to minimise failing test cases. There are numerous techniques, like delta debugging [62] or program slicing [58], which can reduce the debugging effort, and integrating them into SpecTest would be interesting for future work.

3.3   Threats to Validity

A threat to the validity of our evaluation might be that we did not show a comparison to other compiler testing methods. A comparison might be interesting, but our main goal was to show the general applicability and usefulness of SpecTest for different compilers. It would not be fair to compare SpecTest to other testing techniques that focus on different types of bugs, e.g., it might be much easier to find simple parsing errors caused by unusual characters (with techniques, like fuzzing).

One might argue that the test size we used is too limited, which might be a potential threat to the validity of our evaluation. It is true that it would make sense to apply more seed programs and to continue mutating and testing for an extended period of time. However, due to restrictions of KSolidity and K-Java, a larger set of seed programs was not supported, and due to a limited time and computing budget, we did not execute more tests. Nevertheless, we believe that our test size was reasonable, since it allowed us to reveal various issues and bugs.

Another threat to the validity of our evaluation might be that we should not have just relied on existing specifications, where we cannot be sure about their quality. It is true that we might have more confidence in a specification that we created, but since SpecTest checks the correctness of compilers as well as specifications, we have trust that our specifications had a reasonable quality.

4   Related Work

Compiler testing is a broad research field with a range of techniques that target, e.g., the test case generation [49,31,23] or the oracle problem [22]. Several surveys give an overview of these methods [56,26,39,25]. Our study however shows that existing approaches suffer from two weaknesses. They do not apply a test case generation that can extensively cover rare language features, and they often rely on weak or limited test oracles. The test case generation often works with standard code coverage criteria concerning compiler components. For example, Zelenov and Zelenova [61] applied a BNF grammar as a model and produced test cases according to, e.g., code or functional coverage of a syntax analyser. A method based on the coverage of context-free grammar rules was presented by Purdom [49], but it only targets the parser of the compiler. Kalinov et al. [35,36] defined coverage criteria based on a statement machine specification. In contrast to our work, they do not identify rare language features by analysing semantic rule coverage, and they do not construct their test programs via code mutation.

Various compiler testing methods work without any coverage by just randomly generating test cases according to a grammar, which defines valid programs [52,60]. There are also techniques that use mutation for producing test cases [38,41,55]. For example, Le, Sun, and Su [41] produced mutants that should have the same behaviour as the original programs in order to find cases where the behaviour diverges. However, in contrast to our work, they are not considering a semantic coverage for less used language features.

Several attempts have been presented to answer the oracle problem for compiler testing. In the simple case of positive/negative testing, an oracle only tells whether a program is compilable. When a test program is compiled, the result is checked to see if it matches the expectation of the oracle. A match means a successful compilation. Otherwise, there may be a bug. For example, Zelenov and Zelenova [61] illustrated a specification-based approach for generating positive and negative tests. Such approaches are limited to testing the syntax parser.

In the line of work on differential testing compilers [45], the oracle is defined as consistency among two or more compilers for the same language. In this method, the same test programs are given to multiple compilers and the results are compared. If there is a difference then a bug in one of the compilers or an ambiguity in the language is found. There exist different versions of differential testing as explained by McKeeman [45]. Cross-compiler testing [52] is a technique that works by contrasting a new compiler against a pre-existing compiler that has the same specification. When the same test programs are executed with both compilers, a different result can reveal a fault in the new or pre-existing compiler. Sometimes this technique is also called randomised differential testing [60], because the test programs are usually generated randomly, e.g., based on a grammar. Another differential testing technique is cross-optimisation testing, where programs compiled with different optimisations implemented for the same compiler are contrasted to find bugs. Le, Sun, and Su [42] presented such a technique for stress testing link optimisers. Their method generates random test programs and injects various function calls into different code regions in order to increase dependencies between procedures, and it also randomly selects different optimisation levels to produce challenging tests for the optimiser. Cross-version or regression testing is another differential testing method that tries to find bugs by comparing different versions of the same compiler. For example, Sun, Le, and Su [54] developed Epiphron, a tool that generates random test programs to find inconsistencies with the debug information, like missing warning messages, in different versions of the same compiler. Such approaches work only if there are multiple relatively mature compilers for the same language. In contrast to these techniques, SpecTest works with a formal language specification which is especially useful when no compilers could be used as a reference. Moreover, different compilers or compiler versions for the same language might still suffer from the same bugs, which is unlikely for an independent specification.

There are approaches that assume the existence of a reference compiler, i.e., the oracle is an existing formally proven compiler. For example, Leroy [43] presented CompCert, a compiler for a subset of C, which was verified with the proof assistant Coq. However, there are usually no such compilers for a newly developed language and the existing ones cover only subsets of languages since formally proving a compiler is extremely challenging.

For metamorphic testing [57], the oracle is defined as certain algebraic properties of the compiler. For instance, one such property explored in the compiler testing technique called equivalence modulo inputs (EMI) [40,55] is that a modification on a program part which is never executed should not alter the result.

Based on this simple oracle, EMI works by randomly pruning dead code (i.e., code which is not executed given a certain program input) or by randomly inserting or removing instructions from dead code based on a Markov Chain Monte Carlo method. Such approaches are limited to identifying bugs which violate the algebraic properties. Hence, they are not able to find deep semantic errors.

The closest related work to SpecTest was proposed by Kalinov et al. [35,36], where a language specification in the form of abstract state machines and montages is used as an oracle. With this specification, they compare the expected output from the specification to that of a compiled program in order to check whether there are compiler bugs. This approach is limited by the choice of the specification language and it quickly becomes infeasible, because the computation time is too high. Moreover, it is not concerned with semantic coverage.

To demonstrate the limitations of the closely related methods, we come back to the example of Sect. 2, i.e., we discussed a bug with the increment operator that we discovered during our analysis of the Solidity compiler.

```
int a = 1;      int result = a + a++; //produces 3, but it should be 2
```

In this example, the compiler had an issue with the computation order, which resulted in wrong results. Existing approaches, like EMI or differential testing might be able to detect such issues, but with EMI it is difficult to find mutations that lead to such cases. The same is true for differential testing and there is also a high chance that different compiler versions have the same faulty behaviour for such a case (e.g., all versions of the Solidity compiler had this issue).

5   Conclusion

We have demonstrated our novel compiler testing technique called SpecTest that targets less-used language features. SpecTest is based on three components: an executable language specification, a fuzzer for generating test inputs, and a mutator which generates new programs by injecting rare language features. Comparing the abstract execution of the specification to the concrete execution of a compiled program enables our method to find deep semantic errors as well as inconsistencies and issues in the specification.

We evaluated SpecTest by applying it to two programming languages: Java and Solidity. The results are encouraging. We discovered various issues concerning the compilers and the language specifications. Some of them helped to improve the quality of the compilers and many will enhance the specifications.

In the future, we plan to further explore the generality of SpecTest for other languages, and we intend to consider different types of executable specifications.

Acknowledgments

This research is supported by the National Research Foundation Singapore under its NSoE Programme (Award Number.: NSOE-TSS2019-03).

References

1. Casting a floating-point number to an integer, https://github.com/kframework/java-semantics/issues/64
2. Casting double to int and long to int produce different results, https://bugs.java.com/bugdatabase/view_bug.do?bug_id=JDK-8246334
3. Division by zero exception, https://github.com/kframework/java-semantics/issues/63
4. Incorrect output from bitwise and unary operation function call, https://github.com/Conflux-Chain/conflux-rust/issues/988
5. Minus sign issues for hex octal and binary literals, https://bugs.java.com/bugdatabase/view_bug.do?bug_id=8236406
6. Missing error message incompatible types: possible lossy conversion, https://bugs.java.com/bugdatabase/view_bug.do?bug_id=JDK-8244681
7. More specific error message for division by zero, https://github.com/ethereum/solidity/issues/8064
8. New string leads to timeout, https://github.com/kframework/java-semantics/issues/62
9. Octal values in double/float arrays, https://github.com/kframework/java-semantics/issues/61
10. Out of bounds array access, https://github.com/ethereum/solidity/issues/8364
11. Parsing issue for hexadecimal, https://github.com/kframework/java-semantics/issues/60
12. Type error for short computations, https://bugs.java.com/bugdatabase/view_bug.do?bug_id=JDK-8240371
13. Typeerror too restrictive or inconsistent?, https://github.com/ethereum/solidity/issues/8139
14. Wrong modulo computation for negative doubles, https://github.com/kframework/java-semantics/issues/58
15. Wrong precision for float variables, https://github.com/kframework/java-semantics/issues/59
16. Wrong representation of floating point numbers, https://github.com/kframework/java-semantics/issues/66
17. Conflux: High-efficiency public blockchain (2019), https://www.conflux-chain.org
18. Remix: Ethereum ide and tools for the web (2019), https://remix.ethereum.org
19. Specify and enforce evaluation order on sub-expressions (2019), https://github.com/ethereum/solidity/issues/7820
20. Discover, track and compare open source (2020), https://www.openhub.net
21. Truffle suite: Sweet tools for smart contracts (2020), http://truffleframework.com
22. Barr, E.T., Harman, M., McMinn, P., Shahbaz, M., Yoo, S.: The oracle problem in software testing: A survey. IEEE Trans. Software Eng. **41**(5), 507–525 (2015)
23. Bauer, J.A., Finger, A.B.: Test plan generation using formal grammars. In: Proceedings of the 4th International Conference on Software Engineering, Munich, Germany, September 1979. pp. 425–432. IEEE Computer Society (1979), http://dl.acm.org/citation.cfm?id=802969

24. Bogdanas, D., Rosu, G.: K-Java: A complete semantics of java. In: Proceedings of the 42nd Annual ACM SIGPLAN-SIGACT Symposium on Principles of Programming Languages, POPL 2015, Mumbai, India, January 15-17, 2015. pp. 445–456. ACM (2015). https://doi.org/10.1145/2676726.2676982

25. Boujarwah, A.S., Saleh, K.: Compiler test case generation methods: a survey and assessment. Information & Software Technology **39**(9), 617–625 (1997). https://doi.org/10.1016/S0950-5849(97)00017-7

26. Chen, J., Hu, W., Hao, D., Xiong, Y., Zhang, H., Zhang, L., Xie, B.: An empirical comparison of compiler testing techniques. In: Proceedings of the 38th International Conference on Software Engineering, ICSE 2016, Austin, TX, USA, May 14-22, 2016. pp. 180–190. ACM (2016). https://doi.org/10.1145/2884781.2884878

27. Chen, Y., Su, T., Su, Z.: Deep differential testing of JVM implementations. In: Proceedings of the 41st International Conference on Software Engineering, ICSE 2019, Montreal, QC, Canada, May 25-31, 2019. pp. 1257–1268. IEEE / ACM (2019). https://doi.org/10.1109/ICSE.2019.00127

28. Cummins, C., Petoumenos, P., Murray, A., Leather, H.: Compiler fuzzing through deep learning. In: Proceedings of the 27th ACM SIGSOFT International Symposium on Software Testing and Analysis, ISSTA 2018, Amsterdam, The Netherlands, July 16-21, 2018. pp. 95–105. ACM (2018). https://doi.org/10.1145/3213846.3213848

29. Ellison, C., Rosu, G.: An executable formal semantics of C with applications. In: Field, J., Hicks, M. (eds.) Proceedings of the 39th ACM SIGPLAN-SIGACT Symposium on Principles of Programming Languages, POPL 2012, Philadelphia, Pennsylvania, USA, January 22-28, 2012. pp. 533–544. ACM (2012). https://doi.org/10.1145/2103656.2103719, `https://doi.org/10.1145/2103656.2103719`

30. Fowler, T.: How many computer languages are there? (2020), `https://careerkarma.com/blog/how-many-coding-languages-are-there`

31. Hanford, K.V.: Automatic generation of test cases. IBM Systems Journal **9**(4), 242–257 (1970). https://doi.org/10.1147/sj.94.0242

32. Jackson, D., Damon, C.: Elements of style: Analyzing a software design feature with a counterexample detector. In: Proceedings of the 1996 International Symposium on Software Testing and Analysis, ISSTA 1996, San Diego, CA, USA, January 8-10, 1996. pp. 239–249. ACM (1996). https://doi.org/10.1145/229000.226322

33. Jia, Y., Harman, M.: An analysis and survey of the development of mutation testing. IEEE Trans. Software Eng. **37**(5), 649–678 (2011). https://doi.org/10.1109/TSE.2010.62

34. Jiao, J., Kan, S., Lin, S., Sanan, D., Liu, Y., Sun, J.: Semantic understanding of smart contracts: Executable operational semantics of solidity. In: 2020 IEEE Symposium on Security and Privacy, SP 2020, San Francisco, CA, USA, May 18-20, 2020. IEEE (2020), accepted for publication

35. Kalinov, A., Kossatchev, A., Posypkin, M., Shishkov, V.: Using ASM specification for automatic test suite generation for mpC parallel programming language compiler. Action Semantics AS 2002 p. 99 (2002)

36. Kalinov, A., Kossatchev, A.S., Petrenko, A.K., Posypkin, M., Shishkov, V.: Coverage-driven automated compiler test suite generation. Electr. Notes Theor. Comput. Sci. **82**(3), 500–514 (2003). https://doi.org/10.1016/S1571-0661(05)82625-8

37. Klein, C., Clements, J., Dimoulas, C., Eastlund, C., Felleisen, M., Flatt, M., McCarthy, J.A., Rafkind, J., Tobin-Hochstadt, S., Findler, R.B.: Run your research:

on the effectiveness of lightweight mechanization. In: Proceedings of the 39th ACM SIGPLAN-SIGACT Symposium on Principles of Programming Languages, POPL 2012, Philadelphia, Pennsylvania, USA, January 22-28, 2012. pp. 285–296. ACM (2012). https://doi.org/10.1145/2103656.2103691

38. Köroglu, Y., Wotawa, F.: Fully automated compiler testing of a reasoning engine via mutated grammar fuzzing. In: Proceedings of the 14th International Workshop on Automation of Software Test, AST@ICSE 2019, May 27, 2019, Montreal, QC, Canada. pp. 28–34. IEEE / ACM (2019). https://doi.org/10.1109/AST.2019.00010

39. Kossatchev, A.S., Posypkin, M.: Survey of compiler testing methods. Programming and Computer Software **31**(1), 10–19 (2005). https://doi.org/10.1007/s11086-005-0008-6

40. Le, V., Afshari, M., Su, Z.: Compiler validation via equivalence modulo inputs. In: ACM SIGPLAN Conference on Programming Language Design and Implementation, PLDI '14, Edinburgh, United Kingdom - June 09 - 11, 2014. pp. 216–226. ACM (2014). https://doi.org/10.1145/2594291.2594334

41. Le, V., Sun, C., Su, Z.: Finding deep compiler bugs via guided stochastic program mutation. In: Proceedings of the 2015 ACM SIGPLAN International Conference on Object-Oriented Programming, Systems, Languages, and Applications, OOPSLA 2015, part of SPLASH 2015, Pittsburgh, PA, USA, October 25-30, 2015. pp. 386–399. ACM (2015). https://doi.org/10.1145/2814270.2814319

42. Le, V., Sun, C., Su, Z.: Randomized stress-testing of link-time optimizers. In: Proceedings of the 2015 International Symposium on Software Testing and Analysis, ISSTA 2015, Baltimore, MD, USA, July 12-17, 2015. pp. 327–337. ACM (2015). https://doi.org/10.1145/2771783.2771785

43. Leroy, X.: Formal verification of a realistic compiler. Commun. ACM **52**(7), 107–115 (2009). https://doi.org/10.1145/1538788.1538814

44. Lin, S.W.: KSolidity semantics (2018), https://github.com/kframework/solidity-semantics

45. McKeeman, W.M.: Differential testing for software. Digital Technical Journal **10**(1), 100–107 (1998), http://www.hpl.hp.com/hpjournal/dtj/vol10num1/vol10num1art9.pdf

46. Nguyen, D.T., Pham, L.H., Sun, J., Lin, Y., Tran, M.Q.: sFuzz: An efficient adaptive fuzzer for solidity smart contracts. In: Proceedings of the 42nd International Conference on Software Engineering, ICSE 2020. IEEE / ACM (2020)

47. Park, D., Stefanescu, A., Rosu, G.: KJS: a complete formal semantics of javascript. In: Grove, D., Blackburn, S. (eds.) Proceedings of the 36th ACM SIGPLAN Conference on Programming Language Design and Implementation, Portland, OR, USA, June 15-17, 2015. pp. 346–356. ACM (2015). https://doi.org/10.1145/2737924.2737991, https://doi.org/10.1145/2737924.2737991

48. Prechtel, D., Groß, T., Müller, T.: Evaluating spread of 'gasless send' in ethereum smart contracts. In: 10th IFIP International Conference on New Technologies, Mobility and Security, NTMS 2019, Canary Islands, Spain, June 24-26, 2019. pp. 1–6. IEEE (2019). https://doi.org/10.1109/NTMS.2019.8763848

49. Purdom, P.: A sentence generator for testing parsers. BIT Numerical Mathematics **12**(3), 366–375 (1972)

50. Rosu, G., Serbanuta, T.: An overview of the K semantic framework. J. Log. Algebr. Program. **79**(6), 397–434 (2010). https://doi.org/10.1016/j.jlap.2010.03.012

51. Sewell, P., Nardelli, F.Z., Owens, S., Peskine, G., Ridge, T., Sarkar, S., Strnisa, R.: Ott: Effective tool support for the working semanticist. J. Funct. Program. **20**(1), 71–122 (2010). https://doi.org/10.1017/S0956796809990293

52. Sheridan, F.: Practical testing of a C99 compiler using output comparison. Softw., Pract. Exper. **37**(14), 1475–1488 (2007). https://doi.org/10.1002/spe.812

53. Su, Z., Sun, C.: Emi-based compiler testing (2018), `https://web.cs.ucdavis.edu/~su/emi-project`

54. Sun, C., Le, V., Su, Z.: Finding and analyzing compiler warning defects. In: Proceedings of the 38th International Conference on Software Engineering, ICSE 2016, Austin, TX, USA, May 14-22, 2016. pp. 203–213. ACM (2016). https://doi.org/10.1145/2884781.2884879

55. Sun, C., Le, V., Su, Z.: Finding compiler bugs via live code mutation. In: Proceedings of the 2016 ACM SIGPLAN International Conference on Object-Oriented Programming, Systems, Languages, and Applications, OOPSLA 2016, part of SPLASH 2016, Amsterdam, The Netherlands, October 30 - November 4, 2016. pp. 849–863. ACM (2016). https://doi.org/10.1145/2983990.2984038

56. Tang, Y., Ren, Z., Kong, W., Jiang, H.: Compiler testing: A systematic literature analysis. CoRR **abs/1810.02718** (2018), `http://arxiv.org/abs/1810.02718`

57. Tao, Q., Wu, W., Zhao, C., Shen, W.: An automatic testing approach for compiler based on metamorphic testing technique. In: 17th Asia Pacific Software Engineering Conference, APSEC 2010, Sydney, Australia, November 30 - December 3, 2010. pp. 270–279. IEEE Computer Society (2010). https://doi.org/10.1109/APSEC.2010.39

58. Tip, F.: A survey of program slicing techniques. J. Prog. Lang. **3**(3) (1995), `http://compscinet.dcs.kcl.ac.uk/JP/jp030301.abs.html`

59. Wang, C., Kang, S.: ADFL: an improved algorithm for american fuzzy lop in fuzz testing. In: Cloud Computing and Security - 4th International Conference, ICCCS 2018, Haikou, China, June 8-10, 2018, Revised Selected Papers, Part V. Lecture Notes in Computer Science, vol. 11067, pp. 27–36. Springer (2018). https://doi.org/10.1007/978-3-030-00018-9_3

60. Yang, X., Chen, Y., Eide, E., Regehr, J.: Finding and understanding bugs in C compilers. In: Proceedings of the 32nd ACM SIGPLAN Conference on Programming Language Design and Implementation, PLDI 2011, San Jose, CA, USA, June 4-8, 2011. pp. 283–294. ACM (2011). https://doi.org/10.1145/1993498.1993532

61. Zelenov, S.V., Zelenova, S.A.: Automated generation of positive and negative tests for parsers. In: Formal Approaches to Software Testing, 5th International Workshop, FATES 2005, Edinburgh, UK, July 11, 2005, Revised Selected Papers. Lecture Notes in Computer Science, vol. 3997, pp. 187–202. Springer (2005). https://doi.org/10.1007/11759744_13

62. Zeller, A., Hildebrandt, R.: Simplifying and isolating failure-inducing input. IEEE Trans. Software Eng. **28**(2), 183–200 (2002). https://doi.org/10.1109/32.988498

PASTA: An Efficient Proactive Adaptation Approach Based on Statistical Model Checking for Self-Adaptive Systems

Yong-Jun Shin[(✉)] [iD], Eunho Cho [iD], and Doo-Hwan Bae [iD]

Korea Advanced Institute of Science and Technology (KAIST)
Deajeon, Republic of Korea
{yjshin, ehcho, bae}@se.kaist.ac.kr

Abstract. Proactive adaptation, in which the adaptation for a system's reliable goal achievement is performed by predicting changes in the environment, is considered as an effective alternative to reactive adaptation, in which adaptation is performed after observing changes. When predicting the environmental changes, the prediction may be uncertain, so it is necessary to verify and confirm an adaptation's consequences before execution. To resolve the uncertainty, probabilistic model checking (PMC) has been utilized for verification of adaptation tactics' effects on the goal of a self-adaptive system (SAS). However, PMC-based approaches have limitations on the state-explosion problem of complex SAS model verification and the modeling languages supported by the model checkers. In this paper, to overcome the limitations of the PMC-based approaches, we propose an efficient Proactive Adaptation approach based on STAtistical model checking (PASTA). Our approach allows SASs to mitigate the uncertainty of the future environment, faster than the PMC-based approach, by producing statistically sufficient samples for verification of adaptation tactics based on statistical model checking (SMC) algorithms. We provide algorithmic processes, a reference architecture, and an open-source implementation skeleton of PASTA for engineers to apply it for SAS development. We evaluate PASTA on two SASs using actual data and show that PASTA is efficient comparing to the PMC-based approach. We also provide a comparative analysis of the advantages and disadvantages of PMC- and SMC-based proactive adaptation to guide engineers' decision-making for SAS development.

Keywords: Self-adaptive system · Proactive adaptation · Statistical model checking · Environmental uncertainty

1 Introduction

As the complexity of an environment that affects a system's goal achievement increases, analyzing the environment becomes important for reliable goal achievement. The environment, such as user traffic and outdoor temperatures, can change over time [15,29]. Full anticipation of environmental changes at the system design time is challenging and often impossible [6,9]. Systems are required

© The Author(s) 2021
E. Guerra and M. Stoelinga (Eds.): FASE 2021, LNCS 12649, pp. 292–312, 2021.
https://doi.org/10.1007/978-3-030-71500-7_15

to be self-adaptive so that they change their behaviors and structures according to the environmental changes at runtime. To realize this, numerous design approaches [11,13,14,16] have been proposed based on the MAPE feedback loop [18]. These adaptation processes involve the continual monitoring and analysis of the environment as well as the planning and execution of the adaptation.

For most existing approaches, adaptation has been reactively triggered by system failures or changes in the environment [12,31,33]. Other adaptation approaches, known as proactive or predictive adaptation, have emerged, which have proven to be more effective than reactive adaptations in a changing environment by predicting changes in advance [2,24,26]; however, the prediction of environmental changes is uncertain, so the uncertainty affects the consequences of proactive adaptation. To resolve the uncertainty, probabilistic model checking (PMC) was utilized in some studies for the verification of adaptation tactics and their effects on the system's adaptation goal [5,26,27,28].

PMC-based approaches are a major method used for proactive adaptation; however, PMC may be not appropriate for the verification of large and complex self-adaptive system (SAS) models due to the state explosion problem. PMC requires a high verification cost in time and memory to fully examine the given probabilistic models, so the verification of complex SAS models and adaptation tactics may fail due to time and memory constraints. In addition, modeling languages supported by probabilistic model checkers must be used for the modeling of the SAS and the environment. Engineers must be familiar with modeling languages, such as Markov chains, Markov decision processes, or automata, that model checkers can interpret [21]. To overcome the limitations, we propose an efficient proactive adaptation approach based on statistical model checking (SMC) that consumes a smaller verification resource than PMC and only requires simulation results of system models without limiting languages.

Our Proactive Adaptation approach based on STAtistical model checking (PASTA) offers the following contributions:

- We propose a proactive adaptation approach utilizing SMC to eliminate the uncertainty of the future environment faster than PMC for the verification of adaptation tactics.
- We provide algorithmic processes, a reference architecture, and an open-source implementation skeleton of PASTA for developers who will apply PASTA to SAS development.
- Based on evaluations using actual data, we also provide a comparative analysis of the advantages and disadvantages of PMC- and SMC-based proactive adaptation to guide engineers' decision making.

The remainder of this paper is organized as follows. Section 2 introduces related work of proactive adaptation. Section 3 provides the background knowledge of SMC. Section 4 presents an illustrative example. Section 5 introduces our PASTA approach. Section 6 evaluates PASTA based on two SASs with actual data. Section 7 reveals the threats and validity of our work. Section 8 concludes the paper.

2   Related Work: Proactive Adaptation

Numerous studies on proactive or predictive adaptation have been conducted to address issues related to changing environments [3,20,24,25]. As opposed to reacting to changes in the environment or system, predicting and responding to the predicted situations could be more difficult but more effective in preventing system failures and meeting requirements. Many case studies on proactive adaptation have been conducted, and it has been demonstrated that proactive adaptation outperforms reactive adaptation in terms of the system's adaptation goal [2,10,20]. For proactive adaptation, the prediction of the future environment is uncertain, so approaches utilizing probabilistic model checking (PMC), which verifies the property satisfaction of probabilistic model, have been proposed to provide verified and trustworthy proactive adaptation results [5,26,27,28]. The main process of PMC-based proactive adaptation is illustrated in Fig. 1. Core of the process are the formal modeling of the future environment, system, and adaptation tactics, and the verification of the models to identify an optimal adaptation tactic for adaptation goal achievement. However, PMC is not appropriate for the verification of large and complex models due to its state explosion problem. It requires exhaustively examining all possible states of SAS models to verify adaptation tactics. It also requires engineers to develop SAS models written in modeling languages that model checkers can support. To tackle the limitations, as an alternative to PMC-based approaches, which have been the major trend of proactive adaptation, in this paper, we propose a statistical model checking (SMC)-based proactive adaptation approach [19,23,34].

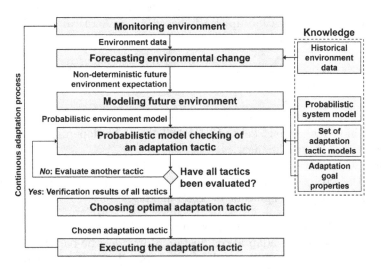

Fig. 1. PMC-based proactive adaptation process

3   Background: Statistical Model Checking (SMC)

We have utilized statistical model checking (SMC) to verify adaptation tactics at runtime under an uncertain environment. SMC is an efficient technique for verifying a stochastic model [22,23]. Although PMC exhaustively examines the model, SMC simulates the model to obtain samples and provides statistical evidence of the satisfaction or violation of the given property using hypothesis testing for the samples. In fact, SMC requires only a set of simulation results, so it can be applied to an executable black-box model or to only a set of simulation results. The fact that the verification results depend on the quality of the model is the same as PMC. However, as it is a simulation-based approach, it is known to be an efficient alternative to PMC in terms of time and memory, performing verification with a certain confidence [1,19]. In this regard, SMC can be used effectively for the runtime verification of SAS adaptation tactics with uncertain environments. The following examples of SMC algorithms are widely used:

- *Simple Monte Carlo Simulation (SMCS).* This is the simplest and most intuitive SMC algorithm [1,4]. It estimates the quantitative satisfaction of a property according to the ratio of samples that satisfy the property in the overall samples. It requires a fixed number of samples from the user.
- *Single Sampling Plan (SSP).* The SSP [34] tests a hypothesis $H : p \geq \theta$ with fixed-size samples, where p is the probability that a system meets a given property and θ is the verification threshold of p. The user provides two error bounds α ($0 \leq \alpha \leq 1$) and β ($0 \leq \beta \leq 1$) of false negatives and false positives, respectively. Within the given error bounds, the SSP estimates p to accept or to reject H. The detailed algorithm can be found in [19,23,34].
- *Sequential Probability Ratio Test (SPRT).* Similar to the SSP, the SPRT [32] tests a hypothesis H within the given error bounds, but the number of samples is determined automatically. It simulates the target system to obtain a sample, and iterates the simulations to generate sufficient samples until it can accept or reject H within a given error bound. The detailed algorithm can be found in [19,23,34].

For the PASTA approach, an SMC algorithm is selected and used to obtain statistical evidence of an adaptation tactic's performance in a future environment to evaluate possible tactics and to identify the optimal tactic at runtime.

4   Illustrative Example

We illustrate PASTA using an adaptive air condition control system as an example. The system monitors indoor and outdoor air conditions, including temperature and humidity, and adaptively controls the indoor condition for a given target condition. Planning an adaptive air condition control with an immediate reaction to the monitored indoor condition can aid the system in achieving its goal; however, the indoor air conditions may change over time due to the influence of the outdoor air conditions, as shown in Fig. 2. If the adaptation plan is made without taking the environmental change into account, the adaptation consequences may differ from the expectations, and thus there could have been a better adaptation tactic that was not chosen. The air condition control system developed by the PASTA approach forecasts future air condition changes and selects an optimal adaptation tactic whose adaptation consequences are verified by SMC at runtime. Throughout this paper, we will describe our approach using this example.

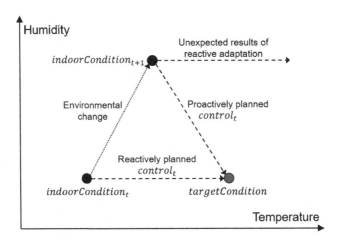

Fig. 2. Adaptive air condition control system

5   Proactive Adaptation Based on Statistical Model Checking

5.1   PASTA overview

We propose the PASTA approach, which is a proactive adaptation, using SMC. Fig. 3 presents the overall adaptation process. The aim of the approach is to provide efficient proactive adaptation based on the prediction of environmental changes and the verification of the adaptation tactics of the SAS. (Step 1) Initially, PASTA continuously monitors the environment to capture its change at runtime. (Step 2) It analyzes the monitored (historical) environment data and forecasts future environmental changes based on its forecasting algorithm. The prediction or expectation of the future environment is in the form of nondeterministic possibility, such as the probability density function of future environmental conditions. (Step 3) Based on the prediction, a sample of the possible future environment is made and given to the simulation engine as a simulation environment. (Step 4) In the given environment, an adaptation tactic is applied to the system model and simulated to make a sample evaluation of the tactic's performance. The simulations are repeated until the system obtains the statistically sufficient number of samples for the verification of the tactic's performance for the adaptation goal in the expected future environmental change. (Step 5) Based on the accumulated samples, the performance of an adaptation tactic is verified. All adaptation tactics are evaluated repeatedly in the same manner, and the SAS statistically guarantees the effects of its adaptation tactics. (Step 6 and 7) When all possible adaptation tactics have been evaluated, an optimal adaptation tactic is chosen and executed. This adaptation process is continuously repeated to respond to continuous environmental changes. We describe the PASTA approach in detail based on this adaptation process in the subsequent sections.

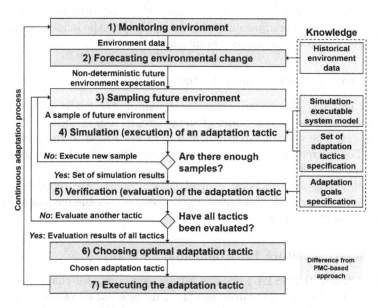

Fig. 3. Overall PASTA process

5.2   Knowledge

Principle. The PASTA approach requires an SAS to accumulate the monitored environment data. The accumulated historical environment data is analyzed to predict environmental changes. Furthermore, the system has its current system model that is an abstraction of the system behavior executable by a simulator. The model in PASTA is user-specific, and although the modeling language and system information to be modeled are selected by the engineer, the only requirement is that the model is executable to generate simulation logs. The system model also contains a finite set (space) of possible adaptation tactics that will be verified. An adaptation tactic is a specification of an adaptation that can be applied to the SAS and its model, such as a set of configurations. The adaptation goal is also specified in the knowledge. Thus, the optimal tactic for the adaptation goals will be selected and executed.

Example. The environmental factors of interest in the adaptive air condition control system are the indoor/outdoor temperature and humidity; therefore, the monitored environment data at a specific time include values of four factors. The simulation models imitate the changes of the indoor temperature and humidity affected by outdoor conditions and the air condition control system's control values. The system's possible adaptation tactics are defined by the system capabilities of each temperature and humidity control capability. For example, the system can increase or decrease the temperature and humidity in $0.1°C$ and 0.1% increments up to $5°C$ and 5%, respectively, in a discrete simulation time unit. The tactic space is a Cartesian product of the possible temperature and humidity controls. The adaptation goal is to manipulate the indoor temperature and humidity to the user's desired conditions.

5.3   Monitoring Environmental Changes

Principle. (Step 1) The system constantly monitors the environment. The environment is measured as the values of the environmental conditions observable by the sensors. The current environmental data are added to the environment database. The current state of the system is also monitored, and the system model is kept up to date.

Example. The air condition control system constantly monitors the indoor/outdoor temperature and humidity. It accumulates the environment data in its environment database.

5.4   Forecasting Future Environmental Change

Principle. (Step 2) PASTA forecasts future environmental changes based on the accumulated historical environment data using a data analysis or forecasting techniques. As the given historical environmental data consist of time-series data, a time-series analysis and forecasting methods, such as random walk [30], errortrend-seasonal [17], autoregressive integrated moving average model [7], or any machine-learning techniques, can be applied, and the choice of the forecasting methods depends on domain engineers. What is important here is that the predictions of future environmental changes based on historical data are uncertain, so the results of the forecasting are non-deterministic expectations, such as the probability density function of future environmental conditions. This uncertainty will be resolved by SMC.

Example. The system predicts the outdoor temperature and humidity changes, which exhibit distinct repetitive patterns (seasonality) at 24-hour intervals. As the environmental data of this system exhibit distinct seasonality, they can be predicted naively with a random walk model using seasonal differencing [17]. Based on the historical temperature data and the forecasting algorithm, the temperature change from the present to a few hours later can be predicted using the probability density function. For example, if the current temperature at 2 p.m. is $24°C$, the temperature at 3 p.m. can be expected to change according to the uniform distribution between $24°C$ and $30°C$.

5.5 Planning Adaptation Using SMC

Algorithm 1: PASTA adaptation planning

Input : *envPrediction, sysModel, tacticSpace, goalProp*
Output: *optimalTactic*
Procedure

    evaluationSheet = [];
    foreach *tactic* **in** *tacticSpace* **do**
        simulationResultList = [];
        while *!***samplesSufficient**() **do**
            *envSample = ***makeSample***(envPrediction);*
            *simResult = ***simulate***(envSample, sysModel, tactic);*
            addElement(*simulationResultList, simResult*);
        end
        *evaluationResult = ***verify***(simulationResultList, goalProp);*
        addElement(*evaluationSheet, (tactic, evaluationResult)*);
    end
    *optimalTactic = ***getOptimalTactic***(evaluationSheet);*
end

Principle. The adaptation planning of the PASTA approach involves searching for the optimal tactic among possible adaptation tactics using SMC, as shown in Algorithm 1. Evaluating an adaptation tactic using SMC consists of three steps: sampling environmental changes, simulating adaptation tactics, and verifying the simulation results. (Step 3) The forecasting result is non-deterministic, so the sample generator produces a deterministic sample of possible future environmental conditions based on the forecasting result. SMC eliminates the uncertainty of the nondeterministic future environment by producing statistically sufficient samples, while PMC probabilistically verifies a stochastic model. The number of samples is determined depending on the SMC algorithms, as explained in the background section. (Step 4) The simulator takes the sample environment, the system model, and an adaptation tactic as inputs. It applies the given tactic to the system model, simulates the system in the sample of the future environment, and returns a simulation result logs that represents the effects of the adaptation tactic in the future environment. (Step 5) The verifier receives the numerous simulation results and evaluates the tactic's performance for the adaptation goal represented as a verification property. This process is performed for all adaptation tactics, and (Step 6) the optimal tactic is selected based on all evaluation (verification) results. Therefore, the planning time required for an adaptation depends on the number of tactics, the number of required samples, and the time for a single simulation of the model.

Example. Based on the predicted range of the temperature change at 3 p.m. ($24°C \sim 30°C$), the samples of the future outdoor temperature (for example, $25°C$, $27°C$, and $29°C$) are randomly selected by an SMC algorithm. The system model and an adaptation tactic (for example, lower the indoor temperature by $3°C$) under the current evaluation are simulated with the sample environments, respectively. Based on the simulation results, the verifier evaluates the adaptation results of the indoor temperature control. In this example, the average distance between the target condition and the current condition is used as a verification property representing an adaptation goal, but the maximum distance indicating the worst case, the presence or absence of events occurring with small probabilities, or any temporal logic can be used as verification properties [19,23,34]. When all possible temperature and humidity control tactics are verified (evaluated), the optimal one is selected.

5.6   Executing Adaptation

Principle. (Step 7) The chosen optimal adaptation tactic is applied to the managed system by the actuators of the system.

Example. The adaptive air control system operates the selected optimal temperature and humidity control. The controls affect the indoor conditions through the system's actuators.

5.7   PASTA Implementation

We also provide a PASTA reference architecture in Fig. 4 for the implementation of this approach. It is a layered architecture of an SAS with the PASTA approach. In the interaction layer, PASTA monitors the environment and managed system through the sensor and affects them through the actuators, like typical SASs. In the data analysis layer, there is a forecasting engine for the prediction of environmental changes and a knowledge management module for keeping the knowledge of the system up-to-date at all times. In the adaptation planner layer, a module searches for the optimal adaptation tactic through interactions with the adaptation verification layer. In the adaptation verification layer, the SMC module verifies an adaptation tactic governing the sample generator, the simulator, and the verifier.

The sample generator produces samples of the future environment based on the prediction of the forecasting engine. The simulator simulates the system model with an adaptation tactic in the given sample future environment. The verifier analyzes the simulation results to check the adaptation goal achievement, such as quality of service or invariant properties. In the knowledge layer, there is an environment database, a system model manager, an adaptation tactic repository, and an adaptation goal manager. This layer interacts with the others, providing and updating the knowledge of the SAS. This architecture is a reference, so it includes the essential components of an SAS with the PASTA approach and can be extended.

Fig. 4. PASTA reference architecture

In addition, to support engineers who develop SASs based on the PASTA approach, which was explained in the previous sections, we implemented a PASTA skeleton based on the reference architecture with guiding comments and released the source code on an open-source repository[1]. The skeleton is available in Java and Python. Engineers should write application-specific codes following comments tagged with *"todo"*. The class diagram of the skeleton is presented in Fig. 5. An adaptation is activated by the *"adaptManagedSystem"* operator. It promotes easier PASTA implementation, allowing for the utilization of third-party libraries or tools for some components, such as the forecasting engine or the SMC module.

6 Evaluation

6.1 Research Questions

We demonstrate the feasibility of applying the PASTA approach as one efficient alternative to PMC-based proactive adaptation to SAS development. There are three research questions addressed.

RQ1: (Cost efficiency of PASTA) How fast is PASTA's adaptation planning? PASTA leverages SMC for efficient adaptation verification at runtime. Although almost all existing proactive adaptation approaches utilize PMC for the runtime verification of adaptation tactics, the PASTA approach is one of the most efficient alternatives to PMC-based proactive adaptation approaches. To determine the efficiency of PASTA, we compare the application planning time of PASTA and the PMC-based adaptation. We confirm the differences in time consumption between SMC- and PMC-based approaches in solving proactive adaptation problems of the same complexities.

RQ2: (Adaptation planning accuracy of PASTA) How accurately does PASTA search for the optimal adaptation tactic? PMC formally examines a probabilistic model and verifies whether it satisfies the given properties; however, SMC examines the given model with numerous sample simulation

---

[1] https://github.com/yongjunshin/PASTA

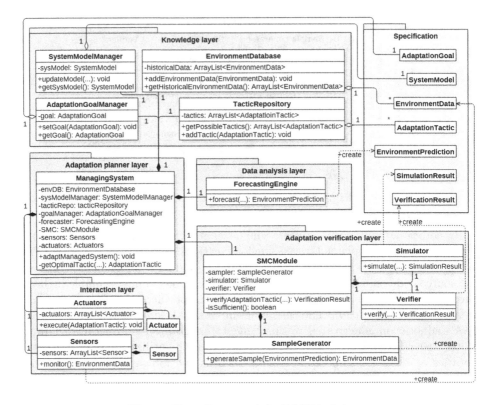

Fig. 5. Class diagram of the PASTA skeleton

results, so it returns the statistical evidence of the model's properties and thus has the inevitable limitation that it can return inaccurate verification results limited to the finite number of samples. It is known that SMC can produce results similar to PMC [19,23,34], and for this research question, we compare the similar proactive adaptation planning results of PASTA with the planning results of the PMC-based approach. We determine how much accuracy has been lost by the cost savings identified in RQ1 as well as whether the loss of accuracy is acceptable.

RQ3: (Adaptation performance of PASTA) How effective is the adaptation goal achievement performance of PASTA? For research question 3, we examine whether the PASTA approach is actually effective in achieving the adaptation goals of SASs. To evaluate the adaptation performance of PASTA, we compare the simulation execution results of approaches taking no adaptation, reactive adaptation, PMC-based proactive adaptation, and PASTA.

6.2   Evaluation Setup

We evaluate the PASTA approach using two example SASs. One is the adaptive air condition control system, the illustrative example of this paper, and the

Traffic Signal Pattern						
Duration	d_1	d_2	d_3	d_4	d_5	d_6
Rule: $d_i \geq 0, \sum d_i = 12$			**Tactic Space Size:** $\frac{17!}{5!} = 6{,}188$			

Fig. 6. Adaptation tactic of traffic signal controller

other is an adaptive traffic signal controller of an intersection. The flow of cars in cities changes with the passage of time, which causes traffic congestion. A smart traffic signal controller that automatically controls traffic flow is a good example of applying proactive adaptation because changes in traffic conditions can be predicted based on historical data. Our signal controller predicts the traffic volume in an intersection and identifies an optimal configuration of signal patterns that minimizes the number of waiting vehicles. An actual signal controller is abstracted, and durations of signal patterns are dynamically controlled, as shown in Fig. 6. We applied PASTA to the two cases of different complexities and simulated them based on actual data acquired from public data repositories to make them realistic. Detailed descriptions of the two SASs and the evaluation setup are provided in Table 1.

We compared the adaptation cost, accuracy, and performance of the PASTA approach with the PMC-based proactive adaptation approach. The PMC-based proactive adaptation approach was implemented following a pioneering paper [26]. PRISM, a widely used probabilistic model checker, was utilized in the implementation [21]. We used default hybrid computation engine. The models of environments, systems, and tactics were specified in Markov decision processes (MDPs), and the adaptation goals were specified in the reward-based properties of the MDPs. As in paper [26], the following environmental changes have been predicted based on the data, and the PRISM modules have been constructed and verified based on the prediction. Thus, the optimal adaptation tactic has been found. In addition to the PMC-based approach, non-adaption and reactive adaptation approaches were also compared in terms of a system's goal achievement. For the PASTA approach, SMCS, the naivest SMC algorithm as explained in the background section, was implemented and evaluated by varying the number of samples used for the verification from 10 to 10000 (10, 100, 1000, 2000, ..., 9000, 10000).

6.3 Evaluation Results

RQ1: We measured and compared the time spent on adaptation planning for both case systems using the PASTA and PMC-based approaches. The adaptation planning time includes modeling or sampling time and probabilistic or statistical verification time to identify the optimal tactic. Figs. 7 and 8 show the

Table 1. SASs for evaluation

	Adaptive air condition control system	Adaptive traffic signal controller
Environment	Temperature and humidity condition	Car inflow to an intersection
Environment complexity	2 environmental factors (temperature, humidity)	12 environmental factors (the number of car inflow from 4 source roads to other 3 destination roads: 12 directions)
Source of real environmental data	Open weather data portal of - South Korea (https://data.kma. go.kr) - 2018 hourly weather data of Seoul	Open traffic data of Daegu, South Korea (https://car.daegu.go.kr) - 2018 Daily&Hourly Traffic data of an intersection in Daegu
System	Indoor air condition controller	Traffic signal controller
System model	Model of changing indoor temperature and humidity affected by environment conditions and the system's control	Model of changing the number of waiting cars in the intersection affected by car inflow and traffic signals
Sensors	Temperature sensor, humidity sensor	Traffic flow sensors for each 12 directions
Actuators	Temperature control actuator, humidity control actuator	Traffic lights
Adaptation tactic	Temperature control value, humidity control value	Configuration of traffic signal pattern duration
Size of the adaptation tactic space	101 possible control values for each temperature and humidity by the system capability (-5, -4.9, ... +4.9, +5 ($^{\circ}C$, %))	6,188 possible configurations of traffic signal pattern duration (Fig. 6)
Adaptation cycle	1 hour	1 hour
Adaptation goal	Target air condition (25, 50) - following ASHRAE comfort zone [8]	Minimizing the number of waiting cars
Tactic evaluation criteria	Average difference between controlled indoor condition and target condition	Average of the number of waiting cars
Forecasting method	Random walk model with seasonal differencing [30]	Polynomial regression

evaluation results for each system. The reported planning time is the average of 100 repeated experiments. The adaptation planning time for the PMC-based approach is constant, but the time for PASTA increases in proportion to the number of samples used for the SMC because the time for a single simulation is almost constant. Unfortunately, the traffic signal controller was not able to obtain adaptation planning results using PMC with a 2G memory because its models and tactics were more complex than the air condition control system so consume larger verification resource. Therefore, for the traffic signal controller,

Fig. 7. Adaptation planning cost - Air condition control system

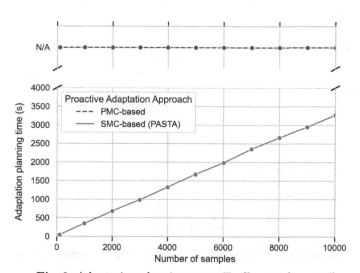

Fig. 8. Adaptation planning cost - Traffic signal controller

the adaptation planning time for the PMC-based approach was not assigned; however, both systems confirmed that PASTA would complete adaptation planning much faster than the PMC-based approach. It was also confirmed that the adaptation planning time of PASTA is proportional to the number of samples and the complexity of the adaptation problem.

RQ2: To confirm the similarity of the optimal tactics that the PASTA and PMC-based approaches found, we compared the optimal tactics returned by the PASTA and PMC-based approaches in the same situation. To quantify the similarity, we defined two criteria. If the two tactics were the same, they were defined as *identical*, and if they were adjacent in terms of the tactic specifications, they were defined as *similar*. For example, for the air condition control system, temperature control tactics $+3°C$ and $+3.1°C$ were adjacent because the temperature control unit is 0.1C based on the system's capability, and the probability that arbitrarily two tactics are adjacent is less than 2%. Because the samples used by SMC are randomly generated, we repeated the PASTA experiments 100 times and report the percentage of identical or similar tactics compared to the tactic returned by the PMC-based approach. Because the traffic signal controller could not find the optimal tactic utilizing PMC, only the experimental results of the air condition controller are shown in Fig. 9. We could see that PASTA always found the same or similar optimal tactic as the PMC-based approach except when using 10 samples; however, one limitation of utilizing SMC is that regardless of how many samples we increased, we could not always obtain the same results as the PMC-based approach's results, which is considered an oracle. This case system returned accurate results at approximately 50% on average.

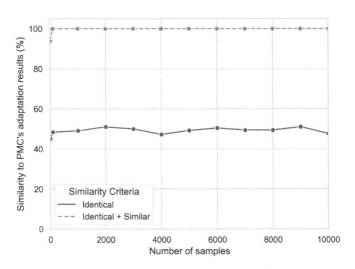

Fig. 9. Adaptation planning accuracy - Air condition control system

RQ3: For RQ1 and RQ2, we showed that PASTA can quickly find a suboptimal adaptation tactic that is similar to the PMC-based approach's result. For RQ3, we obtained simulation results to confirm the adaptation performance of the PASTA approach in comparison with non-adaptation, reactive adaptation, and PMC-based proactive adaptation. As shown in Fig. 10, the goal of the air condition control system was to keep the temperature at $25°C$, and proactive adaptation approaches showed a better adaptation performance than other strategies. In addition, the PASTA and PMC-based approaches exhibited a similar performance because PASTA has always made similar adaptation decisions to

Fig. 10. Adaptation performance - Air condition control system

Fig. 11. Adaptation performance - Traffic signal controller

the PMC-based approach. In Fig. 11, the goal of the traffic signal controller was
to reduce the number of vehicles waiting at the intersection as much as possible,
and proactive adaptation using PASTA showed the best performance. These two
results demonstrate that proactive adaptation outperforms reactive adaptation
and PASTA shows similar adaptation performance to the PMC-based approach
with smaller verification cost.

Table 2. Comparison of proactive adaptation approaches

	PMC-based approach	SMC-based approach (PASTA)
Adaptation cost	Forecasting time	Forecasting time
	Modeling time (relatively high)	Sampling time (relatively low)
	Probabilistic verification time (relatively high)	Statistical verification (Simulation + hypothesis testing) time (relatively low)
Adaptation accuracy and performance	Regarded as an oracle (high, limited to the quality of the models)	Provides similar adaptation results to PMC-based adaptation (relatively low, limited to the quality of the samples and models)
Pros	The optimal adaptation tactic can be found.	A sub-optimal adaptation tactic can be found with a lower adaptation cost. If the model can be simulated, it is not limited to a particular modeling language.
Cons	High adaptation cost is required. Modelling language is dependent on the model checker.	The adaptation result is not fully trustworthy.
Proper application	Safety-critical system	Real-time system

We compared two approaches of proactive adaptation: PMC-based and SMC-based (PASTA) approaches. As we confirmed in our evaluation, the two approaches have their own advantages and disadvantages, so engineers should carefully decide which to choose for their SAS development. We summarized our insights regarding their characteristics in Table 2 to guide engineers' decision making. As we emphasized, the SMC-based approach makes adaptation decisions, verifying a system's adaptation tactics faster than the PMC-based approach. In addition, if it is possible to generate simulation results from the given models, the modeling language is not limited to the model checker; however, it is indubitable that an adaptation decision made by the SMC-based approach may not be globally optimal. Therefore, the SMC-based approach may not be suitable for some safety-critical systems, and the PMC-based approach could be the better choice if the trustworthiness of the system is the most important concern. For SASs requiring a lower adaptation cost, such as real-time systems, PASTA is more appropriate than the PMC-based approach.

7 Threats to Validity

One threat is the selection of the SMC algorithm. We selected SMCS to demonstrate the adaptation performance when selecting the simplest SMC algorithm. SMCS is suitable for explicitly indicating SMC-based adaptation costs affected by the number of samples, and all other SMC algorithms have similar characteristics. To reduce this threat, we also implemented SSP and SPRT and compared them to the PMC-based approach, and both showed similar cost, accuracy, and performance differences. Therefore, for this paper, only SMCS was selected and explained by varying the number of samples.

Another threat is the implementation of the PMC-based adaptation approach. We implemented the PMC-based approach directly following paper [26]. This threat was reduced because the authors published all the structures and codes of the PRISM module for the implementation of the approach. We implemented two case systems according to the PRISM module code shown in the paper. For a fair comparison, environment, system, and adaptation tactic spaces of the same complexities were given to both the PMC-based and PASTA approach.

8 Conclusion

We have proposed PASTA, a proactive adaptation approach using SMC, that is one efficient alternative to PMC-based proactive adaptation. We applied the PASTA approach to two realistic SASs. Through experiments based on actual data, we confirmed that PASTA would make an adaptation decision similar to the PMC-based proactive application approach in a shorter time. We then confirmed that the adaptation decision is more effective in achieving the system's goals than non-adaptation, reactive adaptation, and the PMC-based approach. Currently, PMC-based approaches are considered the major trend in proactive adaptation, but in this paper, we showed that the SMC-based proactive adaptation approach can be an efficient alternative. In addition, the algorithmic processes, reference architecture, and open-source skeleton of PASTA proposed in this paper will be of substantial help to developers who wish to apply PASTA to SAS development. This study was primarily conducted to validate the PASTA approach, but in the future, we plan to study methods such as effective sampling and adaptation space reduction for a more effective PASTA approach, and we also plan to apply PASTA to actual running systems.

Acknowledgement

This research is partly supported by the MSIT(Ministry of Science and ICT), Korea, under the ITRC(Information Technology Research Center) support program (IITP-2020-2020-0-01795) supervised by the IITP(Institute of Information & Communications Technology Planning & Evaluation). This research is partly supported by IITP grant funded by MSIT (No. 2015-0-00250, (SW Star-Lab) Software R&D for Model-based Analysis and Verification of Higher-order Large Complex System). This research is partly supported by Next-Generation Information Computing Development Program through the National Research Foundation of Korea(NRF) funded by MSIT (2017M3C4A7066212).

References

1. Aichernig, B.K., Schumi, R.: Statistical model checking meets property-based testing. In: 2017 IEEE International Conference on Software Testing, Verification and Validation (ICST). pp. 390–400. IEEE (2017)
2. Anaya, I.D.P., Simko, V., Bourcier, J., Plouzeau, N., Jézéquel, J.M.: A prediction-driven adaptation approach for self-adaptive sensor networks. In: Proceedings of the 9th International Symposium on Software Engineering for Adaptive and Self-Managing Systems. pp. 145–154. ACM (2014)
3. Angelopoulos, K., Papadopoulos, A.V., Silva Souza, V.E., Mylopoulos, J.: Model predictive control for software systems with cobra. In: Proceedings of the 11th international symposium on software engineering for adaptive and self-managing systems. pp. 35–46. ACM (2016)
4. Boyer, B., Corre, K., Legay, A., Sedwards, S.: Plasma-lab: A flexible, distributable statistical model checking library. In: International Conference on Quantitative Evaluation of Systems. pp. 160–164. Springer (2013)
5. Calinescu, R., Ghezzi, C., Kwiatkowska, M., Mirandola, R.: Self-adaptive software needs quantitative verification at runtime. Communications of the ACM **55**(9), 69–77 (2012)
6. Cheng, B.H., de Lemos, R., Giese, H., Inverardi, P., Magee, J., Andersson, J., Becker, B., Bencomo, N., Brun, Y., Cukic, B., et al.: Software engineering for self-adaptive systems: A research roadmap. In: Software engineering for self-adaptive systems, pp. 1–26. Springer (2009)
7. Dagum, E.B.: The X-II-ARIMA seasonal adjustment method. Statistics Canada, Seasonal Adjustment and Time Series Staff (1980)
8. De Dear, R.J., Brager, G.S.: Thermal comfort in naturally ventilated buildings: revisions to ashrae standard 55. Energy and buildings **34**(6), 549–561 (2002)
9. De Lemos, R., Giese, H., Müller, H.A., Shaw, M., Andersson, J., Litoiu, M., Schmerl, B., Tamura, G., Villegas, N.M., Vogel, T., et al.: Software engineering for self-adaptive systems: A second research roadmap. In: Software Engineering for Self-Adaptive Systems II, pp. 1–32. Springer (2013)
10. De Matteis, T., Mencagli, G.: Proactive elasticity and energy awareness in data stream processing. Journal of Systems and Software **127**, 302–319 (2017)
11. Elkhodary, A., Esfahani, N., Malek, S.: Fusion: a framework for engineering self-tuning self-adaptive software systems. In: Proceedings of the eighteenth ACM SIGSOFT international symposium on Foundations of software engineering. pp. 7–16. ACM (2010)
12. Fredericks, E.M., Ramirez, A.J., Cheng, B.H.: Towards run-time testing of dynamic adaptive systems. In: Proceedings of the 8th International Symposium on Software Engineering for Adaptive and Self-Managing Systems. pp. 169–174. IEEE Press (2013)
13. Garlan, D., Cheng, S.W., Huang, A.C., Schmerl, B., Steenkiste, P.: Rainbow: Architecture-based self-adaptation with reusable infrastructure. Computer **37**(10), 46–54 (2004)
14. Gerostathopoulos, I., Skoda, D., Plasil, F., Bures, T., Knauss, A.: Tuning self-adaptation in cyber-physical systems through architectural homeostasis. Journal of Systems and Software **148**, 37–55 (2019)
15. Giese, H., Bencomo, N., Pasquale, L., Ramirez, A.J., Inverardi, P., Wätzoldt, S., Clarke, S.: Living with uncertainty in the age of runtime models. In: Models@ run. time, pp. 47–100. Springer (2014)

16. Hielscher, J., Kazhamiakin, R., Metzger, A., Pistore, M.: A framework for proactive self-adaptation of service-based applications based on online testing. In: European Conference on a Service-Based Internet. pp. 122–133. Springer (2008)
17. Hyndman, R.J., Athanasopoulos, G.: Forecasting: principles and practice. OTexts (2018)
18. Kephart, J.O., Chess, D.M.: The vision of autonomic computing. Computer **36**(1), 41–50 (Jan 2003)
19. Kim, Y., Kim, M., Kim, T.H.: Statistical model checking for safety critical hybrid systems: An empirical evaluation. In: Haifa Verification Conference. pp. 162–177. Springer (2012)
20. Krupitzer, C., Pfannemüller, M., Kaddour, J., Becker, C.: Satisfy: Towards a self-learning analyzer for time series forecasting in self-improving systems. In: 2018 IEEE 3rd International Workshops on Foundations and Applications of Self* Systems (FAS* W). pp. 182–189. IEEE (2018)
21. Kwiatkowska, M., Norman, G., Parker, D.: Prism 4.0: Verification of probabilistic real-time systems. In: International conference on computer aided verification. pp. 585–591. Springer (2011)
22. Larsen, K.G., Legay, A.: Statistical model checking past, present, and future. In: International Symposium On Leveraging Applications of Formal Methods, Verification and Validation. pp. 135–142. Springer (2014)
23. Legay, A., Delahaye, B., Bensalem, S.: Statistical model checking: An overview. In: International conference on runtime verification. pp. 122–135. Springer (2010)
24. Metzger, A.: Towards accurate failure prediction for the proactive adaptation of service-oriented systems. In: Proceedings of the 8th workshop on Assurances for self-adaptive systems. pp. 18–23. ACM (2011)
25. Metzger, A., Neubauer, A., Bohn, P., Pohl, K.: Proactive process adaptation using deep learning ensembles. In: International Conference on Advanced Information Systems Engineering. pp. 547–562. Springer (2019)
26. Moreno, G.A., Cámara, J., Garlan, D., Schmerl, B.: Proactive self-adaptation under uncertainty: a probabilistic model checking approach. In: Proceedings of the 2015 10th Joint Meeting on Foundations of Software Engineering. pp. 1–12. ACM (2015)
27. Moreno, G.A., Cámara, J., Garlan, D., Schmerl, B.: Efficient decision-making under uncertainty for proactive self-adaptation. In: 2016 IEEE International Conference on Autonomic Computing (ICAC). pp. 147–156. IEEE (2016)
28. Moreno, G.A., Cámara, J., Garlan, D., Schmerl, B.: Flexible and efficient decision-making for proactive latency-aware self-adaptation. ACM Transactions on Autonomous and Adaptive Systems (TAAS) **13**(1), 3 (2018)
29. Shin, Y.J., Baek, Y.M., Jee, E., Bae, D.H.: Data-driven environment modeling for adaptive system-of-systems. In: Proceedings of the 34th ACM/SIGAPP Symposium on Applied Computing. pp. 2044–2047 (2019)
30. Spitzer, F.: Principles of random walk, vol. 34. Springer Science & Business Media (2013)
31. Sykes, D., Corapi, D., Magee, J., Kramer, J., Russo, A., Inoue, K.: Learning revised models for planning in adaptive systems. In: 2013 35th International Conference on Software Engineering (ICSE). pp. 63–71. IEEE (2013)
32. Wald, A.: Sequential tests of statistical hypotheses. The annals of mathematical statistics **16**(2), 117–186 (1945)
33. Xu, C., Yang, W., Ma, X., Cao, C.: Environment rematching: toward dependability improvement for self-adaptive applications. In: Proceedings of the 28th IEEE/ACM International Conference on Automated Software Engineering. pp. 592–597. IEEE Press (2013)

34. Younes, H.L.: Verification and planning for stochastic processes with asynchronous events. Ph.D. thesis, Carnegie Mellon University (2005)

Understanding Local Robustness of Deep Neural Networks under Natural Variations

Ziyuan Zhong⊙✉, Yuchi Tian⊙, and Baishakhi Ray⊙

Columbia University, New York, NY, USA {ziyuan.zhong,
yuchi.tian}@columbia.edu, rayb@cs.columbia.edu

Abstract. Deep Neural Networks (DNNs) are being deployed in a wide range of settings today, from safety-critical applications like autonomous driving to commercial applications involving image classifications. However, recent research has shown that DNNs can be brittle to even slight variations of the input data. Therefore, rigorous testing of DNNs has gained widespread attention.

While DNN robustness under norm-bound perturbation got significant attention over the past few years, our knowledge is still limited when natural variants of the input images come. These natural variants, e.g., a rotated or a rainy version of the original input, are especially concerning as they can occur naturally in the field without any active adversary and may lead to undesirable consequences. Thus, it is important to identify the inputs whose small variations may lead to erroneous DNN behaviors. The very few studies that looked at DNN's robustness under natural variants, however, focus on estimating the overall robustness of DNNs across all the test data rather than localizing such error-producing points. This work aims to bridge this gap.

To this end, we study the local per-input robustness properties of the DNNs and leverage those properties to build a white-box (DEEPROBUST-W) and a black-box (DEEPROBUST-B) tool to automatically identify the non-robust points. Our evaluation of these methods on three DNN models spanning three widely used image classification datasets shows that they are effective in flagging points of poor robustness. In particular, DEEPROBUST-W and DEEPROBUST-B are able to achieve an F1 score of up to 91.4% and 99.1%, respectively. We further show that DEEPROBUST-W can be applied to a regression problem in a domain beyond image classification. Our evaluation on three self-driving car models demonstrates that DEEPROBUST-W is effective in identifying points of poor robustness with F1 score up to 78.9%.

Keywords: Deep Neural Networks · Software Testing · Robustness of DNNs.

1 Introduction

Deep Neural Networks (DNNs) have achieved an unprecedented level of performance over the last decade in many sophisticated areas such as image recognition [38], self-driving cars [5] and playing complex games [65]. These advances

© The Author(s) 2021
E. Guerra and M. Stoelinga (Eds.): FASE 2021, LNCS 12649, pp. 313–337, 2021.
https://doi.org/10.1007/978-3-030-71500-7_16

(a)   0°, (b) +6°, (c) +24°, (d)   -9°, (e)   0°, (f)   +6°, (g) +24°, (h)   -9°,
bird   airplane   cat   dog   bird   bird   bird   bird

Fig. 1: **(a)-(d) A well-trained Resnet model [14] misclassifies the rotated variations of a bird image into three different classes though the original un-rotated image is classified correctly. (e)-(h) The same model successfully classifies all the rotated variants of another bird image from the same test set. The sub-captions consist of rotation degrees and the predicted classes.**

have also motivated companies to adapt their software development flows to incorporate AI components [3]. This trend has, in turn, spawned a new area of research within software engineering addressing the quality assurance of DNN components [11, 20, 32, 36, 40, 42, 55, 57, 73, 74, 91, 92].

Notwithstanding the impressive capabilities of DNNs, recent research has shown that DNNs can be easily fooled, i.e., made to mispredict, with a little variation of the input data [14, 23, 73]—either adding a norm-bound pixel-level perturbation into the original input [9, 23, 71], or with *natural* variants of the inputs, e.g., rotating an image, changing the lighting conditions, adding fog etc. [14, 52, 55]. The natural variants are especially concerning as they can occur naturally in the field without any active adversary and may lead to serious consequences [73, 92].

While norm-bound perturbation based DNN robustness is relatively well-studied, our knowledge of DNN robustness under the natural variations is still limited—we do not know which images are more robust than others, what their characteristics are, etc. For example, consider Figure 1: although the original bird image (a) is predicted correctly by a DNN, its rotated variations in images (b)-(d) are mispredicted to three different classes. This makes the original image (a) very weak as far as robustness is concerned. In contrast, the bird image (e) and all its rotated versions (generated by the same degrees of rotation) in Figure 1:(f)-(h) are correctly classified. Thus, the original image (e) is quite robust. It is important to distinguish between such robust vs. non-robust images, as the non-robust ones can induce errors with slight natural variations.

Existing literature, however, focuses on estimating the overall robustness of DNNs across all the test data [4, 14, 88]. From a traditional software point of view, this is analogous to estimating how buggy a software is without actually localizing the bugs. Our current work tries to bridge this gap by localizing the non-robust points in the input space that pose significant threats to a DNN model's robustness. However, unlike traditional software where bug localization is performed in program space, we identify the non-robust inputs in the data space. As a DNN is a combination of data and architecture, and the architecture is largely uninterpretable, we restrict our study of non-robustess to the input space. To this end, we first quantify the local (per input) robustness property of a DNN. First, we treat all the natural variants of an input image as its *neighbors*. Then, for each input data, we consider a population of its neighbors and measure the fraction of this population classified correctly by the DNN - a high fraction of correct classifications indicates good robustness (Figure 1:e) and vice versa (Figure 1:a). We term this measure *neighbor accuracy*. Using this metric, we study different local robustness properties of the DNNs and analyze how the weak, *a.k.a.* non-robust, points differ characteristically from their robust counterparts. Given that the number of natural neighbors of an image can be potentially infinite, first we performed a more controlled analysis by keeping the natural variants limited to spatially transformed images generated by rotation and translation, following the previous work [4, 14, 88]. Such controlled experiments help us to explore different robustness properties while systematically varying transformation parameters.

Our analysis with three well-known object recognition datasets across three popular DNN models, i.e., a total of nine DNN-dataset combinations, reveal several interesting properties of local robustness of a DNN *w.r.t.* natural variants:

- The neighbors of a weaker point are not necessarily classified to one single incorrect class. In fact, the weaker the point is its neighbors (mis)classifications become more diverse.
- The weak points are concentrated towards the class decision boundaries of the DNN in the feature space.

Based on these findings, we further develop two techniques (a black-box and a white-box) that can localize the points of poor robustness, thereby providing a means of, input-specific, real-time feedback about robustness to the end-user. Our white-box and black-box detectors can identify weak, *a.k.a.* non-robust, points with f1 score up to 91.4% and 99.1%, respectively, at neighbor accuracy cutoff 0.75. To further check the generalizability of our technique, we aim to detect weak points *w.r.t.* a self-driving car application where we generated natural input variants by adding rain and fog. Note that these are more complex image transformations, and also the model works in a regression setting instead of classification. These models take an image as input, and output a driving angle. Our white-box detector can identify weak points with f1 score up to 78.9%.

In summary, we make the following contributions:

- We conduct an empirical study to understand the local robustness properties of DNNs under natural variations.
- We develop a white-box (DEEPROBUST-W) and a black-box (DEEPROBUST-B) method to automatically detect weak points.
- We present a detailed evaluation of our methods on three DNN models across three image classification datasets. To check the generalizability of our findings, we further evaluate DEEPROBUST-W in a setting with non-spatial transformations (i.e., rain and fog), a different task (i.e., regression), and a safety-critical application (i.e., self-driving car). We find that DEEPROBUST can successfully detect weak points with reasonably good precision and recall.
- We made our code public at https://github.com/AIasd/DeepRobust.

2   Background: DNN Testing

Existing studies have proposed different techniques to generate test data inputs by perturbing input images for a DNN and use them to evaluate the robustness of the DNN. Depending on how the input image is perturbed, the techniques for generating DNN test data can be classified into three broad categories:

i) Adversarial inputs are typically generated by norm-based perturbation techniques [9, 23, 39, 46, 53, 85] where some pixels of an input image (I) are perturbed by norm-based distance (l_1, l_2 or l_{inf}) such that the distance between the perturbed image and I is $\leq \epsilon$, where ϵ is a small positive value. These adversarial examples are used to expose the security vulnerabilities of DNNs.

ii) Natural variations are generated through a variety of image transformations, and are used to evaluate the robustness of DNNs under such variations [13, 14, 73]. Sources of these variations include changes in camera configuration, or variations in background or ambient conditions. The transformations simulating these variations could be spatial, such as rotation, translations, mirroring, shear, and scaling on images, or non-spatial transformations, such as changes in the brightness or contrast of an image. Here we first focus on spatial transformations as opposed to adversarial one for two reasons. First, compared with adversarial examples, which is fairly contrived, spatial transformations are more likely to arise in more benign environments. Second, using simple parametric spatial transformations like rotations and translations, it is easier to systematically explore the local robustness properties. Later, to emulate a more natural variation we add fog and rain on the images of self-driving car dataset and evaluate our method's generalizibility.

iii) GAN-based image generation techniques use Generative Adversarial Network (GAN) to synthesize images. GAN is one class of generative models trained as a minimax two-player game between a generative model and a discriminative model [22]. GAN-based image generation has been successfully used to generate DNN test data instances [92, 93].

Standard Accuracy vs. Robust Accuracy. Standard accuracy measures how accurately an ML model predicts the correct classes of the instances in a given test dataset. Robust, *a.k.a.* adversarial accuracy, estimates how accurately an ML model classifies the generated variants [76]. In this paper, we adopt a pointwise robust accuracy measure, *neighbor accuracy*, to quantify the robustness of a DNN for the neighbors around each data point.

3   Methodology

3.1   Terminology

Original Data Point: An original data point represents an original un-modified data instance (image in our case) in the studied dataset. The original data points can come from training, validation, or testing dataset, depending on the experimental setting. In Figure 2, the triangle in the center is an original data point.

Neighbors: Neighbors are images generated by the natural variations, e.g., spatial transformations applied to an original image. Since the transformation parameters are continuous (e.g., degree of rotations), there can be an infinite number of neighbors per image. In Figure 2, the small circles around an original data point represent its neighbors.

Neighbor Accuracy: We define *neighbor accuracy* as the percentage of its neighbors, including itself, that can be correctly classified by the DNN model. Figure 2 illustrates this; here, red small circles indicate misclassified neighbors, while the green small circles are correctly classified ones. The figure shows that there are only five neighbors per original data point. In the left-hand-side diagram, four out of five neighbors are correctly classified by the given DNN model. If the original data point is correctly classified as well, the neighbor accuracy of the original data is (5/6=) 83.3%. Similarly, in Figure 2 (right), four out of the five neighbors have been misclassified by the model; if the original data point is misclassified, the neighbor accuracy is (1/6=) 16.6%.

Robustness. An original data point is strong, *a.k.a.* robust, w.r.t. the DNN model under test if its neighbor accuracy is higher than a predefined threshold. Conversely, a weak, *a.k.a.* non-robust, point has the neighbor accuracy lower than a pre-defined threshold. For example, at 0.75 neighbor accuracy threshold, the black triangle in Figure 2 is a strong point, and the grey triangle is a weak point.

A region contains an original point and all of its neighbors. If the original point is strong (weak), we call the cor-

Fig. 2: **Illustrating our terminologies. The triangles are original points, and the small circles are their neighbors generated by natural variations. The light-green region is robust with higher neighbor accuracy, while the light-red region is vulnerable. The corresponding original points are robust and non-robust accordingly.**

responding region as a robust (weak) region. In Figure 2, the light green region is robust while the light red region is weak.

Neighbor Diversity: For multi-class classification task, different neighbors of an original point can be mis-classified to different classes. Neighbor Diversity score measures how many diverse classes a point's neighbors are classified, and is formally computed using Simpson Diversity Index (λ) [67]: $\lambda = \sum_{i=1}^{k} p_i^2$ (1)

where k is the total number of possible classes and p_i is the probability of an image's neighbors being predicted to be class i. Large Simpson Index means low diversity. Let's consider we have three possible classes A, B, and C. Assume an image has 4 neighbors. Including the original image, there are 5 images in total. If two of the five images are classified as A, and rest are classified as B, then $\lambda = (2/5)^2 + (3/5)^2 + (0/5)^2 = 0.52$. In contrast, if two of them are classified as A, and two are classified as B, and one is classified as C then $\lambda = (2/5)^2 + (2/5)^2 + (1/5)^2 = 0.36$. Clearly, the latter case is more diverse and thus, has a lower λ score.

Feature Representation: In a DNN, the neurons' output in each layer capture different abstract representation of the raw input, which are commonly known as features, extracted by the current layer and all the preceding layers. Each layer's output forms the corresponding feature space. For a given input data point, we consider the output of the DNN's second-to-last layer as its feature representation or feature vector.

3.2   Data Collection

Neighbor Generation: For the image classification tasks, for each original image point, we generate its neighbors by combining two types of spatial transformations: rotation and translation. We carefully choose these two types as representatives of non-linear and linear spatial transformations, respectively, following Engstrom et al. [14]. In particular, following them, we generate a neighbor by randomly rotating the original point by t ($\in [-30, 30]$) degrees, shifting it by dx (about 10% of the original image's width i.e. $\in [-3, 3]$) pixels horizontally, and shifting it by dy (about 10% of the original image's height i.e. $\in [-3, 3]$) pixels vertically. It should be noted that for image classification it is standard in the literatures [14, 15, 86] to assume that the transformed image has the same label as the original one. As the transformation parameters are continuous, there can be infinite neighbors of an original data point. Hence, we sample m neighbors for each original data point. We explore the impact of m in RQ2.

For the self-driving-car task where the model predicts steering angle, for each original image point, we generate 50% neighbors with rain effect and the rest 50% with fog effects. We adopt a widely used self-driving car data augmentation package, Automold [60], for adding these effects where we randomly vary the degrees of the added effect. For the rain effect, we set "rain_type=heavy" and everything else as default. For the fog effect, we set everything as default.

Estimating Neighbor Accuracy: To compute the neighbor accuracy of a data point for a given DNN model, we first generate its neighbor samples by applying different transformations—spatial for image classification and rain or fog for self-driving-car application. Then we feed these generated neighbors into the DNN model and compute the accuracy by comparing the DNN's output with the label of the original data point. For self-driving-car application, we follow the technique described in DeepTest [73]. More specifically, if the predicted steering angle of the transformed image is within a threshold to the original image, we consider it as correct. This ensures that any small variations of steering angle are tolerated in the predicted results. We then compute $neighbour\ accuracy = \frac{\#correct\ predictions}{original\ point + \#total\ neighbours}$.

3.3   Classifying Robust vs. Weak Points

We propose two methods, DEEPROBUST-W and DEEPROBUST-B, to identify whether an unlabeled input is strong or weak *w.r.t.* a DNN in real time. If a test image is identified as a weak point, although it may be classified correctly by the pre-trained model, this image is in a vulnerable region where a slight change to this image may cause the pre-trained DNN to misclassify the changed input.

(a) workflow - training   (b) workflow - testing

Fig. 3: **Workflow of DEEPROBUST-W**

DEEPROBUST-W: White-box Classifier This is a binary classifier designed to classify an image (in particular, image feature vector) as a strong or weak point. Here, we assume that we have white box access to the DNN under test to extract the feature vectors of the input images from the DNN. These feature vectors are given as inputs to DEEPROBUST-W. Figure 3 shows the workflow.

Training: During training of DEEPROBUST-W, we first feed all the original training images and their neighbors to the DNN under test. From the DNN outputs, we compute the neighbor accuracy for each data point in the training set and label each point strong/weak depending on whether its neighbor accuracy is higher/lower than a predefined threshold. For each original data point, we also extract the output of the DNN's second-to-last layer as its feature vector. We use these vectors as inputs to train DEEPROBUST-W and the outputs are the corresponding strong/weak labels.

Testing: Given a test input, we extract its feature vector by feeding the test image to the DNN under test and then feed the extracted feature vector to the trained DEEPROBUST-W, which predicts if the input is a strong or weak point.

DEEPROBUST-B: Black-box Classifier This is also a binary classifier that is intended to classify an image to strong/weak point. However, here the user does not have white box access to the DNN under test. Figure 4 shows the workflow.

Fig. 4: **Workflow of DEEPROBUST-B**

Given a test input, we first randomly generate some of its neighbors. We then query the DNN under test with all these neighbors and compute the diversity score, as per Equation 1. If the neighbor diversity score (inversely correlated with neighbor diversity) is greater than a given diversity score threshold, the given test input is classified as a strong point; otherwise, a weak point.

Notice that, in this method, we do not need a training step. We only need the diversity score threshold, which can be empirically set using a ground-truth data set. In particular, we first calculate the neighbor accuracy and diversity score of each pre-annotated point. Next, based on a given neighbor accuracy threshold, we identify the weak points, as the ground truth. The highest diversity score among these weak points is chosen as the diversity score threshold.

Usage Scenario DEEPROBUST-W/B works in a real-world setting where a customer/user runs a pre-trained DNN model in real-time which constantly receives inputs and wants to test if the prediction of the DNN on a given input can be trusted. DEEPROBUST-W assumes that the user has white-box access to DNN under test and all the training data used to train the DNN. DEEPROBUST-W leverages the feature vector and neighbor accuracy of the training data to train the classifier, which can notify the user if the current input is a strong point or weak point. If the input is classified as strong point, the user can give more trust to the original DNN's prediction. On the other hand, if the point is classified as a weak point, the user may want to be more cautious about the DNN's prediction and conduct additional inspections.

In the blackbox setting, DEEPROBUST-B assumes the user does not have white-box access to DNN under test. DEEPROBUST-B comes with a small overhead of transforming the input multiple times to get some neighbors and querying DNN under test on them to estimate the diversity score.

4   Experimental Design

4.1   Study Subjects

Image Classification Similar to many existing works [36, 41, 61, 73, 74, 92] on DNN testing, in this work, we use image classification application of DNNs as the basis of our investigation. This is one of the most popular computer vision tasks, where the model tries to classify the objects in an image or video.

Datasets: We conduct our experiments on three image classification datasets: F-MNIST [87], CIFAR-10 [37], and SVHN [89].

- **CIFAR-10**: consists of 50,000 training and 10,000 testing 32x32 color images. Each image is one of ten digit classes.
- **F-MNIST**: consists of 60,000 training images and 10,000 testing 28x28 grayscale images. Each image is one of ten fashion product related classes.
- **SVHN**: consists of 73,257 training images and 26,032 testing images. Each image is a 32x32 color cropped image of house numbers collected from Google Street View images.

Architectures: The popular DNN-based image classifiers are variants of convolutional neural networks (CNN) [28, 38, 79]. Here we study the following three architectures for all the three datasets:

- **ResN**: Following Engstrom *et al.* [14], we use ResN model with 4 groups of residual layers with filter sizes 16, 16, 32, and 64, and 5 residual units each.
- **VGG**: We use the same VGG architecture as proposed in [66].

– **WRN**: We use a structure with block type (3, 3) and depth 28 in [90] but replace the widening factor 10 with 2 for less parameters and faster training.

We train all the models from scratch using widely used hyper-parameters and achieve accepted level of validation natural accuracy). When training models on CIFAR-10, we pre-process the input images with random augmentation (random translation with $dx, dy \in [-2, 2]$ pixels both horizontally and vertically) which is a widely used preprocessing step for this dataset. When training models on the other two datasets, plain images are directly fed into the models. The natural accuracies and robust accuracies of the models are shown in Table 1.

Steering Angle Prediction We further evaluate DEEP-ROBUST-W in a self-driving car application to show that it can be applied into a regression task. These models learn to steer (i.e., predict steering

Table 1: **Study Subjects (values are in percentage)**

Dataset	CIFAR-10			SVHN			F-MNIST		
Model	VGG	ResN	WRN	VGG	ResN	WRN	VGG	ResN	WRN
nat acc'	89.0	89.3	90.6	94.5	95.3	95.2	93.4	93.5	93.6
rob acc*	75.5	68.5	74.8	78.1	78.9	81.	61.1	63.0	64.2

'Natural accuracy. *Robust accuracy is estimated as the average neighbor accuracy for test data points.

angle) by taking in visual inputs from car-mounted cameras that record the driving scene, paired with the steering angles from a human driver.

Datasets: We use the dataset by Stocco *et al.* [68], which is collected by the authors driving on three tracks of different environments in the Udacity Simulator [77]. It consists of 37888 central camera training images and 9427 central camera evaluation images. Each image is of size 320x120.

Architectures: We evaluate our method on the three pre-trained DNN models used in [68]: NVIDIA DAVE-2 [6], Epoch [2], and Chauffeur [1]. These models have been used by many previous testing works on self-driving car [55,68,73].

4.2 Evaluation

Evaluation Metric. We evaluate both DEEPROBUST-W and DEEPROBUST-B for detecting weak points under twelve and nine different DNN-dataset combinations, respectively, in terms of precision, recall, and F1 score. Let us assume that E is the number of weak points detected by our tool and A is the the number of true weak points in the ground truth set. Then the precision and recall are $\frac{|A \cap E|}{|E|}$ and $\frac{|A \cap E|}{|A|}$, respectively. F1 score is a single accuracy measure that considers both precision and recall, and defined as $\frac{2 \times precision \times recall}{precision + recall}$. We perform each experiment for two thresholds of neighbor accuracy that defines strong vs. weak points: 0.75 and 0.50.

Baselines. We compare DEEPROBUST-W and DEEPROBUST-B with two baselines. One naive baseline (denoted *random*) is randomly selecting the same number of points as detected by our proposed method to be weak points. Another baseline (denoted *top1*) is based on prediction confidence score—if the confidence of a data point is higher than a pre-defined cutoff we call it a strong point, weak otherwise. This baseline is based on the intuition that DNNs might not be confident enough to predict the weak points.

5   Results

In this section, we elaborate on our results. In our preliminary experiments, we have two findings regarding neighbor accuracy. First, the neighbor accuracy vary widely across data points and there is a non-trivial number of points having relatively low neighbor accuracy. For example, for all the models trained on CIFAR-10 dataset, 40% of training data and 42% of testing data have neighbor accuracy <0.75, and 16% of training data and 20% of testing data have neighbor accuracy <0.50. These points degrade the aggregated spatial robustness of the model. The same finding holds for the other two datasets. Second, the distribution of neighbor accuracy for a dataset is similar across different models. For CIFAR-10, F-MNIST and SVHN, 60%, 76%, and 81%, respectively, of data points have neighbor accuracy change < 0.2 across any two models on the same dataset. This implies that a large portion of data points' neighbor accuracy is independent of the model selected.

The first observation shows that neighbor accuracy is a distinguishable measure for local robustness for the datasets and models we study. The second observation implies that the properties of points of low neighbor accuracy may be similar across models for each dataset. Following these two observations, we dive deeper and explore the characteristics of data points with different neighbor accuracy in RQ1. We then evaluate the performance of DEEPROBUST-W and DEEPROBUST-B which are developed based on the observations from RQ1 in RQ2 and RQ3, respectively. Finally, in RQ4, we evaluate the generalizability of our method by applying DEEPROBUST-W in a regression task for self-driving cars under more complex transformations.

RQ1. What are the characteristics of the weak points?

We explore the characteristics of robust vs. non-robust points in their feature space. In particular, we check the difference in feature representations between: a) robust and non-robust points, and b) points with different degrees of robustness.

RQ1a. Given a well trained model, do the feature representations of robust and non-robust points vary? In this RQ, we first explore how robust (i.e., strong) and non-robust (i.e., weak) data points are distributed in the feature space.

We apply t-SNE[44], a widely used visualization method, to visualize the distribution of points of different neighbor accuracy in the representation space for all three datasets when using ResN as the classifier. Figure 5 shows the visualization of feature vectors from two randomly picked classes with colors indicating the neighbor accuracy of each point. The darker a point's color is, the lower its neighbor accuracy is. It is evident that most points of low neighbor accuracy tend to be further away from the class center.

To numerically verify this observation, first, we define a class center c_k for each class k as the median value of the feature vectors of all the points from class k. Thus, if f_i is the feature of a point at i^{th} dimension and $\hat{f}_{ik}$ is the median of the ith dimension features for all the points in class k, c_k is defined to be $(\hat{f}_{1k}, ..., \hat{f}_{jk}, ..., \hat{f}_{nk})$.

(a) CIFAR-10   (b) F-MNIST   (c) SVHN

Fig. 5: **The t-SNE plots of data points from two randomly chosen classes across three datasets using ResNet. Darker color indicates lower neighbor accuracy.**

The reason we take median rather than mean is that it is a more statistically stable measure and is less likely to be heavily influenced by outliers in the representation space. Then, for every point p, we define a ratio:
$r^{(p)} = \dfrac{d^{(p)}_{same\_class}}{d^{(p)}_{nearest\_other\_class}}$, where $d^{(p)}_{same\_class}$ is the distance of the p-th point's feature vector to its own class center and $d^{(p)}_{nearest\_other\_class}$ is the distance of the p-th point's feature vector to the class center of its closest other class. A small $r^{(p)}$ means that the point p is close to its own class center while far from other classes, i.e., p is far from the decision boundary. In contrast, a larger $r^{(p)}$ indicates that the point p is closer to some other classes, i.e., it is closer to the decision boundary.

We then measure the average $r^{(p)}$ among the weak points (denoted as r_w) and among strong points (denoted as r_s) for all three datasets across three models. Besides, we also calculate mann-whitney wilocox test[47] and cohen's d effect size [10] between the two ratios to test if the two ratios indeed have statistically significant difference and how large the difference is.

Table 2: **Weak and strong points ratio, and cohen's d effect size**

Dataset	CIFAR-10			SVHN			F-MNIST		
Model	ResN	WRN	VGG	ResN	WRN	VGG	ResN	WRN	VGG
Neighbor Accuracy Cutoff=0.5									
r_w	0.915	0.955	1.004	1.046	1.103	0.997	0.746	0.734	0.976
r_s	0.609	0.584	0.975	0.294	0.309	0.977	0.297	0.293	0.930
d*	1.368	1.736	1.163	2.077	2.428	1.420	1.426	1.312	1.332
Neighbor Accuracy Cutoff=0.75									
r_w	0.778	0.796	0.992	0.604	0.671	0.983	0.516	0.496	0.953
r_s	0.588	0.558	0.973	0.260	0.274	0.977	0.253	0.257	0.918
d*	0.786	1.040	0.749	0.860	1.111	0.401	0.749	0.642	0.937

*Cohen's d effect size of 0.20 = small, 0.50 = medium, 0.80 = large, 1.20 = very large, and 2.0 = huge [10, 59].

As shown in Table 2, for both the neighbor accuracy cutoff (0.5 and 0.75), except one setting, the cohen's d effect size for every setting is larger than 0.50, which implies a medium to very large difference. Besides, for every setting, the mann-whitney wilocox test value (not shown in the table) is smaller than $1e^{-80}$, which implies the difference is indeed statistically significant.

The visualization and numerical results imply that most weak points are close to the decision boundaries between classes. Note that similar observation was also observed by Kim et. al. [36] in case of adversarial perturbation. In particular, they find that adversarial examples tend to be closer to class decision boundaries. In contrast, we focus on spatial robustness and find that spatially non-robust points are closer to decision boundaries.

RQ1b. Given a well trained model, do the feature representations of the data points vary by their degree of robustness? By analyzing the classifications of the neighbors of weak vs. strong points, we observe that the weaker a point is, its neighbors are more likely to be classified in different classes. We quantify this observation by computing diversity of the outputs a point's neighbor; We adopt Simpson Diversity Index (λ) [67] as defined in Equation (1).

Table 3 shows the Spearman correlation between neighbor accuracy and λ on the three datasets and three models for each. Note that while calculating the correlation, we remove points with neighbor

Table 3: **Spearman Correlation between Neighbor Accuracy and Simpson Diversity Index. All coefficients are reported with statistical significance ($p < 0.05$).**

Dataset	CIFAR-10			SVHN			F-MNIST		
Model	ResN	WRN	VGG	ResN	WRN	VGG	ResN	WRN	VGG
corr.coeff.	0.853	0.909	0.946	0.970	0.984	0.983	0.923	0.962	0.8947

accuracy 100% since there are many points having 100% neighbor accuracy and tend to bias upward the Spearman Correlation; if we include points with neighbor accuracy 100%, the correlations become even higher. We notice that for any setting, the Spearman Correlation is never lower than 0.853. This indicates that neighbor accuracy and diversity are highly correlated with each other. For example, the bird image in Fig.1a has neighbor accuracy 0.49 and diversity 0.36, while the bird image in Fig.1e has neighbor accuracy 1 and diversity 1. This shows, the classifier tends to be confused about weak points and mispredicts them into many different kinds of classes.

> **Result 1:** *In the representation space, weak points tend to lie towards the class decision boundary while the strong points lie towards the center. The weaker an image is, the model tends to be more confused by it, and classify its neighbors into more diverse classes.*

RQ2. Can we detect the weak points in a white-box setting?

We explore this RQ using DEEPROBUST-W, as discussed in Section 3.3. DEEPROBUST-W takes the feature vector of a data point as input and classifies it to a strong/weak point. We implement DEEPROBUST-W with a simple 4-layer, fully connected neural network architecture with hidden layer dimensions 1500, 1000, and 500, respectively.

Table 4 shows the result. At 0.75 setting, DEEPROBUST-W has F1 up to 91.4%, with an average of 76.9%. At 0.50 setting, DEEPROBUST-W detects weak points with average F1 of 61.1%, while it can go up to 79.1%. DEEPROBUST-W consistently performs significantly better than the baseline methods.

The top1 has very good precision, since a mis-classified image with low confidence tends to have very poor local robustness. However, there also exist many images that are correctly classified with high confidence yet have poor local robustness. The miss of these points leads the top1 to have very poor recall and thus even worse F1 compared with the random baseline. Our method comes to aid by providing high recall at the same time of decent precision.

Table 4: **Performance of DEEP-ROBUST-W and the baseline methods for predicting weak points.**

dataset	model	method	0.75 neighbor acc.			0.50 neighbor acc.		
			f1	tp	fp	f1	tp	fp
CIFAR-10	ResN	ours	0.79	3844	764	0.581	1290	664
		top1	0.376	1218	206	0.182	255	120
		random	0.488	2372	2236	0.233	520	1445
	WRN	ours	0.747	2901	906	0.56	947	610
		top1	0.35	889	222	0.183	189	90
		random	0.395	1534	2273	0.154	261	1296
	VGG	ours	0.654	2222	938	0.493	747	543
		top1	0.439	1070	153	0.266	278	106
		random	0.332	1127	2033	0.132	200	1090
SVHN	ResN	ours	0.755	6814	2530	0.577	1414	674
		top1	0.315	1665	142	0.267	452	122
		random	0.343	3095	6249	0.086	210	1878
	WRN	ours	0.709	5062	2143	0.582	1404	1055
		top1	0.292	1238	130	0.203	229	85
		random	0.28	2000	5205	0.095	229	2230
	VGG	ours	0.595	5214	3367	0.498	1272	911
		top1	0.172	840	67	0.139	221	52
		random	0.341	2986	5595	0.094	240	1943
F-MNIST	ResN	ours	0.914	6034	873	0.791	2144	556
		top1	0.124	428	11	0.039	57	7
		random	0.657	4340	2567	0.263	712	1988
	WRN	ours	0.896	5743	652	0.76	2033	641
		top1	0.144	490	14	0.045	63	8
		random	0.638	4093	2302	0.281	752	1922
	VGG	ours	0.864	6348	1231	0.654	1895	1082
		top1	0.104	392	5	0.028	39	5
		random	0.734	5393	2186	0.295	854	2123

Notice that DEEPROBUST-W's performance depends on the training data selection, mainly (a) how many weak vs. strong points are used to train the model, and (b) how many neighbors are generated per point to decide if it is strong/weak. To investigate (a), we assign a weight to each input point, indicating how likely it gets selected to train DEEPROBUST-W. In particular, for an input i, a weight $w_i := \frac{1+(1-n_i)^m \times 100^m}{1+100^m}$ is computed, where n is its neighbor accuracy, and m is a configurable parameter; with larger m, more weak points are sampled and DEEP-ROBUST-W will be trained with more weak points, and vice versa.

Table 5A shows the performance: as m increases, the detector trades precision for recall. In this way, choosing different values of m, the precision-recall trade-off of the detector can be adjusted according to a user's need. From a different perspective, this way of oversampling weak points also addresses the potential problem of imbalanced data when the weak points are much less than the strong points.

Table 5: **DEEPROBUST-W performance using different sampling strategies for training**

A: with varying number of strong/weak points

dataset	m	prec	recall	tp	fp	f1
CIFAR-10	0	**0.660**	0.518	1290	664	0.581
	1	0.615	0.599	1490	932	0.607
	2	0.544	**0.699**	1740	1460	**0.612**
SVHN	0	**0.677**	0.502	1414	674	0.577
	1	0.575	0.653	1837	1357	**0.612**
	2	0.332	**0.767**	2160	4356	0.463
F-MNIST	0	**0.794**	0.787	2144	556	**0.791**
	1	0.746	**0.839**	2284	777	0.79
	2	0.712	**0.871**	2372	962	0.783

B: with varying number of neigbours

dataset	#neighbors	prec	recall	tp	fp	f1
CIFAR-10	6	0.662	0.389	967	493	0.49
	12	0.685	0.384	955	440	0.492
	25	0.665	0.502	1250	629	0.572
	50	0.660	0.518	1290	664	0.581
	200	0.683	0.507	1261	585	0.582
SVHN	6	0.723	0.403	1136	436	0.518
	12	0.672	0.527	1483	725	0.59
	25	0.619	0.629	1771	1090	0.624
	50	0.632	0.605	1703	993	0.618
	200	0.667	0.550	1550	774	0.603
F-MNIST	6	0.817	0.727	1981	443	0.77
	12	0.784	0.790	2153	592	0.787
	25	0.773	0.787	2143	629	0.78
	50	0.836	0.727	1981	390	0.778
	200	0.778	0.812	2211	632	0.794

Next, we check how DEEPROBUST-W's performance is dependent on the number of sampled neighbors, because a data point can potentially have infinite neighbors. Table 5B shows that the number of neighbors does not have much influence on the performance of the detector once it goes beyond some value (F1 score change less than 3.5 percentage point between 25 and 200 samples) for all the three datasets. Thus, we choose 50 for all of our experiments. For future work, a statistical bound with confidence intervals for neighbor accuracy can be estimated by modeling neighbor accuracy using distributions like folded normal.

Result 2: DEEPROBUST-W *can identify weak points with reasonably high F1 score: on average* 76.9%, *at* 0.75 *neighbor accuracy cut-off.*

RQ3. Can we identify the weak points in a black-box setting?

We explore this RQ using DEEPROBUST-B, as discussed in Section 3.3. We assume only having access to unlabeled testing data and the model under test as a black-box. To evaluate DEEPROBUST-B, we spatially transform each test input m times by randomly applying $d\omega \in [-30, +30]$ degrees rotation, $dx \in [-3, +3]$ pixels horizontal translation, and $dy \in [-3, +3]$ pixels vertical translation. We then calculate the output diversity score (λ) based on Equation (1) and rank the test images based on λ. Finally, we mark top k images as potential most non-robust points. The parameter k is chosen according to users' need.

Fig. 6: **The spearman correlation coeff. between diversity score (λ) and neighbor accuracy, with varying #neighbors (m).**

Fig. 7: **AUC-ROC curve with neighbor accuracy cutoff at 0.75. The red vertical line indicates when the diversity score threshold is chosen from training data.**

With each test data, DEEP-ROBUST-B queries the model with m neighbors to compute λ. Since querying the classifier comes with an overhead, our goal is to achieve an optimal accuracy with minimal queries (i.e., m). To determine an optimal m value, we explore the spearman correlation between diversity score and neighbor accuracy, with varying m, when running ResN on all the three datasets (see Figure 6). The correlation increases as m increases, as with more query λ becomes more accurate, and so the neighbor accuracy. We notice that at $m = 15$, the correlation coefficients across all the experimental settings reach above 0.8, and the rate of increase begins to slow down significantly. The results for the other two architectures are highly similar. Thus, we set $m = 15$ as default for DEEPROBUST-B.

Next, we evaluate DEEPROBUST-B's performance. We plot AUC-ROC by changing $top - k$ at $m = 15$ and compare our method with the random baseline and the top1 baseline as before. As shown in Figure 7, our method performs much better than the random baseline. In particular, our proposed method achieves AUC higher than 0.87 for all settings when neighbor accuracy cutoff is 0.5 and 0.97 when neighbor accuracy cutoff is 0.75.

Instead of above ranking based scheme, DEEPROBUST-B can also be used as a classifier if a diversity threshold is given (see Section 3.3). Here, we estimate the threshold using pre-annotated training data.

Table 6: **Performance of DEEP-ROBUST-B and the baseline methods for predicting weak points.**

dataset	model	method	75%			50%		
			f1	tp	fp	f1	tp	fp
CIFAR-10	ResN	ours	0.939	4714	257	0.622	1454	801
		top1	0.376	1218	206	0.182	255	120
		random	0.501	2516	2455	0.234	549	1706
	WRN	ours	0.938	3657	171	0.585	986	604
		top1	0.35	889	222	0.183	189	90
		random	0.383	1494	2334	0.182	307	1283
	VGG	ours	0.945	3397	148	0.682	1087	390
		top1	0.439	1070	153	0.266	278	106
		random	0.36	1296	2249	0.153	244	1233
SVHN	ResN	ours	0.956	8371	365	0.67	1845	858
		top1	0.315	1665	142	0.267	452	122
		random	0.336	2944	5792	0.102	280	2423
	WRN	ours	0.963	6827	227	0.718	1602	514
		top1	0.292	1238	130	0.203	275	85
		random	0.275	1950	5104	0.085	191	1925
	VGG	ours	0.976	8608	144	0.779	2138	454
		top1	0.172	840	67	0.139	221	52
		random	0.339	2997	5755	0.102	279	2313
F-MNIST	ResN	ours	0.987	6422	81	0.802	2316	546
		top1	0.124	428	11	0.039	57	7
		random	0.655	4265	2238	0.289	835	2027
	WRN	ours	0.989	6246	70	0.857	2297	360
		top1	0.144	490	14	0.045	63	8
		random	0.631	3987	2329	0.274	736	1921
	VGG	ours	0.991	7078	60	0.847	2393	418
		top1	0.104	392	5	0.028	39	5
		random	0.711	5084	2054	0.277	784	2027

We evaluate precision and recall of DEEPROBUST-B in the nine DNN-dataset combinations under neighbor accuracy cutoffs 0.5 and 0.75. Table 6 shows the result. At 0.75 setting, DEEPROBUST-B has f1 up to 99.1%, with an average of 96.5%. At 0.50 setting, DEEPROBUST-B detects weak points with average f1 of 72.9%, while it can go up to 85.7%. It consistently produces better estimation than the top1 baseline and the random baseline. This shows that our black-box method can effectively identify weak points.

Note that, generating the spatial transformations and querying the model with it under black box setting is fast. Previous black box methods for adversarial perturbation work in such fashion [26,51]. For example, using CIFAR-10 , when we use a batch with size 100, the average transformation+query time for one image is 0.031 ± 0.015 ms. For the other two datasets, the overhead is similar. Thus, to for $m = 15$ queries, it takes only 0.465 ± 0.225 ms, which is a negligible overhead for most real-world DNN based vision applications. This implies that our black-box method can also be used in real time for many applications.

Result 3: *Given only black-box access to the DNN classifier, DEEPROBUST-B can identify weak points with f1 that are much better than those of using top1 method or random method.*

RQ4. How generalizable are these findings?

The local robustness issues also exist in more critical applications like self-driving-car. Here we explore more complex transformations, i.e., adding rain and fog to the driving scenes. As shown in Figure 8, among those correctly classified data points, there is a non-trivial portion (45.8%) of them (in the heatmap, more red signified weaker) suffer from low (<0.75) neighbor accuracy.

Note that, here, we test regression models, which take images of driving scenes as inputs and output the corresponding steering angles.

Let a set of outputs predicted by a DNN be denoted by $\{\hat{\theta}_{o1}, \hat{\theta}_{o2}, ..., \hat{\theta}_{on}\}$, and ground truth labels for the original (unmodified) image points be $\{\theta_1, \theta_2, ..., \theta_n\}$. If the difference between predicted steering angle $\hat{\theta}_{oi}$ of a transformed image and the ground truth label of the original image θ_i is above a threshold, we consider it as incorrect.

The threshold λMSE_{orig} is defined following DeepTest's [73] as $MSE_{orig} = \frac{1}{n}\sum_{i=1}^{n}(\theta_i - \hat{\theta}_{oi})^2$. MSE is the Mean Square Error between the outputs and the manual labels, and λ is a positive coefficient that is chosen to reflect a user's tolerance on the deviation. Note that there is no softmax layer (and thus no confidence score) in these regression models so the top1 baseline method cannot be used here.

Table 7 shows the result when $\lambda = 3$. At 0.75 setting, DEEPROBUST-W has f1 score up to 78.9%, with an average of 58.2%. At 0.50 setting, DEEPROBUST-W detects weak points with an average f1 of 47.9%, while it can go up to 68.2%. It consistently produces better estimation than the random baseline under all the settings. It should be noted that our observation is valid for all the λ used in [73] from λ equal to 1 to 5. This shows that our proposed method DEEPROBUST-W can be applied to regression problems with more complex natural transformations.

Fig. 8: **The t-SNE plot of correctly classified data points from Self-Driving dataset by the epoch model. data points are colored based on neighbor accuracy.**

model	method	0.75 neighbor acc.			0.50 neighbor acc.		
		f1	tp	fp	f1	tp	fp
chauffeur	ours	0.417	555	547	0.346	339	384
	random	0.146	194	908	0.096	94	629
epoch	ours	0.789	4354	1112	0.682	2641	1127
	random	0.586	3234	2232	0.411	1592	2176
dave2	ours	0.541	979	471	0.409	475	246
	random	0.193	350	1100	0.121	141	580

Table 7: **Performance of DEEP-ROBUST-W for predicting weak points of Self-Driving dataset**

It should also be noted that it is unrealistic to use DEEPROBUST-B for this task for two reasons: It is impractical to try different variations of an image in real-time for a self-driving car, which is a time-sensitive application. Further, DEEPROBUST-B requires the calculation of neighbor diversity score. For a regression problem, the predicted values are continuous, so there is a very low probability for any two predictions being equal. Thus, the neighbor diversity score for every data point will be the same and cannot be used for identifying the weak points.

Result 4: DEEPROBUST-W *can detect weak points of a self-driving car dataset with f1 score up to 78.9%, with an average of 58.2%, at neighbor accuracy cutoff 0.75.*

6   Related Work

Adversarial examples. Many works focus on generating adversarial examples to fool the DNNs and evaluate their robustness using pixel-based perturbation [9, 17, 23, 25, 31, 36, 48, 49, 54, 63, 80–83]. Some other papers [14, 15, 86], like us, proposed more realistic transformations to generate adversarial examples. In particular, Engstrom et al. [14] proposed that a simple rotation and translation can fool a DNN based classifier, and spatial adversarial robustness is orthogonal to l_p-bounded adversarial robustness. However, all these works estimate the overall robustness of a DNN based on its aggregated behavior across many data points. In contrast, we analyze the robustness of individual data points under natural variations and propose methods to detect weak/strong points automatically.

DNN testing. Many researchers [16, 21, 29, 36, 41, 55, 69, 70, 74, 94] proposed techniques to test DNN. For example, Pei et al. [55] proposed an image transformation based differential testing framework, which can detect erroneous behavior by comparing the outputs of an input image across multiple DNNs. Ferit et al. [16] used fault localization methods to identify suspicious neurons and leveraged those to generate adversarial test cases.

In contrast, others [8, 29, 64, 73, 78, 92, 94] used metamorphic testing where the assumption is the outputs of an original and its transformed image will be the same under natural transformations. Among them, some use a uncertainty measure to quantify some types of non-robustness of an input for prioritizing samples for testing / retraining [8] or generating test cases[78]. We follow a similar metamorphic property while estimating neighbor accuracy and our proposed DEEPROBUST-B also leverages an uncertainty measure. The key differences are: First, we focus on estimating model's performance on general natural variants of an input rather than the input itself or only spatial variants. Second, we focus on the task of weak points detection rather than prioritizing / generating test cases. We also give detailed analyses of the properties of natural variants and propose a feature vector based white-box detection method DEEPROBUST-W. Further, we show that our method works across domains (both image classification and self-driving car controllers) and tasks (both classification and regression). Other uncertainty work complement ours in the sense that we can easily leverage weak points identified by DEEPROBUST-W and DEEPROBUST-B to prioritize test cases or generate more adversarial cases of natural variants.

Another line of work [18, 19, 27, 33, 34, 58, 72] estimates the confidence of a DNN's output. For example, [19] leverages thrown away information from existing models to measure confidence; [27] shows other NN properties like depth, width, weight decay, and batch normalization are important factors influencing prediction confidence. Although such methods can provide a confidence measure per input or its adversarial variants, they do not check its natural robustness property, i.e., with natural variations how will they behave.

DNN verification. There also exist work on verifying properties for a DNN model [7, 12, 24, 30, 56, 62, 83]. Most of them focus on verifying properties on l_p norm bounded input space. Recently, Balunovic et al.[4] provides the first verification technique for verifying a data point's robustness against spatial transformation. However, their technique suffers from scalability issues.

Robust training. Regular neural network training involves the optimization of the loss for each data point. Robust training of neural network works on minimizing the largest loss within a bounded region usually using adversarial examples [15, 35, 43, 45, 50, 75, 81, 83, 84]. While both robust training methods and our work generate variants of data points, instead of training a model with these variants to improve robustness, we use them to estimate the robustness of unseen data points. The relation between robust retraining and our work is similar to bug fixing vs. bug detection in traditional software engineering literature.

7   Threats to Validity

We adopt rotation and translation as transformations for image classification tasks and rain and fog effects for the self-driving car task. There are many more natural variations such as brightness, snow effect etc. However, rotation and translation are representative of spatial transformation and used by many paper in evaluating robustness of DNN models[14, 55]. Rain and fog effects are also widely leveraged in many influential studies on testing self-driving cars [55,73,92].

Besides, for some of the experiments we did not show all the combinations under both neighbor accuracy cutoffs (i.e. 0.5 and 0.75). However, we note that the observations are consistent and we did not include them purely because of space limitation. Another limitation is that for both DEEPROBUST-W and DEEPROBUST-B, we need to decide the number of neighbors to use for training a classifier and estimating λ, respectively. We mitigate it by selecting the neighbor numbers that give stable performance in terms of precision and recall.

8   Conclusion and Future Work

In this work, we involve the data characteristic into the robustness testing of DNN models. We adopt the concept of neighbor accuracy as a measure for local robustness of a data point on a given model. We explore the properties of neighbor accuracy and find that weak points are often located towards corresponding class boundaries and their transformed versions tend to be predicted to be more diverse classes. Leveraging these observations, we propose a white-box method and a black-box method to identify weak/strong points to warn a user about potential weakness in the given trained model in real-time. We design, implement and evaluate our proposed framework, DEEPROBUST-W and DEEPROBUST-B, on three image recognition datasets and one self-driving car dataset (for DEEP-ROBUST-W only) with three models for each. The results show that they can effectively identify weak/strong points with high precision and recall.

For future work, other consistency analysis methods [18] e.g. variation ratio, entropy can be tried. We can potentially attain statistical guarantee for our black-box method by modeling the neighbor accuracy distribution and assume certain level of correlation between neighbor accuracy and complexity score. Besides, other definitions of robustness like consistency can be explored. We can also leverage ideas from [8,78] to easily prioritize test cases or generate more hard test cases based on identified weak points. Further, we can potentially modify existing fixing methods such as [20] targeting the weak points to fix them.

9   Acknowledgement

We thank Mukul Prasad and Ripon Saha from Fujisu US for valuable discussions. This work is supported in part by NSF CCF-1845893 and CCF-1822965.

References

1. Chauffeur model. https://github.com/udacity/self-driving-car/tree/master/steering-models/community-models/chauffeur (2016)
2. Epoch model. https://github.com/udacity/self-driving-car/tree/master/steering-models/community-models/cg23 (2016)
3. Amershi, S., Begel, A., Bird, C., DeLine, R., Gall, H., Kamar, E., Nagappan, N., Nushi, B., Zimmermann, T.: Software engineering for machine learning: A case study. In: Proceedings of the 41st International Conference on Software Engineering: Software Engineering in Practice. pp. 291–300. ICSE-SEIP '19, IEEE Press (2019). https://doi.org/10.1109/ICSE-SEIP.2019.00042, https://doi.org/10.1109/ICSE-SEIP.2019.00042
4. Balunovic, M., Baader, M., Singh, G., Gehr, T., Vechev, M.: Certifying geometric robustness of neural networks. In: Advances in Neural Information Processing Systems. pp. 15287–15297 (2019)
5. Bojarski, M., Del Testa, D., Dworakowski, D., Firner, B., Flepp, B., Goyal, P., Jackel, L.D., Monfort, M., Muller, U., Zhang, J., et al.: End to end learning for self-driving cars. arXiv preprint arXiv:1604.07316 (2016)
6. Bojarski, M., Testa, D.D., Dworakowski, D., Firner, B., Flepp, B., Goyal, P., Jackel, L.D., Monfort, M., Muller, U., Zhang, J., Zhang, X., Zhao, J., Zieba, K.: End to end learning for self-driving cars. CoRR abs/1604.07316 (2016), http://arxiv.org/abs/1604.07316
7. Bunel, R., Turkaslan, I., Torr, P.H., Kohli, P., Kumar, M.P.: A unified view of piecewise linear neural network verification. In: Proceedings of the 32nd International Conference on Neural Information Processing Systems. p. 4795–4804. NIPS'18, Curran Associates Inc., Red Hook, NY, USA (2018)
8. Byun, T., Sharma, V., Vijayakumar, A., Rayadurgam, S., Cofer, D.: Input prioritization for testing neural networks (01 2019)
9. Carlini, N., Wagner, D.: Towards evaluating the robustness of neural networks. In: Security and Privacy (SP), 2017 IEEE Symposium on. pp. 39–57. IEEE (2017)
10. Cohen, J.: Statistical Power Analysis for the Behavioral Sciences. Lawrence Erlbaum Associates (1988)
11. Du, X., Xie, X., Li, Y., Ma, L., Liu, Y., Zhao, J.: Deepstellar: Model-based quantitative analysis of stateful deep learning systems. In: Proceedings of the 2019 27th ACM Joint Meeting on European Software Engineering Conference and Symposium on the Foundations of Software Engineering. p. 477–487. ESEC/FSE 2019, Association for Computing Machinery, New York, NY, USA (2019). https://doi.org/10.1145/3338906.3338954, https://doi.org/10.1145/3338906.3338954
12. Ehlers, R.: Formal verification of piece-wise linear feed-forward neural networks. In: International Symposium on Automated Technology for Verification and Analysis. pp. 269–286. Springer (2017)
13. Engstrom, L., Tran, B., Tsipras, D., Schmidt, L., Madry, A.: A rotation and a translation suffice: Fooling cnns with simple transformations. arXiv preprint arXiv:1712.02779 (2017)
14. Engstrom, L., Tran, B., Tsipras, D., Schmidt, L., Madry, A.: Exploring the landscape of spatial robustness. In: International Conference on Machine Learning. pp. 1802–1811 (2019)
15. Engstrom, L., Tran, B., Tsipras, D., Schmidt, L., Mądry, A.: A rotation and a translation suffice: Fooling cnns with simple transformations. In: Proceedings of the 36th international conference on machine learning (ICML) (2019)

16. Eniser, H.F., Gerasimou, S., Sen, A.: Deepfault: Fault localization for deep neural networks. In: Hähnle, R., van der Aalst, W. (eds.) Fundamental Approaches to Software Engineering. pp. 171–191. Springer International Publishing, Cham (2019)

17. Feinman, R., Curtin, R.R., Shintre, S., Gardner, A.B.: Detecting adversarial samples from artifacts. arXiv preprint arXiv:1703.00410 (2017)

18. Gal, Y.: Uncertainty in Deep Learning (2016)

19. Gal, Y., Ghahramani, Z.: Dropout as a bayesian approximation: Representing model uncertainty in deep learning. In: Balcan, M.F., Weinberger, K.Q. (eds.) Proceedings of The 33rd International Conference on Machine Learning. Proceedings of Machine Learning Research, vol. 48, pp. 1050–1059. PMLR, New York, New York, USA (20–22 Jun 2016), http://proceedings.mlr.press/v48/gal16.html

20. Gao, X., Saha, R., Prasad, M., Roychoudhury, A.: Fuzz testing based data augmentation to improve robustness of deep neural networks. In: Proceedings of the 42nd International Conference on Software Engineering. ICSE 2020, ACM (2020)

21. Gerasimou, S., Eniser, H.F., Sen, A., Çakan, A.: Importance-driven deep learning system testing. In: International Conference of Software Engineering (ICSE) (2020)

22. Goodfellow, I., Pouget-Abadie, J., Mirza, M., Xu, B., Warde-Farley, D., Ozair, S., Courville, A., Bengio, Y.: Generative adversarial nets. In: Advances in neural information processing systems. pp. 2672–2680 (2014)

23. Goodfellow, I.J., Shlens, J., Szegedy, C.: Explaining and harnessing adversarial examples. In: International Conference on Learning Representations (ICLR) (2015)

24. Gross, D., Jansen, N., Pérez, G.A., Raaijmakers, S.: Robustness verification for classifier ensembles. In: Hung, D.V., Sokolsky, O. (eds.) Automated Technology for Verification and Analysis. pp. 271–287. Springer International Publishing, Cham (2020)

25. Gu, S., Rigazio, L.: Towards deep neural network architectures robust to adversarial examples. In: International Conference on Learning Representations (ICLR) (2015)

26. Guo, C., Gardner, J., You, Y., Wilson, A.G., Weinberger, K.: Simple black-box adversarial attacks. In: Chaudhuri, K., Salakhutdinov, R. (eds.) Proceedings of the 36th International Conference on Machine Learning. Proceedings of Machine Learning Research, vol. 97, pp. 2484–2493. PMLR, Long Beach, California, USA (09–15 Jun 2019), http://proceedings.mlr.press/v97/guo19a.html

27. Guo, C., Pleiss, G., Sun, Y., Weinberger, K.Q.: On calibration of modern neural networks. In: Precup, D., Teh, Y.W. (eds.) Proceedings of the 34th International Conference on Machine Learning. Proceedings of Machine Learning Research, vol. 70, pp. 1321–1330. PMLR, International Convention Centre, Sydney, Australia (06–11 Aug 2017), http://proceedings.mlr.press/v70/guo17a.html

28. He, K., Zhang, X., Ren, S., Sun, J.: Deep residual learning for image recognition. In: Proceedings of the IEEE conference on computer vision and pattern recognition. pp. 770–778 (2016)

29. He, P., Meister, C., Su, Z.: Structure-invariant testing for machine translation. In: International Conference of Software Engineering (ICSE) (2020)

30. Huang, X., Kwiatkowska, M., Wang, S., Wu, M.: Safety verification of deep neural networks. In: International Conference on Computer Aided Verification. pp. 3–29. Springer (2017)

31. Ilyas, A., Santurkar, S., Tsipras, D., Engstrom, L., Tran, B., Madry, A.: Adversarial examples are not bugs, they are features (2019), http://arxiv.org/abs/1905.02175

32. Islam, M.J., Nguyen, G., Pan, R., Rajan, H.: A comprehensive study on deep learning bug characteristics. In: Proceedings of the 2019 27th ACM Joint Meeting

on European Software Engineering Conference and Symposium on the Foundations of Software Engineering. pp. 510–520. ESEC/FSE 2019, Association for Computing Machinery, New York, NY, USA (2019). https://doi.org/10.1145/3338906.3338955, https://doi.org/10.1145/3338906.3338955

33. Jha, S., Raj, S., Fernandes, S., Jha, S.K., Jha, S., Jalaian, B., Verma, G., Swami, A.: Attribution-based confidence metric for deep neural networks. In: Advances in Neural Information Processing Systems. pp. 11826–11837 (2019)

34. Jiang, H., Kim, B., Gupta, M.: To trust or not to trust a classifier. In: Advances in Neural Information Processing Systems. pp. 5541—5552 (2018)

35. Katz, G., Barrett, C., Dill, D.L., Julian, K., Kochenderfer, M.J.: Reluplex: An Efficient SMT Solver for Verifying Deep Neural Networks, pp. 97–117. Springer International Publishing, Cham (2017)

36. Kim, J., Feldt, R., Yoo, S.: Guiding deep learning system testing using surprise adequacy. In: Proceedings of the 41st International Conference on Software Engineering. pp. 1039–1049. IEEE Press (2019)

37. Krizhevsky, A.: Learning multiple layers of features from tiny images. University of Toronto (05 2012)

38. Krizhevsky, A., Sutskever, I., Hinton, G.E.: Imagenet classification with deep convolutional neural networks. In: Advances in neural information processing systems. pp. 1097–1105 (2012)

39. Kurakin, A., Goodfellow, I., Bengio, S.: Adversarial examples in the physical world. arXiv preprint arXiv:1607.02533 (2016)

40. Li, Z., Ma, X., Xu, C., Cao, C., Xu, J., Lü, J.: Boosting operational dnn testing efficiency through conditioning. In: Proceedings of the 2019 27th ACM Joint Meeting on European Software Engineering Conference and Symposium on the Foundations of Software Engineering. p. 499–509. ESEC/FSE 2019, Association for Computing Machinery, New York, NY, USA (2019). https://doi.org/10.1145/3338906.3338930, https://doi.org/10.1145/3338906.3338930

41. Ma, L., Juefei-Xu, F., Sun, J., Chen, C., Su, T., Zhang, F., Xue, M., Li, B., Li, L., Liu, Y., et al.: Deepgauge: Comprehensive and multi-granularity testing criteria for gauging the robustness of deep learning systems. arXiv preprint arXiv:1803.07519 (2018)

42. Ma, S., Liu, Y., Lee, W.C., Zhang, X., Grama, A.: Mode: automated neural network model debugging via state differential analysis and input selection. In: Proceedings of the 2018 26th ACM Joint Meeting on European Software Engineering Conference and Symposium on the Foundations of Software Engineering. pp. 175–186. ACM (2018)

43. Ma, X., Li, B., Wang, Y., Erfani, S.M., Wijewickrema, S., Schoenebeck, G., Song, D., Houle, M.E., Bailey, J.: Characterizing adversarial subspaces using local intrinsic dimensionality. In: International Conference on Learning Representations (ICLR) (2018)

44. van der Maaten, L., Hinton, G.: Visualizing data using t-SNE. Journal of Machine Learning Research 9, 2579–2605 (2008), http://www.jmlr.org/papers/v9/vandermaaten08a.html

45. Madry, A., Makelov, A., Schmidt, L., Tsipras, D., Vladu, A.: Towards deep learning models resistant to adversarial attacks. In: International Conference on Learning Representations (ICLR) (2018)

46. Madry, A., Makelov, A., Schmidt, L., Tsipras, D., Vladu, A.: Towards deep learning models resistant to adversarial attacks. In: International Conference on Learning Representations (ICLR) (2018)

47. Mann, H.B., Whitney, D.R.: On a test of whether one of two random variables is stochastically larger than the other. Annals of Mathematical Statistics **18**(1), 50–60 (1947)

48. Mao, C., Zhong, Z., Yang, J., Vondrick, C., Ray, B.: Metric learning for adversarial robustness. In: Advances in Neural Information Processing Systems. pp. 478–489 (2019)

49. Metzen, J.H., Genewein, T., Fischer, V., Bischoff, B.: On detecting adversarial perturbations. In: International Conference on Learning Representations (ICLR) (2017)

50. Mirman, M., Gehr, T., Vechev, M.: Differentiable abstract interpretation for provably robust neural networks. In: International Conference on Machine Learning. pp. 3575–3583 (2018)

51. Moon, S., An, G., Song, H.O.: Parsimonious black-box adversarial attacks via efficient combinatorial optimization. In: Chaudhuri, K., Salakhutdinov, R. (eds.) Proceedings of the 36th International Conference on Machine Learning. Proceedings of Machine Learning Research, vol. 97, pp. 4636–4645. PMLR, Long Beach, California, USA (09–15 Jun 2019), http://proceedings.mlr.press/v97/moon19a.html

52. Ozdag, M., Raj, S., Fernandes, S., Velasquez, A., Pullum, L., Jha, S.K.: On the susceptibility of deep neural networks to natural perturbations. In: AISafety@IJCAI (2019)

53. Papernot, N., McDaniel, P., Jha, S., Fredrikson, M., Celik, Z.B., Swami, A.: The limitations of deep learning in adversarial settings. In: 2016 IEEE European Symposium on Security and Privacy (EuroS&P). pp. 372–387. IEEE (2016)

54. Papernot, N., McDaniel, P., Wu, X., Jha, S., Swami, A.: Distillation as a defense to adversarial perturbations against deep neural networks. In: Security and Privacy (SP), 2016 IEEE Symposium on. pp. 582–597. IEEE (2016)

55. Pei, K., Cao, Y., Yang, J., Jana, S.: Deepxplore: Automated whitebox testing of deep learning systems. In: Proceedings of the 26th Symposium on Operating Systems Principles. pp. 1–18. ACM (2017)

56. Pei, K., Cao, Y., Yang, J., Jana, S.: Towards practical verification of machine learning: The case of computer vision systems. arXiv preprint arXiv:1712.01785 (2017)

57. Pham, H.V., Lutellier, T., Qi, W., Tan, L.: Cradle: Cross-backend validation to detect and localize bugs in deep learning libraries. In: Proceedings of the 41st International Conference on Software Engineering. p. 1027–1038. ICSE '19, IEEE Press (2019). https://doi.org/10.1109/ICSE.2019.00107, https://doi.org/10.1109/ICSE.2019.00107

58. Qiu, X., Meyerson, E., Miikkulainen, R.: Quantifying point-prediction uncertainty in neural networks via residual estimation with an i/o kernel. In: International Conference on Learning Representations (2020), https://openreview.net/forum?id=rkxNh1Stvr

59. Sawilowsky, S.: New effect size rules of thumb. Journal of Modern Applied Statistical Methods **8**, 597–599 (11 2009). https://doi.org/10.22237/jmasm/1257035100

60. Saxena, U.: Automold. https://github.com/UjjwalSaxena/Automold--Road-Augmentation-Library/

61. Sen, K., Marinov, D., Agha, G.: CUTE: A concolic unit testing engine for C. In: FSE (2005)

62. Seshia, S.A., Desai, A., Dreossi, T., Fremont, D.J., Ghosh, S., Kim, E., Shivakumar, S., Vazquez-Chanlatte, M., Yue, X.: Formal specification for deep neural networks. In: International Symposium on Automated Technology for Verification and Analysis. pp. 20–34. Springer (2018)

63. Shaham, U., Yamada, Y., Negahban, S.: Understanding adversarial training: Increasing local stability of neural nets through robust optimization. arXiv preprint arXiv:1511.05432 (2015)

64. Shankar, V., Dave, A., Roelofs, R., Ramanan, D., Recht, B., Schmidt, L.: A systematic framework for natural perturbations from videos (06 2019)

65. Silver, D., Huang, A., Maddison, C.J., Guez, A., Sifre, L., van den Driessche, G., Schrittwieser, J., Antonoglou, I., Panneershelvam, V., Lanctot, M., Dieleman, S., Grewe, D., Nham, J., Kalchbrenner, N., Sutskever, I., Lillicrap, T., Leach, M., Kavukcuoglu, K., Graepel, T., Hassabis, D.: Mastering the game of go with deep neural networks and tree search. Nature **529**, 484–503 (2016), http://www.nature.com/nature/journal/v529/n7587/full/nature16961.html

66. Simonyan, K., Zisserman, A.: Very deep convolutional networks for large-scale image recognition. In: International Conference on Learning Representations (ICLR) (2015)

67. SIMPSON, E.H.: Measurement of diversity. Nature **163**(4148), 688–688 (1949), https://doi.org/10.1038/163688a0

68. Stocco, A., Weiss, M., Calzana, M., Tonella, P.: Misbehaviour prediction for autonomous driving systems. In: Proceedings of 42nd International Conference on Software Engineering. p. 12 pages. ICSE '20, ACM (2020)

69. Stocco, A., Weiss, M., Calzana, M., Tonella, P.: Misbehaviour prediction for autonomous driving systems. In: International Conference of Software Engineering (ICSE) (2020)

70. Sun, Y., Wu, M., Ruan, W., Huang, X., Kwiatkowska, M., Kroening, D.: Concolic testing for deep neural networks (2018)

71. Szegedy, C., Zaremba, W., Sutskever, I., Bruna, J., Erhan, D., Goodfellow, I., Fergus, R.: Intriguing properties of neural networks. In: International Conference on Learning Representations (ICLR) (2014)

72. Teye, M., Azizpour, H., Smith, K.: Bayesian uncertainty estimation for batch normalized deep networks. In: Dy, J., Krause, A. (eds.) Proceedings of the 35th International Conference on Machine Learning. Proceedings of Machine Learning Research, vol. 80, pp. 4907–4916. PMLR, Stockholmsmässan, Stockholm Sweden (10–15 Jul 2018), http://proceedings.mlr.press/v80/teye18a.html

73. Tian, Y., Pei, K., Jana, S., Ray, B.: Deeptest: Automated testing of deep-neural-network-driven autonomous cars. In: International Conference of Software Engineering (ICSE), 2018 IEEE conference on. IEEE (2018)

74. Tian, Y., Zhong, Z., Ordonez, V., Kaiser, G., Ray, B.: Testing dnn image classifier for confusion & bias errors. In: International Conference of Software Engineering (ICSE) (2020)

75. Tramèr, F., Kurakin, A., Papernot, N., Goodfellow, I., Boneh, D., McDaniel, P.: Ensemble adversarial training: Attacks and defenses. arXiv preprint arXiv:1705.07204 (2017)

76. Tsipras, D., Santurkar, S., Engstrom, L., Turner, A., Madry, A.: Robustness may be at odds with accuracy. In: International Conference on Learning Representations (ICLR) (2019)

77. Udacity: A self-driving car simulator built with Unity. https://github.com/udacity/self-driving-car-sim (2017), online; accessed 18 August 2019

78. Udeshi, S., Jiang, X., Chattopadhyay, S.: Callisto: Entropy-based test generation and data quality assessment for machine learning systems. In: 2020 IEEE 13th International Conference on Software Testing, Validation and Verification (ICST). pp. 448–453 (2020)

79. Wang, F., Jiang, M., Qian, C., Yang, S., Li, C., Zhang, H., Wang, X., Tang, X.: Residual attention network for image classification. In: Proceedings of the IEEE Conference on Computer Vision and Pattern Recognition. pp. 3156–3164 (2017)

80. Wang, J., Dong, G., Sun, J., Wang, X., Zhang, P.: Adversarial sample detection for deep neural network through model mutation testing. In: Proceedings of the 41st International Conference on Software Engineering. p. 1245–1256. ICSE '19, IEEE Press (2019). https://doi.org/10.1109/ICSE.2019.00126, https://doi.org/10.1109/ICSE.2019.00126

81. Wang, S., Chen, Y., Abdou, A., Jana, S.: Mixtrain: Scalable training of formally robust neural networks. arXiv preprint arXiv:1811.02625 (2018)

82. Wang, S., Pei, K., Whitehouse, J., Yang, J., Jana, S.: Efficient formal safety analysis of neural networks. In: Proceedings of the 32Nd International Conference on Neural Information Processing Systems. pp. 6369–6379. NIPS'18, Curran Associates Inc., USA (2018), http://dl.acm.org/citation.cfm?id=3327345.3327533

83. Wang, S., Pei, K., Whitehouse, J., Yang, J., Jana, S.: Formal security analysis of neural networks using symbolic intervals. USENIX Security Symposium (2018)

84. Wong, E., Schmidt, F., Metzen, J.H., Kolter, J.Z.: Scaling provable adversarial defenses. In: Advances in Neural Information Processing Systems. pp. 8400–8409 (2018)

85. Xiao, C., Li, B., Zhu, J.Y., He, W., Liu, M., Song, D.: Generating adversarial examples with adversarial networks. In: 27th International Joint Conference on Artificial Intelligence (IJCAI) (2018)

86. Xiao, C., Zhu, J.Y., Li, B., He, W., Liu, M., Song, D.: Spatially transformed adversarial examples. In: International Conference on Learning Representations (ICLR) (2018)

87. Xiao, H., Rasul, K., Vollgraf, R.: Fashion-mnist: a novel image dataset for benchmarking machine learning algorithms (2017)

88. Yang, F., Wang, Z., Heinze-Deml, C.: Invariance-inducing regularization using worst-case transformations suffices to boost accuracy and spatial robustness. In: Advances in Neural Information Processing Systems 32. pp. 14757–14768 (2019)

89. Yuval Netzer, T.W., Coates, A., Bissacco, A., Wu, B., Ng, A.Y.: Reading digits in natural images with unsupervised feature learning. In: NIPS Workshop on Deep Learning and Unsupervised Feature Learning (2011)

90. Zagoruyko, S., Komodakis, N.: Wide residual networks. In: BMVC (2016)

91. Zhang, H., Chan, W.K.: Apricot: A weight-adaptation approach to fixing deep learning models. In: 2019 34th IEEE/ACM International Conference on Automated Software Engineering (ASE). pp. 376–387 (Nov 2019). https://doi.org/10.1109/ASE.2019.00043

92. Zhang, M., Zhang, Y., Zhang, L., Liu, C., Khurshid, S.: Deeproad: Gan-based metamorphic autonomous driving system testing. arXiv preprint arXiv:1802.02295 (2018)

93. Zhao, Z., Dua, D., Singh, S.: Generating natural adversarial examples. In: International Conference on Learning Representations (ICLR) (2018)

94. Zhou, H., Li, W., Kong, Z., Guo, J., Zhang, Y., Zhang, L., Yu, B., Liu, C.: Deepbillboard: Systematic physical-world testing of autonomous driving systems. In: International Conference of Software Engineering (ICSE) (2020)

Test-Comp Contributions

Status Report on Software Testing: Test-Comp 2021

Dirk Beyer

LMU Munich, Munich, Germany

Abstract. This report describes Test-Comp 2021, the 3rd edition of the Competition on Software Testing. The competition is a series of annual comparative evaluations of fully automatic software test generators for C programs. The competition has a strong focus on reproducibility of its results and its main goal is to provide an overview of the current state of the art in the area of automatic test-generation. The competition was based on 3 173 test-generation tasks for C programs. Each test-generation task consisted of a program and a test specification (error coverage, branch coverage). Test-Comp 2021 had 11 participating test generators from 6 countries.

Keywords: Software Testing · Test-Case Generation · Competition · Program Analysis · Software Validation · Software Bugs · Test Validation · Test-Comp · Benchmarking · Test Coverage · Bug Finding · Test-Suites · BENCHEXEC · TESTCOV

1 Introduction

Among several other objectives, the Competition on Software Testing (Test-Comp [4, 5, 6], https://test-comp.sosy-lab.org/2021) showcases every year the state of the art in the area of automatic software testing. This edition of Test-Comp is the 3rd edition of the competition. It provides an overview of the currently achieved results by tool implementations that are based on the most recent ideas, concepts, and algorithms for fully automatic test generation. This competition report describes the (updated) rules and definitions, presents the competition results, and discusses some interesting facts about the execution of the competition experiments. The setup of Test-Comp is similar to SV-COMP [8], in terms of both technical and procedural organization. The results are collected via BENCHEXEC's XML results format [16], and transformed into tables and plots in several formats (https://test-comp.sosy-lab.org/2021/results/). All results are available in artifacts at Zenodo (Table 3).

This report extends previous reports on Test-Comp [4, 5, 6].
Reproduction packages are available on Zenodo (see Table 3).
Funded in part by the Deutsche Forschungsgemeinschaft (DFG) – 418257054 (Coop).
✉ dirk.beyer@sosy-lab.org

E. Guerra and M. Stoelinga (Eds.): FASE 2021, LNCS 12649, pp. 341–357, 2021.
https://doi.org/10.1007/978-3-030-71500-7_17

Competition Goals. In summary, the goals of Test-Comp are the following [5]:

- Establish *standards* for software test generation. This means, most prominently, to develop a standard for marking input values in programs, define an exchange format for test suites, agree on a specification language for test-coverage criteria, and define how to validate the resulting test suites.
- Establish a set of *benchmarks* for software testing in the community. This means to create and maintain a set of programs together with coverage criteria, and to make those publicly available for researchers to be used in performance comparisons when evaluating a new technique.
- Provide an overview of *available tools* for test-case generation and a snapshot of the state-of-the-art in software testing to the community. This means to compare, independently from particular paper projects and specific techniques, different test generators in terms of effectiveness and performance.
- Increase the visibility and credits that *tool developers* receive. This means to provide a forum for presentation of tools and discussion of the latest technologies, and to give the participants the opportunity to publish about the development work that they have done.
- Educate PhD students and other participants on how to set up performance experiments, package tools in a way that supports reproduction, and how to perform *robust and accurate research experiments.*
- Provide *resources* to development teams that do not have sufficient computing resources and give them the opportunity to obtain results from experiments on large benchmark sets.

Related Competitions. In the field of formal methods, competitions are respected as an important evaluation method and there are many competitions [2]. We refer to the previous report [5] for a more detailed discussion and give here only the references to the most related competitions [2, 8, 32, 39].

Quick Summary of Changes. As the competition continuously improves, we report the changes since the last report. We list a summary of five new items in Test-Comp 2021 as overview:

- Extended task-definition format, version 2.0: Sect. 2
- SPDX identification of licenses in SV-Benchmarks collection: Sect. 2
- Extension of the SV-Benchmarks collection by several categories: Sect. 3
- Elimination of competition-specific functions `__VERIFIER_error` and `__VERIFIER_assume` from the test-generation tasks (and rules): Sect. 3
- CoVeriTeam: New tool that can be used to remotely execute test-generation runs on the competition machines: Sect. 4

2   Definitions, Formats, and Rules

Organizational aspects such as the classification (automatic, off-site, reproducible, jury, training) and the competition schedule is given in the initial competition definition [4]. In the following, we repeat some important definitions that are necessary to understand the results.

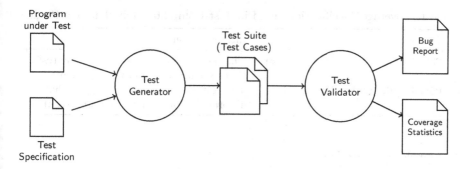

Fig. 1: Flow of the Test-Comp execution for one test generator (taken from [5])

Test-Generation Task. A *test-generation task* is a pair of an input program (program under test) and a test specification. A *test-generation run* is a non-interactive execution of a test generator on a single test-generation task, in order to generate a test suite according to the test specification. A *test suite* is a sequence of test cases, given as a directory of files according to the format for exchangeable test-suites.[1]

Execution of a Test Generator. Figure 1 illustrates the process of executing one test generator on the benchmark suite. One test run for a test generator gets as input (i) a program from the benchmark suite and (ii) a test specification (cover bug, or cover branches), and returns as output a test suite (i.e., a set of test cases). The test generator is contributed by a competition participant as a software archive in ZIP format. The test runs are executed centrally by the competition organizer. The test-suite validator takes as input the test suite from the test generator and validates it by executing the program on all test cases: for bug finding it checks if the bug is exposed and for coverage it reports the coverage. We use the tool TESTCOV [15][2] as test-suite validator.

Test Specification. The specification for testing a program is given to the test generator as input file (either `properties/coverage-error-call.prp` or `properties/coverage-branches.prp` for Test-Comp 2021).

The definition `init(main())` is used to define the initial states of the program under test by a call of function `main` (with no parameters). The definition `FQL(f)` specifies that coverage definition `f` should be achieved. The FQL (FSHELL query language [28]) coverage definition `COVER EDGES(@DECISIONEDGE)` means that all branches should be covered (typically used to obtain a standard test suite for quality assurance) and `COVER EDGES(@CALL(foo))` means that a call (at least one) to function `foo` should be covered (typically used for bug finding). A complete specification looks as follows: `COVER( init(main()), FQL(COVER EDGES(@DECISIONEDGE)) )`.

---

[1] https://gitlab.com/sosy-lab/software/test-format/
[2] https://gitlab.com/sosy-lab/software/test-suite-validator

Table 1: Coverage specifications used in Test-Comp 2021 (similar to 2019, 2020)

Formula	Interpretation
COVER EDGES(@CALL(reach_error))	The test suite contains at least one test that executes function reach_error.
COVER EDGES(@DECISIONEDGE)	The test suite contains tests such that all branches of the program are executed.

```
1   format_version: '2.0'
2
3   # old file name: floppy_true—unreach—call_true—valid—memsafety.i.cil.c
4   input_files: 'floppy.i.cil—3.c'
5
6   properties:
7     — property_file: ../properties/unreach—call.prp
8       expected_verdict: true
9     — property_file: ../properties/valid—memsafety.prp
10      expected_verdict: false
11      subproperty: valid—memtrack
12    — property_file: ../properties/coverage—branches.prp
13
14  options:
15    language: C
16    data_model: ILP32
```

Fig. 2: Example task definition file floppy.i.cil-3.yml for C program floppy.i.cil-3.c (format version and options are new compared to last year)

Table 1 lists the two FQL formulas that are used in test specifications of Test-Comp 2021; there was no change from 2020 (except that special function __VERIFIER_error does not exist anymore).

Task-Definition Format 2.0. The format for the task definitions in the SV-Benchmarks repository was extended by options that can carry information from the test-generation task to the test tool. Test-Comp 2021 used the format in version 2.0 (https://gitlab.com/sosy-lab/benchmarking/task-definition-format/-/tree/2.0).
The options now contain the language (C or Java) and the data model (ILP32, LP64, see http://www.unix.org/whitepapers/64bit.html, only for C programs) that the program of the test-generation task assumes (https://github.com/sosy-lab/sv-benchmarks#task-definitions). An example task definition is provided in Fig. 2: This YAML file specifies, for the C program floppy.i.cil-3.c, two verification tasks (reachability of a function call and memory safety) and one test-generation task (coverage of all branches). Previously, the options for language and data model where defined in category-specific configuration files (for example c/ReachSafety-ControlFlow.cfg), which were deleted before Test-Comp 2021.

License and Qualification. The license of each participating test generator must allow its free use for reproduction of the competition results. Details on qualification criteria can be found in the competition report of Test-Comp 2019 [6]. Furthermore, the community tries to apply the SPDX standard (`https://spdx.dev`) to the SV-Benchmarks repository. Continuous-integration checks based on REUSE (`https://reuse.software`) will ensure that all benchmark tasks adhere to the standard.

3 Categories and Scoring Schema

Benchmark Programs. The input programs were taken from the largest and most diverse open-source repository of software-verification and test-generation tasks [3], which is also used by SV-COMP [8]. As in 2020, we selected all programs for which the following properties were satisfied (see issue on GitHub [4] and report [6]):

1. compiles with `gcc`, if a harness for the special methods [5] is provided,
2. should contain at least one call to a nondeterministic function,
3. does not rely on nondeterministic pointers,
4. does not have expected result 'false' for property 'termination', and
5. has expected result 'false' for property 'unreach-call' (only for category *Error Coverage*).

This selection yielded a total of 3 173 test-generation tasks, namely 607 tasks for category *Error Coverage* and 2 566 tasks for category *Code Coverage*. The test-generation tasks are partitioned into categories, which are listed in Tables 6 and 7 and described in detail on the competition web site.[6] Figure 3 illustrates the category composition.

The programs in the benchmark collection contained functions `__VERIFIER_error` and `__VERIFIER_assume` that had a specific predefined meaning. Last year, those functions were removed from all programs in the SV-Benchmarks collection. More about the reasoning is explained in the SV-COMP 2021 competition report [8].

Category Error-Coverage. The first category is to show the abilities to discover bugs. The benchmark set consists of programs that contain a bug. Every run will be started by a batch script, which produces for every tool and every test-generation task one of the following scores: 1 point, if the validator succeeds in executing the program under test on a generated test case that explores the bug (i.e., the specified function was called), and 0 points, otherwise.

---

[3] `https://github.com/sosy-lab/sv-benchmarks`
[4] `https://github.com/sosy-lab/sv-benchmarks/pull/774`
[5] `https://test-comp.sosy-lab.org/2021/rules.php`
[6] `https://test-comp.sosy-lab.org/2021/benchmarks.php`

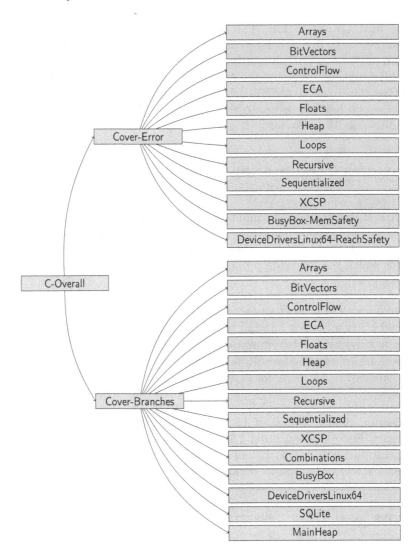

Fig. 3: Category structure for Test-Comp 2021; compared to Test-Comp 2020, there are three new sub-categories in *Cover-Error* and two new sub-categories in *Cover-Branches*: we added the sub-categories *XCSP*, *BusyBox-MemSafety*, and *DeviceDriversLinux64-ReachSafety* to category *Cover-Error*, and the sub-categories *XCSP* and *Combinations* to category *Cover-Branches*

Category Branch-Coverage. The second category is to cover as many branches of the program as possible. The coverage criterion was chosen because many test generators support this standard criterion by default. Other coverage criteria can be reduced to branch coverage by transformation [27]. Every run will be started by a batch script, which produces for every tool and every test-generation task the coverage of branches of the program (as reported by TESTCOV [15]; a value between 0 and 1) that are executed for the generated test cases. The score is the returned coverage.

Ranking. The ranking was decided based on the sum of points (normalized for meta categories). In case of a tie, the ranking was decided based on the run time, which is the total CPU time over all test-generation tasks. Opt-out from categories was possible and scores for categories were normalized based on the number of tasks per category (see competition report of SV-COMP 2013 [3], page 597).

4 Reproducibility

In order to support independent reproduction of the Test-Comp results, we made all major components that are used for the competition available in public version-control repositories. An overview of the components that contribute to the reproducible setup of Test-Comp is provided in Fig. 4, and the details are given in Table 2. We refer to the report of Test-Comp 2019 [6] for a thorough description of all components of the Test-Comp organization and how we ensure that all parts are publicly available for maximal reproducibility.

In order to guarantee long-term availability and immutability of the test-generation tasks, the produced competition results, and the produced test suites, we also packaged the material and published it at Zenodo (see Table 3). The archive for the competition results includes the raw results in BENCHEXEC's XML exchange format, the log output of the test generators and validator, and a mapping from file names to SHA-256 hashes. The hashes of the files are useful for validating the exact contents of a file, and accessing the files inside the archive that contains the test suites.

To provide transparent access to the exact versions of the test generators that were used in the competition, all test-generator archives are stored in a public Git repository. GITLAB was used to host the repository for the test-generator archives due to its generous repository size limit of 10 GB.

Competition Workflow. As illustrated in Fig. 4, the ingredients for a test or verification run are (a) a test or verification task (which program and which specification to use), (b) a benchmark definition (which categories and which options to use), (c) a tool-info module (uniform way to access a tool's version string and the command line to invoke), and (d) an archive that contains all executables that are required and cannot be installed as standard Ubuntu package.

(a) Each test or verification task is defined by a task-definition file (as shown, e.g., in Fig. 2). The tasks are stored in the SV-Benchmarks repository and maintained by the verification and testing community, including the competition participants and the competition organizer.

(b) A benchmark definition defines the choices of the participating team, that is, which categories to execute the test generator on and which parameters to pass to the test generator. The benchmark definition also specifies the resource limits of the competition runs (CPU time, memory, CPU cores). The benchmark definitions are created or maintained by the teams and the organizer.

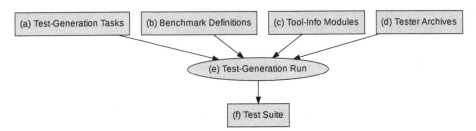

Fig. 4: Benchmarking components of Test-Comp and competition's execution flow (same as for Test-Comp 2020)

Table 2: Publicly available components for reproducing Test-Comp 2021

Component	Fig. 4	Repository	Version
Test-Generation Tasks	(a)	github.com/sosy-lab/sv-benchmarks	testcomp21
Benchmark Definitions	(b)	gitlab.com/sosy-lab/test-comp/bench-defs	testcomp21
Tool-Info Modules	(c)	github.com/sosy-lab/benchexec	3.6
Test-Generator Archives	(d)	gitlab.com/sosy-lab/test-comp/archives-2021	testcomp21
Benchmarking	(e)	github.com/sosy-lab/benchexec	3.6
Test-Suite Format	(f)	gitlab.com/sosy-lab/software/test-format	testcomp21

Table 3: Artifacts published for Test-Comp 2021

Content	DOI	Reference
Test-Generation Tasks	10.5281/zenodo.4459132	[9]
Competition Results	10.5281/zenodo.4459470	[7]
Test Suites (Witnesses)	10.5281/zenodo.4459466	[10]
BenchExec	10.5281/zenodo.4317433	[43]

(c) A tool-info module is a component that provides a uniform way to access the test-generation or verification tool: it provides interfaces for accessing the version string of a test generator and assembles the command-line from the information given in the benchmark definition and task definition. The tool-info modules are written by the participating teams with the help of the BENCHEXEC maintainer and others.

(d) A test generator is provided as an archive in ZIP format. The archive contains a directory with a README and LICENSE file as well as all components that are necessary for the test generator to be executed. This archive is created by the participating team and merged into the central repository via a merge request.

All above components are reviewed by the competition jury and improved according to the comments from the reviewers by the teams and the organizer.

Table 4: Competition candidates with tool references and representing jury members

Tester	Ref.	Jury member	Affiliation
CMA-ES Fuzz	[33]	Gidon Ernst	LMU Munich, Germany
CoVeriTest	[12, 31]	Marie-Christine Jakobs	TU Darmstadt, Germany
FuSeBMC	[1, 25]	Kaled Alshmrany	U. of Manchester, UK
HybridTiger	[18, 38]	Sebastian Ruland	TU Darmstadt, Germany
Klee	[19, 20]	Martin Nowack	Imperial College London, UK
Legion	[37]	Dongge Liu	U. of Melbourne, Australia
LibKluzzer	[35]	Hoang M. Le	U. of Bremen, Germany
PRTest	[14, 36]	Thomas Lemberger	LMU Munich, Germany
Symbiotic	[21, 22]	Marek Chalupa	Masaryk U., Brno, Czechia
TracerX	[29, 30]	Joxan Jaffar	National U. of Singapore, Singapore
VeriFuzz	[23]	Raveendra Kumar M.	Tata Consultancy Services, India

Due to the reproducibility requirements and high level of automation that is necessary for a competition like Test-Comp, participating in the competition is also a challenge itself: package the tool, provide meaningful log output, specify the benchmark definition, implement a tool-info module, and troubleshoot in case of problems. Test-Comp is a friendly and helpful community, and problems are reported in a GitLab issue tracker, where the organizer and the other teams help fixing the problems.

To provide participants access to the actual competition machines, the competition used CoVeriTeam [13] (https://gitlab.com/sosy-lab/software/coveriteam/) for the first time. CoVeriTeam is a tool for cooperative verification, which enables remote execution of test-generation or verification runs directly on the competition machines (among its many other features). This possibility was found to be a valuable service for trouble shooting.

5   Results and Discussion

For the third time, the competition experiments represent the state of the art in fully automatic test generation for whole C programs. The report helps in understanding the improvements compared to last year, in terms of effectiveness (test coverage, as accumulated in the score) and efficiency (resource consumption in terms of CPU time). All results mentioned in this article were inspected and approved by the participants.

Participating Test Generators. Table 4 provides an overview of the participating test generators and references to publications, as well as the team representatives of the jury of Test-Comp 2021. (The competition jury consists of the chair and one member of each participating team.) Table 5 lists the features and technologies that are used in the test generators. An online table with information about all participating systems is provided on the competition web site.[7]

---

[7] https://test-comp.sosy-lab.org/2021/systems.php

Table 5: Technologies and features that the competition candidates used

Participant	Bounded Model Checking	CEGAR	Evolutionary Algorithms	Explicit-Value Analysis	Floating-Point Arithmetics	Guidance by Coverage Measures	Predicate Abstraction	Random Execution	Symbolic Execution	Targeted Input Generation	Algorithm Selection	Portfolio
CMA-ES Fuzz			✓	✓		✓		✓				
CoVeriTest		✓		✓	✓		✓					✓
FuSeBMC	✓				✓	✓				✓		✓
HybridTiger		✓		✓	✓		✓					
Klee						✓			✓	✓		
Legion			✓			✓		✓	✓	✓		
LibKluzzer						✓			✓	✓		
PRTest								✓				
Symbiotic						✓			✓	✓		✓
TracerX	✓								✓	✓		
VeriFuzz	✓		✓	✓		✓		✓				

Computing Resources. The computing environment and the resource limits were the same as for Test-Comp 2020 [5]: Each test run was limited to 8 processing units (cores), 15 GB of memory, and 15 min of CPU time. The test-suite validation was limited to 2 processing units, 7 GB of memory, and 5 min of CPU time. The machines for running the experiments are part of a compute cluster that consists of 168 machines; each test-generation run was executed on an otherwise completely unloaded, dedicated machine, in order to achieve precise measurements. Each machine had one Intel Xeon E3-1230 v5 CPU, with 8 processing units each, a frequency of 3.4 GHz, 33 GB of RAM, and a GNU/Linux operating system (x86_64-linux, Ubuntu 20.04 with Linux kernel 5.4). We used BenchExec [16] to measure and control computing resources (CPU time, memory, CPU energy) and VerifierCloud[8] to distribute, install, run, and clean-up test-case generation runs, and to collect the results. The values

---

[8] https://vcloud.sosy-lab.org

Table 6: Quantitative overview over all results; empty cells mark opt-outs; label 'new' indicates first-time participants

Participant	Cover-Error 607 tasks	Cover-Branches 2566 tasks	Overall 3173 tasks
CMA-ES Fuzz new	0	411	254
CoVeriTest	225	1128	1286
FuSeBMC new	**405**	1161	**1776**
HybridTiger	266	860	1228
Klee	339	784	1370
Legion	35	651	495
LibKluzzer	**359**	**1292**	**1738**
PRTest	79	519	526
Symbiotic	314	**1169**	1543
TracerX	246	1087	1315
VeriFuzz	**385**	**1389**	**1865**

for time and energy are accumulated over all cores of the CPU. To measure the CPU energy, we use CPU ENERGY METER [17] (integrated in BENCHEXEC [16]). Further technical parameters of the competition machines are available in the repository which also contains the benchmark definitions. [9]

One complete test-generation execution of the competition consisted of 34 903 single test-generation runs. The total CPU time was 220 days and the consumed energy 56 kWh for one complete competition run for test generation (without validation). Test-suite validation consisted of 34 903 single test-suite validation runs. The total consumed CPU time was 6.3 days. Each tool was executed several times, in order to make sure no installation issues occur during the execution. Including preruns, the infrastructure managed a total of 210 632 test-generation runs (consuming 1.8 years of CPU time) and 207 459 test-suite validation runs (consuming 27 days of CPU time). We did not measure the CPU energy during preruns.

Quantitative Results. Table 6 presents the quantitative overview of all tools and all categories. The head row mentions the category and the number of test-generation tasks in that category. The tools are listed in alphabetical order; every table row lists the scores of one test generator. We indicate the top three candidates by formatting their scores in bold face and in larger font size. An empty table cell means that the test generator opted-out from the respective main category

---

[9] https://gitlab.com/sosy-lab/test-comp/bench-defs/tree/testcomp21

Table 7: Overview of the top-three test generators for each category (measurement values for CPU time and energy rounded to two significant digits)

Rank	Tester	Score	CPU Time (in h)	CPU Energy (in kWh)
Cover-Error				
1	FuSeBMC	**405**	22	0.26
2	VeriFuzz	385	2.6	0.031
3	LibKluzzer	359	90	0.99
Cover-Branches				
1	VeriFuzz	**1389**	630	8.1
2	LibKluzzer	1292	520	5.7
3	Symbiotic	1169	440	5.1
Overall				
1	VeriFuzz	**1865**	640	8.1
2	FuSeBMC	1776	410	4.8
3	LibKluzzer	1738	610	6.7

(perhaps participating in subcategories only, restricting the evaluation to a specific topic). More information (including interactive tables, quantile plots for every category, and also the raw data in XML format) is available on the competition web site [10] and in the results artifact (see Table 3). Table 7 reports the top three test generators for each category. The consumed run time (column 'CPU Time') is given in hours and the consumed energy (column 'Energy') is given in kWh.

Score-Based Quantile Functions for Quality Assessment. We use score-based quantile functions [16] because these visualizations make it easier to understand the results of the comparative evaluation. The web site [10] and the results artifact (Table 3) include such a plot for each category; as example, we show the plot for category *Overall* (all test-generation tasks) in Fig. 5. All 11 test generators participated in category *Overall*, for which the quantile plot shows the overall performance over all categories (scores for meta categories are normalized [3]). A more detailed discussion of score-based quantile plots for testing is provided in the previous competition report [6].

Alternative Rankings. Table 8 is similar to Table 7, but contains the alternative ranking categories *Green Testing* and *New Test Generators*. Column 'Quality' gives the score in score points (sp), column 'CPU Time' the CPU usage in hours (h), column 'CPU Energy' the CPU usage in kilo-watt-hours (kWh), and column 'Rank Measure' reports the values for the rank measure, which is different for the two alternative ranking categories. (An entry '–' for 'CPU Energy' indicates that we did not measure the energy consumption for technical reasons.)

---

[10] https://test-comp.sosy-lab.org/2021/results

Fig. 5: Quantile functions for category *Overall*. Each quantile function illustrates the quantile (*x*-coordinate) of the scores obtained by test-generation runs below a certain number of test-generation tasks (*y*-coordinate). More details were given previously [6]. The graphs are decorated with symbols to make them better distinguishable without color.

Table 8: Alternative rankings; quality is given in score points (sp), CPU time in hours (h), energy in kilo-watt-hours (kWh), the first rank measure in kilo-joule per score point (kJ/sp), and the second rank measure in score points (sp); measurement values are rounded to 2 significant digits

Rank	Test Generator	Quality (sp)	CPU Time (h)	CPU Energy (kWh)	Rank Measure
Green Testing					(kJ/sp)
1	TRACERX	1 315	210	2.5	6.8
2	KLEE	1 370	210	2.6	6.8
3	FUSEBMC	1 776	410	4.8	9.7
worst					51
New Test Generators					(sp)
1	FUSEBMC	1 776	410	4.8	1 776
2	CMA-ES FUZZ	254	310	–	254

Green Testing — Low Energy Consumption. Since a large part of the cost of test generation is caused by the energy consumption, it might be important to also consider the energy efficiency in rankings, as complement to the official Test-Comp ranking. This alternative ranking category uses the energy consumption per score point as rank measure: $\frac{\text{CPU Energy}}{\text{Quality}}$, with the unit kilo-joule per

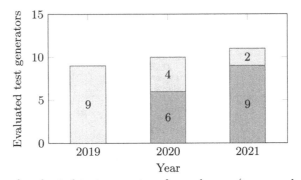

Fig. 6: Number of evaluated test generators for each year (top: number of first-time participants; bottom: previous year's participants)

score point (kJ/sp).[11] The energy is measured using CPU ENERGY METER [17], which we use as part of BENCHEXEC [16].

New Test Generators. To acknowledge the test generators that participated for the first time in Test-Comp, the second alternative ranking category lists measures only for the new test generators, and the rank measure is the quality with the unit score point (sp). For example, CMA-ES FUZZ is an early prototype and has already obtained a total score of 411 points in category *Cover-Branches*, and FUSEBMC is a new tool based on some mature components and became second place already in its first participation. This should encourage developers of test generators to participate with new tools of any maturity level.

6   Conclusion

Test-Comp 2021 was the the 3rd edition of the Competition on Software Testing, and attracted 11 participating teams (see Fig. 6 for the participation numbers and Table 4 for the details). The competition offers an overview of the state of the art in automatic software testing for C programs. The competition does not only execute the test generators and collect results, but also validates the achieved coverage of the test suites, based on the latest version of the test-suite validator TESTCOV. As before, the jury and the organizer made sure that the competition follows the high quality standards of the FASE conference, in particular with respect to the important principles of fairness, community support, and transparency.

Data Availability Statement. The test-generation tasks and results of the competition are published at Zenodo, as described in Table 3. All components and data that are necessary for reproducing the competition are available in public version repositories, as specified in Table 2. Furthermore, the results are presented online on the competition web site for easy access: https://test-comp.sosy-lab.org/2021/results/.

---

[11] Errata: Table 8 of last year's report for Test-Comp 2020 contains a typo: The unit of the energy consumption per score point is kJ/sp (instead of J/sp).

References

1. Alshmrany, K., Menezes, R., Gadelha, M., Cordeiro, L.: FuSeBMC: A white-box fuzzer for finding security vulnerabilities in C programs (competition contribution). In: Proc. FASE. LNCS 12649, Springer (2021)
2. Bartocci, E., Beyer, D., Black, P.E., Fedyukovich, G., Garavel, H., Hartmanns, A., Huisman, M., Kordon, F., Nagele, J., Sighireanu, M., Steffen, B., Suda, M., Sutcliffe, G., Weber, T., Yamada, A.: TOOLympics 2019: An overview of competitions in formal methods. In: Proc. TACAS (3). pp. 3–24. LNCS 11429, Springer (2019). https://doi.org/10.1007/978-3-030-17502-3_1
3. Beyer, D.: Second competition on software verification (Summary of SV-COMP 2013). In: Proc. TACAS. pp. 594–609. LNCS 7795, Springer (2013). https://doi.org/10.1007/978-3-642-36742-7_43
4. Beyer, D.: Competition on software testing (Test-Comp). In: Proc. TACAS (3). pp. 167–175. LNCS 11429, Springer (2019). https://doi.org/10.1007/978-3-030-17502-3_11
5. Beyer, D.: Second competition on software testing: Test-Comp 2020. In: Proc. FASE. pp. 505–519. LNCS 12076, Springer (2020). https://doi.org/10.1007/978-3-030-45234-6_25
6. Beyer, D.: First international competition on software testing (Test-Comp 2019). Int. J. Softw. Tools Technol. Transf. (2021)
7. Beyer, D.: Results of the 3rd Intl. Competition on Software Testing (Test-Comp 2021). Zenodo (2021). https://doi.org/10.5281/zenodo.4459470
8. Beyer, D.: Software verification: 10th comparative evaluation (SV-COMP 2021). In: Proc. TACAS (2). LNCS 12652, Springer (2021), preprint available.
9. Beyer, D.: SV-Benchmarks: Benchmark set of 3rd Intl. Competition on Software Testing (Test-Comp 2021). Zenodo (2021). https://doi.org/10.5281/zenodo.4459132
10. Beyer, D.: Test suites from Test-Comp 2021 test-generation tools. Zenodo (2021). https://doi.org/10.5281/zenodo.4459466
11. Beyer, D., Chlipala, A.J., Henzinger, T.A., Jhala, R., Majumdar, R.: Generating tests from counterexamples. In: Proc. ICSE. pp. 326–335. IEEE (2004). https://doi.org/10.1109/ICSE.2004.1317455
12. Beyer, D., Jakobs, M.C.: CoVeriTest: Cooperative verifier-based testing. In: Proc. FASE. pp. 389–408. LNCS 11424, Springer (2019). https://doi.org/10.1007/978-3-030-16722-6_23
13. Beyer, D., Kanav, S.: CoVeriTeam: On-demand composition of cooperative verification systems. unpublished manuscript (2021)
14. Beyer, D., Lemberger, T.: Software verification: Testing vs. model checking. In: Proc. HVC. pp. 99–114. LNCS 10629, Springer (2017). https://doi.org/10.1007/978-3-319-70389-3_7
15. Beyer, D., Lemberger, T.: TestCov: Robust test-suite execution and coverage measurement. In: Proc. ASE. pp. 1074–1077. IEEE (2019). https://doi.org/10.1109/ASE.2019.00105
16. Beyer, D., Löwe, S., Wendler, P.: Reliable benchmarking: Requirements and solutions. Int. J. Softw. Tools Technol. Transfer 21(1), 1–29 (2019). https://doi.org/10.1007/s10009-017-0469-y
17. Beyer, D., Wendler, P.: CPU Energy Meter: A tool for energy-aware algorithms engineering. In: Proc. TACAS (2). pp. 126–133. LNCS 12079, Springer (2020). https://doi.org/10.1007/978-3-030-45237-7_8

18. Bürdek, J., Lochau, M., Bauregger, S., Holzer, A., von Rhein, A., Apel, S., Beyer, D.: Facilitating reuse in multi-goal test-suite generation for software product lines. In: Proc. FASE. pp. 84–99. LNCS 9033, Springer (2015). https://doi.org/10.1007/978-3-662-46675-9_6

19. Cadar, C., Dunbar, D., Engler, D.R.: KLEE: Unassisted and automatic generation of high-coverage tests for complex systems programs. In: Proc. OSDI. pp. 209–224. USENIX Association (2008)

20. Cadar, C., Nowack, M.: KLEE symbolic execution engine in 2019. Int. J. Softw. Tools Technol. Transf. (2020). https://doi.org/10.1007/s10009-020-00570-3

21. Chalupa, M., Novák, J., Strejček, J.: SYMBIOTIC 8: Parallel and targeted test generation (competition contribution). In: Proc. FASE. LNCS 12649, Springer (2021)

22. Chalupa, M., Strejček, J., Vitovská, M.: Joint forces for memory safety checking. In: Proc. SPIN. pp. 115–132. Springer (2018). https://doi.org/10.1007/978-3-319-94111-0_7

23. Chowdhury, A.B., Medicherla, R.K., Venkatesh, R.: VERIFUZZ: Program-aware fuzzing (competition contribution). In: Proc. TACAS (3). pp. 244–249. LNCS 11429, Springer (2019). https://doi.org/10.1007/978-3-030-17502-3_22

24. Cok, D.R., Déharbe, D., Weber, T.: The 2014 SMT competition. JSAT **9**, 207–242 (2016)

25. Gadelha, M.R., Menezes, R., Cordeiro, L.: ESBMC 6.1: Automated test-case generation using bounded model checking. Int. J. Softw. Tools Technol. Transf. (2020). https://doi.org/10.1007/s10009-020-00571-2

26. Godefroid, P., Sen, K.: Combining model checking and testing. In: Handbook of Model Checking, pp. 613–649. Springer (2018). https://doi.org/10.1007/978-3-319-10575-8_19

27. Harman, M., Hu, L., Hierons, R.M., Wegener, J., Sthamer, H., Baresel, A., Roper, M.: Testability transformation. IEEE Trans. Software Eng. **30**(1), 3–16 (2004). https://doi.org/10.1109/TSE.2004.1265732

28. Holzer, A., Schallhart, C., Tautschnig, M., Veith, H.: How did you specify your test suite. In: Proc. ASE. pp. 407–416. ACM (2010). https://doi.org/10.1145/1858996.1859084

29. Jaffar, J., Maghareh, R., Godboley, S., Ha, X.L.: TRACERX: Dynamic symbolic execution with interpolation (competition contribution). In: Proc. FASE. pp. 530–534. LNCS 12076, Springer (2020). https://doi.org/10.1007/978-3-030-45234-6_28

30. Jaffar, J., Murali, V., Navas, J.A., Santosa, A.E.: TRACER: A symbolic execution tool for verification. In: Proc. CAV. pp. 758–766. LNCS 7358, Springer (2012). https://doi.org/10.1007/978-3-642-31424-7_61

31. Jakobs, M.C., Richter, C.: COVERITEST with adaptive time scheduling (competition contribution). In: Proc. FASE. LNCS 12649, Springer (2021)

32. Kifetew, F.M., Devroey, X., Rueda, U.: Java unit-testing tool competition: Seventh round. In: Proc. SBST. pp. 15–20. IEEE (2019). https://doi.org/10.1109/SBST.2019.00014

33. Kim, H.: Fuzzing with stochastic optimization (2020), Bachelor's Thesis, LMU Munich

34. King, J.C.: Symbolic execution and program testing. Commun. ACM **19**(7), 385–394 (1976). https://doi.org/10.1145/360248.360252

35. Le, H.M.: LLVM-based hybrid fuzzing with LIBKLUZZER (competition contribution). In: Proc. FASE. pp. 535–539. LNCS 12076, Springer (2020). https://doi.org/10.1007/978-3-030-45234-6_29

36. Lemberger, T.: Plain random test generation with PRTEST. Int. J. Softw. Tools Technol. Transf. (2020)
37. Liu, D., Ernst, G., Murray, T., Rubinstein, B.: LEGION: Best-first concolic testing (competition contribution). In: Proc. FASE. pp. 545–549. LNCS 12076, Springer (2020). https://doi.org/10.1007/978-3-030-45234-6_31
38. Ruland, S., Lochau, M., Jakobs, M.C.: HYBRIDTIGER: Hybrid model checking and domination-based partitioning for efficient multi-goal test-suite generation (competition contribution). In: Proc. FASE. pp. 520–524. LNCS 12076, Springer (2020). https://doi.org/10.1007/978-3-030-45234-6_26
39. Song, J., Alves-Foss, J.: The DARPA cyber grand challenge: A competitor's perspective, part 2. IEEE Security and Privacy **14**(1), 76–81 (2016). https://doi.org/10.1109/MSP.2016.14
40. Stump, A., Sutcliffe, G., Tinelli, C.: STAREXEC: A cross-community infrastructure for logic solving. In: Proc. IJCAR, pp. 367–373. LNCS 8562, Springer (2014). https://doi.org/10.1007/978-3-319-08587-6_28
41. Sutcliffe, G.: The CADE ATP system competition: CASC. AI Magazine **37**(2), 99–101 (2016)
42. Visser, W., Păsăreanu, C.S., Khurshid, S.: Test-input generation with Java PATHFINDER. In: Proc. ISSTA. pp. 97–107. ACM (2004). https://doi.org/10.1145/1007512.1007526
43. Wendler, P., Beyer, D.: sosy-lab/benchexec: Release 3.6. Zenodo (2021). https://doi.org/10.5281/zenodo.4317433

CoVeriTest with Adaptive Time Scheduling (Competition Contribution)*

Marie-Christine Jakobs[1]**(✉) and Cedric Richter[2]

[1] Technical University of Darmstadt, Department of Computer Science,
Darmstadt, Germany, jakobs@cs.tu-darmstadt.de
[2] Paderborn University, Paderborn, Germany, cedricr@mail.upb.de

Abstract. CoVeriTest, which is integrated in the analysis framework CPAchecker, adopts verification technology for test-case generation. It encodes individual test goals as reachability queries, which are then processed by verifiers. To increase the effectiveness on a broad class of testing tasks, CoVeriTest leverages the strengths of two different analyses: an explicit value analysis and predicate abstraction. Similar to TestComp'20, the two analyses are interleaved and the time duration of an interleaving segment is calculated dynamically. However, the calculation of the time duration focuses on the predicted future performance instead of the past performance, thus, rewarding analyses that likely cover open test goals.

Keywords: Test-case generation · Cooperative Verification · CPAchecker

1 Test-Generation Approach

Generating test-cases for a diverse set of tasks like in TestComp is challenging and often cannot be performed effectively by a single approach. Therefore, cooperative approaches that combine the strengths of multiple test-case generators frequently show superior performance as long as they do not spend too much time in unproductive test-case generators. To avoid unproductive test-case generation, we equip our CoVeriTest submission with a novel learning-based scheduler that considers the expected productiveness of a test-case generator.

CoVeriTest is a hybrid approach based on the concept of cooperative, verification-based testing [5], which combines complementary verifiers. In our current instantiation, we iteratively run two verification algorithms, namely value analysis [4] and predicate analysis [3]. In each iteration, the analyses proceed their exploration until they hit their time limit. The time limit of an analysis is computed dynamically at the beginning of each iteration round using our novel learning-based time scheduler. To generate test cases, we encode the (open) test

---

* This work was funded by the Hessian LOEWE initiative within the Software-Factory 4.0 project and it was partially supported by the German Research Foundation (DFG) within the Collaborative Research Centre "On-The-Fly Computing" (SFB 901) (grant number 160364472).

** jury-member

E. Guerra and M. Stoelinga (Eds.): FASE 2021, LNCS 12649, pp. 358–362, 2021.
https://doi.org/10.1007/978-3-030-71500-7_18

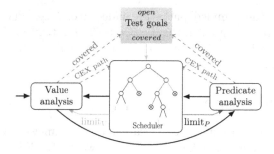

Fig. 1. Our adaptive scheduler integrated in the workflow of CoVeriTest

goals, which are shared between the analyses, as unreachability queries and let the analyses prove the unreachability of those goals. A reported counterexample proves the reachability of a test goal. Therefore, the counterexample is converted into a test [1] and the test goal is removed from the set of open test goals.

Time Scheduling. Our time scheduler limits the time per iteration round to 100 s[3] and distributes the 100 s based on the expected contribution of the individual analyses. The idea is that an analysis gets more time if there exists more paths to open test goals that the analysis is expected to handle well.

Figure 1 shows the integration of our time scheduler into the CoVeriTest workflow. First, the scheduler samples a set of syntactical counterexample paths ρ, which starts at the beginning of the program and ends in an open test goal. Then, it estimates for each path ρ the probability $P(V_i \mid \rho)$ that analysis i detects ρ as a real counterexample[4]. We estimate the probability $P(V_i \mid \rho)$ using an uni-gram language model [9] in combination with the approach of Richter et al. [10] for the abstraction of the syntactical paths ρ. Finally, the scheduler assigns a time budget to analysis i in proportion to the average probability of detecting a counterexample path on a testing task T (program plus open test goals):

$$\text{limit}_i^{\text{new}} = 10s + 80s * \mathbb{E}_{\rho \in T}[P(V_i \mid \rho)] \tag{1}$$

Learning Probability Distribution. The probability distribution $P(V_i \mid \rho)$ is unknown. Thus, we aim to learn the distribution. To this end, we executed the value and predicate analysis separately on the TestComp'20 category coverage-branches and used the reported counterexamples, which are obviously counter-examples that can be decided by the reporting analysis, to pre-train our unigram language model [9]. At the beginning of each CoVeriTest execution, we load the pre-trained model and use the reported counterexamples to improve it during

---

[3] We choose the same iteration time limit as in TestComp'20 [8], which has been established by extensive evaluation of CoVeriTest [5].

[4] Note that it is not important that ρ is a real counterexample. We rather model the probability that the analysis i can decide whether ρ is a counterexample than to decide whether ρ is a counterexample.

execution. When the sampled paths are indecisive, $\mathbb{E}_{\rho \in T}[P(V_i \mid \rho)]$ becomes the normalized progress used in the TestComp'20 strategy [8]. The normalized progress describes the relative contribution of an analysis to the goals covered in the last iteration.

2 Tool Architecture

COVERITEST is an extension of the software analysis framework CPACHECKER [2] (version 2.0) and is written in Java. For parsing, we use the Eclipse CDT parser[5]. For test-case generation, we rely on two instances of CPACHECKER's test-case generation algorithm, which extracts test cases from counterexamples [1]. One instance generates test cases based on CPACHECKER's value analysis [4] and the other instance uses CPACHECKER's predicate analysis [3]. Both analyses apply counterexample-guided abstraction refinement [7] and use the SMT solver Math-SAT5 [6]. We interleave the two instances and determine their time slices based on their expected success on the set of open test goals. To determine the time slices, we added the adaptive scheduler described in the previous section.

3 Strengths and Weaknesses

The main difference between COVERITEST versions in Test-Comp'20 and Test-Comp'21 is the distribution of the 100 s per round. Our own experiments with the Test-Comp 2020 benchmark set revealed a small advantage for our new distribution with respect to the coverage-branches category. Comparing the competition results against a COVERITEST configuration using the time distribution from Test-Comp'20 shows that the new distribution performs slightly worse in the coverage-error category. In total, 13 errors are missed, 8 of them are missed in the subcategory Floats. Overall, an advantage of the new distribution is scarcely noticeable on the Test-Comp 2021 benchmark set. The unigram language model does not generalize well.

Since the underlying analyses remain the same, COVERITEST still generates a small number of test cases. Also, the problems with tasks using large arrays and the subcategories BusyBox-Memsafety and SQLite-Memsafety remain. Additionally, COVERITEST performs poorly on the new ntdrivers tasks and the new subcategory Combinations. While finding the error in the new nla-digbench tasks is difficult, covering branches works well for these tasks. Moreover, COVERITEST deals well with the new category XCSP and the remaining new tasks.

4 Setup

We develop our extension of COVERITEST in a fork[6] of CPACHECKER and submitted revision 970d550, which participated in all categories. To run COVERITEST

---

[5] https://www.eclipse.org/cdt/
[6] https://github.com/cedricrupb/cpachecker

on program **program.i**, one requires a Java 11 runtime environment and must execute the following command line:

```
scripts/cpa.sh -testcomp21 -setprop log.consoleLevel=SEVERE -stats
   -benchmark -heap 10000m -spec property.prp program.i
```

Note that **property.prp** is a place marker for the test specification (**coverage- -error-call.prp** or **coverage-branches.prp**). Tests are generated for programs assuming a 32-bit environment. To support 64-bit environments, one needs to add the configuration option -64. The generated tests are written to the folder **output/test-suite** and adhere to the XML format demanded by the Test-Comp rules. Additionally, the folder contains the mandatory metadata file.

5   Project and Contributors

CoVeriTest is an extension of the CPAchecker project[7] and is developed as a joint, open source project between research groups of Paderborn University and TU Darmstadt. Contributors are Marie-Christine Jakobs and Cedric Richter. We also like to thank all developers of CPAchecker.

References

1. Beyer, D., Chlipala, A.J., Henzinger, T.A., Jhala, R., Majumdar, R.: Generating tests from counterexamples. In: Proc. ICSE. pp. 326–335. IEEE (2004), https://doi.org/10.1109/ICSE.2004.1317455
2. Beyer, D., Keremoglu, M.E.: CPAchecker: A tool for configurable software verification. In: Proc. CAV. pp. 184–190. LNCS 6806, Springer (2011), https://doi.org/10.1007/978-3-642-22110-1_16
3. Beyer, D., Keremoglu, M.E., Wendler, P.: Predicate abstraction with adjustable-block encoding. In: Proc. FMCAD. pp. 189–197. FMCAD (2010), http://ieeexplore.ieee.org/document/5770949/
4. Beyer, D., Löwe, S.: Explicit-state software model checking based on CEGAR and interpolation. In: Proc. FASE. pp. 146–162. LNCS 7793, Springer (2013), https://doi.org/10.1007/978-3-642-37057-1_11
5. Beyer, D., Jakobs, M.: CoVeriTest: Cooperative verifier-based testing. In: Proc. FASE. pp. 389–408. LNCS 11424, Springer (2019), https://doi.org/10.1007/978-3-030-16722-6_23
6. Cimatti, A., Griggio, A., Schaafsma, B.J., Sebastiani, R.: The MathSAT5 SMT solver. In: Proc. TACAS. pp. 93–107. LNCS 7795, Springer (2013), https://doi.org/10.1007/978-3-642-36742-7_7
7. Clarke, E.M., Grumberg, O., Jha, S., Lu, Y., Veith, H.: Counterexample-guided abstraction refinement for symbolic model checking. J. ACM **50**(5), 752–794 (2003), http://doi.acm.org/10.1145/876638.876643
8. Jakobs, M.: CoVeriTest with dynamic partitioning of the iteration time limit (competition contribution). In: Proc. FASE. pp. 540–544. LNCS 12076, Springer (2020), https://doi.org/10.1007/978-3-030-45234-6_30

---

[7] https://cpachecker.sosy-lab.org/

9. Jurafsky, D.: Speech & language processing. Pearson Education India (2000)
10. Richter, C., Hüllermeier, E., Jakobs, M.C., Wehrheim, H.: Algorithm selection for software validation based on graph kernels. JASE **27**(1), 153–186 (2020), https://doi.org/10.1007/s10515-020-00270-x

FuSeBMC: A White-Box Fuzzer for Finding Security Vulnerabilities in C Programs (Competition Contribution)

Kaled M. Alshmrany[(✉)1] *, Rafael S. Menezes[2], Mikhail R. Gadelha[3], and Lucas C. Cordeiro[4]

[1] University of Manchester, Manchester, UK
Institute of Public Administration, Jeddah, Saudi Arabia
kaled.alshmrany@manchester.ac.uk
[2] Federal University of Amazonas, Manaus, Brazil
[3] SIDIA Instituto de Ciência e Tecnologia, Manaus, Brazil
[4] University of Manchester, Manchester, UK

Abstract. We describe and evaluate a novel white-box fuzzer for C programs named FuSeBMC, which combines fuzzing and symbolic execution, and applies Bounded Model Checking (BMC) to find security vulnerabilities in C programs. FuSeBMC explores and analyzes C programs (1) to find execution paths that lead to property violations and (2) to incrementally inject labels to guide the fuzzer and the BMC engine to produce test-cases for code coverage. FuSeBMC successfully participates in Test-Comp'21 and achieves first place in the `Cover-Error` category and second place in the `Overall` category.

Keywords: Automated Test-Case Generation · Symbolic Execution · Bounded Model Checking · Fuzzing · Security.

1 Test Generation Approach

Automated test-case generation is a method to check whether the software matches expected requirements [2]. It involves the automated execution of software components to evaluate intricate properties and achieve code coverage metrics (e.g., decision, branch, instruction). Here, we describe and evaluate a novel white-box fuzzer, FuSeBMC, capable of automatically producing test-cases for C programs. FuSeBMC provides an innovative software testing framework that detects security vulnerabilities in C programs by using fuzzing and symbolic execution in combination with Bounded Model Checking (BMC) (cf. Fig. 1). FuSeBMC builds on top of clang [1] to instrument the C program, uses Map2check [8] as a fuzzing engine, and ESBMC (Efficient SMT-based Bounded Model Checker) [4,5] as BMC and symbolic execution engines, thus combining dynamic and static verification techniques.

---

* Jury Member

© The Author(s) 2021
E. Guerra and M. Stoelinga (Eds.): FASE 2021, LNCS 12649, pp. 363–367, 2021.
https://doi.org/10.1007/978-3-030-71500-7_19

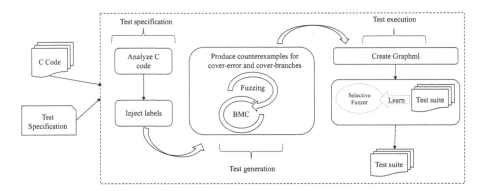

Fig. 1: FuSeBMC: a white-box fuzzer framework for C Programs.

FuSeBMC takes a C program and a test specification [3] as input. In the Cover-Error category, FuSeBMC invokes the fuzzing and BMC engines sequentially to find a path that violates a given property. It uses an iterative BMC approach that incrementally unwinds the program until it finds a property violation or exhausts time or memory limits. FuSeBMC uses incremental BMC to explore the program state space searching for a property violation since all programs in Test-Comp'21 are known to have issues. In the Cover-Branches category, FuSeBMC explores and analyzes the target C program using the clang compiler to inject labels incrementally. FuSeBMC will compute all branches of the C code and inject the labels for each branch by adding the label GOAL-N, where N is the goal number. Both engines will check whether these injected labels are reachable to produce test-cases for branch coverage.

FuSeBMC analyzes the counterexamples and saves them as a *graphml* file. It checks whether the fuzzing and BMC engines could produce counterexamples for both categories Cover-Error and Cover-Branches. If that is not the case, FuSeBMC employs a second fuzzing engine named selective fuzzer which produces test-cases for the rest of the labels. The selective fuzzer produces test-cases by learning from the two engines' output: it analyzes the range of the inputs that should be passed to examine the target C program and then produces different test-cases. Lastly, FuSeBMC prepares valid test-cases with metadata to test a target C program using TestCov [3] as a test validator.

FuSeBMC sets a 150 seconds limit for the fuzzing engine and a 700 seconds limit for the BMC engine and sets a 50 seconds limit for the selective fuzzer. These numbers were obtained empirically by analyzing the Test-Comp'21 results.

2   Strengths and Weaknesses

Incremental BMC allows FuSeBMC to keep unwinding the program until a property violation is found or time or memory limits are exhausted. This approach is advantageous in the Cover-Error category as finding one error is the primary goal. Another strength of FuSeBMC is that it can accurately model C programs that use the IEEE floating-point arithmetic [6,7]. The floating-point encoding layer in our BMC engine extends the support for the SMT FP theory to solvers that do not support it natively. FuSeBMC can test programs with floating-point arithmetic using all currently supported solvers in BMC engine (ESBMC), including Boolector [9], which does not support the SMT FP theory natively.

In both Cover-Error and Cover-Branches categories, various test-cases produced by FuSeBMC are validated successfully. The majority of our test-cases were produced by the BMC engine and the selective fuzzer; our fuzzing engine did not produce many test-cases because it does not model the C library, so it mostly guesses the inputs. For example, in the Cover-Error category, TestCov confirms 500 test-cases produced by FuSeBMC, where our fuzzing engine produces 13 (Map2Check), BMC engine produces 393 (ESBMC), while our selective fuzzer produces 94 test-cases (selective).

However, note that our fuzzing engine is not limited to only produce test-cases. It helps our selective fuzzer by providing information about the number of inputs required to trigger a property violation, i.e., the number of assignments required to reach an error. In several cases, the BMC engine can exhaust the time limit before providing such information, e.g., when there are large arrays that need to be initialized at the beginning of the program. For example, consider the following code fragment extracted from the standard_copy1_ground-2.c benchmark, as illustrated in Fig. 2.

```
1  #define N 100000
2  ...
3  int a, a1[N], a2[N];
4  for (a = 0 ; a < N ; a++) {
5      a1[a] = __VERIFIER_nondet_int();
6      a2[a] = __VERIFIER_nondet_int();
7  }
8  ...
9  for (int x = 0 ; x < N ; x++)
10     __VERIFIER_assert(a1[x] == a2[x]);
```

Fig. 2: Code fragment that contains a large array.

In this particular example, ESBMC exhausts the time limit before checking the assertion $a1[x] == a2[x]$. Apart from that, our employed verification engines also demonstrate a certain level of weakness to produce test-cases due to the many optimizations we perform when converting the program to SMT. In particular, two techniques affected the test-case generation significantly: *constant folding* and *slicing*. *Constant folding* evaluates constants (which includes nondeterministic symbols) and propagates them throughout the formula during encoding, and *slicing* removes expression not in the path to trigger a property violation. These two techniques can significantly reduce SMT solving time. However, they can remove the expressions required to trigger a violation when the program is compiled, i.e., variable initialization might be optimized away, forcing FuSeBMC to generate a test-case with undefined behavior.

Regarding our fuzzing engine, we identified a limitation to handle programs with pointer dereferences. The fuzzing engine keeps track of variables throughout the program but has issues identifying when they go out of scope. When we try to generate a test-case that triggers a pointer dereference, our fuzzing engine provides thrash values, and the selective fuzzer might create test-cases that do not reach the error.

3   Tool Setup and Configuration

In order to run our `fusebmc.py` script,[5] one must set the architecture (*i.e.*, 32 or 64-bit), the competition strategy (i.e., k-induction, falsification, or incremental BMC), the property file path, and the benchmark path, as:

```
fusebmc.py [-a {32, 64}] [-p PROPERTY_FILE]
                [-s {kinduction,falsi,incr,fixed}]
                [BENCHMARK_PATH]
```

where `-a` sets the architecture, `-p` sets the property file path, and `-s` sets the strategy (e.g., `kinduction`, `falsi`, `incr`, or `fixed`). For Test-Comp'21, FuSeBMC uses `incr` for incremental BMC.

When choosing the fuzzing engine, we set the following options when executing Map2Check: timeout of 150 seconds for Map2Check in `Cover-Error`, and a timeout of 70 seconds in `Cover-Branches`; `--fuzzer-mb` 1000 limits memory to 1000 MB; `--target-function-name reach−error` defines the function name to be searched; `--target-function` checks whether the target-function is reachable; `--nondet-generator fuzzer` uses only fuzzing; `--generate-witness` sets the witness output path.

By choosing incremental BMC, the following options are set when executing ESBMC: `--no-div-by-zero-check` disables the division by zero check (required by Test-Comp); `--force-malloc-success` sets that all dynamic allocations succeed (a Test-Comp requirement); `--floatbv` enables floating-point SMT encoding; `--incremental-bmc` enables incremental BMC; `--unlimited-k-steps` removes the upper limit of iteration steps for incremental BMC; `--witness-output` sets the witness output path; `--no-bounds-check` and `--no-pointer-check` disable bounds-check and pointer-safety checks, resp., since we are only interested in finding reachability bugs; `--k-step 5` sets the incremental BMC to 5; `--no-allign-check` disables pointer alignment checks; and `--no-slice` disables slicing of unnecessary instructions.

The Benchexec tool info module is named `fusebmc.py` and the benchmark definition file is `FuSeBMC.xml`.

---

[5] https://gitlab.com/sosy-lab/test-comp/archives-2021/-/blob/master/2021/FuSeBMC.zip

4 Software Project

The FuSeBMC source code is written in C++ and it is available for downloading at GitHub,[6] which includes the latest release of FuSeBMC v3.6.6. FuSeBMC is publicly available under the terms of the MIT License. Instructions for building FuSeBMC from the source code are given in the file README.md (including the description of all dependencies).

References

1. Clang documentation. http://clang.llvm.org/docs/index.html.
2. Anand, S., Burke, E.K., Chen, T.Y., Clark, J.A., Cohen, M.B., Grieskamp, W., Harman, M., Harrold, M.J., McMinn, P.: An orchestrated survey of methodologies for automated software test-case generation. J. Syst. Softw. **86**(8), 1978–2001, 2013.
3. Beyer, D.: Second competition on software testing: Test-Comp 2020. In FASE, LNCS 12076, pp. 505–519, 2020.
4. Gadelha, M.R., Monteiro, F.R., Morse, J., Cordeiro, L.C., Fischer, B., Nicole, D.A.: ESBMC 5.0: An industrial-strength C model checker. In ASE, pp. 888–891, 2018.
5. Gadelha, M.R., Monteiro, F.R., Cordeiro, B., Nicole: ESBMC v6.0: Verifying C Programs Using k-Induction and Invariant Inference - (Competition Contribution). In TACAS, LNCS 11429, pp. 209–213, 2019.
6. Gadelha, M.R., Menezes, R., Monteiro, F.R., Cordeiro, L.C., Nicole, D.A.: ESBMC: scalable and precise test generation based on the floating-point theory - (competition contribution). In FASE, LNCS 12076, pp. 525–529, 2020.
7. Gadelha, M.R., Cordeiro, L.C., Nicole, D.A.: An Efficient Floating-Point Bit-Blasting API for Verifying C Programs. In VSTTE, LNCS 12549, pp. 178–195, 2020.
8. Menezes, R., Rocha, H., Cordeiro, L., Barreto, R.: Map2check using LLVM and KLEE. In TACAS, LNCS 10806, pp. 437–441, 2018.
9. Niemetz, A., Preiner, M., Biere, A.: Boolector 2.0 system description. Journal on Satisfiability, Boolean Modeling and Computation **9**, 53–58 (2014)

Symbiotic 8: Parallel and Targeted Test Generation
(Competition Contribution)

Marek Chalupa[✉], Jakub Novák, and
Jan Strejček

Masaryk University, Brno, Czech Republic

✉ Jury member and the corresponding author: chalupa@fi.muni.cz.

Abstract. The setup of SYMBIOTIC 8 for Test-Comp 2021 brings radical changes in the test generation for `coverage-branches` property. Similarly as in SYMBIOTIC 7, we generate tests by running our fork of symbolic executor KLEE on the analyzed program. SYMBIOTIC 8, however, runs several instances of KLEE in parallel. We run one instance of KLEE on the original program and, simultaneously, we create one (intentionally unsound) program slice for every program-terminating instruction in the program and run KLEE on these slices. Apart from this principal change, we also improved other components of the tool, mainly the program slicer. Further, our fork of KLEE now supports symbolic pointer arithmetics and comparison of symbolic addresses.

1 Test-Generation Approach

SYMBIOTIC [3,2] is an open-source program analysis framework that combines static analyses with code transformations in order to enable faster analysis of the code. In the setup for Test-Comp 2021, SYMBIOTIC uses *program slicing* [6] in combination with *symbolic execution* [5].

Static (backward) program slicing [6] is a technique that removes program instructions that have no influence on reachability or the effect of selected parts of the program. In Test-Comp, we use program slicing for all properties. For `coverage-error-call` property, we slice the program to remove instructions that cannot affect reachability of the error location. For `coverage-branches` property, we use program slicing to create modified versions of the program on which we are likely to quickly generate tests that reach hard-to-cover parts of the program.

Symbolic execution [5] is a program analysis technique that enumerates all possible execution paths of a program. For every path, it computes its corresponding *path condition*, which is a collection of constraints on program inputs that forms the necessary and sufficient condition to follow the path. Each path condition is then used to create a test that makes the program execute the given path.

© The Author(s) 2021
E. Guerra and M. Stoelinga (Eds.): FASE 2021, LNCS 12649, pp. 368–372, 2021.
https://doi.org/10.1007/978-3-030-71500-7_20

1.1   Workflow of Symbiotic 8

The workflow of Symbiotic 8 in Test-Comp 2021 for the property `coverage-error-call` is the same as in Symbiotic 7: we slice the analyzed program with respect to calls of the error function and run Klee on this sliced program. If Klee finds a feasible path that calls the error function, we attempt to replay this path in the unsliced program to fill in the possibly missing values returned from calls to functions `__VERIFIER_nondet_*` that may have been sliced away.

The workflow for the property `coverage-branches` changed significantly in Symbiotic 8. For this property, we run several instances of Klee in parallel: one instance on the original program and other instances on slices generated for every terminating location in the program.

More precisely, we create a pool of processes that keeps running at most 8 processes at the same time (on the first-come-first-served basis). We start an instance of Klee on the original program and add it to the pool. Then we identify instructions in the program that terminate the execution (further referred to as *targets*). For each target, we create a slice and queue a run of Klee on this slice.

These slices are *unsound* in the sense that they do not preserve all execution paths to the targets. A slice is constructed in two steps:

1. We gather all instructions that are backward-reachable from the target in the target's function and recursively in the callers of the target's function. However, we move only up the call stack and do not submerge into procedures during this process.
2. After we gather all such instructions, we replace all other instructions with a call to `abort` and apply standard program slicing with respect to the target.

For example, consider the code on the left in Figure 1. It contains three possible targets, namely `error()` (line 7), `abort()` (line 13), and `return 0` (line 17). If we slice with respect to the target `error()`, we start searching the program backwards from this target and get all instructions in the body of function `foo`. Then we pop up from the call to line 16 and collect all instructions of function `main` except the call to `abort` (from which the call to `foo` is unreachable). All instructions except the gathered ones are replaced with a call to `abort`. Standard program slicing then produces the program depicted in the middle in Figure 1 (in this case, it just removes the `return`). The slice for the target `abort()` preserves only three first lines of `main` as depicted on the right in Figure 1.

Whenever the *main* instance of Klee finishes tests generation, we have tests for all feasible execution paths of the program. Therefore, we kill all other running instances of Klee and discard tests that were not generated by the main instance to reduce the size of the test suite. If the main instance does not finish before timeout, we keep all generated tests.

Using the unsound slices aims only to help reaching hard-to-cover places in the program. In particular, potentially expensive detours are replaced by `abort` and symbolic execution thus does not waste resources to discover them (see line 2 in the middle in Figure 1). The current construction of unsound slices

```
1   int inc(int x) {          int inc(int x) {
2       return x + 1;            abort();
3   }                         }
4
5   void foo(int x) {         void foo(int x) {
6       if (x > 0)                if (x > 0)
7           error();                  error();
8   }                         }
9
10  int main() {              int main() {           int main() {
11      int y = nondet();         int y = nondet();      int y = nondet();
12      if (y < 0)                if (y < 0)             if (y < 0)
13          abort();                  abort();               abort();
14      if (y == 0)               if (y == 0)
15          y = inc(y);               y = inc(y);
16      foo(y);                   foo(y);
17      return 0;
18  }                         }                      }
```

Fig. 1. And example of a program (left) and its unsound slice with respect to the call of error() (middle) and abort() (right).

guarantees that if a test covers a target in the corresponding slice, then it covers the same target also in the original program. The opposite implication does not hold due to the unsoundness. Note that tests generated from the slices may not and usually do not cover all branches in the original program, therefore we still need to run KLEE on the original program.

2   Software Architecture

All parts of SYMBIOTIC 8 use LLVM 10 [7]. We compile the analyzed program into LLVM bitcode by the compiler CLANG.

To carry out symbolic execution, we use our fork of the open-source symbolic executor KLEE [1]. The fork has several modifications compared to the mainstream KLEE. The main modification is the representation of pointers as segment-offset pairs that enables symbolic-sized allocations. Since this year, our fork KLEE also supports comparison of and arithmetic on symbolic pointers. We use Z3 [4] as the SMT solver in KLEE. The components of SYMBIOTIC are programmed in C++ and the scripts that schedule and control running these components are written in Python.

3   Strengths and Weaknesses

Although symbolic execution is very good in generating test-cases, it suffers from the *path explosion* problem. This problem emerges on programs that contain many branching instructions or loops with the number of iterations dependent on the input and may hinder symbolic execution from exploring "deep" parts of the

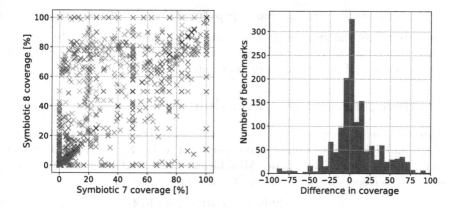

Fig. 2. The coverage achieved by SYMBIOTIC 8 and 7 on individual benchmarks of the *Cover-Branches* category

program. Using unsound program slices for terminating instructions attempts to alleviate this problem. Although the slice is not guaranteed to preserve paths to the target for which it was created, there are programs where this technique helps symbolic execution to cover substantially more instructions. However, there are also many cases where the technique worsens the coverage alike.

Figure 2 illustrates the overall positive and negative effect of this approach. The scatter plot on the left compares the coverage achieved by SYMBIOTIC 8 and the coverage achieved by SYMBIOTIC 7 on individual benchmarks that were used in both Test-Comp 2020 and 2021.[1] The scatter plot shows that the behavior of the tool changes dramatically. To summarize the data, we compute the difference between the two coverages on each benchmark (for example, if SYMBIOTIC 8 achieves 80% and SYMBIOTIC 7 60% coverage, the difference is +20%). The histogram on the right indicates that the overall effect of unsound slices is positive as the distribution is skewed to positive values. Indeed, SYMBIOTIC 8 won the 3rd place in the category *Cover-Branches* (corresponding to `coverage-branches` property) in Test-Comp 2021 which is a big improvement over the previous Test-Comp, where SYMBIOTIC was 8th out of 9 participants in this category.

The workflow of SYMBIOTIC on `coverage-error-call` did not change from the last year and thus the results are similar.

4 Tool Setup and Configuration

The archive is available at https://doi.org/10.5281/zenodo.4491729. Run SYMBIOTIC with the following command

---

[1] The use of unsound slices is not the only difference between SYMBIOTIC 8 and 7, but we believe that it has the biggest impact on the presented results.

```
bin/symbiotic --test-comp --prp <prpfile> [--32] <source>
```

where `--prp` sets the verified property and `--32` tells SYMBIOTIC to assume 32-bit architecture (64-bit architecture is assumed by default). The generated test-cases are stored in the directory `test-suite`.

5   Software Project and Contributors

SYMBIOTIC 8 as it competes in Test-Comp 2021 has been developed by Marek Chalupa and Jakub Novák under the supervision of Jan Strejček. The tool and its components are available under MIT License. LLVM, KLEE, and Z3 are also available under open-source licenses. The project web page is:

https://github.com/staticafi/symbiotic

References

1. C. Cadar, D. Dunbar, and D. Engler. KLEE: Unassisted and automatic generation of high-coverage tests for complex systems programs. In *OSDI*, pages 209–224. USENIX Association, 2008. http://www.usenix.org/events/osdi08/tech/full_papers/cadar/cadar.pdf.
2. M. Chalupa, T. Jašek, L. Tomovič, M. Hruška, V. Šoková, P. Ayaziová, J. Strejček, and T. Vojnar. Symbiotic 7: Integration of predator and more (competition contribution). In *TACAS*, volume 12079 of *LNCS*, pages 413–417. Springer, 2020. doi: 10.1007/978-3-030-45237-7_31.
3. M. Chalupa, M. Vitovská, T. Jašek, M. Šimáček, and J. Strejček. Symbiotic 6: generating test cases by slicing and symbolic execution. *International Journal on Software Tools for Technology Transfer*, 2020. doi: 10.1007/s10009-020-00573-0.
4. L. de Moura and N. Bjørner. Z3: an efficient SMT solver. In *TACAS*, volume 4963 of *LNCS*, pages 337–340. Springer, 2008. doi: 10.1007/978-3-540-78800-3_24.
5. J. C. King. Symbolic execution and program testing. *Communications of ACM*, 19(7):385–394, 1976. doi: 10.1145/360248.360252.
6. Mark Weiser. Program slicing. *IEEE Transactions on Software Engineering*, 10(4):352–357, 1984. doi: 10.1109/TSE.1984.5010248.
7. LLVM. http://llvm.org/.

Author Index

Printed in the United States
by Baker & Taylor Publisher Services